D1645329

Colección Támesis

SERIE A: MONOGRAFÍAS, 266

A COMPANION TO SPANISH CINEMA

Fernán Gómez in Juan Estlerich's *El anacoreta* (1976)

In memoriam
Fernando Fernán Gómez
Lima, 28 de agosto de 1921
fallecido la semana después de que se acabó este libro
21 de noviembre de 2007

Para Sheila
quien sabe mejor que yo
cuánto le debo

BERNARD P. E. BENTLEY

A COMPANION TO SPANISH CINEMA

TAMESIS

First published 2008 by Tamesis, Woodbridge

ISBN 978–1–85566–176–9

Tamesis is an imprint of Boydell & Brewer Ltd
PO Box 9, Woodbridge, Suffolk IP12 3DF, UK
and of Boydell & Brewer Inc.
668 Mt Hope Avenue, Rochester, NY 14620, USA
website: www.boydellandbrewer.com

A CIP catalogue record for this book is available
from the British Library

This publication is printed on acid-free paper

Printed in Great Britain by
CPI Antony Rowe Ltd, Chippenham, Wiltshire

CONTENTS

List of illustrations   vii

Acknowledgements   ix

Abbreviations   x

Introduction   xiii

1   The Silent Reels of the Photographers (1896–1918)   1

2   The Silent Films of the Directors (1918–1930)   27

3   The Cinema of the Republic (1931–1939)   49

4   Years of Autarchy, Silence and Hunger (1940–1951)   77

5   The Establishment, the Cold War and the Dissidents (1951–1961)   116

6   Opening out to Europe, the EOC and a New Cinema (1961–1969)   156

7   The Last Years of the Regime and a Middle Path (1969–1975)   198

8   End to Censorship and Transition to Democracy (1976–1982)   225

9   A Democratic Spain and Socialist Cinema (1982–1989)   255

10   New Departures (1989–1996)   282

Coda: Into the Twenty-First Century   317

Filmography: Alphabetically by directors   353

             Alphabetically by original titles   400

Bibliography   449

Index of Names and Subjects   477

ILLUSTRATIONS

Frontispiece: Fernán Gómez in Juan Estelrich's *El anacoreta* (1976)
Bulbeck & Mas

1a The crowded set of Gelabert's *Amor que mata* (1909)   14
2a Chiaroscuro of Rey's *La aldea maldita* (1930)   39
    Filmoteca Española
3a Double exposure of Perojo's *La verbena de la Paloma* (1935)   68
    Video Mercury Films SA / Filmoteca Española
4a The strength of the family in Sáenz de Heredia's *Raza* (1941)   91
    Filmoteca Española
4b Creationism in Neville's *La torre de los siete jorobados* (1944)   110
    Video Mercury Films SA / Filmoteca Española
5a Visual ironies in Berlanga's *Plácido* (1961)   136
    Sogepac SA
5b The bullfighter in Vajda's *Mi tío Jacinto* (1956)   143
    Video Mercury Films SA
6a Cross-dressing in Fernán Gómez's *El extraño viaje* (1964)   178
    Impala SA
6b The delicate touch of Miguel Picazo's *La tía Tula* (1964)   187
    Video Mercury Films SA
7a Sexual repression in Grau's *La trastienda* (1976)   211
    José Feade PC
7b The allegorical ending of Saura's *El jardín de las delicias* (1970) 215
    Manga Films SL / Querejeta PC
8a The child's perspective in Gutiérrez Aragón's *Demonios en*   245
    El Jardín (1982)
    Luis Megino Producciones
9a The excesses of Almodóvar in *¿Qué he hecho yo para merecer*   272
    esto!! (1984)
    El Deseo / Antonio de Benito
9b The strength of traditions in Armendáriz's *Tasio* (1984)   278
    Manga Films SL / Querejeta PC
10a Emblems/icon in Bigas Luna's *Jamón, Jamón* (1992)   298
    Manga Films SL

10b Female solidarity in Bollaín's *Hola ¿estás sola?* (1995)   310
       Fernando Colomo PC SL
11a Mental loneliness in Amenábar's *Abre los ojos* (1997)   322
       Universal Pictures Video SA/ Sogepac SA
11b The transnationalism of Coixet's *La vida secreta de las palabras*   349
       (2005)
       El Deseo/Kiko García

Every effort has been made to identify and contact copyright holders of the above stills. Confirmation is being sought from El Deseo SA, Bulbeck & Mas, Fernando Colomo PC SL, Filmoteca Española, José Feade PC, Quere-jeta PC, Impala Films SA, Luis Megino Producciones, Manga Films SL, Universal Pictures Video SA, Video Mercury Films SA.

I apologise for any apparent negligence, and any omissions or corrections brought to my attention will be remedied in future editions.

ACKNOWLEDGEMENTS

I would not have been able to write this book without the help of many people, and I need to thank all those who have been with me economically, intellectually and emotionally on this journey. There is the family, who put up with so much, and knowing me at my worse encouraged me. Graham, Jamie and especially Sheila Bentley who, as if her care were not enough, proofread so many versions of each chapter. Secondly, there are my colleagues at the University of St Andrews, above all Nigel Dennis and Belén Vidal, whose support, discussions and occasional reading of chapters has been invaluable. To my students' enthusiasm, interest and questions, I owe a debt of gratitude for the way I have organised this book. Jennie Holmes should be singled out for reading, commenting, suggesting and amending so much, and participating so fully in this book that the final chapter into the twenty-first century is almost a joint effort. Outside the University I must recall Celestino Deleyto who, throughout the 1980s from Zaragoza, would tape me one or two films a week; Montserrat Lunati, who read some of the early chapters, provided me with books and the VHS of *Morena Clara* that I could not locate; and both Peter Evans and Isabel Santaolalla, who have always been so generous with their advice and moral support. At the Filmoteca Española in Madrid I owe a lot to Marga Lobo and Trinidad del Río for their help on my only too brief visits, when they had ready all the tapes that I needed to view. These visits were enabled by a research grant in July 2002 from the Russell Trust for Fife in Scotland, and subsequently from the School of Modern Languages at the University of St Andrews. Natalia Bilestka has been a patient and informed IT adviser, and I would also like to thank Carol Crawford for her cheerful eight o'clock smiles and daily encouragements as I arrived in the Department. There is also Elspeth Ferguson whose faith and determined patience was a great support while this companion to Spanish cinema was being written, but most of all I thank Sheila Bentley, my companion of so much of my life.

I would be very grateful to receive comments and information about anything important that I have taken for granted and omitted from this book.

BPEB

ABBREVIATIONS

AACC	Academia de las Artes y Ciencias Cinematográficas [Spanish Film Academy]
AP	Alianza Popular [Popular Alliance]
ATA	Aberri ta Askatasuna [Homeland and Freedom]
BFI	British Film Institute
CCC	Comisión de Censura Cinematográfica [Film Censorship Commission]
CEA	Cinematográfica Española Americana [Spanish and American Cinema]
CEC	Círculo de Escritores Cinematográficos [Screenwriters' Circle]
CIFESA	Compañía Industrial Film Español Sociedad Anónima [Industrial Spanish Film Company Limited]
DGC	Director General de Cinematografía [Managing Director of Cinema]
DGCPE	Dirección General de Cultura Popular y Espéctaculos [Popular Culture and Performance Department]
DNC	Departamento Nacional de Cinematografía [National Film Department]
ECESA	Estudios Cinema Español Sociedad Anónima [Spanish Cinema Studios Limited]
EEC	European Economic Community
EOC	Escuela Oficial de Cinematografía [Official Film School]
ETA	Euskadi ta Askatasuna [Basque Land and Liberty]
EU	European Union
Fs (Three)	Faith, Fatherland and Family
FORTA	Federación de Organismos o Entidades de Radio y Televisión Autonómicos [Federation of Regional Radio and Television Organisations or Entities]
FRAP	Frente Revolucionario Antifacista y Patriótico [Anti-Fascist and Patriotic Revolutionary Front]
FRIPESCI	Fédération Internationale de la Presse Cinématographique [International Federation of Film Critics]
GAL	Grupos Antiterroristas de Liberación [Anti-Terrorist Liberation Squads]

GATT	General Agreement on Tariffs and Trade
HFP	Hispano-Film-Produktion [Hispano-Film Productions]
ICAA	Instituto de la Cinematografía y de las Artes Audiovisuales [Institute for Film and Audiovisual Arts]
IE	de interés especial [of special interest]
IFISA	Ignacio Ferrer Iquino Sociedad Anónima [Limited]
IIEC	Instituto de Investigaciones y Experiencias Cinematográficas [Institute for Cinema Research and Experiments]
IM	de interés militar [of military significance]
IMDb	*Internet Movie Database*
IN	de interés nacional [of national significance]
JSCC	Junta Superior de Censura Cinematográfica [Supreme Board of Film Censorship]
JSOC	Junta Superior de Orientación Cinematográfica [Supreme Board for Film Guidance]
MATESA	Maquinaria Textil del Norte Sociedad Anónima [North Textile Tools Limited]
MCU.es	Ministerio de Cultura [Internet page of the Spanish Ministry of Culture]
MGM	Metro-Goldwyn-Mayer
MIT	Ministerio de Información y Turismo [Ministry of Information and Tourism]
NATO	North Atlantic Treaty Organisation
NCE	Nuevo Cine Español [New Spanish Cinema]
NO-DO	Noticiarios y Documentales Cinematográficos [Film News and Documentaries]
OCIC	Organisation Catholique Internationale du Cinéma et de l'Audiovisuel [World Catholic Association for Communication]
PCE	Partido Comunista Español [Spanish Communist Party]
PNC	Premios Nacionales de Cinematógrafía [National Film Awards]
PP	Partido Popular [People's Party, former AP]
PRISA	Promotora de Informaciones Sociedad Anónima [Information Promoters Limited]
PSOE	Partido Socialista Obrero Español [Spanish Socialist Workers' Party]
RCA	Radio Corporation of America
RTVE	Radio Televisión Española [Spanish National Television Broadcast]
'S'	Films: from 1978 to 1984 films 'classified' as containing too much sex or violence required an 'S' [never spelt out] certificate with restricted exhibition in special theatres
SEAT	Sociedad Española de Automóviles de Turismo [Spanish Company for Tourist Class Vehicles]

Seminci	Semana Internacional de Cine de Valladolid [Valladolid International Cinema Week]
UCD	Unión del Centro Democrático [Union of the Democratic Centre]
UFA	Universum Film Aktiengesellschaft [Universal Film Corporation]
UNINCI	Unión Industrial Cinematográfica [Industrial Film Union]
USSR	Union of Soviet Socialist Republics
VCE	Viejo Cine Español [Old/Traditional Spanish Cinema]

INTRODUCTION

> – Del cinema al aire libre
> vengo, madre, de mirar
> un mar mentida y cierta,
> que no es la mar y es la mar
> Rafael Alberti, *Marinero en tierra*[1]

There are as many ways of structuring a *Companion to Spanish Cinema* as there are of preparing a Spanish stew or *cocido*. There are opportunities for different combinations, but these must be substantial, tasty, and should above all leave you wanting more at a later stage. Many ingredients must also be left out, and the hope is that the present *cocido* will leave most readers wanting to see more Spanish Cinema. This book is in fact addressed to English-speaking readers who are either film students or students of Spanish who are interested in Spanish Cinema.[2] It is organised chronologically to enable readers to contextualise their own individual viewing and reading. The suggested references inserted after a film is mentioned and the further reading included at the end of each chapter are therefore predominantly from English sources, although the interested reader will find plenty of references to sources in Spanish and other languages in the bibliographies of the recommended texts. All Spanish quotations have been translated, and the original has been included in the footnotes. For the titles of films, the English version found on the *Internet Movie Database* [*IMDb*] is used, even if some of these are at first sight surprising, in order to facilitate IMDb searches for cross-references. If a title in English is preceded by an asterisk '*' it is my own translation when none was found on the *IMDb*. The translated titles are included in square brackets the first time the film is mentioned in a chapter but thereafter the original title is used and both titles are included in the filmography. The year

---

1   '– From the open-air cinema / I'm back, mother, from watching / a sea that is false and definite, / which is not the sea and is the sea.' Rafael Alberti was 22 when his collection of poems, *The Grounded Sailor*, was first published in 1924.

2   It is for this reason that I have kept in mind Carlota Larrea's 2001 film survey, 'Spanish film within the UK and Irish HE system', published in *Vida Hispánica*.

given with each film is that of the first release, which at times differs from the film's licence.

The history of Spanish cinema is, however, still incomplete and problematic. Within Spain not much attention had been given to an historical perspective of its cinematographic legacy until the early 1950s when, among other developments, the *Filmoteca Nacional* [National Film Archives; now the *Filmoteca Española*] was established in February 1953, by which time much material and many reels had been lost or destroyed during Spain's turbulent and fractured past. Throughout the three and a half decades of the Franco regime (1939–1976) Spanish directors were either in tension with the values of the regime and its socio-political agenda or, if critical, they were concerned about the reception of their work and their message. It is these dissidents from the establishment who produced the more interesting cinema. Until the closing decades of the twentieth century, for various reasons, which range from the very specificity of the narratives within their national context to ignorance or prejudice from outsiders, little interest was manifested by international popular audiences (Kinder, 1993: 289 and 484 n.15, 450 n.1). The same was true for academics. Whereas Thompson & Bordwell hardly mention Spain in the 788 pages of their *Film History* (2003), Sorlin's *European Cinemas* (2001) deliberately leaves Spain out of the discussion because 'it is different' (pp. 20–1). Spanish Cinema is European and in the days of the silent 'movies' before the Civil War (1936–39) it had a European market while its directors were equally happy filming in France or Germany. Sorlin's exclusion, given his starting point of representations of the 1914–18 War in the 1930s, may be because Spain was not involved in that war and therefore it need not be included; but this is not a valid reason to exclude Spanish Cinema from its European context. In fact the differences shown by Spanish Cinema, such as the predominance of spectacle and song, or difficulties of production, need to be spelt out within the framework of its European context. If one argues it is too different to be European, then it should at least be dealt with as a national cinema, but here again it is excluded from Hjort & Mackenzie's *Cinema and Nation* (2000).

Fortunately, informed and specialised film critics were aware of those Spanish directors critical of the establishment, appreciating and validating their films at international film festivals (Luis Buñuel, Luis G. Berlanga and Juan Antonio Bardem in the 1960s, Carlos Saura in the 1970s), but it was a restricted public until the Almodóvar phenomenon of the late 1980s. Other Spanish achievements were seen as flashes in the pan undeservedly forgotten by the general public, although three Spanish productions have so far won Oscars as best foreign films: José Luis Garci's *Volver a empezar* [1982 *Begin the Beguine*]; ten years later, Fernando Trueba's *Belle époque* [1992 *The Age of Beauty*]; and more recently Almodóvar's *Todo sobre mi madre* [1999 *All About My Mother*]. With similar neglect, British terrestrial television now rarely broadcasts a subtitled Spanish-language film, but over the Christmas week of 2001 four Almodóvar films were shown late at night by Channel 4, and his latest features now regularly appear on the cover of *Sight and Sound*.[3] But this is privileging one director over many other talented filmmakers. The acting successes of Antonio Banderas or Penélope Cruz in Hollywood, or the remake of Alejandro Amenábar's *Abre los ojos* [1997 *Open Your Eyes*] as *Vanilla Sky* [2002 Cameron Crowe] with Mateo Gil involved in both scripts, demonstrate that perceptions are changing. However, just as this year's best-sellers do not necessarily become tomorrow's classics, so film critics do not frequently agree with the spectators who pay for their own tickets and make this year's box-office successes. Nonetheless Spanish Cinema has much to offer, and readers will be able to decide for themselves as they follow up the present suggestions. Rafael Alberti's stanza, on the first page, is an expression of my own enthusiasm for Spanish Cinema, certainly shared with all the names cited in the concluding bibliography. Alberti's choice of a medieval poetic form[4] roots this interest in Spanish Cinema in its own traditions, back to the time before the medium was developed. The focus on the sea, which is and is not, is a terse way of conveying the fact that cinema is but an illusion with a narrative that has the capacity to move and mesmerise.

In the last twenty years the situation has changed radically with the proliferation of film festivals dedicated to Spanish language films, more adventurous distributors and the interest of foreign critics and academics. Publications in English have multiplied exponentially in the last decade, and in 2004 the first journal in English dedicated to Spanish films was launched, *Studies in Hispanic Cinemas*. Nonetheless the history of Spanish Cinema is constantly changing and still provisional, not just because its compilation started late, and because fashions change as each epoch refashions its perception of the past but, in the particular case of Spain, old films thought to be lost forever are sometimes rediscovered in personal collections or distant film libraries and occasional patiently restored copies are made available by the regional Filmotecas; a key example is *Raza*, discussed in chapter 4.

For the present overview a rough chronological perspective has been chosen as, ultimately, the most coherent manner of organising the rich and varied materials to be gathered. By coincidence, technological and political developments facilitated this particular fragmentation. Many details have been included on the first sixty years of Spanish Cinema because this is an area

---

3   Most recently *Volver* [2006 *To Return*], and previously *Kika* [1993], *Carne trémula* [1998, *Live Flesh*], *Hable con ella* [2002 *Talk to Her*], and *La mala educación* [2004 *Bad Education*]; *Sight and Sound*, 16 June 2006, 4 January 1994, 8 April 1998, 12 July 2002 and 14 June 2004 respectively.

4   Four octosyllabic lines with an alternate rhyme, expressing a child's comment to its mother.

not generally covered in existing anglophone surveys, and it is hoped that this book will contribute to redress the past marginalisation of Spain in more general studies of cinematographic achievements. This account is necessarily selective, and many names are missing, but it also attempts to avoid the danger of becoming a chronological catalogue, even if it only reflects one enthusiast's view of the situation. It focuses on the directors as a means of identifying the films and regretfully misses out on other individuals involved in filmmaking. However, unlike previous accounts in English, it does not overlook the more popular films to concentrate on films that have attracted foreign audiences and critics, and it includes examples of documentaries and films aimed at children, not forgetting animations.

Viewing and General Reading

For accessing currently available DVDs of Spanish films with subtitles, one place to start is the link on the Internet Movie Database (www.imdb.com), and another is to type the title for an Internet search (using Google Image has been very useful). A new webpage was launched at www.filmotech.com on 27 March 2007, allowing the legal downloading of films for as little as one euro. The British Film Institute (www.bfi.org.uk) will also offer links at 'Film Links Gateway' to open up other possibilities. There are at present very few VHS or DVDs of films before 1940, after which they are becoming more readily available. In my experience these are soon out of stock; the best selection to buy in person is usually offered in the video section of the meagre Spanish film rack of the large department stores, the *Corte Inglés* or FNAC, both also available online.

The reading suggestions, which follow each chapter, have been restricted to books and articles written in English, hopefully currently available in most university libraries and even in specialised bookshops like Grant & Cutler. Each book consulted will also provide its own bibliography to expand the reading suggestions into a variety of other languages. The full references can be found in the selected bibliography at the end of the book. The most useful general introduction at present on the market is Barry Jordan & Mark Allinson's *Spanish Cinema. A Student's Guide* (2005). Two equally recent publications are Rob Stone's *Spanish Cinema* (2002) and the clearly focused *Spanish National Cinema* by Núria Triana Toribio (2003). Before, there was Caparrós Lera's brief *Spanish Cinema* (1987), which covers the years 1896 to 1975 in 57 pages, with notes on individual films made between 1939 and 1975 (pp. 73–131), and Augusto Torres's *Spanish Cinema 1896–1983* (1986), but neither are easily accessible. Marvin D'Lugo's *Guide to the Cinema of Spain* (1997) is a reference book comprising a brief historical outline (pp. 1–28) and some 260 films covering alphabetically 1935 to 1995 (pp. 29–114), directors and critics (pp. 115–208), and actors (pp. 209–64). In Spanish, however, there are many histories of Spanish Cinema, and the following have been the most comprehensive and readable: Román Gubern *et al.*, *Historia del cine español* (1995); Emilio C. García Fernández, *Historia ilustrada del cine español* (1985) because of its illustrations and wide coverage; and the *Antología crítica del cine español 1906–1995* (1997) edited by Julio Pérez Perucha, which provided a tempting model for organising the present companion. For those who read French there is Emmanuel Larraz's *Le Cinéma espagnol* (1986) or Jean-Claude Seguin's succinct *Histoire du cinéma espagnol* (1994), also translated into Spanish. It is also strongly recommended to run a name or a title through the ever-expanding *Internet Movie Database* (*IMDb*), where so much can be cross-referenced, and the complementary but less user-friendly Spanish site provided by the Ministry of Education, Culture and Sports (mcu. es), and then to look for corroborating evidence. Both sites will usually link to the official site of the films concerned if available and, in the case of the *IMDb*, to possible DVD sources. To provide the necessary historical and social context for these films there are useful complementary and systematic collections of articles, each one with brief sections on Spanish Cinema: Helen Graham & Jo Labanyi, *Spanish Cultural Studies* (1995), David T. Gies, *The Cambridge Companion to Spanish Culture* (1999), and John Hooper's books on modern Spanish Society (1987 and 1995). Jill Forbes & Sarah Street's *European Cinema* (2000) will contextualise the present book in its European setting and in contrast to Hollywood and 'classic' cinema. The first 50 pages are a useful introduction, raising many questions albeit with too few references to Spain. The rest of the book is dedicated to 12 specific films as case studies, including Buñuel's *Viridiana* (1961) and Saura's *Carmen* (1983). For students who actually have to prepare assignments on Spanish Cinema, Timothy Corrigan's *A Short Guide to Writing About Film* (reprints, with improvements) is strongly recommended. Jordan & Allinson, Thompson & Bordwell, and Monaco all provide a glossary of technical terms at the end of their respective books introducing cinema studies.

The Silent Reels of the Photographers (1896–1918)

Sunrise: the initial impetus

In May 1896, during the week's celebrations for St Isidro, Madrid's patron saint, not everyone went to the daily bullfights. Five months after Louis and Auguste Lumière's first experiments in Paris, and those of Georges Méliès, the Lyonnais Alexandre Promio first presented the Cinematograph to the Spanish press on 13 May and to the general public on 14 May, at the Madrid Hotel de Rusia. On behalf of his employers, the Lumière brothers of Lyon, Promio projected the 20-minute show of eight to ten reels that had first been exhibited in Paris on 28 December 1895 and subsequently in London in March 1896.[1] While preparing his display of French reels, or after, he also shot some footage of his own, thus probably becoming the first person to film in Spain. He included his *Salida de las alumnas del Colegio de San Luis de los franceses* [*Pupils leaving the French Girls' School*] in the exhibition and the pupils, together with the French ambassador who had been so helpful to Promio, were invited. The new technology of presenting photographs that appeared to move attracted some attention in that first year; even the Royal Family was charmed. Not that it was the only system on show in Madrid at the time. Since 11 May Erwin Rousby had been displaying the Animatograph in a circus rather than a hotel.[2] Edison's Kinetoscope had also been on display for a whole year, but was unable to compete for popular attention perhaps because, unlike the collective experience offered by Promio or Rousby, the inquisitive viewer had a long wait in a queue before finally peering through the slits of the apparatus. The first Barcelona presentation of the Cinematograph in December 1896 is even less well documented but may have involved the Lumière brothers in person (Porter i Moix, 1992: 41).

Before long the new technology was being displayed by travelling photographers in Catalonia and other Spanish regions, not always with a Cinemato-

---

[1] Nancy Membrez offers more details of these events with slightly different dates (1989: 540).

[2] Pérez Perucha explains that it may not necessarily have been a Robert W. Paul machine (Gubern, 1995: 24), although it was in 1896 that Paul filmed his *Tour through Spain and Portugal* (Christie, 1994: 24 and 91).

graph since other systems were still competing for the projection market. By 1897 Promio had filmed subjects both of general interest and commercial potential for his French employers (Talens, 1998: 35). With royal approval he filmed the Queen's Guards in front of the Royal Palace, and later bull-fighters and flamenco dancers, *Sevillanas*. According to the titles listed on the *IMDb*, he must also have followed this with a filming trip to Belgium and the Netherlands where he recorded ships, docks and city sights. Some reels, such as the arrival of the bullfighters, *Llegada de los toreros a la plaza*, capture a moment without any warning. The camera with its back to the bullring already has an impressive depth of field; one man is seen to duck in front of the camera as he tries to restrain another walking unconcerned in front of it. Other reels betray the complicity of the participants, *Carga de los lanceros de la Reina* [*Charge of the Queen's Lancers*] begins as a cloud of dust in the distance and ends as the horses halt metres in front of the camera. Similarly, in *Maniobras de la artillería en Vicálvaro* [*Artillery Manoeuvres at Vical-varo*], the camera is positioned on its tripod and as the horses arrive from right to left, the gun carriage is unharnessed in the centre of the frame, the gun is loaded, aimed and fired, all in 39 seconds. Some of the unrehearsed reels are interesting social documents. One can contrast, for example, the 40 seconds looking down on the bustling traffic, collective transport and affluent ladies and gentlemen in hats strolling in Madrid's Puerta del Sol, with the 45 seconds filmed at eye level showing mules, donkeys, carts and people at work in the crowded Puerta de Alcalá. None of these early reels are more than a minute long, but it is not possible to be exact as each copy of the same reel consulted in the Filmoteca Española (Madrid) is of a slightly different length; and one copy of the same film may have a Spanish title while another has a French title registered to 'Lumière, Paris', which all indicates foreign interest for the exotic Spain.

The Spanish pioneers

Meanwhile Eduardo Jimeno Correas and his father, who had been in Madrid in May 1896, were exhibiting French reels in Zaragoza, with a genuine Lumière camera finally bought in Lyon.[3] On 11 October 1896 they filmed the first reel identified as Spanish, *Salida de misa de doce del Pilar de Zaragoza* [*Leaving the Midday Mass on the Feast of Our Lady of Zaragoza*],[4] from a raised posi-

---

3 Méndez-Leite has interesting anecdotes about the purchase of this camera (1965: I, 31–5). The film has been restored by the Filmoteca in Zaragoza. José Luis Borau recreated the occasion on 11 October 1996.

4 Seguin proposes a different first reel, shot on 11 September 1896, as the first autoch-thonous reel: *Llegada de un tren de Teruel a Segorbe* [*Arrival of the Teruel Train at Segorbe*]

tion in front of the cathedral. However, the film was a little dark, so father and son returned the following Sunday on 18 October to make a second reel, *Saludos* [*Greetings*], but this time the parishioners were camera-conscious. In the following years numerous reels of parishioners leaving churches were filmed and competition, using the new technology, was at hand from other photographers such as Baltasar Abadal, Antoni Pàdua Tramullas, Àngel García Cardona and Estanislao Bravo. In 1897, Louis Joseph Sellier was also filming reels in A Corunna such as *Fábrica de gas* [*Gas Factory*] and *Plaza de Mina* [*Mina Square*]. The moving photographs also reached the Canary Islands that same year. All these reels would be shown at country fairs by the travelling photographers and even in makeshift booths [*barracas*] in some cities, as recreated in Lorenzo Llobet Gràcia's *Vida en sombras* [1948 *A Life in Shadows* – released briefly in 1953].

The social context

Nevertheless, only in Barcelona and Valencia did the enthusiasm and interest in this new form of entertainment match the excitement and investment that prevailed in other European cities during these first two decades. Spain in 1896 was still a predominantly rural economy, ruled by a reactionary government. Many agrarian problems needed to be resolved as most of the land was still owned by a privileged minority, while famines persisted. There were few exports apart from wines, oranges and cork, and hardly any industry away from Barcelona and Bilbao. Only about 9% of the population lived in cities of more than 100,000 inhabitants, and transport was problematic. The first Education Minister was not appointed until 1900, and compulsory education to the age of 12 only became law in 1908, and illiteracy still continued to prevail.[5] Under these circumstances Spain could not support the industrial development of this new entertainment technology. Luis Buñuel recalled:

> in my own village of Calanda, where I was born on the twenty-second of February, 1900, the Middle Ages lasted until World War I. It was a closed and isolated society, with clear and unchanging distinctions among the classes. (1987: 8)

(not in Seguin's French original, but included on p. 8 of the translated book), but the cameraman is unnamed; see as well Pérez Perucha (in Gubern, 1995: 25). García Fernández dates the Jimeno reels at 1899 (2002: 22) and as 1897 (2002: 44) – thus begin the problems of chronicling Spanish Cinema.

5   For more information on education, see José Álvarez Junco (in Graham & Labanyi, 1995: 45–51).

Spain suffered greatly from civil unrest and political strife, which intensified its social problems; and certain intellectuals and authors, subsequently
known as the Generation of '98, were concerned with questions of national
identity as they experienced a crumbling society.[6] In 1898, not long after the
conclusion of the Carlist wars in 1876, the nation was again in conflict. Now
against the USA, Spain was defeated over Cuba and also lost its last colonies
of Puerto Rico and the Philippines, retaining just a few territories in North
Africa, which would require further financial and military commitments it
could ill afford. These historical upheavals would later become the context
of many feature films, but meanwhile the loss of these colonies was a loss
for the country's economy, fuelled class struggles and inspired profound self-
doubts as young Spaniards were killed in vain.

Fructuós Gelabert i Badiella (1874–1955)

In Barcelona, Fructuós Gelabert was one of the many photographers fascinated by the potential of moving pictures. He was a talented autodidact, and
to chronicle his progress is to exemplify the development of the medium in
Spain during its first twenty years. With a static camera of his own design
Gelabert started filming many subjects, such as workers leaving factories,
trains arriving at stations, ships in Catalan harbours and, of course, parishioners coming out of church. *Procesión de las hijas de María de la parroquia
de Santa María de Sans* [1902 *Procession of the Daughters of Mary from
the Parish of Santa María de Sans*] shows the young girls in procession with
white dresses, gloves and veils, while the nuns in black make sure they keep
up and stay in line. Some girls fall behind and have to catch up, others wave
to relatives in the crowd. It starts to rain and they are given umbrellas, while
some spectators try to attract the camera's attention.[7] Some reels clearly take
the form of news items and documentaries, such as *Visita de doña María
Cristina y don Alfonso XIII a Barcelona* [1898 *Doña María Cristina and
(her young son) Don Alfonso's Visit to Barcelona*], or the visit of the British
Navy to Barcelona Harbour [1901]. The latter shows careful editing and
structuring of shots: the opening panning shot of a destroyer with breakwa-
ters in the foreground is repeated in the penultimate scene, which precedes
another panning shot of the ship, this time including the first glimpse of the
Royal Navy ensign. The version viewed is 45 seconds long, but as with all

---

6   Illiteracy is an important element for Pilar Miró's *El crimen de Cuenca* [1979 *The
Cuenca Crime*] and the Generation of '98 is evoked in her film *El pájaro de la felicidad* [1993
The Bird of Happiness].

7   The copy viewed in the Filmoteca Española (A 2006) is 1.40 minutes long, but does
show occasional jumps, perhaps indicating small cuts.

these early reels it is impossible to know if they correspond exactly to what was originally filmed.[8] Gelabert's *Barcelona en 1908* is 4.23 minutes and was filmed from the top of a moving tram as it travelled through five different districts. It also shows considerable editing and reveals interesting reactions from the crowds, suggesting that traffic accidents were just as likely to occur in those days as now. Was this camera travelling on a tram a primitive example of a high-angle tracking shot? Gelabert also filmed sporting events: *Carreras de caballos en el hipódromo de Barcelona* [1902 *Horses at the Barcelona Race Course*] or *Carreras de bicicletas en el parque* [1903 *Bicycle Races in the Park*], as well as bullfighting scenes that soon became very popular exports. There is no known coverage by Gelabert of the violent social disturbances in Barcelona during the General Strike of 1902, the disturbances of 1906, or the Tragic Week of July 1909. However, these were covered by other photographers, such as Josep Gaspar i Serra's *Los sucesos de Barcelona* [*The Barcelona Incidents*], many copies of which were exported, and Ricard de Baños who, with his brother Ramon, also filmed the events as well as some of the Moroccan conflict in 1909.[9]

Gelabert acquired a taste for recording more than slices of life. In August 1897 he had already made the earliest surviving Spanish film with a rudimentary story line, *Riña en un café* [*Brawl in a Café*], in line with the Lumières' *L'Arroseur arrosé* [1895 *The Sprayer Sprayed*] shown at Promio's first display. It is only 48 seconds long, though one copy viewed is preceded by a brief moment of Gelabert himself filmed a few months before his death, some 58 years later, with no more context than the fact he is sitting down, enclosed in an iris, holding his walking stick and then rolling it across his lap. Filmed outdoors with a static camera, *Riña* presents on the right of the screen six young, well-dressed men sitting at two round tables, in front of a house with a large barred window. One of them claps his hands to call the waiter, who arrives from the left of the screen, takes the order and leaves. A young lady comes down the steps, from the top left of the screen, to say something to the only young man not wearing a jacket in the foreground on the right. She then continues her journey off screen and a jealous (?) young man in a black suit, hat and no tie, comes round the corner of the house, or café, to challenge his rival in shirt sleeves. Provoked, the latter stands up, only to be pushed back. He takes a swing with a closed fist at his challenger, and both spin round by which time three of their friends are restraining them. A fourth

---

[8]   This version is part of a tape entitled, not surprisingly given what has been lost or still needs to be restored, *Imágenes perdidas* [*Lost Frames*].

[9]   These ten years of Catalan history were filmed as *La ciutat cremada* [1976 Antonio Ribas *La ciudad quemada/The Burned City*]. The historical context can be followed up in Álvarez Junco (Gies, 1999: 76).

friend steps in to keep them apart. He addresses the two rivals, gets them to shake hands, after which they both take a step back, and cut.

From the start Gelabert had engaged with special effects films like *Choque de dos transatlánticos* [1899 *Colliding Liners*], and went on to film more extended comedies including *Cerveza gratis* [1906 *Free Beer*], *Guardia burlado* and *Los competidores* [both 1908 *The Tricked Guard*, *The Rivals*]. In the last two he filmed the actors enunciating their words very clearly, and the dialogue would be repeated aloud behind the screen during the projection. A taste for practical jokes may have given rise to the first candid camera, *Los guapos de la vaquería del parque* [1907, *The Dandies at the Park Dairy*]. The same year he filmed his first literary adaptation, *Terra Baixa* [*The Lowlands*] based on a play by Àngel Guimerà, and he was the first to be prosecuted (unsuccessfully) for plagiarism because of his *Mala raza* [1911 *Bad Blood*], based on 1904 Nobel Prize Winner José Echegaray's play *De mala raza*. Many of his reels were sold abroad, mostly to Pathé. Gelabert did not amass a fortune, but earned enough to carry on experimenting. The *IMDb* records 111 titles for Gelabert, including *La Dolores* [1908], a folkloric melodrama based on a popular song sung diegetically in the film, but as films were soundless the words are included as intertitles: 'If you're going to Catalayud / Ask for Dolores / She is a very beautiful girl / And fond of granting favours.'[10] Other verses are also included as intertitles, dramatised by the action: 'Where there are flowers there are thorns / Where there are wolves you find lambs / Where there are doves you find hawks / And where there's love there is jealousy.'[11] This use of intertitles for songs in silent films became common practice, though the spectators would usually be able to hear the live accompaniment of a gramophone, musician or small orchestra, which was just as well given the 63% illiteracy rate in Spain at the time. An 18-minute fragment of *La Dolores* remains, and it is already quite sophisticated, using crosscutting to narrate individual sequences and different camera angles within a single scene. It includes a bullfight in the main square, a constructed set, introduced by a slow panning shot, which moves from the spectators on the rooftops down to the square to evoke, with an impressive number of extras, a vast crowd. Links are made with irises either opening out or closing in as well as fades and dissolves, and linking intertitles. There is an example of a superimposed image of Dolores on a statue of the Virgin Mary to convey one of the lover's thoughts and give an ironic twist to another verse that appears in the intertitles: 'It is the Virgin of Zaragoza / Who has the most altars / And there is not a single Aragonese

---

[10] 'Si vas a Calatayud / pregunta por la Dolores / que es una chica muy guapa / y amiga de hacer favores.'

[11] 'Donde hay flores hay espinas / Donde hay lobos hay corderos / Donde hay palomas hay halcones / Y donde hay amores hay celos.'

heart / Who does not have one in his heart.'[12] One also notices that the film is longer than usual for the period, and as the narrative moves forward at a very brisk pace there is an increase in the frequency of intertitles, a feature that would stay with the industry. This popular story would be filmed again by Maximiliano Thous Orts in 1924, Florián Rey in 1940 and Benito Perojo in 1947. It was clearly a favourite, demonstrating Spanish taste for musicals as the audience frequently participated vocally. Also very successful was the 1915 *El nocturno de Chopin* [*Chopin's Nocturne*] made with Adrià Gual and starring Margarita Xirgú, remade in 1932 by Ramón Martínez de Rivas. Gelabert was 23 when he filmed his first reel in 1897 and, although he died aged 81 in 1955, his last film, *La puntaire* [*La encajera*/*The Lacemaker*] was made in 1928, coinciding with the arrival of sound on the world's screens. He stayed with photography.[13]

Segundo de Chomón y Ruiz (1871–1929)

Perhaps the most important pioneer of the period was Segundo de Chomón, an Aragonese like Florián Rey and Luis Buñuel. After working in Paris for Méliès, colouring films, he experimented back in Barcelona with his own trick photography and creative montage. His first films used models, *Choque de trenes* [1902 *Train Crash*], and double exposures for *Pulgarcito* [1904 *Tom Thumb*] or *Gulliver en el país de los gigantes* [1905 *Gulliver in the Land of the Giants*].[14] From 1905 to 1909 Chomón was back in Paris employed with his wife by Pathé to compete with Méliès's special effects films. With *Los guapos del parque* and *El hotel eléctrico* [1904 **The Park Dandies* and 1905 *The Electric Hotel*], he had reached a considerable level of technical sophistication with his cinematographic experiments. *El hotel ...* is 4.45 minutes long and is said to be the first shot with single-frame exposures after the objects have been moved (stop-motion) to give the illusion of continuous movement as in a cartoon, although credit for this innovation is usually attributed to J. Stuart Blackston's 1907 *The Haunted Hotel* (Thompson, 2003: 52). *El hotel eléctrico* is technically impressive, using a static camera and judicious cuts that toggle between full shots of the rooms and close-ups. A couple, said to be

[12] 'Es la virgen del Pilar / la que más altares tiene / y no hay pecho aragonés / que en su fondo no la tiene.'

[13] Jordan & Allinson mention a sound remake of *Riña en un café* in 1952, but I have not seen it 2005:4.

[14] As in the case of Gelabert, different sources indicate different dates for these reels, which confirms how much work is still needed in order to establish the early history of Spanish cinema. These dates are cited from Gubern (1995: 40), but see conflicting dates in Porter i Moix, 1992: 71, or Jordan & Allinson, 2005: 4, or the *IMDb*; the same is true for *El hotel eléctrico*.

played by Chomón himself and his wife Jeanne Mathieu, arrives in the lobby of an automated hotel where everything is done for the guests by the power of electricity, controlled by switches mounted on a table. The humorous tone is set right from the beginning, the gentleman having bushy sideburns and a checked suit that bring to mind a Harlequin's costume. As they register with the receptionist their suitcases slide along the floor into the lift, move to the bedroom where they glide around the furniture in a circular dance until one, in the fifth cut and close-up, finds its place in front of a chest of drawers. It opens by itself, and brushes rise from the case into a drawer that opens on its own; then cuffs, collars, bibs, tartan handkerchiefs and striped socks, all find their way into different drawers; shirts and nightshirts fold themselves before resting in their respective drawers. The lady's case is not unpacked, and the sixth cut takes us back to the landing where the lift is seen arriving and the guests enter the bedroom. They walk round the room in appreciation, sit and clap for service, as usual in Spain. A table slides in front of them with its selection of levers. The husband mimes that they need to smarten up. He sits down, and the film cuts to a close-up of his shoes and gaiters that unbuckled by themselves are brushed clean. Back to a medium shot of the room, showing the husband impressed by this automated service. He pulls another lever and his wife's handbag and coat fly away. She sits, her hair is brushed and combed, the chair turns so that the spectators can see the back of her head brushed and her hair reset in a plait. The wife pulls another lever and, in a close-up of the husband's face, we see him receiving a quick and clean shave, and his hair and sideburns are brushed. It is time to write a letter, and as the husband takes out notebook and pen from his pocket, a writing-desk slides in from the back of the room. A close-up shows a sheet of paper coming out of the centre drawer and a letter is written for him in a beautiful script, and although the margin is cut off on the left of screen the spectator can read: 'Chers parents, [In]stalles confortablement [the acute accent is added at this stage on *installés*; new line] [No]us accomplissons simplement [un] voyage des plus charmants. [M]eilleurs baisers, Laure et Bertrand.'[15] The letter in French reflects the fact that these reels had an international market; *El hotel eléctrico* was available in the USA by 1908 (*IMDb*). An unseen address is written on the envelope, the letter folds itself and the writing desk slides out of the room. Laure then rests on the bed and Bertrand lights up a cigarette, sitting with his feet up on the sofa. Cut to a wall with a number of switches where a uniformed employee, not too steady on his feet (drunk?), starts pulling the switches before falling and sliding down the wall out of the frame. Cut to a large turbine turning round with large flashes of elec-

---

[15] 'Dear Parents, Comfortably settled. We are simply having a most pleasant journey. Best kisses, Laure and Bertrand.'

tricity drawn onto the negative, while in the background the same uniformed attendant strikes his head in despair with his cap. In the bedroom all the furniture moves wildly round the room, and the wife is thrown out of bed. Cut to the lobby where the furniture is also sliding round in a chaotic dance. *Fin* [End].[16] The film demonstrates the dangers of modern technology which is far from foolproof. Judging by other film fragments showing dancing suit-cases and furniture, this type of frequently copied creative montage must have pleased spectators.

Referred to as the Spanish Méliès, one could argue George Méliès was the French Chomón (Hopewell, 1986: 10). His reels are full of cinematographic tricks, such as stopping the camera to delete or add an element, and create the magic shows that were great favourites at the time. *Les Kiriki*, given the Spanish title of *Juegos chinos* [1908 *Chinese Games*], presents with a fixed camera oriental magicians on a traditional Serlian stage complete with curtains, still a frequent frame for films in those years. The painting of a Geisha comes alive to walk round the stage with the magician. She steps onto a dais, centre-stage, to be covered by a sheet, which when removed reveals she has been changed into a large flame, into which the magician jumps. He appears to walk out of the flame with his partner, each holding a paper parasol. They bow and straighten up, holding two parasols each; another bow and they have three parasols each; a fourth bow and each of the six parasols is held by a different Geisha; with the final bow the Geishas disap-pear and the parasols float up out of the frame. These films, imitating and rivalling Méliès, are beautifully choreographed and projected at speed. One of the copies viewed (A 2006) reveals that some of the acrobats' clothes were tinted in yellow, while other reels available through Google Video have a lot more colour. *Les Vêtements cascadeurs* [1908 *Transformaciones* (*Metamor-phoses*)] presents an early example of teleportation.[17] A man in dinner jacket and his partner walk on-stage, and she then throws his head, trunk, arms and legs from one side of the stage to the other. He remains standing as himself on the left, while a mannequin is assembled on the lady's right. When she throws his clothes onto the mannequin, he becomes a mannequin and the mannequin becomes a moving railway porter. She dances and then throws the costume onto the left-hand mannequin who becomes a dancing farmer (?) as she dances a very clumsy flamenco with him. After further similar metamorphoses from left to right, the original mannequin becomes a soldier presenting arms, the one on the left a Napoleonic drummer in bearskin, and

---

[16] A Google Video search for *Segundo Chomón* will reveal a number of his reels, albeit poor copies within a reduced frame. A search for *Méliès* shorts will also be productive.

[17] I am thinking here of *Star Trek* [the TV series], and *The Fly* [1986 David Cronenberg]. Kinder refers to this reel as a 'castrating image [...] emblematic of the regional filmmaker's plight' (1993: 407).

finally the soldier on the right is changed into Napoleon himself, while she waves a French flag. All are early examples of trick photography to amaze the spectators. Hopewell relates that formal complaints were raised at Chomón's cruelty when he filmed a ballerina and her horse falling off a highwire in *Atracción de circo* [n.d. *Circus Act*], and he had to explain the trick photography and how the models were used (1986: 11). Perhaps more ambitious was the 6.5 minutes of *Viaje a Jupiter* [1909 *Journey to Jupiter*], a humorous film without intertitles that tells the story of a king, identified by his ermine collar and cloak with fleurs de lys, who, in spite of his wizard and his jester, wishes to visit the planet Jupiter. He does so, only to receive a good beating before being thrown off the planet by Jupiter himself. He discovers at the end of his fall back to earth that it was only a dream. This is achieved by a cut to clouds which, following a frame of painted stars, move from right to left and then thin out to reveal the king's four-poster bed in his chamber, where he had fallen asleep. The film multiplies the links between sequences, which previously had been of one cut. For instance, the king wishes his wizard to see the planets more clearly, and they leave his study; cut as the two cross to the front porch of a cathedral and disappear round the corner; cut to a balcony seen from inside a full-length window; cut to a low-angle shot of the balcony as the two come out and the wizard hands over his telescope to the king.

Chomón continued to develop special effects, worked on colour processing, which Pathé was anxious to improve commercially, and refined the presentation of credits and intertitles on the screen. After his return to Barcelona in 1910, he made *Soñar despierto* [1911 *The Daydream*] in cinemacoloris, with some very effective editing and special effects. Like Gelabert, he also filmed a few *zarzuelas*: *El pobre Valbuena* and *Carceleras* [both 1910, *Poor Valbuena* and *Carcelera, Prison Songs*], and the following year *El puñado de rosas* [*The Handful of Roses*].[18] Perhaps because the cinema industry was not as developed in Spain, in 1912 he accepted a contract from Itala Film of Turin. There he worked with Giovanni Pastrone (aka Piero Fosco) on six films including the Punic epic *Cabiria* [1914], for which he developed what is credited as a moving camera, and the puppet animation *La guerra e il sogno di Momi* [1916 *Momi Dreams of the War*]. Both worked with Luigi Borgnetto on his war film *Maciste Alpino* [1916 *The Warrior*]. He returned to Paris in 1924 and worked out the special effects of, among other films, Benito Perojo's *El negro que tenía el alma blanca* [1927 *The Black Man With a White Soul*] and Abel Gance's *Napoléon* [1926/7], but died in 1929 after contracting a fever whilst filming in Morocco.[19]

---

[18] These are the light operettas described more fully in chapter 2.

[19] Almodóvar's sequence 'El amante menguante' in *Hable con ella* [2002 *'The Shrinking Lover' in *Speak to Her*] can be considered a twenty-first-century tribute to Chomón's inventive work, as well as Jack Arnold's 1957 *The Incredible Shrinking Man*.

Film companies and the blind man

By the beginning of the twentieth century there were already a number of foreign distributors with offices in Barcelona, set up to satisfy the appetite for the moving images: Pathé in 1900, Diorama in 1902 and Gaumont in 1904. Gaumont, through their agents Antoni Pàdua Tramullas and his son Antoni Tramullas Beltrán, had first tried their Chronophone in Zaragoza, an early attempt to synchronise sound with picture, placing the apparatus behind the screen. Contracted by Pathé, Ferdinand Zecca had made the first known adaptation of Cervantes's novel *Don Quichotte* in 1903, filmed in Spain for authentic local colour, and Gaumont immediately followed with their own version; Méliès made his adaptation in 1908. These foreign films were competing with local productions, and the first Spanish adaptation was Narciso Cuyàs's *Don Quijote* of 1908. Many narrative reels were being made, their length gradually increasing and involving growing numbers of actors and technicians.

Antonio Cuesta's *El ciego de la aldea* [1906 *The Village Blind Man*], filmed by Àngel Garcia Cardona and Ángel Huerta for Cuesta Films of Valencia, is a good example of the small but active companies busy at the time. To minimise expenses they filmed on location and thus preserved interesting images of contemporary rural Spain. There are fragments missing from *El ciego de la aldea*, but the present reconstructed reel is 11 minutes long and maintains a coherent narrative. It uses a fixed camera and is filmed mostly in very long takes by today's standards, with four outside locations and one painted set. The fragments begin with a two-shot close-up of a little girl talking to a smiling blind man, clearly identifying them as the central characters, although they are actually marginal to the action that follows: a suspense of abduction and violence. This is the Spanish ballad tradition whereby blind men recite ballads [*romances de ciego*] on fictional, historical or news items in order to earn their alms, as illustrated in the pre-credit and concluding sequence of Pilar Miró's *El crimen de Cuenca* [1979 *The Cuenca Crime*]. Students of literature will recall the sixteenth-century masterpiece *Lazarillo de Tormes*, but in this case the relationship is very different and the two characters are here presented positively, an image that Buñuel will subvert later in *Los olvidados* [1950 *The Forgotten Ones*]. The blind man and his guide will be the only witnesses to the crime. The first cut is to one side of a street lined by orange trees (?). The blind man and small girl are seen walking from the top left of the screen to the bottom right, where five thugs are loitering with probable intent. The diagonal angle of the camera is interesting as it avoids the two-dimensional effect of the right-angled shot standard at the time. The little girl asks for alms, and is refused. A wealthy couple, given their costumes, appear on screen from the bottom right of the frame, and the gentleman also refuses alms until his wife persuades him to be more generous before moving on. The girl informs her blind man and jumps with joy. As they move off screen the thugs take an interest and vote to see which pair they will follow, deciding to follow wealth rather than poverty. Cut to outside the village where the young girl sits the blind man at the foot of a column or 'rollo', that frequently commemorate an event in the Spanish countryside; behind them across the road is a shrine. After they hug each other, the blind man gives the girl a piece of bread, which she is about to devour but then decides to share with her blind man. An ubiquitous dog, which intrudes in various frames, is seen for the first time. When the blind man decides to move and is helped up, the camera pans slightly to keep them in the centre of the frame, and the five thugs arrive. Two take the girl to one side and the other three are shown wondering whether to threaten the blind man. They decide to let them be and move off screen. Cut to another location, in front of a long wall, where the bearded leader of the ruffians arrives to search the landscape as he faces the spectators. He is joined by his four companions and tells them where to hide. A shadow is seen on the road in the bottom right-hand frame, followed by a horsedrawn coach. The wealthy couple get out of the coach and, when it leaves, they are gagged from behind by the four thugs, this time holding revolvers. The lady is taken away by two of the kidnappers, whilst the gentleman is made to sign a ransom note before he is blindfolded and taken in the opposite direction. The bearded leader goes off in a third direction with his ransom note. Cut to the fourth outside location with another wall in the background and in the mid-ground a door that leads to an underground dwelling, or furnished cave. The blind man arrives with his guide and they sit outside in the foreground beside a century plant, which actually masks them from anyone coming into the frame, except from the front. They both panic as two of the thugs come on screen carrying a body wrapped in a blanket into the underground dwelling. They shut the door and the young girl rushes to look through the keyhole. Cut to the inside room: a painted set filmed in the open air, but seen from the little girl's point of view. The body is left in the room and the ruffians make for the door. Cut to the outside as they come out of the dwelling and leave the frame. The young girl leads her blind man into the cave and they discover the body. While they are trying to help, the gentleman arrives outside with three Civil Guards. The young girl, who has come out again, calls them inside where the blind man is trying to remove the body's blindfold. The husband unties the knots and recognises his wife. The guards search the dwelling, but the young girl has heard a noise outside. All hide and the five kidnappers enter to find the room empty. They are arrested at gunpoint and led out by the guards. Husband and wife hug each other, safe and reunited, while the young girl jumps for joy clapping her hands and is then hugged by the reunited couple. They then search for the blind man who is still hiding, and after more hugs all leave the dwelling. Crime does not pay and virtue brings its own joy and rewards, a very different theme from the 1554 *Lazarillo de Tormes*.

This set a trend for what were to be defined as rural (melo)dramas, such as Cuesta's *El pastorcito de Torrent* [1908 *The Little Shepherd from Torrent*] or Codina's *El tonto de la huerta* [1912 *The Orchard Idiot*] based on a Blasco Ibañez novel. In contrast, Cuesta Films' main productions were news features and bullfighting sequences to satisfy the export market. These last newsreels led to the first bullfighting farce *Benítez quiere ser torero* [1910 *Benítez Wants to Be a Bullfighter*], also directed by Àngel Garcia Cardona, in which after causing havoc an overgrown Benítez is finally arrested and given a good spanking by his mother. This was filmed one year before Mack Sennett's first Keystone comedy and four years before Charles Chaplin was signed up.

Melodramas and Spanish exports

Very few of the early reels have survived, many are incomplete and most have been reconstructed; Pérez Perucha states that only 35 films dated between 1897 and 1931 have been identified as complete copies (Gubern, 1995: 13).[20] Many of these reels were made for both the European and American markets, and the copy of *El ciego de la aldea* viewed in Madrid has a French title: *L'Aveugle du village*. Another curious example is *Amor que mata* [*Lethal Love*] [1a]. The first version was made in 1908 by Gelabert in a greenhouse so that he could film inside with the maximum sunlight, probably the first studio used in Spain – a necessity as films became longer and more complicated, requiring more shooting time (Gorostiza, 1997: 18–19). It was refilmed in 1911 by Josep Maria and Joan Maria Codina, with Gelabert at the camera. The 11-minute fragment of this melodrama of love, jealousy and revenge held by the Filmoteca Española has a number of intertitles, signed Tibadabo Films, with written correspondence also shown on the screen to intensify and complicate the situation. In the copy viewed these are all in English, thus underlining the importance of the export market for films made in Spain. The first surviving sequence shows the hand of a lady writing an envelope to 'Jacob de Lara esq / Savoy Hotel / London', which she hands over to a young black bellboy, before starting a second letter. Cut to a hotel where the bellboy delivers the letter. It is important that the spectators read the letter with Jacob de Lara: 'A Gentleman cannot take in marriage the daughter of a sinful woman. Naturally you do not know the family Velez

---

[20] At present one cannot even be certain of the dates of some existing films or of other details. Perhaps owing to the inaccuracies of the original press reports, there are therefore considerable discrepancies in the sources quoted for further reading in the Introduction and at the end of the chapter.

1a The crowded set of Gelabert's *Amor que mata* (1909)

as you have only shortly been introduced into Society, but if you care to inform yourself about them you will surely renounce the love of Martha, which would be a stain and a dishonour to you. A friend.' Stilted English apart, the deep focus, which includes people and carriages as well as palm trees outside the window of the hotel, belies the Savoy in London. Jacob de Lara, esquire, leaves the hotel and gets into a horsedrawn carriage, tracked by a high angle from a moving vehicle immediately in front of the carriage, which is followed by a motor car. Cut to a stationary camera as the carriage arrives at its destination. Jacob gets out and the camera follows him round to the notice he reads by the door of a building 'Centro de Informaciones Prinp.ᵃˡ'. Cut to the lady we left writing the second letter. She is now writing the address 'Miss Martha de Velez / 56 Broad Street / London'. This letter is given to a white maid in uniform who delivers it to a young lady in her own sitting room. The young lady reads her letter: 'You cannot possibly marry Jacob. Your mother's past raises up like an infrangible barrier between you and an honourable man. A good friend.' The next intertitle states that 'A few hours afterwards, the terrible truth.' There follow two shots of another letter delivered outside the hotel and then a cut to the bar-restaurant where it will be read. This shot includes the open door in the background, through which Mr de Lara enters while the hotel personnel can be seen in the hall behind him. There is a slight pivot of the camera to keep him in frame as he sits at a table. Behind him there is a mirror, fragmented by a decorative inner frame, in which can be seen a painting on the opposite wall, a vase and a man sitting down at another table: a mise-en-scène that gives the image greater depth. The letter is from the private detective of the previously contracted 'Information Agency', dated 'London the 15th. March 1914'. It informs him that 'Mrs de Velez life during her widowhood has been extremely gallant until her daughter, having finished her education, came out of School three months ago' and that Martha was possibly not Mr de Velez's daughter. Jacob stands, and the intertitle reads: 'I want to see her again.' Meanwhile the first woman is at home reading a newspaper and comes across a social announcement: 'Miss de Velez is laid up in account of a sport accident. We sincerely wish her a soon recovery.' The penultimate intertitle reads: 'The end of a vengeance', as Martha is seen to swoon and die in front of the doctor and Mr de Lara, after her mother admits in the last intertitle 'It is true… Forgive ne! This is the punishment of my sin!'[21] The first woman, who wrote the two cruel letters, is seen in hat and coat behind a glass door at the back. Given the lack of motivation for the letter-writing woman, who caused young Martha to die of grief at the revelation and confession of her mother's mistake and the consequences for her own future, one can only presume that the film asks for sympathy for the innocent and sensitive victim of the revenge.

Historical and literary inspirations

By this stage melodramas and comedies were not the only topics for these early reels. In the search for new plots, historical subjects also became favourite narratives. To the creationist approach implicit in comedies, and the realist approach of other stories,[22] these early historical films adapted theatrical conventions as the cameramen-directors started hiring theatre companies to perform their scripts. In 1909 Gelabert had already made the historical film *Guzmán, el Bueno* [*Guzman, the Good*] about a father who sacrifices his own son rather than surrender the city to the Moors, starring the famous stage actress Margarita Xirgú and the Señora Guerra, who had appeared in *Amor que mata*. The film is credited with the first use of three-dimensional constructed scenery (Gorostiza, 1997: 19). Another example of such historical films is the remaining 14-minute fragment of *Don Pedro el cruel* [1911 *King Peter the Cruel*] made by Albert Marro and Ricard de

---

[21] All these stilted English quotations are from the intertitles read on the copy stored in the Filmoteca Española, including the 'Forgive ne!' for 'me!'

[22] The term 'realist' is used to describe films that attempt to recreate a slice of life in the Lumière tradition, and 'creationist' to refer to films that exploit all the cinematographic possibilities of the moving images in the Chomón/Méliès innovation.

Baños for their company Hispano Films, with brother Ramon de Baños at
the camera. The film is a page of Castilian history that had been a great
favourite through the many medieval ballads that were written down in the
late fifteenth century, and frequently put on the stage in the seventeenth
century, the Golden Age of Spanish literature, thus indicating a literary precedent and courting for cinema a respectability denied by some intellectual
critics. Marro and Baños's film presents certain conventions, initiated by
Gelabert, that were becoming current practice. For instance, after the title,
the main actors (in this case five) come out in front of a curtain and bow to
the left, right and centre, as they would in a stage performance. The actors
can appear as themselves, in dinner suits or long dresses, or in character
wearing their costume: in this case King Pedro comes through the curtain
sullen and threatening. The first intertitle, 'First Part', appears, while other
films may start with a 'Prologue'. This intertitle is followed by the subject
of the first part 'The Anonymous Letter', all printed in upper case.[23] Some
intertitles are here also presented in fifteenth-century printed Gothic script on
what is clearly a hand-drawn unrolled parchment with a seal, all to enhance
the ambience. After the initial intertitles, the curtain is raised, revealing the
sumptuous painted set of a gothic chamber with table and chair in the centre.
The set is clearly attempting to be realistic, creating a perspective with doors
and a window. King Don Pedro paces across the screen, stops at his table
and reads a letter: 'I warn your Grace that the three illegitimate brothers
are conspiring against your life.'[24] Other sequences are filmed outside, and
show cinematographic development as a number of scenes are edited together
to present more continuous movement. The camera is still basically static,
although there are on occasions slight pans to keep the actor within the frame,
and there is in the fragment one example of an inserted close-up, although
it is not related to a point of view shot. Full use is made of the frame as,
on some occasions, related activities simultaneous to the central action are
included in the margin of the frame. In spite of the growing use of intertitles,
the characters are seen to speak for a lot longer than their attributed statement, although in this film much of the information is conveyed by exaggerated theatrical gestures, eye and mouth movements. Indeed, whereas some
directors filmed with their friends or emerging film actors, others, as in this
case, contracted theatrical companies for their films.

Albert Marro and Ricard de Baños, not forgetting brother Ramon at the
camera, made a productive partnership during the second decade of the twentieth century, investing into subsequent projects the profits from documentaries
and reels sold. But it was never enough money! Ricard de Baños had acquired

[23] 'PRIMERA PARTE', 'PRÓLOGO', 'EL ANÓNIMO'.
[24] The Spanish is deliberately stilted to look old-fashioned: 'Prevengo á vos que los tres
hermanos bastardos conspiran contra vuestra vida.'

his skills working for Gaumont in Paris. They had started off with documentaries in 1905 and 1906 respectively, including the Moroccan campaign and the Barcelona street unrests of 1909. They soon moved on to literary adaptations of nineteenth-century plays such as *Don Juan Tenorio* [1908],[25] *Locura de amor* [1909 *The Mad Queen*], *Don Juan de Serrallonga, o los bandoleros de las Guillerías* [1910], *Los amantes de Teruel* [1912 **The Lovers of Teruel*], *La fuerza del destino* [1913 **The Power of Fate*]. They also adapted, with the authors' enthusiastic and active participation, successful contemporary plays like Benavente's *La malquerida* [1914 **The Ill-Loved*], and even novels like Blasco Ibáñez's *Entre naranjos* [1914 **In the Orange Grove*] and *Sangre y arena* [1916 *Blood and Sand*]. It is a measure of the films' appeal that some would be remade more than once.[26] By 1916 the brothers had split from Marro and founded their own company, Royal Films.

Both Jacinto Benavente and Vicente Blasco Ibáñez were great enthusiasts of the developing entertainment technology. Subsequently seventeen of Benavente's plays were turned into Spanish films (*IMDb*), and eleven of Blasco Ibáñez's novels were filmed, including the Rudolph Valentino classics, *The Four Horsemen of the Apocalypse* [1921 Rex Ingram; 1961 Vicente Minnelli] and *Blood and Sand* [1922 Fred Niblo; 1941 Rouben Mamoulian]. Greta Garbo started her US career in 1926 in two films based on Blasco Ibáñez's novels, *The Torrent* [*Entre naranjos*] directed by the uncredited Monta Bell, and *The Temptress* [*La tierra de todos*] directed again by Fred Niblo just after his *Ben Hur* of 1925. These received implicit praise in terms of parodies, such as Gilbert Pratt's 1922 *Mud and Sand* with Stan Laurel, or Mack Sennett's 1924 *Bull and Sand*, while the University of George Washington honoured Blasco Ibáñez with an honorary degree in 1920.

Adrià Gual, painter and all-round theatre man from Barcelona, also took to cinema and with support from friends founded the Barcinógrafo in 1913. In 1914 he adapted and filmed Calderón de la Barca's seventeenth-century stage masterpiece *El alcalde de Zalamea* [**The Mayor of Zalamea*], casting his stage actors and Joaquim Carrasco, who had gone straight into film acting. In the same year he made the first version of *La gitanilla* [*The Gypsy Girl*] based on Cervantes's short story, and *Misterio de dolor* [**Mystery of Grief*], directing his own script adapted from his own play, and for which he designed sets and costumes, and did his own editing. This rural melodrama, reflecting careful framing and composition, has been praised for its paced editing from general to medium shots to psychological close-ups (Miquel

---

[25] They remade the film two years later in 1910 with the same actors. See also García Fernández (1985: 30–1), for the intertitles of Baños's third remake of the film in 1922.

[26] For instance, *Locura de amor* was remade in 1948 by Juan de Orduña, starring Aurora Bautista and Fernando Rey, and as *Juana la loca* in 2001 by Vicente Aranda with Pilar López de Alaya and Daniele Liotti.

Porter i Moix, in Pérez Perucha, 1997: 34–6). It was in those years that the Barcinógrafo contracted Margarita Xirgú to act in five melodramas directed by Magí Murià between 1915 and 1917. Ten years before she had acted in two of Gelabert's historical films, and she would return to the cinema once more in 1938 to act in García Lorca's *Bodas de sangre* [*Blood Wedding*] directed by Edmundo Guibourt in his only recorded film; this was in Argentina where she had emigrated before the Nationalist uprising. She obviously preferred the stage to the screen.

A frustrated film industry

However, despite these early talents mostly centred on Barcelona, a city looking forward and to the rest of Europe, the interest in cinema in Spain did not match that of the rest of Europe. This was probably related to a fragmentation of energies as well as lack of substantial capital investments, firm commercial organisation and industrial planning (Pozo Arenas, 1984: 21; Jordan & Allinson, 2005: 5); one could also add 'an indifferent government, [and] a meddling Church' (Stone, 2002: 15). Over the years numerous small companies were created.[27] These included Macaya y Marro (1902, with Chomón), Films Barcelona (1906, originally Diorama), Hispano Films (1906, whose large glass gallery to film indoors with maximum sunlight was destroyed in a fire in 1918), Iris Films (1907), Tibidabo (1913), Barcinógrafo (1913), Boreal Films (1914), Royal Films (1914), Condal Films (1915), Falcó (1915), Studio Films (1915, perhaps the best equipped but no competition for other European studios), Dessy Films (1917), etc. Few lasted a decade, some no more than a year, and Dessy just made one film, *El golfo* [1917 Josep de Togores i Muntades, *The Vagrant*]. All these companies were based in Barcelona, with the exception of Cuesta Films in Valencia (1904). Madrid still showed no comparable interest, and audiences there seemed to prefer live entertainment on stage with, perhaps, a reel or two as part of the variety show (Pérez Perucha, in Gubern, 1995: 82–3). Exceptions were Iberia Films and Ángel Sáenz de Heredia's Chapalo Films, both in 1913, Segre 1914, and Benito Perojo's Patria Films founded on the profit of his first short *Fulano de Tal se enamora de Manón* [1914 *Mr Someone Falls in Love with Manon*] filmed with his brother at the camera in the Retiro Park. In 1915 an attempt was made to strengthen the various dispersed interests into the Mutua de Defensa Cinematográfica [Association for the Protection of Cinema].

---

[27] As for the reels, dates cannot be certain and discrepancies are found even within the pages of the same book (García Fernández, 2002: 45–7 and 66).

Cinemas and legislation

By this time there were cinemas in a number of towns, but they were still not really respectable. As Buñuel recalls in his memoirs:

> I think I was about eight years old when I discovered the cinema,[28] at a theatre called the Farrucini. There were two doors, one exclusively for exiting, one for entering, set in a beautiful wooden façade. Outside, a cluster of lemonade sellers equipped with a variety of musical instruments hawked their wares to passersby.[29] In reality, the Farrucini was little more than a shack; it had wooden benches and a tarpaulin roof. […] The sound came from a record player hidden behind the screen. […] Movies then were little more than a curiosity, like the sideshow at a county fair.[30] They were simply the primitive product of a newly discovered techn[ology] (1987: 31; for other recollections, see Membrez, 1989: 541).

The first legislation, regulating the hygiene, furnishings and fire regulations of projection halls, appeared in 1908 after a number of accidents. In 1910 a 5% tax was imposed on entrance tickets in order to help charity funds for child protection and beggars (Pozo Arenas, 1984: 23). This was reminiscent of the licences regulating the Madrid theatres of the seventeenth century to fund the hospitals of the capital. As in those old theatres for a few years men, women and couples were segregated in different sections. Film censorship was actually established by the Royal Decrees of 28 November 1912 and 19 October 1913, at the request of Barcelona's Civil Governor to protect young people (for this legislation, see Pozo Arenas, 1984: 23–4; García Fernández, 2002: 275–7). The decrees confirm Catalonia as the most important centre of film activity at the time, the 'motor-centre from where radiates all cinematographic developments in the whole of Spain'.[31] The Governor's request was not provoked by salacious films, such as those alluded to in Ramón Gómez de la Serna's *Cinelandia* (p. 111),[32] but by the inclusion of too much violence in a film called *La posada sangrienta* [*The Bloody Inn*] (Pérez Bowie, 1996: 65–7). The projectionist had acted as self-imposed censor by placing his hand

---

[28] The original reads: 'En 1908, encore enfant, je découvris le cinema', and the following 'theatre' translates the pejorative 'l'établissement' (p. 40).

[29] The original refers to 'les cinq automates d'un limonaire', and 'passersby' translates the pejorative 'badauds' (p. 40).

[30] The original reads 'il ne s'agissait que d'une simple attraction de foire' (p. 41).

[31] Quoted from Pérez Bowie (1998: 68): 'centro motriz de donde irradia todo el movimiento cinematográfico de España entera y donde seguramente será confiado el papel de censores a personas de amplio espíritu, perfectamente capacitadas […]'.

[32] Published in 1923, *Cinelandia* is an imaginative novel, with little plot, that revels in its linguistic evocation of imagined (Hollywood) film studios. Diez Puertas mentions King Alfonso's interest in such films (2003: 297).

over the lens to blank out an image as he cranked the projector (Membrez, 1989: 542). For comparison, the USA National Board of Censorship dates from 1909, and in the UK the British Board of Censors was also established in 1912.

Fostering viewing habits

Audiences were still not all familiar with this new art of storytelling and many were unable to read the intertitles. Buñuel tells us that in Zaragoza:

> By 1914, there were actually three good theatres. [...] There was a fourth, on the Calle de los Estebanes, but I've forgotten the name. My cousin lived on that street, and we had a terrific view of the screen from her kitchen window. [...] In addition to the traditional piano player, each theatre in Zaragoza was equipped with its *explicador*, or narrator / commentator, who stood next to the screen and 'explained' the action to the audience. [...] It's hard to imagine today, but when the cinema was in its infancy, it was such a new and unusual narrative form that most spectators had difficulty understanding what was happening [on the screen]. Now we're so used to film language [Nous nous sommes habitués inconsciemment au language cinématographique], to the elements of montage, to both simultaneous and successive action, to flashbacks, that our comprehension is automatic; but in the early years the public had a hard time deciphering this new pictorial grammar. They needed an *explicador* to guide them from scene to scene (Buñuel, 1987: 32–3; see also Méndez Leite, 1965: I, 65–70 for amusing anecdotes).

These 'commentators' were also known as *picoteros* (Membrez, 1989: 542). The first magazine exclusively devoted to the new art, *Arte y cinematografía*, was nonetheless founded in Barcelona in 1910, with the first issue appearing on 25 September and publication lasting until the beginning of the Civil War in July 1936. It was followed the next year by *El cine* and *El mundo cinematográfico* (for other titles, see García Fernández, 1985: 42–3, or 2002: 301–3). Films were growing longer (3000 to 4000 metres), and by 1915 some had full-page advertisements in the daily press (Pérez Bowie, 1996: 26). Cinematography was becoming increasingly complex, evolving from the original static camera framing a long take in a medium shot that only changed for a new location. At first one can discern slight pivoting of the camera to keep the subject in the centre of the frame, thus initiating panning shots. Occasional close-ups were added within the context of a medium shot, and functioned as point of view shots as one realised the close-up was what the actor was pointing to; eventually a look sufficed to indicate the point of view. The scenes were gradually filmed from two, then more angles. At the same time intertitles became more numerous and verbose, even unnecessary to modern eyes as the action on screen had already conveyed the information, but they were frequently used to announce new sequences when scenes began to be shot from more than one angle.

The subtle vagrant

An interesting example is the 1917 *El golfo* [*The Vagrant*], the story of an orphan who makes good morally, financially and emotionally, after dire beginnings. It is the last known film directed by Togores and the only one produced by Dessy Films of Barcelona; very well received at the time, it did not unfortunately recover its vast production costs. González López also suggests that the many production difficulties were aggravated by Togores's insistence that the actors should use a more natural acting style than usual at the time (Pérez Perucha, 1997: 37–9). While taking up the popular theme of rewards for the hardworking underprivileged, it strove to incorporate new cinematographic techniques. It begins with a symbolic pre-credit sequence of a young boy looking down on a beach followed by a cut to other boys enjoying themselves as a group on that same beach, thus conveying the loneliness of the protagonist. The two popular stars of the time, Ernesto Vilches and Irene López Heredia, are then introduced followed by Artemio Pérez Bueno, standing small beside a horse, but the villain of the story, played by José Olózaga, is left out of the introduction. The story, which encompasses Spain and the steel furnaces of the State of Nebraska, is spread out in four units over a number of years announced by intertitles: Prologue in 1899 (boyhood), 1907 (youth), 1916 (maturity), and an Epilogue in 1919 (happy future). The narrative also includes unannounced flashbacks to the Prologue and parallel montage. Despite being produced by a Barcelona company, most of the film was shot on the Cantabrian coast and the ending was refilmed in Valencia. Using a predominantly static camera, long takes and slow panning shots are lavished on the Bilbao Bessemer converters spouting flames into the night sky or on waves breaking on the beach, to create a mood rather than move the narrative forward. There are interesting uses of the screen frame, and frames within frames, with contrasts of strong lighting on the actors' faces, even if one presents a moneylender characterised as a stereotypical Shylock with goatee, cap and rubbing his hands. A few sequences begin with close-ups, thus denying the immediate contextualisation of an establishing shot. The plot is also used as another erotetic device, creating suspense by extending and complicating the events with unexpected twists. The intertitles are not only very long, taking up at times two frames, but they have also become very literary and guide the spectators' response: 'A few days later, parting the mists with its majestic progress, there set sail from New York

harbour a liner...', followed by a long take of the ship sailing away.[33] By
the end of the film the sybaritic and deceiving aristocrat is punished, class
barriers are dissolved to promise a glorious industrial prosperity, and diligent
work and honesty are rewarded with love and money, thus giving the lie to the
title of the film – unless 'golfo' is transferred as a metaphor to the villainous
Marqués de Olaye.

Serial films

In these early days of cinema Hollywood did not yet dominate the film world;
D.W. Griffith's *Birth of a Nation* and *Intolerance* date from 1915 and 1916
respectively. Before that the film market within Europe was actually much
more flexible and free than it is today and, as suggested above, Catalonia
had a contribution to make to the international scene, which was dominated
by France. The years 1905 to 1919 saw considerable activity, which included
very successful serial films, following the French models like Louis Feuillade's *Fantômas* [started in 1913], and the following examples captured
Spanish audiences (C. Morris, 1980: 67–9): Joan and Josep Maria Codina's
El signo de la tribu [1915 *The Sign of the Tribe*] for Condal Films; or tales
of revenge following the model of the Count of Montecristo for the rival
Hispano Films, Marro's *Barcelona y sus misterios* [1916 *Barcelona and its
Mysteries,* although no copies have survived] and its sequel *El testamento de
Diego Rocafort* [1917 *The Testament of Diego Rocafort*]; Baños's *Fuerza y
nobleza* [1918 *Strength and Nobility*]; Abadal's *¿Sueño o realidad?* [1919
Dream or Reality?]. In this early competition with US imports, the serial
film was an excellent way of ensuring returning spectators for Spanish
productions, like television series today.

The impact of the Great War

In the rest of Europe, the involvement in and then the devastation of the
First World War (1914–18) changed the situation. Spain was too preoccu-
pied with its own unsettled affairs and had too much to lose economically
to get involved in the Great War (Álvarez Junco, in Gies, 1999: 77). Catalan
filmmakers were productive during this period, which Jean-Claude Seguin
refers to as a Golden Age of Cinema: 28 production companies, 165 films
and 77 documentaries (pp. 11–14 in French original (1994), or pp. 11–13 in

---

[33] 'Pocos días después, rompiendo las brumas con su andar majestuoso, zarpaba del puerto
de Nueva York un transatlántico ...'

Spanish translation (1995)). The industry benefited for a while from its film exports, and in the version of *Amor que mata* mentioned above one letter is dated 'London the 15th. March 1914' (see pp. 13–15); this in turn stimulated home production. Spain also continued to be exploited for its images of bullfighting, flamenco dancers and *bandoleros* [bandits], a popular construct from the French Romantics known as the 'espagnolades' or 'españoladas' in Spanish.[34] This type of film was ubiquitous and the genre was popular for both foreign and Spanish filmmakers, who continued to thrive on it during the Franco years. Foreign directors had come and gone since Promio made his first reels, and Spain became host to other directors, technicians and actors who passed through during the Great War.[35] Giovanni (Juan) Doria, an Italian who arrived to film bullfighting reports and melodramas, stayed in Spain and was the cameraman for *El golfo*. With Augusto Turchi (Turquí) directing, Doria also filmed one of the six versions of *Carmen* made in 1913, starring Margharita Silva, Andrea Habay and Juan Rovira,[36] two years before Cecil B. DeMille and Raul Walsh provided their own versions. The Italian Godofredo Mateldi filmed at least eight sentimental melodramas between 1915 and 1918. However, the most notorious motion picture filmed in Spain during this period was the epic *La vida de Cristóbal Colón* [*The Life of Christopher Columbus*] directed by Charles J. Drossner, who had come to Barcelona in 1916 and founded Films Cinématographiques with Émile Bourgeois for this purpose. In a Prologue and Five Parts, it was the biggest production to date and the first to be subsidised by the Spanish government, persuaded to lend museum pieces as well as contribute to the one million peseta budget, when the average Spanish film cost around 20,000 pesetas (Besas, 1995: 4). According to Méndez Leite, who praises the film very highly, there were ten French actors from the Comédie Française but the others and the crew were all Spanish (1965: I, 146–9), with Josep Maria Maristany, Ramon de Baños

---

[34] 'This patently false image of Spain was gladly accepted by the Spanish themselves' (Aranda, 1975: 108). Triana Toribio rightly addresses the term in her book (2003: 7, 19, 22–3, 43–4, 62–4). The label 'españolada/folclórica' is problematic inasmuch as some critics use it inclusively whereas others use it specifically to distinguish between further subgenres that inevitably overlap (Pineda Novo, 1991: 7–8; Lázaro Reboll, 2004: 7–10).

[35] García Fernández has compiled a list of directors, 1913–18, which can all be traced on the *IMDb* (2002: 89–90).

[36] The Filmoteca copy has French intertitles, and although it states that it is 'L'oeuvre célèbre de Mérimée apportée à l'écran d'après le livre' [The famous work of Mérimée brought to the screen according to the book] the intertitles quote directly in French from the Meilhac and Halévy libretto. The film begins with a game of 'pelota/chistera' with Don José wearing a Basque costume, while the spectators are dressed as Andalusian. For the many versions of *Carmen*, consult the *Carmen Project* on the Internet directed by Powrie and Perriam; there were 75 different versions accounted for in 2001, and Vicente Aranda released another version in 2003.

and the Frenchman Edouard Renault at the cameras. The press was rapturous, but the general public did not eventually share this enthusiasm.

Marketing an exotic Spain

Spaniards also made their reputation abroad. Raquel Meller, stage name for Francisca Marqués López, was a popular singer well known on both sides of the Atlantic. Just turned 31, she starred in Ricard de Baños's *La gitana blanca* [1918–19 *The White Gypsy Girl*] for Royal Films. It is a full melo-drama set against the Moroccan military campaign, blending Cervantes's short story 'La gitanilla' ('The Gypsy Girl') welded to a bullfighting plot including telltale birthmarks at the end to confirm identities. This film was actually collated fragments, with new scenes added, put together from the four-hour episodic series in three parts written by Josep Amich i Bert, *Los arlequines de seda y oro* [1918 *The Harlequins of Silk and Gold*]. The frag-ments viewed reveal a frequent technical problem of the time, which is the uneven quality of footage, due partly to the varying intensity of light at the time of filming and partly to the different quality of reels used. The shorter film was redistributed throughout Europe so as not to lose out on Meller's international reputation as a popular diva,[37] incorporating actual documen-tary footage of the Moroccan war and real bullfights, as well as Meller's flamenco performances. The copy viewed in the Filmoteca [A 3595] was actually distributed in Rotterdam in 1925 as *De Zigeurnerin van Barcelona* [*The Gypsy from Barcelona*], with Dutch intertitles. Meller went on to make a number of very popular films in France during the 1920s, returning to Spain (see the following chapter) with the Belgian Jacques Feyder to film in Ronda the location shots for the 1926 *Carmen*, in which Luis Buñuel appeared as one of the smugglers (Buñuel, 1987: 90). The success of the film both at home and abroad encouraged the production of more films involving gypsies and bullfighters, to the regret of Spanish critics and intellectuals. It is no surprise that the first Spanish cartoon distributed in 1917 by Fernando Marco was a bullfighting parody, *El toro fenómeno* [*The Phenomenal Bull*].

Competition from the USA

In 1917 Spain had to face up to a general strike in August, pressures that had been building up for some time for Catalan and Basque regional autonomy,

---

[37] For Meller's particular fame as a singer of 'cuplé', and this genre of song in general, see Serge Salaün (in Graham & Labanyi, 1995: 90–4), and Woods, 2004a: 43–4. She made it to the cover of *Time Magazine* on 26 April 1926.

and frequent changes of ministers until the government fell in December 1921 after the routing defeat of the Moroccan war (Álvarez Junco, in Gies, 1999: 78–80). France had lost its cinematographic predominance, despite its efficient organisation exemplified by Charles Pathé's company. The USA, given its remoteness from the areas of conflict, had been able to develop its production uninterrupted on the West Coast, improving technologically and, once the patent trust disputes were settled, organising itself commercially to outdo other national cinemas as a form of entertainment that did not depend on language. The USA became the most important purveyor of entertainment, escapism and dream on the silver screen, and in Spain it had taken 50% of the market by 1918 (Forbes & Street, 2000: 4–5). After the war, the roaring twenties was a period of growing prosperity for all, except Spain, but Europe did not regain its cinematographic predominance. Spain was hindered by the fact that it had no laboratories to manufacture film stock, was short of necessary capital investments to create a viable industry and in any case lacked an infrastructure to give it a competitive edge, in spite of some interesting technical developments and innovations (Jordan & Allinson, 2005: 5 and 6).

Further reading

The reason for the extended descriptions of the above examples is that not much information is available in print, and much less in English. Even if considerable work and research still needs to be done, general works on the history of cinema appear to ignore Spain. A specialised book on the first decade of cinema, like Christie's *The Last Machine* (1994), only mentions Segundo de Chomón, in passing on page 37, for his work in Pathé's special effects department, and it does not even include him or Gelabert in the index. For books in English that have a whole chapter on the early cinema, there is Caparrós Lera's *The Spanish Cinema* (1987), which is concise but not easily available, Besas (1985) and Higginbotham (1988). We now have Stone's *Spanish Cinema* (2002), a very readable text that does not identify all its sources for these early years, Jordan & Allinson's *Guide* (2005) and Triana Toribio's *Spanish National Cinema* (2003), which approaches the topic from a problematic perspective. Many of the books whose titles focus on a specific later period of Spanish cinema, to be recommended in subsequent chapters, frequently begin their accounts with reference to these early years. Membrez's article (1989) actually contains a lot of information in spite of its brevity. The journal *Film-Historia* (1991, online since 2001) has published articles on the early Spanish Cinema in English. In Spanish, Méndez Leite's *Historia del cine español* (vol. I) is very detailed and rich in anecdotes but sources are not quoted and, published in 1965, many assertions must now be corrected from the more reliable and academic *Historia* edited by Gubern (1995). Buñuel's autobiography ghosted by Jean Claude Carrière, *My Last Breath*, originally published in French in 1982, is also full of interesting anecdotes and descriptions of these early years but in view of its free translation it is worthwhile to check the French original even if this last does not have an index. For the ideological and cultural context, there is Graham & Labanyi (1995, part I: 25–94), and Gies (1999). Forbes & Street offer a brief but useful contextualisation of the development of European cinema in parallel to the USA, but with few references to Spain (2000, part I: 1–50).

The films themselves are not easily accessible and need to be watched in specialised institutions like the Filmotecas, although a Google Video / YouTube search will reveal pleasant surprises in spite of the poor quality of these copies. One approach to these early films is to study them with an eye to establishing more accurate facts, as well as examining innovations and the development of film narrative, as well as how films are introduced or the evolution of intertitles, while comparing them with other national productions; but basically the early history of Spanish Cinema is incomplete and needs further research centred on the contemporary press and archives.

2

The Silent Films of the Directors (1918–1930)

The Sun also rises: Madrid awakes with the rest of Spain

By the 1920s Madrid and other cities had slowly but haphazardly woken up to the potential of the cinema and started producing films in competition with Barcelona and Valencia. This was in spite of much political unrest and many social disturbances, which led to the military coup of 13 September 1923 and General Primo de Rivera's dictatorship, which remained in place until 1930 (Álvarez Junco, in Gies, 1999: 77–81). These upheavals, which may have hindered the development of the film industry, did not prevent other technological breakthroughs of social importance: in 1919 the Madrid metro was inaugurated; in 1923 the autogiro took flight; in 1924 a National Telephone Company was created, and in September of the same year the first wireless broadcast was made by Radio Barcelona. The British Broadcasting Corporation, which received its charter in 1927, had started to make informal broadcasts in 1922. For Fernando Méndez Leite, 1918 was the year that cinema in Spain blossomed as mass entertainment (1965: I, 159). By 1920 the country had some 900 to 1000 cinemas.[1] Madrid had some 30 cinemas; El Cine Doré was built in 1923 but still stands as the film house for the Filmoteca Española.[2] Barcelona had more than 50, and others were rapidly being built in the larger cities to a better standard than those remembered by Luis Buñuel (1987: 31–3).

A strong promoter of cinema, expanding as an industry, was the popular playwright and 1922 Nobel Prize winner, Jacinto Benavente, who, after the failure of his *Los intereses creados* [1918 *Vested Interests*] in the hands of Ricardo Puga,[3] founded Madrid-Cines in 1919 to film his script of *La Madona de las rosas* [*The Rose Madonna*], which he directed with Fernando Delgado. Ricard de Baños had already made a successful version of Benavente's *La*

---

[1] Pozo Arenas, 1984: 21; but figures consulted do not always agree. For 1925 Gubern has 1497 theatres (1995: 88); García Fernández 1818 (2002: 224); and Diez Puertas 1350 (2003: 40).

[2] Calle de Santa Isabel 3, the nearest metro station is Antón Martín which also serves for the Filmoteca at Calle Magdalena 10. The building is captured briefly with a low-angle shot in Almodóvar's *Hable con ella* (2002).

[3] Méndez Leite has some interesting anecdotes about this production (1965: I, 162–6).

malquerida in 1914, which was remade in 1940 by José López Rubio and as a Mexican production in 1949. However, the four directors who dominated the decade, certainly in terms of the number of films made and popularity, were José Buchs [Echandía] (1893–1973), Benito [González] Perojo (1893–1954), Fernando Delgado [Valverde] (1891–1950) and Florián Rey (Antonio Martínez del Castillo, 1894–1962). All entered the profession by acting in film, unlike the Catalan pioneers who were mostly photographers.

Madrid productions

In Madrid production companies started small and failed, as they had done in Barcelona, not through lack of talent but through lack of adequate financial investments, which partly explains the poor visual quality of their films (Pérez Perucha, in Gubern 1995: 89–94; Pozo Arenas, 1984: 29). Many companies also started by filming news items, such as reels of the Moroccan campaign and bullfighting reports, and then moved on to short comedies. These were modelled on traditional *sainetes*, very popular short urban comedies written for the popular stage and bordering on farce, usually but not always set in Madrid and exploiting local colour (*costumbrismo*). They often included songs, following the equally popular example of the *zarzuelas* (very light operettas with linking spoken scenes), which also became favourites in cinemas. Both genres reinforced comforting stereotypes (Lázaro Reboll, 2004: 8) with their sense of fun, songs, positive attitude and feel-good escapism, at a time when the social and political situation was difficult. This may account for Spanish popular taste and the success of subsequent musical films (Talens, 1998: 36). Artists and intellectuals had their own favourites, as Buñuel recalled musing over his student days in the 1920s:

> During these years, movie theatres were sprouting all over Madrid and attracting an increasingly faithful public. [...] When we went en masse from the Residencia, however, our preferences ran to American comedy. We loved Ben Turpin, Harold Lloyd, Buster Keaton, and every one in the Mack Sennett gang. Curiously, Chaplin was our least favourite (1987: 75).

This enthusiasm for Buñuel's favourites and even more for Chaplin himself, *pace* Buñuel is certainly reflected in the written works of the young poets and authors in Madrid at the time (C. Morris, 1980: 14–15, 159–63).

Chaplin and his imitators

Chaplin, or Charlot as he was called in Spain, soon became very popular when his films were exported from the USA. The first was *A Busy Day*, shown on 1 December 1914, earlier than in France. Studio Films in Barcelona immediately made short comedies with Chaplin lookalikes, and ten titles directed by Domènec Ceret appeared in that first year, collectively entitled *Serie excéntrica* [*Excentric Series*]. This was followed by José Carreras's *Charlot II y su familia* [1916 *Charlie II and His Family*] for Argos Films. There were already local comic characters, like the previously mentioned *Benítez quiere ser torero* [1910], and others like *Linito se hace torero* [1915 Adrià Gual, *Linito Becomes a Bullfighter*], or Juan Oliver's shorts with Joaquín Martínez Palomo 'Palomeque'.

In 1912, Benito Perojo, a young man who was sent with his older brother to boarding school in Hastings, England, returned to Madrid and, after his *Fulano de Tal* shorts, he created a character called Peladilla in the clear image of Chaplin. In 1915, he directed and acted in five short films as Peladilla with María Moreno, although only *Clarita y Peladilla en el fútbol* [1915 *... At a Football Match*] and *Clarita y Peladilla van a los toros* [1915 *... Go to the Bullfight*] have survived with meaningful footage. His company Patria Films, created that year in Madrid, made the Peladilla reels at the cost of 700 pesetas each, subsequently sold at 4000 pesetas per reel (Gubern, 1994: 38–46). In 1916, he passed the company on to Julio Roesset while he went to Paris where he acquired more film experience before returning in 1923.

Some twelve years later the actor Pedro Elviro developed another comic character in *Pitouto, fabricante de suicidios* [1928 *Suicide Manufacturer*] directed by Francisco Elías, just back from eight years in the USA where he wrote intertitles in films for the Spanish-speaking markets. This was followed by *Pitouto, mozo de granja* [1930 Florián Rey, *Farm-Hand*], *Tiene su corazoncito* [1930 Florián Rey, *With His Little Heart*], and many others. The Pitouto films were subsequently post-synchronised in Paris. Suffering from lack of work in Spain when sound films arrived, Pedro Elviro went to France in 1931 to act in French and Spanish films, and then moved to Mexico where he appeared in his last comedy in 1970; in all these countries he occasionally represented his comic creation Pitouto, including Buñuel's dark comedy *Subida al cielo* [1952 *Mexican Bus Ride*].

Child stars

Spain also had its own child star, Alfredo Hurtado, known as Pitusín. Before his seventh birthday he was credited in the cast of *La revoltosa* [*The Mischief-Maker*] and in *La medalla del torero* [*The Bullfighter's Medal*], both directed by Florián Rey in 1924. The same year he appeared as Pitusín in *Los granujas* [Fernando Delgado *The Little Rascals*] and in *La buenaventura de Pitusín* [Luis Alonso *Pitusín's Luck*]. The following year he starred in Florián Rey's *El Lazarillo de Tormes*, only very loosely based on the sixteenth-century classic tale.

Bullfighting

The bullfighting burlesques mentioned above demonstrate the popularity of
the subject both in Spain and with the export markets. Films range from
the 'documentaries' on the death of José Gómez 'Gallito' in the bullring
at Talavera de la Reina, *La muerte de Joselito* [*The Death of Joselito*], of
which at least four films were made in 1920, one of which was by Gelabert,
to Alejandro Pérez Lugín's *Currito de la Cruz* [1925 *Currito of the Cross*],
based on the director's own successful novel.[4] Bullfighting is also the subject
of the first recorded film by a Spanish woman, Helena Cortesina, dancer,
actress and director: *Flor de España o la leyenda de un torero* [1921 *The
Flower of Spain or the Legend of a Bullfighter*], in which she also acted with
her two sisters Ofelia and Angélica.[5] In the same years Jeanne Roques, known
as Musidora, scripted, produced, directed, and acted in four films in Spain,
including *Vicenta* [1919] and *Tierra de los toros* [1924 *The Land of Bulls*]
described by Pérez Perucha as 'a strange and avant-garde experiment'.[6]

Musicals

Filmed versions of *zarzuelas*, despite the obvious limitations of silent screens,
were made on the reputation of their stage performances, and like the comic
sainetes were a great favourite. These were the dominant genres of the 1920s
although already tried by Gelabert, Chomón and, with acclaim, Baños's *Bohemios* [1905 *Bohemians*].[7] The lack of a soundtrack was no problem as the
spectators knew the originals and, in towns, could rely on musicians, phono-
graph or gramophone placed behind the screen to accompany the projections.
In more luxurious cinemas the projection might even pause to allow a choir
to sing. Many were filmed but the most endearing was probably *La verbena
de la Paloma* [1921 *The Fair of the Dove*], directed by the indefatigable José
Buchs from Santander, starring Florián Rey, and first seen accompanied by
a 60-piece orchestra. The *verbena* itself would become an important motif
and location for the burgeoning of love or brewing of disasters in Spanish

---

[4]   *Currito de la Cruz* was remade in 1936 by Fernando Delgado, in 1949 by Luis Lucia,
and in 1965 by Rafael Gil.

[5]   The *IMDb* states that it was Cortesina's only film, with a company set up by Helena
herself (?). That she is the first woman director is questioned by Martin-Márquez, who laments
the state of research on the subject and mentions the case of Elena Jordi and the film *Thais*
[1918] (1999a: 6–7).

[6]   'Curiosa y vanguardista experiencia' in Gubern (1995: 75). For Musidora's *Sol y sombra*
[1924 *Sun and Shadow*], see Méndez Leite (1965: I, 197).

[7]   Remade in Mexico (1935, Rafael Portas), Francisco Elías in 1939, and Juan de Orduña
in colour for TVE in 1962.

films. Buchs filmed this for a new company funded in 1920 by conservative industrialists and other magnates close to the King: Atlántida amalgamated Perojo's Patria Films with Benavente's Cantabria Cine, which had made *Los intereses creados*, in which Buchs had participated both as a technician and with a minor part. Following his initial success, Buchs was entrusted with more *zarzuelas* the following year: the very successful *Carceleras* [1922 *Carcelera/Prison Songs*], enjoyed by the Royal Family, and *La reina mora* [*The Moorish Queen*], followed by *Doloretes* in 1923, and *Mancha que limpia* in 1924 [*The Cleansing Stain*]. Like his father, a famous tenor, he had studied at the Music Academy and filmed these musicals to schedule and with the minimum of fuss, allowing appreciated savings on production costs. In the 1920s he made at least two but usually three films a year, leaving his mark on Spanish films:

> I consider it an error to spurn the exploitation of local colour and traditions that differentiate between nations. We have themes that are so exclusively Spanish, like bullfighting, so full of fascinating possibilities, and Andalusian banditry. Ours is one of the most enthralling cultures in the world. We are compelled to use it as one of the strongest inspirations for Spanish Cinema. I accept and exploit the superficiality of narratives that are intrinsically so, like the so-called 'sentimental' genre or sub-genre.[8]

The number of his films subsequently remade bears witness to the popularity of his tastes. Of those mentioned, *La verbena* was refilmed in 1934 with a soundtrack by Benito Perojo, and in full colour in 1963 by Luis Sáenz de Heredia; in 1932, he remade *Carceleras*, already filmed by Chomón in 1910; and *La reina mora* was redirected in 1936 by Eusebio Fernández Ardavín and again in colour by Raúl Alfonso in 1955. Buchs is also credited with Spain's first war film, *Alma rifeña* [1922 *Moroccan Soul*], shot on location in Morocco, which up to then had only been the subject of documentaries or in the background of other narratives. Unfortunately, Atlántida, like Film Española, which also specialised in *zarzuelas*, and other smaller companies, all disappeared through lack of proper planning and financial backing but not without producing memorable films (Pérez Perucha, in Gubern, 1995: 89–96).

---

8 'Considero un error desdeñar el costumbrismo, que diferencia unos pueblos de otros. Contamos con temas exclusivos nuestros, como la fiesta brava, riquísimas en fascinantes sugestiones, y el brigandaje andaluz. Nuestra historia es una de las más apasionantes del mundo. Estamos obligados a utilizarla como uno de los más sólidos sustentos del cine español. Acepto y empleo la superficialidad en relatos que en sí lo son, como el género o subgénero llamado "rosa",' quoted by García Fernández (1985: 32). This attitude was the subject of much criticism at the time, but it was one that proved commercially successful (Triana Toribio, 2003: 25–7).

Regional melodrama

Another box-office success, which made Carmen Viance one of the stars of the decade, was *La casa de la Troya* [1925 *College Boarding House* – the building is still standing in Santiago de Compostela], directed by Manuel Noriega and Alejandro Pérez Lugín. Pérez Lugín wrote the original best-selling novel and to film it he set up his own production company, Troya Films.[9] Manuel Noriega was born in Asturias, and the *IMDb* has him directing 11 films in Spain between 1923 and 1927, and then acting in the USA and Mexico until 1957. The film represents those sentimental productions set among the upper classes and dealing with a young man 'alone and wealthy, Gerardo Roquer [Luis Peña], law student at Madrid University, game for anything except his studies',[10] who consequently gets into debts. His father decides to send him to the quietest university on earth, in Santiago de Compostela, so that he might concentrate on his degree. An intertitle describes Santiago as 'the bottom of the terrible well',[11] as the Madrid playboy's carriage arrives in a downpour. The intertitles are, through their use of adjectives, very literary, frequently ironic and humorous. The story revolves around a proverb, known to the audience but only spelt out in an intertitle towards the end of the film: 'Come to Galicia with tears and leave it with sorrow.'[12] Indeed, the young student, wet, cold and expecting to be bored, soon makes friends and falls in love with the ravishing and graceful Carmiña de Castro Retén [Carmen Viance]. However, the film is more a tribute to Galicia and its capital city than the retelling of good-humoured student pranks. This is established by the credit sequence, which introduces the author and his book, and when the intertitle spells out the protagonists, it is 'The Landscape'.[13] This is followed by a screen split vertically in three equal sections showing different views of the region and concluding with a street in Santiago where a woman is walking alone through the rain. There follows the actual cast list, and the narrative begins. Every opportunity is taken to present views of Galicia: during Gerardo's

---

[9]   Adolfo Aznar and Joan Vilà Vilamala remade the film with a soundtrack in 1936, now lost; there is also a 1948 Mexican version by Carlos Orellana, as well as Rafael Gil's colour version of 1959.

[10]   First intertitle: 'solo y rico, Gerardo Roquer, estudiante de derecho en la universidad de Madrid, lo hace todo menos estudiar', First act, chapter I. At this time films were frequently divided in chapters or acts, in an attempt to associate the cinema with the more respectable art form of the theatre.

[11]   'El fondo del terrible pozo.'

[12]   'A Galicia se entra llorando y se sale con pena': the tears are related to the fact it is the last place you want to be, because it rains so much, but you leave with sorrow because you have learned to love it, or have fallen in love!

[13]   'Protagonistas / El Paisaje.'

journey to the end of the earth; as he moves through the provincial capital and surrounding areas to court his lady: meeting her at a market, filmed on the day of a local holiday with all the locals in traditional costumes. Although the narration is filmed with a static camera, the shoreline and countryside show careful panning shots and editing. The evocation of Galicia is even achieved linguistically, through quotations of Rosalía de Castro's poems with Galician intertitles followed by their Castilian translation. But all these regional refer-ences, executed with pride and confidence, are integrated into the narrative, the humour and the romantic plot. The film certainly pleased, and like *Rob Roy* [1995 Michael Caton-Jones], it must have worked wonders to attract visi-tors and pilgrims. Today's students will also be surprised by the appearance, behaviour and expectations of the residents of the Casa de la Troya.[14] Among these students one finds Pedro Elviro as Pitouto, Augusto played by Juan de Orduña acting in his first film eleven years before his directing debut and Panduriño played by Florián Rey who also started his cinematographic career in 1920 as an actor with José Buchs. This would be Rey's last acting part as the following year he directed *La revoltosa,* which he produced with Juan de Orduña, for their newly created company Goya Films. Galicia was a favourite location for atmospheric rural melodramas like Rino Lupo's *Carmiña, flor de Galicia* [1926 *Carmiña, The Flower of Galicia*]; or José Buchs's adaptation of Galdós's *El abuelo* [1925 *The Grandfather*] with its use of the sea as the background for the Grandfather's changing emotions,[15] followed in 1927 by his period costume drama *El conde de Maravillas.*

Other melodramas

Also memorable and highly praised at the time was Joan Vilà Vilamala's *Nobleza baturra* [1925 *Rustic Chivalry/Aragonese Virtue,* remade in 1935 by Florián Rey and in 1965 by Juan de Orduña]. Virtue is rewarded in this bucolic romance of traditional songs and dances where the idealised coun-tryside of plentiful harvests actually negates the harsh rural reality of the times. In Madrid the projection of the film included dancers and orchestra to perform some of the *jotas* [traditional Aragonese dances]. Made for 55,000 pesetas, twice the average budget, it grossed 1,500,000 pesetas.[16] The Basque

---

14   A new restored tinted version of the film, which I have not seen, was released in 2003 by the Filmoteca.

15   Originally in seven parts, lasting two hours with tinted negatives, all but six minutes of the film were restored in 1992 and are available on DVD from Divisa. The same is true for Buchs's 1926 *Pilar Guerra.*

16   See Pozo Arenas (1984: 21). For comparison, here in pesetas is the budget for an average film: *Rosa de Levante* [1926 *Valencian Rose,* Mario Ronconori], adding the percentage of the

landscape is also prominent in Telesforo Gil's *Edurne, modista bilbaína* [1924 *Edurne, Dressmaker from Bilbao*] and Mauro Azkona's *El mayorazgo de Basterretxe* [1929 *The Basterretxe Inheritance*] or Francisco Camacho's *Zalacaín el aventurero* [*Zalacaín The Adventurer*, 1929], based on Pío Baroja's action novel of the Carlist wars and taken up by MGM to be distributed in the USA (Besas, 1985: 6–7; Gubern, 1999: 289–91).[17] Spectators appreciated these rural and sentimental melodramas, many of which were adapted by the Álvarez Quintero brothers, Serafín and Joaquín, from their own plays, like the 1926 *Malvaloca* [Benito Perojo, *Hollyhock*]. The second of five reels is lost, but the film was remade in 1942 by Luis Marquina, and in 1954 by Ramón Torrado. In Perojo's version, Lydia Gutiérrez, with Pitusín at her side, played the part of the single mother, or prostitute with a heart of gold, who is reintegrated into society. Much of the film was shot on location in Malaga and Seville and it also includes sequences of the Moroccan War. The 1927 screenings of the film in Madrid's Callao cinema were also programmed to allow singers and dancers live performances (Gubern, 1994: 108–17). Another popular and perhaps more concerned playwright, also engaged in the transfer of his plays to the screen, was Carlos Arniches, whose name is associated with some 50 films according to the *IMDb*. Good examples might be *Los granujas* [1924 *The Little Rascals*], which was Fernando Delgado's second film, or *Don Quintín el amargao* [*The Embittered Don Quentin*] directed in 1925 by Manuel Noriega, and then remade in 1935 and credited to Luis Marquina by Buñuel (1987: 202), subsequently adapted in 1951 as *La hija del engaño* [*Daughter of Deceit*] by Buñuel himself (P. Evans, 1995a: 36). The Quintero Brothers and Arniches were also well known for their comedies of local manners, *sainetes*.

It is the Moroccan War, rather than the Great War, that figures in Spanish film, including Perojo's *Malvaloca* or *La condesa María* [1928], celebrated for its editing.[18] On the other hand, *El héroe de Cascorro* [*The Hero of Cascorro*], directed by Emilio Bautista in 1929, lost and then rediscovered in the archives of the Uruguayan film library, was banned in Spain under Primero de Rivera's dictatorship and not released until the following Republic

---

budget for each item to Pozo Arenas's table (p. 26), a more detailed budget can be found in García Fernández (2002: 283–87):

Actors	5730	(24.4%)	Board and lodging	1548.40	(6.6%)
Technicians	6750	(28.7%)	Transport	1155.80	(4.9%)
Reels and laboratories	6402.30	(27.3%)	Miscellaneous	728.10	(3.1%)
Sets	570	(2.4%)	Minor expenses	333.50	(1.4%)
Costumes	265.90	(1.1%)	Total 23,484 pesetas.		

[17] The first acknowledged Basque fiction is Alejandro Olavarría's 40 minutes' *Un drama en Bilbao* [1924 *A Drama in Bilbao*].

[18] The original play about the lost son was remade by Gonzalo Delgrás in 1942, and this time using the Second World War as the background.

in 1932. This is because it dealt with the Cuban defeat of 1898, even though the Spanish soldiers were all presented as heroes following the example of patriotic Eloy Gonzalo.

A didactic impulse

Some films encouraged a more realistic and critical look at society, though in the view of the contemporary press there were not enough of them (Triana Toribio, 2003: 26–7). *Las de Méndez* [1927 *The Mendez Women*] starring Carmen Viance and directed by Fernando Delgado, although lost, is remembered for its portrayal of middle-class pride and hypocrisy (Méndez Leite, 1965: I, 274–5). *Rosa de Madrid* [1928 *The Rose of Madrid*] directed by Fernández Ardavín, with Pedro Larrañaga and Conchita Dorado as the couple, is a contemporary melodrama that brings up the issues of rape and women's position in society. *La terrible lección* [1927 *The Terrible Experience*], also directed by Delgado, was an attempt backed by the government to use cinema and melodrama educationally, to inform audiences about venereal diseases. It was not a box-office hit in spite of being banned as pornographic by a number of provincial governors, in those days responsible for censorship. Also lost is Camacho's *Zalacaín el aventurero*, an action film that reflected Pío Baroja's liberal concerns and the grim rural reality, although set in the historical context of the Carlist wars. Baroja was one of the authors of the so-called Generation of '98 who was positively involved in the cinema, collaborating with script-writers and contributing two articles on film for *La Gaceta Literaria*. Three of his novels were turned into films, and *Zalacaín* was remade in 1954 by Juan de Orduña, and also turned into a TV series in 1968. In the 1929 version Pedro Larrañaga was cast as Zalacaín and paired with María Luz Callejo, with a cameo appearance by the novelist himself. *La malcasada* [1927 *The Mismatched Bride*], adapted from a true case history, directed by Francisco Gómez Hidalgo and filmed by Josep Gaspar, must also have been a most unusual film. Not only did it broach the theme of divorce during Primo de Rivera's reactionary dictatorship, but it also included him as a 'militar', together with José Millán Astray and Francisco Franco. In fact the cast list of 'other performers' is as vast as it is impressive for the number of actual politicians, engineers, scientists, authors, journalists, artists, bullfighters, etc., who all participated to give their opinion on divorce (Manuel Palacio, in Pérez Perucha, 1997: 58–9). The plot is, however, a bullfighting melodrama set in Mexico and Spain based on an actual event into which a good dose of comedy has been inserted. As a film it was criticised for its mise-en-scène but praised for its editing, which kept the spectators interested even though it was 158 minutes long. In Madrid the police had to intervene during the ticket sales, and in Barcelona it was applauded by the women in the audience when the protagonist was told in the film by the author Concha Espina: 'men rarely deserve that we suffer for them'.[19] Educationally, a number of these films coincide with Carmen de Burgos's literary output and social concerns (Louis, 1999: 49–63).

Production problems

Lack of organisation and leadership within the film industry continued to result in small and short-lived companies scattered throughout the country, in competition with imported films, especially from the USA (Forbes, 2000: 7–8). Statistically, in 1928 film production was beginning its decline with only 58 films made in Spain: Madrid 44, Valencia 7, Asturias 4, Barcelona 2, Bilbao 1 (Pozo Arenas, 1984: 21); against 1000 imported titles (Pérez Perucha, in Gubern, 1995: 102). Concerns had already been voiced in 1915 when the Cámara Española de Cinematografía [Spanish Film Council] was established in an attempt to organise and develop the industry and face the issue of foreign competition. The Gaumont, in particular, persistently filmed popular folkloric films in Spain ['espagnolades'], many by Louis Feuillade, such as La Petite Andalouse [*The Girl from Andalusia] or Le Coffret de Toledo [*The Toledo Chest] both of 1924. Perhaps most memorable was Marcel L'Herbier's El Dorado [1921] with its cultivated stereotypes, even if the dancing of Eve Francis lacks the conviction of Spanish actresses, and where, because of the many location shots in Granada and Seville, the city becomes an important protagonist. The Gaumont's man in Spain had been Enrique Blanco; he had started filming and projecting in Pamplona in 1911, making his reputation with bullfighting and other news reports before moving on to Madrid to take charge of Madrid Films. He directed a few films and was the cinematographer for many more.[20] General frustration probably led to the First Spanish Film Conference of October 1928, organised by the film magazine La Pantalla, which petitioned the government to intervene in support of Spanish Cinema (García Fernández, 2002: 279–80). The Royal Decree of 26 February 1929 put in place a public inquiry, which in turn recommended a film projection quota: (a) five Spanish films to be projected in a cinema for every one foreign film allowed; (b) for every 25 films a foreign distributor exhibited in Spain, one Spanish film had to be distributed abroad by that company (Pozo Arenas, 1984: 24). However, nothing was moving fast and

---

[19] 'Los hombres rara vez merecen que suframos por ellos.' All this information is from Manuel Palacio (in Pérez Perucha, 1997: 58–61), and Caparrós Lera (1981: 75–7).

[20] Already mentioned: La Madona de las rosas, Flor de España, Los granujas, Currito de la Cruz, Las de Méndez, La terrible lección, and in future Madrid en el año 2000, Prim, Fermín Galán.

little happened. To protect itself Germany had already imposed similar restrictions during the war in 1916 and then again in 1921; the British Cinematograph Act followed with its own quota law on the import of foreign films in 1927 (Forbes, 2000: 7). But urban audiences were enjoying the cinema, and even formed sufficient readership for such magazines as *La Pantalla* created in Madrid in 1927 after *Popular Films* and *Fotogramas* in 1926, in Barcelona and Madrid respectively. *La Gaceta Literaria*, started in January 1927 under Giménez Caballero, would for a few years be an influential literary magazine for the film world (Jordan & Allinson, 2005: 175–8).

Imperio Argentina and Benito Perojo

1927 was the year Magdalena Nile del Río, who on Jacinto Benavente's advice had taken the stage name of Imperio Argentina, acted in her first film, now lost, *La hermana San Sulpicio* [*Sister San Sulpicio*] directed by Florián Rey. He promptly cast her again the following year in his *Los claveles de la Virgen* [1928 *The Virgin Mary's Carnations*]. She starred in another nine films with Rey, and married him during the remake of *La hermana San Sulpicio* in July 1934 when she was the brightest star of Republican cinema. In 1926 she had been turned down by Perojo for his *Malvaloca,* but in 1928 she went to Munich with Valentín Parera, the young Alfredo Hurtado and other actors, to be directed by Benito Perojo and Gustav Ucicky in *Corazones sin rumbo* [1928 *Herzen ohne Ziel/*Aimless Hearts*]. The fragments held by the Filmoteca in Madrid [A2007] include an unforgettable sequence that conveys a young woman's distress when she is thrown out of her Barcelona hotel and wanders aimlessly through the city. It is an extended sequence masterly filmed and edited with double exposures that are constantly changing, high-angle shots on heads and hats juxtaposed to close-ups of feet, fragmented bodies, reflections in shop windows, a camera making a full 360-degree circle around a tramway, all to convey and emphasise the distress of feeling alone and bereft in a crowded city. The fact that it was a co-production means that we cannot give Perojo absolute credit for this sequence, but he had already directed the celebrated but now lost *Boy* [1925, remade in 1940 by Antonio Calvache] filmed with some colour sequences and starring Juan de Orduña. Also of importance were *El negro que tenía el alma blanca* [1927 *The Black Man With a White Soul*], a film about the making of a star, which launched Conchita Piquer's career in Spain and paired her with the Egyptian actor Raymond de Sarka, and *La condesa María* mentioned above.[21] The success

---

[21] See Joaquín Cánovas Belchí (in Pérez Perucha, 1997: 71–3), who has little space and much to say about the thematic and technical merits of this film; see also Gubern (1994: 138–52).

of these films contributed to Perojo's credibility as a director even though he
was greatly criticised at the time for using foreign studios. *El negro que...*, is
a film about love, dance, jazz and racial tension, which includes a nightmare
sequence with special effects by Segundo de Chomón; the film was released
in France as *Le Danseur de jazz* (Gubern, 1994: 125–37). Much more meticulous and demanding than Buchs, Perojo filmed his exteriors on location in
Spain and his interiors in French studios. He always picked his crew carefully
and used Albert Duverger as a cameraman before Buñuel. According to the
IMDb, Duverger also worked with Perojo on the two Benavente adaptations,
Para toda la vida [1923 *For Ever*] and *Más allá de la muerte* [1924 *Beyond
Death*], as well as on *Boy* [1925] and a version of Blasco Ibáñez's novel *La
bodega* [1929 *Wine Cellars*]; Pierre Schild[knecht] was the chosen decorator.
La bodega, with its Andalusian setting, became the greatest Spanish international success to date, and was subsequently post-synchronised in Paris.
Más allá de la muerte showed what Perojo was capable of, developing a lot
of camera movements throughout the film, beginning with a close-up of a
pair of hands leafing through a book, cutting to a smiling young woman in a
framed photograph and then to the reflection of the man looking at her with
sadness. The use of close-ups for point of view shots or as a means of starting
a film or linking sequences became a Perojo trademark. *Más allá ...* also
included Gaston Modot, who would subsequently become Buñuel's leading
man in *L'Âge d'or* [1930, see pp. 44–5], as the villain in this high-society
melodrama of intrigue.

The cursed village

This leads on to an acknowledged masterpiece of the silent cinema: Florián
Rey's *La aldea maldita* [1930 *The Cursed Village*],[22] produced by Rey and
Larrañaga, which Rey remade in 1942. Rey had studied law, which he gave
up for journalism, and then started acting for José Buchs before directing
his own films; as well as *La casa de la Troya* he can be seen in *La verbena
de la Paloma* and *Alma rifeña*. *La aldea maldita* is a great rural melodrama
presenting a conflict of honour and values – 'in Castile, he who stains the name
he bears is never forgiven'[23] – set against destructive droughts, hailstorms and
the hardships of agricultural economy. These endemic disasters led to the

---

[22] The only film made before 1947 to be on the list of the 50 best Spanish films voted
by directors, actors and critics in the survey prepared by Cecilia Ballesteros for *Revista de El
Mundo* celebrating the first centenary of the cinema (17/12/1995), pp. 42–5. See also below, p.
320.

[23] 'En Castilla no se perdona nunca al que mancha el nombre que lleva' is one of the
intertitles.

2a Chiaroscuro of Rey's *La aldea maldita* (1930)

rural migrations that the country was constantly experiencing, and yet the film only suggests the consequent urban problems that would be explored in later films. Hopewell describes the film as a complex moral drama (1986: 11–12), where the miserly Tío Lucas [Uncle Lucas, Ramón Meca] turns out to be the positive reconciling agent in contrast to the Abuelo [Grandfather, Víctor Pastor], who is more than visually blind and incarnates family values of racial purity. The curse on the village is not just its dependence on precarious weather and harvests, but its blind belief in honour. The protagonist, appropriately named Juan Castilla, is defined by an intertitle as 'a poor peasant, with the aspirations and feelings of a great landowner'.[24] The use of shadow and light is extremely well worked out, with a number of scenes shot with a source of light concealed within the frame, reminiscent of Caravaggio or Georges de La Tour. It is a film that, through its use of lighting and its meticulous compositions within the frame,[25] leaves haunting images in the specta-

---

[24] 'Juan, un pobre campesino con ideas y sentimientos de gran señor.'

[25] A frequent shortcoming in other films of the period, which, although they usually handled crosscutting between general and medium shots with close-ups successfully and meaningfully, the use of a static camera often meant that the actors were not always where they should be within the frame of the screen.

tor's mind, like the distraught mother being stoned by children or rocking an empty cradle. The montage is also powerful in its economical presentation of information. The opening sequences establishing the village, for example, juxtapose the father tilling the arid land, the attractions of the city, the blind Abuelo's confidence that his genes have been passed on, the mother caring for her baby, the hailstorm and the prayers of impotent villagers. Rural migration is memorably depicted, in Biblical proportions as an intertitle announces 'Exodus'. The village is practically abandoned as the caravan sets off with close-ups, low and high-angled shots, through the streets to end as a snake winding its way across the screen into the distance, and concluding with a high-angle shot on the caravan disappearing into the centre of the frame to face the hardships of urban survival. This effect is lost in the 1942 remake, which cuts where Acacia's and Luisa's cart parts company with the rest of the caravan. The remake is not as concise as the first version; the lighting does not offer as many contrasts; the opulence of the sets and the folkloric costumes jar with the impact of famine in the village; Church values are ever-present through the iconography on the sets and the characters' gestures; Juan is more affluent; the Abuelo is not so imposing although on his shoulders and blindness rests the weight of patriarchal honour; Tío Lucas is no longer instrumental to the plot; the characters are flatter and their decisions not so well motivated.[26] The 1930 tragedy is personalised through the contrasting individual fortunes of Juan Castilla [Pedro Larrañaga] and his wife Acacia [Carmen Viance], portraying women's difficult social position when they are denied a voice in a patriarchal society. This is poignantly presented through a silent film that deprives the woman of intertitles, and where her silence is taken as proof of guilt. This powerful use of silence is perhaps an example of why many, including Chaplin and Hitchcock, felt something had been lost with the coming of sound in 1927, but fortunately for Florián Rey Spanish cinemas were not yet equipped for the projection of talking pictures. The film was taken to Paris where sound was added with some dialogue and a few extra scenes before it was shown as *Le Village maudit* to an excellent critical and popular reception for a whole year.[27]

Avant-garde cinema

In October 1928 the first Spanish film club, Cineclub Español, was founded in Madrid by Ernesto Giménez Caballero to show more unusual films, better described as artistic, experimental or provocative (Edwards, 2005: 20). It

---

[26] See Sánchez Vidal (2005: 13–21) for a more detailed comparison of the two versions.

[27] The Paris version is now lost, but the 1930 version was released as a DVD by Divisa in 2003.

projected many diverse films such as *Nanook of the North* [1920–2 Robert Flaherty], *Greed* [1923 Erich Von Stroheim], *La Fille de l'eau* [1924 Jean Renoir, *Whirlpool of Fate*], *Tartüff* [1925 Murnau], *L'Étoile de mer* [1928 Man Ray, *The Starfish*], *La Chute de la maison Usher* [1928 Jean Epstein, *The Fall of the House of Usher*, on which Buñuel had worked as an assistant (1987: 89)], and of course Buñuel's own film *Un Chien andalou* [1928 *An Andalusian Dog*].[28] The Cineclub, like the Residencia de Estudiontes, was one of the focal points of the Generation of '27 poets, who had rediscovered the merits of the seventeenth-century poet Luis de Góngora. It was supported by the literary journal *La Gaceta Literaria*, founded the year before, and also directed by Giménez Caballero, who in fact commissioned Buñuel as special correspondent to write on cinema from Paris (Buñuel, 1987: 75–6).[29] Barcelona followed suit in 1929 with the Mirador Cineclub, supported by the magazine of the same name under the direction of Sebastià Gasch. Both generated much interest among young artists whose techniques were influenced by those of filmmaking. The Cineclub soon had many branches throughout the country (for its achievements, see C. Morris, 1980: 14).

In contrast to the imaginative work produced by other European avant-garde cinematographers, little remains in Spain of a similar experimental cinema, which is now mostly known through written testimonies.[30] The most frequently mentioned film is perhaps *Madrid en el año 2000* [1925 *Madrid in the Year 2000*], of which there are no known surviving copies. Produced by Madrid Films under Enrique Blanco and directed by Manuel Noriega, it was partly intended as a technical demonstration of what the studio could achieve, perhaps inspired by the orchestrated publicity surrounding the filming of Fritz Lang's *Metropolis* in Berlin during that year (Gubern, 1999: 160–4). The *Historia de un duro* [1928 *The History of a Five Peseta Coin*], directed by Sabino Antonio Micón who defined his film as a 'película de vanguardia', is also lost although there is a decoupage describing the journey of the coin from hand to hand without revealing the faces of the owners (published by Gubern, 1999: 165–75). The films of the Basque Nemesio Manuel Sobrevila, described at the time as reflexive satires, were denied commercial release. *Al Hollywood madrileño* [1927 *To the Madrid Hollywood*; renamed in 1928 *Lo más español, *Absolute Spanish*] presented seven parodies of existing

---

28 Gubern has a detailed account of the 21 sessions of the Cineclub, Madrid (1999: 279–389).

29 Gubern also provides a list of published articles on cinema sorted by contributors, and another list by films (1999: 202–59).

30 Gubern labels these films as 'slightly eccentric', and gives seven reasons why in his opinion there was no true experimental cinema in Spain (1999: 154–60) in his very informative chapter of *Proyector de luna* (1999): 'Una vanguardia sin cine' [An avant-garde without films], chapter 7, pp. 146–201.

cinema genres, including a sketch based on a Pío Baroja play. Sobrevila was a trained architect, and at the time his imaginative sets were compared to those of *Metropolis*. *El sexto sentido* [1929 *The Sixth Sense*] is the only one of Sobrevila's films to have survived: Kamus, philosopher and alcoholic, claims he can ascertain the scientific truth through a sixth sense, which is in fact the cine-camera, although the narrative demonstrates that even this scientific truth is open to misinterpretation.[31] *Esencia de Verbena* [1930 *The Essence of the Fair*] is a documentary directed by Giménez Caballero, which attempts to capture the fun and spirit of the popular Madrid summer fairs through images and montage to allow surprising associations. It was first shown at the Cineclub on the same night as Buñuel's *Un Chien andalou,* with an entertaining and witty commentary read by Ramón Gómez de la Serna acting as *explicador.*[32] Two unrealised film scripts, which might have altered Spanish Cinema, were Federico García Lorca's *Viaje a la luna* [1929 *Trip to the Moon*] and Salvador Dalí's *Babaouo,*[33] subsequently made in 1998 by Manuel Cussó-Ferrer.

Luis Buñuel (1900–1983)

This chapter cannot conclude without mentioning Buñuel and his first two films, *Un Chien andalou* and *L'Âge d'or* [1930 *The Age of Gold*], on which there is a great deal published. It is true that neither film was made in Spain and that Buñuel was immediately claimed by the French Surrealists, and much later by French cinema. After 1975, and even before, however, Spaniards also claimed him as their own, 'the key to Buñuel remained his *Spanishness,* in the sight of the world' (Aranda, 1975: 190, see also p. 130). In Spain he only made one documentary (*Tierra sin pan, Las Hurdes* [1933 *Land Without Bread*]) and directed two films (1961 *Viridiana*, 1970 *Tristana*), as well as some sequences for a couple of the French productions (*La Voie lactée* [1969 but not in Spain, *The Milky Way*] and *Cet Obscur Objet du désir* [1977 *That Obscure Object of Desire*]), but there is something indelible about

[31] The version viewed, reconstructed by the Filmoteca and distributed by Divisa, has scrambled sequences leaving the viewer to reconstruct the chronology of the narrative, thus providing a further ironic comment on the reliability of cinematic narrative; see Ginger, 2007: 69–78.

[32] The copy viewed has a later soundtrack and voice-over recorded by Giménez Caballero. This paragraph relies on Gubern (1999: 175–95, 430–45), and Luis Fernández Colorado (in Pérez Perucha, 1997: 74–6).

[33] C.B. Morris (1980: 127–34), but Monegal (1994) needs to be consulted for the original script. Dalí was later called in by Hitchcock to design Gregory Peck's nightmare in the 1945 *Spellbound.*

Buñuel's vision of the world and understanding of society that both connect him with his Aragonese origins and allow his films to transcend his personal context.[34]

Un Chien andalou was filmed in Paris in 1928 and was actually funded, under false pretences, by Buñuel's mother (1987: 104; Baxter, 1994: 75). The precise facts of its conception are unclear, partly because of the subsequent break-up and blurring of the relationship between Buñuel and Salvador Dalí, and the identification of a number of in-jokes shared among the students in the Residencia de Estudiantes (Gubern, 1999: 391–4).[35] Buñuel's written testimony is that it 'came from an encounter between two dreams [...] a long, tapering cloud sliced the moon in half, like a razor blade slicing through an eye. Dalí immediately told me that he'd seen a hand crawling with ants in a dream he'd had the previous night' (1987: 103–4).[36] The film presents the juxtaposition of images, scenes and sequences that allow a narrative to be inferred, but it has the consistency of dreams where the situation is constantly changing through associations and without apparent causal relationships. Furthermore each frame is full of details that do not immediately match our experience of a coherent reality, and the film is punctuated by ironic intertitles that cluster the scenes into sections, a disorientating device also exploited in *L'Âge d'or*. Nonetheless the spectator's mind strives to establish and impose some sort of causality, order and meaning, which are bound to be as different as the individual viewers' personal experiences and knowledge. Many images build up to an expression of repressed sexual desire and its destructive consequences on the individual (Sánchez Vidal, 1984: 63), reflected in Buñuel's choice of musical accompaniment. On a gramophone Buñuel alternated excerpts from Wagner's tragic tale of *Tristan and Isolde* and tangos, whose predominant themes are frustrated love, themes found in Salvador Dalí's 'The Great Masturbator' and other paintings executed in the summer of 1929, whereas in *L'Âge d'or* that desire is seen in the context of

34   See also P. Evans (1995: 2–12 especially p. 6), where the problem is discussed as a question of authorship; see also Kinder (1993: 286–92 and 319–38), and Fuentes (2004: 159–72). Like these critics I do not hesitate in considering Buñuel as a Spaniard in exile; from personal experience, even after adopting the nationality of one's host country, those closest will still perceive you as from another land.

35   A selective student residence in Madrid founded in 1910 with liberal and progressive ideas on education, from where blossomed a number of Spain's intellectuals and artists, including Salvador Dalí, Federico García Lorca, Rafael Alberti and Ramón Gómez de la Serna, as well as a number of future politicians of the Second Republic. See e.g. Aranda (1975: 22–4, 28–9) or Baxter (1994: 19–20, 25–30).

36   The original reads: 'd'un nuage effilé coupant la lune et d'une lame de rasoir fendant un oeuil. De son côté il [Dalí] me raconta qu'il venait de voir en rêve, la nuit précédente, une main pleine de fourmis' (p. 125). The juxtaposition of the two images has been translated as a simile by Abigail Israel.

and in collision with society. But then Buñuel's 'films are not answers, but questions' (Aranda, 1975: 146).

According to Buñuel, the success of *Un Chien andalou* was unexpected when it was first shown on 6 June 1928 in the Studio des Ursulines in Paris (1987: 106), and André Breton claimed it as the first Surrealist film. Adverse publicity led the studio to cancel subsequent projections, but these were taken over by Studio 28 in Montmartre where it was projected for another nine months (Baxter, 1994: 86–8, 93–4). It was a commercial success that undermined Buñuel's status as a newly recruited Surrealist. Buñuel wanted to shock and provoke and subsequently wrote: 'the foolish crowd has found beautiful and poetic what is, in effect, only a despairing, passionate call to murder'. For his part, Dalí stated: 'We believe, however, that the spectators who applauded *Un Chien andalou* are spectators made mindless by avant-garde journals and promotions who applaud out of snobbism what to them appears to be new and unusual.'[37] In Spain the film was first shown on 24 October 1929 at the Mirador in Barcelona. It was then shown as part of the eighth session of the Cineclub in Madrid in December 1929, introduced by Giménez Caballero, when Buñuel repeated his statement to be published in the *Révolution Surréaliste*. There was some unrest during the projection and the police threatened to close the Cineclub. There were more projections the following year, when it was also chosen for the inauguration of the Cineclub in Zaragoza (Gubern, 1999: 322–7).

L'Âge d'or was financed by the Vicomte de Noailles as a birthday present for his spouse (Buñuel, 1987: 114–16), and again there is much of Dalí in the script (Gubern, 1999: 394–416). It was accepted by the Parisian censors on 1 October, providing one of the intertitles was removed. After two private showings it opened on 28 November at the Studio 28 who were hoping to repeat the financial success of *Un Chien* (Buñuel, 1987: 117–18). *My Last Sigh* states that Dalí's intentions 'were to expose the shameful mechanisms of contemporary society. For me [Buñuel], it was a film about *l'amour fou*, the irresistible force that thrusts two people together, and about the impossibility of their ever becoming one' (p. 117).[38] The spectators were not as enthusiastic as they had been for *Un Chien...* and, as the word spread, some right-wing groups (extreme Catholics, as well as patriotic and anti-Semitic

---

[37] Buñuel: 'la foule imbécile a trouvé beau et poétique ce qui, au fond, n'est qu'un désespéré, un passioné appel au meurtre' in *Révolution Surréaliste* 12 (15 December 1929), p. 34; and Dalí: 'Creemos, sin embargo, que el público que ha aplaudido *Un Chien andalou* es un público embrutecido por las revistas y divulgaciones de vanguardia que aplaude por esnobismo lo que le parece nuevo y extraño' in *Mirador*, 39 (24 October 1929), p. 6 (quoted in Gubern, 1999: 324–5). See C.B. Morris (1980: 82–3) for the poet Rafael Alberti's reaction.

[38] The original does not establish a mutually exclusive contrast: 'Pour moi il s'agissait *aussi – et surtout –* d'un film d'amour fou [...]' (p. 141, with my italics).

organisations) took exception to the film and organised a riot in the cinema during the performance of 3 December, causing considerable property damage (Edwards, 1982: 63–4; Baxter, 1994: 117–22). The French national daily, *Le Figaro,* renamed it *The Age of Filth/HardGold,* 'Family and religion are dragged through the filth/hard gold'.[39] The film was banned on 10 December, the Vicomte de Noailles was ostracised from his social club, and Buñuel partly achieved the reaction he wanted although he was not there to witness it since he had left for Hollywood at the invitation of L.L. Laurence of MGM, who had viewed the film before the scandal occurred (Buñuel, 1987: 127). There was only one private projection of the film in Madrid, on 22 November 1931, but it was rejected by Giménez Caballero who by this stage was consolidating his right-wing tendencies (Gubern, 1999: 251–2, 257). Subsequently it was only tolerated at private functions and in cinema clubs; the first UK projection was on 2 January 1931, in the USA in 1980, and it was only allowed back in France in 1981.

Both films demonstrate the importance of the initial sequence of a film (Bentley 1995b: 259–73). *Un Chien andalou*'s opening shot is one that still affects today's spectators, with Buñuel's razor assaulting the eye staring out at the spectators.[40] It is a challenge to each individual viewing experience, to the very medium of the cinema and source of its pleasure and satisfaction, scopophilia (Mulvey, 1989 or Easthope, 1993: 111–34), right at the beginning of the tale 'Once upon a time …'.[41] Seeing it again still affects me today after many viewings, even though I now know it was the eye from a heifer's carcass (Aub, 1985: 59 and 69). The initial sequence of *L'Âge d'or* with the close-ups of fighting scorpions, presented like an entomological documentary, is also very powerful and makes a telling commentary on human behaviour as developed by the film.

Opposition to the cinema

These two films also remind us that the development of cinema was not without protest and that many objected to the medium itself, regardless of the content of the films. Two chapters in C.B. Morris's *This Loving Dark-*

---

[39] Richard Bodin, 7 December 1930: *L'Âge d'ordure,* 'la famille, la religion y sont trainées dans l'ordure' – a comment to remember for future chapters.

[40] Given the fact that this is a very personal film, it is unlikely that the friends who viewed it in 1930 could escape identifying the character who slices the eye with the film's creator, just as those who watched *L'Âge d'or* could not avoid the social irony linking the scorpions, the poisoned rat, the bishops, the smugglers and the artists who played them, Max Ernst and Pierre Prévert. Both films question normal viewing experience (Bentley, 1995a,: 3–5).

[41] 'Il était une fois', the traditional beginning of a fairy tale in French.

ness summarise both the condemnations, ethical and aesthetical, as well as
the enthusiasm generated by the cinema in those early years (1980: 16–41).
Interestingly, vocabulary aside, many of the arguments had been heard and
read before with reference to seventeenth-century drama; both were criticised for enticing immorality and corrupting the minds of weaker individuals.
Although cinema criticism also included the new question of the relative
merits of film and theatre, since so many more film scripts were adapted from
the theatre than from novels (Triana Toribio, 2003: 24–5).[42] The traffic went
both ways since films were also rewritten as novels and published in weekly
magazines (for instance, *La Novela Semanal Cinematográfica* or *La Novela
Cinematográfica del Hogar* [*The Weekly Film Novel/The Home Film Novel*]);
novels were inspired by the film world; new plays were written adapting
cinematographic techniques, and poets demonstrated their enthusiasm for
the medium in their work.[43] Many older intellectuals and academics sneered
at the cinema, from Francisco Rodríguez Marín and Miguel de Unamuno to
Antonio Machado, for whom cinema that showed 'how the man who arrives
through a chimney, leaves by a balcony and paddles about in a pond, is of
no more interest to us than a ball bouncing off the cushions of a billiard
table'.[44] The debate opposes High Art to popular entertainment. However, it
also gained many supporters, including Machado's brother Manuel, and to
praise cinema became a way to criticise the establishment, something that
Buñuel exploited to an extreme.

Codicil

Many interesting titles have been omitted from this brief survey, but during
these years more films were lost than preserved, making judgement difficult

---

[42] José Antonio Pérez Bowie's *Materiales para un sueño* (1996) is a very useful complement to C.B. Morris, chapters 2–3, since it brings together contemporary documents from 1896
to 1936, linked by brief comments.

[43] Pérez Bowie (1996: 131–58). Among the novels, see Ramón Gómez de la Serna's
sparkling evocation of cinema studios in *Cinelandia* (1923), and Andrés Carranque de Ríos's
Cinematógrafo (1936) for using the underside of the film world as the context for the plot of
his grim realist novel, building on his own experience as an actor (*Al Hollywood madrileño, Es
mi hombre, La del Soto del parral, El héroe de Cascorro, Zalacaín, Doña Francisquita*).

[44] 'El cine nos enseña como el hombre que entra por una chimenea, sale por un balcón y se
zambulle en un estanque, no tiene para nosotros más interés que una bolla de billar rebotando
en las bandas de una mesa,' quoted from Pérez Bowie (1996: 29). Rodríguez Marín was an
impressive scholar of the works of Miguel de Cervantes; Miguel de Unamuno was professor
of philosophy at Salamanca University and a novelist; the Machado brothers were subtle but
very different poets with the power to move their readers through words, two of their co-written
plays being filmed in the 1940s; see also Caparrós Lera (1981: 230–40) and Pérez Bowie (1996:
29–44).

and any survey provisional; of course, better organisation and greater investments would have allowed the potential to flourish. Many of these films are only available at second hand through press reviews and magazine articles. In 1929, however, the future looked very uncertain. In Spain Primo de Rivera resigned, universities were closed for opposing the regime, from October all were experiencing the after-effects of the Wall Street crash, and in December a Republican uprising was crushed. Screen sound had also been added to the 'movie experience', but Spanish cinemas were unable to take advantage of it for some years.

Further reading

Caparrós Lera (1987), Jordan & Allinson (2005), Stone (2002: 20–7) and Triana Toribio's more focused discussion (2003: 19–24) are, at the moment, the main sources of information in English for the period. For a brief overview, Peter Besas (1985) and John Hopewell (1986) offer perceptive comments from different perspectives. In Spanish, Méndez Leite (1965) hardly misses a film and continues to provide interesting anecdotes to complement Gubern's *Historia* (1995). Morris's *This Loving Darkness* (1980) will add many details on the reception of cinema in the 1920s and how it affected the young poets of the time. Sánchez Vidal provides a reading of *La aldea maldita* and its remake (2005). On Buñuel a great deal has been published, see e.g. Baxter (1994), Evans & Santaolalla (2004) and Edwards (1982 and 2005). As well as his 'autobiography' (1982), a good start on *Un Chien andalou* would be the monograph by Jenaro Talens, *The Branded Eye* (1993), and Phillip Drummond's article for *Screen* (1977), which both include detailed descriptions of each shot and consecutive stills from the film. Paul Hammond has a monograph on *L'Âge d'or* (1997, 2004), and Linda Williams's *Figures of Desire* gives both films a psychoanalytical reading (reprinted 1992). Graham & Labanyi (1995), part I, pp. 25–94, and Forbes & Street (2000), part I, pp. 1–50, continue to offer brief but useful contextualisations. Ginger has recently published an article on Baños, Sobrevila and Elías (2007).

The films that have survived need to be watched in special institutions, like the Filmotecas, apart from Buñuel's *Un Chien andalou* [1928] and *L'Âge d'or* [1930], which are both available on video/DVD. Divisa have released a few of the Filmoteca's restoration on DVD, like *El abuelo*, *Pilar Guerra* and *El sexto sentido*, which engages the power and limitations of cinema within its diegesis, but their stock is rapidly exhausted. An interesting angle from which to study the decade, of relevance to the future of Spanish Cinema, would be press and film magazines for spectator reception, to confirm that what encouraged producers was the popular preference even in the age of the silent movies for spectacles, with music and song, rather than narratives.

Among the contributors to these reviews, María Luz Morales seems to be a very interesting case. The concept of a Spanish avant-garde cinema is also one that warrants further investigation. Other subjects might the debate between High Art and popular entertainment, the relationship of theatre to cinema, the exoticisation of Spain and Spanish themes in both foreign and Spanish cinema; the 'blackmail' motif also keeps recurring in plots, is intriguing and could be investigated. Salacious photography and reels are another topic that remains to be explored methodically.

3

The Cinema of the Republic (1931–1939)

Beginning again: the political context

Concluding the previous chapter with Luis Buñuel's *L'Âge d'or* brought in the sound era. 1931 also saw a radical change in Spain as the Second Republic was proclaimed following landslide results at the local elections that took place throughout the country. Primo de Rivera had already resigned from office in January 1930, a financial scandal breaking the camel's back, and Dámaso Berenguer, another military man, was unable to mitigate the economic difficulties during his *Dictablanda*,[1] which for pragmatic reasons exercised a more gentle form of government. Following the April elections King Alfonso XIII abdicated. A tradition going back centuries has it that there were two ideological Spains: the Black Spain associated with the reactionary values of Church and military, representing wealth and land, the substance of the Black Legend, repressing the Red Spain, which promoted democratic progress, liberal and socialist ideals. The distinction between Progressive Liberals and Conservative Catholics is too blunt to reflect the facts (Hopewell, 1986: 25–6), but this is the distinction most frequently evoked during the Franco regime (*Rojo y negro* [1942 Carlos Arévalo, *Red and Black*]) and in many subsequent films revisiting the past; Giménez Rico's *El disputado voto del Sr Cayo* [1986 *Mr Cayo's Contested Vote*] set during the 1977 elections still has a red campaign car for the Socialist party while the extreme right have a black one. With the Second Republic the Red Spain was again in ascendance, but while its supporters, encompassing many different ideologies, did not feel changes were happening fast enough, the Black Spain believed these changes were far too extreme. With its constitution approved in December 1931, parliament under the presidency of Manuel Azañas represented the interests of 26 parties and was restrained from passing the reforming laws on its agenda by the opposition's vociferousness and its own beliefs in free speech. Nonetheless women were given the vote in December 1931 and divorce laws were in place by February 1932. Many other social, agrarian, employment and judiciary reforms were frustrated as the Socialists

---

[1] The 'Soft Dictatorship', a pun based on the Spanish *dictadura* (*dura* means hard, and *blanda* soft).

lost control of the cabinet in the November 1933 elections and the reactionary government of Alejandro Lerroux took over. Civil unrest increased and the right-wing government aggravated the situation by using the military and Civil Guards to suppress demonstrations and riots, at their worst in Asturias in 1934 when General Franco was called in to suppress the miners and their supporters (Álvarez Junco, in Gies, 1999: 81–4).

The arrival of sound on screen

Against the background of political and social upheavals the 1930s also experienced many changes in film production. *The Jazz Singer* [1927 Alan Crosland] is credited as the first film with a soundtrack, although it was Brian Foy who directed the first full talking movie in 1928 with *Lights of New York*. On 26 January 1929, at the second session of the Cineclub in Madrid, *The Jazz Singer* was shown four days before the Paris presentation, without the soundtrack but with a small orchestra and an introduction by Ramón Gómez de la Serna who blackened his face for the occasion (Gubern, 1999: 285–7). It would be released in 1931 as *El ídolo de Broadway* [*The Idol of Broadway*]. It took a number of years before European cinemas could actually project these sound films, and even later in Spain where the capital investment was very slow to manifest itself. Only one film was made in Spain in 1931 while foreign films flooded in to satiate appetites. The development of the talkies required restructuring the film industry, building appropriate studios, developing new skills and refurbishing the theatres. Foreign companies were interested in the Spanish market, and the Phonofilm sound system, which prevailed at first, was initially displayed in Barcelona in June 1927. The pioneering Barcelona Coliseum was fitted for sound by Western Electric in time to show on 19 September 1929 *Innocents of Paris* [Richard Wallace] with Maurice Chevalier's songs, and Madrid's Real Cinema installed the RCA Photophon for its October opening.

Early Spanish-language films from abroad

As the necessary infrastructure was being put in place many film professionals left the country to make sound films in newly equipped studios in the UK, Germany and France, leaving J.E. Delgado in Spain to make sound interviews with his Fox Movietone camera. In 1929 Saturnino Ulargui had *La canción del día* filmed in the Elstree studios by George Samuelson, who also made an English version, *Spanish Eyes*, using the locations previously shot in Madrid. Benito Perojo had always preferred foreign studios and in 1930, with location shots in Seville, he started on the now lost *El embrujo de Sevilla*

[*The Sevilian Spell] in Berlin, and he completed it in Paris where a French version was also made as L'Ensorcellement de Séville [1931] (Gubern, 1994: 188–95). Also in 1930 the Gaumont studios in Paris made Cinópolis, a satirical comedy about the cinema industry directed by José María Castellví and Francisco Elías, with Imperio Argentina and Valentín Parera in the lead.

As the technology was not yet available for dubbing or subtitles but the potential for Spanish audiences in America and Europe was vast, companies in the USA reshot their own scripts in Spanish for Hispanic consumption. To begin with these versions were made with Spanish-speaking actors of different nationalities but, together with the sets and situations, these did not feel right in Spain and gave rise to an 'accent war' in the press,[2] even though the films could not always be projected with their soundtrack. Buñuel was there:

> When talkies first appeared in 1927, the movies instantly lost their international character; in a silent film all you had to do was change the titles, but with talkies you had to shoot the same scenes with the same lighting, but in different languages and with actors from different countries. This, in fact, is one of the reasons so many writers and actors began their hegiras to Hollywood (Buñuel, 1987: 28)

Edgar Neville, a keen participant of the Cineclub in Madrid, was a diplomat appointed to Washington who then moved on to Los Angeles.[3] In 1929 he was asked by MGM to translate and adapt George Hill's The Big House as the Presidio, which he also supervised. The following year he translated Way for a Sailor [1930 Sam Wood] filmed by the Chilean director Carlos Borcosque as En cada puerto un amor [1931 *Love in Every Port]. Partly through his friendship with Irving Thalberg, director of MGM, Neville was also influential in getting other Spanish professionals to Hollywood. For instance, in 1931, on the international reputation of the postsynchronised La bodega [1929 Wine Cellars], Fox Film invited Perojo to make Mamá [*Mother!] in Hollywood, not a Hollywood remake but an original Spanish film, adapting a play credited to Gregorio Martínez Sierra.[4] It was a high society comedy with

---

[2]   It made no sense to portray a family with a Spanish father, Argentine mother and Mexican child. There were parallel tensions in the UK: 'American idioms initially proved incomprehensible (they would not be today, thanks to the mass media), but on the other hand, audiences in the north of England and in Scotland preferred the apparently "classless" accents of American actors to the relentlessly upper middle-class southern English accents of most British screen actors' (Forbes, 2000: 32).

[3]   1899–1967; he was Conde de Berlanga de Duero, a title inherited from his mother since his father had been an English engineer.

[4]   His wife, María Lejárraga y García, is now recognised as the author of most of his plays.

an incipient feminist flavour, very successful on both sides of the Atlantic and billed at the time as 'the first Spanish film from Hollywood'.[5]

Paramount actually set up their own studios in Joinville, on the outskirts of Paris, where they filmed in 14 European languages. They contracted Buñuel (1987: 143) to remake and dub their own films in a way that would appeal to the Spanish market. Perojo directed his first film for Paramount in 1930, *Un hombre de suerte* [*A Lucky Man*], with Roberto Rey and Rosario Pino, a Spanish version now lost of *Un Trou dans le mur* [René Barbéris *A Hole in the Wall*, not to be confused with Robert Florey's 1929 film of the same name]. Florián Rey adapted Frank Turtle's *Her Wedding Night* as *Su noche de bodas* [1931], with Imperio Argentina and Miguel Ligero, first shown in Spain on the night the new Republic was proclaimed on 14 April 1931; Louis Mercanton was in charge of the French version, *Marions-nous*. In the same year Rey directed at least two other films in the Joinville studios, *Lo mejor es reír* [*Laughter's the Best Remedy*] and his only film at the time without Imperio Argentina, *La pura verdad*, a remake of Victor Schertzinger's 1929 *Nothing but the Truth*. Spaniards were picking up the technical skills to make talking pictures. In 1933 Imperio Argentina acted and sang with Carlos Gardel for Paramount in *Melodía de arrabal* [Louis Gasnier *Suburban Melody*, supervised by Florián Rey].

Filming in Spain

An alternative to foreign travel was to remain in Spain and have a soundtrack recorded abroad, usually in Paris. Initially synchronised records were used, but these did not prove satisfactory as the grooves wore out after two dozen projections or synchrony was lost when snapped reels were repaired. José Buchs used this system to film for Diana Exclusivas's *Prim* [1930, released in January 1931 *General Prim*], a monarchist historical costume drama with locations in Morocco and involving some 2000 extras. He also directed *Isabel de Solís, reina de Granada* [1931, *Isabel de Solís, Queen of Granada*]. Other directors did the same, like Sabino Micón for his *La alegría que pasa* [1930 *The Joy that Passes*], or Edgar Neville, just back from the USA, for his satire on Hollywood magnetism, *Yo quiero que me lleven a Hollywood* [1931 *I Want to be Taken to Hollywood*], commissioned by Rosario Pi (Martín-Márquez, 1999a: 56–60). In 1933 Buñuel also returned to make his documentary, *Tierra sin pan* (*Las Hurdes*) [*Land without Bread*], and continued to shock. Las Hurdes is an arid mountainous region sixty miles south-west of Salamanca, practically forgotten through lack of communication. Because of its isolation, in the land without bread, incest was rife and the population

[5] 'La primera película española de Hollywood'; see Gubern on Perojo (1994: 196–208).

subject to all sorts of congenital diseases, not to mention malaria, cholera and malnutrition (Buñuel, 1987: 139–42; Baxter, 1994: 142–6; Edwards, 1982: 37–45).[6] It is difficult to know how much the inhabitants realised the implications of being recorded on camera while they posed, or how many incidents were manipulated for the impact of the documentary. The film has also been carefully edited at different times to provoke specific reactions (Hopewell, 1986: 17–19; Ibarz, 2004: 27–42).[7] The music acts as an ironic comment on the reality captured by the camera, contrasting an inhospitable aridness with affluent sophisticated culture, Brahms' *Fourth Symphony*, and the indifferent tone of Abel Jacquin's voice-over. The soundtrack was finalised in Paris in 1936, but it was projected once in Madrid in 1933 when a text was read and music played on a gramophone. Although obviously not immediately responsible for the fact the region had been isolated for centuries, and the situation had been assessed in 1922, the newly elected right-wing cabinet felt that the documentary was too powerful and provocative, undermined its reluctant agrarian and education policies. The film was banned, together with the projection of Soviet films (Pérez Bowie, 1996: 69–77; Triana Toribio, 2003: 26–7). Intellectuals were recognising the educational and emotional power of the cinema.

The first Spanish sound film

There are disagreements over which Spanish film was the first to use sound, given those made abroad and those filmed in Spain but whose soundtracks were recorded in France. Totally 'made in Spain' could be Francisco Elías's satire of spectators' tastes and aspirations to the film world, *El misterio de la Puerta del Sol* [1930 *The Mystery of the Puerta del Sol*], which used the unsuccessful Phonofilm system.[8] It was first shown in Burgos on 11 January 1929 and then in Zamora on 4 February, but could not be released commercially since none of the theatres had the necessary equipment. The camera used by the newly created company Phonofilm was so heavy that it was easier to move the set than the camera (Gorostiza, 1997: 31). The sound is frequently used impressionistically, and for the spectators' delight it included

[6] As Sánchez Vidal documents, the project was to some extent inspired by the 1927 PhD thesis of a French ethnologist, Maurice Legendre (1984: 88).

[7] Because of changing political circumstances there are various Spanish and French versions with different ideological agendas, of which I have seen three.

[8] Like *The Jazz Singer* only parts of the film were sonorised, and Pozo Arenas therefore describes it as a silent film (1984: 22). It was restored by the Filmoteca Española in 1995, although some of the present silences are a result of the quality of the only surviving copy. It is available from Divisa on a DVD, which also includes *El orador* and *Esencia de verbena* with its interesting montage of popular entertainment; see Ginger, 2007: 69–78.

a few songs and edited in some aerial photography from a draughty plane. Using the same system Ramón Gómez de la Serna had recorded the year before not a film but a four-minute comic speech, *El orador* [*The Orator*], sometimes called *La mano* [*The Hand*] because of one of the amusing props used (Gubern, 1994: 350–2). But the first Spanish sound film is usually identified as the now lost *Fermín Galán*, a biopic directed by Fernando Roldán. It was the only film made entirely in Spain in 1931, but was not well received partly because of the deficiencies of post-synchronisation on records and perhaps because of its political commitment, celebrating the Republican hero executed by firing squad after the unsuccessful coup of 1930, at a time when audiences went to the cinema to escape and dream.

A nascent industry

With the continued and increasing influx of foreign films, which also affected Spanish-speaking America, Spanish filmmakers were seriously concerned and called the first Hispanoamerican Film Conference in 1931. This brought together professionals from 14 countries, who had strong reactions against the patronising attitude of US producers. They discussed many issues but were actually powerless to do anything. The government was criticised for doing so little for the emergent industry. In March 1934, however, a law was passed to have all foreign films dubbed into Spanish, and it also tried to levy a tax of 7.5% on each film presented, but in the face of objections this was subsequently reduced to 1.5% for Spanish films and 4.5% for foreign films (Pozo Arenas, 1984: 30–2). In spite of this local film production was increasing. Caparrós Lera identifies 74 Spanish language films made outside Spain in 1930 and 1931, but there were less than nine a year made abroad in each of the following four years to 1935 as the Spanish studios hired out their facilities to production companies (1981: 16–19). Productions were forthcoming, and until 1934 were still concentrated in Barcelona, although not sufficient at first to compete effectively with all the foreign imports. Cinema was generating its audiences, and the general public was voting with its feet, preferring a talking picture, ideally with songs. This was true in spite of the very poor initial sound quality if the facilities were available, and even if some films not in Spanish required intertitles to summarise the incomprehensible drawls of the foreign actors. Intellectuals were more critical of the new talkies, not just because of the poor sound quality but also aesthetically: it was felt that with dialogue cinema was moving towards the theatre rather than concentrating on its individual visual strengths (Pérez Bowie, 1996: 85–95). Despite this in June 1932 Western Electric celebrated fitting out its first hundred sound cinemas in Spain, at the same time as film crews and actors were returning home.

Exploiting the soundtrack

In these early years of sound, intertitles were at first still very much in evidence, as in *L'Âge d'or,* and, as a continuation of the live music that often accompanied the silent reels, silences tended to be avoided by a continuous musical background. However, for some directors the soundtrack was not specifically used to include dialogue but exploited to create mood; like lighting and framing, it was another element to convey the film's narrative. As in *El misterio...*, Von Sternberg's *The Blue Angel* [1929] or Hitchcock's *Blackmail* [1929], which uses voices and sounds to suggest the victim's sense of persecution and consequent panic, so in *L'Âge d'or* Buñuel exploits the soundtrack. For instance at the beginning of the film, except for a repeated 'Emmenez-le!' [Take him away!], Buñuel distorts the voices of the crowd on the beach, as well as the Governor's speech before cementing the foundation stone of Rome, to convey the nonsense of many political speeches when the respectful and hypocritical listeners are not really paying attention. The music is constant but interrupted for diegetic sound effects (waves, flushing toilet, bird songs) and dialogue; sometimes the characters are seen to speak but are not heard on the soundtrack, as in the sequence of the cow on the bed where only the bell is heard; the Calanda drumbeat[9] is first heard to convey the Conductor's headache and carries on to the end of the film with a final ironic snippet of Van Parys' light music. In *La hija de Juan Simón* [1935 *Juan Simon's Daughter*] a photograph and the sound of the fair trigger the heroine's flashback; in *Don Quintín el amargao* [1935 *The Embittered Don Quentin*] an offensive song is introduced through a diegetic gramophone and then a radio being switched on, with which the whole café gradually starts singing. With Buñuel, both dialogue and music are in fact frequently used for irony, to qualify the image projected on the screen, rather than to convey literal information (Aranda, 1975: 83–4; and Kinder, 1993: 292–4, 298–300).

Barcelona's Orphea Studios

The new technology required reorganisation and capital. As well as cinemas with sound recording equipment, new soundproof studios were needed for the microphones and heavy cameras. The first sound studios, and soon the busiest, were Orphea Films opened in Barcelona in 1931, built in the empty

---

[9]   The Calanda drums and their connection with the Passion of Christ are explained in Buñuel's *Last Breath*, 1987: 19–21. The drum beats are juxtaposed to the Christ-like presentation of the Duc de Blangis [Lionel Salem] who is identified by the intertitles as a depraved and jaded reprobate (Buñuel, 1987: 117).

Pavilion of Chemical Industries set up for the Barcelona 1929 World Fair. Six months after its opening five films were being shot simultaneously. Catalonia was once again taking the lead even if it was Francisco Elías and Camille Lemoine who took the personal initiative. Their first film, now lost, was actually in French, *Pax* [1932], with the Swiss cinematographer Arthur Pochet and René Renault as sound engineer, but no one was found to invest in the distribution of a Spanish pacifist narrative about the overthrow of a dictator. The first Spanish film with direct sound recording was José Buchs' remake of his 1922 musical *Carceleras* [1932] in the same studio and with location filming in Granada, for Diana Exclusivas; now also lost it is described by Gubern as very mediocre (1994: 217). Buchs persevered right into the Franco era but never mastered sound films.

Perojo returned to Spain in 1932 and hired the studio to make another of his high society satirical comedies, *El hombre que se reía del amor* [*The Man Who Laughed at Love*], also with Arthur Pochet at the camera and René Renault on sound; it was commissioned by Rosario Pi of Star Films. It is a film which, like Pedro Mata's novel on which it is based, was considered erotic and ironically critical of the new permissiveness through its presentation of the love life of Juan Herrero [Rafael Rivelles] pursuing women throughout European capitals. This Don Juan finally gets caught at his own game, as he falls in love and is left frustrated and alone at the end. The film, now lost, was subsequently banned in 1943 by the Franco censors, in spite of its moralising ending. The following year Perojo made the satirical musical comedy of intrigue, again set among high society and with luxurious sets, *Susana tiene un secreto* [*Susana has a Secret*]; her secret is that she is a somnambulist and does not want to let her intended know! There followed *Se ha fugado un preso* [*A Prisoner has Escaped*], the first Spanish film to be invited to the Venice Film Festival, inaugurated in 1932, and the first musical farce comedy, topical and critical since Spanish jails were at the time overcrowded.[10]

In 1933 Florián Rey completed, after location shooting in the mountains around Ronda, his now lost *Sierra de Ronda* about Andalusian bandits in the mould of Robin Hood: heroic, sentimental and well-meaning.[11] Also in 1933, in these same studios, Ricard Baños made his last film, *El relicario* [*The Locket*], a remake with songs of a 1927 bullfighting melodrama first directed by Miguel Contrera Torres.[12] Popular taste dictated a predominance of these folkloric themes with songs, already referred to pejoratively in the

---

[10] Again it is unfortunately lost. Detailed accounts of Perojo's lost films can be found in Gubern, who has retrieved the information from contemporary cinema magazines and other sources (1994: 214–34).

[11] For Florián Rey's lost film consult Sánchez Vidal's 1991 monograph.

[12] Consult Caparrós Lera 1981 for all known surviving copies of films up to 1981, made

previous decades as 'españoladas' (D'Lugo, 1997: 7; Lázaro Reboll, 2004: 7–8; Carranque, 1997: 78). Francisco Elías also directed the musical romance *Boliche*, which opened on Christmas Day 1933, making a lot of money subsequently invested and lost in his 1935 crime spoof *Rataplán* – both films are now lost. He then directed a film a year until, as a Nationalist supporter in Republican Barcelona, he left for Mexico in 1938 where he worked until 1954 making eight more films, before returning to Spain and making his last, *Marta* [1955], a disaster at the box-office.

Cinematográfica Española Americana

In 1932, spurred on by the Hispanoamerican conference held the previous year and with financial backing from the Madrid Chamber of Commerce, CEA was set up on the initiative of writers including Benavente, the Quintero brothers, Carlos Arniches, Pedro Muñoz Seca, and other important directors and personalities (Besas, 1985: 8). Shares in the new company did not sell particularly well but six sound stages were built at Ciudad Lineal just outside Madrid, and Tobis-Klangfilm sound equipment was installed. The first film, made in 1933 and distributed by the new company CIFESA, was *Agua en el suelo* [*Water in the Ground*] directed by Eusebio Fernández Ardavín who, back from Joinville, was named the studio's executive producer. It was the first Quintero brothers' script written specifically for the cinema rather than a stage adaptation, and proved itself a successful clergy melodrama dealing with an irresponsible press slandering a priest and his ward, who are both eventually vindicated.[13] Ardavín subsequently directed two folkloric musicals in 1935, *Vidas rotas* and *La bien pagada* [*Broken Lives, *She Who is Well Paid*], as well as contributing the script of Santiago Ontañón's 1936 *Los claveles* [**The Carnations*]. In the same studios Perojo also directed his 1934 *Crisis mundial* [*World Crisis*], of which only a fragment remains: another of his high society romantic and satirical comedies set mostly in a Swiss hotel against the background of the Wall Street Crash and sumptuous *art déco* sets, starring Antoñita Colomé, Miguel Ligero, both already favourite stars of the Republic, and Ricardo Nuñez. This box-office success must have been a great contrast to CEA's second hit in 1934, the adaptation of *La Dolorosa* [**Our Lady of Sorrows*], a *zarzuela* directed by the Frenchman Jean Grémillon,

in Spain during the Second Republic; since then other copies have been restored. He includes credit acknowledgement as well as plots and commentaries.

[13] It is one of those films tagged here as a 'clergy film' that were going to reappear frequently in the following thirty years of Spanish Cinema, the 'cine de curas', which present narratives involving at least one member of the Catholic clergy, obviously not the exclusive prerogative of Francoist film production.

with Rosita Díaz Gimeno, Agustín Godoy, Ramón Cebrián, and some 1500 extras on location in Aragon, a melodrama exuding folkloric atmosphere and latent sensuality.

Estudios Cinema Español, Sociedad Anónima

ECESA followed in 1933, building their studios near Aranjuez with the best equipment available to date. In 1934, for their first film, Perojo remade *El negro que tenía el alma blanca* [*The Black Man with a White Soul*], as a luscious musical, making many changes to the 1927 plot, and casting the Cuban pianist and singer Marino Barreto, Antoñita Colomé and the flamenco singer Angelillo (Ángel Sampedro Montero). Only a fragment remains of this great success, which included 15 separate numbers.[14] When the film was re-released in 1948, one of the songs was censored out together with a swimming-pool scene, where an actress takes a shower, and singer Angelillo's name was also deleted from the credits as one who had emigrated to America with other Republican artists. The other great success of the year was Francisco Gargallo's *Sor Angélica* [*Sister Angelica*]. The same year Florián Rey filmed the very successful frivolous *El novio de mamá* [*Mother's Boyfriend*], again lost.

Compañía Industrial Film Española, Sociedad Anónima

More studios were opened in the next two years, as well as dubbing companies like Trilla-La Riva, Fono España, MGM and Acustic, created to deal with all the foreign imports (Ávila, 1997: 73–5 and *passim*). In 1934 when Buñuel left the Joinville Paramount studios, he supervised the Warner Brothers' dubbing operations in Madrid for about ten months (Buñuel, 1987: 143).

By 1935 the Valencian CIFESA, controlled by the Casanova family, started producing its own films, on the strength of its experience and success as distributors of Spanish films, and importers of Columbia Pictures since 1932 (Jordan & Allinson, 2005: 8–9). Besas explains that CIFESA's distribution of Capra's *It Happened One Night* in 1934 made the company enough money to follow through with their project (1985: 11). CIFESA had offices in Madrid, Barcelona, Bilbao, Seville and Majorca, with good connections throughout Europe and many American countries. Learning from Hollywood they contracted directors, technicians and stars, like Imperio Argentina and

---

[14] Homaged in a sequence of Farida Ben Lyziad's *La vida perra de Juanita Narboni* [2005 *Juanita Narboni's Dirty Rotten Life*].

Miguel Ligero. They played a conservative card making popular musicals and clergy films, establishing themselves as the strongest production company. Their first contract was for Florián Rey, who had returned from Paris in 1933. He directed a number of successive remakes like his 1927 box-office success *La hermana San Sulpicio* [1934], which exploited regional interests as a Galician doctor [Miguel Ligero] courts a flamenco-singing Sevilian novice [Imperio Argentina]; slow in its editing pace but with good framing, the dialogue gently questions the position of women in society. It combined what the audience wanted, folkloric elements and songs, with very little non-diegetic music. Other clergy films and melodrama followed from CIFESA, including *El cura de aldea* [1936 *The Village Priest*] directed by Francisco Camacho, a remake of Florián Rey's silent 1927 film, which for Caparrós Lera brings out the hunger, pride and religiosity of the Castilian land (1981: 140–1). In 1935 there was also José Buchs' *Madre Alegría* [*Mother Happiness*], set in 1918 Madrid to deal with abandoned children, and his remake of the 1925 *El niño de las monjas* [*The Convent Child*] who becomes a bull-fighter. Directed in 1935 for Diana Exclusivas and distributed by CIFESA, both films reveal antifeminist fears brought about by the current emancipation of women.[15] CIFESA also signed up the cosmopolitan polyglot Benito Perojo in 1935 to make four films, including the musical *Rumbo al Cairo* [*The Road to Cairo*] and a remake of José Buchs' 1921 *La verbena de la Paloma* [*The Fair of the Dove*], frequently singled out as one of the most accomplished films of the period. *Rumbo al Cairo*, of which the final reel is still missing, was another very successful romantic musical following the Hollywood pattern, with Miguel Ligero, Ricardo Nuñez and the then unknown Mary del Carmen Merino, where the journey of the title ends short and happily in Majorca. Carmen Merino, the daughter of a Madrid taxi driver, chosen from 85 aspirants for her blue eyes and fair hair, received a contract that reveals how CIFESA wanted to control its employees following the successful Hollywood studios: 'For the duration of this contract, the said young lady binds herself not to put on weight, not to have a boyfriend, not to alter the present colour of her hair, not to go outside on foot, and not to stay up all night, except with permission from the management.'[16] The witty script was written by Edgar Neville and Alfredo Miralles. In 1936 the company contracted Eduardo García Maroto who directed his first feature film, *La hija del penal* [*The Daughter of the Penitentiary*], a gentle comedy satire on the

---

[15] The latter was remade in colour by Ignacio F. Iquino in 1958, and in a Mexican version in 1944.

[16] 'Durante la vigencia de este contrato, dicha señorita, se compromete a no engordar, a no tener novio, a no cambiar el color actual de su pelo, a no pasear a pie por la calle y a no trasnochar, salvo permiso de esta dirección.' Gubern, 1994: 252–9, 255.

prison service scripted with Miguel Mihura, but now lost. On the strength of this film Maroto signed a contract to make two films a year for CIFESA.

Filmófono

In 1929, like CIFESA, Filmófono started by distributing films, specialising in selective non-commercial 'Art' films. It was responsible for the only projection of *L'Âge d'or* in Spain and for showing Soviet films. To balance the accounts it also distributed the early Disney cartoons, but its elitist choice of films made it difficult for its cinemas to return a profit. In 1930 the company also attempted to make sound films with its own system, and distributed Florián Rey's now lost *Fútbol, amor y toros* [*Football, Love and Bullfighting*]. It was owned by the Urgoiti family from the Basque country who already controlled two liberal newspapers (*El Sol* and *La Voz*), and a publishing firm (Espasa). Ricardo Urgoiti managed Unión Radio Madrid, set up in 1924, which also explains the early interest in sound films. In 1935 Filmófono decided to counterbalance its Art Films by producing popular entertaining films as economically as possible. Buñuel, who was then working for Warner's, proposed, or agreed, to be executive producer as long as his name did not appear in the credits; he even invested some of his mother's money into the venture (Buñuel, 1987: 143). With values very different from CIFESA, Filmófono set out to create 'a contemporary and progressive reinterpretation of particular traditional themes from Spanish popular culture',[17] and 18 films were produced in two years (Edwards, 2005: 6). The films were planned on a tight schedule to keep the budget low, with a predetermined crew including José María Beltrán on camera and Fernando Remacha as musical director. There is a focus on melodramatic plots, where interest and irony is provided by excess, female victims, songs and happy endings. Aranda argues that Buñuel was much more involved in the planning and directing of the films than he cared to admit (1975: 100–15). The first was a remake of Noriega's 1925 *Don Quintín el amargao* [1935], adapted from a sentimental melodramatic *sainete* by Carlos Arniches, which Buñuel enjoyed hamming up (1987: 144) adding a number of passing references to the contemporary cinema and actors. Perojo was to have been the original director, but since he was contracted by CIFESA, the direction was passed on to the sound engineer Luis Marquina.[18] The film

---

[17] 'Una relectura moderna y progresista de ciertos temas tradicionales de la cultura popular española' (Perucha, 1992: 44), also quoted by Triana Toribio, 2003: 21–2; Hopewell describes the difference in other words (1986: 19–20).

[18] Luis Marquina (1904–1980) went on to write and direct his own films. Buñuel reworked this film in México as *La hija del engaño* [1951 *Daughter of Deceit*]; see P. Evans, 1995: 36–48, as Buñuel's Mexican films will not be included here.

made enough money to allow the next production, *La hija de Juan Simón* [1935 *Juan Simon's Daughter*; remade in 1957 by Gonzalo Delgrás], starring Pilar Muñoz and singer Angelillo, who had a great screen presence. This is a melodrama based on a Sobrevila script and play itself based on a song; but then many people went to the cinema to hear the songs in a context and, here, to see one sequence of Carmen Amaya's dancing. The film was first directed by Nemesio Sobrevila, who had written the original play and designed the sets; but he was sacked for not working fast enough and replaced by José Luis Sáenz de Heredia, out of work since *Patricio miró a una estrella* [1934 *Patricio Looked at a Star*] failed at the box-office.[19] In keeping with the company's proletarian ideals, *La hija ...* opened on the same night in 14 cinemas, both in prestigious and working-class districts (Kinder, 1993: 297). 'Audiences, however, were so delighted to see Spanish stories and *Madrileño* actors on the screen rather than American comedies remade by Frenchmen with Mexican actors that the first two [films] were as successful on film as on stage' (Baxter, 1994: 151–2). This success assured Sáenz de Heredia his next film *¿Quién me quiere a mí?* [1936 *Who Loves Me?*], an attempt to launch Mari-Tere Pacheco, a child star billed as the Spanish Shirley Temple, in a sentimental comedy. The topical plot explored the question of which divorcing parent should care for the child (divorce laws were in place since February 1932), but it was the least successful of the Filmófono productions: 'My only commercial failure, and a pretty dismal one at that' (Buñuel, 1987: 144). Lively Mari-Tere was also included in the next film *¡Centinela alerta!* [1936 *Sentry, Keep Watch!*], another adaptation of an Arniches *sainete* with Jean Grémillon directing, although Buñuel had to take over when his friend was indisposed. A comedy about two recruits adopting a single mother and her daughter, with Angelillo once again making a success with his singing. It became Filmófono's biggest box-office hit even if it was completed after the Nationalist uprising and only released a year later, on 12 July 1937, without directing credits (Buñuel, 1987: 145). These films were not devoid of social criticism, as the lower classes are shown exploited by the socially more fortunate, women dependent on sometimes brutal men, with the inclusion of contemporary allusions in the dialogues and small subversive details in the sets, this last taking a satirical perspective on the army recruits. Filmófono announced sixteen films to be made in the following year (Aranda, 1975: 115), but the consequences of the military coup put an end to the projects. It started production again in 1940 with Ricardo Quintana's *Jai-Alai* [*Basque*

---

[19] The film satirises the appeal of the cinema with a touch of pathos and irony, as a film star comes to the shop where Patricio works and his so-called friends play a joke on him. It was the first time the inside of a studio was included in a Spanish film, and for Caparrós Lera it presents its characters very persuasively (1981: 279), but Sáenz de Heredia believed it lacked the popular appeal of the *folclóricas* (Mortimore, 1975: 181).

Pelota] and closed down six films later in 1951 with Luis Suárez de Lezo's *Servicio en la mar* [**Service at Sea*]; this was without Ricardo Urgoiti who had left for Argentina with Angelillo and made a few more films there before returning to Spain in 1943.

Rosario Pi's Star Films

These successful companies were not the only ones that contributed to the blossoming of cinema in Spain during the short-lived Republic. Already mentioned is Rosario Pi, one of the founders of Star Films, producing Neville's 1931 *Yo quiero que me lleven a Hollywood*, followed by Perojo's *El hombre que se reía del amor* in 1932. It is also known that she wrote two film scripts: *Doce hombres y una mujer* [1934 *Twelve Men and a Woman*] directed by Fernando Delgado but now lost, and, very different in setting and theme, *El gato montés* [1936 **The Wildcat*] which she directed herself in the Barcelona Orphea studios including numerous exterior locations. It is a tragic musical melodrama again opposing social classes and raising both gender and racial issues, where the gypsy, the bandit and the wealthy bullfighter all die (Martin-Márquez, 1999a: 65–82). It was a new adaptation with the author of the original *zarzuela* Manuel Penella, which had been filmed in Hollywood twelve years earlier as *Tiger Love* by George Melford. The second film she directed was another *zarzuela*, also lost, *Molinos de viento* [1937 *Windmills*], for which she recreated a Dutch village in Barcelona in order to explore gender relationships when a crew of sailors arrives at a coastal village. It was not shown in Spain until 1939, when it also received a New York screening.

Visitors from abroad

Most companies had no chance to last long. Inca Films, for instance, was started by Géza Pollatschick and Erich Darmstaedler, Jewish cineasts who fled Nazi persecutions, and with an international crew produced Ardavín's *Vidas rotas* [1935] in the CEA studios. It is a psychological melodrama adapted from a novel by Concha Espina, which presented a very different interpretation of life on Spanish screens (J.B. Heinink, in Pérez Perucha, 1997: 97). Wilhelm Goldberg was the cameraman, and he then worked on Edgar Neville's comedy of intrigue *El malvado Carabel* [1935 **The Evil Carabel*], a kind heart who never manages to become a true criminal.[20] Hein-

---

[20] As from 1941 credits acknowledge him as Guillermo Goldberg. This comedy was remade in 1956 by Fernando Fernán Gómez, who also took the main part, and in 1962 in Mexico.

rich Gärtner, who signed himself Enrique Guerner, arrived in 1934 with 97 films to his credit, the most recent filmed in Portugal. He was the cameraman for *La hermana San Suplicio*, *Vidas rotas*, *Nobleza baturra*, *Morena Clara*, and some further 80 titles. Max Nosseck was in a similar position when he founded Ibérica Films but only made three films in Spain: *Una semana de felicidad* [1934 *One Week of Happiness*], *Poderoso Caballero* [*A Big Guy*] and *Aventura oriental* [**Eastern Adventure*], these last two in 1935.

Animation

One company that lasted as long as the Republic was the Sociedad Española de Dibujos Animados [Spanish Animation Company], founded in 1930 by Joaquin Xaudaró and Ricardo García López, aka K-Hito. Their first release *El rata primero* [**The Rat First*] was made in 1932, and their first talking animation followed the next year, *La novia de Juan Simón* [*Juan Simón's Girl*].

Production and projection

By 1935 there were eleven studios in Spain, which as well as making their own films would hire out their facilities to independent producers, of which there were more than twenty, some of them only managing one film; and there were eighteen film laboratories. Curiously, in spite of the need for soundproof studios, a lot more location filming took place than in the silent era as film production increased steadily throughout the Republican years (Caparrós Lera, 1981: 313 and 326). Gubern has tabulated 6 films in 1932, 17 in 1933, 21 in 1934, 37 in 1935, and 28 by the middle of July 1936, most of these in Barcelona (1995: 129), statistics demonstrating the rapid growth of an emerging industry that was to be shattered by political events, which would also destroy most of its achievements. Caparrós Lera lists 95 titles of the 109 films, some incomplete, made between 1932 and 1936 that were lost (1981: 337–40), and the Filmoteca is patiently restoring what it can. During the same years the number of Spanish films made abroad was decreasing rapidly (see Caparrós Lera's table in 1981: 16; reproduced in Pozo Arenas, 1984: 30). By 1935, Spain had a population of 24 million and 3300 cinemas; 1739 (over 52%) of these were on the east coast and, whereas just over half of these could screen a sound film, in the rest of the country less than half of the halls had sound facilities. In Barcelona all but two of the 114 cinemas and in Madrid 58 of its 64 cinemas could project with sound. Although new equipment was being installed, not all cities could afford a cinema, as Laurie Lee recalls of his first evening in Segovia, in July 1935: 'once again, the aqueduct came into use, with a cotton sheet strung from one of its pillars, on to which a pale beam of light, filtering from an opposite window, projected an ancient and jittery melodrama. Half the town it seemed had turned out for the show, carrying footstools and little chairs, while children swarmed on the rooftops' and he goes on to describe the audience's reaction (Lee, 1974: 93–4). A similar experience of the villagers arriving at the town hall with their own chair to watch a film, shared by a number of personal friends, is recorded at the beginning of Víctor Erice's *El espíritu de la colmena* [1973 *The Spirit of the Beehive*], set in the early 1940s.

Some social implications

Employees of the film industry organised themselves into fifteen professional organisations to protect their rights, and the government also passed laws affecting the projection of films. On 27 October 1935 the President of the Republic, Niceto Alcalá Zamora, signed a decree allowing the censorship of films 'which attempt to falsify historical facts or harm the respect owed to the institutions or the personalities of our nation',[21] while previously in April the Governor of Catalonia banned a nudist film *El paraíso recobrado* [Xavier Güell, *Paradise Recovered*]. On 1 May he had decreed that films had to be classified according to their suitability for those aged under fifteen. That same month *L'Âge d'or* was banned from the Surrealist Exhibition in the Canaries, and in October so was *The Devil is a Woman* [1935 Josef von Sternberg] for showing two drunk Civil Guards. The Church had started to colour-code films in 1932 (White: moral and inoffensive, can be watched by children; Blue: moral but not for children; Pink: moral but not suitable for young people; Red: deals with lurid subjects or contains immoral scenes; Green: pornographic; Black: offensive to pious audiences). However, both middle- and working-class enthusiasts found a growing number of film clubs where they could indulge their curiosity and passion for the cinema; Caparrós Lera identifies 29 of them (1981: 29–30). A new film review was launched in 1932, *Nuestro Cinema* [*Our Cinema*], and some 31 academic books on the cinema were published during the period (Caparrós Lera, 1981: 35). Cinema was introduced as a subject at Barcelona's Autonomous University in 1932, and in the Catalan school curriculum of 1934–5.

A brief look at the rise of the studios and their production reveals that the period is dominated by remakes with soundtracks, and plots adapted from other genres, dramatic rather than novels. The film industry was burgeoning even if the government only thought of taxing its earnings in a restless and

---

[21] 'que traten desnaturalizar los hechos históricos o tiendan a menoscabar el prestigio debido a instituciones o personalidades de nuestra patria' (Caparrós Lera, 1981: 37; see also Pozo Arenas, 1984: 34, 38–9).

precarious socio-political climate (Hopewell, 1986: 15 and 22). As in the USA during the Depression, cinema provided an important safety valve and source of escapism for city-dwellers, who shunned serious films that explored contemporary issues, 'to dream a little', as the poet Luis Cernuda put it (C. Morris, 1980: 117–21; Triana Toribio, 2003: 25). In contrast to the critics, the general public voted with its feet, preferring musicals, whether based on *zarzuelas* or in the spirit of Hollywood comedies where Benito Perojo dominated. Perojo was the most prolific director of the period, generally very well received both in Spain and abroad, but attacked by left-wing critics for presenting a fictional world ignoring the Spanish reality that spectators did not really want to watch. His comedies and intrigues tended to be set in cosmopolitan circles and concentrated on entertaining, although some, like *El negro que tenía el alma blanca*, encouraged reflection and others, like *Crisis mundial*, took important world events as their context. For Caparrós Lera these films were ironic and satirical (1981: 277) and their dialogues included plenty of contemporary references. It is a great pity that so many of Perojo's films have been destroyed because visually and on paper he stands out as the most interesting director of the period (Gubern, 1994).

The folkloric appeal and regional colours

Folkloric settings were very popular, with *jotas* or flamenco, referred to pejoratively as *españoladas* or *folclóricas*, sometimes based on *zarzuelas*.[22] These frequently, but not always, focused on an Andalusia that had been exoticised by fascinated foreigners, and included plenty of music, gypsies, and preferably a bullfighter or two. Good examples are Fernando Delgado's remake of the 1925 *Currito de la Cruz* [1936 *Currito of the Cross*], and Francisco Elías's *María de la O* [1936, released in 1939] as a vehicle for the dancer Carmen Amaya and Julio Peña, remade in 1958 by Ramón Torrado. Harry D'Abbadie d'Arrast-Soriano[23] also joined in with the now lost *La traviesa molinera* [1934 *The Miller's Mischievous Wife/Le Tricorne/It Happened in Spain*], scripted by Edgar Neville. Many of these films are set in a *cortijo*

[22] Woods, 2004b: 202–7, and see chapter 1, note 34. As Martin-Márquez argues, the label is still a prickly issue for Spanish critics (1999a: 64–6), as an example, see Caparrós Lera, 1981: 264. The term *folclórica* is frequently used to present this type of film positively when made by a Spanish director. For the *zarzuela*, see Gubern, 1998: 50–1. The *jota* is the traditional Aragonese dance.

[23] In 1935 he made an English version of the story *The Three Cornered Hat*, his last film. The *IMDb* defines him as Argentine, but his parents were French Basques, and he established himself in Hollywood where he made eight films before coming to Europe where he stayed although he made no more films.

[farming estate that usually raises fighting bulls], which provide a kind of microcosm in which a frequently stereotyped or idealised society could sort out its problems. The conflict between the son of the land and the take-it-all-for granted *señorito*[24] could also be used as 'a way of treating class problems while seeming not to' as in Rosario Pi's *El gato montés* (Labanyi, 1997: 226). José Buchs, who had made a film a year, also included farmhands on strike in *El rayo* [1936 *The Lightning Bolt*].

The Galician setting is very prominent in the remake of *La casa de la Troya* [1936 Adolfo Aznar and Joan Vilà Vilamala] or the Peruvian Richard Harlan's *Odio* [1933 *Hatred*], now both lost. But the three most celebrated films of this period, all made by CIFESA in the CEA studios, were: Florián Rey's remake of *Nobleza baturra* [*Aragonese Virtue/Rustic Chivalry*], released with simultaneous second nights on 12 October 1935 in 35 cities; Benito Perojo's *La verbena de la Paloma* [*The Fair of the Dove*], released on 23 December 1935; and *Morena Clara* [1936 *Dark and Bright*] also by Rey, premiered on 11 April 1936 the day before Easter, also with multiple simultaneous releases in major cities (Besas, 1985: 11–12). For once critics and public agreed in praising these films as exceptional.

Nobleza baturra (1935)

Today's spectator may not be enthralled by the plot of *Nobleza baturra* about a rejected wealthy suitor, Marco [Manuel Luna], who launches a libellous song round the village at the expense of María del Pilar [Imperio Argentina] because she prefers Sebastián [Juan de Orduña], a young farmhand her father [José Calle] does not consider appropriate. Pilar would choose her reputation over love, but Sebastián sacrifices himself to prove the song wrong and is then accepted as a son-in-law thanks to the private contrition and attrition of the villain Marco. However, the film provides a wonderful evocation of an idealised rural Aragon, through its locations and images of agricultural plenty, songs, dances, language, humour and stereotypes (including a priest [Juan Espantaleón] who keeps the peace) and the captivating singing of Imperio Argentina. The film is remarkable in the way the music and traditional dances, except for the harvest song that frames the whole film, are naturally integrated into the narrative to convey the characters' emotion.[25]

---

[24] The *cortijo* setting would be pervasive during the Franco years, and a psychological examination of the stereotype can be seen in Antonio Giménez Rico's 1976 *Retrato de familia* [*Family Portrait*].

[25] A skill that some directors had still not acquired in the 1960s, in spite of their desire to continue with the genre.

The scarce non-diegetic music is also essential to the characterisation, like the musical counterpoint that accompanies the parallel montage that conveys Pilar's distraught reaction as the libellous verses are sung. The editing is also unusual for the time since it does away with the expected scene transition of irises and wipes, with one brief exception that shows the town gossiping by using a rapid of sequence of diagonal, anticlockwise, horizontal wipes, a lateral split screen, and finally a dissolve. In contrast it prefers sharp cuts, pans and swift dissolves to black or to another image to convey the passing of the night or the change of location. The pace of the montage also varies with the mood of the sequence, and there is a predominance of close camera work with medium close-ups contrasted with panoramas to present the countryside, all of which contribute to the film's reputation.

La verbena de la Paloma (1935)

La verbena de la Paloma is said to have used colour rather than tinting in one of its sequences (Caparrós Lera, 1987: 36) although the colour must have faded rapidly, but this was in the same year as Mamoulian's *Becky Sharp*, the first colour film. It is an extended adaptation of the popular eponymous one-act *zarzuela*, and successfully transfers the stage performance to a screen experience. It is still set in Madrid on one day established by four close-ups, beginning at 7 a.m. on the feast of Our Lady of the Dove, Tuesday 15 August 1893, the year the original *zarzuela* was composed. Unusually for Perojo it is set in a working-class district, albeit entirely constructed in the CEA studios. Julián a typesetter [Roberto Rey] with a very jealous disposition and Susana the seamstress [Raquel Rodrigo] argue and, encouraged by her trollish aunt Tía Antonia [Dolores Cortés], she decides with her sister Casta [Charito Leonís] to spend the evening at the annual neighbourhood fair with the ridiculous roué of an apothecary, Don Hilarión [Miguel Ligero]. Of course the lovers make up at the end, after a frantic chase in a draper's shop that ends in the police station. Filming entirely in the studio allowed a lot of unexpected camera movements, panning and tracking shots, as well as subjective framing through shelves and other orifices, with angle changes including the vertical top-shot of Julián going up the stairs to the sisters' flat or the panning sequence of the flats across the street, which brings to mind Hitchcock's *Rear Window* [1954], introducing a musical number crosscut with the flamenco being danced and sung in the Café de Manila opposite, where the camera has entered through the door and panned round. For sequence changes straight cuts are preferred, with some close-ups, a few wipes and many blurred pans. The songs are presented in creative and different ways, allowing the spectators to enjoy the fact they are watching the film of a *zarzuela*, with for instance Julián working in the printing room, and as the wheel of the printing

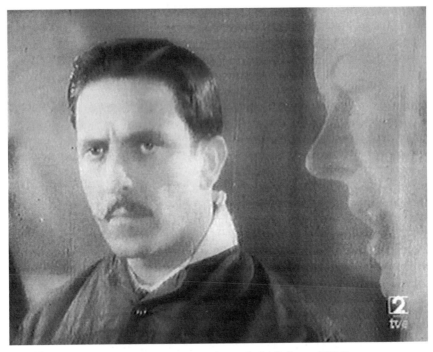

3a Double exposure of Perojo's *La verbena de la Paloma* (1935)

press turns the image dissolves to the wheel of Susana's sewing machine, then there is a superimposition of his face singing, expressing his thoughts, to which is added the superimposition of Susana's profile when she replies, all against the background of the working Julián; and when the final chorus is called it is the other printers who join in as themselves. The crowd scenes are particularly effective, the whole film conveying what Hopewell describes as a strong sense of community and solidarity (1986: 16–17), the festive spirit being expressed by alternating whole groups in general shots with sharp focus on selected faces. Perojo has a fine eye and ear for detail, not just in recreating the end-of-century atmosphere, but also in little humorous touches like the chamber pot under the bed when the sisters are trying to hide Don Hilarión, Tía Antonia sitting on his hat to hide it, or even the inclusion of background noises where necessary to evoke the crowds. Perojo went on to produce a third version of the *Verbena* with Cesáreo González in 1963, in which Miguel Ligero repeated his part of Don Hilarión and the direction was undertaken by Sáenz de Heredia.

Morena Clara (1936)

Morena Clara is the adaptation of a three-act play premiered in March the year before, in 1935, with added songs, which are still sometimes repeated in more recent films. Rey turned it into a busy and light hearted Andalusian comedy about a witty and cheeky gypsy [Imperio Argentina] who challenges her severe and prejudiced prosecutor's rhetoric [Manuel Luna] when he wants to condemn her and her brother [Miguel Ligero] to six months' imprisonment for selling 'subtracted' hams back to their owner. She enters the service of the prosecutor's mother [María Brú], solves the family's problems and wins the prosecutor's heart! The contrasting behaviour of the attractive gypsy and the upper classes is, however, pertinently critical of Spanish society's prejudices against gypsies and the establishment's own hypocrisy. Like *La verbena*, the film allows women a lot more freedom than they will enjoy after the Civil War, and here the siblings are defended by a female barrister [Perfiria Sanchiz].[26] The film celebrates with great enthusiasm, humour and many intrigues, a society that resolves its racial and class differences, at a time when the country is about to tear itself apart. Like the previous two films, it still surprises with its cinematographic achievements, beginning with a long tracking shot into an inn with a pivoting camera. When it was learnt that Rey and his star had gone to Germany to make their next film, and had both met Goebbels and Hitler, this box-office success was banned in Republican Spain where it had been so popular (Kinder, 1993: 460–1). It was remade in 1954 by Luis Lucia with Lola Flores, Fernando Fernán Gómez, Miguel Ligero playing an uncle rather than the brother, Julia Lajos, Ana Mariscal, and Manuel Luna playing the prosecutor's father.

Popular comedies

Other types of comedies were also popular and, given spectator preference, overlapped with the folkloric films. Perojo's cosmopolitan comedies dominated in the bills, like his adaptation of Carlos Arniches's *¡Es mi hombre!* [1935 *He's My Man!*] on how to succeed with wit and kindness. This was his only film that cannot be described as musical, but it is now lost to posterity. The play had already been adapted for the screen in 1927 by Carlos Fernández Cuenca and would have a third remake in 1966 by Rafael Gil. Edgar Neville's *La señorita de Trevélez* [1936 *Miss Trevélez*] was a bittersweet comedy of manners based on another Arniches play, which Bardem took up in 1956 as *Calle Mayor* [*Main Street*]; but whereas Bardem developed

---

[26] For the sexual politics of Spanish society at this time, see Graham, 1995: 99–116, in Graham & Labanyi.

the plot into a dark indictment of provincial gender attitudes, Neville treats the small-mindedness with a lighter touch (Roberts, 1999: 27–9). It was edited by Sara Ontañón.[27] Luis Marquina directed *El bailarín y el trabajador* [1936 *The Dancer and the Worker*], adapting the original play with its author Jacinto Benavente. This sentimental musical comedy, the third from the CEA studios, contrasts the frivolous and wealthy with the conscientious working class as the dancer of waltzes becomes a reliable factory employee. The plot and themes are presented with efficient editing contrasting phoney studio sets with location scenes in a factory. There were also a few army comedies in the style of *¡Centinela alerta!*, like Mariano Lapeyra's *Amor en maniobras* [1935 **Love on Manoeuvres*].

Crime

Not as popular were the suspense thrillers such as *El desaparecido* [1934 Antonio Graciani, *He Who Disappeared*, remade in Mexico in 1989]; *Al margen de la ley* [1935 Ignacio F. Iquino, **On the Margin of the Law*, remade as *El expreso de Andalucía* in 1956 by Francisco Rovira Beleta and in 1990 by Imanol Uribe] based on an actual incident that took place in 1924. With a good dose of comedy the screenwriter José Santugini directed his only film *Una mujer en peligro* [1936 **A Woman in Danger*], which, according to Caparrós Lera, is the first film to have used a zoom shot (1981, p. 326). Others were Juan Faidellá's *Error de juventud* [1935 **A Mistake of Youth*] or Pedro Puche's *Barrios bajos* [1937 **Low Districts*]. On his way to Latin America James Bauer directed *No me mates* [1936 **Don't Kill Me*]. Similarly, there were very few films that demonstrated a more explicit social commitment, and those made were even less successful: *Sobre el cieno* [1933 Fernando Roldán, **In the Mire*] exposing prostitution in Madrid; or Alfonso Benavides's *Madrid se divorcia* [1933 but released in 1935, **Madrid Gets Divorced*].

Siblings divided: the military rebellion

A real film industry was developing, and CIFESA with an eye on international distribution had offices in Paris, Berlin, Jerusalem and some Latin American countries. In 1936, however, when the Popular Front regained the majority in

---

[27] An editor who certainly warrants more attention. *MCU.es* credits her with 42 films between 1937 and 1965, the *IMDb* with 49 films, omitting her first contribution in *La señorita de Trevélez*, *Una mujer en peligro* [1936], *Nuestro culpable* [1938], and how many more? Another editor with 48 titles listed is Margarita de Ochoa.

the February elections, the military reacted with the uprising of 18 July. The government retained control of the major cities of Madrid, Bilbao, Barcelona and Valencia. This, however, initiated a long and bloody Civil War that put an end to the burgeoning film industry and a period sometimes described as the Golden Age of cinema, when Spanish films were more popular in Spain than foreign imports.[28] Raquel Meller had returned from France to make her first sound film in Spain, *Lola Triana*, but it was never completed.[29]

Struggling productions

Some productions nonetheless continued for a while. Iquino made *Diego Corrientes*, a drama about mountain bandits that had already been filmed in 1914 by Alberto Marro, in 1924 by José Buchs, and would have its own colour version in 1959 directed by Isasi-Isasmendi. Perojo's *Nuestra Natacha* [*Our Natasha*, remade in Argentina in 1944] was actually filmed in the summer of 1936 in Barcelona, based on a play by Alejandro Casona premiered in Madrid on 6 February that same year. The film dealt with student protests, significantly motivated by a woman, arguing for the reform of antiquated and oppressive educational methods, and the consequent violent suppression by the establishment. Not released during the war, it was subsequently considered too subversive, labelled 'communist' and banned in 1939. The negatives were deposited in the Riera laboratories in Madrid, which were destroyed in a fire on 16 August 1945, when many other films were also lost. *Nuestra Natacha* would have been interesting as it included Fernando Rey's first acting part, cast as a student while he was studying architecture. Antonio Sau Olite's *Aurora de esperanza* [1937 *Dawn of Hope*] was a committed drama about the frustration and misery of unemployment and social injustice, and a father who while on a hunger march enlists in the Republican militia when the army's rebellion is announced, concluding with an upbeat image of solidarity and the moral superiority of the working class. Commissioned by the entertainment industry's trade union, much of it was filmed in the streets of Barcelona and mostly with unknown actors, but its release was delayed for a year and then it was dismissed as propaganda; audiences preferred 'the "drug" of entertainment instead of the truth about Spain' (Triana Toribio, 2003: 25 and 34). The Union's second commission was a very different project: Pedro Puche's *Barrios bajos* [1937 *Low Districts*], a melodrama set in a bar-hotel in Barcelona's red light district by the harbour, anticipating Marcel Carné's *Quai des Brumes* [1938 *Port of Shadows*] but with a happy

[28] Interesting statistical tables for the period are presented by Caparrós Lera (1981: 347–52) and Gubern (1995: 155–6).

[29] For Raquel Meller, see pp. 24–5, or initiate a Google search.

ending as the lovers sail away from the criminal underworld and dead bodies. It was filmed in two weeks and opened in Barcelona, Valencia and Madrid in May. The Madrid branch of the film union preferred to commission an escapist and subversive musical comedy that nonetheless targeted the judiciary and industrial magnates (Triana Toribio, 2003: 34). *Nuestro culpable* [1938 *Our Guilty Man*] was filmed entirely in the abandoned Madrid CEA studios in spite of falling Nationalist bombs. It was entrusted to the Italian Fernando Mignoni, who also wrote the script even though until then he had been a set decorator for a number of Perojo films, among others. The film, which, like the other two commissions, kept a lot of union members in work, was edited by María Paredes and Sara Ontañón. Not all other films started in 1936 were so lucky. For instance, Fernando Delgado's comedy *El genio alegre* [*A Cheerful Disposition*] was interrupted by the rebellion while on location in Cordoba. The crew was stranded and separated from its studio. The film was completed in 1939 even though a number of actors and technicians had left the country for political reasons; but on its release the exiled actors' names, like Rosita Díaz Gimeno, were removed from the credits (Bonet Mojica, 1996b: 56–7). Some of its original sets were modified for *Nuestro culpable* (Caparrós Lera, 1981: 200). Francisco Elías's musical *Bohemios* [*Bohemians*], or Fernando Roldán's bandit narrative, *Luis Candelas*, both started in 1936, were similarly interrupted and released after the war. Other films and many other projects had to be abandoned, for instance José María Estívalis aka Armand Guerra's *Carne de fieras* [1936 *Flesh for Beasts*], a daring film including the circus act of a topless dancer in a cage of lions.[30]

Newsreels and documentaries

Production emphasis changed during the war and energies were soon concentrated on documentaries and newsreels. These, *Noticario Español*, *Film España*, *Cinespaña*, had been made since 1932, as the government, which criticised the popular films just documented, had recognised the educational potential of cinema for a large illiterate population. Their effort had been centred on the Misiones Pedagógicas [Pedagogical Missions], which used film as an educational medium before the war (Christopher Cobb, in Graham & Labanyi, 1995: 133–8). In fact many documentaries had been produced at the time on a wide range of topics, like Vilà Vilamala's *Cómo nació la República española* [1932 *How the Spanish Republic was Born*], Adolfo Aznar's *Mendicidad y caridad* [1932 *Mendicity and Charity*], Ramon Biadiu's *La*

---

[30] It was never completed and the film was unavailable until 1992, when it was restored by the Zaragoza Filmoteca.

ruta de Don Quijote [1934 **Don Quixote's Journey*], José María Beltrán's *Reforma agraria* or *Siembra* [both 1935, **Agrarian Reform*, **Sowing*], Carlos Velo's *Ciudad y campo* [**City and Country*], *Felipe II y El Escorial* and *Galicia y Compostela*, *Almadrabas* [all four 1935, **Tuna Fishing*], or his *Saudade* [1936], Antonio Román's *Canto a la emigración* [1935 **Hymn to Migration*] about the Galician problem, followed by *La ciudad encantada* [1935 **The Enchanted City*]; José Val del Omar is also said to have made a number, which have unfortunately been lost.[31] So there was plenty of documentary experience to build on when the rebellion started to gain impetus; the problem was finding film stock for the cameras.

Newsreels and documentaries under fire

Barcelona, Valencia, Bilbao and Madrid were still flying a Republican flag, but each city was isolated by the fighting and operated independently. Consequently the ideology of the documentaries depended on the individual political tendencies of cinematographers and producers, which could range from Anarchist, Marxist, Communist, Socialist, Liberal or Republican to Regionalist (Enrique Montero and Alicia Alted, both in Graham & Labanyi, 1995: 123–33 and 152–9). CIFESA remained loyal to the Republic even though its president, Vicente Casanova, promptly left to join the rebels in Andalusia. In December 1936 the autonomous Catalan government fostered Laya Films, promoted by Jaume Miravitlles (friend of Dalí and Buñuel, who had played one of the two priests in *Un Chien andalou*) to produce the weekly newsreel *Espanya al dia* [**Spain Day by Day*]. Five weeks later this was co-edited for a while with Film Popular for the Castilian version, *España al día,* distributed in Republican territory, and as the *Nouvelles d'Espagne* and *Spain Today* beyond the Pyrenees, each with the appropriate voice-over. This went on through to January 1939 when the Nationalists entered Barcelona. As well as newsreels numerous documentaries were produced for home and foreign propaganda, frequently as fund-raisers to attract foreign help. The titles speak for themselves: *Reportaje del movimiento revolucionario en Barcelona* or *Barcelona trabaja para el frente* [both 1936 Mateo Santos, **Report on the Revolutionary Movement in Barcelona* and **Barcelona Working for the Front Lines*], *Julio 1936*, or *Por la unidad hacia la victoria* [Fernando Mantilla, 1936 **July 1936*, 1937 **United to Victory*]; *Defensa de Madrid* [1936 Ángel Villatoro, *The Defence of Madrid*, with Ivor Montagu and including the poet

---

[31] *IMDb* lists *Natación* [**Swimming*] and *Gimnasia* [**Gymnastic*] for 1937. Judging by the few subsequent films that have survived, like *Fuego en Castilla* (1960), it is a great loss to both Spanish and World Cinema. In 1994 Cristina Esteban made a documentary on his surviving work *Ojalá, Val del Omar.*

Rafael Alberti]; *El paso del Ebro, El camino de la victoria* or *Mando único* [all 1937 Antonio del Amo, *Crossing the Ebro, *The Path to Victory* and *Single Command*]; *Sanidad, Resistencia en el Levante* or *Ametralladoras* [Rafael Gil 1937 *Health*, 1938 *Resistance from the East*, and 1939 *Machine Guns* to teach the militias how to use the Soviet weapons], *La mujer y la guerra* [1938 Mauricio Sol(lín), *Woman at War*]. In the Basque Country José María Beltrán took some footage of the still-smoking rubble of Guernica in 1937. This was edited in Paris by Nemesio Sobrevila, with contrasting views of the previously peaceful countryside and rural activities, to make a 20-minute documentary on the destruction of the country, *Guernika*. Sobrevila was also responsible for *Elai-Alai* [1938 *Happy Swallows*] (Zunzunegui, 1985: 23–31). In Paris Buñuel was very much involved with the editing of news footage taken by various cameramen to make *España leal en armas* [*Loyal Spain At War!*], aka *España 1936* or *Madrid 1936,* though details of the production of both Spanish and French versions are rather blurred (Aranda, 1975: 118–22).

Foreign cameras

There were also foreign pro-Republican films made with specific audiences in mind. As well as Ivor Montagu's *Defence of Madrid* [1936], these include Roman Karmen's Soviet *Ispaniya* [1939] and Dutchman Joris Ivens's *Spanish Earth* [1937] scripted by John Dos Passos with a voice-over from Ernest Hemingway although the credits acknowledge Orson Welles (Morgan, 2000: 45–54). Boris Peskine and André Malraux started on *Sierra de Teruel* [*Days of Hope*], adapting with Max Aub a fragment of Malraux's own novel *L'Espoir*. It was filmed as the Republican soldiers were retreating, and the reels managed to escape the Nationalist troops and the Nazi occupation of Paris after it was edited in July 1939, reflecting the new political situation. It was screened twice but not released until 1945 after the conclusion of the Second World War as *Espoir*, and in Spain in 1977 (Talens, 1998: 58–72). This was the last film that the sound engineer René Renault made in Spain: he had been working in the Orphea studios since they opened in 1932 and had contributed to six documentaries during the rebellion, after which he returned to France where he was involved in French cinema, including Alain Renais's 1959 *Hiroshima mon amour*. There were also a few Hollywood action films set against the Civil War, like *The Last Train from Madrid* [1937 James P. Hogan] or *Blockade* [1938 Willian Dieterle], but these are another story (Seguin, 1994: 35 in French or 1995: 28 in Spanish).

Hollywood imports

In spite of the fighting and falling bombs cinemas continued to show films, whether foreign imports or the favourite fare of folkloric and musical comedies, and this wherever possible on both sides of the military front. Hollywood films were the favourites on Spanish screens: 'of the 500 feature films brought into Spain about 300 were sound films of which nearly 80 per cent were American [...]. From 60 per cent to 70 per cent of 200 silent films were American' (Bosch & del Rincón, 1998: 114). As Mortimore (1975) described:

> Cinemas were very popular during the war. People arrived with their sandwiches and stayed to view more than one screening, thus avoiding the dangers in the street. They often refused to leave the cinemas during the bombardments, insisting that the film be continued. The *milicianos* [Republican soldiers] went on carrying their guns and refused to leave them in the cloakroom. The soundtrack was sometimes inaudible due to the sound of *pipas* [dried sunflower seeds being eaten].[32]

Viewing and further reading

A handful of videos and DVDs are at present available, again from Divisa but these without subtitles, while over 86% of the films have been lost or destroyed, so any viewing will have to be mostly in a Filmoteca where slowly and patiently old films are restored even if not in their totality. One frequently needs to refer to the reconstructed descriptions from the contemporary press, now published in specialised extensive monographs like Gubern's work for Benito Perojo (1994), Sánchez Vidal on Florián Rey (1991) and on Buñuel (1984), Pérez Perucha on Edgar Neville (1982), as well as Caparrós Lera's comprehensive *Arte y política en el cine de la República* (1981), and Fanés's book on CIFESA (1982, 1989). For a general perspective in English see the suggestions for the previous chapter: Hopewell (1986: 15–26) D'Lugo (1997: 4–8), and Triana Toribio (2003: 19–37). In addition to Buñuel's *My Last Breath*, Baxter is the latest biography in English (1994). Aranda (1975: 100–22), Mortimore (1975: 180–2), and Kinder (1993: 292–300) are also very useful on Buñuel's contribution to the Filmofóno films, and P. Evans (1995a) covers the Mexican films, which are not part of this survey, while Evans & Santaolla (2004) and Edwards (2005) gather more recent contributions. Ginger has devoted part of an article to Francisco Elías (2007).

---

[32] Quoted twice by Caparrós Lera (1981: and 1983: 20–1), here in the translation by Triana Toribio 2003: 33; see also Esther Gómez Sierra, 2004: 96–7.

Martin-Márquez has a whole chapter dedicated to Rosario Pi (1999a). Talens includes a chapter on Civil War documentaries and on *La verbena de la Paloma* (1998), this last also discussed by Mira (2005). A good start to study exiled directors is the website for Juan Rodríguez.

As for the previous chapters, much of this survey is still provisional and all of it would benefit from detailed revisions. One particularly interesting angle for the study of this decade, especially in contrast to the following years, would be the social implications of the values presented on screen, and especially the positioning of women in the film narratives (Graham: 99–116, in Graham & Labanyi 1995), or even to pursue the careers of Margarita de Ochoa or Sara Ontañón initiated in the editing suites of Republican Spain. Reading about the films of the Republic comparisons are frequently made to Eisenstein, Chaplin, Ernst Lubitsch, Frank Capra, René Clair, Marcel Carné and Busby Berkeley, for which examples and more concrete details would be useful, as one follows through the increasing sophistication of filming techniques of some directors like Perojo or Rey.

4

Years of Autarchy, Silence and Hunger (1940–1951)

The Old Dark House: consolidating authority

If the Republicans under siege were vulnerable partly because of their initial tolerant and multiple points of view, the Nationalists were determined to impose a single perspective from the beginning of their uprising. In November 1936 a Press and Propaganda Office, whose remit also covered radio and cinema, was set up in Salamanca under General Millán Astray. Additional offices were subsequently established in Seville and Corunna on 21 March of the following year to control the isolated Nationalist territories. In November 1937, cinema was identified as needing its own Junta Superior de Censura Cinematográfica [JSCC/Supreme Board of Film Censorship] with four appointments,[1] and in April 1938, with the Nationalist HQ now in Burgos, the Departamento Nacional de Cinematografía [DNC/National Film Department] was created as part of the national propaganda effort, with Manuel García Viñolas as its director. Four priorities were identified: film production cannot be the exclusive concern of the State; the state can only stimulate private initiatives; the state must ensure that films be worthy of the Fatherland's spiritual values; the state reserves for itself the production of newsreels and propaganda (Caparrós Lera, 1983: 23). In addition, the Comisión de Censura Cinematográfica [Film Censorship Commission] was established as a first checkpoint. Ramón Serrano Suñer, Minister of the Interior and Franco's brother-in-law, justified these measures in the Foreword to the 1938 censorship law by explaining that: 'Given the undeniable and profound influence of the cinema in disseminating ideas and educating the masses, it is vital that the State be vigilant wherever there is a danger of deviating from this mission.'[2] The state was vigilant and consequently, as

---

[1] González Ballesteros (1981: 381); pp. 351–508 are an Appendix with transcriptions of decrees passed between 1936 and 1978.

[2] 'Dado que el cinematógrafo ejerce una innegable y enorme influencia sobre la difusión del pensamiento y sobre la educación de las masas, es indispensable que el Estado vigile siempre que haya riesgo que pueda apartarle de su misión', quoted in Caparrós Lera (1983: 22)

from 15 July 1939, all scripts had to be approved before filming could begin (article 2, section 3).[3]

Educating Nationalists

During the conflict the DNC started producing the 23 chapters of the *Noticiario Español* [*The Spanish Newsreel*]. This was at first problematic since studios and laboratories were all in Republican territory. However, the CIFESA crews of both *Asilo Naval* [*Naval Protection*] and *El genio alegre* [*A Cheerful Disposition*] were enlisted in July 1936 when their location filming was interrupted by the Nationalist troups in Cadiz and Cordoba respectively. This included the two directors, Fernando Delgado and Miguel Pereyra, cameramen Alfredo Fraile and Ricardo Torres, as well as the editor Eduardo García Maroto. They were soon joined by Vicente Casanova, president of CIFESA, while his company carried on filming for the Republicans against his wishes. Delgado made a number of short documentaries such as *Hacia una nueva España* [1936 *Towards a New Spain*] and *Bilbao para España* [*Bilbao for Spain*], followed by other titles like *Santander para España* and then *Asturias para España*, *Entierro del General Mola* or *Brigadas de Navarra* [all in 1937, *General Mola's Funeral* and *The Navarrese Brigades*]; Pereyra and Torres filmed titles such as *Con las brigadas de Navarra* [1936 *With the Brigades of Navarre*] or *La toma de Bilbao* [1937 *The Capture of Bilbao*]. In 1937 and 1938 Casanova was responsible for Alfredo Fraile's three-part documentary entitled *Reconstruyendo España* [*Rebuilding Spain*] chronicling the war from a Nationalist perspective. To process the films, Maroto was first sent to use friendly laboratories in Lisbon, and then to Cinecittà in Rome and the UFA [Universumfilm Aktiengesellschaft] in Germany (Gubern, 1995: 177–8). Overall Nationalist production was small, and according to Caparrós Lera there were only 32 Nationalist documentaries to the 220 Republican documentaries (1983: 232), although their titles reveal their perspective. Other directors with right-wing sympathies included Arturo Ruiz Castillo who, after collaborating with Federico García Lorca and the peripatetic theatre of La Barraca, became director, cameraman, editor, set and costume designer for documentaries like *Guerra en el campo* and *Guerra en la nieve* [1936 *War in the Fields* or 1938 *War in the Snow*]; Ricardo Gutiérrez's *Arriba España* or *La reconquista de la patria* [1937 *For Spain* and *The Reconquest of the Fatherland*]; Manuel García Viñolas *Prisioneros de Guerra* [1938 *POWs*]; Joaquín Martínez Arboleya with documentaries like *La guerra por la paz* or *Voluntad* [both 1937,

---

3   González Ballesteros (1981: 389).

*War for Peace and *The Will]; and Edgar Neville who contributed *Ciudad Universitaria, Juventudes de España* [1938 *University City, *Spanish Youth] and ¡*Vivan los hombres libres!* [1939 *Let Free Men Live!*].

Hispano-Film-Produktion [HFP] produced the feature-length documentary, *España heroica* [*Heroic Spain*], which was written, directed and edited in Berlin by Joaquín Reig and others, premiered in Bilbao on 3 August 1938. Using different footage of the conflict from various sources, including German and confiscated Republican reels, it presented the Nationalist justification of the military rebellion. The Republicans are demonised as the victims of sedition instigated by manipulative and greedy International Brigades, in keeping with the Nationalist belief that no true Spaniard could have progressive liberal ideas and that these must be the product of subversive and destructive foreign influences. With little commentary and careful montage it contrasts destructive Republican mobs with the reconstruction efforts of disciplined Nationalist forces; anarchic crowd against orderly rank and file in uniform became the norm of presenting these ideologies on screen (Triana Toribio, 2003: 49). For some reason the copy of *España heroica* released in Spain (86 minutes) ended the 'documentary' in October 1937 whereas the German version *Helden in Spanien* (71 minutes) covered events up to July 1938.[4] In official contemporary documents the insurgence is referred to as the National Revolution, and is linked to the National-Catholicism of the Nationalists. The Bishop of Salamanca Plà y Deniel described it as the Crusade for the Reconquest of Spain – an emotive term that linked the Nationalist movement to the Catholic Monarchs, Ferdinand and Isabel, who unified the peninsula in 1492, and this label stayed. This is the theme of the US *Defenders of the Faith*, filmed in 1939 by Russell Palmer, said to be the first ever war documentary shot in colour.[5] There is also the problematic 82-minute scripted documentary *Romancero marroquí* [1939 *Moroccan Ballads*] directed by Enrique Domínguez Rodiño who adapted some of Carlos Velo's earlier ethnographic film material to create a eulogy to the North African troops that sealed Franco's victories, presented as their debt of gratitude to Spain's colonising protection (Alberto Elena, in Pérez Perucha, 1997: 122–4).

[4] See Ramón Sala Noguer (in Pérez Perucha, 1997: 119–21). The length of the two versions is here quoted with caution from the *IMDb* since every source consulted gives a different length for the films.

[5] Documentary to be contrasted with at least one supporting the legal government, for instance, *The Spanish Earth* (see p. 74).

Open invitations

In 1937 Vicente Casanova and CIFESA, which had an office in Berlin since
May 1936 and was now without access to its studios in Spain, associated
itself with the German UFA to form Hispano-Film-Produktion. UFA also
linked up with Saturnino Ulargui Moreno of Ufilms, the UFA representative
in Spain since 1926 (Gubern, 1994: 291–3). With the participation of the
Galician Noberto Soliño, ex-CIFESA representative in Cuba and now free-
lance impresario, UFA saw an opportunity to establish itself in the lucrative
Latin American market (Triana Toribio, 2003: 35–6). In 1938 while travelling in America, Florián Rey was contracted to make *Carmen, la de Triana*,
although the credit title reads 'Imperio Argentina / in an interpretation of
Carmen (the one from Triana).'[6] It was the first of five Spanish films to be
produced by this new partnership in Germany, an episode of Spanish filmmaking evoked in Fernando Trueba's fiction *La niña de tus ojos* [1998 *The
Girl of Your Dreams*]. Location shots were done in Seville and Ronda in a
freezing winter, and the Spanish version included Rafael Rivelles as the Brigadier José and Manuel Luna as the bullfighter Antonio. On one hand the film,
like many of the period, may seem stilted for today's expectations because
of the Sunday-best folkloric costumes, many parade uniforms, painted back-
drops and theatrical performances that contrast with Argentina and Rivelles's
more natural acting style. However, there is Argentina's performance and
singing (the songs are far removed from Bizet's opera, and this Carmen is
a professional performer rather than a tobacco girl); Florián Rey's direction and his significant use of light and shadows (as in German films of the
period many sequences take place at night); as well as Johanna Rosinski's
editing whether, for instance, in the dancing sequences or the crosscutting
for the bullfight which uses documentary footage. This Carmen, who wears
a much lower *décolleté* and kisses longer than will be permissible in the films
of the Dictatorship, is sacrificed on the altar of the army's honour in this
new ending, and is shown repentant through the last superimposed images
of the film. Argentina also learnt German in order to star in Herbert Maish's
version, *Andalusische Nächte* [*Nights in Andalusia*], which was made with
German actors and a different crew. This taste for an exotic Spain is also
evident in Rey's second film in Germany, *La canción de Aixa* [1939 *Song of
Aixa*], a musical fantasy set in Spanish Morocco, featuring Imperio Argentina
playing opposite Ricardo Merino who replaced Rafael Rivelles as leading
man.[7] For Labanyi 'Arab values here figure an extreme version of patriarchal

---

6   'Imperio Argentina / en una interpretación de Carmen (la de Triana).' Triana was the old
Gypsy ghetto on the south bank of the Guadalquivir river in Seville.
7   After this film Imperio Argentina broke off with Rey, and followed her leading man
Rafael Rivelles.

ethos propounded by early Francoism, but its exaltation requires spectators to identify with Arab culture and to reject European modernity' because it is decadent and alien to Nationalist values (1997: 223). This link between the two cultures is present in the ideology of *Raza* [(1941) 1942, *Race* – PNC], which celebrates, through its hero and the final superimposed shots, the fact that Spain, victim of corrupt Western ideas, was rescued by forces spearheaded by Franco's North African regiment.

Benito Perojo, despite having previously directed ten films in four years, had not worked since *Nuestra Natacha* [1936] and was in France when he was also contracted by UFA. Accustomed to working abroad, he directed three films with German crews, all incorporating numerous songs and set in Andalusia, casting Raquel Rodrigo, the singer Estrellita Castro, Roberto Rey, Miguel Ligero and others. The first was a sumptuous and free adaptation of the Beaumarchais play, *El barbero de Sevilla* [*The Barber of Seville*], which blurred even more the class differences between the Count and Figaro. This was followed by *Suspiros de España* [1938 *Spanish Sighs*] about the success of an exiled Spanish artist [Estrellita Castro] in Cuba, with the exterior locations shot in Seville and two cameras filming simultaneously from different angles. With an equally uplifting rags-to-riches narrative from the Republican years (Woods, 2004a: 56–7), Perojo went on to film *Mariquilla Terremoto* in 1939. All three films were shown first in Nationalist cities throughout Spain before their final release in Madrid that autumn.

The harsh realities

On 1 April 1939 the Republican Government surrendered unconditionally to the Nationalist army. There was some small-scale, but ultimately unsuccessful resistance, including *guerilleros* in the hills until 1951 (*El corazón del bosque* [*Heart of the Forest*], Gutiérrez Aragón 1979]). The new government, a self-proclaimed military dictatorship, assumed the task of purging the nation of any decadent republican ideas as it attempted to rebuild a devastated country whilst legitimising its own authority, but reconstruction did not happen as efficiently as planned (Graham & Labanyi, 1995: 173–82, 237–45). Spain was isolated, at first because the rest of Europe was at war, then because Franco was associated with the losing side despite declaring neutrality, and later as a consequence of the failure of the government's chosen autarchic strategies (*El jardín de las delicias* [*The Garden of Delights*], Saura, 1970). The state's main asset was the mass of unemployed who provided cheap labour; even silenced political prisoners could redeem themselves through forced labour on the construction of the Valle de los Caídos monument or be hired out to private firms (Graham & Labanyi, 1995: 224). Up to 137 work camps and three concentration camps were still operating in 1946 (*Los años bárbaros* [*Barbaric Years*], Fernando Colomo, 1998). The 1940s were marked on one hand by ration books, shortages of raw materials and a thriving black market trade, which made quite a few fortunes, and on the other by the fear of voicing any opinion that could be identified as dissent from the official ideology that was swiftly suppressed. The autarchy of the 1940s thus became known as the years of hunger (*Demonios en El Jardín* [*Demons in The Garden*] Gutiérrez Aragón, 1982) and the times of silence (*El espíritu de la colmena* [*The Spirit of the Beehive*], Erice, 1973). The extent of the politically motivated purges is still not certain and victims are still being counted by forensic archaeologists. The conservative estimate is that over one million Spaniards died between 1936 and 1939, and in the following four years there were some suspected 200,000 executions and disappearances, and 400,000 incarcerations as well as some 400,000 exiles, many of whom were intellectuals and artists. These were years of repression and censorship of all known and unknown dissident voices.

Back to work

So much had been destroyed and lost during the fratricidal war that there was little for cinema to build on, yet people wanted to be entertained and dream for 80 minutes in an attempt to forget their daily misery and hardships. Cinemas provided a warm location where spectators could escape their overcrowded accommodation and eat their sandwiches, as seen in *Esa pareja feliz* [(1951) 1953 J.A. Bardem and L.G. Berlanga *That Happy Couple*]. With the censor's office in place, previous Republican favourites and foreign imports were repeated, joined by the five HFP films, as well as feature-length documentaries and the gradual release of films started in 1936 whose filming had been interrupted by the conflict (see chapter 3). Production of feature films started again under Nationalist control when, in October 1938, Dioniso Ridruejo, head of the Propaganda Office, negotiated an agreement with Italy, since both governments had more in common than either had with Nazi Germany. Consequently Edgar Neville went to Rome in 1939 to direct two films, *Santa Rogelia* and *Frente de Madrid* [*The Madrid Front*]. The latter focused on a couple separated by the war and included a final reconciliation scene between two dying soldiers, which was censored, thus revealing a government policy not to forgive the vanquished. Also in Rome and in 1939, Perojo filmed *Los hijos de la noche* [1940 *The Children of the Night*], a comedy of mistaken identities with social implications in which a wealthy bachelor hires three marginalised youths to act as his children to cover up a lie and deceive his visiting sister. He followed this with the musical *La última falla* [1940 *The Last Carnival*]. Both films were scripted by Miguel Mihura, a popular political satirist who had just started to make his name in the film

world with two shorts for Eduardo García Maroto, which were strongly criticised by the establishment in Italy and Spain, suffering the censors' cuts.

The studios open

Spanish productions gradually picked up again, reaching an average of 39
films per year throughout the 1940s. CIFESA at its zenith dominated, making
41 films during the decade, followed by the new Suevia Films with 38. Films
were identified by actors, the stars' names usually preceding the title on
posters and in the credits, although José Enrique Monterde recommends that
the period be approached by genres rather than directors, even if the generic
tables he offers are open to interpretation given the overlaps evident in the
films themselves (Gubern, 1995: 204–5, 230).

Production started off with remakes. For CIFESA García Maroto, back
from Portugal, remade the comedy *Los cuatro Robinsones* [1939 **The Four
Robinsons*],[8] the first of the eleven films he directed during the 1940s and which
included the folkloric *Canelita en rama* [1943 **Canelita, Cinnamon Stick*]
where the songs are carefully integrated in the plot (González-Medina, 1997:
15–29). Feeling restricted by the constraints of the official ideology Maroto
then left the CIFESA. José Buchs, with a film a year up to 1936, remade his
1929 *zarzuela* of *El rey que rabió* [1939 **The Old King who Raged*]. Back
from Germany and separated from Imperio Argentina, Florián Rey filmed the
second remake of *La Dolores* [1940 – PNC][9] with a fine eye for detail in the
sets and a much terser plot for this tale of sexual politics, casting Conchita
Piquer as his leading lady. He uses music and song to evoke a bountiful rural
Aragon that never existed: a shot of Dolores singing as she milks the cows
is crosscut with a close-up of sows suckling their piglets, implying a prosperity that again contradicts reality as Dolores can move from one employer
to another without even needing a letter of reference. Rey continued to make
one or two films a year until 1956, including a remake of his own 1930 *La
aldea maldita* in 1942 [PNC]. It received a medal at the Venice Film Festival,
but is not as powerful a film as his original (see pp. 38–40): the Church
casts a dark shadow, Biblical references are moral rather than dramatic, the
forgiveness of the repentant Acacia [Florencia Bécquer] can too easily be
read as an allegory for a transgressive Republic returning to the patriarchal
fold, while the sumptuous costumes contradict the visual tragedy presented
and contemporary social reality. Although a great hit at the box-office, the

8   The first is the silent 1926 version directed by Reinhardt Blothner, who only made two
other silent films in Spain, in 1927 and 1928.
9   The original was Gelabert's 1908 version, and the first remake was Thous's in 1924. The
PNC was a newly established prize explained in the following paragraph.

whole is not as effective as his previous *La Dolores*. The following year he filmed another rural drama set in the Aragonese Pyrenees, *Osoria* [1943]. Very successful was Rey's new comedy with a Galician background *¡Polizón a bordo!* [1941 **Stowaway on Board!*] whose profits are said to have established Cesáreo González's Suevia Films as the main competitor to CIFESA. The great success of 1939 was Gonzalo Delgrás's first film, now lost, the adaptation of a feel-good escapist stage comedy *La tonta del bote* [*The Complete Idiot*], which paired Josita Hernán and Rafael Durán for the first time; it was remade in 1970 by Juan de Orduña. Eusebio Fernández Ardavín got started again in 1940 with the musical *La Marquesona* [*The Strange Marchioness*] and in the same year *La florista de la reina* [*The Queen's Flower Girl* – PNC], a very successful melodrama, based on his own play, that discreetly raised the question of adultery by setting the story at the end of the previous century, starring María Guerrero, Alfredo Mayo and Ana Mariscal. This temporal displacement became a possible device for presenting sensitive matters under the dictatorship. Fernando Delgado directed a third version of *La gitanilla* [1940 – PNC], and José López Rubio remade Baños's rural melodrama *La malquerida* [1940 – PNC], a tale of honour where the stepfather is the lascivious predator.[10] Also in 1940, Perojo returned from Italy to direct his fourth film for Saturnino Ulargui in the newly restored Orphea Studios, *Marianela*. It is an adaptation of Benito Pérez Galdós's novel, an unusual choice even though the story was first published in 1878, since in the 1940s Galdós was not sanctioned by the ideological authorities because of his liberal views and anticlericalism (Faulkner, 2004a: 131).[11] Perojo brought the story into the twentieth century and cast 18-year-old Mary Carrillo, said to have had no particularly attractive features, in order to subvert the platonic stereotype that the physically beautiful is morally good. The film received the Biennale cup at the Venice Festival in 1941 despite the eight cuts that were requested from the finished version, including one that showed a dilapidated Spain that the censors were unwilling to accept or reveal.

---

[10] José Luis López Rubio was a Spaniard who went to Hollywood in 1930, aged 27, to translate and adapt films into Spanish. He wrote a number of scripts, and only returned to Spain in 1940.

[11] Pérez Galdós, the giant of the nineteenth-century novel, had inspired two silent films, *El abuelo* [José Buchs 1925, *The Grandfather] and *La loca de casa* [1926 Luis Alonso, **The Mad Woman of the House*]. His novels would not be filmed again in Spain until 1970 when Buñuel directed *Tristana* and in the same year Angelino Fons's *Fortunata y Jacinta*, followed by *Marianela* in 1972. However, Galdós's *Doña Perfecta* was filmed in the USA as *Beauty in Chains* in 1918 by Elsie Jane Wilson, and eight of his novels were adapted for films in Argentina and Mexico, including Buñuel's *Nazarín* [1958]. In Spain this would change in the 1970s (Faulkner, 2004a: 90).

Encouragement and rewards

The film magazine *Primer Plano* [*Close-up*] directed by the head of censorship, M.A. García Viñolas, was first issued on 20 October 1940 to provide a platform for the cinema's official intellectual voice and allow the Delegación Nacional de Cinematografía [DNC/National Film Delagation, previously 'Department'] to publicise its priorities and indirectly legitimise the new order. The regime preferred to suggest, encourage and reward rather than prescribe the films they desired (Triana Toribio, 2003: 38–44). In order to foster 'appropriate' films the DNC, now also responsible for theatre, set up a Classification Board on 11 November of the same year.[12] The so-called Sindicato Nacional del Espectáculo [National Spectacle Union] provided funds and loans for Spanish producers, based on the scrutiny of projected scripts and budgets. To reward the productions that appeared to endorse the values of the regime, official prizes were established [Premios Nacionales de Cinematógrafía, PNC]: two of 400,000 pesetas, four of 250,000, with five of 50,000 pesetas for the best scripts. On 15 June 1944 new awards were created for films deemed of 'interés nacional' [of National Significance], and on 13 May 1946 the category 'interés militar' [of Military Significance] was added. These new prizes did not necessarily coincide with the PNC awards since too many separate government offices had a say in the production and distribution of each individual film (Pozo Arenas, 1984: 48 and 57). In place was a fragmented and clumsy bureaucratic organisation, run by zealous censors with different agendas, who promoted a film culture that corresponded to the propaganda effort:

> Franco behaved like an old soldier. His strategy was not to interfere with the workings of the industry, but merely to ensure the established order. The cinema was farmed out among the victors in the war. The Church took charge of its morality; the state unions got its administration, racketeers and the rich the chances to make a buck. (Hopewell, 1986: 37)

Controls

The Propaganda Department was also very protective of the reputation and authority of the State and Church, guardians of its citizens. For instance, although the script of the pro-Franco *El crucero Baleares* [1940 Enrique del Campo, *Battleship Baleares*] was approved, it is said that the film was banned before its release at the request of the Navy, who found the film not good

---

[12] Dates of legislation are taken from Pozo Arenas's list (1984: 44–9), and these are transcribed in the Appendix to González Ballesteros's book.

enough to be effective propaganda, and all copies subsequently destroyed in 1948. A war romance set in Madrid, *Rojo y Negro* [1942 Carlos Arévalo, *Red and Black*] was also granted permission but this was rescinded after unidentified complaints were made; no reasons were given but, according to the restored copy, it may have been because it presented the love of a 'good' and repentant communist for a national falangist. Names of artists with known Republican sympathies who had emigrated, like Angelillo or Rosita Díaz Gimeno, were removed from the credits of old films. In *Alas de paz* [1942 Juan Parellada, *Wings of Peace*] twelve cuts were requested including a dance that revealed too much flesh. In *Viejo Smoking* [1942 Eduardo Morera, *Old Tuxedo*] a phrase, where the word 'revolutionary' is used by Carlos Gardel's friend, was excised, and the trailer for *The Prisoner of Zenda* [1937 John Cromwell, released dubbed in 1942] had to delete the photograph of Douglas Fairbanks Jr because of his known Republican sympathies, shared with Chaplin.[13]

Informing the nation

To control public information and the dissemination of the official interpretation of home and external affairs the NO-DO (short for *Noticiarios y Documentales Cinematográficos* [*Film News and Documentaries*]), directed by Alberto Reig (brother of Joaquín), was set up on 29 September 1942. From January 1943 it produced the only authorised newsreel in Spain, screenings of which were compulsory in every licensed cinema until 1978 (Sheelagh Ellwood, in Graham & Labanyi, 1995: 201–3). It had a good start having appropriated some 90,000 metres of Laya's archive footage in 1939. Documentaries continued to flourish, and were used to redefine regional ethnicity according to the values of the regime, expressed through voice-overs and camera angles. Examples include Juan de Orduña's *Suite Granadina* and *Feria en Sevilla* [both 1940 *Granada Suite* and *Fair in Seville*, the second with Rafael Gil]; Antonio Román's *Merida, De la Alhambra al Albaicín*, or *El hombre y el carro* [*Merida*, *From the Alhambra to the Albaicín*, and *The Man and his Cart*, all from 1940]; Neville's 1941 *Verbena* [*Madrid Carnival*]; Ruiz Castillo's *Jardines de España* or *Vino y otras bedidas* [1941 *Gardens of Spain* and 1944 *Wine and other Beverages*]; or García Viñolas's

---

13   These random examples for the year 1942 are from González Ballesteros (1981: 221–3). Further examples of the censors' cuts and objections can be found in Besas (1985: 18–19 and 25); Bosch (1998: 116–17 and 121–4;) Graham & Labanyi (1995: 210); Higginbotham (1988: 11 and 16); Kinder (1993: 33); Molina Foix (1977: 5); Stone (2002). González Ballesteros (1981) has a wide-ranging account in Spanish of censors' instructions, for both Spanish and foreign films released in Spain between 1936 and 1977. At present work is being done in the newly released censors' archives.

Boda en Castilla [1942 **Castilian Wedding*]. Many of these included traditional dances and songs performed by the local groups of *Coros y danzas*
[*Choirs and Dances*], who also participated in a number of feature films like
Ladislao Vajda's very successful *Ronda española* [1951 **Spanish Serenade*
– PNC]. This ensured that regional energies were channelled into safe folkloric settings, which could be easily integrated into the image of a united
nation by the propaganda office.[14]

Official criteria

Although scripts had to obtain official permission to be filmed since 15 July
1939, no official document detailing what could or not be shown was published
until the 1960s. Censors were notoriously subjective, their meetings were
secret and by keeping their criteria vague they gave themselves the power to
reject anything they felt could be subversive. These norms were only printed
in a decree of 9 February 1963, which contains nineteen articles identifying
various potentially 'dangerous' situations, another ten applicable to younger
viewers, and a further nine referring to exceptional circumstances (González
Ballesteros, 1981: 422–8). However, these were still subject to interpretation,
and the implications of some articles were so wide-ranging that they could
be used to justify almost any objection. For example article 17 states: 'Will
be prohibited whatever may threaten in any way: 1st The Catholic Church,
its dogma, its morals and its practice; 2nd The fundamental values of the
State, and national dignity, as well as the internal and the external security
of the country; 3rd The person of the Head of State.'[15] I refer to these as
Franco's three 'F's: Faith, Fatherland and Family. The Catholic Church was
the guardian of social behaviour and education, enforced by the civil law, and
the state controlled everything including the trade unions (the term Fatherland is used to reflect both its patriarchal values and the fact that official
propaganda presented Franco as the father of his people). The family was
institutionalised as the most important social nucleus of the regime, since in
the aftermath of the war the country needed to be repopulated and orphans,
maimed, sick and elderly, all had to be cared for by the extended family
where the father's word was literally the law. Many films, including *Raza*
(see pp. 90–1), depict the family as a microcosm of the Nation and establish

---

[14] Triana Toribio (2003: 59–62); another useful gauge of the regime's propaganda machine
is philately, but that would be another book.

[15] 'Se prohibirá cuanto atenten de alguna manera contra: 1° La Iglesia Católica, su dogma,
su moral y su culto; 2° Los principios fundamentales del Estado, la dignidad nacional y la segu-
ridad exterior o interior del país; 3° La persona del Jefe del Estado.' Transcribed by González
Ballesteros (1981: 425); see also Graham & Labanyi (1995: 207–14).

the models of masculinities dedicated to the state with a self-sacrificing wife who bears children and minds the home.[16] Carlos Saura's *Ana y los lobos* [1973 *Anna and the Wolves*] can be viewed as an allegorical representation of these three Fs of the Franco regime.

Imports and quotas

In the five years between 1939 and 1944 some 185 Spanish films were made in contrast with the following imports: 340 from the USA, 180 from Germany, 95 from the UK, 90 from Italy, 55 from France, 30 from Argentina, 15 from Mexico and maybe five from Portugal.[17] Cinema in those difficult years was a 'haven in a heartless world [...] one of the few means of escape open to Spaniards' (Bosch, 1998: 113–15), and the pre-war American Dream prevailed, elliptically illustrated in Fernando Trueba's *El embrujo de Shanghai* [2002 *The Shanghai Spell*]. Import licences linked to the production of new Spanish films were imposed from 28 October 1941 in order to stem the flood of old foreign films (Besas, 1985: 25). On 1 January 1942 the quota was regularised to one week of Spanish Cinema for six weeks of imported films. However, this was no incentive for quality cinema since some companies rushed out very cheaply produced films just to obtain the necessary import licences and thus show guaranteed foreign box-office successes. To combat this practice new classification norms were set up on 18 May 1943: films judged to be First Class would receive three to five import licences, a Second Class could obtain two to four licences, whereas a Third Class qualification was denied a licence.

Dubbing

Thought to be useful as an ideological prophylactic, dubbing laws for foreign films were passed on 23 April 1941: no original sound versions were allowed and only films with Castilian dialogue dubbed in Spain could be projected. This fitted in with the regime's policy to centralise the country in every possible ways, including language. As the Nationalist forces had marched

---

[16] Whether single or married, women's energy was channelled and organised through the Sección Femenina, founded in 1934, a sort of blend of the Girl Guides and Women's Institute to support the values of the regime and its practical work in health and education (Graham & Labanyi, 1995: 182–95).

[17] These rough figures, based on the records Pozo Arenas had available (1984), are for comparison and can be found on p. 62, see also pp. 72–3. Caparrós Lera (1983: 232–3) has separate tables of imported films by year and country from 1946 to 1973.

through the peninsula during the war, regional languages had been successively prohibited: Galician in July 1936, Basque in April 1937, and Catalan in June 1939. Dubbing enabled the censors to alter titles and include new dialogues as well as voice-overs, in order to alter narratives considered politically or morally subversive. Such changes could, for instance, turn a lover into a brother or a comrade into a friend if it was felt that the original identities would threaten the values of State, Church or Family. These measures would, however, be counterproductive as far as fostering Spanish Cinema was concerned. As Perojo put it in an interview: 'We sold out our language and mortgaged our freedom. And that is how we axed our own cinema.'[18] The dubbing laws meant that every import was readily accessible when distributed in Spain, undermining locally made films (Jordan & Allinson, 2005: 15–16). However, with the censors watching closely, producers carried on making films, in spite of difficult economic and working conditions, which did not guarantee quality in this Spain of ration books. Nonetheless on 17 April 1941 new studios at Charmatín, Madrid, were opened and by the end of the decade there would be eighteen productive studios.

Rewriting the Civil War

A tragedy as great as a civil war could not leave a nation untraumatised; the experience needed to be explained and even purged. While the rest of Europe was at war a number of films provided just this type of catharsis for the victors, however more than half the nation was denied this healing experience; for them the humiliation of defeat was the least of their sufferings as the government embarked on a policy rejecting any reconciliation (Talens, 1998: 86–8).[19] The victors' films, setting out their own deeds and values, became known as the *cine cruzada* [crusading films] and celebrated the Fatherland with the rewritten achievements of the Nationalist forces; a genre highly commended in numerous articles of *Primer Plano* (Triana Toribio, 2003: 46–51), often acknowledging military and religious advisers in their credits. The first, *Sin novedad en el Alcázar* [1940 *The Siege of the Alcazar*], written and directed by Augusto Genina, was filmed in Rome as a Hispano-Italian 'superproduction', with equipment unavailable in Spain. It reconstructed the survival of Nationalist soldiers, women and children in the Toledo fortress and army barracks besieged by what is depicted as a disorganised Repub-

---

[18] 'Vendimos nuestro idioma e hipotecamos nuestra libertad. Y ahí le dimos el hachazo al cine,' quoted in Gubern (1994: 357). Even the contributors to *Primer Plano* objected to compulsory dubbing.

[19] A suppressed perspective is well dramatised in Agustí Villaronga's *El mar* [2000 *The Sea*].

lican rabble often with an iconic bottle in hand. This assault-and-siege film, which received the Mussolini Cup for best Italian film at the Venice Festival in 1940, presents all the Francoist values that would be reiterated during the decade, articulating Spain's isolation and autarchic policies while celebrating glorious military sacrifices and National Catholicism. Carlos Arévalo's first film, ¡Harka! [1940, harkas were detachments of Berber recruits led by Spanish officers], was released five months later, the second of Arévalo's ten films. The film exemplifies the regime's slogan 'Todo por la patria' [All for the Country] and is dedicated to the officers and casualties of the Nationalist forces, even if it appropriates documentary footage previously taken by Republican Carlos Velo. It is an uncluttered story set mostly in the desert where an officer [Luis Peña] learns the value of comradeship and stoic loyalty to the harka[20] and the Nation at the expense of his personal fulfilment as a husband. In fact women have very little screen space; the fiancée [Luchy Soto] is presented as a dangerous distraction who belongs to a frivolous Madrid of nightclubs and restaurants, ready to sap the virile virtues that the state strove to foster (Peter Evans in Graham & Labanyi, 1995: 218–19).

The most important 'crusade' film was Raza [1941 PNC; the literal translation is Race, but *Pure Blood might be more appropriate],[21] based on a text by Franco himself. It uses autobiographical references to chronicle the lives of the fictional and emblematic Churruca family who find that the sacrifices made at Trafalgar, in Cuba and during the Civil War, are vindicated by the recent victory: implying that even though the colonies were lost through previous political mismanagement, at least the country was finally safe with the military, therefore justifying 'the Nationalist rebellion before God and History' (Hopewell, 1986: 34). After a number of documentaries and the comedy A mí no me mire usted [1941 *Don't You Look at Me] about a most unusual school teacher oblivious of the fact that the World War was in its second year, José Luis Sáenz de Heredia was selected to write the shooting

---

[20] Because of their military experience these soldiers were essential to the Nationalist victory as acknowledged in Raza.

[21] The Spanish National Day, on 12 October (when Columbus first saw Caribbean land), was popularly called 'El día de la raza' [Day of the Race] although later officially named 'día de la Hispanidad' [day of the Hispanic Community]. Franco used the name Jaime de Andrade as his pseudonym. Vernon describes the text as 'a study in compensatory fantasy [... and] self-idealization' (1986: 28–9). Franco is said to have enjoyed the cinema, especially zarzuelas and westerns, which he would view privately, every night, according to Augusto Torres (in Graham & Labanyi, 1995: 369; see also Preston (1993: 52, 352, 488, 549, and for Raza, see pp. 417–18; Diez Puertas (2003: 297–304)). Regueiro's 1993 Madregilda [*Mother Gilda] is a comedy based on these rumours (Vernon, 1997: 47–61, 54). Judging by his alleged reaction to the later Surcos and Viridiana scandals, Franco appears more broadminded than the censors appointed in his name.

4a The strength of the family in Sáenz de Heredia's *Raza* (1941)

script for *Raza* with Antonio Román's cooperation, and then once approved he was granted government funds to direct it (Besas, 1985:19–22). The film is important as it reflects the political paranoia of the early 1940s through its plot, clichéd characters and platitudes defining idealised attitudes towards the nation and family, based on absolute loyalty and personal sacrifice (Kinder, 1993: 152). It was reissued in 1951 as *Espíritu de una raza* [*The Spirit of a Race*], which was the only version known until 1993 when a damaged copy of the original was discovered in Germany; subsequently a complete version of the original was found in the Berlin UFA archive in 1995. As the political climate had changed, the original loaded rhetoric, general xenophobia, the strong anti-Semitic and US references, the evocation of international Masonic plots, all had to be altered with cuts, added voice-overs and dubbing of the original, which was done with the same voices used to dubbed *Gone with the Wind*. The new dialogues were focused on a strong anti-communist dialogue reflecting the hardening of the Cold War and lifting of the UN diplomatic boycott of Spain on 5 November 1950 (Talens, 1998: 65–9).

Antonio Román went on to direct *Escuadrilla* [1941 *The Squadron* – PNC] celebrating the Nationalist aircrews with a romantic narrative. Another film to take up the virile crusading values was the actor Juan de Orduña's second feature film, ¡¡A mí la legión!! [1942 Follow the Legion!! – again a more accurate title might be With Me, Legionaires!!], which, with the Peña-Mayo tandem of ¡Harka!,[22] reflected the same values of duty to the Fatherland. It presents strong male bonding but trivialises the spirit of ¡Harka! with a fantasy plot that begins with the Legion as a refuge away from women, uniting all classes beneath one flag, and moves to the fictional Kingdom of Eslonia, concluding with the re-enlistment of its King and his friend into the Legion in July 1936 for that glorious death and fulfilment (D'Lugo, 1997: 29–30). Demonstrating an even stronger note of latent homoeroticism in its gestures and photography than ¡Harka! (Hopewell, 1986: 34–6) the excesses of the film almost qualify it as a parody. These last four films all contributed to the typecasting of Alfredo Mayo as the archetypal Franco hero, and generated other adventures like Legión de héroes [1942 Juan Fortuny and Armando Seville, *Legion of Heroes].

Los últimos de Filipinas [1945 Antonio Román, *Last Stand in the Philippines – PNC] shot in the CEA Madrid studios, also reiterates all the values of the cine cruzada as it rewrites the loss of the Spanish colony in 1898 (Santaolalla, 2005a: 50–9). The film portrays the united soldiers as victims of diseases as much as of their enemy,[23] presented again as a preying rabble, and it celebrates the courage, loyalty, stoicism and sacrifices of the stubborn detachment besieged in a church for almost a year with repeated high-angle shots of the bell-tower flying the flag to provide a concise visual reminder of Church and country. In the light of Tolentino's suggestion (1997) that 'Spanish national masculinity is recuperated for 1945 audiences through the valorization of the heroism of its colonial past' (1997: 146) it is significant that the only female character [Nani Fernández playing a Tagalog in love with a Spanish soldier, Fernando Rey] unwittingly causes a disaster for the garrison (Labanyi, 1997: 218). The film has been read as an allegory of Spain's political and economic isolation in these early years of the Dictatorship (Tolentino, 1997: 143), but times were changing, and in 1945 the USA was to be courted rather than insulted. It is therefore not surprising that Los últimos... acknowledges the help given by the US Embassy, since in 1898 Spain had capitulated to the USA for the second time.

That same year Sáenz de Heredia even directed a musical war film, Bambú [1945 *Bamboo – PNC; edited by Sara Ontañón] set against the Cuban war

---

[22] Luis Peña (1918–1977) had started his acting career as a child on the stage, and moved to film with the 1925 La casa de la Troya. Alfredo Mayo (1911–1985) also started on the stage, had been in two films before the Civil War and had just acted in La florista de la reina, becoming the heartthrob of the decade. Orduña (1907–1974), as evident from chapter 3, was a star of the silent screen and filmed a few documentaries during the war.

[23] 'La epidemia es peor que las balas' [The diseases are worse than the bullets].

of 1898, in which Imperio Argentina, opposite Luis Peña, once again plays a mixed-race heroine (as in *Morena Clara* and *Aixa*) who dies with her lover fighting for the honour of Spain 'explicitly linking the genre to an imperial model of nationhood' (Labanyi, 1997: 224). The fashion for this type of war film declined as the Second World War concluded and new political lines were drawn.

To escape a harsh reality, and dream a little

Although criticised by *Primer Plano*, which hoped for more edifying narratives (Triana Toribio, 2003: 39–41), the paying public's favourites were still musicals, comedies and Andalusian settings; preferably all three together (Woods, 2004a: 52–3). Credit sequences frequently began with a soundtrack that is a musical overture. Many such hybrids were produced blurring the generic distinctions that a tidy mind would wish to impose. For instance, the entertaining *Alma de Dios* [1941 Ignacio F. Iquino, **Heart of Gold*; starring Amparo Rivelles, and a remake of Manuel Noriega's silent 1922 title], covers the whole range from farce to melodrama, includes gypsies and songs, as well as a couple of luxurious sets contrasted with location shots in the streets of Madrid, thus allowing views of a contemporary Spain in need of much rebuilding and evoking the corruption of city life. Following the Italian model, films such as Perojo's *Héroe a la fuerza* [1941 **The Reluctant Hero*, starring Miguel Ligero], or Fernando Delgado's *Fortunato* [1942], were called 'white telephone comedies' because the prop only occurred in this context. Some consider *Fortunato* to be Delgado's swan song, in spite of two films in 1943 and two more in 1947. It was based on a play by the Quintero brothers, and presents Fortunato, a character prone to misfortunes who, made redundant by the insurance company for which he worked, has to find jobs, which he can never keep; but he perseveres, remaining hopeful and virtuous until a permanent post provides closure. It is a reflection of 1941 when unemployment was high, but the film was approved without cuts since it is set in the dissolute Republican year of 1934 and denigrates wealthy and decadent liberals taking drugs. Despite not mentioning the Second World War, even when other European cities were featured, such passing subversive references to contemporary difficulties demonstrate that these feel-good films were not always devoid of social commentary (Marsh, 1999: 65–75).

In the first half of the decade CIFESA was still very much in control, and produced all the following examples of escapist wish-fulfilment. Orduña, claiming Ernst Lubitsch as his model but without the budget or the studio resources, consolidated his reputation with comedies set among the very wealthy that invariably included sentimental male leads. He directed escapist plots like *Deliciosamente tontos* [1943 **Delightfully Foolish*] with Amparo

Rivelles[24] and Alfredo Mayo, *La vida empieza a medianoche* [1944 *Life begins at Midnight*] with Marta Santaolalla and Armando Calvo, where the 'mujeres independientes' [independent women] do end up with a romantic husband, and *Ella, él y sus millones* [1944 *She, He and His Millions*], again pairing Josita Hernán with Rafael Durán, and José Isbert playing his supporting roles in the last two.[25] After documentaries, at first for the Rebublican cause, Rafael Gil directed his first full-length comedies *El hombre que se quiso matar* [1942 *The Man Who Wanted to Kill Himself* – which he remade in 1970; cf. Capra's 1946 *It's a Wonderful Life*] and *Huella de luz* [1943 *Traces of Light* – PNC]. Contrary to received opinions of the 'white telephone' comedies, it can be observed that in spite of the required happy closure through marriage, the implications are that the fictional brides do not always conform to the regime's ideal image of womanhood (Graham, 1995: 182–95; Donapetry, 1998: 37–40). As in many seventeenth-century Spanish plays, these resourceful women marry sentimental and at times inept suitors. Both Gil's comedies, casting Antonio Casal opposite Rosita Yarza in the first and Isabel de Pomés in the second, also make passing comments on the hard times of unemployment, albeit with humour. Gil would still be at it in 1958 with the sentimental *Camarote de lujo* [*Luxury Cabin*], which reflects the economic migrations of the 1950s.

Everyone had forgotten *Cinópolis* [1930] but José María Castellví remade his reputation with five post-war comedies, including his last *El hombre que se las enamora* [1944 *The Man Who Makes Them Fall In Love*]. The Hungarian Ladislao Vajda (1906–1965), having directed over twenty films in Hungary, France, Italy, Portugal and the UK, made his first Spanish film in 1943, *Se vende un palacio* [*A Palace for Sale*], unfortunately lost. Luis Marquina's romantic intrigue set in high society, *Vidas cruzadas* [1942 *Lives Entwined*], was so politically correct that 'seven red' at the roulette table is a 'siete encarnado'; however, it is not devoid of social implications and criticism as Eugenia [Ana Mariscal] has to negotiate the patriarchal environment. The same can be said of *La chica del gato* [1943 Ramón Quadreny, *The Girl with the Cat*], which launched Fernando Fernán Gómez's film career[26] opposite Josita Hernán. The following year Quadreny directed *Una chica de opereta* [*An Operetta Girl*], which could equally well be classified as a musical,

---

[24] Born in 1925, she dominated the screen with twenty-one films during this decade. The daughter of actors Rafael Rivelles and María Fernanda Ladrón de Guevara, at 17 she had signed a three-year contract with CIFESA. From 1959 to 1974 she lived and worked in Mexico.

[25] These scripts frequently followed the theatre's typecasting tradition that goes back to the seventeenth-century stage: leading man [*galán*], ladies [*damas*], funny man [*gracioso*], old man [*barba*], and added more mature actresses to the cast, like Julia Lajos.

[26] Born in Lima in 1921; by 2004 he had acted in 193 films, directed 30 and written 25 scripts. Fernando Fernán Gómez died on 21 November 2007, just after this book was completed.

given the frequent overlap between the genres. Gonzalo Delgrás also flourished with fifteen films during the decade, nine of them written or adapted by his wife Margarita Robles, who also acted in most of them, like the taming of the shrew comedy *Un marido a precio fijo* [1942 *A Fixed Price Husband*]. This film, like their next, a romantic melodrama, *La condesa María* [1942], paired off Lina Yegros and Rafael Durán, with Margarita Robles as the Countess. In contrast to Perojo's more animated 1930 original where Luis [José Nieto] is the long- lost son of the Moroccan wars and which included documentary footage, Delgrás's remake now presents a Luis [Vicente Vega] who returns from the Eastern Front where the Spanish División Azul was fighting against the Soviets, without any war footage except for one superimposition of flying planes. Delgrás's version retains its stage origins, adds references to the 'war of liberation' and comments on the glory of dying for Spain and God, presenting the matriarch as one of the many incarnations of Spanish virtues to be seen on screen (another version of Marsha Kinder's patriarchal mothers [1993]: 199–200). Luis Lucia, who started off in this decade, also directed his share of comedies and intrigues, like *Dos cuentos para dos* [1947 *Two Stories for Two*], which, in spite of being distributed by CIFESA, was by implication critical of the upper classes and employment anomalies.

Ignacio F[errés] Iquino (1910–1994)

Highly productive was the Catalan Ignacio F. Iquino who made thirty films during the decade, most of them comedies, like the crime spoof *Los ladrones somos gente honrada* [1942 *We Thieves Are Honourable* – remade in 1956 by Pedro L. Ramírez], or the absurd case of mistaken identities between two sets of twins *Un enredo de familia* [1943 *Family Confusion*]. Seven of these films were for Campa-CIFESA, sixteen for Emisora Films, and then he started his own company IFI(SA).[27] For Emisora he made the crime films *Hombres sin honor* [1944 *Men Without Honour*], *Una sombra en la ventana* [1944 *A Shadow at the Window*], and *¡Cupable!* [1945 *Guilty!*]. His first for IFI was *La familia Vila* [1950 *The Vila Family* – starring José Isbert, Maruchi Fresno and Juana Solé], a melodrama reflecting patriarchal family structures and featuring a comforting priest, which pleased the censors since 'the script never loses its moralising outlook',[28] but also referring to the black market and the 'sardana', a Catalan folkdance only just decriminalised for public performances. In 1948, Emisora Films was responsible for the first

---

27 These details are collected from the *IMDb* and the *MCU.es*. His film career started in 1934 and concluded in 1984, with 102 films as screenwriter and 88 as director.

28 'El guión no pierde en ningún momento la tónica moralizadora' (Casimiro Torreiro, in Pérez Perucha, 1997: 256).

Spanish colour system, cinefotocolor, and in 1949 released *En un rincón de España* [*In a Corner of Spain* – PNC] directed by Jerónimo Mihura with Isidoro Goldberger at the camera, about Polish asylum seekers and an exiled Republican sailor stranded on the Costa Brava.

Darker intrigues

There were darker melodramas, like Antonio Román's *Boda en el infierno* [1942 *Marriage in Hell* – PNC] with a film to denigrate Soviets and Republicans. It begins in Odessa in 1935 as the captain of a Spanish tanker [José Nieto] marries Blanca [Conchita Montenegro], the daughter of the last Tsar's ambassador, in order to rescue her from a communist hell. They divorce in Paris and meet up by accident in a Spain torn apart by the war. The dialogues by Miguel Mihura are not without humour and the cast includes Manolo Morán, who was usually typecast as the funny man even in serious films like *Escuadrilla* or *Los últimos...* Another Román film, *La casa de la lluvia* [1943 *The House of Rain*], a melodrama evoking Galicia, was a personal film, which, like his comic detective in *Intriga* [1943 *Intrigue*], did not satisfy the spectators. Other dramas of intrigue were Gonzalo Delgrás's *Cristina Guzmán* [1943, remade in 1968 by Luis Amadori] based on the novel by Carmen de Icaza set in Madrid and Paris, or his *Altar mayor* [1944 *The High Altar*] based on a novel by Concha Espina and set in rural Asturias. Claudio de la Torre created a psychological intrigue with *Misterio en la marisma* [1943 *The Wetland Mystery*] set among otiose aristocrats hunting on their estate, including a female protagonist [Conchita Montes] who determines the course of the plot and the brief appearance of a 'girl jazz band'.

Two great box-office successes were based on a novel and a short story by Pedro de Alarcón. The first, *El escándalo* [1943 Sáenz de Heredia, *The Scandal* – PNC, remade in 1964 by Javier Setó], was set in 1860 and concerns the redemption of a Don Juan [Armando Calvo]; it was the first film under Franco to deal with adultery, skilfully edited by Julio Peña to create a clear sense of suspense.[29] Sáenz de Heredia had learnt much from Buñuel at Filmófono, and certainly knew how to please the spectators. He also managed to impress the establishment as he earned PNCs for all his films in this decade. The second film was Gil's *El clavo* [1944 *The Nail* – PNC] with Amparo

---

[29] This is the second of 70 films he edited. He acted in 97 films starting in 1930 in Spanish language films from the USA. He also produced two films directed by Jerónimo Mihura, *Confidencia* [1947 *Confidences*] and *Siempre vuelven de madrugada* [1949 *They Always Return at Dawn*].

Rivelles and Rafael Durán.[30] Both films allowed CIFESA to import no less than fifteen foreign films each. One could add *Mariona Rebull* [1947 Sáenz de Heredia – PNC], which, using flashbacks, captures nineteenth-century Barcelona and its social upheavals, including the 1893 anarchist bomb in the Opera House that destroys the fictional lovers. Building on the possibilities of *La florista de la reina*, distancing narratives from the contemporary period, usually through a nineteenth-century setting, allowed screenwriters to explore through their dialogues a more subversive sexual content and suggest issues that would otherwise have been censored, albeit with compensating moral comments and conclusions (Labanyi, 2000: 176–8).[31] Enough films were made in this context for them to be identified as 'cine de levita' [frock-coat films], including Neville's biopic *El marqués de Salamanca* [1948], the railway builder, and the commercial tale *El señor Esteve* [released in Barcelona on 30 December 1948].

Fostering the young

In 1940 cartoon production started again in Barcelona, and in 1945, while the rest of Europe was at war, Spain produced the first European feature-length colour animation *Garbancito de la Mancha* [*Don Chickpea of La Mancha*[32] – PNC], with echoes of the Disney aesthetic and Quixotic references. Given working conditions and lack of materials, this production from Ramón Balet and José María Blay, directed by Arturo Moreno, is worth registering. Garbancito is knighted by a good fairy, given a magic sword and the ability to change himself into a chickpea [*garbanzo*] while his faithful goat Peregrina's horns can glow when danger is present. Thus armed and learning to use his wits, after a number of adventures pious Garbancito frees the country from the evil witch Tía Pelocha and the child-eating ogre Caramanca. The fable was well received in other European cities recovering from the World War, and it could be given differing allegorical readings as it includes in its conclusion the reconciliation of Garbancito with the three inept villains who have made his mission much more difficult. This was followed in 1948 by *Alegres vacaciones* [*Happy Holidays*], also based on Arturo Moreno's drawings, and in 1951 by *Los sueños de Tay-Pi* [*The Dreams of Tay-Pi*]. Another

---

[30] Gil included a few clips of *El clavo*'s opening night in his 1980 generational-conflict film, *Hijos de papá* [*Spoilt Brats*].

[31] The displacement was not guaranteed, as exemplified by the brilliant comedy satire *La corte de faraón* [1985 José Luis García Sánchez, *The Court of the Pharaoh*]. The original *zarzuela*, written by Guillermo Perrín and Miguel Palacio in 1910, based on the story of Joseph and Potiphar, was actually banned by the censors in 1940.

[32] Title as released in the UK, not on *IMDb*.

feature-length animation from Estela Films was *Érase una vez* [1950 Alexandre Cirici Pellicer, **Once upon a time*], originally to be called *Cinderella*
until the Disney Studios released their own version of the fairy tale that same
year. Animation then declined for a while, unable to compete with Disney
and other US imports.

Mid-forties Crises

1945 was a critical year for CIFESA, who only produced one film, *Un
hombre de negocio* [Luis Lucia **A Business Man*], and none in 1946. In
spite of the respite and financial success of the subsequent historical cycle
CIFESA would lose its domination of the market to Suevia Films by the
1950s (Besas, 1985: 26–7). On 16 August 1945 a fire in the Madrid Riera
Laboratories, never fully investigated (Gubern,1995: 14), destroyed many
unique copies of films stored on the premises, thus compounding the losses
incurred during the Civil War and before. The summer of 1945 experienced
the end of the Second World War, the negotiation of peace settlements and
the consequent readjustment of Franco's policies now that his allies had
been defeated. A number of changes took place in the DNC, which included
placing censorship and cinema under the responsibility of the Ministry of
Education. The JSCC was renamed the Junta Superior de Orientación Cinematográfica [JSOC], replacing the word 'censura' by the seemingly more
benign 'orientación'. Film import regulations were modified on 31 December
1946 to reduce the number of licences conceded, although they could now be
sold and transferred to another producer. The compulsory dubbing laws were
repealed on 25 January 1947, but the damage had been done and viewing
habits had become too engrained for subtitles to become a viable commercial
alternative, and illiteracy was still an educational problem. When Humphrey
Bogart visited Madrid, spectators refused to believe he was the real Bogart
because of the contrast between his voice and his dubbed voice. Film clubs,
which had flourished before and during the Republican years, were reinstated
in 1946 and thus allowed some spectators to view some films in their original
version. A decree on 26 February 1947 confirmed that a film school able to
confer degrees, the Instituto de Investigaciones y Experiencias Cinematográficas [IIEC/Institute for Cinema Research and Experiments], was to be set up
under Victoriano López García,[33] who had been responsible for a film course
in the Madrid Engineering Faculty since 1941. Education, however, remained

---

[33] Its official remit is described in the Oficina Informativa Española's *El cine español*
(pp. 119–240, translated in 1950 (pp. 125–30); significantly the book only devotes one page
to censorship (p. 106, trans. 112). The impact of the School's graduates will be elaborated in
chapter 5.

mainly in the hands of the Church (Alicia Alted, in Graham & Labanyi, 1995:
196–9), and government ministers began to experience the influence of the
secular organisation dedicated to promoting National-Catholicism, the Opus
Dei (Graham & Labanyi, 1995: 423 and 421).

Rewriting Spanish history

By the mid-1940s the taste for 'crusading films' had waned and Vicente
Casanova pushed CIFESA into a new venture, the historical epics (Mira,
2005: 61–2). A few historical films had already appeared, such as Eusebio
Fernández Ardavín *El abanderado* [1943 *The Standard Bearer* – PNC], one
of Suevia Films' first productions. The story was set during the Napoleonic
wars, included the slaughter of the Madrid citizens on 2 May 1808, and capi-
talised on Alfredo Mayo's screen image as he learns to rise above his love
for Isabel de Pomés to fight for Spain, so that both courage and virtue are
eventually rewarded. The historical epic received the full rhetorical approval
of *Primer Plano*:

> The primacy and responsibility of the historical film is such that it cannot
> be compared to any other genre [...]. The significance of the historical
> genre on the screen is such, in fact, that it affects the actual development
> of the National Spirit [/national identity]. There is no other moment like
> this one – when the fundamental and irrevocable duty of all Spaniards is
> the exaltation of the essence of the Nation – when producers and directors
> should feel as an irrefutable imperative the obligation to teach, within and
> outside our commonwealth, what was the magnificently glorious trajectory
> of Spain throughout the centuries.[34]

It was also hoped that such films would inscribe and legitimise the new
regime as an intrinsic part of Spain's historical destiny as, for instance, the
initial voice-over of *Agustina de Aragón* [1950 Juan de Orduña – PNC] makes
clear:

> to the glorious heroes of Spanish Independence [and of the Civil War] we
> dedicate this film which does not attempt to be an exact and detailed histor-

---

[34] 'La altura y responsabilidad del cine histórico es tal que con ningún otro género puede
compararse [...] La importancia del género histórico en la pantalla alcanza, pues, a la forma-
ción misma del espíritu nacional [...] Ningún momento como éste – en que la exaltación de las
esencias nacionales es deber primordial e ineludible de todo español – para que productores y
realizadores sientan como imperativo indeclinable la obligación de enseñar, dentro y fuera de
nuestras fronteras, cuál fue la trayectoria magníficamente gloriosa de España a través de los
siglos.' *Primer Plano*, 9 August 1942, p. 95, quoted by Monterde (in Gubern, 1995: 234).

ical reconstruction [...] but rather a passionate and rousing commentary on the courage and valour of her [Spain's] children embodied in the incomparable figure of Agustina de Aragón, symbol of the courage of the Nation and the indomitable spirit and of the independence of all Spaniards.[35]

The agenda behind these films was clearly to strengthen national resolve against foreign pressure as Spain was being ostracised by other nations, and, at the same time, imply that the regime was following in the footsteps of these heroes.

Most of these films are melodramas set in a historical context, and those best remembered turn a historical moment into a melodrama dependent on its stars, with costumes, action and romance. Ana Mariscal, whose screen performances started with the costume drama *El último húsar* [1940 Luis Marquina, *The Last Hussar*] shot in Rome and included *La florista de la reina* and *Raza*, starred in Luis Lucia's first substantial breakthrough, *La princesa de los Ursinos* [1947 *The Princess of the Ursinos* –PNC], which dealt with political intrigues at the court of Philip V in seventeenth-century Madrid, under French threats on a question of legitimate succession. Mariscal was also in Iquino's *El tambor del Bruch* [1948 *The Bruch Drum*] where Napoleon's army is fighting in Catalonia and defeated by the drummer boy.[36] José Luis López Rubio's 1944 *Eugenia de Montijo* [PNC] relates how the lady [Amparo Rivelles] finally weds Napoleon III [Mariano Asquerino] in spite of all opposition. M.A. García Viñolas and J.M. Leitão de Barros directed a co-production on a romanticised episode of fourteenth-century Portuguese history, *Inés de Castro* [1945 – PNC], which had already been dramatised for the Madrid stage by Luis Vélez de Guevara [c. 1630–40] and the French stage by Henry de Montherlant [1942]. Eusebio Fernández Ardavín's *El doncel de la reina* [1946 *The Queen's Little Soldier*] combines adventure with the conquest of Granada in 1492 and leads to the colonisation of America, whereas Rafael Gil's *Reina santa* [1947 *The Holy Queen* – PNC] is set a century earlier, with Maruchi Fresno as Isabel de Aragón opposite Antonio Vilar as the Portuguese King Dionís, and Fernando Rey as the Infante Alfonso. Luis Marquina's *Doña María la brava* [1948 *Doña María the Brave*] deals with the political intrigues and succession of Juan II in the fifteenth century.

The two most successful historical films at the box-office were both Orduña melodramas for CIFESA, and this new formula restored the compa-

---

[35] 'A los héroes gloriosos de la independencia de España dedicamos esta película que no pretende ser un exacto y detallado proceso histórico [...] sino la glosa ferviente y exaltada del temple y valor de sus hijos reunidos de la impar figura de Agustina de Aragón, símbolo del valor de la raza y del espíritu insobornable y de la independencia de todos los españoles.'

[36] Film remade in 1981 by Jordi Grau as *El timbaler del Bruc/La leyenda del Bruc*.

ny's fortune for a while after their mid-decade crisis (Hopewell, 1986: 42–3). Both films cast Aurora Bautista opposite Fernando Rey, and both narratives were presented as flashbacks. *Locura de amor* [1948 *The Mad Queen* – PNC], which also included Sara Montiel (María Antonia Abad), is not the only film of the life of Juana the Mad, daughter of Isabel la Católica (Martín Pérez, 2004: 71–85).[37] Adapting the nineteenth-century play by Tamayo y Baus, this version presents foreign plots against the legitimate succession and the victimised Spanish Queen, framed by the past glory of the Catholic Monarchs and the future Empire of Charles V (the disruption of the Second Republic followed by rehabilitation with the Franco regime). The initial flashback in *Agustina de Aragón* [1950 – PNC; Florián Rey directed a first version in 1929] is crucial in creating a positive gloss over the failed defence of Zaragoza from Napoleon's troops and appraising the value of devotion and sacrifice to the nation (Labanyi, 2004: 45–9), and it benefited from the massive participation of the standing cavalry. Orduña followed these two fictionalised historical accounts with another about María Pacheco, *La leona de Castilla* [1951 *The Lioness of Castile*], this time subject to foreign plots at the time of Charles V. The blending of history and melodrama continued: compare, for instance, Ruiz Castillo's *Catalina de Inglaterra* [1951 – PNC] and its strong anti-British agenda with Marquina's *El capitán Veneno* [1951 *Captain Poison*, based on a novel by Pedro de Alarcón], where melodrama is blended with humour and Fernán Gómez is cast as a misogynist reformed by Sara Montiel, and images of cackling women are juxtaposed with inept politicians, albeit at the Court of Isabel II. Mira sees the musical *Lola la piconera* [1952 Luis Lucia, *Lola the Coalgirl*, starring Juanita Reina] with its flamenco, folkloric and gypsy costumes, presenting the Napoleonic siege of Cádiz, as the last success of the CIFESA cycle (2005: 60–9).

In spite of the bad press these films receive from Hopewell as cinema (1986: 42–3), they are interesting because of their attempt to use historical events to comment on the present, justify the Nationalist rebellion and explain Spain's isolation. They implicitly reflect the political climate and social circumstances of the 1940s (Mira, 2004: 60–75),[38] and on occasions explicitly demonstrate the shortage of facilities and materials that led them to being labelled as papier-mâché sets, 'de cartón-piedra' [of cardboard stone]. Some historical films were denigrated in this way because the sets were so

37 Ricard de Baños 1909 with the same title, and Vicente Aranda 2001 as *Juana la Loca* [*Mad Love*].

38 As a parallel, in 1995 three unusual films were produced without any ideological directives but in tune with the political discussions of the time: *Rob Roy* [Michael Caton-Jones], *Braveheart* [Mel Gibson], and *The Bruce* [Bob Carruthers, the only autochthonous production]; in 1997 the Scots were given a second referendum on devolution, and their Parliament was reconstituted in 1999.

cheap that they stood out as fake, as parodied at the beginning of *Esa pareja feliz*; for instance, the credits of *Inés de Castro* are presented as carvings on the wall of the castle. The rhetoric of these films presents Spaniards united by the same language and the same concept of 'España' as understood by the Franco regime, reducing regional diversities to different costumes and different accents (Peter Evans, in Graham & Labanyi, 1995: 216–17). Furthermore, even when not based on historical figures, these narratives present a Spain that is physically or intellectually under siege or involved in questions of succession. Both reflect the political imperative of the regime to legitimise itself historically and voice its preoccupations over its self-imposed policy of political and economic isolation before 1945, and then its ostracisation after 1946 when refused membership of the UN. Their extreme Manichean discourses also suggest the diplomatic vulnerability experienced at a time when foreign ambassadors left the country and France closed its borders for a year (Bonaddio, 2004: 24–9). Triana Toribio goes further: 'the [siege] metaphor also allows for a reinterpretation of the country's recent violence against itself as the product of the attack of an evil and external force, thus legitimising the violence as self-defence' (2003: 49). The aggressors are presented as foreigners assailing Spanish lives and values, or treacherous and ambitious Spaniards misled by reading Voltaire and respecting the democratic ideals of the French Republic. A third element is that they nearly all present a strong female protagonist, a consecrated star representing a personal experience, to captivate the spectator and inspire a sense of pride in the nation personified as a strong woman and challenging males into action (Gómez, 2002: 579; Peter Evans, in Graham & Labanyi, 1995: 222), they 'represent Spanish virtues' (Mira, 2005: 67).[39] Labanyi proposes an additional hypothesis: 'as in contemporaneous Hollywood *film noir*, [...] this served as a way of helping men negotiate the transition from the "tough guy" of wartime to the "family man" of peace time' (2000: 164).

Actors in cassocks

Another genre, already exploited during the days of the Republic and which blossomed in the second half of the decade, was the 'cine de cura' [clergy

---

[39] The question is more complex, and needs more study on the spectators' response and identification; see also Jesús González Requena (1988: 91) and Labanyi (2000: 165–6, 173–6, 181). There is also an important precedent in Lope de Vega's seventeenth-century *Fuenteovejuna* (Act III, lines 1723–1818) where Laurencia insults patriarchal values and male pride, haranguing the villagers to rebel against the official but unworthy figure of authority. In both *Rob Roy* and *Braveheart* the female figure also gains symbolic connotations to convey the rape of Scotland in the first and its international appeal in the second, which visually also equates the hero's execution with Christ's crucifixion.

films], which broadens out to include missionary films and historical dramas. This comes as no surprise in 1946 when films celebrating military triumphalism were no longer appropriate after the defeat of Fascism and that the existing national prizes linked to funding were now under the growing influence of the Opus Dei. These films could visually demonstrate Spain's contribution to the Catholic cause, which had always supported the regime, given that the Vatican had been the first political entity to recognise Franco's government in March 1941. Generally they are melodramas with a strong plot that emphatically presents Catholic values. They start with Orduña's *Misión blanca* [1946 *White Mission* – PNC], actually filmed on location in Spanish Guinea although the extras had to wear supplementary clothing to appease the Spanish censors. In Gil's *La fe* [1947 *The Faith* – PNC], again conveniently set in the previous century, the village priest [Rafael Durán] successfully resists the temptations of the flesh [Amparo Rivelles]. Sáenz de Heredia, now with his own production company Chapalo Films, produced and directed *La mies es mucha* [1948 *The Harvest is Rich* – PNC], 142 minutes of missionary zeal set in India with Fernán Gómez cast as the priest competing with Anglican missionaries, pressgang labour bosses and diseases. *Balarrasa* [1951 José Antonio Nieves Conde, *Reckless*] starts with Fernán Gómez, once again a missionary but this time literally freezing to death in Alaska, and considering in flashback the changes he has experienced from his dissolute life as a legionnaire who, remorseful, espouses the cloth and rescues his wealthy family from the consequences of crime; the Fatherland almost loses out to the Family and Faith.[40] The narrative, in spite of its religious motivation, presents a tight gangster film drama undermined by Aspa Films imposing luxurious sets rather than the middle-class context that was originally scripted. Arturo Ruiz Castillo's *La manigua sin Dios* [1949 *The Godless Swamp*, edited by Sara Ontañón] is more historical and deals with eighteenth-century Jesuits in Paraguay and their subsequent expulsion leaving the Guarani Indians to be exploited; it is a film that includes songs and dances, and a narrative taken up in *The Mission* [1986 Roland Joffé]. There are also straight hagiographies like José Díaz Morales's *El capitán de Loyola* [1948 *Loyola the Soldier Saint*] with the gallant Rafael Durán as Ignatius, the founder of the Jesuit Order. Orduña's superproduction *Pequeñeces* [1950 *Trifles* – PNC] is not a clergy film but a very costly yet successful overloaded historical melodrama. Based on Fr Coloma SJ's novel, it encompasses the First Republic and the subsequent restoration of the monarchy, starring the same actors as *Locura...* Aurora Bautista, Jorge Mistral, Sara Montiel, but without Fernando Rey. Pedantically didactic as Currita de Albornoz

---

[40] The film begins its flashback with the Civil War; and just as Captain Mendoza, aka Balarrasa, leaves the barracks for the seminary, so film plots would replace the military uniforms by cassocks.

repents for her adulteries and many sins, the script had to be toned down to
be allowed a release.

The authority of literature

The adaptation of literary masterpieces to link the regime's values to the past
may have motivated a similar sense of pride and continuity as the historical
epics discussed above, but there were surprisingly few at first. Antonio Román
adapted Lope de Vega's early seventeenth-century play *Fuenteovejuna* [1947
The Sheepwell], where the rebellion of a whole town against its demonised
Comendador [Governor] is finally legitimised by the Catholic Monarchs,
figures of ultimate authority equated to Franco; the changes made by Román
were not all cinematographically necessary but do reflect the values of the
regime.[41] It was also time to reappropriate one of Cervantes's masterpieces,
already filmed by many foreigners (Seguin, 1994: 44–5 in French or 1995:
35–6 in its Spanish translation), so CIFESA as part of the fourth centenary of Cervantes's birth contracted Rafael Gil to tackle *Don Quijote de la
Mancha* [1948 – PNC] with a star-studded cast that included Rafael Rivelles
as Quixote, Juan Calvo as Sancho, Sara Montiel as Antonia [sic], Manolo
Morán as the barber, Fernando Rey as the graduate Sansón Carrasco, and
Juan Espantaleón as the priest.[42] Two years earlier Luis Arroyo had directed
Dulcinea [1947, adapted from a play by Gaston Baty and remade in 1963 by
Vicente Escrivá] presenting the consequences of the Hidalgo Quejana's boasts
on the simple minded Aldonza Lorenzo, played by Ana Mariscal. Another
Spanish icon taken to the screen was *Don Juan* [1950 Sáenz de Heredia
– PNC], which cast Rosa María Salgado as Doña Inés opposite Antonio Vilar,
and blends more elements of José Zorrilla (nineteenth century) than of Tirso
de Molina (seventeenth century) in a very free adaptation by Carlos Blanco,
also responsible for the script of *La princesa de los Ursinos* and *Locura de
amor* (Wright, 2005: 415–31).

   More recent novelists, now part of the literary canon, were also adapted
for the screen, whereas the silent cinema looked more frequently but not
exclusively to dramatists for its adaptations. Examples would be Pío Baroja's
Las inquietudes de Shanti Andía [1947 Ruiz Castillo, *The Preoccupations
of Shanti Andía*], or Unamuno's *Abel Sánchez* [1947] in Carlos Serrano de
Osma's first feature, on a screenplay by Pedro Lazaga, which was far too

---

[41] P. Evans (1997) and Bentley (2004, contribution to be amplified and published in English
to develop this argument). In 1972 there was a film adaptation for Italian television, and two
more in 1974 for Portugal and Belgium in Dutch.

[42] A search on the *IMDb* for 'Quijote' or 'Quichotte' will reveal numerous adaptations of
the novel, both silent and in many languages.

experimental with its use of lighting. Neither of these authors were endorsed by the establishment, especially as the second film deals with two rival brothers. Emilia Pardo Bazán's *La sirena negra* [1947 *The Black Siren*] was Serrano de Osma's third film, and there was as well Blasco Ibáñez's *Mare nostrum* [1948 Rafael Gil, *Our Sea* – PNC], Armando Palacio Valdés's *Las aguas bajan negras* [1948 Sáenz de Heredia, *The Waters Run Black* – PNC], *El huésped de las tinieblas* [1948 Antonio del Amo, *The Guest of the Mists*] inspired by Gustavo Adolfo Bécquer, and Washington Irving's *Cuentos de la Alhambra* [1950 Florián Rey, *Tales of the Alhambra*]. The most cooperative novelist was probably Wenceslao Fernández Flórez, who had frequently collaborated with directors ever since he first adapted his work *Una aventura de cine* [Orduña, *A Film Adventure*] in 1928.

The exotic folkloric

Together with Hollywood comedies it was, however, the many folkloric comedies and melodramas that continued to provide the local escape from reality, and although they were still criticised by the establishment they were lucrative, and popular with the public (Triana Toribio, 2003: 62–5). Their temporal context is often undetermined, and Eva Woods describes them as offering 'spaces where alternative forms of identity could be imagined and in this sense they challenged prevailing hegemonic norms' (2004a: 52; see also Vernon, in Gies, 1999: 249–54). Examples of this genre are Marquina's 1942 remake of *Malvaloca* with Alfredo Mayo and Amparo Rivelles where, significantly, the question of the single mother so important to Perojo's earlier version is left in the background (Hopewell, 1986: 33 and 248); *La blanca paloma* [1942 Claudio de la Torre, *The White Dove*], based on a Pérez Lugín novel, which resolves the situation with a miracle and launched Juanita Reina's career; *Macarena* [1944 Antonio Gúzman Merino], with Juanita Reina and Miguel Ligero. In 1941, José López Rubio cast Miguel Ligero as *Pepe Conde* in a comedy of false identity and opposing social classes set in Andalusia, making the sequel, *El crimen de Pepe Conde* [*Pepe Conde's Crime*] in 1946. The latter, perhaps because it is more of a farce as Pepe Conde's superstitious nature is magnified, made twice as much at the box-office. Although there is a continuity of settings with the Republican folklorics, which 'had chiefly used the genre's reliance on lower-class characters to air issues of social injustice' (Labanyi, 1997: 221), the Francoist folklorics tend to show a female gypsy, often brought up by bandits, falling in love with a member of the establishment and thus presenting 'the political subtext of the need for national unification' as the heroine is integrated into patriarchal society and therefore 'the racial conflict dramatized in the vast majority of *folclóricas* is a way of treating class problems while seeming not to' (Labanyi, 1997: 224 and 226; and 2000: 169–70). There were of course variations: in Florián Rey's *Carmen, la de Triana* Don José dies to save his regiment, in *Filigrana* [1949 Marquina, starring Conchita Piquer and with Carmen Sevilla making her billed debut[43]] the heroine turns the tables on her seducer once she has found fame and fortune through her singing; something similar happens in Orduña's *La Lola se va a los puertos* [1947 *Lola Leaves for the Ports* with Juanita Reina, Manuel Luna and Ricardo Acero – remade in 1993 by Josefa Molina] where the emotional conflict is resolved as Lola stays with her own kind.

Historical displacements were frequent and *La Lola* was set in 1860. *Goyescas* [1942 – PNC and a Venice Award] is a sumptuous costume musical, a tribute to the painter Goya and the composer Granados that had been maturing for over ten years on Perojo's desk. Its plot may appear trivial as the flighty Condesa de Gualda and the loyal Petrilla, a singer of much lower social standing, are rivals for the same honourable soldier [Rafael Rivelles]. Imperio Argentina plays both women, which allows in the context of 1942 an implicit social reading criticising a society being remodelled from above (Labanyi, 2004: 41–5). The censors gave the script a cautious endorsement since the action unfolds by means of amorous situations, and Perojo was warned that official approval would depend on the final screening so that any vulgarity or suggestion of voluptuousness ['a la crudeza o a la sugestión voluptuosa'] should be avoided; in the meantime he was to delete from the script a sequence containing a misplaced prayer (Gubern, 1994: 362).[44] The dual-role device was repeated in Lucia's historical adventure *La duquesa de Benamejí* [1949 *The Duchess of Benamejí*], a CIFESA superproduction on a play by the Machado brothers, where Amparo Rivelles played the Countess and the gypsy Rocío. This film had to be rewritten to gain approval, adding a punishment for the nineteenth-century bandits too easily identified with the remnants of left-wing guerrillas (Luis Fernández Colorado, in Pérez Perucha, 1997: 253–4).

Bullfighters still had their place as protagonists, as in José Buchs's *Un caballero famoso* [1942 *A Famous Gentleman*] with Alfredo Mayo and Amparo Rivelles in her fourth film; Florián Rey's *Ídolos* [1943, *Idols*] about a French actress [Conchita Montenegro] and a bullfighter [Ismael Merlo], excellent for tourist propaganda; Neville's more critical *El traje de luces*

---

[43] She was christened María del Carmen García Galisteo and took her stage name from her birthplace, Seville. Her first part was in *Serenata española*. On most Saturday evenings she now presents on Spanish television a retrospective popular Spanish film. Many films discussed in this book were viewed through this series, known as *Cine de barrio*, previously hosted by José Manuel Parada from 1995 to 2003.

[44] After this film Perojo left for Argentina where he made nine films in the next six years.

[1947 *The Bullfighter's Suit]; Enrique Gómez's La fiesta sigue [1948 *The Party Goes On]; and Florián Rey's biopic Brindis a Manolete [1948 *A Toast for Manolete]. There was also the third remake of Currito de la Cruz [1948 Lucia – PNC][45] set in 1835, where dialogue, narrative closure and 'baroque framing devices of grilles and windows and doorway' return Rocío, 'an independent, self-assertive woman', to domesticity (Peter Evans, in Graham & Labanyi, 1995: 219–20). According to Carranque de los Ríos's cynical but entertaining Cinematógrafo, a novel about the underside of film production, bullfighting and regional settings also had commercial advantages when marketing exports to America, a point exploited at the end of the novel (1997: 262–6, 381).

The sound of music

Consistent with the popular taste of the Republic, very few comedies or adventures did not include a song or three. This makes it impossible to use the label restrictively and to distinguish musicals from the many folkloric or rural and urban dramas already mentioned above, and the genre could perhaps be limited to those films that protagonise professional singers. Luis Marquina's 1941 Torbellino [Whirlwind, with Estrellita Castro and Manuel Luna] highlights the importance of radio and popular music at the time (Woods, 2004b: 201–18). La patria chica [1942 Fernando Delgado *Our Homeland, a comedy based on a Quintero brothers' plot starring Estrellita Castro] relates how two small groups of performers are stranded by a fraudulent impresario on the run in a Paris oblivious of the Second World War. Typically they sing to a couple of diegetic guitars and a full non-diegetic orchestra; and although they keep bickering about the relative merits of their native Andalusia or Aragon, they finally work together to perform a spectacle to the glory of Spanish unity, for which they are joined by a crowd of unexplained extra dancers and earn enough to pay their fare back home. There is Antonio Román's Lola Montes [1944 – PNC, starring Conchita Montenegro], a fantasised melodramatic biopic of the singer who, on one of her international tours, had an affair with Ludwig I of Bavaria; the story was retold in 1955 by Max Ophüls with Martine Carol and Peter Ustinov. Serenata española [1947 Orduña, Spanish Serenade – PNC] is a biopic of the composer Isaac Albéniz starring Julio Peña and Juanita Reina. A variation on this theme were musicals like Carlos Serrano de Osma's second film, Embrujo [1947 *The Spell, also written with Pedro Lazaga], which starred and focused on the lives of performers like Lola [Flores] and Manolo [Ortega] Caracol in a disturbing plot about two doomed

---

45   There have been four versions to date: Pérez Lugín in 1926, Fernando Delgado in 1936, Luis Lucia in 1949, and Rafael Gil in 1965.

professionals, but with too many complex point of view shots and apparently surreal touches to be enjoyed by the audiences of the time, supported by the now- married Fernando Fernán Gómez and María Dolores Pradera. Florián Rey's *La cigarra* [1948 for Filmófono, **Soledad, the Cicada*] did not help his waning reputation during the decade, despite reuniting with Imperio Argentina in his ninth and last film with her. The film also starred Miguel Ligero in a plot that moves from Seville to Buenos Aires, and includes flamenco and tango. *El sueño de Andalucía* [1951 Lucia, **Dream of Andalusia*] is a co-production based on a French operetta celebrating the genre by filming the making of a folkloric musical in a Paris studio, thereby blurring on screen the characters' public performances and their fictional reality. It starred Carmen Sevilla and Luis Mariano, who made his career in France. They would make two more French co-productions in the 1950s: *Violetas Imperiales* and *La bella de Cádiz* [1952 Richard Pottier **Imperial Violets*; 1953 Raymond Bernard and Fernández Ardavín **The Beauty from Cadiz*]. Songs, dances and spectacle are the great attraction of these films and, like Bollywood film,s they should not be judged by their narrative or psychological interest.

Of course these musical films did not always revolve around flamenco. Another great success of the time, which recovered the loss Suevia made on Gil's *Reina santa*, was *Botón de ancla* [1948 Ramón Torrado, **Anchor Button*[46] – PNC], light-hearted adventures about three cadets' promotion in the Navy Academy [Antonio Casal, Jorge Mistral and Fernán Gómez whose character sacrifices himself], which blend Galician local colour with a positive image of the Navy. Armed forces cadets would reappear in a number of films; for instance, Torrado recast the three male leads in *La trinca del aire* [1951 **The Threesome of the Air*], and in his remake of the original as *Los caballeros del botón de ancla* in 1974, after Miguel Lluch had also remade it in 1960 using the pop singers El Dúo Dinámico.

Crime and intrigue

There had been straightforward crime films in addition to the comic and historical hybrid previously mentioned, for example, Ramón Quadreny's *Sangre en la nieve* [1942 **Blood in the Snow*] about smuggling, Carlos Fernández Cuenca's *Los misterios de Tánger* [1942 **Tanger Mysteries*] about arms trafficking, Luis Lucia's *El trece-trece* [1943 *The Thirteen-Thirteen*] spy thriller, or Ricardo Gutiérrez's *El secreto de la mujer muerta* [1945 **The Secret of the Dead Woman*]. In the second half of the decade detective narra-

---

[46] The reference is to the anchor on the brass button of the navy cadets' uniform; the film consolidated Suevia's success over CIFESA.

tives were brought up to date with contemporary Spanish settings, inspired by and yet in contrast to US imports. Nieves Conde started with three crime films with a difference: *Senda ignorada* [1946 *Path Unknown*] set in the USA, *Angustia* [1948 *Anxieties*], which blends the detective story with psychological drama, and *Llegada de noche* [1949 *Night Arrival*]. Gil's *La calle sin sol* [1948 *The Sunless Street* – PNC], takes up plot elements of Pedro Puche's *Barrios bajos* [1937] but required some rewriting because of the censor's objection to the plot's resolution that depended on a divorce. Gil followed this with *Una mujer cualquiera* [1948 *Just Any Woman*], which builds on Mexican María Félix as a femme fatale and becomes the victim of handsome Antonio Vilar who reveals himself involved in black-market-eering, cocaine trafficking and murder, all with fine location shots of Madrid at night. The more unequivocal detective films that would proliferate in the 1950s made their first appearance with Ladislao Vajda's *Barrio* [1947 *The Neighbourhood*] based on a Simenon novel, for which he also directed a Portuguese version. Julio Salvador's *Apartado de correos 1001* [1950 *P O Box 1001*] announced its novelty in the initial voice-over, consolidating a more realistic setting in the streets of Barcelona. Iquino made the well-paced suspense *Brigada criminal* [1950 *The Criminal Brigade* – PNC], blending *film noir* techniques in contemporary Madrid locations, where only the enco-miastic voice-overs about the merits of the Spanish police detract from the final product, but one suspects that these were imposed and that the main impulse was suspense, although one knew the police would always resolve its case. Paco [Francisco] Rabal and Mayra O'Wisiedo made their debuts as protagonists in *La honradez de la cerradura* [1950 Luis Escobar, *The Honesty of the Keyhole*], a blackmail thriller based on a Benavente play that promotes the influence of Church values and equates police intervention with divine providence. Although crime films are associated with the Barcelona studios, Madrid also made its contribution with, for instance, Pedro Laza-ga's second film[47] *El hombre acosado* [(1950) 1952 *The Hounded Man*], in which Alfredo Mayo is cast as the villain who traffics in false passports for his clients whom he then kills and robs as they leave the country.

---

[47] After learning his trade as assistant director with *Abel Sánchez, Embrujo, La sirena negra* and *Vida en sombras*, he went on to direct 94 films, dominating the popular home production of the 1960s and 1970s. In 1955 he made an unusual film *Cuerda de preso* [*The Prisoners' Rope*], about a prisoner being transferred on foot to the provincial capital in the company of two Civil Guards, but the film was not released until March 1962, despite its narrative displacement to 1878.

4b Creationism in Neville's *La torre de los siete jorobados* (1944)

In need of reassessment

Although Edgar Neville did not have much of a following at the time, he directed a number of innovative crime films that often went against the prevalent grain, presenting imaginative solutions that exploited the resources of cinema with humour or irony, thus causing the censors serious concern. *La torre de los siete jorobados* [1944 **The Tower of the Seven Hunchbacks*], a gripping gothic mystery full of atmosphere set in nineteenth-century Madrid, involving a community of hunchbacks led by a megalomaniac in hiding within a seventeenth-century tower that does not rise but sinks underground.[48] The film echoes Robert Wiene's imaginative cinema and reflects *ad absurdum* the regime's political paranoia with its use of light and shadows,

---

[48] The tower was designed by Pierre Schild, Francisco Escriña and Antonio Simont. Pierre Schild[knecht] left Russia after the 1917 Revolution, worked in France with Perojo, Abel Gance, Buñuel and Marcel l'Herbier, before coming to Spain in 1940 (Gorostiza, 1997: 315).

identified by Steven Marsh as the first in the Madrid trilogy (Marsh, 2006: 63–96). His next film, *La vida en un hilo* [1945 *Her Life on a Thread*], is more realistic in its presentation but just as creationist in its conception as a 'what if' film, full of irony, as we are shown what happens to a young widow, Mercedes [Conchita Montes], when she chooses to share a taxi with Ramón [Guillermo Marín] and what would have happened had she chosen to accept the first offer from Miguel Ángel [Rafael Durán], implying a criticism of the boorish middle-class values endorsed by the regime (Marsh, 2006: 41–62).[49] A parallel case of metacinema released three months earlier was Sáenz de Heredia's *El destino se disculpa* [1945 *Fate Apologises* – PNC] with Rafael Durán, and Fernán Gómez as the voice of his conscience providing in this case clear moral commentaries. Neville went on to make *Domingo de carnaval* [1945 *Carnival Sunday*], a more straightforward detective story set against the lively background of the fair and evocation of working-class Madrid told with humour and references to Nick Carter to mark the contrast with US films.[50] *El crimen de la calle de Bordadores* [1946 *The Embroiderer Street Murder*] set in the nineteenth century was his third crime film (Kinder, 1993: 459). Initial jumpcuts slide into a flashback, which is then followed by contradictory point of view reports revealing various motives for perjury and a crime, leaving the spectator to deduce the identity of the culprit, who may have got away with the murder. The film also includes a critical presentation of the press and gullible public opinion. In spite of its humour and some excellent flamenco singing, it may have been a little too complex and ambiguous for the contemporary spectators more at ease with linear narratives (Marsh, 2004a: 27–41).

In 1947, Neville filmed Carmen Laforet's prize-winning novel *Nada* [*Nothing*], reflecting a grim picture of the Spanish extended family, middle-class hypocrisy, and women's position in society where the house and especially the staircase, designed by Sigfrido Burmann,[51] play an important role (Gorostiza recalls Orson Welles' 1942 *Magnificent Ambersons* [1997: 60] and the use of the staircase certainly anticipates Hitchcock's atmospheric bell tower in the 1958 *Vertigo*). The censors requested numerous cuts to minimise the impact of the depressing images of Spanish daily life. Three films later, in 1950, he directed the satirical comedy *El último caballo* [*The Last Horse*]

---

[49] It was remade in 1992 by Gerardo Vera as *Una mujer bajo la lluvia* [*A Woman in the Rain*] with Ángela Molina, Antonio Banderas and Imanol Arias.

[50] Nick Carter was a favourite of silent films, and two episodes with Walter Pidgeon had just been directed in 1939 and 1940 by Jacques Tourneur.

[51] Burmann's first credits are for Perojo's *Barbero de Sevilla* in Berlin, and he came to Spain that year to work on the sets of *Los cuatro Robinsones*, *La Dolores*, *La gitanilla*, *Raza*, etc. (for more details consult the *IMDb*), establishing himself as one of the most wanted set designers.

with Fernán Gómez, concerning a trooper who completes his military service and buys his horse to save it from the bullring when he learns his regiment is to be motorised. This captivating film was denied permission to represent Spain at the Cannes Festival, even though the references to contemporary Spanish problems like job insecurities and exploitation, wage freezes and rising inflation, the black market and ration books, are all very mild and used for comic effect, and a good example of Neville technique, which frequently includes amusing little vignettes.

Late war films

The glorious spirit of the defence of Spanish (i.e. Francoist) values returned briefly in the late 1940s. *Héroes del 95* [1947 Raúl Alfonso, **Heroes of 95*] featured Alfredo Mayo under siege in Cuba. *Alhucemas* [1948 López Rubio – the Alhucemas being Spanish islands off the coast of Morocco] returned to the earlier colonial war as the setting for a conflict of loyalty between the family and the military nation, with Julio Peña and Nani Fernández. Ruiz Castillo's Civil War episode *El santuario no se rinde* [1949 **The Sanctuary Does Not Surrender* – PNC, edited by Sara Ontañón] about the besieged civil guards and civilians in the sanctuary of Santa María de la Cabeza in Jaen, surrounded by undisciplined International Brigades, offers some Republicans [Fernán Gómez] the possibility of redemption and reconciliation (Hopewell, 1986: 40–1). The film recovers Alfredo Mayo as a character who has much of Ruiz Castillo's *alter ego*,[52] and the events are remembered through voice-over of the female protagonist, Beatriz de Araña (Labanyi, 2000: 172).

Unusual experiments

As the decade drew to a close, further interesting experiments were made. *Vida en sombras* [**A Life in Shadows*], made in 1948 by Lorenzo Llobet Gràcia, casting Fernán Gómez, María Dolores Pradera and Isabel de Pomés, is a unique film not just because it manages to encapsulate a history of cinema in Spain and, according to Marsha Kinder, 'offers a model for how to use a personal romantic/sexual discourse to talk about political topics that were otherwise suppressed' (1993: 409), among them the Civil War from the losers' perspective. It is the fascinating work of an amateur cinephile with a very modest budget yet offering reflections on the cinema and the point of

---

[52] Like Antonio del Amo, Rafael Gil and Carlos Serano de Osma, Arturo Ruiz Castillo had started his film career making Republican documentaries and had difficulties in resuming a cinematographic career.

view shot with particularly effective clips from Cukor's 1936 *Romeo and Juliette* and Hitchcock's 1940 *Rebecca*. It was only released in 1953 with a Third Class qualification, described by the censors as 'uninteresting in every respect [...] inconceivable, unacceptable, inadmissible, unpresentable'.[53] Lost, it was rediscovered in the late 1970s and has become a cult film (D'Lugo, 1997: 109–10). *De mujer a mujer* [1950 Lucia, *From Woman to Woman*] sets up the bond between the wife, Isabel [Amparo Rivelles], and the mistress, Emilia [Ana Mariscal], in what Martin-Márquez calls 'an overdetermined woman's film', which considers adultery and suicide and displays to excess many plot elements typical of Hollywood (1999a: 101–3). Once again the action is displaced to the previous century and the anticipated final medical authority is replaced by that of the Church, for 'in Spain, the conventional emotional excesses of melodrama were inflected with a specifically Catholic sadomasochistic discourse, which merged with Fascist rhetoric in fetishizing suffering and death' (Kinder, 1993: 73). After scripting for Antonio del Amo *Alas de juventud* and *Noventa minutos* [both 1949, *Wings of Youth*, *Ninety minutes*], Manuel Mur Oti directed his first films *Un hombre va por el camino* and *Cielo negro* [both 1949, *A Man on the Road* – PNC, *Black Sky* not released till 1951 with a PNC after being cut first from 115 to 110 and then to 90 minutes]. This last, about the cumulative disasters that push Emilia [Susana Canales] to the point of contemplating suicide, exploits effectively point of view shots of the girl's dream and myopia.

Balance sheet

Comparative production (and spectator) figures for the year 1951 are revealing: the UK produced 102 films (recorded audience of 1365 million), Italy 104 (705.7 million), France 94 (372.8), and West Germany 57 (554.8). In Spain the recorded audience was 315 million, and 37 films were made, which was ten less than for 1950, although still twice as many as the output of remaining European countries (Vincendeau, 1995: 464 and 466). It is remarkable that Spanish Cinema was able to reconstruct itself as the fifth strongest in Europe in spite of the constraints of censorship, production difficulties, shortage of materials and lack of resources, frequent power cuts, as well as its weak socio-political situation aggravated by international isolation and competition from foreign film imports. During the 1940s the veteran directors of the silent era, José Buchs, Fernando Delgado and Florián Rey were on the wane despite a

---

[53] 'sin interés en ningún aspecto [...] inconcebible, inaceptable, inadmisible, impresentable', quoted by José Luis Castro de Paz (in Pérez Perucha, 1997: 240).

few box-office hits. Benito Perojo, after directing the comedy *Yo no soy la Mata-Hari* [1949 *I'm not Mata Hari*] and the Napoleonic drama *Sangre en Castilla* [1950 **Blood in Castile*], initiated a new career as a producer with Luis G[arcía] Berlanga's *Novio a la vista* [1954 *Boyfriend in Sight*]. Edgar Neville consolidated his talents even if spectators did not appreciate his ingenuity or variety (see also chapter 3). The generation of directors whose career had started during the Republican years, like Marquina (1904–1980), Sáenz de Heredia (1911–1992) and Iquino (1910–1994), consolidated their reputation following the fallow war years, and were joined by those who established themselves through documentaries in spite of their early Republican credentials: Orduña (1900–1974), Román (1911–1989), Gil (1913–1986) and Del Amo (1911–1991). There was also a new generation who began directing in the 1940s like Luis Lucia (1914–1984), Nieves Conde (1915–2006), Pedro Lazaga (1918–1979), and latecomer Mur Oti (1908–2003).

Viewing and further general reading

Viewing films of this decades is still very restricted. Of the general books, Caparrós Lera (1987) if accessible, Besas (1985), Hopewell (1986: 33–43), Higginbotham with a whole chapter on censorship (1988: 7–23), D'Lugo (1997: 9–12), and Stone (2002: 37–9) all cover the period briefly, and Triana Toribio's thesis comes into its own as she examines government policies on the margin of cinema (2003). Bosch & del Rincón discuss the social importance of cinema, the regime and audiences' reactions to Hollywood imports (1998). Graham & Labanyi (1995) and Gies (1999) continue to provide important contextualisation and brief bibliographies.

More specific discussions can be found in Talens (1998) with contributions on Civil War documentaries, *Raza, Carmen, la de Triana*, Orduña's early films and *Vida en sombras*, also considered by Kinder (1993: 401–12), whereas her 1992 article deals with this last film from the perspective of regional cinema. Lázaro Reboll (2004) includes four contributions on the period. Kinder (1993), Tolentino (1997) and Santaolalla (2005a) discuss *Los últimos de Filipinas* and the crusading epics. González-Medina's discussion of *Canelita en rama* examines why critics and audiences rarely share the same reaction to a film and how some folkloric musical comedies negotiate the official ideology (1997), a subject taken up by Labanyi (1997, 2003 rpt), who also discusses the strong women protagonists of the second half of the decade (2000). Triana Toribio (2000a) and Martin-Márquez (1999a) provide some very pertinent re-evaluations of Ana Mariscal's acting career, melodrama and the position of women in society. Perojo and Neville as the most innovative directors of this decade (Marsh 2004a, 2006) warrant closer studies, and I could not find any full-length study of the prolific Ignacio F.

Iquino or Juan de Orduña (Llinás's disparaging analysis [1998] would be a fertile starting point – see also Wright, 2005: 415–31). Individual studies on comedies and melodramas would also add to our collective knowledge.

An interesting angle for these films is the 'patterns of contradiction and resistance' to the official ideology of the regime, often emerging out of the blurring of genres and conventions (Peter Evans, in Graham & Labanyi, 1995: 222; P. Evans, 2000: 77–88), examples of which are the presentation of the family, visual references on the screen or a remark in the dialogue, the inclusion of a regional language, or even at times the excesses of the official rhetoric. Labanyi's hypotheses on female contemporary audiences are particularly illuminating especially with reference to the strong heroines (2000, 2004). Dapena asks if the presence of foreign film technicians working in Spain, fleeing Nazi persecutions in the forties or either pro- or anti-Peronist governments in the 1950s, also undermines a monolithic film production (2004), a comment implicit in Labanyi (2004). Labanyi (1995) and Bentley (2004) offer examples of how cinema conventions can alter literary adaptations and rewrite historical incident to reflect the contemporary political and social agenda. A motif-index à la Stith Thompson would have been very useful to discuss the musical, folkloric films and comedies, including not just plot elements but characters and cinematographic devices. Labanyi (1997), Vernon (1999), Marsh (1999) and Woods (2004a and b) have all made a start. The whole question of the predominance of song, dance and spectacle over narrative is worth examining for the 1940s and subsequent decades of Franco cinema. The implicit values of crime and detective narratives also beg a systematic investigation. Labanyi has announced *An Oral History of Spanish Cinema-Going in 1940s and 1950s Spain*, in which a number of the above academics are participating; see also Gómez Sierra (2004) and volume 2, part 2 of the new journal *Studies in Hispanic Cinemas* (2005). The opening up of the censors' archive should also provide some interesting information.

The Establishment, the Cold War and the Dissidents (1951–1961)

Against all odds: Spain opens up

During its first ten years the Franco regime, locked in on itself, consolidated its authority by balancing the interests of the armed forces, the Church and the capitalist investments of industrialists and landowners, suppressing any dissenting voices to unify conservative interests under the three Fs of Faith, Fatherland and Family.[1] The so-called Law of Succession, defining Spain as a Catholic State and Kingdom to be administered during his lifetime by the Caudillo Francisco Franco de Bahamonde was passed on 6 March 1947. However, the Cold War conflict of the 1950s altered priorities and required the realignment of international politics. The passionate Spanish anti-communist agenda in defence of the faith attracted the diplomatic recognition of Western nations and thus enabled the economic expansion of the regime, albeit at the expense of any democratic progress. UN sanctions were lifted on 4 November 1950 and foreign ambassadors returned to Madrid; full integration to the UN followed in December 1955, but full membership of NATO and the Common Market would be denied for another thirty years as a dictatorship would not be admitted. Rationing had stopped in 1952 and wheat loans from the USA were starting to filter through, to be followed in 1954 by economic aid in return for the construction of military air bases. A political facelift was necessary and consequently there were important government reshuffles in July 1951. Strong conservative Catholic influences came to the fore with the appointment of Admiral Gabriel Carrero Blanco as Franco's right-hand man and Joaquín Ruiz Giménez as the minister for education. On 19 July a new Ministry linking Information and Tourism was created under the leadership of hardliner Gabriel Arias Salgado with the remit of controlling the official representation of the country within and outside its territories. The responsibility of Información y Turismo [MIT] was to attract potential foreign currency and investments while internally it was accountable

[1] For the three Fs, see pp. 87–8 and their allegorical presentation in Saura's *Ana y los lobos* [1973 *Anna and the Wolves*].

for propaganda, censorship and public events, therefore subsuming the JSOC. This government's concern for a national image allowed lasting stereotypes and myths of Spain to be (re-)created and (re-)enforced (Hopewell, 1986: 48–51; Kinder, 1993: 19–22). The reshuffle had important consequences for Spanish Cinema, and in August 1951 the more liberal José María García Escudero was appointed Director General de Cinematografía, previously the responsibility of the education minister. García Escudero had a strong desire to improve cinema in Spain but his first appointment lasted only seven months (Triana Toribio, 2003: 65–9).

A first error of judgement

The ultimate failure of CIFESA, supportive of the regime through its ideologically motivated historical films, was a blow to the government propaganda effort. After the company had distributed some very successful films, *Alba de América* [1951 Juan de Orduña, *Dawn of America* – PNC, IN] is said to have been its swan song. Described as the reaction of wounded national pride to David MacDonald's *Christopher Columbus* [1949], which presented him as achieving only some of his goals, and these in spite of the Catholic Monarchs, in *Alba...* Columbus is cast as the single-minded discoverer of a continent for the glory of Queen Isabel of Castile, for Spain's triumphant future as fulfilled by Franco, and for the greatness of the Catholic Church (Donapetry, 1998: 50–1; Peter Evans in Graham & Labanyi, 1995: 217–18). Costing over ten million pesetas, nationally subsidised as part of the 500th anniversary celebrations of the Catholic Monarchs and strongly endorsed by Admiral Carrero Blanco and Franco himself,[2] the film did not fulfil its financial ambitions, in spite of its 53 days' run, or its artistic aspirations, as it lacked the melodramatic tension of previous historical films. Stone dismisses it as a 'didactic pantomime' (2002: 40), neither film nor documentary (Mira 1999: 136).

Another film, *Surcos* [*Furrows*], also made news in 1951 and was locked into competition with *Alba de América*. Radically different from the idealised escapist productions of the time, it was also a new departure for its right-wing director José Antonio Nieves Conde. It is described as 'a curious graft of American gangster thriller and neo-realism. It is also a Falangist thesis drama' (Hopewell, 1986: 56), presenting closely observed reality with touches of humour (Vernon, in Gies, 1999: 256–7). It dealt with contemporary social issues: rural poverty, housing problems, unemployment and crime,

---

2   Mira argues that it was a state project (1999: 128–31), and Heredero that Carrero Blanco wrote the original draft to be converted into a film script (1993: 175).

as migrants flocked from village to city in the hope of betterment in the wake
of economic difficulties and the 1947 law, which finally allowed Spaniards to
move within the territory. It develops latent implications of Florián Rey's *La
aldea maldita*, and the crowded frames with deep-focus long shots suggest a
Madrid teeming like a nest of hungry grubs. To show the hidden and harsher
side of Spanish society the film relates the gradual breakdown of a family
after its arrival in Madrid and traces the varied experiences as each one tries
to survive while sharing overcrowded accommodation. The microcosm of the
family, once again a metaphor for the macrocosm of society, is used to convey
the patriarchal values of the regime, here undermined by the mother figure,
thus enabling the representation of the conflicts and tensions between the
impoverished traditional rural life and illusory urban development (Kinder,
1993: 43 and 72; Richardson, 2002: 29–48). *Surcos* did not shy away from
topics and scenes that were shocking at the time, whether of black-market
trade leading to prostitution and crime or the lack of social welfare and security. The original circular ending had been censored as too negative when the
script was approved, on the understanding that situations and language would
be toned down, but the opening pessimistic intertitle remains to contrast with
the final return to the village accompanied by upbeat music. The visual style
of *Surcos* was also different, with numerous street shots, often from a high or
unusual angle creating, in retrospect, a sense of visual documentary for which
there had been precedents[3] but which nonetheless frequently earns *Surcos* the
reputation of being the first Spanish neo-realist film. It does stand as a useful
social comment on the period, and its artistic merits were acknowledged by
García Escudero with the award of a National Interest prize at the expense
of the more artificial *Alba de América*. This bold gesture in recognition of a
superior film, against ministerial and clerical opinions, cost García Escudero
his job. He was forced to resign in March 1952 and Joaquín Argamasilla,
who had held the post from 1943 to 1945, took over, awarding the National
Interest prize to *Alba*. Nieves Conde went on to make seven films during the
decade, some of which are interesting and not devoid of irony and criticism,
such as *Los peces rojos* [1955 *Goldfish* – PNC] about a deception that runs
out of control. Rural migration continued and the theme was preferred with
the positive filter of the Cinderella dream, as used in Rafael Gil's sentimental
De Madrid al cielo [1952 *From Madrid to Heaven*]. The title is taken from
an old proverb probably dating back to the seventeenth century when Spain
experienced similar rural depopulation and misplaced hopes: 'Del infierno
a Madrid y de Madrid al cielo' [From Hell to Madrid and from Madrid to
Heaven] (Bentley, 1995b: 268–70).

---

[3] For instance, *Aurora de esperanza, Barrios bajos, Vida en sombras, Las aguas bajan
negras, Calle sin sol, La familia Vila, Apartado de correos 1001* and *El último caballo*, to
mention just a few from previous chapter.

Distribution, screening and productions

As part of the new reforms film classifications were revised on 16 June 1952 into six categories (Interés Nacional [IN], 1A, 1B, 2A, 2B, 3); these were linked to a possible maximum subsidy of 50% for the best and none for the worst, which were not even permitted a Madrid or Barcelona release. Appeals were allowed, as happened in the case of *Alba* … against *Surcos*. The classifications were, however, no longer linked to import licences, which were now correlated to distribution and screening rather than production. In 1955, a law was passed obliging distributors to show one Spanish film to every four imports. Subsidies were also granted for film exports, as Spanish directors started to participate more frequently in international festivals (Pozo Arenas, 1984: 83–7). The JSOC's censorship practices and norms carried on from the previous decade, that is, with no further explanatory details other than that the films were not to offend the moral, social or political beliefs of the nation (the three Fs). Since the reopening of the Madrid and Zaragoza Cineclubs in the winter of 1945, these proliferated throughout the decade, allowing a restricted but varied projection of values and ideologies. On 21 March 1953, the Filmoteca was founded as the Filmoteca Nacional and given a tiny budget, but it was an important first step for the belated creation of a film archive as well as the subsequent restoration and preservation of films (Prado, 2005: 9–18). The same year saw the initiation of the San Sebastián Film Festival as a showcase for national cinema to international distributors, followed in 1956 by the Valladolid Film Festival, at first devoted to religious cinema. The number of cinema theatres also continued to expand even if they showed mostly foreign films in dubbed and sanitised versions.[4]

Gradually throughout the 1950s production circumstances slowly improved, in terms of equipment, working conditions and even a reduction of power cuts after the years of hunger and ration books. The number of co-productions increased throughout the decade, mostly with Italy (79) but also with France (32) and Mexico (21).[5] These often led to two versions being distributed as the Spanish censors required cuts for home screening, usually to tone down possible erotic suggestions.[6] In 1955 Joaquín Argamasilla resigned his post as

---

4   Table in Gubern (1995: 263). With a presumed need for 250 films a year, García Escudero negotiated an annual 100 US film imports, 60 through US distributing offices and 40 through national distributors.

5   These will not be mentioned in the text, but scrutiny of the *IMDb* will identify them and provide much more information, and easily accessible cross-references not available on *MCU. es*.

6   These were rather puerile, but it mattered to cut kisses and paint in decolletages considered too revealing. In *Esa pareja feliz* [*That Happy Couple* – p. 133] when Juan and Carmen are having their sandwiches and keeping warm in the cinema while watching a Hollywood melodrama, a spectator shouts '¡Han cortado el beso!' [Kiss cut!].

Director General de Cinematografía over the scandal caused by the exposure
of these double versions with the case of the Hispano-British co-production
directed by Terence Young, *La princesa de Éboli* [1954, *That Lady* – PNC],
where the export presentation of sixteenth-century Spain had been modified
negatively (Heredero, 1993: 64–6).

Spanish films and co-productions 1951–61[7]

Year	National productions	Co-productions	Total
1951	36	8	44
1952	33	9	42
1953	37	10	47
1954	53	16	69
1955	46	15	61
1956	54	23	77
1957	50	26	76
1958	47	25	72
1959	51	17	68
1960	55	16	71
1961	70	21	91

It was in the second half of the decade that US production companies started
to film in Spain. Simultaneously, after the years of silence, voices of dissent
started to express themselves cautiously through films and more violently in
street marches and demonstrations. ATA [Aberri ta Askatasuna/Homeland
and Liberty, a Basque separatist organisation] took shape in October 1952.

Clergy films and Catholic cinema

The regime's shift from its military values towards National-Catholicism
(Gómez, 2002: 588–9) is neatly reflected in Nieves Conde's *Balarrasa* [1951
Reckless] where Javier Mendoza [Fernán Gómez] replaces his legionnaire
uniform with a cassock. The large variety of increasing clergy-related films,
which reinforced the official ideology through the use of endemic authoritative voice-overs, found approval from the public and the establishment, as
reflected by the awards of the National Interest prizes. Also greatly appreciated in other Catholic countries, *La señora de Fátima* [1951 Rafael Gil, *Our
Lady of Fatima* – PNC, IN] related the Portuguese visitation of 1917, as

---

[7] This table is taken from Heredero (1993: 435–8), and does not match the information
in Gubern (1995: 256) or Caparrós Lera (1983: 230); this is because no reliable statistics were
taken at the time. All these historians lament the discrepancies.

careful with its point of view shots as it is with the title, which refers to *The lady...* rather than the *Our Lady...* of the international release. The film offers the clear message that all are to pray for the conversion of the Soviet Union to Catholicism. There was Luis Lucia's *Cerca de la ciudad* [1952 **On the Edge of the City* – PNC, IN] about a parish priest's redeeming work with street adolescents, reminiscent of MGM's Father Flanagan [Spencer Tracy] series with the Dead End Kids of *Boys' Town* [1938 Norman Taurog] or *Angels Wash their Faces* [1939 Ray Enright]. In Lucia's film there is, however, some irony at the expense of both the genre and neo-realist films (Labanyi, 1997: 220–1). Ignacio Iquino's *El Judas* [1952 *The Judas* – PNC, IN], planned to coincide with the 35th International Eucharistic Conference celebrated in Barcelona in May 1952, parallels Judas's betrayal and the Passion of Christ with the life and redemption of the protagonist [Antonio Vilar] through his performance of the Easter pageant in the narrative. The film was also released in a cut Catalan version. Another attempt to inscribe a Catalan presence on the screen, produced by Iquino's IFI, was Antonio Momplet's melodrama *La hija del mar* [1953 **The Daughter of the Sea*], a play by Àngel Guimerà already adapted by Adrià Gual for the silent cinema in 1917; it was Momplet's first film after returning from exile in America. *La guerra de Dios* [1953 Rafael Gil, *I Was a Parish Priest* – PNC, IN, Venice OCIC and San Sebastián] deals with labour conflicts, as the newly appointed Father Mendoza helps the miners obtain fairer working conditions. It was set in 1930 to gain the censors' approval and by contrast implies the excellence of the regime's vertical trade unions. The script was written by Vicente Escrivá and the priest, Padre Mendoza, was played by Claude Laydu, the protagonist of Bresson's *Le Journal d'un curé de campagne* [1951 *Diary of a Country Priest*], which was banned in Spain because of its more problematic theme. Escrivá actually wrote ten scripts for Rafael Gil between 1951 and 1956,[8] including other clergy-related narratives such as the singing nun who becomes a missionary in *Sor Intrépida* [1952 *The Song of Sister Maria* – PNC, IN], *El beso de Judas* [1954 *Judas's Kiss* – IN, Venice Honourable Mention], or *Un traje blanco* [1956 *A Communion Suit – PNC, IN, Venice Honourable Mention] with the young actor Miguelito Gil. At the end of the decade a number of hagiographies were also released: Luis Lucia's *Molokai* [1959 – PNC, IN], the name of an Indonesian island where Father Damian de Veuster ran a leper colony and died; Ramón Torrado's *Fray Escoba* [1961 *Brother Broom – PNC] based on the life of Brother

---

8   Vicente Escrivá (1913–1999) was a journalist who moved into radio and, after writing a few novels, specialised in clergy films, starting in 1948 with *La mies es mucha*. He also scripted *Balarrasa, Pequeñeces, Agustina de Aragón* and *La leona de Castilla*, all mentioned in chapter 4. With *Balarrasa* he started his own production company, Aspa Films, with the blessing of Pope Pius XII, which later moved on to produce comedies for the home market until 1976, at first distributed by CIFESA.

Martín de Porres in Peru, who was actually canonised a few months before the film was released; and, the same year, Juan de Orduña's hagiography of Spain's most important nun *Teresa de Jesús* [PNC, IN] with Aurora Bautista as the reformer and mystic. Set in the same period, and more accurately described as the last of the historical epics distributed by CIFESA, was Luis Lucia's pious fiction about Charles V's illegitimate son and defender of the faith *Jeromín* [1953]. All rewarded with financial prizes of the DGC.

One endearing clergy film is Ladislao Vajda's *Marcelino, pan y vino* [1955 *The Miracle of Marcelino* – PNC, IN, Berlin Silver Bear, Cannes OCIC] with six-year-old Pablito Calvo, which relates the brief life of an abandoned baby brought up by twelve good Franciscan monks, his literal belief in what he is being told about Christianity and a forbidden attic full of sharp tools. Given the narrative frame of the film, which is the visualisation of a story told by a monk [Fernando Rey] to comfort a terminally ill little girl, we are offered a parable on the acceptance of death in the context of a Christian faith. Vajda captured world audiences with his command of the point of view and focalising shots to create a very atmospheric film exploiting and overriding the conventions of the horror genre.[9] Another very popular film was José Eliorreta's *Canción de cuna* [1961 *Cradle song*], which involved nuns that are bringing up a little girl. Both films were remade in the 1990s, *Marcelino* in 1991 by Luigi Comencini, and the *Canción* in 1994 by José Luis Garci, although there had already been Argentine [1941] and Mexican [1953] black and white versions of *Canción*.

The anti-communist discourse

These strong Catholic values spilt over into other genres, including thrillers, war and disaster films such as *Vuelo 971* [1953 Rafael Salvia, *Flight 971*], where the passengers are saved by the strength of their faith. This ideology was at first bound to a strong anti-communist rhetoric evident in Rafael Gil's melodrama *Murió hace quince años* [1954 *He Died Fifteen Years Ago* – PNC, IN], starring Paco Rabal as one of the Republican children sent to the USSR for safety in 1937 who returns as a communist agent to assassinate his father, or the most unusual adaptation of Wagner through Daniel Mangrané's production and direction with Carlos Serrano de Osma of *Parsifal* [1952 *The Evil Forest* – PNC]. These films spilled over into more blatant explorations of the Catholic crusade against communism following Gil's *El canto del*

---

[9]   Fracisco Llinás recalls that seeing the film as a child he remembered it more as a nightmare (1997: 105); it was my first personal contact with Spanish Cinema but I remember reacting much more positively. The film is given a psycho-political reading in Kinder (1993: 242–7); but there is probably more satisfaction in accepting a literal reading.

gallo [1955 *The Cock Crow* – PNC, IN] again with Paco Rabal but this time as a fearful priest who recants his calling, or Antonio Isasi-Isasmendi's *Rapsodia de sangre* [*Blood Rhapsody* – IN], both evoking the Hungarian repressions, or César Fernández Ardavín's *Y eligió el infierno* [*And She Chose Hell* – PNC, IN] about East Germany, both of 1957. As always satirical comedies and parodies also followed, such as Eduardo Manzanos' *Suspenso en comunismo* [1956 *A Fail in Communism*] scripted by Miguel Mihura, or Antonio Román's subversive *Bombas para la paz* [1958 *Peace Bombs*] with Fernando Fernán Gómez as the young scientist who designs gas bombs that predispose individuals to understanding and tolerance, not war.

Revisiting the Civil War

Films dealing with the Civil War occasionally reappeared, usually reinter- preting the past bloodshed as an anti-communist crusade for Catholicism against atheism,[10] and the regime thus presented itself anachronistically as the first to react against Soviet intervention in anticipation of the Cold War. This political strategy may explain the re-release of *Raza* [1942] as *Espíritu de una raza* in 1951, with cuts and rewritten dubbed dialogues with new voice-overs (pp. 90–1; Talens, 1998: 65–9). The sacrifices endured for the Faith and Fatherland against communism are revisited with a strong reli- gious agenda in the biopic *Cerca del cielo* [1951 Domingo Viladomat & Mariano del Pombo, *Close to Heaven* – PNC, IN], which tells the story of Bishop Polanco of Teruel executed by firing squad, or Pedro Lazaga's *Frente infinito* [1956 *The Infinite Front*], which focused on Padre Herrera [Adolfo Marsillach] caught in the middle of the fratricide. In April 1954 the last 248 soldiers of the Blue Division, the División Azul that Franco volunteered to fight for Hitler and which was sent to the Eastern front, were returned to Spain from the Soviet prison camps. Only three films dealt with these prisoners. Pedro Lazaga, who like Luis G[arcía] Berlanga had served with the Division, made the first, *La patrulla* [1954 *The Platoon* – PNC, IN], and both released in 1956 were *La espera* [Vicente Lluch, *The Wait*] and *Embajadores en el infierno* [*Ambassadors in Hell* – PNC, IN]. This last was the most explicit, and therefore suffered a lot more interference from the censors; it nonethe- less became José María Forqué's first success. In 1959 Lazaga filmed *La fiel infantería* [*The Proud Infantry*, literally 'loyal' – PNC] to celebrate the twen- tieth anniversary of Franco's victory in colour. This film takes the reasons for the conflict for granted without presenting any anti-communist agenda.

---

10 Franco signed the Concordat with Pius XII in 1953, and the Vatican had been the first international institution to recognise his government.

It occasionally shows Republicans in uniforms that are far too clean and only as depersonalised enemy fire, but never demonises them as in previous films. It prefers to focus on personal relationships and with its concluding sequence of slaughter and death together with the final intertitle manages to acknowledge regrets for all those who had died. Klimovsky carried on with the conflict into the 1960s with *La paz empieza nunca* [1960 *Peace Never Starts* – PNC, IN] about Juan [Adolfo Marsillach], who infiltrates a cell of Republican *maquis* by renewing contact with his pre-war sweetheart Paula, of Republican tendencies [Concha Velasco], and betrays all to the authorities.

The return of exiles can be seen *Servicio en la mar* [1951 Luis Suárez de Lezo, *Service at Sea*] and *Rostro al mar* [1951 Carlos Serrano de Osma, *Facing the Sea*]. Both include the conflict of duty or family, and are examples of possible redemption for those who recant their Republican values. Arturo Ruiz Castillo's *Dos caminos* [1953 *Two Paths* – PNC, IN] presents two alternative paths, which are literal, metaphorical and ideological, and Margarita Alexandre and Rafael Torrecilla's *La ciudad perdida* [1954 *The Lost City*] makes similar propositions, although in this film the possibility of reconciliation required much rescripting to satisfy the censors. Other films followed, such as Forqué's *La noche y el alba* [1958 *Night and Dawn*] or Isasi's *Tierra de todos* [1961 *A Land for All* – PNC], and Ana Mariscal's *Con la vida hicieron fuego* [1957 *They Fired with Their Lives* -released in 1960]. The latter integrated explanatory flashbacks to the Civil War into the narrative, which as Martin-Márquez proposes 'constructs a public space representative of the post-war nation and imbued with Francoist values' (1999a: 127). There were also gentler ways of evoking the past, such as Edgar Neville's last film *Mi calle* [1960 *My Street*], a series of amusing vignettes filmed entirely in the Madrid Sevilla Films studios, which look at the varied residents of the street in 1906, 1916, 1936 and in the 1950s, in order to chronicle developments without bluntly spelling them out. He had used a similar format for the screen adaptation of his play *El baile* [1959 *The Ball*], which concerns one single and privileged household, and totally ignores the conflict.

Popular folkloric musicals

Much more popular and lucrative were musical and folkloric productions (Woods, 2004a: 40–59), usually focusing on a lively female lead, who is often a gypsy and therefore a social outcast and vulnerable before the male, who tends to represent the establishment and its prejudices as well as its desire to possess and dominate. These women, exuding a sensuality that they must protect, usually win through by the strength of their personality and artistic talent, generating near complete audience identification with the seductive lower-class female protagonist played always by a big name star. [...] It allowed the victims of Francoist repression a cathartic release from their own relations of dependency, while allowing members of the establishment the illusion of 'loving' (literally 'patronising') the lower classes. (Labanyi, 1997: 225 and 226)

Songs and dances erupt on the most tenuous of pretexts, as settings for or as commentaries on the narrative, as monologues, dialogues, spontaneous expressions of feelings, performances within the narrative, or just because; and if at times the singer or dancer is accompanied diegetically by an unexplained guitar or two, the non-diegetic soundtrack will contribute a full orchestra. So Lola Flores, Carmen Sevilla and Paquita Rico were topping the billboards, often with remakes of previous successes. The Argentine Luis Saslavsky, in exile from the Perón government, managed to cast the three of them in his 1962 musical comedy *El balcón de la luna* [*The Balcony Beneath the Moon*]. Most of these musicals were now in colour as Emisora films had first introduced cinefotocolor in 1948 (Pozo Arenas, 1984: 70); thus emphasising the primacy of spectacle, music and dance over realistic concerns that were preferred in black and white owing to the lack of subtlety of the early colour processing systems (Bordwell, 1990: 200; Monaco, 1981: 93).

    The plots came with different contexts but with similar situations, often a fragmented family where mother or father is absent. Whichever generic category one may choose to describe these films, there are overlaps. They frequently contrasted gypsies and *payos* (those who are not gypsies) such as Lucia's *Un caballero andaluz* [1954 *An Andalusian Gentleman* – PNC, IN], labelled by Heredero as the paradigm of the folkloric (1993: 184–5). Starring Carmen Sevilla as the blind Colorín Esperanza and Jorge Mistral as Don Juan Manuel de Almodóvar, it is a feel-good and patronising narrative blessed by the prudent priest Don Elías played by Manuel Luna. Other examples are Ramón Torrado's *La niña de la venta* [1951 *The Girl at the Inn*] with Lola Flores, or his remake of *Malvaloca* [1954 *Hollyhock*] starring Paquita Rico. There were others set among *bandoleros,* mountain bandits and smugglers, such as *La estrella de Sierra Morena* [1952 Torrado, *Estrella, the Star of the Sierra Morena*] with Lola Flores. *Estrella* was set in the previous century, as was *Lola la piconera* [1952 Lucia, *Lola, the Coalgirl*] with Juanita Reina, reiterating the struggle against Napoleonic troops (Mira, 2005: 61–9). León Klimovsky's *La pícara molinera* [1955 *The Cheeky Miller's Wife*], starring Carmen Sevilla, is a remake of the 1934 *La traviesa molinera* [*The Miller's Mischievous Wife*] but by changing the wife's adultery into a misunderstanding, not a reality, he satisfied the censors. These films have also been defined as 'españoladas históricas' (Triana Toribio, 2003: 62–3). The clergy were sometimes involved in these plots. Lucia's remake of *La hermana San Sulpicio* [1952 – PNC] with Carmen Sevilla, which contains a good dose of self-irony but lost its note of anti-clericalism, was followed by *Hermana Alegría* [1955 *Sister Happiness*] with Lola Flores. Luis Marquina's *La viudita naviera* [1961 *The Ship Company Widow*] is the story of a court-ship to allow Paquita Rico to sing in the context of the Cadiz carnival of 1895. Everything was tried, even a pantomime ghost story in the *zarzuela* of *La reina mora* [1955 Raúl Alfonso, *The Moorish Queen*] with Antoñita Moreno.[11] There were also self-reflexive folklorics that enjoyed being just that, and focused on their own genesis, such as Lucia's *El sueño de Anda-lucía* [1951 *Dream of Andalusia*] with Carmen Sevilla and Luis Mariano (chapter 4; Triana Toribio, 2003: 64–5). Lucia went further into meta-cinema with his ironic and convoluted remake of *Morena Clara* [1954] featuring Lola Flores, Fernando Fernán Gómez and a few of the original cast (p. 69); this time the plot revolves around the prosecutor surviving a millennium gypsy curse with a dialogue peppered with references to the cinema of the 1940s. Lola Flores was also greatly appreciated in Mexico, and in Miguel Zacarías's *Maricruz* [1957], a Hispano-Mexican production distributed by Suevia Films, although set in a Mexican village she manages to include a very full anthology of Mexican and Iberian regional dances.

It was women's voices that attracted the public, and although Luis Mariano could also be at the top of a poster, male singers were not as popular. Antonio Molina sang in a few films such as *El pescador de coplas* [1954 Antonio del Amo, *The Fisher of Songs*], *Esa voz es una mina* [1955 Luis Lucia, *That Voice is a Gold Mine*], in which he plays a miner who becomes a singer. There were also documentaries, the most committed and sensitive of which was Edgar Neville's 85-minute *Duende y misterio del flamenco* [1952 *Flamenco*, Cannes Honourable Mention], an attempt to remove flamenco from its commercial exploitation, filming numerous dancers, singers and musicians, in colour and edited by Sara Ontañón.

Zarzuelas

Zarzuelas were no longer as popular, and *La reina mora* was a parody. Vajda's reworking of *Doña Francisquita* [1953 – PNC, IN; already filmed in 1934 by Hans Behrendt] is worth a mention for its adaptation of the operetta for the screen as it presents the effects of Amadeo Vives' original music, actu-ally written in 1923 for a plot inspired from the seventeenth-century play *La discreta enamorada* [*The Wise Lover*] by Lope de Vega, but here reset in the nineteenth century. This interesting film disappointed many who felt cinema should limit itself to reproducing the stage work rather than reworking it with

---

[11] This is actually the third adaptation, following José Buchs's silent 1922 version and the 1937 remake by Eusebio Fernández Ardavín.

the same music. Vajda went on to make the *Aventuras del barbero de Sevilla* [1954 *The Adventurer of Seville*], a costume musical with Luis Mariano and Lolita Sevilla that was not as successful. Both films were produced by Benito Perojo, who had spent six years in Argentina (1942–8) and returned to produce many more musicals and other films until his death in 1974.

Rural dramas

Related to the folkloric films, because of accompanying songs and frequent Andalusian settings, is the rural drama, which tends to deal with issues of sexuality, motherhood and awakening desires usually tamed through marriage or repressed through punishment. Rewarding examples are Manuel Mur Oti's tale of jealousy *Condenados* [1953 **Condemned*], noted as a rare example of an unpunished crime, and the family feud *Orgullo* [1955 *Pride* – PNC], followed by *Fedra* [1956 *Fedra, The Devil's Daughter*] loosely based on Seneca's play, or Antonio del Amo's melodrama, *Sierra maldita* [1955 *Cursed Mountain* – San Sebastián],which, set among charcoal burners who believe in an infertility curse, explores sexual repression and consequent sexual violence. *La gata* [1956 *The Cat*] was the last of three films the Margarita Alexandre and Rafael Torrecilla tandem-made in Spain before leaving for Cuba and producing three of Gutiérrez Alea's films.[12] Two years after *The Robe* [1953 Henry Koster], *La gata* was the first Spanish Cinemascope–stereophonic production and, like *El gato montés* [1936 Rosario Pi, **The Wildcat*], was set in the *cortijo* of a bullfighting estate. In a personal interview with Martin-Márquez, Alexandre describes it as an attempt to revise the clichés of gender representations in folkloric films, presenting the woman, here played by Aurora Bautista and called María/*la gata*, both as subject and sexual object of the farmworker Juan [Jorge Mistral] (1999a: 250–64). The censors asked for their cuts, but allowed a more explicit international release, demonstrating that they were becoming more conscious of foreign attention through burgeoning international festivals.

Bandolero films, often described as Spanish westerns, linked thematically to the above and to the gypsy context, increased in popularity with films such as Forqué and Lazaga's *María Morena* [1951], which was made in colour when most were still in black and white. Vajda was quick to demystify these narratives with his black and white *Carne de horca* [1953 **Meat for the Gallows* – PNC, IN], still a costume drama but full of suspense and surprises where the genre and myth of the generous *bandolero*, presented through the *romances* [ballads] of the initial sequence and non-diegetic soundtrack, are

---

12 Like Ana Mariscal's *Misa en Compostela* [**Mass in Santiago*], their first film was also a religious documentary *Cristo* [**Jesus* – PNC, IN]; both documentaries were made in 1954 and in black and white.

contradicted by the images and events on the screen. In colour, José María Forqué presented Paco Rabal as the good bandit Juan Cuenca in *Amanecer en Puerta Oscura* [1957 *Whom God Forgives* – PNC, Berlin Special Prize] in a story of nineteenth-century miners in conflict with an English mining company. The script, co-written with the playwright Alfonso Sastre, was greatly diluted at the censors' instructions. Another film, compared to a western, was the patriotic spy fiction *La llamada de África* [1952 César Fernández Ardavín,[13] *The Call of Africa* – PNC, IN] which re-explores the North African settlements, in full support of the present regime, with the Germans cast as the aggressors (Zumalde Arregi, in Pérez Perucha, 1997: 309–11).

Popular comedies

Social comedies were the staple diet, although there were many very different types ranging from the frivolous 'comedias rosas [pink comedies]' with family or professional settings, to satirical comedies;[14] but in fact most films included elements of humour and, usually, a song or three. These comedies often chronicle the social changes of the decade, albeit indirectly or distorted by the filter of sentimentality and feel good escapism, which for some 'risked mocking the regime's principles' and for others 'did not challenge them far enough and were opium for the masses' (Triana Toribio, 2003: 63; P. Evans, 2000: 77–88), that is until the release of Luis G. Berlanga's wit and talent, which deserve a chapter of their own. *Habitación para tres* [1951 'Tono' Antonio de Lara, *A Room for Three*] was based on a stage bedroom farce of Marx Brothers' dimensions, subversive because of its excess; it also included references to football, now making occasional filmic appearances as a growing popular mass spectacle that challenged bullfighting. Centred on football Iquino made the gentle satire *El sistema Pelegrín* [1951 *The Pelegrín Combination*] and Francisco Rovira Beleta, using actual players, *Once pares de botas* [1954 *Eleven Pairs of Boots*].[15]

In the early 1950s comedies were many and varied, for example: *Así es Madrid* [1953 Marquina, *Such is Madrid*]; *El diablo toca la flauta* [1953 Forqué, *The Devil Plays the Flute*]; *Buenas noticias* [1954 Eduardo Manzanos, *Good News*], reflecting the world of the press; *Los gamberros*

---

[13] César started his film career working for his uncle Eusebio Fernández Ardavín.

[14] Spanish film historians tend to subdivide the genre into more varieties, in spite of the frequent and contentious overlaps. See Heredero, 1993: 163–4.

[15] More serious treatment of football was the biopic of the Hungarian Barcelona player Ladislav Kubala *Los ases buscan la paz* [1955 Arturo Ruiz Castillo, *Aces looking for Peace*], which appropriated the anti-communist cold war agenda (see pp. 122–3), or Alfredo di Stéfano in Javier Setó's *Saeta rubia* [1956 *Blond Arrow*].

[1954 Juan Lladó, *The Louts*]; El padre pitillo [1954 Juan de Orduña, *Father Cigarette*], taking up the clergy setting and not the only comedy or drama where the Church's good advice is crucial to the plot; or Todo es posible en Granada [1954 Sáenz de Heredia, All is Possible in Granada – PNC, IN] remade as a musical in 1982 by Romero Marchent with Manolo Escobar. Recognised by Berlanga as one of his models, Eduardo García Maroto directed his last feature film in 1955, Tres eran tres [Three Were Three], so-called because four film genres presented in the form of three sketches parodying the western, Spanish comedy, the folkloric and horror, are on trial before the spectators. These are parodies of Mel Brooks proportions. Films incorporating a number of stories were a frequent formula, such as Lucia's Aeropuerto [1953 *Airport*], a comedy with four different plots beginning in Barajas airport, which with time has gained value as a satirical presentation of contemporary Madrid. One of the most endearing comedies is Historias de la radio [1955 Sáenz de Heredia, *Radio Stories* – PNC, IN], made at a time when the radio was still the most influential means of mass communication and popular entertainment. Presenting five integrated stories, it follows three individuals, with very different motivations, as they attempt to make it to a live radio broadcast to collect the prizes on offer. Ten years later Sáenz de Heredia revisited the idea with the less successful Historias de la televisión [1965 *Television Stories*], chronicling how times had changed although the competitions remained. In between came El grano de mostaza [1962 *The Mustard Grain*], a showcase for its large cast.

Crime

The taste for police and crime thrillers, which had blossomed in Barcelona with Ignacio F. Iquino during the previous decade, continued to flourish with a variety of plots and situations, even if the words 'thriller/suspense' do not exist in Spanish and the English is used (Jordan & Morgan, 1998: 86–8). The genre includes one of Sáenz de Heredia's best efforts Los ojos dejan huellas [1952 *Eyes Leave Prints* – PNC], Javier Setó's Mercado prohibido [1952 *Forbidden Trade*] on penicillin trafficking, and Enrique Gómez's Persecución en Madrid [1952 *Persecution in Madrid*] about an escapee from a Polish prison camp who finally finds refuge in Madrid, and also includes the return of a Republican exile [Manolo Morán]. In César Fernández Ardavín's ¿Crimen imposible? [1954 *An Impossible Crime?*] it was the censors who requested the interrogative for the title. This is said to be the only example of a police officer covering up some of the evidence and includes a sequence in red monochrome. Nieves Conde's Los peces rojos [1955 *Goldfish* – PNC], set on a windy Asturian coast, presented a complex plot with a flashback where reality catches up with the fiction created by a failed novelist and an aspiring actress, too sophisticated for the general public.[16] There were plenty more, including Iquino's *Camino cortado* [1955 **Closed Exit*] about the chase after a robbery goes wrong. Given the popular taste for songs, hybrids such as Antonio Román's *Último día* [1952 **Last Day*] were perhaps inevitable. It is a whodunit set in a theatre company specialising in *zarzuelas,* starring José Isbert as the inspector in charge; it was a formula repeated by Feliciano Catalán in *Intriga en el escenario* [1954 **Plot on the Stage*].

Neorealism or neo-realism

Meanwhile in Italy Neorealism had made its point and moved on, leaving its mark. Neorealism has been defined as

> a generic term applied to the cinema which emerged in Italy immediately following the liberation [after 1945 …]. Although the expression has been understood in many different ways, the core characteristics of Neorealism can be defined in terms of a method (a preference for location filming and the use of non-professional actors), attitude (a wish to get closer to everyday reality), subject matter (the life of the popular classes in the aftermath of the war), and ideology/politics […] (Vincendeau, 1995: 302)

to which one can add a visual style that preferred ellipses and contrasting continuity editing, long takes, as well as a marked emphasis on visual narration, letting the images speak for themselves, with socio-political implications. One of the important topics of Spanish Cinema history is the extent of Neorealism's influence on Spanish directors, attributed to the Italian Cultural Institute's promotion of Neorealist films in its cinema weeks of November 1951 and March 1953, together with the fact that the National Film School owned a copy of *Ladri di biciclette* [1948 Vittorio de Sica, *Bicycle Thieves*] (Faulkner, 2006: 91). However, caution needs to be exercised with these received opinions, and it is important to distinguish between the Italian films as Neorealism and neo-realism as a style. The most frequently quoted first Spanish example is Nieves Conde's *Surcos* although also mentioned is Buñuel's *Los olvidados* [1950 *The Forgotten Ones*], problematic because it both exploits surrealist techniques and was made in Mexico; but neither director attended the Film School. Furthermore numerous earlier Spanish films have been identified as sharing many but not always all of the identifying characteristics, and these can often be attributed to financial restrictions over aesthetic considerations as well as a committed personal agenda from the directors. This was the case with Manuel Mur Oti's *Un hombre va por el camino* [1949 *A Man on*

---

[16] It was remade in 2003 by Antonio Giménez Rico as *Hotel Danubio*.

the Road]; Antonio del Amo's *Día tras día* [1951 *Day by Day*] about street children; or Ana Mariscal's first feature as a director, with her newly founded production company, Bosco Films, *Segundo López, un aventurero urbano* [1953 **Segundo López, Urban Adventurer*]. This last example was originally classified as a Third Class that was renegotiated the following year (Martin-Márquez, 1999a: 113–22); it employed a most unusual blend of different genres, tones and techniques, featuring unknown actors, using the streets and other real locations thereby revealing the destitution of the period, and adding reflections on cinema and filmmaking. But to attribute these innovations to two weeks of restricted cinema viewing, and the limited commercial release of Italian films, often late and censored (Heredero, 1993: 288–9), seems to be overstating the case, especially as the so-called influences are only partially manifest in those Spanish films identified as neo-realist. The only exception, perhaps, some ten years later, is Saura's *Los golfos* [1959 *The Delinquents*]. Furthermore, while Neorealism was free to react against Fascism in Italy, this was not the case in Spain where the censors were vigilant. As Triana Toribio points out, the Church, which had the right of veto in the JSOC, had already clashed with Neorealism in Italy and was consequently on its guard (2003: 58–9).

It may be more accurate to attribute this fresher and more realistic expression of Spanish Cinema to a natural progression made by filmmakers, whose original impulses will have been stimulated and reaffirmed by exposure to Neorealism. The new aesthetic can also be linked to the prior development of the Spanish post-war novel. It is notable that whilst acknowledging the literary precedents, Nieves Conde also denied any Neorealist influence (Heredero, 1993: 295). Nonetheless there are many affinities and there were plenty of public and academic discussions about Neorealism, whether in the press, journals, among directors, even references within films themselves, and especially in the left-wing and politically committed film magazines *Objetivo* and *Cinema Universitario* (Jordan & Allinson, 2005: 182–4, which offers a different perspective on the situation). Kinder argues that there was a cross-fertilisation, 'a dialectic of opposition', 'associated with Hollywood and contrasted to Neorealism' that produced an 'absurdist neo-realism' (1993: 36–40, 54; see also Heredero, 1993: 287–301). The ambivalent relationship is evoked as a joke in *Surcos*, where the mobster's mistress suggests, 'Why don't you take me to the pictures? They're showing a psychological thriller.' 'That's already out of date. What's on now are neo-realist films.' 'And what's that?' 'Well, social problems, ordinary folks …';[17] or in its integration in the

---

[17] '¿Por qué no me llevas al cine? Echan una psicológica.' 'Esto ya está pasado. Ahora lo que se llevan son las neorrealistas.' '¿Y eso qué es?' 'Pues, problemas sociales, gente de barrio …'.

plot of the traditional comedy *El deseo y el amor* [1951 Henry Decoin & Luis María Delgado, *Le Désir et l'amour/Love and Desire*].[18]

The National Film School

By 1951 some of the students admitted to the National Film School, founded in 1947 [Instituto de Investigación y Experiencias Cinematográficas, IIEC], had graduated with degrees in different aspects of film production. Considered by some as an unnecessary expense, the School had been set up by the Sub-Secretariat for Popular Education to foster an autochthonous cinema and provide young talents with the technical expertise to create rousing films that would promote the values of Faith, Fatherland and Family. They were taught by a few industrious film professionals, who were subsequently assisted by recent graduates (Pozo Arenas, 1984: 75–9). Although short of funds and frustrated by too much theory, some students organised themselves into a production company, Altamira, led by the experienced Antonio del Amo who taught montage.[19] Altamira's first production was *Día tras día* filmed, mainly for financial necessity, in Madrid's streets and flea market, about a Father José [José Prada] doing good works with adolescents, anticipating another Father José [Adolfo Marsillach] in Lucia's *Cerca de la ciudad* – both optimistic plots given the lie in Buñuel's *Los olvidados*.

At first there was some resentment between the young academically trained filmmakers and those who had learned their trade on the sets of the Spanish film studios (Gómez Rufo, 1990: 242–3), but there was an even stronger rift. The school, in spite of its right-wing president Alberto Reig, did not actually produce the type of professionals that the funding authority had hoped for, and many of its graduates subsequently undermined the establishment's aspirations and were critical of the regime and its perceived hypocritical values. They became the first open dissidents who also re-established Spain's place in the context of international cinema (Schwartz, 1991: xi–xiii). Those best remembered from the 1950s are the two angry young men, Juan Antonio

---

[18] This French co-production starred Martine Carol and Françoise Arnoul alongside Carmen Sevilla and Antonio Vilar. The film begins as a NO-DO report in the Gare d'Austerlitz, Paris, as the French crew leaves to make a film in Spain, travelling by train to Madrid and coach to Málaga. A local fisherman [Antonio Vilar] is persuaded to act as stuntman for the leading man, who cannot swim, and ends up playing the lead 'according to the latest fashions, films are all made with people from the streets' [una película moderna; se hacen todas con gente de la calle], but Antonio Vilar was not plucked from the streets since he had started his acting career in Portugal in 1931 and moved to Spain in 1947 with *Reina Santa*.

[19] Del Amo was initiated through the Filmófono studios and had been involved in Republican documentaries including the filming of Malraux's *Espoir*; he also had a number of publications to his name and worked in film crews before directing his own films.

Bardem and Luis G. Berlanga. These two directors are seen by Hopewell as the initiators of the 'Modern Spanish Cinema' (1986: 44). In the words of Higginbotham 'they pioneered *la estética franquista*, the ironic film style' (1988: 29), using humour and cynicism to identify certain misrepresented aspects of their social context.

Bardem and Berlanga in tandem

Although their names go together they actually only co-directed one film, *Esa pareja feliz* [*That Happy Couple*]. Produced by Altamira in 1951, it is a satirical comedy, full of inventive visual gags and situations. It presents the aspirations of a conscientious working-class couple, Carmen and Juan [Elvira Quintillá and Fernando Fernán Gómez], who accept the official propaganda and promises made on national radio, contrasting their different illusions and shared aspirations with their real-life hardships and insecurities. Even the dreams and escapism that the cinema offered are presented as illusions by Juan,[20] who works as a gaffer in a film studio, and feels compelled to explain a tracking shot in the middle of the film he and Carmen are watching to have a little privacy away from their sublet overcrowded flat. Spectators, however, wanted and needed the illusion of the American dream (Vernon, in Gies, 1999: 257–8). In their initial desire to get something for nothing the happy couple is clearly presented as the victim of advertising propaganda, seduced by the promises that will not bring happiness to a nascent consumer society; that is until they both realise that they are being used in advertising campaigns that exploit their dreams and aspirations. Classified as Second Class, the film only received one import licence, which was sold off and hence no one wanted to distribute it until the summer of 1953, when the second and last film they co-scripted, *¡Bienvenido míster Marshall!* [1953 *Welcome Mr Marshall* – PNC, IN, Cannes], proved a financial and international success (Heredero, 1993: 44).

¡Bienvenido ...! was made in 1952 and won the International Prize at the 1953 Cannes Festival. Bardem worked on the script with Berlanga and Miguel Mihura, but left the project for financial reasons before filming began (Besas, 1985: 36). The censors approved the script thinking that it would be a harmless folkloric vehicle for Lolita Sevilla's film debut; she was Carmen Sevilla's sister and had just signed a contract with the producing company

---

[20] The initial sequence of the film is also a brilliant burlesque of the historical genre. The need for escapism is encapsulated in *Surcos* when the mobster's mistress reflects on neo-realism: 'No sé que gusto encuentran con sacar a la luz la miseria. ¡Con lo bonita que es la vida de los millonarios!' [I don't know what pleasure they find in portraying misery, when the life of millionaires is so beautiful!].

UNINCI,[21] together with the comic veterans José Isbert and Manolo Morán. The final version, however, actually exposed the artificiality of such films and the fact that they did not correspond to any Spanish reality; within the fiction of the narrative Andalusian costumes are hired out from Madrid and the Castilian village is refashioned like a film set in order to satisfy the antici- pated expectations of its potential US visitors (Hopewell, 1986: 49; Marsh, 2006: 97–121). The film was edited by Pepita Orduña, who had also just completed *Día tras día* and *Esa pareja feliz* and would work on Berlan- ga's next two films. It is a friendly satire of Spanish characters, where the microcosm of the village stands for the macrocosm of the nation, and it also provides another deconstruction of filmmaking starting from a very contrived opening sequence with its voice-over by Fernando Rey mocking the recur- rent didactic voice-overs of the time, and parodying both Spanish and Holly- wood cinema, integrated into the narrative through dream sequences that also reveals the characters' values and aspirations.[22] The film also includes political commentaries on the regime's negotiations with the USA (Pavlovic, 1992: 171–2).[23]

> *¡Bienvenido Mr Marshall!* soon became landmark and benchmark, demon- strating to other filmmakers the richly provocative possibilities of film comedy as a means of out-manoeuvring censorship and creating a climate of reception in which audiences might be encouraged to reflect on their own experience and to contemplate the extent of their cultural conditioning by ideologies which both informed and dominated their daily experience.
>
> (Rolph, 1999: 3)

The film was invited to represent Spain at the Cannes Festival but Edward G. Robinson, on the jury that year, tried to have it banned as he took it, and its self-publicity stunts, to be a criticism of and insult to the USA (Besas, 1995: 38). More explanations had to be offered as the Madrid release and its posters coincided with the installation of the new US ambassador. Berlanga

---

[21] Started in 1949, UNINCI [Unión Industrial Cinematográfica] was a small company with strong left-wing tendencies that attracted the young hotheads of the IIEC, including Jorge Semprún (see pp. 282–3). Its two worthy successes were *Bienvenido ...* and Buñuel's *Viridiana* in 1961. For more information, see Heredero (1993: 287–316), who also covers Spanish neo- realism, the IIEC, Altamira and UNINCI; see also Besas (1985: 35–9).

[22] See Vernon (in Gies, 1995: 258–9, and 1997: 40–2). The fifth dream sequence of the schoolteacher Eloisa [Elvira Quintillá] was not filmed, but a rough script can be found in the film magazine *Contracampo* 24 (1981), pp. 23–6. In 2002 Berlanga made a thirteen-minute short entitled *El sueño de la maestra* [*The Teacher's Dream*].

[23] George Marshall was the US Secretary of State who proposed the European Recovery Plan (Marshall Plan, 1948–52) for the economic reconstruction of post-war Europe from which Spain was excluded. As mentioned, Spain was later granted a separate aid package in return for three US air bases on its territory.

and his crew shrugged their shoulders and went on with their next film, very pleased with all the publicity.

Luis García Berlanga (Valencia, 1921)

Berlanga was then contracted by Perojo to make the generation-gap satire, *Novio a la vista* [1954 *Boyfriend in Sight*], a Tati-esque summer vacation story set in a seaside resort in 1914. Based on a script by Edgar Neville, reworked with Bardem and Juan Colina (Hernández-Les, 1981: 49–58; Beckwith, 1998: 113–27), it includes the first reference to the Austro-Hungarian Empire, which has become a running joke in Berlanga's filmography. *Calabuch* [the name of a fictitious seaside village – PNC, IN, Venice OCIC] followed in 1956. Like *Bombas para la paz*, it is set against the Cold War tensions to present the unsuccessful attempt of the eminent US scientist Jorge Hamiltón [Edmund Gwenn] to escape international attention and pressure. The little harbour is far from quiet with its petty smuggling and unusual prison arrangements, not to mention the local rivalries for the best annual firework display.[24] Meanwhile the rest of the world looks for the missing scientist and the full might of the US fleet is sent to 'rescue' him. Berlanga continues to make constant references to previous cinema, including the song 'Soy un pobre presidario [I am an unfortunate prisoner]' from *La hija de Juan Simón* and a burlesque bullfight on the beach. Through his films Berlanga established what proved to be a very useful formula to outmanoeuvre the censors and lead the spectators to reflect on their own situation by illustrating through humour 'the disparity between the ideology of fascism and the popular experience of its practice' (Nair, 2000: 90). He focuses on and builds up an illusion, usually motivated by need or greed, which soon becomes contagious and is then deflated with the implicit lesson that anticipated happiness built on the lottery, a soap company competition, or Marshall aid, are illusory solutions to real problems and can only bring disappointment.[25] Humour is often enhanced through small subversive details such as one-liners in the dialogue or an unexpected object located within the frame; at times these are very culturally specific and thus often overlooked by foreign viewers but there is always enough in the

---

24   Berlanga returns to a post-tourist boom Calabuch with a blue European beach flag in 1999 with *París–Tombuctú*. This time it is visited by a stressed and impotent French plastic surgeon played by Michel Piccoli who shares the local life for a week and allows Berlanga to revisit the humour of many of his previous films. It is his cinematographic *envoi*.

25   Films like *Whisky Galore* [1949 Alexander Mackendrick] and *Local Hero* [1983 Bill Forsyth] exploit a similar recipe to frustrate those who, understandably given their situation, want something for nothing. Alex de la Iglesia has made good use of the formula in *La comunidad* [2000 *Common Wealth*].

5a Visual ironies in Berlanga's *Plácido* (1961)

thrust of the narrative and images to provide entertainment and intelligent criticism of the *status quo* (Hopewell, 1986: 62).[26]

In *Los jueves, milagro* [1957 **Thursday Miracles*] Berlanga looks at the exploitation of religious beliefs for economic gain, here to revive a small-town economy, undermining the clergy films that were reaching the end of their popularity. The producers hired the services of a priest, Father Garau, to work on the script so that the false miracles would not appear anti-Catholic, but it was still censored and diminished as a consequence (Hernández-Les, 1981: 72–3). His last film of the decade, after a number of censored and unfilmed scripts, was his personal favourite and not just because it was nominated for an Oscar: *Plácido* [1961, the name of a hardworking and well-meaning self-employed father who is determined to make his first down payment on his three-wheel motorised cart, ubiquitous at the time, before the bank closes for Christmas – PNC]. The film looks satirically at social hypocrisy and institutionalised charity where the poor only exist as commodities to assuage wealthy consciences or to promote pressure-cookers in a campaign that sits 'a beggar

---

[26] E.g. in *Esta pareja feliz* a photograph of García Lorca on a dressing-room wall, in *Bienvenido* ... the town's goal posts are carried off the village football pitch past other villagers being taught how to dance flamenco, in *Calabuch* the US rocket is called 'Marilyn'.

at your table' on Christmas Eve.[27] This subversive comedy, where Berlanga initiates his long-term partnership with screenwriter Rafael Azcona, presents a rich collection of caricatures from many layers of society, displaying a cynical vision of Spain where the interests of the Church and commerce are safeguarded by the state, contradicting the government's social slogan 'Paz y prosperidad [Peace and Prosperity for All]'. It includes an excellent musical score from Manuel Asins Arbó and a Terry Gilliam-type credit sequence, as well as nominations for both an Oscar and the Golden Palm at Cannes.

Juan Antonio Bardem (Madrid, 1922–2002)

Bardem, who did not eventually graduate from the Film School, was a very different director even if he shared Berlanga's critical attitude to the Spanish situation. Bardem was more politically focused and a signed-up member of the Spanish Communist party (PCE), and cinematographically more realist in style. His first solo project was the taut *Cómicos* [1954 *Thespians*, although the script was ready in 1951 – PNC, IN], about the aspirations and hardships of a second-rate and waning touring company performing in provincial towns during the difficult 1950s, seen mostly from the perspective of a young actress Ana Ruiz played by Elisa Galvé (Martin-Márquez, 1999a: 187–9). This world was not unfamiliar to Bardem as his parents, Rafael Bardem and Matilde Sampedro, were both actors.[28] *Felices pascuas* [1954 *Merry Christmas*], which included both his parents in the cast, was a comedy that set a thematic strand for his subsequent films by focusing, through symbolism, on the awakening of a social conscience as Pilar and Juan [Julia Martínez and Bernard Lajarrige] try to rescue the family's free Christmas dinner and Juan learns his lesson (Higginbotham, 1988: 33).

He then directed what are now identified as his two most important films. *Muerte de un ciclista* [1955 *Death of Cyclist* – PNC, Cannes FRIPESCI] starts with an unreported road accident that leaves a cyclist to die on the road, beside a Civil War battle site, and becomes a psychological thriller that examines the hypocrisy and egoism of the establishment. The narrative alternates 'abruptly between Hollywood and neo-realist conventions [...] used as a class discourse to reveal the Hollywood [melodramatic] genre's traditional alignment with the bourgeoisie' (Kinder, 1993: 57, 73–86; J. Evans, 2005a: 253–65). It includes implicit criticism of the university system in crisis at

---

27 'Siente un pobre a su mesa' was the original title but it was prohibited by the censors; and there is only one indigent woman in the film! For Berlanga's use of slogans, and further analysis of his subversive comedy, see Marsh (2004: 113–28).

28 His sister Pilar, his niece Mónica and nephews Javier and Carlos are also actors, and his son Miguel directed his first feature in 1996 *Más que amor, frenesí* [*Not Love, Just Frenzy*].

the time, passing references to the Civil War that destroyed former relationships, the contemporary pandering to US businessmen, who are entertained
with Flamenco spectacles, all contrasted to powerful images of the struggling working classes and student solidarity shown in brief shots of demonstrations. It concludes with a bitter ironical twist after the central character
becomes aware of his social responsibilities. The film also offers careful use
of the soundtrack and silences, as well as sharp connecting editing by Margarita Ochoa, which builds up the tension at first without commentaries, thus
allowing the spectators to decipher the relationships, which with increasing
dialogues assume different points of view as the lovers [Lucia Bosè and
Alberto Closas] shift apart. *Calle mayor* [1956 *Main Street* – PNC, Venice
FIPRESCI[29]] takes up Arniches's farce *La señorita de Trevélez* in earnest,
turning it into an examination of the narrow-minded and asphyxiating provincial life with its patriarchal values that transforms Isabel's life [Betsy Blair]
into the silent tragedy of many single women, while also taking a side-swipe
at the American dream propagated by Hollywood and totally out of reach for
Spaniards in the 1950s (Roberts, 1999: 30–1). Elisa Galvé in *Cómicos*, Aurora
Bautista's even more complex character in *La tía Tula* [1964 Miguel Picazo,
*Aunt Tula – San Sebastián] and even José Luis López Váquez in *Mi querida
señorita* [1972 Jaime de Armiñán, *My Dearest Señorita* – PNC], all depict
subtle female characters as silent victims of this society to present a strong
indictment of its reactionary and patriarchal values (Roberts, 1999: 19–37).

La venganza [1957 *Vengeance* – PNC, Cannes] was another committed
social drama whose initial voice-over roots the film into the Spanish landscape and links it to the international context of migrant labour exploitation (Higginbotham, 1988: 38).[30] It was, however, distorted by the censors'
requirements: the temporal context had to be pushed back to pre-Republican
Spain and it could not use its original title *Los segadores* [*The Harvesters],
although the theme, with echoes of the Civil War, remains through this melodrama of a family feud at the expense of working-class solidarity (Besas,
1985: 44–5). Like Berlanga, Bardem received close scrutiny from the censors
and decided to use different narratives to convey the same themes. In *Sonatas*
[1959 – PNC] he turned to the literary adaptation of Valle Inclán's *fin de
siècle* prose, but this Mexican co-production filmed in colour failed at the
box-office. The Marqués de Bradomín [Paco Rabal] is shown to acquire a
political conscience as he moves from Galicia (1824) to Mexico (1830) and

---

[29] This is the first recorded Sant Jordi award for best film, although it was then known in
Castilian as San Jorge (Porter i Moix,1992: 274). Unlike the equivalent prize for literature,
awarded annually since 1947 except for 1949 and 1950, the film prize could not be restricted
to Catalan-language films since there were none.

[30] Triana Toribio suggests that these initial voice-overs or prologues are at times a way of
addressing the censors publicly (2003: 101).

joins in the armed struggle for freedom from tyrannical military controls. This was followed by a critical bullfighting narrative without any bullfighting sequences, *A las cinco de la tarde* [1960 *At Five in the Afternoon*] based on a play by another frequently censored dissident, Alfonso Sastre.

Mid-term manifestos (1954–5)

Midway through the decade more active intellectual debates on the cinema flared up, stirring but not altering the situation. In 1954, the year that Madrid overtook Barcelona in the number of film theatres available, García Escudero, as passionate and as stubborn as ever about the cinema and its values, wrote his negative *The History of Spanish Cinema in 100 Words*:

> Until 1939 there is no Spanish Cinema, neither materially, spiritually/ [intellectually], or technically. In 1929 and 1934 it took its first step. In 1939 it could have walked, but the creation of an industry or the possibility of a committed cinema was obstructed. Castanets and dinner jackets prevailed. Attempts at unpretentious cinema are still overwhelmed by the cinema of ruffs and frock coats, and religious films without any authenticity. Neorealism, which could have been Spanish, was reduced to one late film. But our cinema is better than that of 1936, and one hopes that the young may give it the national style it needs.[31]

Friends from the IIEC, led by PCE collaborators Bardem and Ricardo Muñoz Suay, had founded the film magazine *Objetivo* in May 1953, expressing the parallel but more radical and impatient attitudes of that younger generation and their interest in Neorealism (Kinder, 2003: 26–7). They called for and provoked a formal discussion on the state of Spanish Cinema, which took place in Salamanca from 14 to 19 May 1955. It was organised by Basilio Martín Patino of the Salamanca University Cineclub, who invited all parties interested to discuss the state of the Spanish film industry, whatever their political ideologies. They concluded, in the words of Juan Antonia Bardem, that Spanish Cinema was

---

[31] 'Hasta 1939 no hay cine español, ni material, ni espiritual, ni técnicamente. En 1929 y 1934 da sus primeros pasos. En 1939 pudo echar a andar, pero se frustra la creación de una industria, así como la posibilidad de un cine político. Continúan las castañuelas y el smoking. Sobre los intentos de cine sencillo se desploman el cine de gola y levita, y un cine religioso sin autenticidad. El neorealismo, que pudo ser español, se reducirá a una película tardía. Pero nuestro cine supera al de 1936 y puede esperarse que los jóvenes le den el estilo nacional que necesita.' *La historia en 100 palabras del cine español*,1954: 11.

politically ineffective, socially false, intellectually deficient, aesthetically worthless, and technically stunted. [...] The problem with Spanish cinema is that it does not present any [social] problems, it is not a testimony of our times. [...] It continues to be a cinema of painted dolls.[32]

The establishment took offence and even closed down *Objetivo*, but paternalistically forgave the 'young offenders'. More visible protests also appeared in the form of student demonstrations, which provoked the replacement of the education minister. Labour strikes followed in 1956. One of the conference's minor requests was a national federation of Cineclubs allowed to show a different kind of cinema, unavailable in popular theatres. This was subsequently granted on 11 March 1957 and García Escudero was appointed as its first president. Nonetheless some liberalisation had to be demonstrated after December 1955 when Spain was finally admitted into the UN as a result of Cold War realignments. Franco reshuffled the cabinet in February 1957, bringing in twelve new ministers, who established the Opus Dei[33] as a strong voice within government. In 1959 the important Stabilisation plan for the next decade was announced, but labour protests intensified and ETA [Euskadi ta Askatasuna/Basque Land and Liberty], the underground separatist party, was created in 1959.

Late 1950s musical productions

Meanwhile musical films, relying on the popularity of their singing stars, continued for a while to attract and distract spectators, whether the recycling of previous successes such as Ramón Torrado's 1958 *María de la O* with Lola Flores, where the honest and patronised gypsy sings 'You'll be more than a Queen, / promised the white man / and I believed him',[34] or Serrano de Osma's last film *La rosa roja* [1960 *The Red Rose*], which combined flamenco, bandits and patriots in an Andalusian setting. There were expensive costume melodramas such as *Venta de Vargas* [1959 *Vargas's Inn*] with Lola Flores and María Esperanza Navarro, set in 1808 Andalusia during the Napoleonic War and reiterating the patriotic rhetoric of the previous decade: how

---

[32] '[El cine español actual es] políticamente ineficaz, socialmente falso, intelectualmente ínfimo, estéticamente nulo e industrialmente raquítico', 'el problema del cine español es que no tiene problemas, que no es testigo de nuestro tiempo', 'sigue siendo un cine de muñecas pintadas': see Pozo Arenas (1984: chapter 5 (pp. 135–9)) for the transcription of the minutes, although Berlanga later claimed that he did not share this extreme position (Pozo Arenas, 1984: 142; Gómez Rufo, 1990: 161).

[33] A Catholic lay organisation with strong convictions and social commitments (Graham & Labyani, 1995: 423).

[34] 'Será má que reina / me dijo a mí el payo / y me lo creí.'

glorious it is to die for the Fatherland and to put one's trust in God. This film was directed by Enrique Salaberry, an Argentine who, from 1956 to 1964, made ten films in Spain.

The gypsy folklorics were then eclipsed for a while by other varieties of musicals, often involving the adventures of stage performers, starting with Juan de Orduña's *El último cuplé* [1957 *Last Torch Song* – PNC][35] starring Sara Montiel. Made and sold for a pittance, it was distributed by CIFESA and became the most popular Spanish film of the decade with its 24 songs, nostalgic and excessive evocation of pre-Republican popular numbers made famous by Raquel Meller (pp. 24–5, 71; Perriam, 2005: 89–96; Vernon, 2004: 183–99), and generated many 'cuplé' films. An international star after working for six years in Mexico and Hollywood, Montiel returned to Spain for this musical melodrama, which she followed with three others, all produced by Benito Perojo, also box-office hits: *La violetera* [1958 Luis César Amadori, *The Flower Girl* – PNC],[36] *Mi último tango* [1960 Amadori, *My Last Tango*], a feel-good melodrama with humour and pathos, which, as always, served as a vehicle for her voice, a formula repeated with *Pecado de amor* [1961 *A Sin of Love*]. *Carmen la de Ronda* [1959 Tulio Demicheli, *A Girl Against Napoleon*] adapts the Carmen story to the Napoleonic campaign in Andalusia and Montiel recycles Imperio Argentina songs in a way that drives the action forward.

Whereas Demicheli settled in Spain to escape Perón's censorship, Amadori came to Spain when Perón fell from power. The same year as *La violetera* he had another box-office success with a romance and musical page of Spanish history *¿Dónde vas Alfonso XII?* [1958 *Where Are You Going Alfonso XII?* – PNC, IN] with Vicente Parra and Paquita Rico in a melodrama that attempts to blend Spanish history with the costumes, sets and sugar pink success of Romy Schneider's *Sissi* trilogy [1955, 1956 and 1957, Ernst Marischka]. It was perfect for its Christmas Eve première in Alicante. It was followed two years later by the historical sequel and melodrama *¿Dónde vas triste de ti?* [1960 Alfonso Balcázar, *Where Are You Going so Sad?*], where again Guillermo Cases's composing skills were put to good use.[37] Amadori directed sixteen films in Spain, most of them produced by Benito Perojo. He had his finger on the audience's pulse and they enjoyed the spectacle his cinema offered, feel-

---

[35] A 'cuplé' is a popular music hall song with salty *double-entendre*; see also Fernando Gabriel Martín (in Pérez Perucha, 1997: 416–19) for the pre- and post-production problems.

[36] This is actually the third remake; the first two versions are the work of Henri Roussel, *Violettes impériales*, 1924 and in 1932 with sound, both starring Raquel Meller, whose most popular songs punctuate the film, including of course 'La violetera', the melody used by Chaplin in *City Lights* [1931].

[37] Royal matters were in the air. In 1958 Franco announced that the natural successor to his regime would be Alfonso XII's great-grandson Juan Carlos, and in 1960 Prince Baudouin of Belgium married the Spanish aristocrat Fabiola de Mora y Aragón.

good glossy romantic dramas such as *Una muchachita de Valladolid* [1958 *Girl from Valladolid*] set among the new diplomatic circles, and interesting in terms of where and how women are positioned in this conjugal romance.

There were less openings for male leads but Antonio Molina made a number of films: *Malagueña* [1956 Ricardo Nuñez], and *La hija de Juan Simón* [1957 *Juan Simón's Daughter*], *El Cristo de los faroles* [1958 *The Christ of the Lamps*] and *Café de Chinitas* [1960 *Chinitas's Café*], all directed by Gonzalo Delgrás. Juanito Valderrama made his film debut with Juan Fortuny's *El rey de la carretera* [1955, *King of the Road*] followed in 1960 by *El emigrante* [Sebastián Almeida, *The Emigrant*] celebrating the triumph of emigrants who returned to Spain,[38] but principally a vehicle for Valderrama's voice. There were also those happy and overgrown singing student capers such as the remake of *La casa de la Troya* [1959 Rafael Gil – PNC], *Pasa la tuna* [1960 José María Elorrieta, *The University Chorus*] and *Margarita se llama mi amor* [1961 Ramón Fernández, *My Love is called Margarita*], in stark contrast to the protesting students of the time or their reflection in *Muerte de un ciclista*. There were plenty of other musical films such as the ludicrous Italian co-production *Pan, amor y Andalucía* [1959 Javier Setó, *Bread, Love and Andalusia*], where an Italian band wins a Seville Music Festival with the help of Carmen Sevilla dancing the tarantella and including some brightly kilted bagpipers who are also competing.

Bullfighting

Bullfighters figure in some of those favourite musicals such as *Un caballero andaluz* and *El último cuplé*, but fewer films now took up the theme. There was the biopic *El Litri y su sombra* [1960 Rafael Gil, *Litri and His Shadow*] where Miguel Báez 'El Litri' played himself. The more memorable bullfighting films of this period were quite critical of the profession: Vajda's *Mi tío Jacinto* [1956 *My Uncle Jacinto*] through its humour, and *Tarde de toros* [1956 *Bullfighting Afternoon* – PNC, IN] through its more realistic portrayal of the profession, despite its colour. Antonio Román's *Los clarines del miedo* [1958 *Bugles of Fear*] undermines the glory and lustre of bullfighting, as did the aforementioned *A las cinco de la tarde*, both of which underline the exploitation of the bullfighters by the impresarios and the blood-lust of the crowds. Two films that provoked strong public reaction were *Los chicos* [(1959) 1963 Marco Ferreri, *The Lads*] and the even bleaker *Los golfos* [1959 but not released until 1961 in Barcelona and 1962 in

---

[38] The economic emigrant abroad is an aspect of Spanish reality that is barely mentioned in the cinema of the regime; it is briefly raised in the early 1970s.

5b The bullfighter in Vajda's *Mi tío Jacinto* (1956)

Madrid, *The Delinquents*] directed by Carlos Saura. Both exploit the illusions such stardom presented for marginalised youth in their bleak urban settings (Delgado, 1999: 38–54).

Children as protagonists

Films with a child protagonist were not new but became very popular following Vajda's 1955 success for Chamartín with Pablito Calvo as *Marcelino*. He was contracted to make two more with the boy. *Mi tío Jacinto* contrasts the optimism of young Pepote with his disillusioned uncle, a broken and drunk bullfighter who never made it, set in a Madrid that is equally wretched. The more ambitious *Un ángel pasó por Brooklyn* [1957 Vajda, *An Angel over Brooklyn* – IN], which includes the brief appearance of Peter Ustinov promptly metamorphosed into a dog, is another parable with exteriors filmed in Brooklyn's Italian quarters and directed at the Italian market.

Another discovery was Joselito [José Jiménez Fernández, b. 11/02/47?][39]

---

[39] Sources consulted agree his birthday is on 11 February, but the year varies from 1943 to 1948, with 1947 being the most frequently cited.

whose career was established on his exceptional voice and, as a child prodigy, he starred in fourteen films between 1956 and 1969. Antonio del Amo directed the first five of which the first, *El pequeño ruiseñor* [1956, *The Little Nightingale*], is the most endearing. This was followed in 1957 and 1958 by two more, equally sentimental, Little Nightingale films, both in colour and reflecting the popular beliefs of rural devotion. The little shepherd of *El ruiseñor de las cumbres* [1958 *The Nightingale Up High*] after tribulations, minor trials and songs, confirms all the values of the family and faith. In 1960 del Amo put him in a period costume film, *El pequeño coronel* [*The Little Colonel*], where he is a male Snow White to seven stupid *bandoleros*. This was immediately followed by the *Aventuras de Joselito en América* [1960 *Adventures of Joselito and Tom Thumb*] under René Cardona's direction, and back with del Amo in 1961 he appeared alongside Libertad Lamarque in a second Mexican co-production, *Bello recuerdo* [*Beautiful Memory*], still managing to look twelve to pluck heartstrings with another orphan story! Certainly extremely talented, Joselito performed in perfect feel-good escapist narratives, vehicles for his wonderful singing.

There were many more child actors who got started, but with less success, such as Miguel Ángel Rodríguez in *El sol sale todos los días* [1955 Antonio del Amo, *The Sun Rises Every Day*], or Miguelito Gil in Pedro L Ramírez's *Recluta con niño* [1955 *Recruit with a child*] in which José Luis Ozores plays a stuttering country rustic (a *paleto*)[40] who must look after his younger brother while doing his military service, with Manolo Morán as the sergeant major. Then came Marisol, but her films and success will be covered in the next chapter.

Social comedies

The socio-economic progress and growth of consumerism are reflected in the comedies of the late 1950s, which also reveal a slight relaxation of prudish values. Many involve young people courting or just married in the mould of *Esa pareja feliz*, but also draw attention to growing affluence illustrated, for instance, by the arrival of Spanish television in 1956[41] or the SEAT 600 car in 1957, and some early tourists from Northern Europe. Many comedies

[40] Like the *pícaro*, the insignificant opportunist who lives by his wits, the *paleto*, or country yokel, would become a stereotype of Spanish comedies.

[41] In *Atraco a las tres* [1962 José María Forqué, *Hold-Up at Three*] there is an unforgettable sequence where the landlady, who sublets her flat, also charges the other tenants of the building to come and watch her television set, which she is still paying for by instalments. In *La gran familia* [1962 *The Big Family*] the sixteen children and grandfather watch television through the open window of the neighbours' flat across the courtyard.

were built on the Cinderella dream of young women, with a job, wanting to catch or avoid an imposed often incompetent husband, and when the plots are resolved with a Church marriage they comment positively on the experienced social progress. These popular comedies were known as 'comedias de chicas' [chick comedies], focusing on groups of young women and indirectly under-lining the situation of women in society, for example, the air hostesses of *Las aeroguapas* [1957 Eduardo Manzanos, *The Airbeauties*], Pedro Lazaga's *Las muchachas de azul* [1957 *The Girls in Blue*] from a department store, *Ana dice que sí* [1958 *Ana Says Yes*], or his *Luna de verano* [1958 *Summer Moon*] set on a summer course for foreign students. The last three starred Fernando Fernán Gómez and Analía Gadé, and the last two were both written and produced by José Luis Dilbidos. Pedro Masó wrote Rafael Salvia's *Las chicas de la Cruz Roja* [1958 *The Red Cross Girls* – PNC], about four young women of different social backgrounds collecting for the Red Cross, and Fernando Palacios's *El día de los enamorados* [1959 *Valentine's Day*]. José María Forqué's *Maribel y la extraña familia* [1960 *Maribel and the Strange Family*] was another hit of the period.

Other comedies focused more critically on the difficulties faced by young couples, such as León Klimovsky's risqué (for the times) *Viaje de novios* [1956, *Honeymoon*] or Josep Maria Forn's *La vida privada de Fulano de tal* [1961 *The Private life of A. N. Other*], both starring Fernán Gómez, with Analía Gadé in the first and Susana Campos in the second. Fernán Gómez's *La vida por delante* [1958 *Life Ahead*] was his first commercial success as a director and led to the sequel *La vida alrededor* [1959 *Life Around Us*], both produced by Dilbidos, starring Fernán Gómez as Antonio, who reminds us of the Juan he played in *Esa pareja feliz*, partnered by Analía Gadé. Visually very inventive, they also creatively exploit the soundtrack and its relationship to the image as well as using a first-person narration. Through their humour and touches of farce they deal with contemporary social problems and insti-tutions, including the disparity between women's professional restrictions and their unrewarded abilities, but their tone and gentle irony mitigate the criticism. *La vida alrededor* is the more accomplished of the two films, but the sequel does provide an even stronger indictment of an incompetent legal system and the operations of entrepreneurs.

Producers, directors and actors made other urban comedies such as *Manolo, guardia urbano* [1954 Rafael Salvia, *Manolo, Urban Policeman*], which integrates all sorts of anecdotes with a vast cast surrounding Manolo Morán. Many included *pícaros* and *paletos*, trying to survive in their bleak urban settings, such as *Fulano y Menguano* [(1956) 1959 *The Two Nobodies*] with José Isbert and Juan José Menéndez, directed by Joaquín Romero Marchent who went on to make spaghetti-westerns in the 1960s. Some other examples featuring the regular stars of these comedies are: *Los ladrones somos gente honrada* [1956 *We Thieves Are Honourable People*, a reworking of Iquino's

1942 film] with José Isbert, Antonio and José Luis Ozores; *El tigre de Chamberí* [1957 *KO Miguel*], a boxing caper with José Luis Ozores and Tony Leblanc, both directed by Pedro L. Ramírez; *Perro golfo* [1961 Domingo Viladomat, *Mischievous Dog*] where Isbert focuses all his experience on recovering a dog.[42] These low- to medium-budget films often reveal interesting fragments of life in a changing Spain through their mise-en-scène and location shots; for instance, the increase in traffic and type of cars on the road, the corner bar, etc. Examples might be Pedro Lazaga's *Los tramposos* [1959 *The Tricksters*] where Leblanc and Antonio Ozores try unsuccessfully to make money from any scam available until they realise there are tourists to be exploited; *Los económicamente débiles* [1960 *The Economically Handicapped*] with Leblanc, José Luis López Vázquez, Antonio Ozores, and Marisa Paredes's first credited appearance; or *Tres de la Cruz Roja* [1961 Fernando Palacios, *Threesome from the Red Cross*] where Leblanc, López Vázquez and Manuel Gómez Bur join the Red Cross just to be able to watch their football for free.

Now that there were affordable economy cars, they became an important status symbol as in *Ya tenemos coche* [1958 Julio Salvador, *Now We Have a Car*], followed up by the black humour of *El cochecito* [1960 *The Wheelchair* – Venice] a more acerbic comedy directed by Marco Ferreri and confirming Rafael Azcona as a screenwriter.[43] They had already collaborated on *El pisito* [1959 *The Tiny Flat*] (Hopewell, 1986: 58–62) to comment satirically and through humour on the urban housing problem, in which both he and Azcona had cameo parts and so did a young Carlos Saura, according to the *IMDb*. These two comedies, with their frames full of disparate details, are more blatant and biting about exposing the values and hypocrisy of the regime (Kinder, 1993: 111–26). In both films the ending was seriously altered by the censors, although double standards were once again applied for the international release (Larraz, 1986: 146–7). When Ferreri was denied a residence permit he returned to Italy (Higginbotham, 1988: 25).

---

[42]   The reader is reminded to use the *IMDb.com* or the *MCU.es* to look up the credit titles for all these films. The *IMDb* will also allow useful cross-reference. Another personal favourite of these comedies is Rafaela Aparicio (1906–1996) who usually plays maids or mothers and triumphed in Carlos Saura's *Ana y los lobos* [1973 *Anna and the Wolves*] and *Mamá cumple cien años* [1979 *Mama Turns a Hundred*]; her first credited appearance is in the 1935 *Nobleza baturra* and as Gregoria in *La hija de Juan Simón*, resuming her career in 1955 for at least 153 more films.

[43]   Azcona (1926–2008) was already well known for his black humour and contributions to the satirical magazine *La cordoniz*. By 2004 Azcona had 90 scripts to his credit, and a cameo appearance in both *El pisito* and *El cochecito*. Kinder discusses this specific humour and satirical approach with reference to the 'esperpentos', a neologism coined at the beginning of the twentieth century by the dramatist Ramón del Valle Inclán to describe the satirical humour of his own plays (1993: 115–24), see also Hopewell (1986: 59–62) and Marsh (2006: 145–66).

After *Surcos*, Nieves Conde carried on with his socially committed films, albeit from a different perspective, and after *Todos somos necesarios* [1956 *We are All Needed* – San Sebastián Golden Shell] about three ex-prisoners, he directed *El inquilino* [1958 *The Tenant*], which also focused on the continuing housing shortage and unwieldy bureaucracy where, again, the ending was censored and the film was re-released the following year with a more positive conclusion (Higginbotham, 1988: 24–5). An unusual and gentle satirical narrative is Clemente Pamplona's first film, *Farmacia de guardia* [1958 *Duty Pharmacy*].[44] Defined as 'Drama' by the *IMDb*, it is in fact a series of related episodes presenting slices of life set in a chemist's with its night-time emergencies, including the local *sereno* [night street-watchman] who keeps warm in the shop. This indirect tribute to pharmacists is made up of various episodes, very effectively edited by Sara Ontañón, with disparate but intercalated characters that are scripted with gentle humour to reveal a muted criticism of hypocritical values, with sexual implications and plenty of references to contemporary cinema, especially the continuing run of *El último cuplé*.[45]

Darker crime

If comedies, folkloric settings and songs prevailed, there were of course other genres, following the Hollywood example, which continued to please despite being censored and/or dubbed. As Graham and Labanyi phrase it, Spanish isolation in the 1940s and 1950s 'would be mitigated by the influx from the late 1940s of Hollywood movies, and by the arrival in the 1950s of American aid, prefiguring the massification and Americanization of culture that would mark the regime's later decades; (1995: 170). Crime and *noir* are genres where this influence was particularly strong, even if the censors demanded that the police make no mistakes and that criminals be severely punished or confess and repent. In spite of these moralistic stipulations Kinder suggests that these films 'served during this decade as one of the most effective forms of political critique for both the Left and Right. [They] continued to be tolerated by the Francoist regime through the 1960s and 1970s, partly because these films so blatantly imitated American and French action genres [...] and thereby appeared to minimise Spanish specificity' (1993: 60). Yet these generally low-budget films in black and white used the streets of Barce-

---

[44] Pamplona was at the time better known as a screenwriter, with *Agustina de Aragón*, *Cerca del cielo*, *Dos caminos* and *Los ases buscan la paz* to his name.

[45] The formula was developed by Antonio Mercero in a popular television series of the same name, which ran from 1991 to 1995.

lona or Madrid for their settings, therefore unmistakably rooting them in the Spanish 1950s.

José María Forqué, who delighted with his comic treatment of the genre, could also take it seriously as in *091 Policía al habla* [1960 *091 Police On Line*]. Ignacio F. Iquino continued in Barcelona with his companies Emisora Films, Producciones Iquino and IFISA, and was the most prolific provider, as a director and producer (Faulkner, 2006: 98). Films such as *Brigada Criminal* [1950 *The Criminal Brigade*] or *¡Buen viaje, Pablo!* [1959 *Bon Voyage, Pablo!*] both warrant re-evaluation. Julio Coll was a playwright, contracted by Iquino as a screenwriter, who then moved on to direct his own thrillers: *Nunca es demasiado tarde* [1956, *Never Too Late*], *Distrito quinto* [1958 *The Fifth Precinct*] praised for its angle-shots and editing in the Iquino house-style, and the more psychological *Un vaso de whisky* [1959 *A Glass of Whisky*] or *Los cuervos* [1962 *The Crows*], which did not please the critics. Other examples, also produced by Iquino's companies, are Antonio Santillán's *El ojo de cristal* [1955 *The Glass Eye*] where the inspector's son resolves the same crime as his father but by very different means; Juan Bosch with *Sendas marcadas* [1957 *Marked Paths*] or *A sangre fría* [1959 *In Cold Blood*]; Francisco Rovira Beleta's *Los atracadores* [1961, *The Robbers* –PNC], which includes the execution of a criminal, and his *El expreso de Andalucía* [1956 *The Andalusia Express*], which recreates an actual robbery. Ricardo Blasco's *Armas contra la ley* [1961 *Guns against the Law*] or *Autopsia de un criminal* [1962 *Autopsy of a Criminal*] examines how a gambler [Paco Rabal] is driven to crime, with plenty of shadows, a *femme fatale*, and too many verbal explanations after 90 minutes of well-handled suspense. Another very compelling film was Ladislao Vajda's *El cebo* [1959 *It Happened in Broad Daylight*], a tense thriller filmed in Switzerland with an international crew, about the capture of a child murderer and implied paedophile.[46] Of course these films attracted their parodies, including José María Forqué's *Usted puede ser un asesino* [1961 *You Could Be a Murderer*] or his *Atraco a las tres* [1962 *Hold-Up at Three*], or Juan G[arcía] Atienza's undervalued *Los dinamiteros* [1962 *The Dynamiters*].

Literary adaptations

There was a slight growth in literary adaptations, that is, bringing the acknowledged classics of previous centuries to the screen rather than contemporary

---

[46] Some do not consider this a Spanish film, but it does include Spanish actors and crew, and Vajda was naturalised in 1954. His next film was a comedy made in Germany, produced for Karl Ulrich. He came back to Spain in 1960 to make *María, matrícula de Bilbao* [*Maria, Registered in Bilbao*] about a ship-owning family, revealing for its construction of Francoist masculinity.

authors whose plots informed many films already mentioned, including those authors that have since become classics such as Antonio Buero Vallejo's *Historia de una escalera* [1950 Ignacio F. Iquino, *The Story of a Staircase*] and his *Madrugada* [1957 Antonio Román, *Dawn*], as well as Alfonso Sastre's *Un hecho violento* [1958 José María Forqué, *A Violent Fate*], the Italian co-production *Tal vez mañana* [1957 Clauco Pellegrini, *Perhaps Tomorrow*], as well as the aforementioned *Amanecer en Puerta Oscura, La noche y el alba, A las cinco de la tarde* and *Carmen la de Ronda*.

Among the novels adapted were Fernán Caballero's *Luna de sangre* [1950 Francisco Rovira Beleta *Blood Moon*], Concha Espina's *Dulce nombre* [1951 Enrique Gómez, *Sweet Name*], Blasco Ibáñez's *Cañas y barro* [1954 *Reeds and Mud* – PNC] and the second version of Pío Baroja's *Zalacaín el aventurero* [1954 *Zalacaín the Adventurer*], both directed by Juan de Orduña, or Pardo Bazán's *El indulto* [1960 Sáenz de Heredia, *The Reprieve*]. Arturo Ruiz Castillo's film *La laguna negra* [1952 *The Black Lagoon*] is based on a poem by Antonio Machado.

Classical drama also received attention with a seventh version of José Zorrilla's *Don Juan Tenorio* [1952 Alejandro Perla], a second version of Lope de Vega's *La moza del cántaro* [1954 Florián Rey, *The Girl with the Jar*], not forgetting Caderón's *El alcalde de Zalamea* [1954 José Gutiérrez Maesso, *The Mayor of Zalamea*] and, in colour, *El príncipe encadenado* [1960 Luis Lucia, *The Prince in Chains* – PNC, IN] released in the USA as *King of the Vikings* when it is in fact a version of *La vida es sueño* [*Life is a Dream*]. Antonio Román's *La fierecilla domada* [1955] is a reworking of Shakespeare's *The Taming of the Shrew* in colour and with a few surprising cuts and additions, not least only one song by Carmen Sevilla to taunt Alberto Closas who has to tame her.

César Fernández Ardavín's adaptation of *El Lazarillo de Tormes* [1959 – PNC, IN], which received a Gold Bear at the Berlin Festival, was not favoured by the Spanish public but appreciated by the establishment after, at the censors' insistence, it was purged of its satirical bite and given a new moral agenda. As in Franco's Spain the duty of all citizens was to defend the Church and not to criticise its ministers, the narrative is therefore framed by the boy Lazarillo's confession and a symbolic but effective coda beneath a Biblical tree of knowledge (?). Rightly praised for its black and white photography, the better sequences are those not in the original narrative; at times in need of extras for crowd scenes, it presents the new story as a journey between national monuments to awaken the appetite of potential tourists: it is an adaptation that responds to its decade (D'Lugo, 1997: 66–7).[47]

---

[47] As Seguin points out (p. 60 in French original [1994], and p. 49 in Spanish translation [1995]), some sequences like the hidalgo's bath will today raise surprised eyebrows. Florián Rey had filmed a silent version in 1925, and Fernán Gómez and García Sánchez made a third

The IIEC graduates

Meanwhile the National Film School continued to provide courses in unfavourable circumstances owing to lack of adequate funding; some of the lecture rooms did not even have chairs. The enthusiasm and discussions generated did not produce many professionals. Only four directors graduated in this decade: Luis G. Berlanga, José Gutiérrez Maesso, José María Zabalza (aka Joseph Trader and Harry Freeman) and Carlos Saura. Unlike Berlanga, Juan Antonio Bardem did not graduate in 1951 since he received a 'suspenso [fail]' for his final project *Barajas, aeropuerto transoceánico* [*Barajas, Transoceanic Airport*] (Cerón Gómez, 1998: 26–39). Carlos Saura was the only student to graduate in 1957, and he started teaching in the Film School. His first commission was a colour promotion documentary for the authorities of Cuenca Province in 1957 contrasting the old with the new town, a conflict that will be manifest in many films during the next decade, including his own (D'Lugo, 1991: 23–7). Of all the Spanish films I have seen his first feature, *Los golfos* is, in style and ideology, the closest to the Neorealist aesthetics described above, although such a debt is strongly denied by Saura himself (Kinder, 1993: 90–4). Inspired by press articles about a Madrid street gang, moulded by lack of funds and difficult shooting conditions, using a practically unknown cast, the film describes the gang's attempts to raise money through larceny in order to get one of them started on the road to bullfighting success, a possible metaphor for a non-existent 'physical and social mobility' (Kinder, 1993: 103). The camera work and editing, which inhibits identification or condemnation, captures a bleak vision of a deprived Madrid and its outskirts, frequently photographed metaphorically, as the context for the gang's motivation and their failure (D'Lugo, 1991: 29–42). The script offended the censors who kept sending it back for revisions, but they finally gave it a low 2B classification; as a consequence no one was willing to take on the distribution risks and the film was only released in 1961 with 10 minutes' worth of cuts (Higginbotham, 1988: 26–7). It was nonetheless sent to Cannes with *El cochecito* in 1960, the year Fellini won the Golden Palm with *La dolce vita* [*The Sweet Life*], and it received the FIPRESCI prize. Both films were produced by Pere Portabella for Films 59, had the same cinematographer Juan Julio de Baena and the same editor Pedro del Rey; according to Besas, both films may have been chosen because it was the first time the Spanish entries had been selected by film professionals rather than bureaucrats (1985: 48).

---

version in 2001 as *Lázaro de Tormes*, a rewriting that conveys the original irony of Lázaro's narrative.

Experimental cinema

Truly unusual was the experimental work of José Val del Omar in what has been labelled documentary, creating visual moving photographs, distortions and mutations frequently observed in close-up, bordering on the abstract. Much of his work has been lost but throughout the 1950s he worked on his creative *Tríptico elemental de España* [*Elemental Triptych of Spain*] evoking and recalling the natural, cultural and artistic manifestations of Spain (Sánchez, 2000: 105–6).

Buñuel's visit

The perfect film with which to conclude this decade is Buñuel's 1961 *Viridiana*, written in collaboration with Julio Alejandro, which was an artistic success like the 1928 *Un Chien andalou* and caused a cinematographic scandal as *L'Âge d'or* did in 1930–1. The history of the film is as interesting as its story. The momentum for the project started with talks when Buñuel was approached by UNINCI and Bardem filming *Sonatas* in Mexico in 1959. This was followed up with more talks at the Cannes Festival, not that same year when Buñuel's *Nazarín* picked up the international prize, but in 1960 when Buñuel's second film in English, set in the US Deep South, *The Young One*, received a special award for its treatment of racial discrimination (Buñuel, 1987: 192–3). Buñuel met with Pere Portabella and Saura, who were all very keen that he should direct a film in Spain. Buñuel himself recalls a meeting with Mexican financier Gustavo Alatriste, eager to see his wife Silvia Pinal in a film (1987: 232–8). A co-production was therefore set up by Films 59 using UNINCI's name and Alatriste providing most of the money. The censors, wanting to uphold their more liberal image and perhaps hoping to repeat Salvador Dalí's permanent return to the Dictatorship, accepted the script with a few changes: such as softening the Mother Superior's character, being more circumspect with the inclusion and framing of some religious icons, removing the suggestion of rape, and changing the ending. Filming started in February on an estate just outside Madrid, but it was a race against time when finally the reels were taken to Paris for the editing and soundtrack. In order to be complete in time for the 1961 Cannes Festival it was shown to the censors without the music. They were anxious and only approved the film by one vote, because it was expected in Cannes and international opinion was a powerful influence (Besas, 1985: 48–51). The altered ending proved even more powerful than the original (Buñuel, 1987: 237) and, as well as being denied the added irony of the soundtrack, the censors had missed the suggestion of a *ménage à trois*.

Viridiana can be read as the study of the repressive forces of extreme

Catholicism on the character of Viridiana, an orphaned novice out of her convent on her last visit to her uncle and ward Don Jaime, played by Fernando Rey (McDermott, 2000: 108–19). After his suicide she must come to terms with both the guilt she experiences and the values of her cousin, her uncle's illegitimate son Jorge [Paco Rabal] with his plan to modernise the house they have jointly inherited. If Madrid was the metaphor for a struggling Spain in Saura's film, for Buñuel it is the big gothic house, and the film can be given a strong socio-political reading as the ideologies of the two Spains, explained in chapter 3, have to cohabit (Fiddian & Evans, 1988: 60–70). Victor Fuentes detects a deeper allegorical reading suggesting how 'the great sin of fraternal hate would come to be purged and erased' (2004: 167), while both Gutiérrez Albilla and Rodríguez suggest post-Lacanian readings. The film was a triumph and won the Golden Palm. Buñuel was ill or unwilling to leave Paris to receive the prize and so the Director General de Cinematografía, José Muñoz Fontán, was only too pleased to accept the award in the name of Spanish Cinema. Two days later the Vatican press condemned the film as blasphemous and anti-Catholic. The embarrassed Ministry of Information and Tourism sacked Muñoz Fontán, ordered all copies of the film to be burnt, and UNINCI went bankrupt as this just created another problem for the struggling company. However, there was a copy in Paris, which Alatriste was able to distribute to the rest of the world as a Mexican film. It was first screened in Spain in 1977, the same year the Communist party was legalised, and only in 1982 was it recognised as a Spanish film.

Balance sheet

During the 1950s colour film slowly took over from black and white, and more cinema theatres were being built. Production increased steadily during the decade from 41 films in 1951 to 91 in 1961, peaking with 70 films and 21 co-productions.[48] The number of recorded spectators also increased throughout the decade to 370 million in both 1960 and 1961. These statistics for 1961 compare favourably with Europe's busiest film- producing nations. In 1961, 151 films were produced in the UK, a reduction on the 164 films of 1957, and attendances decreased gradually throughout the decade to 449.1 million after the recorded 1365 million in 1951, although UK ticket sales were much greater in the second half of the 1940s. In Italy 117 films and 88 co-productions were released in 1961, with 741 million spectators recorded; production had peaked there in 1954 with 144 films and 46 co-

---

[48] Using Heredero (1993: 435); all other figures are taken from Vincendeau (1995: 464 and 468), but should perhaps be taken for comparative purposes rather than for their numerical accuracy.

productions, and spectators were at their maximum in 1955 at 819.4 million. The same pattern is true for France with 69 films and 98 co-productions, and 328.4 million spectators, whereas production had peaked in 1956 with 90 films and 39 co-productions, and spectators in 1957 at 411.7 million. West Germany produced 69 films and 11 co-productions with 516.9 million spectators; production had peaked in 1955 with 120 films and 8 co-productions, and spectators' attendance was at its highest in 1956 at 817.5 million. This decrease in spectators, which continued in the sixties, is linked to the arrival of television which 'replaced cinema as the mass medium of entertainment' (Forbes, 2002: 20 and 21); this happened during the 1960s in Spain, later than in the other countries. In Spain popular taste favoured entertainment, preferably with a female singer in the lead role, as well as feel-good films where religion upholds positive national values and sentimentality, as the accompanying table demonstrates. In the historical romance ¿Dónde vas Alfonso XII? even the young queen [Paquita Rico] sings and there is a chorus of singing soldiers. Posters still give top billing to the titles and actors, rather than the directors, but it is the decade when young directors start to speak out and, to the establishment's embarrassment, to receive international attention at film festivals.

Spanish films with the longest continuous run in terms of days of exhibition in Madrid[49]

Title	Director	Year	Classification	Days of exhibiton
El último cuplé	Orduña	1957	1A / PNC	325
La violetera	Amadori	1958	1A / PNC	217
¿Dónde vas Alfonso XII?	Amadori	1958	IN / PNC	210
Marcelino, pan y vino	Vajda	1955	IN / PNC	145
Tarde de toros	Vajda	1956	IN / PNC	144
Molokai	Lucia	1959	IN / PNC	105
Historias de la radio	Sáenz de Heredia	1955	IN / PNC	91
La leona de Castilla	Orduña	1951	2	63
La fiel infantería	Lazaga	1959	1A / PNC	62
Balarrasa	Nieves Conde	1951	IN	61
Las chicas de la Cruz Roja	Salvia	1958	1A / PNC	60

49 Table from Gubern (1995: 262), who also laments the lack of accurate statistics. Some dates have been altered to reflect the date of release, as used consistently in this volume in an attempt to resolve the discrepancies found in MCU.es, IMDb and other sources.

IN = National Interest Prize; PNC = National Cinema Prize, awarded by a different body from the IN. There were other film prizes available, for instance, as from 1945 by the Círculo de Escritores Cinematográficos [CEC, Screenwriters' Circle]; as from 1951 the Fotógramas de Plata [Silver Filmstills]; the International Valladolid Film Festival [Seminci] started in 1956 and awarded prizes as from 1958.

Fray Escoba	Torrado	1961	1B / PNC	60
La señora de Fátima	Gil	1951	IN / PNC	56
Un caballero andaluz	Lucia	1954	IN / PNC	56
El ruiseñor de las cumbres	Del Amo	1958	2	56
Alba de América	Orduña	1951	IN / PNC	53
Pecado de amor	Amadori	1961	1B	53
Bienvenido míster Marshall	Berlanga	1953	IN / PNC	51
La guerra de Dios	Gil	1953	IN / PNC	51

Beyond this popular list, also deserving of attention are Ignacio F[errés] Iquino (1910–1994) and Pedro Lazaga (1918–1967), both very prolific and usually working on low budgets; even if plots, dialogues, actors, or sometimes all three fail, both directors are technically very effective in presenting their stories on the screen. José Antonio Nieves Conde (1915–2006) is interesting both for his personal agenda and technique. Edgar Neville (1899–1967) and Ladislao Vajda (1906–1965) are veterans who offer rewarding individual viewing. However, cinephiles identify the decade as belonging to the new generation of Luis G. Berlanga (b. 1921) and Juan Antonio Bardem (1922–2002) for their sharp critical assessment of Spanish society and their presence at film festivals; these were the two directors who placed Spain on the international circuit, in addition one should note Carlos Saura's (b. 1932) first film. Also critical, through their humour, are the films of the prolific actor and director Fernando Fernán Gómez (1921–2007) and the Italian Marco Ferreri (1928–1997), who was unable to spend much time in Spain.

Viewing and further general reading

Graham & Labanyi (1995) and Gies (1999) continue to provide important information and bibliographies on the social context and its consequences. On the Web there is http://www.teacuerdas.com, which contains all sorts of interesting information concerning the fifties and sixties that accompanies the very successful television series 'Cuéntame cómo pasó' [started in 2001, Agustín Crespi & Ramón Fernández, '*Tell Me How It Happened']. In Spanish, Heredero (1993) is the present reference book for the period. If accessible, Vicente Molina-Foix's *New Cinema in Spain* (1977) is the earliest book in English to cover the period but is very brief (27 pages, and 16 pages for a directory of the film directors of the period). The same is true for Caparrós Lera (1987), but there is now of course D'Lugo's *Guide* (1997), Besas (1985), Hopewell (1986: 44–64), Higginbotham (1988: 7–17, 23–49, chapters on censorship, Bardem and Berlanga); Stone is still selective (2002: 27–60); and Triana Toribio discusses the polemics behind folkloric and realist cinema (2003: 54–69). Labanyi (1997 and 2003 rpt article) and Vernon (1999: 249–55) also provide valuable analyses of folkloric musicals in this decade, and Perriam focuses on the Sarah Montiel phenomenon (2005: 89–96). Lázaro Reboll & Willis (2004) and Mira's collection of articles (2005) engage more specifically with the popular cinema. Vernon (1999: 255–60) moves on to neo-realism, to which one should add Jordan (1990: 101–15) and Jordan & Allinson's (2005) last chapter. Kinder (1993, chapters 1 and 2) engages with Neorealism, Hollywood melodrama and their mutual relationship with reference to specific films, and the convergences with Valle Inclán's *Esperpentos*. Martin-Márquez (1999a) writes on Margarita Alexandre and Ana Mariscal, see also Triana Toribio (2000), Richardson on *Surcos* (2002: 24–48), whereas P. Evans's *Auteurist Tradition* (1999) includes three contributions on films of this period, and the recently published *24 Frames* (Mira 2005) includes five. Buñuel has received a lot of attention (see chapter 2; McDermott, 2000; P. Evans, 2005, and included bibliographies). Also of recent publication is Marsh's book examining the critical implications of popular comedies (2006). As well as videos and DVDs, film scripts for films of the period are becoming available (consult the *IMDb* and search links).

The motif-index for the folkloric films suggested for the 1940s (also known pejoratively as 'españoladas' or 'de panderetas' [of tambourines]) would also be useful for the 1950s to identify their development.[50] Individual directors and numerous films are worth revisiting, because they were overlooked at the time or have acquired value-added interest with the intervening years – for example, many of the comedies contain either implicit criticism or blatantly exemplify and extol Francoist values, and the same goes for crime films whether as comedies or taken seriously. Close study of tensions within the family is also one way of examining the legacy of the Civil War on those that survived, and tried to forget. The handling and development of anti-communist rhetoric would also reveal something of the decade. As Triana Toribio phrased it, the criticism levelled at popular Spanish Cinema, whether from García Escudero's right-wing perspective or Bardem's communist views 'does not allow for any measure of agency in its public, nor the pleasures these texts gave, and certainly not for the resistant readings they might conjure up in their audience' (2003: 69).

---

[50] Terenci Moix (1993) provides a very sympathetic examination of the genre in Spanish, in an account structured around the singers themselves.

6

Opening out to Europe, the EOC and a new Cinema (1961–1969)

Tourism is a Great Invention: introducing a New Spain

The stabilisation plans of July 1959 and recognition by the International Monetary Fund would have a profound economic and social impact. By 1962 Spain was able to start negotiating entry into the European Economic Community, even if full integration was denied until June 1986. Economic migrants continued to provide ready currency for families back in Spain where tourism started to bloom, converting some coastlines into permanent construction sites, first for hotels and subsequently for second homes. This provided jobs, brought in foreign income, and thus contributed to the new affluence and a growing consumer society. All this is reflected positively in the typical musical comedy *Una chica para dos* [1966 León Klimovsky, *A Girl for Two*], about overgrown singing students focused on girls rather than their degrees or political issues, who visit tourist sites with plenty of open road in between. These are very different images of Spain from the one recalled in Peter Besas's first impressions in 1959 (1085: 69–72) and the reality presented in films that were labelled subversive. Films now include numerous panning shots of building sites and tourists, at first mature spinsters with an iconic white poodle as, for instance, in Pedro Lazaga's *Martes y trece* [1962 *Tuesday, the Thirteenth*[1]], a Portuguese co-production starring Concha Velasco and José Luis López Vázquez. Consequently wealthy characters in Carlos Saura's films prosper thanks to land speculation and property development. The promises of consumerism, ever present in Hollywood films presenting the American dream, and the actual boom did not favour everyone, and many were exploited by unscrupulous entrepreneurs. Tourism also introduced the aspirations of other European workers, who could now afford to enjoy package holidays abroad, and Spaniards could see that their economic progress was late and not bringing them political changes; Spain was still a

---

[1]   In Spain the unlucky day is Tuesday the thirteenth, and the comedy builds on the proverb 'El martes no te cases ni embarques' [on Tuesdays do not get wed or set out on a journey].

dictatorship. The government's problem was fostering economic development while not extending democratic rights, preserving its paternalistic structures, which suited men and designated women as second-class citizens by maintaining a civil law based on the interpretation of National Catholicism. The younger generation might have heard about the repression and privations of the post-war years but had not experienced the destruction and bloodshed of the Civil War; consequently, the government faced increasing social dissent from workers, students, and Basque nationalists, who all wanted a political voice taken for granted in much of the rest of Europe. During this decade the Church itself was changing and acquiring a more proletarian conscience, distancing itself from the government on some issues. All these changes and tensions had repercussions on the cinema industry, and their influence can be discerned in the films from this decade, sometimes making them opaque to those not aware of the circumstances. It was important for the Ministry of Information and Tourism [MIT] to manipulate both tourist and ideological propaganda because international reactions and opinions were important to Spain's development.

Cinema reforms

As part of the opening-out programme, the *apertura* as it was called, Gabriel Arias Salgado, the conservative minister responsible for MIT, was replaced in the summer of 1962 by the more liberal Manuel Fraga Iribarne, who remained in the post until October 1969. His remit was to present the new face of Spain to the world. He reappointed José María García Escudero as his Director General of Cinema at the JSOC; he was a genuine cinephile who had published on the subject, although perhaps mistaken in the belief that a cultural elite could change popular taste (Triana Toribio, 2003: 65–9). Some of Escudero's reforms included the reorganisation of the Board of Censors in September 1962,[2] and the much-awaited publication of the censorship norms *Normas de censura cinematogáfica* (May 1963, with minor revisions in 1965); while these finally provided some guidelines for screenwriters and directors they were still open to the censors' interpretation. García Escudero modified the funding of productions, in effect a form of state protectionism, that included credit of up to 50% for films designated of 'special interest',[3] and he encouraged co-productions, which led to the exploitation and prolifer-

---

[2] The new board had 26 members, some more liberal but with seven members of the clergy; it finally allowed the release of David Lean's *Brief Encounter* [1945], among other banned classics.

[3] 'De interés especial', which is indicated in the text as IE, although I have not yet been able to identify all the films awarded the prize and financial subsidy. PNC continues to identify

ation of westerns and horror films. He restructured the National Film School (IIEC, founded in 1947) with increased funding and gave it a new name in 1962: the Escuela Oficial de Cinematografía [EOC/Official Film School]. He revitalised the Filmoteca, founded in 1953. Following the French example he instituted box-office controls (1966). Although he never fulfilled his wish to develop a strong cinema for children, he did manage to encourage the spread of Cineclubs and *Salas de Arte y Ensayo*, Art Cinemas where foreign films, including those by Chaplin,[4] could be viewed with subtitles though still subject to the censors' cuts. Towards the end of the decade, however, those who were benefiting from the new-found affluence would be spending their weekends in Perpignan or Biarritz to view the latest films from Europe and the USA, uncensored.

Old and New Cinema

Nonetheless the popular genres, so criticised at the Salamanca talks and by García Escudero, prevailed at the box-office. Employing a commercial formula that fitted in with the censors' requirements, these films were too concerned with pleasing local tastes to be exportable. On the other hand, non-conformist voices became bolder and more frequent, promoting an ethic that prevented escapism while promoting awareness and more direct engagement with social issues (Triana Toribio, 2003: 74). Whether fed by the National Film School or not, these dissident voices soon became known as the *Nuevo Cine Español* [*NCE*/New Spanish Cinema]. Intellectually more elitist and with restricted distribution within Spain, the *NCE* was nonetheless validated at international film festivals, thus falsifying the national picture as cinephiles and intellectuals focused on this more limited production to define Spanish cinema (Triana Toribio, 2003: 81–4). Although not wishing to polarise the two trends, it is wiser to take each in turn and consider cross-references since 'both cinemas shared an obsession with Spain's image outside Spain' (Triana Toribio, 2003: 92) often sharing the same crews and actors (Faulkner, 2006: 7–24); the most explicit example of this crossover between popular and art cinema is Fernando Fernán Gómez's contribution both as actor and director. Furthermore, in the 1980s and 1990s, screenwriters and directors will return more frequently to the popular films of the sixties than to the *NCE*. The decade also experienced other marginalised independent contributions.

films receiving the *Premios Nacionales de Cinematógrafia*, established in 1940. Indirectly this marked a change from propaganda to artistic quality.

[4] His films had been banned in Spain because of his open support of the Republic during the Civil War.

Cine de barrio: popular cinema

The popular cinema, which is sometimes defined as the *Viejo* [Old] *Cine Español* because in contrast to the *NCE* it follows on from the productions of the previous decade, is usually referred to in Spain as *cine de barrio* [neighbourhood or fleapit cinema]. It tended to be shown in *palacios de pipas* [sunflower seed palaces], so-called because of the dry-salted sunflower seeds eaten before popcorn became the norm (Gómez Sierra, 2004: 92–112); one stepped into a noisy chicken-coop and walked over a carpet of discarded shells. These noisy local cinemas carried on from the previous decade, looking for new stars and ingenious plots to tell a straightforward conflict or search narrative, modified to keep up with contemporary fashions filtering into Spain. Singing actors were still preferred and songs were inserted often without warning or motivation, gradually resembling primitive pop videos with changes of clothes and spectacular settings, as well as unnatural acting and diction resulting from post-synchronisation, although at their best the narratives proceed with accomplished editing. Too frequently, especially at the end of the 1960s, supporting actresses appear to be contracted more for their looks and figure than their acting ability, overly made-up even when waking up in bed, and with 1960s' dark eye makeup, heavy eyelashes and wigs, extravagant wardrobes and hats, gradually including the rising mini-skirts to reveal as much thigh as possible, not forgetting the building sites and tourists in the frame.

Song and dances

Well-established singers appeared on screen using previous popular narratives, like Manolo Escobar who sang his way through rags-to-riches musicals directed by Ramón Torrado: *Mi canción es para tí* [1965 *My Song is for You*], *Un beso en el puerto* [1966 *A Kiss in the Harbour*], a comedy of errors with a brief history of tourism in Benidorm, and *El padre Manolo* [1966 *Father Manolo*] about a singing priest in a Father Brown investigation who raises funds for his parish, a plot repeated for Juanito Valderrama in Ramón Comas's *El padre Coplillas* [1968 *The Singing Priest*]. Singing clergy still appealed, and this same year Ramón Fernández brought them up to date with *Sor Ye-Ye* [*Sister Yeah-Yeah*]. During the next five years Manolo Escobar starred in six musicals with Concha Velasco, five of them directed by José Luis Sáenz de Heredia, including *Pero ¿en qué país vivimos?* [1967 *But what sort of a Country are we Living in?*] where the battle of the sexes and flamenco vs pop overlap with the competition between native and imported products, wine or whisky, *Relaciones casi públicas* [1968 *Almost Public Relations*], *Juicio de faldas* [1969 *A Skirt at Court*] and *Me debes un muerto*

[1971 *You Owe Me a Body]. Pedro L. Rámirez also had him singing with
Rocío Jurado in another Napoleonic resistance musical, Escobar's first film,
Los guerrilleros [1963 *The Guerrillas], not the only return to the topic
since Fernando García Vega remade for television Lola la piconera [1969
*Lola the Coalgirl] with the same Rocío Jurado. Peret was another flamenco
singer who occasionally appeared on the screen, in comedies such as Ramón
Torrado's Amor a todo gas [*Love at Top Speed], concerning a Madrid taxi
driver's relationship with a Latin American vedette, and in Antonio Román's
last and most successful film of his waning decade, El mesón del gitano
[*The Gypsy's Inn], both from 1969. The songs were what mattered most.

There were also a few more serious encounters with flamenco. Francisco
Rovira Beleta's Romeo and Juliet conflict adapted Alfredo Mañas's play,
setting it in Barcelona, Los Tarantos [1962 *The Tarantos – PNC, IE], starring Sara Lezana and Rafael Martín as the lovers as well as the dancers
Antonio Gades and Carmen Amaya in her last film. It was praised in its day
for its flamenco and implicit social message blended in with the musical
numbers. The film was nominated for an Oscar in 1964 but lost to Fellini's
8½. In 1967 Rovira Beleta filmed El amor brujo [Bewitched Love – PNC,
also nominated for an Oscar and Moscow Gold Medal], again with Antonio
Gades, who would make another adaptation of this story with Carlos Saura in
1986; there was also Antonio Román's 1949 version. In 1965 Joaquín Bollo
directed more duelling families in Gitana [*Gipsy] with a plot and choreography that echoes West Side Story [1961 Jerome Robbins & Robert Wise],
reconfirming the national taste for music and spectacle. In 1966 Ana Mariscal
produced, scripted and directed Los duendes de Andalucía [The Splendour of
Andalusia], and appeared the following year under her own direction with the
singer Massiel in Vestida de novia [1967 *Dressed as a Bride].

Marisol

Joselito, his youth over, acted in his last film in 1969, Prisionero en la
ciudad [Antonio de Jaén, *Prisoner in the City]; having made his eighth
with Antonio del Amo El secreto de Tomy [1963 *Tommy's Secret] in which
he becomes a jockey, La vida nueva de Pedrito de Andía [1965 Rafael Gil,
*Pedrito de Andia's New Life], with a strong evocation of the Basque coun-
tryside,[5] and Loca juventud [1967 Manuel Mur Oti, *Crazy Youth]. Luis
Lucia was contracted to direct a new child star: Josefa Flores González,
better known as Marisol (b. 1948), 'who refracted in her all-singing, all-

---

[5]   The author of the original novel, Rafael Sánchez Mazas, is the subject of David Trueba's
film Soldados de Salamina [2003 Soldiers of Salamina], based on the novel of the same name
by Javier Cercas.

dancing, all-talking vivacity the hectic expression of a nation's sham illusion of utopian festivity' (P. Evans 2004b: 129). Originally from Málaga, she was spotted by the producer Manuel J. Goyanes's daughter as a talented eleven-year-old in a television competition; blonde and blue-eyed, equally at ease with flamenco or the latest pop song, *yeyé* or *dúa-dúa* as they were called. Lucia directed her as a wilful and charming child in *Un rayo de luz* [1960 **A Ray of Light*], full of life and winning the heart of a grumpy old grandfather after her father's death in an aeroplane crash. In *Ha llegado un ángel* [1961 **An Angel has Arrived*] she is a recent orphan who goes to Madrid to her nearest relatives whom she reforms with her songs, kind heart, old-fashioned country values and the help of the maid Herminia [Isabel Garcés].[6] This was promptly followed by *Tómbola* [1962 **Lottery*], a vehicle for her energy and songs based on her constructed public persona, all optimism and feel-good escapism. Fernando Palacios took her over for *Marisol rumbo a Río* [1963 **Marisol Goes to Río*], where she plays contrasting identical twins, and then in *Búsqueme a esta chica* [1964 *Find That Girl*] she impresses the tourists with her busking as she become a desirable adolescent sought after by an American impresario on the Costa; the film enlisted the participation of the pop group el Dúo Dinámico. In *La nueva Cenicienta* [1964 George Sherman, *The New Cinderella*] both the flamenco dancer and the American singer seek her. This was followed, among other films, by *Cabriola* [1965 Mel Ferrer, *Every Day is a Holiday*]. These films were heavily influenced by Hollywood musical mise-en-scène but produced on much lower budgets, reflecting Spain's economic rapprochement with the USA as much as the public demand for foreign films. Marisol's films were backed by successful record sales and careful marketing of her wholesome cheerful image, which was projected through her films, in commercials and even a fan magazine. As a seductive adolescent with a clean image she starred in two more Lucia films. *Las cuatro bodas de Marisol* [1967 **Marisol's Four Weddings*], is a convoluted episodic narrative involving a Scottish laird, a bullfighter, a 'médecin sans frontières', and a US film director, all to showcase her versatile singing. In *Solos los dos* [1968 **Both Alone*] she is the pop idol who flirts with the real bullfighter, Sebastián Palomo Linares.

Although her early films are inscribed in a conservative ideology where Marisol ingenuously resolves different problems, by the 1970s she had rebelled against the marketing of her personal image, which had culminated in many personal problems for the young actress. Recovering her real name, Pepa Flores, she moved radically to the left with her politics, starring in two psychological thrillers directed by Juan Antonio Bardem, *La corrupción de*

---

6   Isabel Garcés (1901–1981) came late to the cinema at 58, playing similar roles as Rafaela Aparicio. She was cast in five of Marisol's films, and three with Rocío Dúrcal (consulting the *IMDb* is the quickest way to make the links).

Chris Miller [1973 *The Corruption of Chris Miller*] with Jean Seberg, and as the *femme fatale* appropriately named Juna (Janus), braless and with different dark wigs, in *El poder del deseo* [1975 *The Power of Desire*]. As with many other Bardem films, this last contained too many social comments, both in dialogues and mise-en-scène, to please the spectators. In 1978 she appeared in Mario Camus's *Los días del pasado* [*The Days of the Past*] about the *maquis* in 1940s' Spain, and also participated in Carlos Saura's *Bodas de sangre* [1981 *Blood Wedding*] and *Carmen* [1983].

Other child stars

Marisol's early commercial success had put the pressure on to find further youthful singing talent such as the tamer and older twins Pili and Mili, Pilar and Aurora/Emilia Bayona Sarriá (b. 1947), who made seventeen films between 1964 and 1972. They started in 1964 with Perojo Productions, directed by Luis César Amadori's *Como dos gotas de agua* [*Like Peas in a Pod*], then in 1965 Pedro Lazaga directed them in *Dos chicas locas locas* [*Two Mad Mad Girls*] and Fernando Palacios in *Whisky y Vodka* [*Whisky and Vodka*]. The following year they appeared in a musical western *Dos pistolas gemelas* [1966 Rafael Romero Marchent, *Sharp-Shooting Twin Sisters*], a sub-genre that had a brief vogue. In 1970 they made one film together in Mexico; Mili stopped acting and settled there, while Pili made a few more films before returning to Spain where she has carried on acting. There was also Rocío Dúrcal, aka María de los Ángeles de las Heras Ortiz (b. 1944), who also acted in her first two films with Lucia in 1962, *Canción de juventud* [*Song of Youth*] and in 1963 as the orphan in *Rocío de la Mancha* [*Rocío, the Dewdrop of La Mancha*]. *Tengo diecisiete años* [1964 José María Forqué, *I am Seventeen*] is a Christmas musical fantasy with echoes of Snow White, which she followed with *La chica del trébol* [1964 Sergio Grieco, *The Clover-Leaf Girl*], which presents social contrasts and where the Cinderella character makes her final choice singing 'Los piropos de mi barrio' [The flirtatious wisecracks of my neighbourhood / are more sincere...]. She starred in another eleven films through to 1972, including a remake of Delgrás's 1943 *Cristina Guzmán* [1968] with Amadori, where she plays twin sisters Cristina and Mara with very different personalities, as suggested by the contrasting blue and red screens of the credit sequence, which are then followed by a building site in the background. She also starred in the second Spanish version of Galdós's *Marianela* [1972] directed by Angelino Fons. Luis Lucia also directed Ana Belén's film debut, *Zampo y yo* [1965 *Zampo and Me* – PNC], distributed by Perojo Productions and starring Fernando Rey as the eponymous clown, the narrative again presents a young girl without a mother, this time at odds with her wealthy father because she wants to join the circus. Ana Belén's acting career started in earnest in 1971 with Roberto Bodegas's socially engaged *Españolas en París* [*Spaniards in Paris* – PNC].

More musicals

Established pop singers such as the Dúo Dinámico (Ramón Arcusa and Manuel de la Calva) were also recruited. With their guitars they appeared in another remake of *Botón de ancla* [1961 Miguel Lluch], then *Escala en Tenerife* [1964 León Klimovsky, **Stopover in Tenerife*], and helped out Marisol in *Búsqueme a esta chica*, concluding with Klimovsky's *Una chica para dos* in 1966.[7] Raphael was another pop-idol brought to the screen three times from 1966 to 1969 by Mario Camus, recently graduated from the Film School: *Cuando tú no estás* [1966 **When You Are Not Here*], *Al ponerse el sol* [1967 **At Sunset*], and *Digan lo que digan* [1968 *Let Them Talk*]. Raphael was then contracted by Vicente Escrivá who exploited his clean-cut image to make three clergy films in two years. The pop star then left the cinema until his 1973 *Volveré a nacer* [Javier Aguirre, **I Will Be Born Again*]. He subsequently made two television series in 1978 and 1980, and one last film in Argentina in 1981. One of the surprises of the decade, dismissed by public and critics, was the musical comedy in full colour, *Diferente* [1962 *Different*], ascribed to Luis María Delgado, but mostly the work of the Argentine dancer Alfredo Alaria; a surprising homosexual apology, it was passed by the censor's office but suffered in the National-Catholic press.

There were occasional nostalgic *zarzuela* remakes, such as *La revoltosa*, of which two versions were made during the decade, in 1963 by José Díaz Morales and in 1969 for Spanish television by Juan de Orduña. In fact Spanish television commissioned a number of *zarzuelas* during the decade, thirteen by Orduña. The most successful remake was Sáenz de Heredia's 1963 *La verbena de la paloma* [PNC] with Vicente Parra, Concha Velasco, and Miguel Ligero still playing Don Hilarión, produced by Benito Perojo who was very active throughout this decade. The credit and final sequences frame the film in the modern city, suggesting that the love of the genre is part of the essence of Madrid.[8]

Rafael Gil was recycling old genres and themes like *Currito de la Cruz* [1965 *Currito of the Cross*], the fourth remake of the rivalry between two bullfighters for bulls and a woman [Soledad Miranda, Paco Rabal and Manuel Caño 'El Pireo'], or *Sangre en el ruedo* [1969 **Blood in the Bullring*],

---

[7] Pedro Almodóvar's *Átame* [1990 *Tie Me Up!*] concludes with the protagonists singing one of the Dúo's songs 'Resistiré'.

[8] *La revoltosa* was first filmed by Florián Rey in 1929; *La verbena ...* was first directed in 1921 by José Buchs and then in 1934 by Benito Perojo.

Camino del rocío [1966 **The Path of the Rocío Pilgrimage*] this time with
Carmen Sevilla and Paco Rabal opposite the *señorito*, Arturo Fernández. The
following year he made *La mujer de otro* [1967 **Another's Wife* – PNC] where
the ideal Franco family is reconstructed when on the verge of disaster.

Popular comedies: Pedro Lazaga (1918–1979)

Comedies abounded, and it is difficult to know how to present and organise
them; whether classified by directors, screenwriters, actors, themes or
producers, generalisations can be made but complications are encountered.
Directors developed their own style and varied the issues they presented,
and were one criterion for the spectators to choose between films or not
go to the cinema. Pedro Lazaga, with 94 titles from 1948 to 1978, not all
comedies, directed an average of four films a year throughout the decade. His
big successes came in collaboration with José Luis Dibildos in the 1950s and
early 1960s, and then with Pedro Masó and Vincente Coello from 1966 to
1970, using the same range of actors and supporting comedians. With hindsight these comedies have gained value because they captured the obsessions
of the average spectators and the tensions of the time, albeit resolving them
in a conservative ending. The position of women in society and the perceived
sexual limitations of the males, employment and financial difficulties, rural
migration, the relationship between the repressed and backward provincial
attitudes and the city's growing affluence and consumerism, all invite analyses of the influence on traditional social aspirations of the values of the more
prosperous tourists visiting Spain. Lazaga presented topical subjects from
family situations and generational conflicts usually resolved with a patriarchal blessing, such as *¿Qué hacemos con los hijos?* [1967 **What shall we do
with the Children?* – PNC], or *El padre de la criatura* [1972 **The Father
of the Child*], where the grandfather finds out his wife is pregnant again
and not his married daughter. In *Operación Plus Ultra* [1966 **Mission Over
and Beyond*[9]] Alberto Closas acts as the *paterfamilias* who takes a group
of special children to Rome to see the Pope. Social issues are raised in *Las
secretarias* [1969 **The Secretaries*] starring Sonia Bruno, Teresa Gimpera,
Mari Francis, Mari Carrillo and Rafaela Aparicio, which highlights through
its humour the employment anomalies endured by women while indulging
some male viewers with close-ups of secretarial knees; in *Los tramposos*
[1959 **The Tricksters*] or *El turismo es un gran invento* [1968 **Tourism is
a Great Invention*], both films exploit the growing importance of tourism to

---

[9]   'Plus Ultra' was Charles V's personal motto, and used during the Dictatorship to consolidate the link with the Imperial past.

the economy and the need to make money fast. *El dinero tiene miedo* [1970 **Money is Afraid*] is another comedy about small-time confidence tricksters. As the sexual revolution moved on apace north of the Pyrenees so Lazaga became bolder, even if the censors saw to it that by today's standards the films seem amusing rather than sexy and certainly not explicit:[10] *¿Por qué pecamos a los cuarenta?* [1969 **Why do we Sin at Forty?*], a significant title since it clearly indicates the ethical premise on which these films are based, or the failed bedroom farce and comeback for Sara Montiel, *Cinco almohadas para una noche* [1974 **Five Pillows for the Night*]. Each year comedies became gradually more provocative by showing more flesh, but not as much as their advertising posters would suggest. The situation most frequently presented was that of sex-obsessed males who, while avoiding marriage, fantasise that they are everything a woman desires. Since a serious or visual treatment of the subject would be censored, it was more a question of constantly alluding to sex in the context of a musical or a comedy, only suggesting what was denied and prohibited, if need be punishing its consequences or, more frequently, reinserting sex behind the closed door of the conjugal bedroom (Triana Toribio, 2003: 98–9). 'If sex were to be practised it was best for the actress to be foreign, have a foreign name, or play a foreigner"'(Hopewell, 1986: 47). True to this statement, the first bikini in a Spanish film appeared in Juan Bosch's 1962 comedy, *Bahía de Palma* [*Palma Bay*], worn by German Elke Sommer who played opposite Arturo Fernández. The opening sequence of *¿Por qué pecamos...?* captures the consequence of sexual repression as men ogle female knees below mini-dresses as the camera follows their limited and fixated gaze, whereas *Cinco almohadas...* focuses on the bedroom and Sara Montiel's scanty nightdresses, but after due titillation all tension is resolved in harmony with the official repressive attitudes to sex.

Popular comedies: parodies

In those years when big-budget 007 films were so popular, Spanish comedies, unable to compete, went for parodies like Mariano Ozores's *Operación Cabaretera* [1967 **Mission Cabaret*] with the unlikely López Vázquez and Gracita Morales, or Fernando Merino's two 1968 farces, both starring Tony Leblanc, Alfredo Landa and Manolo Gómez Bur: *La dinamita está servida* [**The Dynamite is Served*], and *Los subdesarrollados* [1968 **The Underdeveloped*] about the 'International *Investigación Espanish* Section' and its two

---

10 The same is true of the *Carry On* films, which flourished in the UK during this decade, the first being Gerald Thomas's *Carry On Sergeant* in 1958, and continuing up to the 1991 revival of *Carry on Columbus*. This was not exportable comedy, but reflects much of its time.

incompetent detectives who specialise in conjugal separations. José María Forqué, known for his police thrillers, also used the bank heist in a comic mode. Among the most successful were *Atraco a las tres* [1962 *Hold-Up at Three*], a low- budget film written by Masó and Coello, now considered a classic about the dehumanising dangers of modernisation.[11] In a similar vein is Juan G[arcía] Atienza's only feature film, *Los dinamiteros* [1962, *The Dynamiters*], where the robbers are three septuagenarians played by the irreplaceable José Isbert, the Mexican Sara García and Italian Carlo Pisacane, a film that unfortunately was not appreciated at the time of its release in 1964. Forqué's comedies also took up other topics: the contrast of provincial and Madrid values in *Maribel y la extraña familia* [1960 *Maribel and the Strange Family*]; or the contrast of Spanish and foreign attitudes in *Vacaciones para Ivette* [1964 *A Holiday for Yvette* – PNC] in which a Madrid family arranges a summer exchange for their son Andrés and young Pierre Bernard from Paris, but older sister Yvette turns up instead of the expected Pierre, and once again the foreigner is the temptress. *Un millón en la basura* [1967 *A Million in the Bin*] hinges on whether virtue and honesty will prevail and be rewarded when at Christmas time a night street-sweeper finds a million pesetas in a bin. *Las que tienen que servir* [1967 *Those who have to Serve*] is a farce that uses stereotypes and a Tati-esque mise-en-scène to explore the impact of the social and gender relationships generated between Spaniards and Americans around the US air bases, in this case Torrejón located near Madrid. The clergy and military films are not spared as in *Sor Citroen* [1967 Lazaga, *Sister Citroen*] accident-prone Sister Tomasa [Gracita Morales], with the grudging help of Sister Rafaela [Rafaela Aparicio], finally obtains her licence to drive the orphanage's 2CV. In *Los guardiamarinas* [1966 Lazaga, *The Naval Cadets* – PNC], a patriotic comedy like *El marino de los puños de oro* [1968 Rafael Gil, *The Sailor with Golden Fists*] the Spanish navy comes off better than its boxing champion, in line with *Botón de ancla*. There were farces such as *Las siete vidas del gato* [1970 Lazaga, *The Cat's Seven Lives*], a 'sexy' treatment of the Old Dark House motif. Pedro Masó produced and wrote many of these scripts,[12] although he only started directing in 1971 with *Las Ibéricas FC* [1971] about a women's football team.

Popular comedies: actors

These films tended to use the same actors, because they were popular. Some names, like Lina Morgan, Paco Martínez Soria and Alfredo Landa, are still

[11] Eva Lesmes's *El palo* [2001, *The Hold-Up*] is a clever and enjoyable reworking of the story with female protagonists.

[12] At the beginning of 2004 the *IMDb* listed 64 film-scripts, 38 productions and the personal direction of 20 films. Vicente Coello was his co-writer for many of these.

used as generic markers to identify comedies. Others, like Concha Velasco, Gracita Morales, Rafaela Aparicio, Isabel Garcés, Julia Gutiérrez Caba, María Isbert, Florinda Chico, Laura Valenzuela, Amparo Soler Leal, Laly Soldevila, José Isbert, Tony Leblanc, José Luis López Vázquez, Manolo Morán, Antonio Ozores, Juanjo Menéndez, José Sazatornil, Manolo Gómez Bur, Luis Ciges, Manuel Alexandre, Ángel de Andrés, Xan das Bolas, Casto Sendra 'Cassen' and many more were very effective in supporting roles, some without ever getting a main part. This is how José Sacristán started in 1965, as the failed student in Fernando Palacios's *La familia y uno más* [1965 *The Family Plus One*].

This was one of two sequels to Palacios's very successful *La gran familia* [1962 *The Big Family* – PNC], ideal for Christmas viewing: fifteen children, one living-in grandfather, one paternal salary and an even more overworked mother, an excess implicitly critical of government policy (Faulkner, 2006: 27–48). The film focuses on nicely observed activities (morning wash, meal times, playing with grandfather, watching the neighbour's television, going to bed) and situations (first communion, school results, holiday by the sea, child getting lost). The two sequels, *La familia y uno más*, without the mother or the grandfather[13] and, fourteen years later directed by Pedro Masó himself, *La familia bien, gracias* [1979 *The Family's Fine, Thanks*] the same actors reappear, Alberto Closas as the father and José Luis López Vázquez as the godfather to present a cynical view of changed family values through a bitter-sweet comedy (P. Evans, 2000: 77–88). All three films were scripted and produced by Pedro Masó. López Vázquez (b. 1922), who started his career in 1946 and was still filming in 2007, is credited in 240 films and is a recurrent face in these comedies.

Lina Morgan, aka María de los Ángeles López Segovia, was not so prolific, because she was and is just as interested in theatre, variety shows and television, enjoying her live audiences. In cinema she started in 1961 with *El pobre García* [*Poor García*] directed by Tony Leblanc,[14] and with stuttering Antonio Ozores in *Vampiresas 1930*, a comedy-musical-thriller full

---

[13] Amparo Soler Leal turned down the contract to star in *La familia y uno más*, and José Isbert had died. Fernando Palacios, not yet fifty, died shortly after completing the second film.

[14] Leblanc only directed three films, all in 1961–2, which he also co-scripted and in which he acted. He is mostly remembered paired off with Concha Velasco. He stopped acting in 1975 with *Tres suecas para tres Rodríguez* [Lazaga, *Three Swedish Girls for three Rodríguez*] – a Rodríguez was the name given to those fathers who stayed in Madrid whilst their family went away on holiday to the beach or mountain; readers could view *Cuarenta grados a la sombra* [1967 Mariano Ozores, *Forty Degrees in the Shade*] about three husbands and their summer adventures. Tony Leblanc returned to the screen in 1998 to take part in Santiago Segura's *Torrente, el brazo tonto de la ley* [*Torrente, the Stupid Arm of the Law*] and its two sequels, as well as the popular television series *Cuéntame cómo pasó*.

of surprises in which she steals the show from Mikaela [Wood]. Directed by
Jesús Franco, with an impressive jazz soundtrack, *Vampiresas* presents struggling musicians and film extras in Paris and Cannes in 1930 when the talkies
arrive (joke: the Charles Trenet numbers included are all from the late 1930s).
Visually it reveals Franco's passion for and knowledge of Hollywood cinema.
Lina Morgan sings, dances and is an accomplished gymnast usually taking
on the persona of the golden-hearted fool, as in the nostalgic remake of the
1939 *La tonta del bote* [1970 Juan de Orduña, **The Total Idiot*; the 'bote' is
an empty red capsicum pepper tin in which the orphan collects cigarette ends
for her friend the blind man!] or the clever girl who pretends to be inept in
Mariano Ozores's musical *Dos chicas de revistas* [1972, **Two Chorus Line
Girls*]. Her *Soltera y madre en la vida* [1969 Javier Aguirre, *Unmarried and
Mother in Life*[15]] also starring Alfredo Landa and José Sacristán, was an 18-
rated comedy, presumably because of the situation since, physically, there is
only one kiss on the forehead exchanged on the screen and the couple get
married at the end.

Paco Martínez Soria, who acted in his first film in 1934, excelled on stage
and screen in the part of the *paleto*, the country bumpkin who realises that *La
ciudad no es para mí* [1966 *City Life is not for Me*]. He also starred in *Abuelo
made in Spain* [1969 *Old Man Made in Spain*], and in *El abuelo tiene un plan*
[1973 **Grandpa has a Plan*], all three directed by Pedro Lazaga, the first two
written and produced by Pedro Masó and the third by Mariano Ozores, each
dealing with traditional family values challenged by the expanding urban
consumerism and modernisation; they were 'far from innocent comedies'
(Richardson, 2002: 71–86, 85). Faulkner views the first as 'civilising women'
and 'above all concerned with the control of female sexuality' (2006: 66 and
68).

Popular comedies: productions

All these comedies were produced and distributed with alacrity as crews
worked on more than one film at a time. In 1968, for instance, Javier Aguirre
directed the gangster comedy *Los que tocan el piano* [*They who Play the
Piano*[16]] and *Una vez al año, ser hippy no hace daño* [**Once a Year, Being
a Hippy Is Not Harmful*]. Both were written by Dibildos and starred Tony
Leblanc, Concha Velasco, Alfredo Landa, Manolo Gómez Bur and José Saza-

---

[15] 'En la vida' is actually an idiom meaning 'Never/Not on your life'. Readers are reminded
that an asterisk indicates my own translation; whenever possible the international title given on
the *IMDb* is used to facilitate cross-reference on the website even if the translation is at times
far too literal.

[16] In context 'playing the piano' means having served time in prison.

tornil among others, and were edited by Petra de Nieva, with cinematography by Manuel Rojas, sets by Adolfo Cofiño, and music by Adolfo Waitzman; in fact practically the same crew was involved in both films. One comedy that encapsulates many of these characteristics is the very successful *Abuelo made in Spain*, made in 1969 when Masó scripted seven more films and produced four of them; Lazaga directed six of these films and García Abril composed the music for all six as well as for five more films. Marcelino [Paco Martínez Soria] is the *abuelo* whose three daughters have all left the village for the city, to find a job and a husband. Unexpectedly, the eldest asks him to help out and mind his grandchildren. He arrives in Madrid, with the obligatory suitcase and animal, to find there is no longer any family solidarity among his daughters, and that the grandchildren are being brought up without care, with all the perceived vices of the modern consumer society and foreign influences encapsulated by the bilingual title. He sets out to restore traditional values, accompanied by the expected pop group formed by some of his grandchildren, Los Gritos [The Screams].

More serious concerns

Not all the so-called *VCE* was laughter, song and dance. Some directors explored issues with more gravity and in greater depth, although these films tended not to be great successes at the box-office. Employment difficulties and economic migration, not forgetting sexual repression and double standards, are approached as a harsh and difficult reality in Jesús Fernández Santos's *Llegar a más* [1964 *To Move On*], his only feature film as he was usually engaged with documentaries and in writing novels. These issues are also present in Pere Balañá's *El último sábado* [1965 *The Last Saturday*] and Josep Maria Forn's *La piel quemada* [1965, released 1967 *Burnt Skin*], set in Lloret del Mar. Forn's film presents one day in the life of José [Antonio Iranzo] awaiting his family's arrival from Andalusia; flashback and parallel montage recall their tribulations and the journey, starting with a powerful sequence contrasting bikinis on the beach with labourers on building sites. It is an early example that interrogates Catalan identity and migrant labour during the Franco dictatorship, including some Catalan dialogues as well as an ex-Republican soldier (D'Lugo, 2002: 167–8). Forn's next film, *La respuesta* [*The Response*], also addressed Catalan identity and student demonstrations; although completed in 1969 it was not allowed a release until October 1975 (Besas, 1985: 86–7). A similar attempt to foster Catalan consciousness was Armando Moreno's melodrama *María Rosa* [PNC], an adaptation of an Angel Guimerà novel, starring Nuria Espert and Paco Rabal. Made in 1964, it was released the following year, and a dubbed Catalan version was distributed in 1966. Presenting Basque identity, and also with references to labour migrations, is the 103-minute documentary *Ama lur* [1968 *Tierra Madre/ *Mother Earth*]. Praised for Pedro del Rey's editing, which was subsequently censored, it was funded by public subscriptions raised by Néstor Basterretxea and Fernando Larruquert after their initiation with three short documentaries including *Pelotari* [1964 **The Pelota Players*] (Stone, 2002: 136–7).

The Civil War sometimes resurfaces as in Lazaga's *Posición avanzada* [1965 **Forward Position* – PNC], or as the experience of children evacuated to Belgium during the Nationalist siege of Bilbao in *El otro árbol de Guernica* [1969 **The Other Guernica Tree*] based on Luis de Castresana's novel published in 1967, as well as novelist and screenwriter Rafael García Serrano's only attempt at direction *Los ojos perdidos* [1967 *Lost Eyes* – PNC]. These are films that mention the importance of reconciliation but on Nationalist terms within the dominant ideology. To celebrate the official '25 Years of Peace' under the dictatorship, Sáenz de Heredia was entrusted with the biographical documentary *Franco: ese hombre* [1964 **Franco, The Man* – PNC],[17] to which one could add Santos Alcocer's negative presentation of the Republic in *Las últimas horas* [1966 **The Last Hours*].[18] Mariano Ozores, who worked on Heredia's documentary, made *Morir en España* [1965 *To Die in Spain* – PNC] perhaps as an official reply to Frédéric Rossif's pro-Republican *Mourir à Madrid* [1963 *To Die in Madrid*].

Thrillers and suspense

It was difficult to compete with imported crime and *noir*, even when censored, and national production declined in popularity, stifled by censorship. Even Iquino turned his attention to other genres like the western, but some were still being made such as Forqué's *Accidente 703* [1962 **Accident 703*], Francisco Pérez Dolz's *A tiro limpio* [1963 **A Clean Shooting*[19]], not missing out on lessons learnt from Hollywood, Antonio Santillán's *Senda torcida* [1963 **Twisted Path*], Nieves Conde's *El diablo también llora* [1963 **The Devil also Weeps*], Julio Buchs's *El salario del crimen* [1964 **The Wages of Crime*], Ramón Fernández's *Rueda de sospechosos* [1964 **Line-up of Suspects*] or Lazaga's *El rostro del asesino* [1965 **The Murderer's Face*]. The prolific and always surprising Jesús Franco attracted attention with both *La muerte silba un blues* [1963 **Death Whistles the Blues*] and *Rififí en la ciudad* [1964

---

[17] It has a very positive commentary on the *IMDb*. Faulkner's analysis of the film within the framework of Saura's *La caza* [1966 *The Hunt*] reveals some of its rhetoric (2006: 158–9).

[18] Santos Alcocer produced nine films between 1953 and 1969, scripting eight as from 1958, and directing six from 1959.

[19] Remade in 1996 by Jesús Mora, and relocated in the Canaries.

*Trouble in the City]. It is a tale of political corruption, sex and drugs, set in an undetermined Latin American country at the request of the censors. Accompanied by an excellent musical soundtrack, it has been described as a cinematographic homage to Orson Welles (Andrés Peláez Paz in Pérez Perucha, 1997: 543–5). Julio Coll also developed spy and narcotics plots with *Comando de asesinos* [1966 *High Season for Spies*] or *Persecución hasta Valencia* [1968 *The Narco Men*]. His *Fuego* [1964 *Fire*] is a thriller about a husband taking revenge on the mistress who destroyed his family. Another psychological intrigue is Eugenio Martín's series of murders, which begins with a ventriloquist, *Hipnosis* [1962 *Hypnosis*]. In the wake of the early James Bond, Antonio Isasi-Isasmendi directed *Estambul 65* [1965 *Istanbul 65*], and his *Las Vegas, 500 millones* [1968 *Our Man in Las Vegas* –PNC] was a vast co-production between Spain, France, Italy and West Germany, starring a cohort of international actors headed by Jean Servais from both Jules Dassin's 1955 and Jesús Franco's very different 1964 *Rififí* with Fernán Gómez as the suspended and honest policeman.

Literary adaptations

In contrast to contemporary novels, which formed the plot of many film narratives (Deveny, 1999), literary adaptations still only made a limited appearance on Spanish screens in the 1960s (Faulkner, 2004a), although they would inspire some of the new graduates of the EOC as a means of examining Spanish reality. The first of Miguel Delibes's novels, written in 1950, brought to the screen was *El camino* [1963 *The Journey*], with village life as seen by the boy Daniel 'el Mochuelo' [José Antonio Mejías's only screen appearance]. It was adapted with gentle humour, directed and produced by Ana Mariscal, again with her husband Valentín Javier. Martin-Márquez points out that the film takes advantage of one minor event in the novel to develop an extended comment on censorship, just as Mariscal's *Segundo López* had reflected on the cinematic illusion (1999a: 131–7). Unfortunately, the film passed by unnoticed at the time.

In 1963 Escrivá directed a remake of Gaston Baty's play *Dulcinea* [*A Girl from La Mancha* – PNC, IE], the title role played by Millie Perkins, developing situations from *Don Quixote* using Aldonza's perspective. In keeping with his earlier productions it is steeped in scriptural references, and was effectively photographed in strong foreboding black and white contrasts by Godofredo Pacheco, who went on to make numerous westerns and horror films. César F. Ardavín directed a version of the fifteenth-century masterpiece *La Celestina* [1969 *The Wanton of Spain* – PNC], to be remade more successfully in 1996 by Gerardo Vera. Ercilla's sixteenth-century epic poem *La Araucana*, on the arrival of the Conquistadors in Chile, was adapted in 1971 by Julio

Coll into a cowboy and Indian tale of wrath. Benito Pérez Galdós, an author proscribed in the early years of the regime for his liberal and anti-clerical views, was now adapted for the screen in 1970 with Buñuel's *Tristana* [PNC] and Angelino Fons *Fortunata y Jacinta* [PNC] followed in 1972 by *Marianela* (see *NCE* below, pp. 181–2, 188).

Foreign investment

Important for the home cinema industry was the fact that after Robert Rossen filmed *Alexander the Great* [1955] in Spain other foreign producers followed to take advantage of the economic situation in order to reduce the growing costs of fashionable sandal epics. These productions included part of Orson Welles's *Mr Arkadin* [1955] as well as his *Chimes at Midnight* [1966 – Cannes]. His lifelong project of adapting *Don Quixote* was not realised, until his widow asked Jesús Franco to edit the reels in her possession; this was released in 1992 as *Don Quijote de Orson Welles*.[20] If Spain may have been the obvious location for *The Pride and the Passion* [1957 Stanley Kramer], it was a financial decision in the case of *Solomon and Sheba* [1959 King Vidor]. This generated employment and experience. Eduardo G. Maroto, for instance, found new, and appreciated, engagements as Spanish production manager. Welles specifically requested Jesús Franco's technical participation, and Fernando Rey, José Nieto and other actors were also contracted for his *Chimes*. Many Spaniards looked for employment in these foreign productions, as captured in the plot of Lazaga's nostalgic comedy *Vente a ligar al oeste* [1972 *Get Your Girl Out West*] where Alfredo Landa plays a railway pointsman, Benito, dreaming of fame, money and women on the film sets of Almería, or the more recent *Bala perdida* [2003 Pau Martínez, *Lost Bullet*]. These foreign productions fuelled Samuel Bronston's ambition to establish Spanish studios to rival Hollywood as discussed by Peter Besas (1985: 53–67). Among the Bronston productions are John Farrow's *John Paul Jones* [1959], Nicholas Ray's *King of Kings* [1961] and *55 Days at Peking* [1963],[21] or Anthony Mann's *El Cid* [1961], which was partly motivated to flatter the regime and earn its support. However, the financial failure of Mann's *Fall of*

---

[20] The *IMDb* states that not all the material available was used by Franco and that more reels may exist in private collections. A parallel fate happened to Terry Gilliam when he ran out of funds for his adaptation of the novel, although Keith Fulton and Louis Pepe who were filming for 'The Making of…' made a fascinating documentary of the failure, released in 2002 as *Lost in La Mancha*.

[21] Jacinto Molina, aka Paul Naschi/y, Paul MacKey, James Molin, David Molva etc. (*IMDb*), was an extra in these two films and then moved on. Now a cult figure, he has to date scripted 34 films, directed 13, acted in 85, and earned himself the reputation of the Spanish Werewolf. Carmen Sevilla was cast as Mary Magdalene in *King of Kings*.

the Roman Empire [1964] followed by Henry Hathaway's disastrous *Circus World* [1964] put an end to Bronston's super-productions and his dream of filming *Isabella of Spain*. Nonetheless some foreign productions carried on for a while, and not just because the studios were bought by 20th Century Fox.

Spaghetti and chorizo

Just as Sergio Leone moved from historical sandal epics to establish himself with his own kind of westerns, so the Spanish film industry accommodated itself to film spaghetti westerns that used local crews and extras. After Michael Carreras's *The Savage Guns* [1962 *Tierra brutal*], starring Paquita Rico opposite Richard Basehart, including Fernando Rey and José Nieto, there flourished an autochthonous version referred to as *chorizo* westerns, named after the now ubiquitous Spanish sausage. These were filmed on the sets of Almería, of Torrejón near Madrid, and also in Esplugas, Catalonia, with Alfonso Balcázar and his brother Jaime. According to Casimiro Torreiro, 168 westerns were made between 1962 and 1969 (Gubern, 1995: 334), mostly Hispano-Italian co-productions, with important or waning Hollywood stars cast in the main parts.

Joaquín Romero Marchent had already established a precedent in 1955 and 1956 with his *El Coyote* and the sequel *La justicia del Coyote* [*The Judgment of the Coyote*], using the popular comic-strip character created by José Mallorquí.[22] In 1962 and 1963 he returned with two Zorro films, directing eleven westerns between 1962 and 1965, including *El sabor de la venganza* [1963 *Gunfight at High Noon* – PNC] or *Antes llega la muerte* [1964 *Hour of Death*], which focuses on relationships and the challenge of getting the heroine to a doctor in time. Often under pseudonyms,[23] established directors produced, directed and scripted westerns, such as Iquino's *Oeste Nevada Joe* [1964 *Joe Dexter*] or *Cinco pistolas de Texas* [1967 *Five Dollars for Ringo*]. Ramón Torrado, signing some of his westerns as Raymond Torrad, joined in with titles like *Bienvenido padre Murray* [1964 *Black Angel of the Mississippi*] or *Los cuatreros* [1965 *Shoot to Kill*]. Even Antonio del Amo participated with *El hijo de Jesse James* [1965 *Son of Jesse James*], and Antonio Román's penultimate film was about a milk-drinking, chess-playing, gun-for-hire contracted to protect the ranchers, *Ringo de Nebraska* [1966 *Savage Gringo*], played by Ken Clark. This Italian co-production ran into financial difficulties and it is said that Mario Brava took over the direction; conse-

---

[22] In 1998 Mario Camus offered *La vuelta de el Coyote* [*The Return of El Coyote*].

[23] The *IMDb* is very useful in identifying these multiple pseudonyms.

quently, although filmed in 1966, it was not released until 1968 (Coira, 1999: 239–40). José María Zabalza (aka Harry Freeman or Joseph Trader), who graduated from the IIEC with Berlanga, also provided further titles such as *Las malditas pistolas de Dallas* [1965 *Three Dollars of Lead*] or *Los rebeldes de Arizona* [1970 **The Arizona Rebels*]. Eugenio Martín's[24] *El precio de un hombre* [1966 *The Bounty Killer* – PNC] was the only western to receive a prize. The popularity of the genre is captured in Julio Suárez's comedy *A galope tendido* [2000 *At Full Gallop*] about another railway employee, well-meaning Quixotic Jaime [Aitor Merino], who dreams of being a sheriff but only has his bike to rescue and help others.

Horror and terror

An equally successful cult following was generated by horror films, many of which were the results of co-productions. Even established directors experimented with the genre; Nieves Conde was surprisingly contracted to film the Greek treasure quest *El sonido de la muerte* [1964 *The Prehistoric Sound*], and Eugenio Martín's *Pánico en el transiberiano* [1972 *Horror Express*] starred Christopher Lee and Peter Cushing. The movement seems to be from western to horror, as exemplified by Jesús Luis Madrid's filmography. Jazz-loving Jesús Franco excelled in all the excesses of the genre and the 'sadistic male gaze' (Martin-Márquez, 1999a: 155), as well as creating 'many interesting female figures [...] remarkable and unusual heroines' (Pavlovic, 2004: 138). In 2004 the *IMDb* listed 182 titles and over 35 different pseudonyms for Jesús/Jess Franco/Frank. His *Gritos en la noche* [1961 **Screams in the Night*] gave birth to the abominable Dr Orloff, played by the Swiss actor Howard Vernon, whom he directed in 39 films, including *Miss Muerte* [1965], his last black and white terror, produced by Serge Silberman and scripted with Jean-Claude Carrière. 'With Orloff sex sizzled into the foreground, changing the face of Euro-horror for the next twenty years' (Tohill & Tombs, 1994: 77). He directed Christopher Lee as both Fu Manchu and Dracula, as well as in two films dealing with the Marquis de Sade's Justine and Eugénie; but his excesses, with increasing sadism and exploitation of the female body, could only be distributed abroad.

In 1967 Jacinto Molina, often credited as Paul Naschy, launched his career when he scripted *La marca del hombre lobo* [1967 Enrique Eguiluz, *The*

---

[24] Eugenio Martín (aka Gene Martin or at times Jean Martin) picked up his skills as a crew member of British and US productions in Spain, e.g. *The Seventh Voyage of Sinbad* [1958 Nathan Juran] or *The Worlds of Gulliver* [1960 Jack Sher]. He then made a swashbuckling film, *Los corsarios del Caribe* [*Conqueror of Maracaibo* 1960], to which one could add another adventure, Isasi's *La máscara de Scaramouche* [1963 *The Adventures of Scaramouche*].

Mark of the Wolfman] and, unable to find a suitable actor, he became its protagonist. Numerous Waldemar Daninski films depicting the cursed and tormented Werewolf have since followed; the most recent noted on the IMDb is *Tomb of the Werewolf* from 2003, made in the USA, scripted and directed by Fred Olen Ray, starring Jacinto Molina.[25] These productions represent 'the epitome of "bad sixties" low budget films, but although it lacks in material resources, it oozes in imagination and kitsch' and '[s]exploitation'.[26] According to Joan Hawkins 'Despite the raw visual quality of most of the films, they can still be situated at the intersection of high and mass culture, the place where traditional distinctions between high and low culture become unhelpful, if not completely meaningless' (2000: 113).

Less prolific, but equally famous through his television work and the series 'Historias para no dormir',[27] is Uruguayan-born Narciso Ibáñez Serrador who has, to date, only directed two feature films. *La residencia* [1969 *The Finishing School* – PNC] achieved the greatest international recognition, but loved by the public it was heavily criticised by Spanish critics (Lázaro Reboll, 2004: 152–68). It starred Lilli Palmer as the authoritarian headmistress of a reform school for difficult young women in a very successful blend of Jack the Ripper and Frankenstein, from which a parallel can be established between the house and a closeted Spanish society about to explode if safety valves were not allowed, a clear manifestation of Clemens's return of the repressed (1999). This was followed much later with *¿Quién puede matar a un niño?* [1976 *Would You Kill a Child?*], which, through its excess, explores the hypothetical consequences of the arrogant tourist development with an equally surprising ending. The box-office success of *La residencia* is often credited as the start of the Spanish terror 'boom', although a number of precursors have been mentioned above, and a film festival dedicated to the genre had already been established in Sitges in 1968, and more festivals followed. Of course in most cases only heavily censored versions were released in Spanish cinemas (Lázaro Reboll, 2002: 90–2).

Animation

The Estudios Moro went on producing animated shorts after the 1945 success of *Garbancito de la Mancha* [Arturo Moreno, **Garbancito, the Little Chickpea* – PNC], but there was really no competition for Disney and other US imports. It was the start of television broadcasting in 1957 that

---

25   A brief biography and filmography is offered by Tod Tjersland (2003).
26   Quoted in Lázaro Reboll (2002: 85; for a production chronology see also p. 90).
27   Horror series, *Tales to Keep You Awake* (1964–1982), a similar concept to *The Twilight Zone* or *Tales of the Unexpected*.

gave animation a new impetus, at first for advertising spots and pedagogical materials targeted at children. This generated new blood and a few more feature-length cartoons in the 1960s. In 1966 Francisco Macián, trained in the Moro studios, created Macián Films, and released *El mago de los sueños* [*The Dream Wizard*] after two years' work, using his own animation system, M-Tecnofantasy, which blended animation with photographs. The story was based on the Telerín Family, created by José Luis Moro, which every night concluded children's television viewing with the six children going to bed to the song 'Vamos a la cama / Hay que descansar ...' [Let's go to bed / We have to take a rest...]. Once they are in bed, the Wizard arrives with a fairytale for each, thus endowing each child with a personality. The episodic format allowed the designers to use very different graphic styles for each of the six stories. One of the musical comedies written for Los Bravos, a very popular Beatles-style band, blended Macían's animations in a psychedelic romp, *Dame un poco de amooor* [1968 *Give me a Little Lo-o-o-ving* released the same year as *Yellow Submarine* [George Dunning]. Also producing animation for children were the Estudios Castilla and Salvador Gijón who specialised in shorts with animated puppets. After gathering experience with the Moro Studios, Palomo Cruz Delgado went on to set up his own company to make many shorts, both for entertainment and schools. He also created the feature *Mágica aventura* [1974 *Magic Adventure*], based on Perrault and Andersen tales, before going on to make episodic series in the 1980s. Starting in 1967 with plenty of new episodes until 1971, Rafael Vara Cuervo produced the series of 'Mortadelo y Filemón, agencia de información' [1966–71 *'Mortadelo & Filemón, Private Investigations'] shorts inspired by Francisco Ibáñez's comic-strip. The characters were revived for television in 1994, and in 2003 Javier Fesser directed the live action feature film *La gran aventura de Mortadelo y Filemón* [*Mortadelo and Filemón: The Big Adventure*], casting Benito Pocino and Pepe Viyuela as the two inept secret agents.

The outriders

It seems perhaps misleading, after the previous discussion loosely based on popular genres, to create a section for Fernando Fernán Gómez, Luis G[arcía] Berlanga and Juan Antonio Bardem; but these three directors, although not the only ones, gave the censors great cause for concern, and warrant attention since they are neither thought of as popular *Viejo Cine* or as *Nuevo Cine* (Marsh, 2006). The first two used laughter, or more specifically satire, as a means of reflecting on Spanish reality, while Bardem employed more allegorical narratives (González Requena, 1998: 86–7). Hopewell has identified a formal camera technique that enabled them to convey visually the feeling of repression experienced by many in 1960s Spain: 'deep focus photography but foreshortened interiors [...]. Foreground / background contrasts [...]. Sequence shots [based on extended tracking movements [...]. Diminishing or denial of off-screen space' (1986: 62–3) that all endow the frame with additional information. Some wide panoramas as well as the inclusion of little details in the mise-en-scène contribute to the overall irony for those who can spot them (Peter Evans, in Graham & Labanyi, 1995: 306). In Fernán Gómez's *El extraño viaje*, the credit sequence accompanied by playful music pans over close-ups of local newspapers and international magazines, including a cover photograph of the future Spanish Monarchs' wedding on 14 May 1962, which contrast with the local event of a corset stolen from the small haberdashery appropriately called 'La parisien' [sic] and the broken promises of marriage exploited in the film (Marsh, 2006: 167–88). In Berlanga's *Plácido* each frame is packed with information impossible to take in on first viewing: Plácido's wife, for instance, is the attendant to the public lavatory, which is the family's second home, and in the ladies the walls are covered with ironic posters and amusing instructions while a sink contains the family's Christmas nativity scene; the publicity parade from the railway station has to cross a funeral procession; the corpse of one of the beggars is loaded onto Plácido's three-wheeler in front of a commemorative plaque celebrating one of General Franco's headquarters during the Civil War; this deceased beggar lived in a house leaning against army barracks just beside a church where midnight mass is being celebrated; and not forgetting the non-diegetic Christmas carol solo as the film concludes, and so on (Marsh, 2006: 122–37). In Bardem's *Nunca pasa nada*, the French actress Jacquie [Corrine Marchand] refuses to be entrapped by Spanish society and its provincial values, represented graphically by her stroll through the market stalls where she only buys a toy bull,[28] while the lack of modernisation is evoked by the constant passage through the town of lorries loaded with consumer goods.[29]

Fernando Fernán Gómez, outrider (Lima, 1921–2007)

In the 1960s Fernán Gómez was directly involved in twenty-nine films, directing seven of them. As an actor he participated in many *VCE* comedies, but his screenwriting and directing reflects a much more critical view of Spanish reality. In *Sólo para hombres* [1960 *For Men Only*], based on a Miguel Mihura comedy and building on his success with Analía Gadé in *La vida por delante* [1958 *Life Ahead*], he uses a nineteenth-century setting to

---

28 As Kinder comments (1993: 280–1), Jacquie is played by Corinne Marchand who had shown her modernity in the *Nouvelle Vague* film *Cléo de 5 à 7* [1961 Agnès Varda, *Cléo from 5 to 7*].

29 The image is used frequently with similar effect in Erice's trains of *Espíritu de la colmena* or Bigas Luna's lorries in *Jamón, jamón*, filmed as far apart as 1973 and 1992.

6a Cross-dressing in Fernán Gómez's *El extraño viaje* (1964)

make evident the mismatch between the intellectual capacities of women and their lack of professional opportunities while poking fun at the instability of elected governments to remind Spaniards of their lack. This was quickly followed by a contract to direct and act in the farce *La venganza de don Mendo* [1961 *Don Mendo's Revenge*]. His best and most biting comments came in his following two films. The first was a two-hour-long family melodrama, *El mundo sigue* [1963 **Life Goes On*]. Again, as established by the initial sequence, it explores the difficult socio-economic conditions of the time and lack of opportunities for the lower classes. No producer wanted to touch the film so Fernán Gómez and his friend Juan Esterlich financed it themselves, but the film was denied a Madrid release and was only seen briefly in provincial cinemas. The second was *El extraño viaje* [completed 1964, *Strange Voyage*], a black comedy providing a fictional explanation suggested by Berlanga for a real and unresolved multiple murder, known at the time as the 'Mazarrón Crime'. No reference to the actual case was allowed in the title, and the censored film had to wait until 1967 for its release in Bilbao and 1969 in Madrid. Behind the shutters of respectability, in a dark old provincial house overlooking the main square, the film gradually reveals the moral and social hypocrisy of the tyrannical character of Doña Ignacia [Tota Alba], and her dominance over her two infantilised siblings, Paquita [Rafaela Aparicio] and Venancio [Jesús Franco, no less], including sequences of cross-dressing from Fernando [the leading man Carlos Larrañaga]. The mise-en-scène presents a backward and decrepit Spain, which together with the amusing dialogues, makes explicit references to provincial stagnation and the world beyond Spain where psychological and social freedom is allowed to flourish (Hopewell, 1986: 50). Discouraged, but not beaten, Fernán Gómez directed three less provocative comedies, although the last, *Mayores con reparos* [1966 *For Adults, with Caution*], in which he acted once again opposite Analía Gadé, required 30 minutes of cuts. He concluded the decade by acting in six less contentious films.

Luis G[arcía] Berlanga, outrider (Valencia, 1921)

In spite of the censors, Berlanga directed two of his best subversive comedies during Escudero's decade. *Plácido* [1961], already mentioned (pp. 136–7, 177), was followed by *El verdugo* [1964 *The Executioner* – PNC, Venice FIPRESCI]. This black comedy managed to combine the housing shortage, economic migration and expansion of tourism with a comment on the death penalty, which was pointed since three political prisoners were executed a few months before the film's release. The plot builds on a favourite device of Berlanga's narratives, the needs of those who, however innocently, believe that something can be got for nothing. The film received the international prize in Venice, but was only released in Spain after fourteen more cuts. Sánchez Bella, future Minister of Information and Tourism but at that time ambassador in Rome, described the script as containing: 'all the ingredients of anti-Spanish communist propaganda, presented in a very Spanish way, that is to say almost anarchic'.[30] It was four years later that Berlanga was able to film his next project, and this was in Argentina. A cinematographic disaster, *La boutique/Las pirañas* [1967 *The Piranhas*] explored gender relations, a theme he followed up in the comedy set in Sitges *Vivan los novios* [1970 *Long Live the Bride and Groom*] with its black humour focus on the overpowering mother, who dies on the eve of her infantilised son's wedding, neither of whom can deal with the social progress, contrasting the straitjacket of Spanish hypocritical middle-class obligations with the more liberated and irresponsible tourists usually filmed in their bikinis; 'the comedy arises from the gap between the projections of Francoist society and its popular experience' (Nair, 2000: 96), which wraps and represses the individual in a gigantic spider's web, as suggested by the memorable concluding high-angle shot. Both

---

30 'El guión contiene todos los requisitos de la propaganda comunista en relación con España a través de una versión muy española, que quiere decir casi anarquista,' quoted by Casimiro Torreiro (in Gubern, 1995: 331), letter dated 30/08/1963 to the Minister of Foreign Affairs, Fernando Castiella; see also Marsh (2006: 137–42).

films were written in collaboration with Rafael Azcona and have contributed to Berlanga being labelled 'misogynistic'. The triptych was concluded with his next film *Tamaño natural* [1974 *Love Doll*] with locations shot in Paris, banned in Spain until 1978 (Higginbotham, 1988: 52–4).

Juan Antonio Bardem, outrider (Madrid, 1922–2002)

During the 1960s, in spite of his international profile based on films made in the 1950s, Bardem's films declined in popularity as he pursued his ideological agenda, commenting on women's situation in Spain (Martin-Márquez, 1999a: 187–202), which continued to attract the censors' disapproval. After the bull-fighting *A las cinco de la tarde* [1961], he directed four co-productions. *Los inocentes* [1962 *The Innocents*] received a prize at the Berlin Festival, but the most interesting was *Nunca pasa nada* [1963 and released in Madrid in 1965, *Nothing Ever Happens* – PNC], written with playwright Alfonso Sastre in 1961, but with production delayed when UNINCI was closed after the *Viridiana* scandal. The press at Cannes criticised it for revisiting the narrow mentality of the provincial life of *Calle Mayor*, here perceived by Jacquie the French actress needing an urgent appendectomy followed by a prolonged and enforced convalescence in the little provincial town of Medina. The fourth was *Los pianos mecánicos* [1965 **The Mechanical Pianos*], which examines the behaviour of foreigners on the Costa Brava, and was his most commercially successful despite the censor's cuts.

Luis Buñuel, as an outrider (Calanda, 1900–1983)

In 1969 Buñuel was persuaded to return to Spain to direct the adaptation of a second Galdós novel, *Tristana* [1970 – PNC], a project initiated in 1962 after completing *Viridiana*, which was denied permission by the censors. He set to work with Julio Alejandro[31] with whom he had already collaborated in 1958 to film *Nazarín* in Mexico (Faulkner, 2004a: 126–47). The setting was transferred from Galdós's Madrid to pre-War Toledo with all its connotations of the Black Spain, where the narrative follows the hardening of an innocent mind as the young orphaned Tristana [Catherine Deneuve] seeks to define herself in her society, and as victim becomes the avenging aggressor. The film can be read as 'not only a denunciation of the social backwardness of Spanish society, but also an attack on the hypocrisy of liberal thinkers

---

[31] Buñuel always felt more secure when the dialogues of his films were scripted with someone else.

who adjust their beliefs to suit their own desires', as her guardian Don Lope [Fernando Rey] modifies his values as he grows old (D'Lugo, 1997: 103). In the background the working class remains unable to speak, or is persecuted, thus allowing the identification of the female victim of patriarchal values as a representation of the repressed and oppressed victims of the Franco regime. While discreetly sharing the conventions of the horror film, *Tristana* has been read as a political allegory (Aranda 1975: 242–4; Dongan, 1984), a social criticism (Mellen, 1978: 297–305; Eidsvik, 1981), an indictment of women's situation (Edwards, 1983: 222–46; Miller, 1983), and a psychoanalytical discourse (Kinder, 1993: 316–19; P. Evans, 1995b). It can be viewed as all of these, even if Buñuel always reacted against giving his films a meaning and, like Hitchcock, was fascinated by Tristana/Deneuve's amputated leg, which literalises the Spanish proverb about a respectable woman, safe at home with a broken leg (Buñuel, 1987: 246–7; Labanyi, 1999: 76–81).[32]

The *Nuevo Cine Español*

García Escudero's reforms benefited the new EOC graduates, and the reformed 'Special Interest Prize' potentially provided them with the subsidies to make their own films, which became known as the *Nuevo Cine Español* [New Spanish Cinema]. Even if the new censorship laws were more show than reality, at least there was funding while Escudero was in office between July 1962 and November 1968. According to Casimiro Torreiro, some 48 new directors got started during this period, and were protected by screen quotas in the *Salas de Arte*, which specified one day of Spanish films for every three days of imported cinema. This measure actually undermined general distribution by privileging them in the *salas*, which most spectators avoided as intellectual snobbery (Gubern, 1995: 309 and 339), and these films viewed at international festivals presented an image of Spanish Cinema that did not reflect the cinema that Spanish spectators were actually enjoying and paying for at the box-office. These new 'young' directors were all born just before the Civil War and all bring a critical assessment of their post-war upbringing mingled with their aspirations of creating *auteur* cinema by filming more realistic narratives, preferably in black and white to contrast with the happy-ending and feel-good escapism of the colour *VCE*. They were also keen to make their own cinema different, emulating in their own very different ways the critical success of the *Nouvelle Vague* and the film magazine *Les Cahiers du Cinéma* as well as other European experiments in film narrative (Forbes, 2000: 21). The left-wing film magazine *Nuestro Cine*, founded in 1961,

---

[32] 'Mujer honrada, en casa y pierna quebrada', according to one of the many versions of the proverb.

defended the new cinema, and so did *Film Ideal*, founded in 1956 as the voice of National-Catholicism, with their new perspective as from 1962. Their critical perspective could not be expressed openly and could only be manifested indirectly and elliptically, through allusions and consequences, metaphor and allegory (Hopewell, 1986: 75–7). The initial opacity of meaning would lead spectators to reflection and thus to unravel the symbols. In spite of the official support from Escudero's department and its official prizes, geared to promote a national cinema, most of these films had the opposite effect and actually experienced considerable problems with the censors; they were cut, mutilated, and often released much later in Spain.

Carlos Saura (Huesca, 1932; graduated IIEC, 1955)

Made before the cinema reforms, Saura's 1959 *Los golfos* was finally released in 1961, as part of Escudero's liberalisation policy. Like other graduates, Saura went back to teach at the IEEC and, according to Gutiérrez Aragón, put his students off by insisting on photographs when they wanted to make films. Saura's second film, *Llanto por un bandido* [1963 *Lament for a Bandit*], written with Mario Camus, was an Italian co-production radically different from *Los golfos,* with a much bigger budget and filmed in colour. It uses a *bandolero* narrative set in the aftermath of the Napoleonic War and, with its visual allusions to Goya paintings, presents two opposing Spains, a device already exploited in earlier films to avoid direct references to the present. On the surface it attempts to demystify the legend of El Tempranillo [Paco Rabal], as Vajda had done in 1953 with *Carne de horca*. The film, which includes cameo appearances from Buñuel as an executioner and dissident playwright Antonio Buero Vallejo, was marred by censors' cuts to minimise parallels with the Civil War.[33] Saura then teamed up with Elías Querejeta's production company, which provided him with an excellent technical crew with which he worked on some very provocative films until *Dulces horas* [1982 *Sweet Hours*]. *La caza* [1966 *The Hunt* – Berlin Best Director, Sant Jordi for best film], written with Angelino Fons and filmed on a much lower budget in austere high-contrast black and white, was a very successful meditation on unresolved tensions of the Civil War with its suppressed consequences always about to erupt, in which both the landscape and the characters bear the scars of the war (Hopewell, 1986: 63 and 71–7).[34] Faulkner adds that it is

---

[33] See Buñuel (1987: 225); Kinder (1993: 156–60); and for the censors' cuts to the initial sequence and other dissident writers that participated D'Lugo (1991: 48).

[34] Hunting was not just one of Franco's favourite pastimes, but is also an important social marker, which had, since the Middle Ages, been acknowledged as a necessary preparation of the nobility for warfare. It becomes an important motif in subsequent films such as Borau's

a powerful examination of the ageing male, and the ageing dictatorship as it celebrates its propaganda of twenty-five years of peace (2006: 145–73).

If Saura's first three films highlighted men and their relationships, the focus now shifted to gender and sexual relationships. *Peppermint frappé* [1967 – IE; Berlin Best Director; the title refers to the drink, with its strong French connotations and a supposed aphrodisiac] can be viewed as a Hitch-cock-style suspense film that also questions the impact of modern European values on the mind of its provincial protagonist, Julián [José Luis López Vázquez, associated with the popular comedies and values but equally at ease in a dissident film]. As in *La caza,* the film exploits Alfredo Mayo's star image from the 1940s as leading man and young Francoist hero; here he plays Julián's childhood friend, who has taken advantage of the tourist boom and prospered through land speculation, on a return visit to Cuenca with his foreign girlfriend. Perhaps even more than it would in *Cría cuervos* [1976 *Raise Ravens*], the musical soundtrack pertinently juxtaposes traditional and modern Spain. A hymn from the *Misterio de Elche* [*Mystery of Elche* to celebrate the Virgin Mary] accompanies the objectification of women in the opening credit sequence in which cover-girls' photographs are cut up, contrasting with the contemporary pop music that is inserted in the film as a way of characterising male constructions of femininity according to the medieval palindrome of AVE–EVA.[35] It was the first of his collabora-tions with Geraldine Chaplin, which were to last until 1979. At this point she was still bathing in the limelight of playing Tonya from David Lean's *Dr Zhivago* [1965], some of which had been filmed in Spain, and she thus gave the film an international dimension.[36] Chaplin plays two women, Ana and Elena, Christian and pagan names that emphasise their contrasting personali-ties and values. It is characteristic of Saura to dedicate his films and this one, with its reference to the Calanda drums (Buñuel, 1987: 19–21; Kinder, 1993: 165–72) and its setting in an old dark house, is appropriately dedicated to Buñuel. The less commercially successful *Stress es tres tres* [1968 *Stress is Three*] takes up again from a different perspective the problems of the rapidly modernising consumer society in Spain, land speculation and the construc-tion trade, adapting an affective situation that refers back to Cervantes's and Calderón's seventeenth-century jealous husbands, with more than passing

---

Furtivos [1975 **Poachers*] or Berlanga's *La escopeta nacional* [1978 *The National Shotgun*], demonstrating how little things had changed in spite of the rise of Catalan values. Kinder examines repressed and physical violence as a political comment in films by Saura and others (1993: 150–83).

35 Woman as either virgin or whore, actually the choice for women was traditionally encap-sulated as 'virgen, madre o puta' [virgin, mother or whore].

36 Chaplin has remained very involved in Spanish Cinema, more recently in Antonio Hernán-dez's *En la ciudad sin límites* [2002 *The City of no Limits*] and *Oculto* [2005 **Hidden*].

echoes of Buñuel's *El* [1953 *This Strange Passion*, made in Mexico].[37] *La madriguera* [1969 *Honeycomb*], Saura's second film written with Rafael Azcona and which also acknowledges Chaplin as co-writer, further explores gender relationships as affected by the weight of paternal–Catholic indoctrination and its contradictions as Spain modernised (D'Lugo, 1991: 85–91). The title literally means 'warren', and refers to the ultra-modern house, which confines the couple and provides the spaces where they act out their games and memories; this symbolism has given rise to different translations for the title: *Honeycomb, Bunker, Den, Warren.*

Mario Camus (Santander, 1935; graduated EOC, 1963)

Camus, who co-scripted Saura's first two films, directed his first two films thanks to Ignacio Iquino. *Los farsantes* [1964 *Frauds*] presents his views on Spanish provincial values and explores the contrast between reality and performance as a travelling troupe ends up spending Easter Week in Valladolid (Faulkner, 2006: 73–100). *Young Sánchez*, also produced by Iquino, followed in 1964 with the flavour of *Rocco e i suoi fratelli* [1960 Luchino Visconti, *Rocco and His Brothers*] in presenting the ambiguous hero played by Julián Mateos (Triana Toribio, 2003: 126–7). It deals with the shattered illusions of a boxer as a parallel for aspiring young Spaniards with no real connections, wanting to assert themselves but betrayed by the system. *Con el viento solano* [1966 *With the East Wind*] follows an outlawed gypsy trying to overcome his intolerant and prejudiced environment, and counted on the flamenco dancers Vicente Escudero and Antonio Gades in his third film with a comeback for Imperio Argentina. Lack of success at the box-office led Camus to direct more popular films and musicals, with stars such as Raphael, Sara Montiel in *Esa mujer* [1969 *That Woman*], a court-room melodrama with a singing nun, and later Marisol.

José Luis Borau (Zaragoza, 1929; graduated IIEC, 1960)

Borau was accepted on his second attempt to study at the then IIEC in 1957 and graduated in 1960 with his compulsory short *En el río* [1960 *In the River*]. In spite of his present reputation and status he has made very few films, nine including the most recent *Leo* in 2000. In the 1960s he seemed

---

[37] Fiddian & Evans add Bergman and Godard as other points of cross-reference (1988: 73–82). Furthermore, as Galt points out, 'since Buñuel's films were banned in Spain at the time, his influence via foreign film festival screenings was, in itself, a political statement' (2007: 207).

set for a very different career; after two documentaries his first two features were contracts for commercial cinema: a spaghetti western, *Brandy* [1963], followed by a crime film *Crimen de doble filo* [1964 *Double Edged Crime*], which brought in a pay cheque but little personal satisfaction, although it is a tense psychological film with a number of surprises. That same year he returned to the Film School, now the EOC, to teach screenwriting, and made a further three documentaries. In 1966 he started his own production company, El Imán, and would resurface with more creative control to produce and direct *Hay que matar a B* [*B Must Die*] and *Furtivos* [**Poachers*], both released in 1975.

Manuel Summers (Seville, 1935–1993; graduated IIEC, 1959)

Many of Summers's films explore more unusual emotional relationships, starting with the evocation of childhood and old age in *Del rosa... al amarillo* [1963 *From Pink... to Yellow* – IE, San Sebastián Silver Shell] in two beautifully observed stories, filmed in Toledo. In the first a boy still wearing short trousers falls in love with an older girl, and this is followed by a shorter unconnected romance in an old people's home (Martin-Márquez, 1999b: 56–75). There was a third story for a planned triptych, which Summers used for his second feature *La niña de luto* [1964 *The Girl in Mourning* – Cannes]. This film also explores the weight of outmoded traditional, and often hypocritical, values and how these can destroy relationships, here depicted by three consecutive mourning periods for Rafael's fiancée Rocío. Summers filmed in his own village with the participation of the villagers who play themselves and support Alfredo Landa and María José Alfonso. *El juego de la oca* [1966 *Snakes and Ladders*, co-scripted with Pilar Miró], which opens with a close-up of Borau trying to tell a joke in a café, failed to attract spectators in spite of dealing with the prickly topic of adultery. It was followed by *Juguetes rotos* [1966 *Broken Toys* – IE], an ironic montage from Pedro del Rey, who had edited the two previous films, of interviews and archive materials of forgotten stars (singers, boxers, footballers, bullfighters), that undermined the gloss of the present official reality and consequently the documentary suffered numerous cuts before its release. It was not a commercial success despite its many merits, and consequently Summers then directed two commercial comedies starring Alfredo Landa: *No somos de piedra* [1968 *We Are Not Made of Stone* – PNC] and *¿Por qué te engaña tu marido?* [1969 *Why Does Your Husband Deceive You?*]. These were followed by *Urtain, el rey de la selva* [1970 *Urtain, King of the Mountains*] with Marisol and Basque European heavyweight champion José Manuel Ibar, known as Urtain and then at the height of his boxing career.

Francisco Regueiro (Valladolid, 1934; graduated EOC, 1963)

Regueiro also focused on problems dealing with emotional and sexual rela-tionships. He started with *El buen amor* [1963 *The Good Love*] about two students spending the day together in Toledo to get away from their Madrid surroundings and family pressures, but the oppressive atmosphere of the city prevents any warmth.[38] It was well received in Cannes but the success was not repeated with his subsequent features: *Amador* [1965 **Lover*], a black comedy involving sexual violence, which had to be rewritten three times; *Si volvemos a vernos* [1967 *Smashing Up*] about racism as a white prostitute falls in love with a black soldier on the US base; and *Me enveneno de azules* [1969 **I Poison Myself with Blues*]. He directed another four films but would have to wait until 1985 for financial success, which he finally achieved with the irreverent comedy satire *Padre nuestro* [*Our Father*].

Miguel Picazo (Cazoria, Jaen province, 1927; graduated IIEC, 1960)

Picazo was another whose first film, *La tía Tula* [1964 **Aunt Tula* – IE, San Sebastián Best Director, Sant Jordi for best film[39]], based on Unamuno's novel, showed promise that was not subsequently realised, not even with *Extramuros* [1985 *Beyond the Walls*], a period melodrama set in a sixteenth-century convent that does leave room for thought. Both these films in their different ways explore the female situation in patriarchal societies and feature a star of the 1940s, Aurora Bautista. In *La tía Tula* the confining and stifling values are appropriately conveyed through a careful mise-en-scène and camera work in black and white, with very significant silences (Faulkner, 2004a: 101–24). An excellent understated drama, it presents the contradic-tions of the devoted aunt, like a virgin mother repressed by her religious beliefs (Hopewell, 1986: 66), whereas *Extramuros* is a much more sensa-tional exploration of female desire. *La tía Tula* became the biggest commer-cial success of the *NCE*, very different from his heavily censored second feature, *Oscuros sueños de agosto* [1967 *Obscure August Dreams*], which did not fare well with critics or spectators.

---

[38] With colour film still strident in its contrast, a number of films were still made in black and white and thus created a cinematic impression of greater 'stark' realism.

[39] According to the *IMDb*, this is the second recorded Sant Jordi award for best film. Unlike the equivalent literary prize, the film prize was at first very sporadic: 1957, 1959, 1965, 1967, 1972, 1977, 1979 and annually since 1984.

6b The delicate touch of Miguel Picazo's *La tía Tula* (1964)

Basilio Martín Patino (Salamanca, 1930; graduated IIEC, 1960)

Another key film of the *NCE* was Patino's first feature film *Nueve cartas a Berta* [*Nine Letters to Bertha,* released in 1967 – San Sebastián Best Director], filmed in his native Salamanca. It is an epistolary film with a voice-over confession from Lorenzo [Emilio Gutiérrez Caba] who writes to Berta, the daughter of an exiled Republican intellectual whom he met in London, while he courts his girlfriend Mari-Tere [Elsa Baeza]. Edited using short freeze frames, slow motion and interesting camera angles, it comments with discreet irony through its voice-over and contrasting images on the claustrophobia and stagnation of provincial towns, the apathy and lack of commitment of its generation (Hopewell, 1986: 66–8); 'defeat and impotence pervade in the ending' (Triana Toribio, 2003: 94).[40] His next film was more commercial given the circumstances of its Italian star Lucia Bosè, just separated from her bullfighting husband Dominguín, *Del amor y otras soledades* [1969 *Love and Other Solitudes*], showing two people trapped in a broken marriage with no possible divorce, was also well censored and consequently did not fare well with critics or spectators.

---

[40] Triana Toribio establishes interesting links between this film and Marisol's musicals (2003: 92–5); see also Faulkner for other ironic comments (2006: 125–44).

Angelino Fons (Madrid, 1935; graduated IEEC, 1960)

Fons had already collaborated on three film scripts (*Amador, La caza* and *Peppermint frappé*) before turning to direction. He also questioned Spain's present reality and at first he showed 'the will to articulate opposition through literary adaptation' (Faulkner, 2004a: 11 and chapter 4). He directed three literary adaptations. The first was Pío Baroja's very pessimistic *La busca* [1967 *The Search* – IE], which follows Manuel [Jacques Perrin, criticised for being too handsome for the part] as he seeks to better himself but instead falls into delinquency. Using sets that deliberately avoid making references to Baroja's turn-of-the-century Madrid the narrative succeeds in commenting on the Dictatorship. Fons was also commissioned to adapt two novels by Benito Pérez Galdós, *Fortunata y Jacinta* and *Marianela* in 1970 and 1972, both perhaps over-determined in different ways by the leading ladies, Emma Penella and Rocío Dúrcal respectively (Faulkner, 2004a: 89–97). A similar error of judgement occurred with the musical *Cantando a la vida* [1969 *Singing to Life*], starring Massiel the year after she won the Eurovision Song contest, with a clichéd plot revolving around the disappearance of a Eurovision winner.

Other Film School students

But not all these recent graduates made a financially successful first film. Antxon Eceiza, who was at the IIEC from 1958 to 1962 without completing his degree, was involved in many collaborations and active as a film critic. His first feature film, *El próximo otoño* [*Next Autumn*], was filmed in 1963 but only released in 1967. His next three films were produced by Querejeta, the first two released three months apart in 1967, *Último encuentro* [*Last Meeting*] and *De cuerpo presente* [*Lying in State*] based on Gonzalo Suárez's novel. These were followed in 1970 by *Las secretas intenciones* [*Secret Intentions*], questioning Spain's superficial material modernisation through adultery and suicide, 'a delight in elliptical editing for insinuation, economy and wit' (Hopewell, 1986: 71), it was, however, another financial failure. For political reasons Eceiza left for Paris and then Mexico where he made two films in the 1970s, returning at the end of that decade to make two more features. Julio Diamante's first film *Los que no fuimos a la guerra* [*We Who Did Not Go to War*], based on Fernández Flores's novel, was presented in Venice in 1962, but had problems with the censors and was not released in Spain until 1965 after his next film. *Tiempo de amor* [1964 *Time for Loving*] presents three different episodes: the first deals with premarital sex between a young couple who are engaged but unable to marry until he passes the exams he keeps failing, in the second a young and naïve shop-assistant is seduced by a wealthy student,[41] and the third presents the matrimonial difficulties of a hard-working couple. It did please audiences by dealing with situations in a manner that was recognisable to them. This success was not followed by *El arte de vivir* [1965 *The Art of Living*], which like *Tiempo de amor* was written in collaboration with Elena Sáez, his wife. Javier Aguirre, after starting with about thirteen experimental shorts, was encouraged to make the comedy *Los oficios de Cándido* [1965 **Candido's Jobs*], which was not even released. He subsequently established himself in popular cinema where he has been very productive across a wide range of genres.

Elías Querejeta, producer (Hernani, Guipúzcoa province, 1935)

A key figure for the *NCE* is the producer Elías Querejeta, who had played football for the Santander Real Sociedad. He entered the IIEC with his friend Antxon Eceiza, and became involved in production, starting with UNINCI before setting up on his own when the company was closed down after the *Viridiana* scandal. Not only did he possess the acumen to exploit the new financing measures put in place by Escudero, but also to back talented directors and some excellent scripts with a clear focus to appeal to home and international audiences, playing the censors off against the official policy to present a liberalising attitude abroad (Stone, 2002: 5–10). He produced eleven of the films just mentioned, including Eceiza's four and four by Saura, using an excellent team of professionals, including Primitivo Álvaro as production manager, the cinematographer Luis Cuadrado, Teo Escamilla on the second camera, Pablo G[onzález] del Amo as editor, and the composer Luis de Pablo.

The children of Franco

All the above, associated with the *NCE* and Madrid because of the Film School and the centralised structure of the regime, actually come from different regions of Spain. Only Fons is from Madrid. Borau and Saura come from Zaragoza and Huesca in Aragon, Patino from Salamanca and Regueiro from Valladolid. Summers is from an English family settled in Seville, Picazo from Cazoria near Jaen and Diamante from Cadiz, all different parts of Andalusia. Aguirre, Camus, Eceiza and Querejeta are all from the Basque Country. Marsha Kinder dubbed them the 'Children of Franco' (1983: 57–76), as they were all brought up and endured under the repression of the Dictatorship.

---

41 For a popular treatment of the same situation, see *La chica del trébol*.

They fulfilled the rebellious potential of the Spanish proverb that describes difficult children: 'cría cuervos, y te sacarán los ojos'.[42]

The Catalan connections

As in the days of the silent cinema, there was also plenty of activity in Barcelona, not just from Iquino's production companies, which for the most part identified the main distribution markets in national terms. There was also an impulse, seen in the evolution of Jordi Grau and Jaime Camino's cinema, to make films different from the Madrid productions both visually and in terms of the concerns explored. It would be just as critical of the establishment, albeit from the Catalan perspective overlooked by Madrid (Hopewell, 1986: 69–70), enhanced, as Galt puts it, by 'the European and outward-looking nature of Catalan culture' (Galt, 2007: 210).

Jordi Grau (Barcelona, 1930)

Jordi Grau, who came from a strong Catholic background, started in theatre and was also a painter with a number of exhibitions to his name when he received a bursary to study direction in Rome. His first feature, *Noche de verano* [1963 *Summer Night* – IE], was partly funded by *NCE* subsidies, backed by the Opus Dei, and yet took a critical look at the Barcelona middle class. This was followed by the socially committed *El espontáneo* [1964 *The Rash One*]. The title refers to those young men who jump into the bullring in order to be noticed and earn themselves a bullfighting career in illusion of escaping their wretched circumstances without opportunity of employment. Like Saura's *Los golfos*, it is a powerful metaphor to explore social issues; also set in Madrid, it uses a touch of colour in a black and white context. Next came the experimental *Acteón* [released in 1967], which updated Ovid's story. After this Grau adopted a more straightforward narrative style returning to middle-class Barcelona in *Una historia de amor* [released in 1968, *A Love Story* – San Sebastián Best Actress for Serena Vergano], describing the tensions arising between a young couple when the wife's sister stays with them to help during a pregnancy and is physically attracted to her brother-in-law. He directed the musical *Tuset Street* [1968], co-scripted with Azcona and produced by Sara Montiel in another personal effort to relaunch her own career. However, the film was completed by Luis Marquina because of disagreements with the producing actress about Grau's unconventional

---

[42] 'Raise ravens, and they'll pluck out your eyes', equivalent of biting the hand that feeds you.

aesthetics. He then moved to direct *Historia de una chica sola* [1969 *Story of a Girl Alone*]. The documentary director Josep Lluis Font also examined the Catalan middle-class hypocrisy that collaborated with the dictatorship in the inheritance drama *Vida de familia* released in 1965 [*Family Life*].

Jaime Camino (Barcelona, 1936)

Jaime Camino was self-taught and made his debut with *Los felices sesenta* [1963 released in 1969, *The Happy Sixties*], produced by his own production company, Tibidabo Films. Set against the modernisation of the Costa Brava, it deals with the frustrations of middle-class Catalans engaged on summer seductions, beginning with a provocative soundtrack of folk singer Raimón in Catalan. *Mañana será otro día* [1967 *Tomorrow is Another Day*], filmed in a style that did not appeal because it moved away from the prevailing realist narratives, takes up the consumer discourse and the difficulty of employment using the context of the film world and advertising. *España otra vez* [1968 *Spain Again* – PNC] touched on a difficult subject for its time by introducing a doctor and former Lincoln Brigade volunteer returning to Barcelona, which became the first positive image of the defeated tolerated by the censors. Together with *La piel quemada* and *María Rosa* it was one of the first films to include Catalan dialogues on the soundtrack to mark the cultural differences that had been officially suppressed. It was written in collaboration with Román Gubern and Alvah Bessie, away from Hollywood because of McCarthy purges. The success of the film would lead Camino, after the dissolution of the Dictatorship, to direct many other films about the Civil War. His next film, *Un invierno en Mallorca* [1969 *A Winter in Mallorca* – PNC], was based on George Sand's account of her stay on the island with Frédéric Chopin developing his taste for historical narratives.

The Barcelona aura

Other Catalan directors manifested more radically their dissatisfaction with both the centralised political and economic control from Madrid and the dominance of the dissident *NCE* filmmakers from the EOC. Their films are interesting precisely because they manifest their difference through a totally different visual style and cinematographic premise. In a climate of renovation, also found in the *Nouvelle Vague*, *Cinema Nôvo* and *Free Cinema*, each experimented with individual styles, breaking away from narrative continuity and realism, using images and montage to communicate in a more abstract and even surrealist manner.

The essence of that critique was the ideological cleavage between cosmopolitan, universalist culture in Barcelona, strongly identified with the intellectual and artistic currents of the rest of Europe, and the Francoist Castilianism of Spanish culture and film which was, in their eyes, provincial and anachronistic (D'Lugo, 2002: 169).

Although some films did receive special subsidies, most had to be self-financed, hence the participation of non-professional actors. Collectively they became known as the Barcelona School, a label first used by Ricardo Muñoz Suay[43] in the April 1967 issue of film magazine *Fotogramas* (Casimiro Torreiro, in Gubern, 1995: 321–6; Besas, 1985: 85–91 for personal testimonies). In many cases these films were not released until some time after they were made, and mostly in restricted theatres.

Vicente Aranda (Barcelona, 1926)

Vicente Aranda is named as the precursor of the 'Barcelona School' on the reputation of his second film *Fata Morgana* [1965, released 1967, *Left-Handed Fate*[44]], scripted with Gonzalo Suárez. It is an experimental thriller, which used its elliptical surrealistic narrative and strong visual impact to manipulate established genres, mixing science fiction, comics and pop-art with dry humour, presented from the perspective of a model's personal fears [Teresa Gimpera, one of the best-known models of the time], who seems to voice the apprehensions of a whole region (D'Lugo, 2002: 169–70; Galt, 2007: 201–10). This came as a surprise after his first film *Brillante Porvenir* [1965 *Brilliant Future*], which was a more conventional realist search-for-a job and place-in-the-city narrative, scripted and directed in collaboration with Román Gubern on his return from a seven-year exile in Venezuela. His next film, the psychological feminine thriller *Las crueles/El cadáver exquisito* [1969 *The Cruel Women/The Exquisite Corpse,* the alternative title being the original denied by the censors], also co-scripted with Suárez, where a mysterious woman [Capucine] takes revenge on a philandering publisher [Carlos Estrada]. As it manipulates the suspense with a skill as surprising as Claude Chabrol's, it also makes 'a scathing critique of Spanish machismo, linking it to the established male social order of Franco's Spain' (Willis, 2003: 77).

---

[43] Muñoz Suay started as assistant director for *Esa pareja feliz* and other Berlanga films, then became executive producer for *Viridiana* and other films, directing three films of his own in the mid-1950s (for details, see *IMDb*).

[44] This is the *IMDb* international title. It also lists five very different films with the title *Fata Morgana*.

Gonzalo Suárez (Oviedo, 1934)

Asturian-born Gonzalo Suárez, who denied adhesion to the movement, was then living and writing in Barcelona but his short stories 'Fata Morgana' and 'El cadáver exquisito', as well as his more experimental *Ditirambo* [1967, released 1969] link him to Aranda. Suárez not only wrote and directed *Ditirambo*, but he also played the eponymous journalist with a contract to kill, in a film that springs from the *noir* genre but questions traditional narrative assumptions, which for Hopewell exploit generic conventions to convey socio-political comments (1986: 70). Suárez followed this with *El extraño caso del Dr Fausto* [1969 *The Strange Case of Dr Faustus*], showing an interest in reworking universal myths, to which he would return in subsequent films. Although *Faustus* was not successful, like Aranda he has moved on to develop a substantial filmography with fascinating intrigues.

A Barcelona School

1967 is said to be the year of the Barcelona School, following Joaquim Jordà's pronouncement at the Sitges festival and then published in *Nuestro Cine* (Molina Foix, 1977: 23; Galt, 2007: 193–210), but the directors who collaborated did not all go on to direct very much. Their filmic manifesto was *Dante no es únicamente severo* [1967 *Dante is not Only Severe*] in which five of them were to participate. Antoni de Senillosa, Ricardo Bofill and Pere Portabella pulled out one by one to make their own shorts, leaving Jacinto Esteva Crewe and Joaquim Jordà to direct the same actors and crew separately in nine different sequences, with a prologue and epilogue, which were then put together by Juan Luis Oliver, who died on the job which was then completed by Ramón Quadreny. The film favours the visual over narrative coherence, and owes much to *Un Chien andalou* [1928 Buñuel]. Esteva went on to direct the even more puzzling *Después del diluvio* [1968 *After the Flood*] and *Metamorfosis* [1970], with no commercial success. In 1970 he filmed and edited his last work *Lejos de los árboles* [released 1972 *Far from the Trees*]. Jordà pursued an active career in screenwriting, creating a few documentaries and in 1996 the police thriller *Un cos al bosc* [*A Body in the Woods*]. Carlos Durán's *Cada vez que …* [*Each time that … I fall in love I think it is for ever*], released in 1968, describes a romance, framed in the context of the fashion world and publicity, where little happens in order to focus on a relationship without prejudices, with a touch of Richard Lester and his Beatles films and more than a nod to Jean-Luc Godard's cinema. Durán kept up this style in the 1970 *Liberxina 90,* co-scripted with Jordà, which was heavily censored and never released commercially, perhaps because of the implications of its references to May '68 in France. He remained involved in different aspects of film production, but did not direct his own films. Risk-taking Pere Portabella, producer of Films 59 (*El cochecito, Los golfos, Viridiana*), made and directed the episodic and experimental *Nocturno 29* [*Nocturne 29*] in 1969, replete with political references including the first 29 years of the Dictatorship, which he followed with the equally experimental reflections on cinema and contemporary Spain in the prohibited *Umbracle* [1970 *Trellis*] with Christopher Lee.

The outcome

García Escudero's well-intentioned efforts to determine a new cinema for the regime ended in failure. His subsidies allowed new directors to make a start, but many did not carry on. They enabled Querejeta, Borau, Camino and other directors to set up their own production companies, and thus have more authorial control over their films, but these were too frequently censored. To add insults to Escudero's injuries, at the first International Week of Film Schools, organised in Sitges in the first week of October 1967, he was booed and there were minor riots. His *Salas de Arte* were felt to be another form of state control and the average spectator avoided them. His subsidies created huge debts, as producers learned to exploit the system with inflated budgets and fake co-productions, since no minimum investment was required from foreign co-producers (Higginbotham, 1988: 15–16). In September 1967 the regime decided to tighten the reins and Carrero Blanco was appointed vice-president of the government, which led to the reorganisation of Manuel Fraga Iribarne's department. Escudero's office was replaced by the new Dirección General de Cultura Popular y Espectáculos, and Carlos Robles Piquer was appointed as its director in December, holding the post until October 1969. The EOC teaching was transferred to Madrid University's Faculty of Information Technology in 1971 and renamed 'Ciencias de la Imagen Visual y Auditiva'. Fraga Iribarne was himself replaced during the 1969 cabinet reshuffle by the more conservative and much stricter Alfredo Sánchez Bella (Casimiro Torreiro, in Gubern, 1995: 340).

Balance sheet

At the beginning of the decade recorded audience numbers continued to increase until reaching their maximum figure of 435.2 million in 1965, over-taking the 326.6 million viewers in the UK, which explains the increasing Spanish production figures peaking at 164 films in 1966, in contrast with the 125 films made in 1969. After 1965 spectators gradually decreased, as in the rest of privileged Europe since going out to the pictures became a less popular form of entertainment than the televisions that more and more people were able to hire or purchase (Forbes, 2000: 20–1). In Spain RTVE started its official public broadcasts on 28 October 1956 (Jordan, in Graham & Labanyi, 1995: 361–9),[45] at first limited to Madrid and then reaching other important cities, although it was not until 1970 that the whole peninsula could tune in. The continuous decline in cinema audiences lasted until 1988 when they slumped to 69.6 million, by which time UK figures had increased again, overtaking those in Spain, which also started to increase. However, statistics can be misleading, because in 1962 there were 64 Spanish films and 24 co-productions, whereas in 1966 distribution was made up of 67 Spanish films and 97 co-productions, so that Spanish film production, excluding co-productions, averaged some 60 films per year from 1962 to 1969, whereas co-productions shot up from 24 in 1962 to 98 films in 1965 before starting to drop again. From 1965 to 1970 the distribution of co-productions in Spain greatly exceeded exclusively Spanish films, a situation that was only reversed from 1971 onwards. The dominance of co-productions throughout the decade is naturally also reflected by the other European film producing nations, except the UK.[46]

Viewing and further general reading

The general reading mentioned at the end of the previous chapter will continue to provide further information, and all provide complementary bibliographies to amplify critical scope. One shared problem for the enjoyment of most of these films is that they can be very specifically embedded in their cultural context, and one not personally familiar with Spain would benefit from reading general but informative books like Hooper (1987) or the more academic Graham & Labanyi (1995). Triana Toribio has an important contribution on García Escudero's values and policies throughout the decade, as well as on the representation of sexuality on screen (2003: 54–107), contrasting Patino and Marisol, who is also taken up by P. Evans (2004). Godsland & White (2002), Lázaro Reboll & Willis (2004) and Mira (2005) address some of the popular genres, while the cult horror films are explored by Kinder (1993), Willis (2002, 2003), Tjersland (2003) and Pavlovic (2003, 2004). Faulkner's recent book (2006) examines possible points of contact

---

45 The first experimental broadcasts took place in 1949, limited both in time and to bull-fights and church services. The first football match was transmitted in 1957.

46 The paragraph uses the tables from Vincendeau (1995: 464–8), which do not always match the infomation found in Casimiro Torreiro (in Gubern, 1995: 339) or Caparrós Lera (1983: 231 and 233). Experience shows that these figures should be taken for comparative purposes rather than as factually exact.

between *VCE* and *NCE*. Martín-Márquez is perceptive on the representation of women and female subjectivity, particularly in Bardem (1999a: especially pp. 187–202) and in Manuel Summers (1999b). Richardson examines the growing consumerism and urbanisation of the 1960s from the perspective of *La ciudad no es para mí* and *Tiempo de silencio* (2002). There are considerable commentaries on Berlanga (Nair, 2000; Marsh, 2006). Labanyi (1999), P. Evans & Santaolalla (2004) and Edwards (2005) will bring the reader up to date on Buñuel and *Tristana*. Deveny, starting in 1965, examines films derived from novels (1999), supplemented with greater specificity by Faulkner (2006). D'Lugo has a vital monograph on Saura (1991), though his bibliography will no longer be up to date,[47] and Stone begins his book with an interview with Querejeta. For the Barcelona avant-garde it is useful to consult Molina Foix if available (1977) or the latest revisions from Galt (2007). The new periodical *Studies in Hispanic Cinemas*, with its first number published in 2004 while this book was being written, is now presenting dedicated articles annually. Increasing numbers of DVDs and some film scripts are being released (consult the *IMDb* and *MCU.es* with their changing links).

The many popular comedies reveal much about their context, implying social commentaries that could do with further and new investigations as they strain to different extents against the dominant ideology and patriarchal values. Most of them are very efficiently edited, and some research on these editors, many of them women (e.g. Teresa Alcocer, Mercedes Alonso, Margarita Ochoa, Sara Ontañón, Ana María Romero Marchent, Petra de Nieva, Rosa Salgado, Maruja Soriano), would be rewarding. The number of times child protagonists are presented with one or no parent warrants further enquiry as it could be more significant than an easy appeal to sentimentality or a way of self-defining the protagonist. The representation of the family and gender roles evolved swiftly throughout the decade, blaming or praising the modernising foreign influence for the changes, often through the town–village juxtaposition and the representation of generational tensions or conflicts, as adolescents became freer, wilder or clung on to their complexes according to the screenwriters' and directors' values. The presence of the reprehensible modernising foreigner, whether as tourist, businessman, sexually liberated or perverse individual, would reveal interesting conclusions. A comparison of the *NCE*'s treatment of favourite themes of the *VCE* would be valuable, especially to point out the overlaps, as would an examination of the double-edged Lazaga or Atienza's seriously undervalued satirical comedy, *Los dinamiteros*. The often subversive *crime noir* films, the development of *chorizo* westerns and horror, which Lázaro Reboll defines as 'horrotica' (2002: 93), remain to be developed as a manifestation of the return of the

---

[47] There is, however, a new monograph in English in the pipeline.

repressed (Clemens, 1999). A start has been made on exploring the 'cult' of horror films' 'often low-budget, sleazy, exploitation fare', which could none-theless be subversive and 'served to make political points' (Hawkins, 2000; Willis, 2003: 71 and 75; Lázaro Reboll or Pavlovic, both in 2004). Women are usually presented with reference to their bodies, both as prey to be hunted by the male and as devourers, but 'sexual chauvinism went hand in hand with political and national chauvinism' (Hopewell, 1986: 31). More generally, co-productions and consequent double versions could be usefully compared, both as entertainment and from the perspectives of production and distribu-tion. Foreign directors like Peter Collinson working in Spain also deserve further attention. Of interest to both this decade and the following would be studies of those actors and technicians who moved, apparently easily, between the production of popular films and *auteur* cinema.

7

The Last Years of the Regime and a Middle Path
(1969–1975)

Agony: continued political repression and social demands

In September 1967 the Franco cabinet was modified in an attempt to halt the progressive liberalisation experienced during the decade, but this only aggravated the social situation. The small freedoms recently acquired and their felt potential could not be repressed so easily. Barcelona and Madrid Universities had to be closed a number of times as students and the labour force demonstrated against the establishment, just as their French counterparts would do in May '68. Furthermore in June 1968 ETA carried out their first assassination of a policeman, followed two months later by the murder of a senior police chief, Melitón Manzanas. A state of emergency was imposed and not lifted until August 1969 when senior government officials were implicated in the MATESA and Guerra fraud scandals and had to back down (Hooper, 1987; 177–8). In the subsequent cabinet shake-up conservative ministers predominated and directed the country until 1973, introducing more repressive measures. In July 1969, General Franco officially named Juan Carlos and the Monarchy as his legal successor. The Burgos trial of six ETA militants in 1970 provoked protests both at home and abroad, and another state of emergency was declared in December, lasting a further six months. By June 1973 Franco was 81 and very ill. He appointed hardliner Admiral Luis Carrero Blanco to lead the government, by which time Spanish bishops had distanced themselves from the official repression and voted for a separation of Church and State. However, Carrero Blanco was assassinated on 20 December 1973 in an explosion planned by an ETA squad, an event recreated in the film *Operación Ogro* [1980 Gillo Pontecorvo, *Operation Ogre*]. Carlos Arias Navarro took charge of the cabinet and attempted to control the situation by offering a more liberal government, a promise remembered as the 'spirit of 12 February' 1974 and the *apertura* [opening out].

Repercussions for the cinema

These events had a great impact on Spanish Cinema as ultra-conservative Alfredo Sánchez Bella was appointed as the responsible Minister of Information and Tourism from October 1969, where he was active until January 1974, a period of crisis, according to Casimiro Torreiro (in Gubern, 1995: 246–50). Film production continued to struggle, unable to compete against Hollywood imports while theatres were too big and in need of refurbishment. Ultimately many had to close down owing to decreasing spectators as television sets proliferated in private homes now that broadcasting covered the whole country. The situation was aggravated by the inevitable debts of the Escudero subsidies incurred throughout the previous decade and the fiscal consequences of the MATESA fraud. In October 1969, Carlos Robles Piquer was replaced at the Dirección General de Cultura Popular y Espéctaculos [Department for Popular Culture and Performances, now responsible for cinema] by another ultra-conservative appointment, Enrique Thomas de Carranza, who remained in charge until Rogelio Díaz replaced him in January 1974. Carranza announced the closure of the EOC in 1971 and teaching was transferred to Madrid's Complutense University until 1976. He approved the increase in the price of cinema tickets, and in 1972 re-established the budget of the Filmoteca Nacional so that it was able to resume some of its pre-1967 activities (Santamarina, 2005: 30–1). He changed the 'Special Interest' subsidies to post-production awards so that they no longer contributed to the financing of new films, which further stifled productions; however, the measure was subsequently reversed in 1973.

With the liberalising swing that followed in January 1974 under Arias Navarro, Pío Cabanillas took over from Sánchez Bella as Minister for Information and Tourism to implement more open policies, but this only lasted until the following October. Cabanillas was considered too permissive. His authorisation on 19 February 1975 to modify the censorship norms, in place since 16 February 1963, including a radical change in article 9 stating that 'Nudity will be accepted provided it is required by the thematic integrity of the film, but it will be rejected when it is introduced with the intention to excite the passions of the average spectator or leads to pornography',[1] opened a flood gate. This resulted in the release of many foreign films previously judged too provocative or morally subversive. Consequently the first flash of a naked Spanish breast on the screen was authorised, soon followed

---

1 'Se admitirá el desnudo siempre que esté exigido por la unidad total del film, rechazándose cuando se presente con intención de despertar las pasiones en el espectador normal o incida en la pornografía.'

by a brief instant of frontal female nudity albeit a reflection in a mirror.[2] But these things are relative, and they were very brief takes at a time when European cinema was becoming much more visually explicit: *A Clockwork Orange* [1971 Stanley Kubrick], *The Devils* [1971 Ken Russell] or *La Grande Bouffe* [1973 Marco Ferreri, *Blow-Out*, scripted by Rafael Azcona and Francis Blanche]. Nonetheless what was politically known as the *apertura* [Opening Out] was thus matched by the cinematographic *destape* [taking the lid off], as if compensating for the very slow release of other civil rights. It was also a time when colour photography became more subtle and muted, and thus more convincing as a realistic medium. Politically Pío Cabanillas was also officially criticised for allowing the distribution of Carlos Saura's *La prima Angélica* [1974 *Cousin Angelica*], said to be the first film to refer openly to the Civil War from the losing side and to present Francoist stalwarts in a ridiculous light, thus provoking extreme-right reactions and even riots (Hopewell, 1986: 90–2; Richardson, 2002: 114–38).

During the Sánchez Bella years, 1969–74, double versions were tolerated and soon proliferated, differentiating home from export distribution with greater nudity, the latter also having more than one version depending on their release in the UK and USA, or Germany and other more permissive countries. This gave rise to the scandal caused by Rafael Moreno Alba's *Las melancólicas* [1971 *Women of Doom*] in Santiago de Compostela when the export version of this gothic mental asylum narrative was shown in error instead of the censored home version. At this time of growing affluence there was an increase in weekend trips to Biarritz or Perpignan for uncensored viewing, when busloads of Spaniards would cross the border to be satiated on prohibited films.

> In 1973 five cinemas opened there [Perpignan] and *Last Tango in Paris* [1972 Bernardo Bertolucci], a particularly hot item at the time, was seen by more than 150,000 viewers in the town's cinemas. With a population of 200,000 this is an astonishing figure. The cinemas would open their doors at ten in the morning and show films right up until midnight. Often keen Spaniards would catch three or four films a night.
>
> (Tohill & Tombs, 1994: 64)

---

[2] The first was Carmen Sevilla in Gonzalo Suárez's *La loba y la paloma* [1974 *House of the Damned*], a co-production with Liechtenstein, and the second was María José Cantudo in Jordi Grau's *La trastienda* [1976 *Back of the Store*] where the frame cuts off a few inches below the waist – I report not from memory but from the DVD versions. In between there would be the breasts of Amparo Muñoz, Miss Universe 1974, in Antonio Drove's *Tocata y fuga de Lolita* [1974 **Lolita's Toccata and Fugue*], Ana Belén in Jaime de Armiñán's *El amor del capitán Brando* [1974 *The Love of Captain Brando*], and Alicia Sánchez's fragmented striptease in the woods of José Luis Borau's *Furtivos* [1975 **Poachers*].

These visits are the context for Vicente Escrivá's *Lo verde empieza en los Pireneos* [1973 *Smut Starts at the Pyrenees* – PNC].

Barrio cinema: the old favourites

The popular *cine de barrio* kept up its well-tried genres of musicals and comedies with the experienced pre-EOC directors, using the same crews and exploiting the reputation of the established comedians, some of whom were listed in chapter 6, pp. 166–8. The older directors were still bringing out their feel-good musicals. Juan de Orduña, who in the 1960s had filmed thirteen *zarzuelas* for television, directed two more musicals before he died in 1974: *El caserío* [1972 **The Farmhouse*] and *Me has hecho perder el juicio* [1973 **You've Made Me Lose The Trial*] with Manolo Escobar. Manolo Escobar also starred in Luis Lucia's last film, *Entre dos amores* [1972 **Between Two Loves*] and Sáenz de Heredia's *Cuando los niños vienen de Marsella* [1974 **When the Children Arrive from Marseilles*]. A number of these musicals were remakes of successful films, including the third version of *El relicario* [1970 **The Locket*, also 1927 and 1933] by Rafael Gil, dealing with a mysterious locket that affects a bullfighter's performances, with singer Carmen Sevilla, leading man Arturo Fernández and bullfighter Miguelín; Gil's *El sobre verde* [1971 **The Green Envelope*] about the staging of the musical of the same name; or Ramón Torrado's *Los caballeros del botón de ancla* [1973] about naval cadets and their pranks.[3] Torrado also exploited the Eurovision Song Contest in Dublin with *En un mundo nuevo* [1971 **In a New World*] fictionalising Karina's entry with La Pandilla.[4] Even more traditional is the story of the prize-winning singer with a golden heart, the helpful priest, the orphan needing an operation, radio contests, bulls and flamenco narrative, all in *Españolear* [1969 **Doing it the Spanish Way*] directed by former EOC student Jaime J. Balcázar.

Challenged family values are still the concern of Paco Martínez Soria's comedies, whether directed by Sáenz de Heredia, *Don Erre que erre* [1970 **Mr Goesby Thebook*], Mariano Ozores's *La descariada* [1973 **The Stray Sheep*] or *El calzonazos* [1974 **The Hen-pecked Husband*], Javier Aguirre's *El insólito embarazo de los Martínez* [1974 **The Smiths' Most Unusual Pregnancy*], or Pedro Lazaga's *Hay que educar a papá* [1971 **Educating Father*], *El padre de la criatura* [1972 **The Father of the Child*] or *El abuelo tiene un plan* [1973 **Grandfather has a Plan*]. Other favourite topics surviving

---

3   This remake is the least engaging of the three versions; see p. 108 for Torrado's first version and explanation of the title, and p. 163 for Miguel Lluch's version with the pop group Dúo Dinámico.

4   In 1971 she was the runner-up in the actual contest, and Séverine won for Monaco.

the decades were the *pícaro* narratives like *Enseñar a un sinverguenza* [1970 Agustín Navarro, **Lesson for a Rascal*] echoing the small-time confidence tricksters so well developed in Lazaga's 1959 *Los tramposos*. In spite of improbable plots like Gil's remake of his first comedy *El hombre que se quiso matar* [1942, 1970 **The Man Who Wanted to Kill Himself*] or Lazaga's *El dinero tiene miedo* [1970 **Money is Afraid*], both starring Tony Leblanc, the mise-en-scène in many of these films reveals much about the time when they were made and, with hindsight, its official values. Sometimes the films intuit subsequent social issues behind their puerile humour, like Mariano Ozores's *Señora Doctor* [1973 **Madam Doctor*] with Lina Morgan and José Sacristán, which deals with the prejudice against women now progressing as professionals as well as the lack of gynaecological information given to most women, albeit in the context of a village life. The comic detective or bank heist was another much used motif: Sáenz de Heredia's *La decente* [1970 **The Decent One*], or *La llamaban la madrina* [1973 **They Called Her the Godmother*], with Lina Morgan directed by Mariano Ozores in a farce concerning a family of small-time crooks who are sucked into counter-espionage. Priests and nuns also remained on the posters of some comedies: *¡Se armó el belén!* [1970 Sáenz de Heredia, **What a Fuss of a Nativity!*] about getting the parish nativity pageant broadcast on television and the neighbourhood back in church; *Coqueluche* [1970 Germán Lorente] starring Gracita Morales as a strange nun on the Costa del Sol; or *Una monja y un don Juan* [1973 Mariano Ozores, **A Nun and a Don Juan*], a comedy about the nun Lina Morgan raising money for the convent and provoking catastrophes when she meets the *pícaro* José Sazatornil.

Comedias sexy: negotiating new limits

During the last six years of the Dictatorship the plots dominating popular cinema were those labelled Iberian Sex Comedies (*comedias del destape* or *comedias sexy*), revealing with each film more and more female flesh while dealing with male sexual prowess which was usually undermined, frustrated or re-inscribed within the institution of patriarchal marriage. The most prolific directors of these comedies were Pedro Lazaga,[5] Mariano Ozores[6]

---

[5]   The veteran of the three: the *IMDb* lists 93 films between 1951 and 1978. He died the following year.

[6]   A prolific director from a film family. His father Mariano and mother, Luisa Puchol, two brothers José Luis and Antonio, and two of his nieces, Adriana and Emma, were and are all actors. He started as a screenwriter in the 1950s and has been acting and directing since 1959. At the time of writing the *IMDb* is confusing on his records.

and Pedro Masó,[7] who all frequently collaborated, and Ramón Fernández. Masó wrote and produced many of these narratives and tried more openly to eroticise his films as far as the censors would permit, as revealed by his risqué titles but inoffensive plots: *Una chica y un señor* [1972 **A Girl and a Gentleman* – PNC], *Un hombre como los demás* [1974 **A Man Like All the Others*], *Las adolescentes* [1975 *The Adolescents*].[8] Pedro Lazaga's titles include *Verano 70* [1970 **The Summer of 1970*], in which the mothers and children of four families meet every year for their vacation in Benidorm while the men, full of anxieties at their challenged masculinities, go back to Madrid to play at *rodríguez* (p. 167, n. 14). In another tourist comedy, *El abominable hombre de la Costa del Sol* [1970 **The Abominable Marbella Man*], Juanjo Menéndez plays an inept aristocrat and failed seminarist who is given the public relations post at the Hotel Don Pepe in Marbella. However, by far the most successful comedy of this type was Ramón Fernández's *No desearás al vecino del quinto* [1970 *Thou Shalt Not Covet Thy Fifth Floor Neighbour*], with Alfredo Landa in his first lead role. He had to date appeared most frequently in secondary parts as the shy and blundering *paleto*, but also portrayed another stereotype, that of the shy, sexually repressed individual who is inept in female company, while in other films he is the frustrated 'obseso sexual maníaco'.[9] The character and his situations appealed because of the taboo that the censors had placed on sexuality and in *No desearás...* Fernández exploits both the situation and Landa's screen persona by reversing the anticipated outcome. The film plays on stereotypes that were actually outmoded even for Spain in 1970 but were still present in films, as well as pandering to provincial prejudices which typecast fashion models, gynaecologists and homosexuals,[10] thus revealing that social attitudes still needed to mature (Triana Toribio, 2004: 100–4). The film had considerable problems with the censors, but when released it was for 31 years the biggest national box-office success. The formula was repeated the following year in Fernando Merino's *No desearás la mujer de tu prójimo* [1971 **Thou Shalt Not Covet thy Neigbour's Wife*], and the term 'Landismo', which boosted Landa's

---

7   At the beginning of 2004 the *IMDb* lists Masó 64 film-scripts, 38 productions and the personal direction of 20 films.

8   Masó's most successful box-office comedy as a producer-screenwriter-director came later in 1979 with *La miel* [*Honey*], with Jane Birkin as the single mother of a quick-witted Jorge Sanz in his first film, who disrupts the non-existent sex-life of his school teacher played by López Vázquez.

9   'Sexually obsessed maniac' is the term used in *¿Por qué pecamos a los cuarenta?* to describe López Vázquez's character, but it applies to the other men in the comedy.

10   The film is constructed on the stereotyped caricature that professionals who attend exclusively to female consumers are inevitably represented, in pre-democratic cinema, as homosexuals with affected and camp mannerisms.

screen career,[11] was coined to describe the obsessed and immature individual of these frequently repeated plots. 'Typically low-budget, these shamefully vulgar features focused mainly on the hugely inflated but constantly frustrated libido of the typical, repressed Iberian male' (Jordan & Morgan 1998: 64–6; Jordan, 2003: 167–86).

There were many other films with similar titles, usually produced against the clock. Vicente Escrivá directed *Aunque la hormona viste seda* [1971 *Even if Hormones Wear Silk*], *La Curiosa* [1972 *The Inquisitive One* – PNC] or the successful *Lo verde empieza en los Pireneos* [1973] with López Váquez, José Sacristán and Rafael Alonso as three professional men on a weekend film viewing in Biarritz. Luis María Delgado kept busy with *Guapo heredero busca esposa* [1972 *Handsome Heir Seeks a Bride*], starring Alfredo Landa as the innocent *paleto* who comes to the city to find any bride, needed to receive his inheritance, and during the same year the more self-reflexive *Cuando el cuerno suena* [1972 *When the Horn Sounds*[12]]. Ramón Fernández directed *Simón contamos contigo* [1971 *We're Counting on You, Simon*], *Los novios de mi mujer* [1972 *My Wife's Boyfriends*] and *El adúltero* [1975 *The Adulterer*]. Pedro Lazaga worked within this framework but often added a touch of his own. *El alegre divorciado* [1975 *The Happy Divorcee*] was a co-production, appropriately set in Mexico, that raised the question of divorce between Paco Martínez Soria and Florinda Chico only to conclude that it is not a worthwhile solution to differences.[13] *Vente a ligar al oeste* [1972 *Get a Girl out West*] recalls the impact of US production companies and subsequent westerns filmed in Almería, while in *Vente a Alemania, Pepe* [1971 *Come to Germany, Pepe*] a migrant worker back in his village after working in Germany tells stories of sexual achievements that he could only dream about. Both films starred Landa in his signature role of the sexually repressed *paleto*. According to Barry Jordan, who takes this last film as his example, 'sex and sexual anxieties function as a powerful synecdoche, representing a much wider range of fears, lacks and uncertainties' of Spaniards vis-à-vis the apparently greater freedom offered in other European countries but who, in the end, choose the security of their own known context even if it is repressive (1995: 128–31, 130).

---

[11] Landa would have to wait until the 1980s to break out successfully from this typecasting with films like *El crack* [1981 José Luis Garci, *The Crack*] and *Los santos inocentes* [1984 Mario Camus, *The Holy Innocents*].

[12] In Spanish the reference to *cuerno* immediately brings to mind the horns of the cuckold.

[13] The Catholic context could not allow anything else, but it is important that the question was raised. In Spain the film was originally released as *Casada es mi mujer*. Divorces were legal in Republican Spain from 1932 to 1938, and then reintroduced on 7 July 1981.

Literary adaptations

Rafael Gil was still working hard, with twelve films in these six years, including a number of literary adaptations. In 1972 it was *Nada menos que todo un hombre* [*Nothing Less than a Real Man* – PNC] based on Unamuno's novel *Todo un hombre*, followed by *La duda* [1973 *Doubt* – PNC, San Sebastián Best Actor for Fernando Rey] based on Galdós's *El abuelo*, which has had other adaptations in 1927 and 1998, and the same year *La guerrilla* [*The Guerilla*] from Azorín, an anti-war film set in 1808 during the Napoleonic Wars. In 1974 he adapted Lope de Vega's seventeenth-century play *El mejor alcalde el rey* [*The King is the Best Mayor*] for the screen. There were other literary adaptations such as the actor Adolfo Marsillach's only foray into film direction, *Flor de santidad* [1972 *Flower of Holiness*], based on a Valle Inclán novel; Rafael Moreno Alba's *Pepita Jiménez* [1975 *Bride to Be*] from Juan Valera's novel with Stanley Baker as Pedro de Vargas and Sarah Miles as Pepita, first adapted in 1925 by Agustín Carrasco and with a Mexican version in 1946; or José Jara's adaptation of Unamuno's *Niebla* released as *Las cuatro novias de Augusto Pérez* [1975 *The Four Brides of Augusto Pérez*]. But if serious literary adaptations like Gonzalo Suárez's *La Regenta* [1974 *The Regent's Wife*] or Mario Camus's *Leyenda del alcalde de Zalamea* [1972 *The Legend of the Mayor of Zalamea*] were used to illustrate the repressive power of the Church's hypocritical values or to question authority (Hopewell, 1986: 77), so films can be used to reflect on new sexual attitudes rather than nudity. This is the case with the adaptation of the fourteenth-century classic *El libro de buen amor* [1975 Tomás Aznar, *The Book of Good Love*], a film with good location shots but probably difficult to follow if one does not know the original text, and *El libro de buen amor II* [1976 Jaime Bayarri], which presents a pseudo-biography of the poet rather than the Archpriest as a character. Ramón Fernández also adapted the seventeenth-century satire by Luis Vélez de Guevara into a fantasy comedy starring Landa, *El diablo cojuelo* [1971 *The Limping Devil*].[14] These films actually showed very little nudity or sex, in direct contrast to what the promotional posters promised. Not only were they more talk than action, but they were often very patronising in their attitude towards women, praising them as sexual objects desired without marriage vows.

Dramas and thrillers tackling social realities

Thrillers and dramas from the established directors taking advantage of the *destape* continued at a slower pace. For instance, Ignacio F. Iquino directed

---

[14] In contrast with and reminiscent of *Marcelino, pan y vino* [1954], Fernández also adapted a story by Anatole France, *El Cristo del océano* [1971 *Christ of the Ocean*].

Aborto criminal [1973 **Criminal Abortion* – PNC], *Chicas de alquiler* [1973 **Girls for Hire*] and *Fraude matrimonial* [1976 **Matrimonial Fraud*], exploiting the erotic while managing to raise gender issues, before ending his fifty-year career in 1984, having scripted 102 films and directing 87. José Antonio Nieves Conde's *Más allá del deseo* [1976 **Beyond Desire*] retells with many flashbacks how a car accident leads to a passionate past difficult to understand. The even more prolific José Antonio de la Loma directed *El último viaje* [1974 *The Last Trip* – PNC] dealing with the drug scene. Drugs were also the subject of Rafael Gil's *Novios de la muerte* [1974 **Death's Newlyweds*], an adventure set in the Foreign Legion and resolved to the Legion's credit. However, given the censors' requirement that the representatives of the law should always be shown in their best light not to undermine figures of authority, the police thriller, successful in other countries, was very restricted in Spain (Hopewell, 1986: 37–8). Antonio Isasi's *Un verano para matar* [1972 *Summertime Killer*] was a co-production with Italy and France, originally released in Italian and with an international cast: Christopher Mitchum, Karl Malden, Olivia Hussey, Raf Vallone, and others. Some of the directors coming out of the Escudero stables and new directors to be mentioned below did, however, explore and renew the genre by setting their political intrigues and thrillers in foreign lands or developing narratives that exploit the psychological, the para-normal and terror rather than plausible narratives.[15]

The Civil War

Whereas the young directors and dissidents would allude to the Civil War and approach it indirectly, more established directors were able to deal with it more openly because their political credentials and self-censorship did not threaten the establishment. Ramón Torrado's *La montaña rebelde* [1971 **The Rebel Mountain*] is set in 1936 in the Republican territory of the Asturian mountains, but concerns a civilian doctor and focuses on the melodrama of three men attracted to the same woman. León Klimovsky's *La casa de las Chivas* [1972 **The House of Bitches*, Deveny's translation (1999: 404)] is another melodrama set behind the front lines where things are not as they seem. It stars Simón Andreu as a good Republican and covert priest, and although the values upheld strictly adhere to the Catholic perspective it does not demonise the Republicans. *La orilla* from Luis Lucia [1971 **The River Bank* – PNC], about a Republican officer saved by nuns, also avoids a facile

---

[15] Jordan & Morgan point out that the term 'thriller' does not translate directly into Spanish and the English is frequently used together with 'cine policiaco', 'cine negro' or even 'cine de suspense' (1998: 86–9).

polarisation and offers a message against war and for reconciliation within Franco's Spain, as Lazaga had implied timidly with *La fiel infantería* [1959 *The Proud Infantry* – PNC] or *El otro árbol de Guernica* [1969 *The Other Guernica Tree*].

Horror films

Although the *chorizo westerns* of the 1960s lost favour and were gradually abandoned, many directors carried on with the alternative genre of horror and terror. Jesús Franco and Jacinto Molina's cult status continued and continues to grow, stretching the excesses of their 1960s' 'horrotica' even further with films that could not be released in Spain, and in some countries also included inserted fragments of soft-porn footage (Hawkins, 2000: 96). Jesús Franco made some fifty-five films in the last six years of the Dictatorship, mostly horror and then soft-porn, in Sweden, France, Germany but very few in Spain, and these under many different aliases (see *IMDb*). Being an accomplished musician, he often wrote his own music under one of his pseudonyms. Always surprising (Pavlovic, 2004: 135–50), one could select among his films *99 Mujeres* [1969 *99 Women*], a women-in-prison drama, *El conde Drácula* [1970 *Count Dracula*] with Christopher Lee and Klaus Kinski, to which Lázaro Reboll adds *Las vampiras* [1971 *Vampyros Lesbos*] also with Soledad Miranda and heavily censored in Spain (2002: 83–96).

Between 1967 and 1980, Jacinto Molina, better known as Paul Naschy, scripted and starred in his many films. In nine of these he featured as the aristocratic werewolf Count Waldemar Daninski. The first, *La marca del hombre lobo* [1967 *The Mark of the Wolfman*] was directed by Enrique Eguiluz. This was followed by León Klimovsky's *La noche de Walpurgis* [1971 *Shadow of the Werewolf*], whose success generated many sequels. In Klimovsky's *Dr Jekyll y el hombre lobo* [1972 *Dr Jeckyll and the Wolfman*][16] a more scientific approach is attempted to overcome the curse in a plot that is typically enriched with echoes of Dracula, Justine and Jack the Ripper, characters that Molina had played and would play in other films (Lázaro Reboll, 2005: 129–36). Molina's fifth Daninsky, *La furia del hombre lobo* [1972 *The Fury of the Wolfman*], was directed by José María Zabalza, while Carlos Aured took care of the first of many *El retorno de Walpurgis* [1973 *The Return of Walpurgis*]. Jacinto Molina did not hesitate to direct himself in some of these films, like *Inquisición* [1976 *Inquisition*] or as Daninski again in another *Retorno del*

---

[16] From 1973 to 1977 Klimovsky directed seven more Molina films. The music for both these films, as well as for other Molina productions, is credited to Antón García Abril, who also wrote the music for numerous Lazaga films and other comedies, including a Rocío Dúrcal musical, as well as for Mario Camus and Pilar Miró. In 2005 the *IMDb* listed 166 titles.

hombre lobo [1980 *The Return of the Wolfman*], still presenting the werewolf as persecuted by his unwanted curse and seeking redemption. The Spanish releases of these co-productions were tolerated, subject to numerous cuts, because they presented foreigners in other lands. They contain both the predictable and the surprising, while the shoestring budgets and hasty filming make them quite endearing and are part of Molina's international cult appeal. Molina defines his films (32 films in six years, 1970–6) as 'fantaterror' with traces of the displaced frustrations of his upbringing during the Civil War and the subsequent repressive Dictatorship; he was born in 1934. Daninsky was still going strong in 2003 with *Tomb of the Werewolf* [Fred Olen Ray], but *Licántropo* [1996 Francisco Rodríguez Gordillo, *Lycanthropus: The Moon-light Murders*] is one of the more interesting psychologically. The essential Waldemar returns at 66, now a successful novelist but still a victim of the curse. Through his fevers, nightmares and murders, he seeks release and redemption through the love of a Platonic Lady who might be able to save him. It leaves the gothic setting for a more contemporary mise-en-scène but not without a wink to the audience since the Lady, played by Amparo Muñoz, is called Mina. It is more explicitly metaphorical than other films from the series, since the credit sequence establishes the monster and the *machista* as the product of repressive and intolerant Fascist ideologies with austere patriarchal values, and underlining the plot there is a plea for tolerance and condemnation of discrimination on the basis of gender or race.

Jesús Franco and Molina did not hold a monopoly. Valencian Francisco Lara Polop directed his first film in 1972, *La mansión de la tiniebla* [*Murder Mansion*], followed by the erotic attempts *Cebo para una adolecente* [1973 *Bait for an Adolescent*], *Perversión* [1974 *Perversion*], *Obsesión* [1975 *Obsession*], and the crime thriller *La protegida* [1975 *The Protected One*]. Following a similar trajectory, Catalan José Ramón Larraz, mostly under pseudonyms (*IMDb*), started directing and scripting with his eroticised terror *Whirlpool* [1970], a Danish film set in London. His next four were made in the UK with a fifth in Italy, and he then came to Spain to make *Emma, puertas oscuras* [1974 *Emma, Dark Doors*] and *El fin de la inocencia* [1976 *The End of Innocence*]. More successful was Claudio Guerín Hill's *La campana del infierno* [1973 *A Bell from Hell*] after *La casa de las palomas* [1972 *The House of the Doves*], but he died after falling off the bell-tower on the last day of shooting and the film was completed by an uncredited Bardem (Willis, 2003: 78–82). A similar but less prolific pattern was followed by Galician Amando de Ossorio who after a few *chorizo westerns* in the 1960s directed the successful *La noche del terror ciego* [1971 *Night of the Blind Dead*], presenting excommunicated Templar Knights returning through the centuries on horseback to terrorise professional women with lesbian feelings on their vacation. Narciso 'Chicho' Ibáñez Serrador made his second film in 1976 *¿Quién puede matar a un niño?* [*Would You Kill a Child?*] where the terror is reserved for an English couple wanting a quiet tourist holiday on a Balearic island.

Marsha Kinder argues that the 'eroticised violence could be used so effectively by the anti-Francoist opposition to speak a political discourse, that is to expose the legacy of brutality and torture that lay hidden behind the surface beauty of the Fascist and neo-Catholic aesthetics' (1993: 138). Willis adds that these films reached a popular and young audience in contrast to the more intellectual *auteurist* approach of Saura and the *NCE* (2003: 71–83). However, financial concerns were perhaps the most important motivator, and the pattern for most of the less successful directors following popular taste is from *chorizo western* to horror to soft-porn as Jesús Luis Madrid's filmography illustrates; from *La venganza de Clark Harrison* [1966 *Ruthless Colt of the Gringo*], to *El vampiro de la autopista* [1970 *The Motorway Vampire*] and then *Striptease a la inglesa* [1975 *English Strip-tease*].[17]

The mixed fortunes of the NCE graduates

García Escudero's investment in the *NCE* had left vast debts and did not produce the desired results. A number of the graduates of the EOC disappeared. Julio Diamante tried with one comedy *Sex o no sex* [1974 *Sex or no Sex*] and then a drama, *La Carmen* [1976], before withdrawing from the film world.[18] Others, like Miguel Picazo and self-exiled Antxon Eceiza, were silent and unseen for a number of years. Some had moved into more commercial cinema, like Javier Aguirre with fourteen films and many documentaries released in those six years. Even the titles of his comedies show that he is earning his living by satisfying the popular *cine de barrio* audience: *Vibraciones oscilatorias* [1975 *Oscillatory Vibrations*], *Ligeramente viuda* [1975 *Slightly Widowed*] or the musical *Pierna creciente, falda menguante* [1970 *Waxing Leg and Waning Skirt*]. Francisco Regueiro was also productive with films examining relationships, like *Carta de amor de un asesino* [1972 *Love Letter from a Murderer*], the black farce in the absurd world of *Duerme, duerme mi amor* [1975 *Sleep, Sleep my Love*] and *Las bodas de Blanca* [1975 *Blanca's Weddings*], where Blanca [Concha Velasco] hopes her second husband will not be impotent like the first, but this would be his last film until 1985. Similarly for Angelino Fons who, as well as pursuing his enthusiasm for the novelist Benito Pérez Galdós by filming *Marianela*

---

[17] *Torremolinos 73* [2003, Pablo Berger] is a brilliant evocation, with other twists, of what could have happened on the unseen margin of the exploitation of sex on film.

[18] Some films released in 1976 are included in this chapter on the grounds that they were conceived, if not completed, before Franco's death, but would not have been released had Franco not died in November 1975.

[1972], also explored the strained relationships of couples and families but with more interference from the censors and not much interest from the spectators, *La primera entrega* [1971 *First Surrender*] and *Separación matrimonial* [1973 **Conjugal Separation*].[19] Fons also directed the musical comedy *Mi hijo no es lo que parece* [1974 **My Son is not what he Seems*] where a homosexual tendency is to be cured by a woman, and two films in 1976, *La casa*, and *Emilia... parada y fonda* [**The House* and **Emilia... Road Stop and Inn*]. The latter is more interesting but met with no more success in spite of a strong cast exploring female psychology with a script based on a short story by novelist Carmen Martín Gaite. His next film would be made in Mexico in 1983. Antonio Giménez Rico had started directing in 1966 with a children's comedy, *Mañana de domingo* [**Sunday Morning*], followed by the satirical comedy *El hueso* [1967 *The Bone*], but after the failure of *¿Es usted mi padre?* [1971 **Are You My Father?*], he left the film world to work for television, returning six years later in 1976 with the very successful *Retrato de familia* [*Family Portrait*].

Others directed excellent films that were precisely what the censors did not want released. Basilio Martín Patino's *Canciones para después de una guerra* [1971 **Songs for after a War*] is a documentary montage of 1940s' footage, photographs, press clippings, children's comics, etc. set against the ironic soundtrack of contemporary songs. It thus builds on the collective popular memory of hardships and brief distractions with an efficient and fascinating 'nudging sarcasm' (Hopewell, 1986: 125–7) as it chronicles the years of hunger and silence up to young Juan Carlos's integration into the Franco fold on which the film concludes with a powerful photograph of a melancholic ten-year-old looking at the spectator. The film was banned a few days after its release and was not seen again until September 1976. Similar bans were placed on Patino's next projects, also feature-length documentaries. The first was on General Franco, *Caudillo* [1974 **The Leader*], and another interviewed three official executioners of the Franco regime, *Queridísimos verdugos* [1974 *Dearest Excecutioners*]. These two documentaries, also steeped in irony, were only released in 1977 but Patino did not make another film until 1985. Manuel Summers directed three of the films he scripted at the time, pursuing his concerns for adolescents in *Adios cigüeña, adios* [1971 *Goodbye Stork, Goodbye* – PNC], *El niño es nuestro* [1973 **The Baby is Ours*] and *¡Ya soy mujer!* [1975 *I'm a Woman Already*[20]],

---

[19] As mentioned p. 204, note 13, divorce was illegal in Spain from 1939 to 1981 but legal separations could be arranged and, in the case of this film exposing the hypocrisy, by drastic means.

[20] Better translated as *I'm a Woman Now!* as Celia and her sister have their first period, but 'already' is the title given in English, written in lipstick on a bathroom mirror, behind the Spanish credit title.

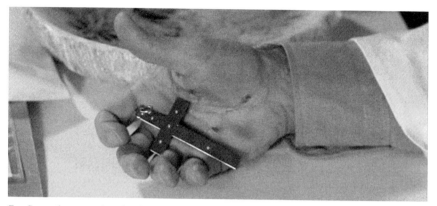

7a Sexual repression in Grau's *La trastienda* (1976)

which in spite of the censors' interference all examine the consequences of not discussing the impact of puberty with youngsters and adolescents. The limited popular knowledge of childbearing and looking after babies is also well illustrated by Javier Aguirre's 1972 comedy *Soltero y padre en la vida* [*Father and Unmarried*], which presents an impossible situation and characters for laughs.[21]

Mario Camus continued to mix commercial cinema like the western *La cólera del viento* [1970 *The Wind's Anger*], which nonetheless raises questions of social justice, with more intellectual films like *La leyenda del alcalde de Zalamea*, adapting into one narrative two seventeenth-century plays about the Mayor of Zalamea, one by Lope de Vega and the other by Calderón de la Barca, to examine civil and military authority. In 1975 he released two very different films, *Los pájaros de Baden Baden* [*The Birds of Baden Baden* – PNC], the end of a summer romance because of social pressures, and *La joven casada* [1975 *The Young Bride*]. Jordi Grau was even more eclectic with a number of documentaries, some experimental films, three horror films and the box-office hit of 1976, *La trastienda* [*Back of the Store*]. Exploiting both the relative freedom of the *destape* and the bullfighting festivities of San Fermín in Pamplona, this strong melodrama about infatuations also makes a critical comment on the powerful Opus Dei overwhelmed by its reputation. José Luis Borau after his initial commercial contracts concentrated on his teaching at the EOC, and also came out with two excellent political intrigues with serious implications (Kinder, 1993: chapter 7). *Hay que matar a B* [1973 *B Must Die*] is a tense, dark political thriller set in a fictional corrupt Latin American country, a tale of betrayals and cover-

---

[21] This is not a sequel to Aguirre's 1969 *Soltera y madre en la vida*, even if José Sacristán is in both films.

ups which manipulates the press, commenting on both 'the political situation in Spain and the [noir] generic conventions themselves' (Kinder, 1993:
351–7). It was made in English as a Swiss co-production with foreign actors
and touches of Jesús Franco's 1963 *Rififí en la ciudad*. It was followed by
Furtivos [1975 **Poachers/*The Furtive Ones* – PNC, San Sebastián]. Both
controversial and critical, it was a box-office success written with Manuel
Gutiérrez Aragón, who also directed the sequences where Borau appears as
the regional governor. It inverts two myths of the popular Spanish Cinema,
that of the country as the space of wholesome traditional values, the Francoist claim that Spain is a large peaceful and fecund forest, and the myth of
the happy and strong family (Hopewell, 1986: 97–104). *Furtivos* presents
a political denunciation of oppressive and hypocritical authority that covers
up incest, two murders and an implicit suicide, a family that destroys itself
against an oppressive backdrop. Peter Evans identifies and describes the film
as the 'Spanish *Psycho*' (1999a: 126), while Robin Fiddian examines the
contemporary socio-political implications by picking up the parallels and
reversals of the Hansel and Gretel archetype (1989: 300). The poster for the
film was designed by Iván Zulueta, who was also an EOC student from 1964
to 1967, and has to date only made some experimental shorts and two equally
unusual feature films. In 1969 he directed *Un, dos, tres, al escondite inglés*
[**What's the Time Mr Wolf?*[22]], an extravagant musical satire on contemporary pop culture, using a World Song Contest but in the zany spirit of
Richard Lester's *Help!* [1965]. Co-written with Jaime Chávarri and produced
by El Imán, José Luis Borau's own producing company founded in 1968, it
featured a part for Antonio Drove with a large cigar and a cameo appearance
from Borau as a moustacheless teacher.

The Barcelona directors

From Barcelona Vicente Aranda offered an excursion into gothic horror.
Pushing *Las crueles* [1969] a little bit further, *La novia ensangrentada* [1972
The Blood-Spattered Bride] is seen as an alternative way of indicting the
regime and its values, where again a woman takes revenge on men (Willis,
2003: 77–8), and the genre allowed for a lesbian subtext (Martin-Márquez,
1999a: 247). This was followed by an erotic comedy-drama with a difference, *Clara es el precio* [1974 *Claire is the Price*], about the double life of
a bored housewife who engages in soft-porn films, starring Amparo Muñoz
in her fourth film. Gonzalo Suárez directed the tense mystery thriller *Morbo*

---

22 It is impossible to translate the playground game with a reference to Britain.

[1971 *Morbidness/*Perversion*[23]] in which Ana Belén and Víctor Manuel go off in their caravan for a honeymoon far away from the city, but under pressure their relationship disintegrates. After this came another thriller, *La loba y la paloma* [1974 *House of the Damned*], about retrieving a lost statue from a mute girl, played by French actress Muriel Catala, combining a sensual Carmen Sevilla with Donald Pleasence and Michael Dunn,[24] a film that could be given an allegorical reading based on a narrative of latent and past violence. Suárez's concise evocative adaptation of Clarín [Leopoldo Alas]'s literary masterpiece[25] *La Regenta* [1974 *The Regent's Wife*], starring Emma Penella, Charo López and Pilar Bardem with English stars Nigel Davenport and Keith Baxter, used the nineteenth century to mark the continuing powerful psychological influence of prudish and hypocritical Church values. Suárez's next film, *Beatriz* [1976], was also a literary adaptation, combining two stories by Ramón del Valle Inclán. Biding his time, Jaime Camino returned with *Mi profesora particular* [1973 *My Private Teacher*], building on his own experience as a former piano teacher.

The usual suspects and identified dissidents

In the last few years of the dictatorship both Fernando Fernán Gómez and Juan Antonio Bardem turned to more commercial scripts but without much popular success. In addition to his busy acting schedule Fernán Gómez directed a number of comedies: *Crimen imperfecto* [1970 **Imperfect Crime*] about a private detective in Madrid with some cross-dressing, *Cómo casarse en siete días* [1971 **How to Get Married in Seven Days*], then *Yo la vi primero* [1974 *I Saw Her First*], which included performances by the directors Manuel Summers, León Klimovsky and Fernán Gómez himself, and *La querida* [1975 *The Mistress*] where he acts opposite the singer Rocío Jurado. Bardem also went for films that included big names, the failed comeback of Sara Montiel in *Variétés* [1970 *Varieties*] as well as the two thrillers with Marisol, *La corrupción de Chris Miller* [1973 *The Corruption of Chris Miller*] and *El poder del deseo* [1975 *The Power of Desire*], mentioned in the previous chapter. The latter, in spite of taking advantage of the *destape,* is an old fashioned romantic thriller with poor continuity and psychology, that contains too many social comments, including references to child abuse and

---

[23] English titles are taken from the *IMDb* for easy cross-referencing. When they are preceded by an asterisk it is my translation in the absence of an *IMDb* title; in this case it is an alternative suggestion.

[24] Post-synchronisation of a film's diegetic soundtrack was still the norm in the 1970s.

[25] This nineteenth-century novel ranks alongside *Madame Bovary*, *Anna Karenina* and *Effie Briest*.

migrants, to appeal to the spectators. There was also an adventure film, *La isla misteriosa* [1971 *The Mysterious Island of Dr Nemo*] with Omar Sharif in the title role.

Berlanga only made one film, *Tamaño natural* [1974 *Love Doll/Life Size*], which examines the individual isolation of Michel [Michel Piccoli] and his relationship with a life-size doll. It could not be filmed in Spain owing to the censors, but even abroad the film shocked. Michel purchases his doll as a silent partner to compensate for his fear of human relationships provoked, it is suggested, by his overpowering mother as in his previous *Vivan los novios* [1970 *Long Live the Bride and Groom*] but with a totally different approach.[26] *Tamaño...* owes a lot to Buñuel, and indeed Berlanga and Rafael Azcona also had the cooperation of Jean Claude Carrière when writing the script, which contains good doses of irony and pathos. However, in spite of the French context the problems presented are evidently those of the repressed and sexually frustrated middle-class Spaniard so often seen in the Iberian comedies.[27] It was released in France in August 1974; in London it was distributed as a porno-film and thus failed to satisfy the targeted audiences; in Italy it provoked violent feminist rejection, and was only released in Spain on 1 December 1977 in Barcelona and 25 February 1978 in Madrid (Hernández-Les, 1981: 119; Higginbotham, 1988: 52–4).

Carlos Saura, the dissenting maverick

Carlos Saura, with Elías Querejeta as his producer, was very active and together they became the recognised face of Spain at international film festivals. Saura's films pursued a narrative style that moved away from social realism to be consciously allegorical, including autobiographic elements and making increasing references to both his own films and those of others, as well as including personal dedications. Saura's films still concern indirectly the couple and the exploration of gender differences but now focus on the family, divided and dysfunctional, as a metaphor for Spanish society, confined to a big house with or without a garden, representing 'private past experience and the collective past of Spain [...] a search that is at once personal and collective' (Kovacs, 1981: 46). *El jardín de las delicias* [1970 *The Garden of Delights* – Sant Jordi for best film and for López Vázquez], a title based on Hieronymus Bosch's painting of 'The Garden of Earthly Delights (and Sin)' in the Prado Museum, develops Saura's growing interest in the workings of

---

[26] Francisco Rovira Beleta's *No encontré rosas para mi madre* [1973 *Roses and Green Pepper*] also examines the dominant mother but from a different angle.

[27] I have only seen the film with a Spanish soundtrack, which somewhat undermines the characterisation, but I suspect that the French dialogue contradicts the motivation.

7b The allegorical ending of Saura's *El jardín de las delicias* (1970)

the individual and collective memory that was still managing to repress the experience of the Civil War and subsequent oppression. In the powerfully symbolic concluding sequence those with money and power are presented as impotent, mindless and wheelchair-bound. There are constant parallels between the formerly authoritarian and abusive Antonio Cano [José Luis López Vázquez], the fictional Charles Foster Kane and the real industrialist Juan March, whose fortune waxed and waned in parallel with the Franco regime. Through the allegorising of individual experiences, Saura attacks the greed and exploitation of the victors of the war. This indictment was reiterated in *Ana y los lobos* [1972 *Anna and the Wolves*] where the English au-pair [Geraldine Chaplin] both identifies and is trapped by the values of the big house, obligatory in so many horror films, where the three brothers [José María Prada, José Vivó and Fernando Fernán Gómez] of the dysfunctional family are grotesque deformations of the military, the *paterfamilias* and the Church.[28] The 1973 *La prima Angélica* focuses on the victims of the war, pursuing the problems of individual memory subject to the dangers of being modified by the experience of the present and censorship. The protagonist tries to come to terms with the psychological scars of his childhood during the Civil War; 'the scenes set in the past in *La prima Angélica* are not flashbacks to the past as it was but recollections of the past remembered' (Hopewell,

---

[28] The three Fs of Francoism identified in chapter 4 (pp. 87–8). Saura identified the three male characters as the three Spanish Juans: Don Juan de Austria, Don Juan Tenorio and San Juan de la Cruz, typifying the three Spanish obsessions of the military, sex and religion, guarded by the censors.

1986: 88) by using the device of letting present and past glide in and out of the same frame without a cut and allowing López Váquez to play Luis/Luisito as both the adult and the child of his memories. Once again actors play more than one part to emphasise the traps of the mind and the tricks of memory started in *Peppermint frappé* [1967]. It is a film that at the time was the most critical of the Civil War's victors and consequently provoked violent reactions from the extreme right, leading to riots in theatres showing the film and pro-Franco demonstrations in the streets.

Concerns with memory are further explored in *Cría cuervos* ... [1975 *Raise Ravens*[29]], announced through the credit sequence of photographs, which the film then reveals do not even present the surface of the experiences lived by the characters. The confused memories of a young woman Ana [Geraldine Chaplin] are retold visually and a-synchronically, blurring one event with another that took place earlier, contextualised in a mise-en-scène, glimpsed four times during the film that suggests an empty future. Ana attempts to understand her feelings as a child [Ana Torrent] growing up in Franco's Spain and her childhood traumas of losing her mother, father and pet hamster. However, the first viewing of the film appears to protagonise the child Ana rather than the adult, and the film presents the young girl's confused experiences within the same frame without indication of time jumps. The film presents three generations of women, each identified by her musical theme, as the victims of hypocritical patriarchal values and of the military since, to the censors' concern, Ana's father [Héctor Alterio] is an army officer. As established in *Viridiana* and *Tristana,* and seen in other films, women are often representative of all the silent victims of the regime.

Saura worked with the same crew, provided by Querejeta's production company, although *Cría* ... was the first script he wrote on his own, severing his partnership with Rafael Azcona but acknowledging Geraldine Chaplin's collaboration (D'Lugo, 1991: 79 and 88). Another change was the substitution of the cinematographer Luis Cuadrado, with his failing eyesight, by Teo Escamilla, previously the second cameraman (Smith, 1999a: 103–6; D'Lugo, 1997: 143–4 and 150–1). It is Saura who earned his generation the label 'Children of Franco' (Kinder, 1983), and interestingly the censors were kinder to him, or more cautious, than they were with other dissident directors. His films were released when Patino's *Canciones* ... and other projects were denied distribution. This was mainly owing to Querejeta's ability to manipulate the international scandal card as a bargaining tool. Strict censorship did attract unwanted negative publicity at a time when the government wanted to present a more open and liberal image of itself, for diplomatic and economic

---

[29] As previously indicated (pp. 189–90), the title is in fact the beginning of a proverb. 'Cría cuervos y te sacarán los ojos', which might be best translated as 'biting the hand that feeds you' as applied to ungrateful and badly behaved children.

reasons. The censors no longer wanted to draw attention to a film that could pass unnoticed by the home viewers. It was felt that Saura's work had become so hermetic and difficult to understand, that it would in any case only appeal to minority groups who were already negative to the regime (D'Lugo, 1991: 114–15). Nonetheless the film was released just days before Franco's death and then put on hold until 26 January 1976.

A third or middle way

Midway between popular cinema, the Iberian Sex Comedies and the more demanding intellectual *auteur* films, there sprung up a third type of film, the so-called *Tercera vía* [Third Way], also seen as a transitional cinema by Hopewell (1986: 83). It was reflective and critical, looking at the new Spain and its concerns, but wanting popular box-office returns at home while keeping an eye on possible foreign distribution. It avoided the stereotypes and caricatures of the comedies but took advantage of the slightly more explicit images allowed on screen to give sex and family relationships a more serious treatment. In 1970, through Agata Films sponsored by José Luis Dibildos, like Querejeta now an influential producer, Roberto Bodegas, who had previous experience as an assistant director mostly acquired in France, made *Españolas en París* [1971 *Spaniards in Paris*; the original title marks the feminine – PNC], casting Ana Belén, five years after her debut in *Zampo y yo*, as a naive teenager arriving in Paris to find employment.[30] An earnest look at economic migrants working abroad in the service sector, a situation also taken up later in Buñuel's *Cet Obscur Objet du désir* [1977 *That Obscure Object of Desire*], the film raises the issue of exploitation and abortion, and included a song written by dissident poet José Agustín Goytisolo sung by Paco Ibáñez. Bodegas went on to make *Vida conyugal sana* [1973 *Healthy Married Life*], examining the legacy of a couple's rigid education and the consequences (Hopewell, 1986: 82–4). The following year brought an entertaining black comedy, *Los nuevos españoles* [1974 *The New Spaniards* – PNC] about a US company taking over a small Madrid insurance firm and refashioning the employees according to the ethos that destroyed Willy Loman in Arthur Miller's *Death of a Saleman*. It concludes ironically with Beethoven's 'Ode to Joy', as five widows collect awards posthumously bestowed on their husbands who worked themselves into early graves. This was followed by *La adúltera* [1975 *The Adulteress*] and *Libertad provisional* [1976 *Out on Parole*], again dealing with couples and their relation-

---

[30] This is an aspect of reality that is conspicuously rare in Spanish Cinema, but a recent if nostalgic treatment of the subject is Carlos Iglesia's *Un franco, 14 pesetas* [2006 *Crossing Borders*] set in the 1960s.

ships. Dibildos also contracted Antonio Drove, a 1967 graduate from the EOC working in television with a few documentaries and film scripts to his name. His first film was *Tocata y fuga de Lolita* [1974 *Lolita's Toccata and Fugue*, starring Amparo Muñoz and Arturo Fernández], which with an ironic disclaimer in its credit sequence relates a generational conflict and the problem of ageing when new freedoms were being found after so many decades of sexual repression. Drove's second film, *Mi mujer es muy decente, dentro de lo que cabe* [1974 *My Wife is Very Respectable, Given the Circumstances*], did not rise above the main commercial productions and put an end to Dibildos's experiment, even though the film starred the now-established Concha Velasco and José Sacristán in their fifth film together.

Pedro Masó, capitalising on his reputation, also took up a topical issue in a simple but serious vein with *Experiencia prematrimonial* [1972 *Premarital Experiment* –PNC], although he had to start with the censors' premise that such an experiment in a Catholic country had to be doomed to failure even if for the best of motives. The young couple wants to see if they are compatible for married life in contrast to their parents' double standards as adultery and the separation law that bypassed the divorce prohibition of the time are introduced at the beginning of the film (Triana Toribio, 2003: 104–7). Unfortunately, the film is somewhat undermined by Augusto Algueró's non-diegetic music too reminiscent of his musicals for Marisol and Dúrcal, poor postsynchronisation, dubbing of Italian actors Ornella Muti and Alessio Orano, in addition to its affluent and filmic social context, which belies the reality it wants to convey.

New directors

In these last years of the Dictatorship a number of new directors, not discouraged by the financial production crisis, appeared on Madrid billboards, some of them with considerable experience in the field of cinema. They too were critical and subversive in their presentation of the repressive society that had marked their adolescence.

Pedro Olea, born in Bilbao in 1938 and EOC student from 1964 to 1967, started his busy career with a romance, *Días de viejo color* [1968 *Days of Faded Colour*], examining the impact of the tourist boom on young affluent Spaniards, which won him the prize for best new director. He followed this with a science-fiction adventure, *En un mundo diferente* [1969 *In a Different World*], for the pop group Los Brincos who had contributed to the soundtrack of his first film. His first big box-office success arrived with an atmospheric tale of presumed lycanthropy in Galicia, using López Vázquez in *El bosque del lobo* [1971 *The Ancines Woods* – PNC], a rational twist to the horror genre. Then came the disastrous *La casa sin fronteras* [1972 *A House without*

Boundaries], a critical allegory of the Opus Dei. However, the year before Berlanga's *Tamaño natural*, his reputation recovered with a psychological thriller, *No es bueno que el hombre esté solo* [1973 *It is not Good for Man to be Alone*], about an apparently shy and repressed married engineer [López Vázquez]. Again set in a big house, this time on the outskirts of Bilbao, without indulging in nudity it is more of an indirect exploration of loneliness than a meditation on sexual frustrations. Developing a taste for period films, he then directed an adaptation of Galdós's *Tormento* [1974 – San Sebastián], with Ana Belén, Paco Rabal and Concha Velasco in a daring plot for the time since the much darker and grubby novel deals with a priest who cannot keep his vow of celibacy. *Pim, pam, pum ¡fuego!* [1975 *One Two Three, Fire!*] is set in the immediate post-war years as chorus girl Paca [Concha Velasco with red hair] is torn between security with an older black market racketeer [Fernán Gómez] and a young Republican soldier on the run [José María Flotats]. Olea's next film, *La Corea* [1976], opens with the arrival of the protagonist at Atocha station where Olea himself is filming *Tormento* and then moves on to explore the sexual underworld of contemporary Madrid. These three films are remembered as the Madrid trilogy, as they chronicle the city in the late nineteenth century, in the 1940s and then in the contemporary 1970s.

Older and from Madrid, Jaime de Armiñán, born in 1927, was an experienced playwright who moved into television scriptwriting in 1958 and started screenwriting in the 1960s, mostly for José María Forqué. He directed his first film in 1969, *Carola de día, Carola de noche* [*Carola by Day, Carola by Night*], another effort to relaunch Marisol in a musical romance, and the following year *La Lola, dicen que no vive sola* [1970 *They Say Lola Doesn't Live Alone*]. It was in 1972 that he presented *Mi querida señorita* [*My Dearest Señorita*[31] – PNC] written in collaboration with and produced by J.L. Borau. Forty-three-year-old Adela [López Vázquez] in her little provincial town where the national flag flies every day, learns that anatomically she is male, the most extreme consequence of overlooking sexual education. Renamed Juan, she eventually leaves town to try to survive in modern Madrid with only the skills that middle-class women were taught in Franco's Spain. He followed this astounding film with a modest comedy, *Un casto varón español* [1973 *A Chaste Spaniard*] and the memorable *El amor del capitán Brando* [1974 *The Love of Captain Brando* – PNC, Berlin]. Using references to the western the film examines an adolescent's infatuation for his understanding teacher [Jaime Gamboa and Ana Belén], and includes the republican memories of a returned exile [Fernán Gómez]; the village and its values serve once again as a microcosm of what is seen as an educational

---

[31] This English title is diegetically inserted in a sequence of *Hay que matar a B.*

problem, the lack of sexual information. Armiñán then directed the difficult *Jo, papá* [1975 *Gosh, Dad*], where the father played by Antonio Ferrandis takes his family on holiday by revisiting places that he remembers from his days as a nationalist soldier.

Another Basque, born in 1944, Eloy de la Iglesia also started his career in 1969 with the melodrama *Algo amargo en la boca* [*Something Bitter in Your Mouth*] and *Cuadrilátero* in 1970 [*Quadrilateral*], which at first made little impact except on the censors. He met his first real success with thrillers that border on the horror film. The success of *El techo de cristal* [1971 *Glass Ceiling*] allowed him to film an earlier and more interesting script, *La semana del asesino* [1972, released in 1974 *Week of the Killer/Cannibal Man*], where after an accident Marcos [Vicente Parra] becomes a serial killer in order to cover up the event. Both films are strong on graphic violence and eroticism, all to become the hallmark of Iglesia's films and cause him censorship problems,[32] since he repeatedly uses sex and violence as socio-political metaphors. Then came *Nadie oyó gritar* [1973 *No One Heard the Scream*], *Una gota de sangre para morir amando* [1973 *Murder in a Blue World*], before the more sexually explicit *Juego de amor prohibido* [1975 *Forbidden Love Game*] earned him the tongue-in-cheek description of 'by no means academically respectable' from P.J. Smith (1992: 129).

Ricardo Franco, born in 1949 in Madrid and nephew of Jesús Franco with whom he acquired his skills, wrote, directed, acted in and produced the historical drama *El desastre de Annual* [1970 *The Annual Debacle*] to revisit the 1921 military defeat in Spanish Morocco, which was unsurprisingly denied a release during the Dictatorship as military ineptitudes were not on the propaganda agenda. His first success was *Pascual Duarte*, another very critical look at Spanish values adapted from Camilo José Cela's *La familia de Pascual Duarte* written in 1942. Focusing on violence brought about by hopeless circumstances, it was filmed in 1975, but not released until 1976 after the Dictator's death (Faulkner, 2004a: 54–9). Alfonso Ungría explored the early post-war years with two films: *El hombre oculto* [1971 *The Man in Hiding*] about those republicans who spent long years in hiding to avoid arrest, and *Tirarse al monte* [1974 *Gone to the Mountain*] about the early *maquis*. Casimiro Torreiro identifies these two directors, adding Álvaro del Amo and Augusto Martínez, as previously involved in clandestine 16mm underground films (in Gubern, 1995: 353). At forty, Nino Quevedo, after a number of shorts and documentaries, directed Paco Rabal in *Goya, historia de una soledad* [1970 *Goya, a Story of Solitude*], which was so modified by the censors that it failed to satisfy anyone. José Luis García Sánchez, who

---

[32] In this case the original script was refused, and a false script was then presented. The censors then required 64 cuts and the refilming of the end (Andrés Peláez Paz, in Pérez Perucha, 1997: 692–4).

during this period was more active as a screenwriter with Gutiérrez Aragón, Francesc Betriu, and Patino, directed his first comedy *El love feroz* [*Ferocious Love*] in 1972, examining the consequences of sexual repression.

Josefina Molina, who in 1969 was the first woman to graduate from the EOC, also came to film from television, directing her first feature film in 1973, *Vera, un cuento cruel* [*Vera, a Cruel Story*] examining the possible drastic consequence of denial, with the concrete case of the death of a loved one. Manuel Gutiérrez Aragón, who graduated from the EOC in 1970, scripted and directed *Habla mudita* [1973 *Speak, Little Dumb Girl*] about an intellectual [José Luis Vázquez] who while on holiday in the mountains attempts to try to teach a dumb girl [a young Kiti Manver] to speak; it is a Pygmalion narrative where silences, as in *El espíritu de la colmena*, echo those years of silence and the difficulty of expressing what is repressed by the norms of the establishment (Peter Evans, in Graham & Labanyi, 1995: 306–7). The village and countryside was now increasingly used not so much to contrast tradition against modernisation but to create a new and more problematic metaphorical space (Richardson, 2002: 178–9). Antonio Mercero had been making documentaries and shorts since 1962, but then made an excellent suspense short in 1972, *La cabina* [*The Phone Box*] with the same López Vázquez caught in what becomes a surreal allegory of human isolation. Mercero followed this up with a psychological thriller, *Una mancha de sangre en un coche nuevo* [1974 *Blood Stains in a New Car*], where López Vázquez's guilty conscience will not give him a moment's peace, calling again for an allegorical reading (Mitchell, 2004: 169–87). Released in 1973, Francesc Betriu's first feature, *Corazón solitario* [*The Lonely Heart*], is described as a black comedy about an ageing bachelor still living with his mother, not so surprising in Spain, but he falls in love with a much younger girl. His second film, *Furia española* [1975 *Spanish Fury*], follows with irony Sebastián [Casto Sendra 'Cassen' of *Plácido*], a ticket collector who moves in the *barrio chino*, the brothel district of Barcelona. Sebastián's passion is Barcelona's football club, the Barça, and he finally marries his pregnant marijuana-growing Julieta [Mónica Randall] whose underwear is in the club colours, humour that proved too provocative for the censors.

But in 1973 the revelation of the year was Víctor Erice's *El espíritu de la colmena* [*The Spirit of the Beehive*]. Produced by Querejeta, it was the first Spanish film to win the Golden Shell at San Sebastián since the 1952 *La guerra de Dios* and *Sierra maldita* of 1953. Erice graduated from the EOC in 1963, but to date he has only made some six shorts (Kinder, 1993: 172–83) and three films, in 1973, 1983 and 1992. He is the only director whose full filmography has been shown on British terrestrial television; indeed, no film has attracted more critical reaction in English than *El espíritu de la colmena* (Higginbotham, 1998; Smith, 1999a). The film has been viewed from many perspectives, but since it is set 'around' 1940 most interpretations are political, inferring a rich web of connections between Fernando (played by Fernán Gómez), Dr Frankenstein and his monster (since the film establishes strong visual and psychological links with James Whale's film), Francisco Franco (the monster never seen), and potentially the mother figure as a monster (Deleyto, 1999a: 39–51). The narrative is presented from the perspective of a little girl [Ana Torrent, before she starred in *Cría cuervos*] who must confront her monsters and make sense of her environment and all that is hidden from her. It thus also offers an insight into childhood and its conflicts, and serves as an example of 'female socialisation in a patriarchal society' (Martin-Márquez, 1999a: 220–31, 222). Young Ana tries to make sense of the beehive, where she does not want to stay for ever, brought up in a family where the parents, victims of their past, are also emotionally trapped. Kinder examines the exploitation/subversion of the melodramatic tradition (1993: 67); Joan Hawkins sees the film in the context of horror films (2000: 97), as does Peter Evans (in Graham & Labanyi, 1995: 309), Xon de Ros regards it as meta-cinema (1999a: 27–37), and García Soza explains its popular appeal (2002) – just to mention some of the critical analysis this very powerful film has received (Stone, 2002: 85–94).

Jaime Chávarri graduated from the EOC in 1968. After a number of shorts, collaboration on film scripts (*Un, dos, tres, al escondite inglés* and *Las vampiras*), small acting parts, editing and other film-related activities, he directed his first film in 1974, *Los viajes escolares* [*School Trip*], using his own experience to examine the dysfunctional family. His critical breakthrough came in 1976 with *El desencanto* [*The Disenchantment*], a documentary that reveals the hypocrisy behind the façade of the respectable establishment, in this case the Panero family. Francesc Bellmunt had also made a number of shorts before his first film, *Robin Hood nunca muere* [1974 **Robin Hood Will Never Die*], using the legendary struggle against abuse of power to facilitate another political reading. His next features were documentaries of actual pop-rock concerts that took place in 1975 showcasing contemporary Catalan youth culture: *Canet Rock* [**Rock from Canet*] and *La nova cançó* [**The New Songs*], which are political gestures since Catalan identity and Rock were demonised by the regime.

An uncertain future

After a long illness, General Franco's death was announced on 20 November 1975. Juan Carlos, who had taken over as temporary Head of State in October, was crowned King of Spain on 22 November 1975. Given that there were fewer monarchists than republicans, tensions ran high as Spain was bound to embark on an important political and social transition; furthermore many recalled the Portuguese revolution of April 1974, albeit with carnations in hand.[33] There was considerable friction and even violence in the streets, not just from ETA.[34] A Prevention of Terrorism Act was passed in August 1975, and used to suppress magazines like *Cambio 16, Destino, Posible* and *Triunfo*.

The last five years had also been difficult for Spanish Cinema even if the 'Spirit of 12 February' had allowed it a little more freedom of expression. According to Vincendeau's comparative tables (1955: 464–8), the trend established in the previous decade continued as audiences carried on decreasing from the 1965 peak of 435.2 million, with the production of 151 films, 98 of them listed as co-productions. By 1970 spectatorship had fallen to 364.6 million and would continue to dwindle gradually to 249 million in 1976, not recovering until 1988 when the nadir of 69.6 million was reached. Production also decreased, with 125 films in 1969, 70 of which were co-productions, reaching its lowest in 1971 with 91 films, but 48 of these were integrally Spanish, thus marking a reduction in the proportion of co-productions. From 1971 onwards overall production started to increase again and the number of co-productions to drop off so that by 1975 there were 89 totally Spanish productions and only 21 co-productions listed. These figures, low as they are, were in fact healthier than those in Britain.

Viewing and further general reading

For overviews of the decade there is helpful reading in Besas (1985), Higginbotham (1988), Stone (2002) and Jordan & Allinson (2005), who all cover the period in English, although the most provocatively stimulating is probably Hopewell (1986). A retrospective focus on the popular comedies is provided by Jordan (2005). Triana Toribio discusses the polemics and politics behind cinema production (2003), and D'Lugo's *Guide* provides valuable information as required (1997). All these texts have ample bibliographies. For the shared problems of these films still frequently embedded in their own cultural context, Hooper (1987) and Graham & Labanyi (1995) are very informative. Critical attention has tended to focus on the dissident directors, and both Luis Buñuel and Carlos Saura have been dealt with in full monographs in English (Edwards, 1982 and 2005; Baxter, 1999; D'Lugo, 1991), as well as collections of articles (Mellen, 1978; P. Evans 1995, 1999 and with Santaolalla, 2004). The new periodical *Studies in Hispanic Cinemas* together with other journals are providing outlets for individual contributions on specific films, as

---

[33] Event chronicled by Maria de Medeiros, of *Pulp-Fiction*-fame, as *Capitães de Abril* [2000 *Captains of April*].

[34] An interesting thriller covering ETA during this period is Miguel Courtois's *El lobo* [2004 *Wolf*].

well as edited volumes like P. Evans (1999) or Mira (2005). Deveny, starting from 1965, examines films derived from novels (1999), and Faulkner, starting with Buñuel, Fons and Suárez takes a more theoretical and selective approach to 'the will to articulate opposition through literary adaptations' (2004a). Kinder comments on many films of the period, and has a chapter on Borau (1993). *El espíritu de la colmena* is the subject of a monograph (Higginbotham, 1998) and of so many articles that the film's reception could also be the subject of investigation. Attention has recently turned to popular cinema (Jordan, 1995; Lázaro Reboll & Willis, 2004) as well as to the 'cult' horror films, 'often low-budget, sleazy, exploitation fare' (Willis, 2003: 71; and see the conclusion to the previous chapter). The number of DVDs allowing these films to be viewed is again increasing annually, although it is not possible to be certain whether one is actually watching the version originally released in Spain as the various sources that can be consulted (*IMDb, MCU.es*, the DVDs themselves or original reels in the Filmotecas) state different lengths and at times different dates. This is particularly frustrating in the case of the Divisa DVD of *La trastienda*. These DVD re-releases come too often without subtitles, either a sign that they target the Spanish-speaking market or that there is not sufficient interest abroad to have them subtitled.

There is still much work to be done on individual films, both as films and to examine the tensions of the time, as politically and socially Spain was experiencing both the fruits of consumerism and the consequences of thirty years of dictatorship, society was changing and the future highly uncertain. Franco was terminally ill, and as changes were anticipated a need was felt to re-examine the past and its legacy, against the will of the censors. With hindsight, popular cinema has value-added information to offer on these changes, which reflect the changes in family values, urban growth and its contrast with the country, increased questioning of authority and consequent repression. An interesting topic would be work on those films that present a 'rite of passage' and how this is treated across the genres and ideologies. The production crisis required a change in marketing strategies in attempts to attract new spectators and both to compete and collaborate with television, all warranting research into audience reception. Other topics for research could be the village as a space for discourse rather than as a place, and, in view of forthcoming concern, the representation of gypsies.

8

End to Censorship and Transition to Democracy
(1976–1982)

Seeking stability: the political transition

Francisco Franco died on 20 November 1975 although, because of Franco's illness, Carlos Arias Navarro had been running the cabinet since December 1973, following Admiral Carrero Blanco's assassination. The King had been the temporary Head of State since July 1974, and on 22 December 1975 he swore allegiance to be King of *all* Spaniards (my italics) and yet continued to appear publicly in military uniform for a number of years in this period now known as the Transition. As a king imposed by Franco he was in a difficult position as there were more closet republicans than monarchists. The autumn of '75 was a time of tightening controls and restrictions owing to public demonstrations and terrorist activities. The country experienced its biggest strikes in January and February 1976, and in July while the left was in the streets requesting political amnesties, Adolfo Suárez was given the reins of government after Arias Navarro's resignation. Suárez promoted a conciliatory policy, agreeing to grant amnesty to those imprisoned for political crimes committed before 15 December 1976. In April 1977 he negotiated the legalisation of the Partido Comunista Español [PCE/Spanish Communist Party], in time for 15 June and the first democratic elections since 1936, in spite of violent provocations from the extreme right. These elections were won by his own Unión del Centro Democrático [UCD/Union of the Democratic Centre] against the right coalition of Alianza Popular [AP/Popular Alliance]. The new 'Cortes' [parliament] was opened on 22 July 1977. Three months later, on 25 October, Suárez negotiated the Moncloa Pact, whereby the opposition agreed to collaborate and compromise in a spirit of reconciliation rather than recrimination over necessary reforms for a democratic constitution. The new constitution was approved by parliament in October 1978 and then confirmed by national referendum on 6 December, effective on 29th. The UCD won the next national election in March 1979, but in the municipal elections the left won significant victories in the main cities. One of the major breakthroughs of the new constitution was the devolution of power to regional autonomies, so both the Basque Country and Catalonia held their own parliamentary elections in February 1980, and by February 1984 all seventeen Autonomies were in place. Now that Spain was no longer a dictatorship, negotiations to join the EEC [European Economic Community, now the European Union] could be taken forward. There were, however, major problems facing the emerging constitutional monarchy, most notably a serious economic crisis and ETA's continuing militancy. Deprived of the necessary co-operation, Suárez resigned in January 1981 and was replaced by Leopoldo Calvo Sotelo. Many social reforms had nonetheless been achieved with the return of democracy and the creation of regional autonomies: the *Permiso Marital* was abolished in 1975; universal suffrage was established in 1976; in 1978 adultery, contraception and homosexuality were all decriminalised and the Church was disestablished; in 1981 divorce laws were finally re-established and the *Patria Potestad* abolished.[1]

The cinema of the Reform

The censors' office was closed by the Royal Decree of 11 November 1977, and films like Buñuel's *Viridiana* [1961], Berlanga's *Tamaño natural* [1974] and Grau's *La trastienda* [1975] could finally be seen in Spain. This did not mean complete freedom. Censorship was replaced by a classification office as from January 1978, so a release licence still had to be obtained for one of five categories: general release, fourteen and older, sixteen and older, eighteen and older, and if these last 'were likely to wound the sensitivity of the average spectator' they were qualified with the letter 'S', only to be viewed in specially licensed theatres.[2] Indirect pressures could still weigh on producers and directors, as demonstrated by Pilar Miró's second film *El crimen de Cuenca* [*The Cuenca Crime*], completed in 1979, which was at first refused a distribution licence. The film narrates the Grimaldos affair: a chain of true events that took place in the province of Cuenca when two men, after false confessions extracted under torture by the local Guardia

---

[1]   From 1939 the Dictatorship's Civil Code imposed the *Permiso Marital* [Conjugal Permission] whereby a married woman could not have a bank account, be employed, travel on her own passport, etc. without her husband's permission, while the *Patria Potestad* gave all legal right and responsibilities to the husband. An unmarried woman did not become legally independent of her father until she was 25, a son at 23. In practice these restrictions may not have been so rigidly enforced after 1961 but they would stand up in court. See pp. 87–8, 214 on the three Fs of the Franco regime, and Hooper (1987: chapter 16; and 1995: chapter 11).

[2]   '[P]udieran herir la sensibilidad del espectador medio [...] que la película sea calificada con la letra "S"': González Ballesteros (1981: 495–508, 499). Just Jaeckin's 1974 *Emmanuelle* was the first film to receive this 'S' with no name.

Civil, were erroneously sentenced for a crime that had not been committed.[3] The pressure to ban the film came from the Guardia Civil who objected to being portrayed in such a negative light, even though the events narrated started in 1910. The film might never have been shown if it were not for the attempted military coup on 23/24 February 1981 when a Civil Guard, Lieutenant-Colonel Antonio Tejero Molina, held the Spanish parliament at gun point in a bid to return to the regime of the Dictatorship. The King stood firm on the side of democracy, the coup was aborted, the insurgents sentenced in June 1982, the Civil Guards were tarnished and the charges against the film were dropped. With all this publicity *El crimen de Cuenca* became one of the box-office successes of the decade.[4]

With the new-found freedom of expression, albeit still curtailed, the issues first and most frequently visited by the directors of the Transition were personal relationships, the historical past, and the present social changes. However, film production continued to slow down, perhaps at first in competition with the release of previously banned foreign films and Spanish features but also in response to the continued financial crisis created by the Escudero debt and the decreasing funding available for new productions (chapter 7). Audiences declined further as television networks showed more and more films. Furthermore the Dirección General de Cinematografía [DGC] was rather disorganised between 1976 and 1982, with six different directors appointed in five years. In 1978 box-office monitoring was imposed and, in an attempt to protect national production, tighter film quotas of two days of imported films for one day of Spanish films were reintroduced, but this was a target that distributors could not actually match. These reforms were strongly opposed at the First Democratic Spanish Film Conference, which took place in December 1978. After protests from the distributors the ratio was first abandoned, and then changed in 1980 to one Spanish film for every three foreign films. In June 1980 the renegotiation of RTVE regulations also set up formal agreements with the film industry securing funding for new films, which in return could be shown on television only two years after release. Consequently production increased again for a few years (Jordan & Morgan, 2000: 179–80). Meanwhile now that the news could be seen to evolve daily on television, the weekly NO-DOs no longer fulfilled their official purpose (p. 86). Their legal monopoly was cancelled in April 1978 and they were finally abandoned in April 1980 (Gubern, 1995: 368).

---

[3]   The film has four brief torture scenes that were enough to turn many sensitive stomachs (eight minutes in the total 93), but just as much violence is conveyed through reaction shots.

[4]   The only Spanish film that made more money was another drama set in the past and based on a Delibes novel, Mario Camus's *Los santos inocentes* [1984 *The Holy Innocents*].

Taking the lid off sex

The *destape* of the early 1970s continued. As more flesh was revealed on screen, narratives moved into soft-porn, which was exhibited in the new 'S' theatres, depending on the amount of simulated sex and/or violence displayed. The first Spaniard to receive an 'S' for his films was new director Enrique Guevara. Starting with *Una loca extravagancia sexy* [1978 **A Wild Sex Extravaganza*], he went on to make ten such films between 1978 and 1982. José [Ramón] Larraz, who had returned from the UK to take advantage of the *destape* with films like *El fin de la inocencia* [1976 **The End of Innocence*] and *Mirón* [1977 **Peeping Tom*], then moved on to more explicit 'S' films like *La visita del vicio* [1978 *The Coming of Sin*], *Polvos mágicos* [1979 **Magic Ejaculations*], or *El periscopio* [1979 *And Give Us Our Daily Sex*]. They were joined unsurprisingly by filmmakers like Jesús Franco, Carlos Aured, Javier Aguirre, Alfonso Balcázar, Juan Bosch, José María Zalbaza and others like Luis María Delgado, Tulio Demicheli, Vicente Escrivá, Ramón Fernández or Ignacio Iquino, who had all been involved in low-budget *chorizo* westerns and horror films (chapter 6). Some freedom had finally arrived for these directors who, for the most part, had lived their life under the sexual repression of the former regime and were reaching the end of their career with comic erotic fantasies.[5] Daniel Kowalsky argues that the sexual liberation presented in the early 'S' films could be seen metaphorically as a statement of socio-political liberation from the Dictatorship, but not so for the later films made after 1980 which moved from soft-porn to 'nearly hardcore' (2004: 199, 191). It was a time when if *Snow White and the Seven Dwarfs* was billed, it was not necessarily the Disney cartoon. Most of these films, whose titles and posters promised more than they delivered, and in spite of their financial contribution to the industry, were for the most part marginalised and ignored by Spanish film critics pushing for a strong and internationally viable cinema (Triana Toribio, 2003: 114–15).

Kowalsky distinguishes the exploitation of sex on screen from a different treatment of perversions by other new directors 'interested in the psychological underpinnings of those forms of sexuality long repressed in Spanish society' (2004: 190–1). José Juan Bigas Luna's first films with nudity, sex and violence, following his early shorts in soft-porn, are all very provocative and raise questions about obsessions that transcend the immediate image rather than titillate the viewer (Stock, 1992: 40). *Tatuaje* [1976 *Tattoo*], based on a Vázquez Montalbán episode of the private detective Pepe Carvalho,[6] involves crimes of passion and filming in Amsterdam, an international dimension

---

5   Pedro Almodóvar inserts a parody clip in his *Laberinto de pasiones* [1982 *Labyrinth of Passions*].

6   *Tatuaje* is the fictional detective's first appearance on screen. He has reappeared played

Bigas Luna consistently seeks. He went on to script and direct *Bilbao* [1978] which explores and questions the conventions of the thriller and sex film, as Leo [Ángel Jovè] endeavours to escape from his hypocritical middle-class Catalan values through his attempts to turn a prostitute he names Bilbao [Isabel Pisano] into an object to possess (Kinder, 1993: 262–75). This was followed by *Caniche* [1979 *Poodle*], a psychological thriller plotted on the sexual obsessions and jealousy of two siblings and their dog.[7] These, and his subsequent films, 'challenge us to examine extant critical categories with which we select, classify and evaluate films' (Stock, 1998: 183).

New attitudes

Sexual relationships portrayed on screen were not all confined to the 'S' theatres and many films had wider distribution. After writing a number of scripts, eventually for José Luis Dilbidos and the so-called *tercera vía* (pp. 217–18), the film critic and self-taught José Luis Garci made his first feature, *Asignatura pendiente* [1977 *Unfinished Business*]. A box-office success, this melancholic comedy set in 1975 at the time of Franco's death examines how the values of the regime had deprived two lovers, now married to other partners, of the relationship they try to recover during this period of uncertainty. A literal translation of the title would be *Subject/Examination Pending*, which the characters cannot take or pass because they cannot recreate their lost opportunities, and so he rides off alone to involve himself in the new politics (Hopewell, 1986: 110–11; Pereira, 1998: 155–70). Garci kept José Sacristán and Fiorella Faltoyano for his next film *Solos en la madrugada* [1978 *Alone in the Dark*], which also examines crises in masculinities through a radio agony uncle dealing with his own failed marriage (Estrada, 2005: 137–50; 2006: 265–80), then cast Alfredo Landa in *Las verdes praderas* [1979 *The Green Pastures*]. The latter two films did not have the same success as *Asignatura* but nonetheless established a personal style that gives Garci's films a traditional Hollywood gloss and a sense of nostalgia that he has kept (D'Lugo, 1997: 33–4; Pereira, 1998: 157–70). Fernando Méndez-Leite's *El hombre de moda* [1980 *Man of Fashion*] presents the new liberal man just divorced and unable to deal with assertive women, or his new social context. Ricardo Franco's third feature, *Los restos del naufragio* [1978 *The Remains from the Shipwreck*], also presents crises in masculinities, exploring through refer-

---

by different actors and in the hands of different directors, and in 1986 he had his own television series.

7   In the 1960s comedies these white poodles were icons for elderly female tourists in Spain: see, for instance, *Martes y trece* [1962 Pedro Lazaga, **Tuesday the Thirteenth*].

ences to different film genres the lost illusions and future dreams of two men, played by himself and Fernán Gómez, in an old people's home.

If films dealing with couples had previously but with notable exceptions[8] focused on the male, an increasing number now approached the couple from the perspective of 'his' partner, examining the legacy of the Dictatorship and how it imposed itself on women through education and socialisation. Patriarchal values are the subject of a number of films and reflections, and not just from the emerging women directors. A graduate of the EOC in 1967 who started her career in RTVE, Pilar Miró's belated first film *La petición* [1976 *The Request*] is a costume drama based on a short story by Emile Zola for which cuts were requested because of its inferred presentation of sadism and eroticism, but it 'was released essentially intact' (Martin-Márquez, 1999a: 151). After *El crimen de Cuenca* and the debacle that followed, her next two films, the very personal *Gary Cooper, que estás en los cielos* [1980 *Gary Cooper Who Art in Heaven*] and *Hablamos esta noche* [1982 **Let Us Talk Tonight – Moscow medal for Mercedes Sampietro*], both look in different ways at how personal problems can influence professional responsibilities. The autobiographical *Gary Cooper* ... presents a television director, played by a still relatively unknown Mercedes Sampietro, who has 48 hours to sort out her affairs before a serious operation, while *Hablamos* ... features an ambitious nuclear power station manager played by Víctor Valverde (Morgan, 1999: 176–93; Martin-Márquez,1999a: 141–82). Josefina Molina was also working in RTVE and her second feature, a bold artistic documentary, *Función de noche* [1981 **Evening Performance*], is set in a theatre greenroom where the characters play themselves, as Lola [Herrera] talks to her estranged husband Daniel [Dicenta] about the many reasons for their failed marriage. To complicate the emotional issues discussed, Lola Herrera is acting in a dramatisation of Miguel Delibes's novel *Cinco horas con Mario*, an ironical interior monologue by a widow who reflects on her unfulfilled life with her recently deceased husband (Martin-Márquez, 1999a: 202–17; Triana Toribio, 2002: 84–90), but one is not to know where Lola and Daniel are acting in front of the cameras. Cecilia Bartolomé, who in the 1960s had made five shorts, directed the first of her two feature films, *Vámonos, Bárbara* [1978 **Lets Go, Barbara*], setting out a feminist agenda in a mother–daughter road movie whose script had been turned down by Miró.[9] Pilar Távora made *Nanas de espinas* [1983 **Lullabies of Thorns*], which, like her 1988 film *Yerma*, is based on Federico García Lorca's theatre.

---

[8]   Among films previously mentioned, *La aldea maldita* [1930], *Calle mayor* [1956], *La tía Tula* [1964], *Mi querida señorita* [1971], *Cría cuervos...* [1975] stand out.

[9]   Bartolomé's second feature was made in 1966 with the collaboration of her brother José Juan, *Lejos de África* (*Black Island*) [*Far from Africa (Black Island)*]. In between there was her documentary work.

During this period Fernán Gómez continued to act in many films and directed three. *Mi hija Hildegart* [1977 *My Daughter Hildegart*] is all the more extraordinary as a narrative because it is based on the strange but true trial of Aurora Rodríguez Caballeira [Amparo Soler Leal], who raised her daughter on her own to be a model of women's emancipation but then in 1933 murdered her when she was just eighteen. Co-scripted with Rafael Azcona, Fernán Gómez addressed the problems of women's education in a provocative way that pleased audiences but was unjustly slated by the critics (Keown, 1999: 147–63). The events are told in long flashbacks from the perspective of Rodríguez Caballeira's biographer, Eduardo Guzmán [Manuel Galiana], which allows a pertinent link with the present situation. Jaime de Armiñán had broached the theme in *Mi querida señorita*, and returned to it with a very different slant in *Al servicio de la mujer española* [1978 *At the Service of Spanish Womanhood*], focusing on a dissatisfied wife. Saura made, without much public success, the very personal and literary film *Elisa, vida mía* [1977 *Elisa, My Life*], which examines a complex daughter–father relationship with voice-overs from the father and a feeling of disillusion [*desengaño*], which goes well beyond the contemporary political climate. It is a film that polarised Saura viewers, and indeed many refer to this period as one where he had lost his way (Stone, 2002: 72–3). *Mamá cumple cien años* [1979 *Mama Turns 100* – San Sebastián Special Jury] was Saura's first comedy. In it the au pair of *Ana y los lobos* [1973] returns to the house of her previous employers and keeps repeating that nothing has changed even though the family structure has been drastically altered by much more authoritative women to reflect changes in contemporary society. There is a plot to kill Mamá, played by Rafaela Aparicio continuing her wonderful role, who does not want to sell her old house and thus lose her memories, so that the family bank balance can be restored. Josep Antón Salgot's *Mater amatísima* [1980 *Mother Dearly Beloved*, based on a story by Bigas Luna] is controversial in its portrayal of the relationship between a mother and her autistic child [Victoria Abril and Julio de la Cruz]. Buñuel's *Cet Obscur Objet du désir* [1977 *That Obscure Object of Desire*], with a few location shots in Seville, presents the power of women and sexuality, as well as a world where terrorists are commonplace and migrant workers can be deported on a whim. The enigmatic protagonist Conchita is played by two actresses [Ángela Molina and Carole Bouquet], emphasising the confused male point of view embodied by Fernando Rey.[10] In *La Sabina* [1979], also starring Ángela Molina, José Luis Borau explores foreigners' fascination for the Andalusian woman through the feelings of an English writer investigating the disappearance of a romantic nineteenth-

---

[10] In *Peppermint frappé*, *Prima Angélica*, *Cría cuervos*, *Elisa*, etc., Saura had also portrayed psychological effects on individuals by using the same actor for different characters and different actors for the same person.

century English poet. Located in a rural setting, evoked as a traditionally patriarchal space, the film exposes the contradictions still enveloping the strong woman (Fiddian, 1989: 301–14), to which Kinder adds a homoerotic backstory (1993: 357–64). Javier Aguirre, who was busy and popular with his commercial cinema, risked much for a more experimental film starring his wife Esperanza Roy. This 95-minute monologue *Vida/Perra* [1981 *A Dog's Life*], which he described as his 'anticine' [anti-cinema], is based on Ángel Vázquez's novel *Juanita Narboni* about a lonely, depressed, alcoholic woman musing over her circumstances. The film pleased the critics but not the box-office.[11] Gerardo Herralde in *Vértigo en Manhattan* [1981 *Jet Lag*] focuses on another protagonist in search of herself in New York. In *El nido* [1980 *The Nest*] Jaime de Armiñán exploits the relationship of a wilful thirteen-year-old [Ana Torrent] with a shy widower [Héctor Alterio]; and, in a comic vein, *Nunca es tarde* [1977 *It's Never Too Late*], starring Ángela Molina, José Luis Gómez and Madeleine Christie, shows a marriage under stress because the husband wants to be a father while the old lady on the floor above wants to be a mother. Jaime Chávarri explores incest and the silences that cover it up in *Dedicatoria* [1980 *Dedicated to …*], for, according to Hopewell 'authority, control and censorship in Spain may have been less intrusive by 1980 but still exercised a crucial behind-the-scenes influence' (1986: 216–17), in the same way that just as many war crimes were left undisturbed to facilitate the transition to democracy.

The Madrid comedies

Growing out of the *tercera vía* experiments (pp. 217–18), a number of new directors, based in Madrid, were now making films examining how couples were renegotiating relationships, often after separation, in this new democratic Spain. These films targeted the 'progres', the progressive urban generation in its twenties and thirties at the time of the Transition, accustomed to smoking marijuana or cannabis and sleeping around. These comedies tended to present entertaining ironies as reflections and counterpoint to the social and political disappointment, 'desencanto', and the consequent apathy 'pasotismo' (Hopewell, 1986: 223–4) 'that both passively reflect and actively respond to the crisis of masculine identity' felt by this generation of young men as women reposition themselves in society (Estrada, 2005: 137). The directors took more care with their films because of their low budget, promoting a more

---

[11] Another version of the novel was released in 2005: *La vida perra de Juanita Narboni*, directed by Farida Ben Lyziad, starring Mariola Fuentes in a Hispano-Moroccan production restoring the social and postcolonial context that had been left out of Aguirre's film.

natural acting style and delivery of lines, as well as witty dialogues recorded directly rather than post-synchronised. They cast the same group of friends who were also new to the profession and had mostly started off making shorts together: Antonio Resines, Óscar Ladoire, Carmen Maura, and where other young actors found their place, like Verónica Forqué, Kiti Manver, Marisa Paredes, etc. The result was a number of films that had enough in common to be labelled *comedias madrileñas* [Madrid comedies; comedies of manner], and injected many new ideas and practices into Spanish Cinema (Jordan & Morgan, 1998: 68–71).

Fernando Colomo's first feature, for which he created his own production company, La Salamandra, was *Tigres de papel* [1977 *Paper Tigers*]. Taking the recent democratic elections as its context, *Tigres* ... examines how those who trumpeted the new liberal attitudes were still restrained and confused by their education. His next film, *¿Qué hace una chica como tú en un sitio como éste?* [1978 *What is a Girl like You Doing in a Place like This?*], was co-scripted with Jaime Chávarri and featured Carmen Maura in her first major role. In this darker, far-fetched comedy nothing is as it should be and the police are more dangerous than the young delinquents. The comedy continued with *La mano negra* [1980 *The Black Hand*], a crime spoof where reality and appearances are contrasted again. His *¡Estoy en crisis!* [1982 *I'm having a Crisis*] is a fast-moving comedy satire on the new executive, played by José Sacristán. A little jewel, still on a low budget, is *La línea del cielo* [1983 *Skyline*], with Antonio Resines. The skyline is that of New York where Gustavo has arrived with high hopes of becoming a photographer for *Life Magazine*. Closely observed and beautifully framed, the film explores and blurs the stereotypes of the USA as seen from a Spanish perspective through Gustavo's frustrations at his own linguistic inadequacies and the clash between his expectations and reality.

Fernando Trueba was another precocious film critic and his first film, *Ópera prima* [*First Work*], was released in 1980. At twenty-five Matías [Óscar Ladoire] is an unemployed divorced journalist trying to write a thriller when he unexpectedly meets his much younger cousin Violeta [Paulina Molina] in Madrid, and although they are chalk and cheese she moves into his flat on the Plaza del Ópera where they met.[12] The film continues with its coincidences as it chronicles the spirit of disillusion voiced by Matías's friend León [Antonio Resines] who states that 'it is perfectly clear that we are living at a time of absolute decadence'.[13] Antonio Resines also acted in José Antonio Pangua's *Crónica de un instante* [1981 *The Chronicle of a Moment*] about an overgrown Madrid student, in Alberto Bermejo's *Vecinos* [1981 *Neighbours*]

---

[12]   To add a further twist, 'prima' is also the Spanish word for a 'female cousin'. The French title focuses on the second suggestion of *Opera prima*: *Cousine, je t'aime*.

[13]   'Está muy claro que estamos en una época ¡de decadencia absoluta!'

caught in a triangular relationship, José Luis Cuerda's *Pares y nones* [1982 *Odd and Even*], and in Óscar Ladoire's *A contratiempo* [1982 *Problems and Mishaps*], where the protagonist played by Ladoire himself feels lost and makes a nostalgic journey to Galicia to find himself, but picks up a young hitch-hiker who complicates everything. These were the directors' first and in the case of Pangua and Bermejo their only film. *Bajo en nicotina* [1984 *Low in Nicotine*] starring Silvia Munt, Óscar Ladoire and Antonio Resines was the last of the three films directed by Raúl Artigot, better known as a cinematographer who made 72 films between 1964 and his last film in 1985 for Betriu's *Réquiem por un campesino español* [*Requiem for a Spanish Farmhand*]. With a different edge and context the actor Antonio del Real also filmed his first comedies *El poderoso influjo de la luna* [1980 *The Powerful Influence of the Moon*] and *Buscando a Perico* [1982 *Looking for Pete*], and so did Javier Maqua with *Tú estás loco Briones* [1980 *You are mad Briones*], whose next film, *Chevrolet,* only came out in 1997.

Families and generational conflicts

Traditional comedies still frequently focused on the family, but the relationships were now much more confrontational, at times from the perspective of the older generation to emphasise the father's loss of authority. *La familia bien, gracias* [1979 Pedro Masó, *The Family, Fine, Thanks*], whose precredit sequence recalls the original *La gran familia* and *La familia y uno más* (p. 167), brings Alberto Closas and José Luis López Vázquez up to date with a cynical look at the new family relationships and allows us to evaluate the change in audience expectations. Masó would return once more to the family in the TV film *La familia... treinta años después* [1999 *The Family... Thirty Years on*], but with only López Vázquez left from the original team it failed to generate the television series it was supposed to pilot. The generation gap is taken up in García Sánchez's *Colorín colorado* [1976 *And They Lived Happily Ever After*], and Rafael Gil's *Hijos de papá* [1980 *Spoilt Brats*] set in 1978 as father José Bódalo observes his children and recalls in flashback his experience as a son in 1946. Antonio Mercero's *La guerra de papá* [1977 *Daddy's War*, starring Héctor Alterio and Teresa Gimpera] is set in 1964 in order to expose the contradictions within the family and the period, through which those of the Civil War can easily be inferred. These tensions are viewed, misunderstood and presented by a three-year-old who is now competing for attention with a newly born sister (Mitchell, 2004: 173–4). After a horror spoof, Mercero then made *La próxima estación* [1982 *The Next Station*] starring Alfredo Landa and Lola Herrera as parents having to deal with a teenage son and his girlfriend. In other films the idealised family under Franco is revealed to be an ideological propaganda construct full of contradictions, as in the failed marriage examined in Emilio Martínez-Lázaro's first feature, *Las palabras de Max* [1978 *What Max Said* – Berlin Gold Bear], produced by Querejeta. His second film, *Sus años dorados* [1980 *Their Golden Years*] is a very busy situation comedy full of coincidences that illustrate the irony of the title. The surprising ending places a price on political apathy, as the protagonists meet at the unemployment exchange and are still searching for a job at the end, after participating in a porno film and having seen *El espíritu de la colmena*.[14] Rafael Moreno Alba's *Mis relaciones con Ana* [1979 *My Liaison with Ana*] is a drama about a weak and selfish man who recounts the breakdown of his relationship. Conflicts within the family are of course present in many other films, and used to suggest other tensions, as in Gerardo García's only film, *Con mucho cariño* [1979 *With Much love*], a satire on the family of a small industrialist, written and set in 1975 during the last summer of the Dictatorship.

Taking the lid off homosexuality

Homosexual relationships were another issue that now received serious treatment, in contrast to the camp stereotypes found in earlier comedies like the often-quoted box-office hit *No desearás al vecino del quinto* [1970 *Thou Shalt Not Covet Thy Fifth Floor Neighbour*] (Triana Toribio, 2003: 100–4). Eloy de la Iglesia is perhaps the first and most consistent director to deal explicitly with the subject. Already present in the violent *Juego de amor prohibido* [1975 *Forbidden Love Game*], the issue is central to *Los placeres ocultos* [1977 *Hidden Pleasures*], the melodrama said to have opened the Spanish closet. This was followed by a study of repressed sexuality in *El sacerdote* [1978 **The Priest*], with a script that was first offered to Pilar Miró. De la Iglesia's *El diputado* [1978 *Confessions of a Congressman*] blends contemporary political references and shots with its fiction, dating it but also exposing a society that presented itself as proudly liberal but which nonetheless persecuted, and in this case manipulated, homosexuals (Melero Salvador, 2004: 87–102).[15] This was followed by *La mujer del ministro* [1981 **The Minister's Wife*], which was classified as pornographic, but also placed corrupt politicians in the frame. In de la Iglesia's films the violence and more graphic sex, set in the context of melodramas at times bordering on horror, are often used to shock popular audiences as they deliver an incisive socio-polit-

---

[14]   Martínez-Lázaro, together with Ricardo Franco, Alfonso Ungría, Paulino Viota and Augusto M. Torres, were among the independent and underground directors of the early 1970s mentioned by Hopewell (1986: 70–1).

[15]   This is de la Iglesia's only film mentioned here that did not cast Simón Andreu; it starred José Sacristán whose star image at the time was, like Spain's, in transition.

ical comment.[16] He adopts this approach to make a powerful indictment of a hypocritical society that previously incarcerated homosexuals, later subjected them to the 1970 Ley de Peligrosidad y Rehabilitación Social [Social Danger and Rehabilitation Law] and now discriminated against them while claiming to be a new liberal society (Smith, 1992: 5–12; Tropiano, 1997: 157–64).

A quieter treatment of the issue and of coming to terms with one's sexuality and loneliness is Jaime Chávarrí's 1977 *A un dios desconocido* [*To an Unknown God*] with its silent homage to García Lorca, jumping from 1936 to the present (Perriam, 1999a: 77–91). A different approach is taken by Vicente Aranda in *Cambio de sexo* [1977 *Change of Sex*], said to be based on a true case and presented as such. Starring Victoria Abril and Bibí Andersen[17] in their first major roles, it fictionalises the newly available sex-change surgery in an informative manner and in the context of a sensitive narrative not devoid of songs and entertainment as well as the violent chauvinistic reaction from the boy's father.[18] Homosexuality was also presented in the context of the historical thriller as in Pedro Olea's *Un hombre llamado Flor de Otoño* [1978 *A Man called Autumn Flower*] in which José Sacristán plays a young lawyer by day and transvestite artiste by night against the backdrop of pre-Republican Barcelona. Sacristán's character comes out both politically and sexually, demonstrating that the situation was not new but had been closeted during the Dictatorship. In fact, the Penal Code of 1932 did not cite homosexuality as a crime unless accompanied by public scandal or the corruption of minors (Smith, 1992: 7). Ventura Pons's first film is an 85-minute documentary, *Ocaña, retrat intermitent* [1978 *Ocaña, An Intermittent Portrait*], where the Andalusian painter and transvestite, well known for his exhibitionism on the Barcelona Ramblas, talks freely about his experiences and fantasies.

Juvenile delinquency

Eloy de la Iglesia's social commitment also led him to make a number of thrillers on other aspects of the transitional society. In *Miedo a salir de noche* [1980 *Afraid to Go Out at Night*], *Navajeros* [1980 *Young Knives*] and *Colegas* [1982 *Pals*] he deals with marginalised and disaffected youths, using graphic images of violence, sex and drugs. Creating a visual style

---

[16] See also *La otra alcoba* [1976 *The Other Bedroom*] or *La criatura* [1977 *The Creature*].

[17] She is sometimes credited as Bibiana (or Manuela) Fernández Chica, b. 1954, not to be confused with Swedish actress Bibi Andersson, b. 1935, who is said to have provided the inspiration.

[18] The film is greatly problematised by Kinder (1999: 128–46).

defined as 'tremendismo',[19] de la Iglesia implies that the contemporary lack of employment opportunities and dysfunctional families can push adolescents into delinquency. A prolific creator of films about street violence was the veteran José Antonio de la Loma who directed *Perros callejeros* [1977 *Street Warriors*] and its 1979 sequel, or the biopic *Yo, el Vaquilla* [1985 *I, The Vaquilla*]. Saura's *Deprisa, deprisa* [1980 *Fast, Fast* – Berlin Gold Bear] was another take on the disaffected youth, although a little too sanitised, which he had visited twenty years earlier in *Los golfos*. The four mates are metaphorically 'completely surrounded'[20] by the wastelands on the outskirts of Madrid, with no way to progress as the trains noisily pass by their high-rise flat, and so they turn to crime and drugs. Also presented at the 1981 Berlin Festival and sharing the same context of juvenile delinquency, drugs and a dysfunctional family but very different in tone and genre is Gutiérrez Aragón's *Maravillas* [1981 Maravillas is the name of the eponymous heroine and also means 'Wonders/Marvels']. It is a film that transcends the immediate situation to explore as a fable a more comprehensive Spanish reality, especially its Hebrew past ever present in the non-diegetic soundtrack, which was now allowed to resurface in democratic Spain (Kercher, 1995: 86–95). Generational conflict and the links with the past are emphasised in *Maravillas* by having established actors like Fernando Fernán Gómez and Francisco Merino acting opposite the new young faces of Cristina Marcos and Miguel Molina in their first film; significantly the film does not really offer a sense of closure.

Satire and exaggerations, the *esperpento*

Another way of handling reality and social problems was through humour, and one particularly Spanish approach is through exaggeration, the use of the grotesque and at times the absurd, with a frequent touch of black humour. This type of humour, referred to as the 'esperpento' (p. 146, n.43) had started to flourish again in the late 1950s and 1960s, especially in the films of Neville, Ferreri and Berlanga, as well as in the scripts of Azcona.[21] Berlanga's *La escopeta nacional* [1978 *The National Shotgun*], about a Catalan industrialist who organises a hunting party in order to promote his new electronic doors, and its two sequels all chronicle with biting satire the socio-political changes

---

[19] A term borrowed from literary criticism to describe an exaggerated realism that focuses on the grimmer aspects of life (Prout, 2005: 166).

[20] This is a quotation from the film as a huge police detachment locates one of the four friends.

[21] Azcona co-scripted 15 of Ferreri's 28 films and 11 of Berlanga's 18 features (*IMDb* search)

and the consequences for the fortunes of those that the Franco regime had blessed as the Marqués of Leguineche and his son, played by Luis Escobar and José Luis López Vázquez, have to start earning their living in the new democratic society (Jordan & Morgan, 1998: 75–6). In Juan Esterlich's *El anacoreta* [1976 *The Anchorite*[22]] where, through the experience of a Fernán Gómez whose character has not left his bathroom for eleven years, the implications of the consumerism to which Spain had been aspiring since the beginning of the 1960s are satirised more harshly than in so many of the popular *barrio* comedies of Pedro Lazaga and others (chapters 6–7). Fernán Gómez also directed *Cinco tenedores* [1979 *Five Forks*] to undermine old-fashioned attitudes to hunting, eating and cuckolds (Fiddian 1995). José Luis García Sánchez's third film, *Las truchas* [1978 *Trout* – Berlin Gold Bear], is set in another restaurant but this time with an association of anglers at their annual banquet. More traditional as a comedy was Jesús Yagüe's *Cara al sol que más calienta* [1977 **Facing the Sun that Warms You Best*[23]], a satire on Opus Dei scandals, starring López Vázquez who appeared at ease with whatever political view or genre he worked in.

From Barcelona and in the same spirit, after his musical documentaries, Francesc Bellmunt directed three hippie satirical comedies: *L'orgia* [1978 **The Orgy*],[24] *Salut i força al canut* [1979 *Cuernos a la catalana/Catalan Cuckold*], films that had to be dubbed into Castilian in order to reach wider audiences,[25] and *La quinta del porro* [1980 **The Stoned Recruits*], which dealt with the question of compulsory military service.[26] After his *Furia española* [1975] Francesc Betriu directed *Los fieles sirvientes* [1980 **The Loyal Servants*] using role reversals to suggest the impossibility of changing attitudes; he then turned his skills to literary adaptations. Very anti-Catholic, because of the Church's association with the repression of the Dictatorship, Valencian Carles Mira used history as the vehicle for his satires, contrasting Castilian austerity with his exuberant and exaggerated celebration of the body. *La portentosa vida del pare Vicent* [1978 *The Prodigious life of Father*

---

[22] Like the Berlanga triology mentioned, this film was also scripted by Azcona, and it is worth consulting the *IMDb*.

[23] 'Cara al sol ...' are the first words of the Nationalist anthem, and can be heard at http://www.himnonacional.org/caraalsol.htm.

[24] This film gave Assumpta Serna, Silvia Munt and Juanjo Puigcorbé their first foot on the ladder.

[25] The problem is still relevant today as Catalan television funds many films that have to be dubbed for wider release in Spain. However, this often spoils the film as the characters lose their personality when not speaking in their own voice. At this time to support the Catalan language the new Autonomy funded Catalan television and invested considerable sums to have foreign films dubbed into Catalan.

[26] Compulsory military service was abolished on 31 December 2001, when the Spanish military became a professional army.

Vincent] is an irreverent and racy biopic of Vicente Ferrer, patron saint of Valencia. Mira followed this with *Con el culo al aire* [1980 *Caution to the Wind*], set in an asylum run by nuns where Juan [Ovidi Montllor] is locked up after losing his virginity and where the inmates pretend to be the historical figures so dear to the Dictatorship's propaganda; then came *Jalea real* [1981 *Royal Jelly*] set at the court of Carlos II, the 'Bewitched'. Vicente Escrivá (chapters 5 and 6), who had moved into erotic farces like *La lozana andaluza* [1976 *The Lascivious Andalusian*[27]] or *Niñas ... ¡al salón!* [1977 *Girls ... To the Drawing Room!*], also joined the Valencian revelry with *El virgo de Visanteta* [1978 *Visanteta's Virgin*] and its sequel *Visanteta, esta-te queta* [1979 *Visanteta, Be Still*].[28]

Reactionary reactions

Other criticisms of the Transition and its changes also came from the more conservative directors. Rafael Gil teamed up with popular novelist Fernando Vizcaíno Casas who scripted his last six films. In *La boda del señor cura* [1979 *Father Cami's Wedding*] a priest loses his faith with the changing times. With *Y al tercer año, resucitó* [1980 *And in the Third Year, He Rose Again*] everyone needs to reconsider their ideological position, investments or cinematographic production when an elderly gentleman looking just like Franco is spotted hitching a lift away from the Valle de los Caídos and the French Franc ['el franco'] recovers on the Stock Exchange. *De camisa vieja a chaqueta nueva* [1982 *From the Old Shirt to a New Jacket*] is a not-so-veiled allusion to Adolfo Suárez, accused of changing his allegiance from the blue fascist shirt to a neat new jacket of democratic and corrupt progress. While in Gil's penultimate film, *Las autonosuyas* [1983 *The Autonothemselves*] the village mayor, Alfredo Landa, champions local autonomy. Pedro Lazaga kept directing until he died in 1979, seven years before Gil, but not before making *Vota a Gundisalvo* [1978 *Vote for Gundisalvo*], a satirical and cynical portrayal of the electoral campaign of the Concordia Democrática del Estado Español [Democratic Harmony for the Spanish State] party. He had already directed Paco Martínez Soria in eight films and he concluded with two more. In *Estoy hecho un chaval* [1977 *I Feel as Young as a Lad*] Martínez Soria's character retires as a modest accountant to be replaced by a less efficient computer and learns that his wife is expecting twins, while in *Vaya par de gemelos* [1978 *What a Pair of Twins!*] Martínez Soria plays three different parts, for laughs rather than social criticism. Equally prolific was Mariano Ozores who in

---

[27] Based on Francisco Delicado's 1526 satire of the same name, set among prostitutes in Rome.

[28] Escrivá then moved on to writing and filming for television until 1997.

1982, for instance, scripted seven films and directed five of them, some with explicitly political titles. *¡Todos al suelo!* [*On the Floor!*] is about a botched bank heist but echoes Tejero's failed coup. In *¡Qué vienen los socialistas!* [*The Socialists are coming!*], set on the eve of the elections in a provincial town, the voters fear, among other disasters, the nationalisation of all private enterprises.[29] In *Los autonómicos* [José María Gutiérrez Santos, *The Auto-nomicals*] another mountain village makes a bid for autonomy. Other than *La familia bien...,* Pedro Masó's most successful comedy as a director was *La miel* [1979 *Honey* (p. 203, n.8)], an ingenious twist to the generation conflict and attitudes to sex exploited for comedy. However, he also took on politically sensitive topics in *El divorcio que viene* [1980 *The Forth-coming Divorce*] and *127 millones libres de impuestos* [1981 *127 Million, Tax-Free*], both of which he co-scripted with Azcona and produced himself. Javier Aguirre's *El consenso* [1979 *The Consensus*] and Ramón Fernán-dez's *El gran mogollón* [1982 *The Great Big Fuss*] are other examples of conservative political comedies. Rafael Gordon's *Tiempos de constitución* [1979 *Times of the Constitution*] is more a collection of vignettes with an early sequence showing the skyline of Madrid to suggest the whole city is as indifferent to the reforms as the various characters presented; although Juana and Luisón [Verónica Forqué and Francisco Algora] do eventually get married, nothing much happens in this film, but that is the point to describe the 'pasotismo' of the time.

Taking the lid off the past

The lifting of censorship also gave filmmakers more freedom to explore social and political subjects that had previously been suppressed or only alluded to indirectly. Officially the war crimes of the victors were left buried and uninvestigated, to avoid recriminations and accusations that might have prevented the transition to democracy to proceed as smoothly as it did, but cinema did start to speak out even if the testimonies were personal, partial and manipulated by the montage and soundtracks. This is evident in the style of the new documentaries and, after thirty-five years of the patronising voice-overs of the NO-DOs, it was a welcome change (Hopewell, 1986: 172–3). Basilio Martín Patino's documentaries were finally released: *Canciones para después de una guerra* in September 1976, and in 1977 both *Caudillo* and *Queridísimos verdugos* (p. 210). Jaime Camino's *La vieja memoria* [*The Old Memory*] was made in 1977, released the following year in Barcelona and

---

[29] *¡Qué vienen ...* features Antonio Ozores, brother of the director; for Mariano's other family relations in the cinema, see p. 202, n. 6.

in 1979 in Madrid. Cross-cutting archival footage with present interviews of politicians and personalities from different persuasions discussing their memories of the Republican years, the Civil War and its consequences, it is edited with (false) reaction-shots in such a way as to suggest conversations that never took place, thus eliciting numerous contradictions on which to reflect. Diego Abad de Santillán, a former anarchist interviewed by Camino, also filmed his own reflections in ¿Por qué perdimos la guerra? [1977 *Why Did We Lose The War?]. In Dolores [1980] García Sánchez interviewed Dolores Ibárruri, known as la Pasionaria, a communist MP in the Republican Cortes, re-elected in 1977 but remembered for her '¡No pasarán!' [They shall not pass!] to the Nationalist armies encircling Madrid during the Civil War. Gonzalo Herralde's Raza, el espíritu de Franco [1977 Race, The Spirit of Franco – written with Román Gubern] is a clever montage of interviews with Pilar Franco de Bahamonde, the Dictator's sister, and Alfredo Mayo, the leading film star of the early Dictatorship, as they react to fragments of Raza, the big success of the early 1940s with a story line written by Franco himself (pp. 87–8, 90–1). In 1976 Jaime Chávarri interviewed the widow and three sons of Franco's poet laureate, Leopoldo Panero, who died following a heart attack in 1962. He edited this footage into a 97-minute documentary, El desencanto [The Disenchantment – produced by Querejeta], which reveals the deep cracks within Francoist values and the idealised family.[30] Made in 1981 but only released in 1983, Cecilia and José Juan Bartolomé's two-part documentary of 90 and 93 minutes, Después de ... [*And After ... Franco's death], draws on interviews of various prominent figures from politics, the arts and so forth to investigate the possible reasons for the apathy of the period. There is also Ángel García del Val's experimental documentary Cada ver es ... [*Each Viewing Is .../Corpses]. Made in 1981, it encountered great difficulties in its release, finally being premiered in Valencia in 1983. This was related to its subject matter, work in the Valencia morgue, reflections on death and the Dictatorship, for which it received an 'S', and secondly because as a 16mm film it was not the right format for theatres (Imanol Zumalde Arregi, in Pérez Perucha, 1997: 838–40).

There was considerable activity and funding in the autonomous regions. For instance, in the Basque Country Iñaki Núñez made the 55-minute Toque de queda [1978 *Curfew]. Imanol Uribe's first feature was El proceso de Burgos [1979 The Burgos Trial – San Sebastián Cantabrian Pearl], a 134-minute film comprising interviews with ETA radicals imprisoned in 1970 and released as part of the 1977 amnesty, cross-cut with images of Basque culture and countryside (Stone, 2002: 138–40). Pío and Julio Baroja made a three-

---

[30] In 1994 Ricardo Franco interviewed the three sons again after their mother Felicidad Blanc died, a film released as Después de tantos años [*After so many years ...], this time produced by Imanol Uribe's own company Aiete.

BERNARD P.E. BENTLEY

hour anthropological documentary exploring the roots of Basque values, *Guipuzkoa* [1980]. In Catalonia the Institut del Cinema Català [ICC, Catalan Cinema Institute] was set up in December 1975 to fund brief newsreels and documentaries in Catalan. Longer works were also produced like Pere Portabella's four-hour *Informe general ...* [1977 *General Report ...*] on political opinions for the future, where the mise-en-scène is used to characterise the interviewees; it also included both news footage and brief fictional reconstructions of minor events following the Dictator's death (Torreiro, 1998: 303–18). There were other issues, for instance, Gonzalo Herralde allowed a murderer to explain himself and interviewed those who knew him in *El asesino de Pedralbes* [1978 *The Pedralbes Murderer* – the murder having taken place in 1974], or Fernando Trueba's *Mientras el cuerpo aguante* [1982 *While the Body Lasts*] 85 minutes of 'an engagingly casual documentary of Chicho Sánchez Ferlosio in conversation and song' (Hopewell, 1986: 223). Other regions also funded documentaries, for instance, Fernando Ruiz Vergara's *Rocío* [1980 *Our Lady of the Rocío*] is an 80-minute documentary about the annual feast day in the Province of Huelva, which was also denied classification for a year until certain personal comments were deleted from the film (Torreiro, in Gubern, 1995: 370). With very little funding or means Gonzalo García Pelayo made *Vivir en Sevilla* [1978 *Living in Seville*], an attempt at a fictional narrative but using the real city and its inhabitants. This is a technique that along with a good deal of nudity he would repeat in his subsequent road-type-movies: *Intercambio de parejas frente al mar* [1979 *Exchanging Partners on the Beach*] and *Corridas de alegría* [1982 *Rushes of Joy*], which present his region of Andalusia and take advantage of the *destape*. Manuel Summers, after another exploration of first sexual experiences, *Mi primer pecado/experienca* [1977 *My First Sin*], took a more humorous and candid approach with a hidden camera to present a satirical depiction of youth culture and its disillusion with democracy in *To er mundo é güeno* [*Everybody's Good*], released in 1982. He made a first sequel *To er mundo é ... mejó* [*Everybody's ... Better*] in the same year, and in 1985 *To er mundo é demasiao* [*Everybody's Too Much*]. Also appreciated by the audiences was Antonio Giménez Rico's feature documentary introducing transsexuals in *Vestida de azul* [1983 *Dressed in Blue*] (Garland, 1991: 95–102; Kinder, 1997: 73–82).

Political fictions

Political issues could now be treated more directly, and in some cases they merge with the new documentary styles (Jordan & Morgan, 1998: 22–3). Juan Antonio Bardem made the three-hour pseudo-documentary thriller, *Siete días de enero* [1979 *Seven Days in January* – his second Moscow Gold

Medal] about the assassination by an extreme right terrorist group of five people connected with the Communist party in their legal office in Atocha street on 24 January 1977. This film was made possible by Bardem's unexpected success with *El puente* [1977 *The Long Weekend* – his first Moscow Gold Medal], a satirical motorcycle road movie where Alfredo Landa plays an accident-prone mechanic who by the end of the film has learnt the value of political commitment and working-class solidarity. Imanol Uribe, who was born in El Salvador in 1950 of Basque parents but sent back to boarding school in Madrid, graduated from the EOC in 1974, and became closely associated with the Basque Country. He followed *El proceso* ... with *La fuga de Segovia* [1981 *Escape from Segovia*], another dramatisation,a docufiction of real events concerning ETA radicals but in the shape of a thriller and prison break movie (Stone, 2002: 140–1). Also from the Basque Country was Pedro de la Sota's biopic, *Sabino Arana* [1979], on the founder of the Basque Nationalist Party. In a co-production involving France and Italy, Gillo Pontecorvo directed *Operación ogro* [1980 *Operation Ogre*] chronicling Carrero Blanco's assassination on 20 December 1973 from the perspective of an ETA squad.

Other previously forbidden subjects were fictionalised. Gutiérrez Aragón's *Camada negra* [1977 *Black Litter* – Berlin Best Director, co-scripted and produced by J.L. Borau] focuses on the violence of extreme-right activists and manages to combine all the post-1975 stereotypes of the fascist: apparent respect for a strong mother and the Church, the importance of a virile image and physical courage even if one requires raping and the other murder. The following year *Sonámbulos* [1978 *Somnanbulist*] was released, another study of terrorism and violence, but more complex and too opaque for the average viewer. Saura's *Los ojos vendados* [1978 *Blindfolded Eyes*] was another complex film examining individual and institutional violence, but perhaps more interesting in this case are Saura's reflections on the problems of representing both reality and memory. There were other narratives like Vicente Aranda's *La muchacha de las bragas de oro* [1979 *Girl with the Golden Panties*], which dramatises Juan Marsé's novel where an ex-nationalist tries to reinvent himself in the new democracy by writing his memoirs, a conscious fictionalisation of the unspoken pact not to dig up the real Nationalist past, also using incest as a motif. A more gentle and straightforward narrative would be José Luis Garci's *Volver a empezar* [1982 *Begin the Beguine*], the recipient of Spain's first Oscar, which took as its subject matter the return to Spain of exiled intellectuals, and includes a telephone call from King Juan Carlos as well as a great deal of sugary sentiment.

The Civil War and its aftermath revisited

After forty years with only a reduced number of films dealing with the Civil War, whether from the bias of the National perspective or indirectly through allusions, the new political climate allowed directors to present something different to Spanish audiences, albeit 'an access [to] the past via the personal and private, the domestic and the everyday' (Jordan & Allinson, 2005: 25). The carnage of fratricide was still not always confronted directly and the preferred focus was personal memories rather than history, and this with an eye on the box-office rather than accuracy. Antonio Monegal argues that the film industry became an accessory to the reconciliatory political attitudes of the Transition that 'nobody is guilty [...] and one way to subscribe to the moderate position was to present the events from the viewpoint of the middle-class, as if this group had been the innocent victim of the war' (1998: 212; see also Besas, 1985: 188–9; Gubern, 1991: 103–12). It is, however, the collective trauma viewed as a personal tragedy that allows for moving and persuasive drama.

Jaime Camino, who would make a number of films set during the Civil War, started with *Las largas vacaciones del 36* [1976 *Long Vacation of 36*] and chronicled the events from the periphery through the perspective of two middle-class families who decided to stay in their summer retreat outside Barcelona when the insurrection started, as no one realised it would last three years. Adapted from another Delibes novel, Antonio Giménez Rico's *Retrato de familia* [1976 *Family Portrait*] was a narrative on the generation conflict, at first rejected by the censors but accepted the following year once Franco had died. It begins with the February 1936 elections and reveals in flashbacks why the *señorito* (of the 'cortijo' films, pp. 65–6, 127) is a bully and a coward, as it undermines the declared values of the bourgeois family in whose name the generals rose against the government. Presenting retreating Republican soldiers on their way to Alicante is Alfonso Ungría's *Soldados* [1978 **Soldiers*], an adaptation of Max Aub's novel *Las buenas intenciones* [1954 **Good intentions*] that uses the war as a metaphor for humankind's propensity to destroy itself with or without a war as the film relates the separate misfortunes of five characters; but *Soldados*, like Ungría's other carefully crafted films never received the credit it deserved.[31] Two films revealed to contemporary viewers the existence of the continued Republican armed guerrilla resistance in the 1950s by those who were known as the *maquis*,[32] hiding

---

31 In 1976 he had directed *Gulliver*, starring Fernando Fernán Gómez. Ungría also survived the crisis through television work, including the nine-part series on Cervantes [1980 *Cervantes*].

32 The word, originally French for 'scrub land', was used to describe the French guerrilla resistance during the Nazi occupation, and in which many Spanish Republican soldiers also fought when the Republic was forced to capitulate.

8a The child's perspective in Gutiérrez Aragón's *Demonios en El Jardín* (1982)

in the mountains from the new Nationalist government (Jordan & Morgan, 1998: 46–7). Mario Camus directed *Los días del pasado* [1978 *The Days of the Past*], starring Marisol and Antonio Gades in a sentimental but powerful narrative, while Gutiérrez Aragón made the more complex *El corazón del bosque* [1979 *Heart of the Forest*]. Starring Norman Briski, Ángela Molina and Luis Politti, it has been described as a statement 'against the progressive deterioration that collective memory [...] exercises upon individual memory' (Vilarós, 1998: 191; Hopewell, 1999: 164–75). Gutiérrez Aragón returned to the post-war years of black market profiteering and hunger in *Demonios en El Jardín* [1982 *Demons in The Garden*[33] – San Sebastián FIPRESCI]. Another story of strong women and absent fathers, it became his first real popular triumph as he used a straightforward linear narrative for this film and built a very successful pre-release publicity campaign based on the affected competition between its two stars Ana Belén and Ángela Molina. José María Gutiérrez Santos directed *¡Arriba Hazaña!* [1978 *Long Live Hazaña*], an allegory of a nation set in a boarding-school mutiny that reveals personal memories of religious education during the Dictatorship. Saura, who had not been afraid of making occasional explicit references to the Civil War (*El jardín de las delicias* 1970, *La prima Angélica* 1974 – pp. 214–16),

---

[33] El Jardín is the name of the grocery store from which the black market operation is run by the family, and is a powerful microcosm of the Spain Gutiérrez Aragón presents on screen.

approached it again with an important implicit warning for all such films through the personal *Dulces horas* [1982 *Sweet Hours*]. This film filtered the war through his preoccupation with the dangers of false memories and muddled recollections, and blended it with his fascination for the relationship between life and its representation.

Films in Catalan,[34] a language that had been outlawed, took the revision of the past onto a more epic scale to provide a platform for the resurrected regional enthusiasm. In 1976, Antoni Ribas finally made *La ciutat cremada* [*The Burned City*], a social history from the Cuban debacle of May 1899 to the tragic week of July 1909. The suffering and exploitation of a nation is narrated through the experience of a family, but not without some collective criticism and touches of humour. Many Catalans rushed to be extras in the crowd scenes, but given its use of the vernacular there were problems from beginning (script) to end (distribution) and the versions originally subtitled for wider release had to be dubbed into Castilian. In 1983 and 1984 Ribas extended the continuation of his historical fresco with the three six-hour part *Victòria!* Josep Maria Forn's *Companys, procés a Catalunya* [1979 *Companys, Calatonia on Trial*] is a biopic of Lluis Companys, President of the Republican Generalitat (1933–40), exiled in France and returned to Spain by the Vichy Government to be shot after a Francoist trial. In 1981, Jordi Feliu released *Som i serem* [1981 *We Are and Will Be*], a history of the Catalan parliament, the Generalitat, from its origins in the thirteenth century. In 1976, Feliu made *Alicia en la España de las maravillas* [*Alice in Spanish Wonderland*]. Re-released with a Catalan soundtrack in 1982, it uses Lewis Carroll as a way to structure a historical journey through Franco's Spain, starting with the Civil War. Eugeni Anglada in *La ràbia* [1978 *Rage*] took a much more personal approach as teenager Ferran, played by the director's son Darius, looks back with anger and through flashbacks provided by family films at growing up during the post-war period in rural Catalonia. With a cast led by Fernán Gómez and Charo López, Anglada's second film, *Interior Roig* [1982 *Red Interior*], was a sentimental melodrama in the context of turn-of-the-century political insecurities and unrest.

Thrillers and *noir*

A number of the films explored above exploit the conventions of the thriller and are stylistically influenced by foreign films that the directors had enjoyed, but they also develop their own surprises. The lifting of censorship now allowed

---

[34] One should remember that many Catalan directors made their films in Castilian to enhance distribution. These have been integrated in other paragraphs. For a Catalan perspective, see, for example, Porter i Moix (1992).

police corruption to be explored where it had previously only been alluded to, and the taste for the genre was preceded by the publication boom of such novels, which frequently became film scripts. Antonio Isasi's *El perro* [1977 *The Dog*] is a fugitive narrative set in an unspecified Latin American dictatorship with clear implications for Spain. Paulino Viota's *Con uñas y dientes* [1977 *Tooth and Nail*] is a familiar story of these years about a failed strike and corruption in high places, but told by subverting expectations and genres: constantly blurring the boundaries between *noir*, thriller, detective and soft porn. He has only made one more film, 198s *Cuerpo a cuerpo* [*Hand to Hand*], also experimental in its narrative structure but classified as a comedy about unsatisfied couples, in keeping with the 'desencanto'. In *Demasiado para Gálvez* [1981 *Too Much for Galvez*] about the inept journalist's investigations, Antonio Gonzalo's humour subverts the cover-up of the plot and the genre itself. José Luis Garci created his own production company, Nickel Odeon, and made *El crack* [1981 *The Crack*], which cast Alfredo Landa as a hard-nosed detective in a surprising sidestep from his more trivial 'comedias sexy' but for which he won an acting prize. This box-office success begged a sequel, *El crack* 2 [1983]. There were other suspense thrillers, such as Jordi Cadena's *Barcelona Sur* [1981 *Barcelona South*], a Mexican co-production distributed by Suevia, or Fausto Canel's *Juego de poder* [1982 *Power Game*], which was relatively tame by his previous standards, starring Jon Finch and casting Juan Diego Botto in his first film. Vicente Aranda's *La muchacha de las bragas...* was marketed as a thriller, and two years later again with Victoria Abril he directed *Asesinato en el comité central* [1982 *Murder in the Central Committee*], the second screen appearance of Manuel Vázquez Montalbán's Pepe Carvalho, investigating a murder at a communist conference. José Antonio Zorrilla's first film is a very tense thriller, *El arreglo* [1983 *The Deal*], and much more explicit in dealing with police corruption. José Juan Bigas Luna's *Reborn/Renacer* [1981] is a thriller that exposes the darker side of TV evangelism and the recruitment of unsuspecting victims. It was made in Hollywood and cast Dennis Hopper in an attempt to capture international interest.

Some of the historical films could also be described as variations on the thriller, like *Un hombre llamado Flor de Otoño*, or Antonio Drove's *La verdad sobre el caso Savolta* [1980 *The Truth on the Savolta Affair*]. The latter is politically engaged and set in the labour struggles of 1917–23 Barcelona dealing with exploited factory workers and strikes and corrupt arms deals; although simplifying the references of Eduardo Mendoza's complex novel, it also reflects on present issues. Released earlier and set in 1662, José María Forqué's *El segundo poder* [1976 *The Second Power*] dealt with the Inquisition's investigations and false accusation of a mother and daughter, played by Juliet Mills and Verónica Forqué in her debut, in the company of Jon Finch and Fernando Rey. Set back in the Middle Ages there is Antonio Giménez

Rico's tale of oppression and mute revenge in *Del amor y de la muerte* [1977 *On Love and Death*].

Literary adaptations

In surveying literary adaptations there is a distinction between films using a contemporary novel as story line[35] and those actually billed as literary adaptations. New agreements between RTVE and the film industry produced contracts for series like León Klimovsky's nine episodes of *La barraca* [1979 *The Hut*] from Blasco Ibáñez's novel, or the thirteen episodes of Rafael Moreno Alba's *Los gozos y las sombras* [1981 *Joys and Shadows*] based on Gonzalo Torres Ballester's novel. In 1980 Mario Camus adapted Galdós's *Fortunata y Jacinta* in ten episodes for television; Angelino Fons had already made a film version in 1970. In 1982 it was Camilo José Cela's novel, originally published in Argentina in 1951, that Camus adapted for the cinema, *La colmena* [*The Beehive* – Berlin Gold Bear]. Although the novel is cinematographic in structure Camus chose to turn this 1942 fragmented slice of life in the sordid post-Civil War Madrid into a linear narrative, as a huge cast of well-established actors frequent Doña Rosa's café [María Luisa Ponte] (Faulkner, 2004a: 15–33). He followed this in 1984 with the very successful literary adaptation of Miguel Delibes's *Los santos inocentes* [1984 *The Holy Innocents* – Cannes]. In 1975, Ricardo Franco directed Cela's *Pascual Duarte*, commissioned by Querejeta and conceived as a film, which was finally allowed a release in 1976. Nominated in Cannes for the Golden Palm, it won José Luis Gómez the best actor's award. An austere and elliptical film, it focuses on the mindless violence of the protagonist's despair brought about, so the omissions from the novel and the camera seem to suggest, by circumstances and social environment (Kenworthy,1992: 55–9). Francesc Betriu's *La plaça del diamant/La plaza del diamante* [1982 – the title refers to a square in Barcelona] serialised for television Mercè Rodoreda's novel written in exile. The original four hours were then cut down to 110 minutes for cinema releases in both Catalan and Castilian. As Faulkner explains, it pressed all the right buttons of the Transition: a Catalan setting for some, a female perspective [Silvia Munt's breakthrough], a working-class environment, a new look at twenty-five years of traumas covering Primo de Rivera's dictatorship, the years of hunger and ending in 1952 (2006: 22). Ramón Sender's *Crónica del alba* was filmed by Antonio Betancor in two parts: *Valentina* [1982] and *1919, Crónica del alba* [1983 *1919, Dawn Chronicle*]. Both films begin with 1939 footage of Republican refugees arriving in France

---

35 For a list of post-war narratives adapted for the screen, see Deveny (1999: 414–17).

to be sent to concentration camps on the beaches. *Valentina* then flashes back to 1911 to relate the childhood infatuation of eight-year-old Pepe Garcés [Jorge Sanz] with Valentina [Paloma Gómez], the pranks he played and his memories of his mentor Moisén Joaquín [Anthony Quinn]. *Crónica* is set eight years later and describes the birth of a Republican conscience in the adolescent Pepe [Miguel Molina]. In 1982 Jaime Chávarri directed *Luis y Virginia*, a village comedy for television that contrasted opposing attitudes to the reforms of the Transition. The following year, with a much bigger budget for a glossy epic treatment, Chávarri was commissioned to direct *Bearn o la sala de las muñecas* [1983 *Bearn or the Dolls' Room* – Montreal Special Jury Prize] based on Llorenç Villalonga's Mallorcan family saga, about a patriarch who has dissipated his seed and fortune, starring Fernando Rey, Amparo Soler Leal and Imanol Arias (Perriam, 2003: 17–43). Although set in 1865, a time that the initial intertitles describe as '[...] marked by the restless process of change',[36] it is scripted from present concerns and the secrets of the past are left to be inferred. Not so noteworthy were César Fernández Ardavín's adaptation of Galdós's *Doña Perfecta* [1977], even though it featured Victoria Abril, or Luciano Berriatúa's *El buscón* [1976, released 1979 *The Scrounger*] where Quevedo's Pablos de Segovia [Francisco Algora] is presented as a sympathetic victim and survivor in a truncated plot. A different type of adaptation is Miguel Picazo's graphic hagiography *El hombre que supo amar* [1977 *The Man who Knew Love*[37]], a biopic about the sixteenth-century Juan de Dios and an indictment of self-satisfied hypocrisy, with Timothy Dalton in the title role.

The *déjà passé* musicals

Traditional musicals were not the flavour of the decade, perhaps because they were too closely associated with the Dictatorship,[38] but the musical formula did managed to trail along, appealing to an older generation. Manolo Escobar at forty-five made his last five films singing for directors in their fifties: *Donde hay patrón...* [1978 Mariano Ozores, *What the Skipper Says...*] exploits the tourist sites of Marbella and Estepona; *Préstamela esta noche* [1978 Tulio Demicheli, *Lend Her to Me for the Night*]; *Alejandra mon amour* [1979 Julio Saraceni *Alejandra, My Love*]; *¿Dónde estará mi niño?* [1981 Luis María

---

[36] 'En una época marcada por un agitado proceso de transformación [...]'.

[37] The Spanish 'supo' strongly connotes 'managed to/knew how to love'. The year before Picazo had directed *Los claros motivos del deseo* [*The Clear Motives of Desire*] about two adolescent siblings' desire for the same boy.

[38] Morgan associated the paucity of musicals with the general climate of optimism and change (1995a: 155).

Delgado, *Where Can My Son Be?*], a possible reaction to the divorce laws; and finally *Todo es posible en Granada* [1982 Rafael Romero Marchent, *All Is Possible in Granada*] shows off tourist sites and some of Manolo Escobar's greatest hits (Crumbaugh, 2002: 261–76). Aiming for a box-office hit Javier Aguirre made a children's musical, *La guerra de los niños* [1980 *Children's War*], with a band of five ten-year-old teenyboppers known as Parchís. It spawned three more films in the following three years, and during those same years the group made three more films in Argentina under the direction of Mario Sábato. In spite of its Moscow Special Jury Prize for children's film, Luis María Delgado's *Loca por el circo* [1982 *Circus Mad*] is a disappointing musical comedy. Rafael Gil's last film was a musical comedy set in 1946, *Las alegres chicas de Colsada* [1984 *The Cheerful Colsada Girls*], with a kind priest to help them. Very different were two parodies of the traditional *zarzuela* (pp. 30–1): Fernán Gómez's *Bruja, más que bruja* [1977 *Witch, Nothing but a Witch*], which uses the genre to reflect on cinema, and Francesc Betriu's low-budget and provocative *La viuda andaluza* [1977 *The Andalusian Widow*], inspired by the same text as *La lozana andaluza*. Neither film was popular with audiences, possibly because even as a parody the *zarzuela* was also too closely associated with Franco himself (p. 90, n. 21).

Saura's second wind

The great innovation of the decade was Carlos Saura's collaboration with flamenco dancer and choreographer Antonio Gades, which brought a truly fresh angle on the gypsy films and musicals that had faded out of fashion. The films reinterpret and recontextualise the clichés of twentieth-century tourist propaganda and Spanish *españolada* cinema, thus creating a spectacle that has its own authenticity and integrity, and enabled Saura to attract international art house audiences (McDermott, 2000: 133–42; Fiddian & Evans, 1988: 83–92). *Bodas de sangre* [1981 *Blood Wedding*] is based on Lorca's 1933 play, pruned of dialogue to express emotions and conflicts through the choreography, as the dancers rehearse and perform the ballet that Gades had been presenting on stage for some years (Edwards, 1992: 274–82). *Carmen* [1983 – nominated for an Oscar, Golden Palm, and Golden Globe, it won other awards] is based on Bizet's opera and a re-reading of Mérimée's original novella. Again it relates both the rehearsals and the musicians' efforts to express Bizet's music with an authentic flamenco tonality, as the dancers within the film begin to experience the emotions of the opera characters (Deleyto, 1994: 237–47). Saura worked a third time with Gades for *El amor brujo* [1986 *A Love Bewitched* – three awards] on Manuel de Falla's music for the ballet (D'Lugo, 1991: 192–214), which had already been adapted for the screen by Antonio Román [1949] and Rovira Beleta [1967], in this last also with Antonio Gades. The film begins with a reminder of this cinematic pedigree by making the camera travel through a vast studio set, after the gates are closed, thus secluding the ballet and its gypsies. When the film was presented at the Montreal Festival Saura received the Special Prize for all three films. Although *El amor brujo* was Gades's last film, Saura has continued to bewitch with his own special brand of dance and musicals with such films as *Sevillanas* [1992], *Tango, no me dejes nunca* [1998 *Tango*], *Salomé* [2002], *Iberia* [2005].

Celebrations for non-conformists

With the 1980s the 'movida' arrived, sometimes described as Spain's post-modern popular culture (Jordan & Morgan, 1998: 80–3). The generation coming of age after Franco's death felt they could say anything and did try to do most things to flaunt the new climate of tolerance. The repression and consequent self-imposed guilt of previous decades was replaced by a 'punk' ethic with an emphasis on the present, pleasure, sex and drugs, certainly less aggressive than its UK inspiration (Hooper, 1995: 344–5; Triana Toribio, 2000b: 274–82). It was also a period of value conflicts for some, which Chus Gutiérrez recreates with hindsight in *El Calentito* [2005 – the name of a small night club] in an exciting and pertinent narrative. With reference to cinema it was the self-taught Pedro Almodóvar who best captured the moment and its energy. He had made a few experimental shorts (Sánchez, 2000: 108–10) and came out of nowhere with his first feature film *Pepi, Luci, Bom y otras chicas del montón* [1980 *Pepi, Luci, Bom and Other Girls on the Heap*]. It is a film funded from the participants' own savings, which at the time only had a limited appeal with the young iconoclasts of the 'movida' (Smith, 1995: 25–40). Its wider influence was only duly acknowledged in 2000 (Triana Toribio, 2003: 134–42). Almodóvar followed this with *Laberinto de pasiones* [1982 *Labyrinth of Passions*], exploding traditional sexual attitudes with unexpected elements (Mandrell, 1995: 41–57), while *Entre tinieblas* [1983 *Dark Habits*], with a very strong feminine cast, is an irreverent and amusing thriller about drugs in a convent, and much more (Prout, 1999: 53–66). These first three films liberated sex, reassessed gender issues, presented strong women, played with different genres in an anarchic fashion, and wanted to celebrate and entertain rather than look back at the departed regime, and earned him the label of post-modern (Vernon & Morris, 1995). His subsequent films would gradually modify these elements and yet continue to tell captivating narratives.

There were some even more experimental films. Iván Zulueta, who designed Almodóvar's early posters, made his second film, *Arrebato* [1980 *Rapture*], also on a very low budget and in line with the thought-provoking metacinema of Nemesio Sobrevila (p. 42) and Lorenzo Llobet-Gràcia (pp. 112–13). In *Arrebato* two cinephiles [Eusebio Poncela and Will More] have to deal with drugs and a Canon camera that destroys its subject. Zulueta plays on the low-budget drug/sex/horror films without brutality, but as Vicente Sánchez Biosca suggests, the world viewed on heroin as a plot element is perhaps more surprising than a vampire camera (2005: 169–77). Ten years late Zulueta made *Párpados* [1989 *Eyelids*], a study of the gaze (Sánchez, 2000: 107). Álvaro del Amo, who would become better known in the 1990s as a screenwriter, had only made three shorts when in 1980 he released *Dos* [*Two*], a film devoid of narrative as a couple just talk in their home without a sense of development, and which concludes where it begins. José Luis Téllez describes *Dos* as a fascinating experimental film that was noticed at festivals in Amsterdam, Berlin, Cannes, Montreal, Lisbon and Valencia, but a failure in the theatres; when shown publicly in Valencia the eleven spectators present walked out and the projection was cut short (in Pérez Perucha, 1997: 812–14).

Animation and cartoons

One successful genre of the period was the full-length animation for children. Such films and series transcended all frontiers and were bought by many television channels. Luis Ballester Bustos made two very successful animation series, both Japanese co-productions. Released in 1981 were the 26 episodes of *La vuelta al mundo de Willy Fog* [*Around the World with Willy Fog*] made with Fumio Kurokawa, and in 1986, with Shigeo Koshi, *D'Artacan y los tres mosqueperros* [*Dogtanian and the Three Muskehounds*]. Palomo Cruz Delgado had been making cartoons since 1964 and had three very successful productions: the feature-length *Mágica aventura* [1974 *Magic Adventure*] based on tales by Perrault and Andersen, followed in 1978 by *Don Quijote de la Mancha* in 39 episodes although 52 had been planned, with the voices of Fernando Fernán Gómez as Quixote and Antonio Ferrandis as Sancho; and *Los viajes de Gulliver* [*Gulliver's Travels*] in 1983. He went on to release *Los cuatro músicos de Bremen* [*The Four Musicians of Bremen*] six years later.

Another feature of the *destape* was Jordi Amorós 'Ja's *Historias de amor y de masacre* [1979 *Stories of Love and Massacre*]. This 95-minute animation for adults was made with the collaboration of other cartoonists also well known in the press: Óscar, 'Fer', Chumi Chúmez, Miguel Gila, Ramón Tosas 'Ivá, and Perich. Outrageous and extravagant, these six sketches are certainly not devoid of social satire and film parodies. Ten years later Amorós released *Despertaferro* [1990 *Sparks of the Catalan Sword*], celebrating Catalan history starting with a boy's dream in the Parque Güell in Barcelona as the Gaudi architecture takes on a life of its own and takes him back to the Middle Ages.

Production, figures and spectators

To provide figures for the crisis in cinema experienced at the time (Hopewell, 1986: 217–20; Triana Toribio, 2003: 108–11), Caparrós Lera includes ten different statistical tables for 1975 to 1987 at the end of his book *El cine español de la democracia* (1992: 411–87). Vincendeau's comparative production and spectatorship tables (1995: 464–8) also allow for interesting comparisons between 1975 and 1982. In those seven years when cinemas were closing everywhere in Europe, France produced the most films while Italy had the busiest cinemas and largest box-office returns, but there were actually fewer paying customers in France than in Spain, until 1981 when the French spectatorship increased. In 1981, the comparative figures were 215.2 million in Italy, 189.2 in France, 173.7 in Spain, 141.3 in West Germany, and only 83 million in the UK. In Spain numbers kept falling, from 255.8 million in 1975 to 69.6 million in 1988, which is the lowest recorded number in Vincendeau's table. The quantity of Spanish full-length features fluctuates, decreasing from 89 films and 21 co-productions in 1975 to 56 and 33 co-productions in 1979, when production then increased for three years as a consequence of the 1980 reforms. The paradoxical increase in film production when spectators were diminishing may be explained by the restricted distribution of 'S' films, which were taxed and received subsidies like any other film. In 1981. there were 92 films and 45 co-productions followed by 118 films and 18 co-productions in 1982, which is the highest recorded number of Spanish films distributed according to Vincendeau's table. Kowalsky quotes a figure of 146 films for 1982, stating that 41 of these were classified with an 'S' (2004: 198). In 1983, the number of productions started declining again, but the Miró regulations introduced the X category that same year, in line with other European countries and the USA (pp. 256–7). Home videos started to find their way into Spanish households and so some films were only released in video format. Many directors, film technicians and actors were managing to survive the crisis because of television contracts.

Viewing and further General Reading

John Hooper's *The Spaniards. A Portrait of New Spain* (1987) and *The New Spaniards* (1995) are very readable accounts of the period to add to the general introduction to Spanish cultural studies already mentioned. Both Besas (1985) and Hopewell (1986) conclude with the start of the 1980s, and Jordan & Morgan-Tamosumas's *Contemporary Spanish Cinema* takes over (1998). Kinder's *Refiguring Spain* (1997) contains thirteen essays on the cinema and film industry of the period. Faulkner (2004a) and Deveny's two books (1993, 1999) become very useful as they deal with literary adaptations and films on the Civil War that started to gain in importance during the Transition. For monographs in English on specific *auteurs* there are a number on Buñuel, mentioned in the previous chapter with their bibliographies; there is also D'Lugo's on Saura (1991), although both Hopewell (1986) and Stone (2002, 2004) have individual chapters on him. Stone has a full chapter on Basque cinema, and Smith on Eloy de la Iglesia in particular (1992). Smith introduced Almódovar in 1992, and then several monographs followed: Smith (2000), Allinson (2001), Edwards (2001), D'Lugo (2006), Acevedo Muñoz (2007) and forthcoming from Ann Davies. But most directors are in need of more specific attention, and Saura Transition films warrant a revaluation (Stone, 2004). Many DVDs on films of the period are being made and distributed, but most of them for the Spanish market without subtitles.

Other approaches have been taken, like Kinder's *Blood Cinema* (2003), or Martin-Márquez's *Feminist Discourse* (1999a), which examines Pilar Miró and Josefina Molina films in detail as well as other films that present a 'feminist voice' (p. 291) or privilege 'a specifically female voice and discourse' (Morgan, 1999: 178). This is a theme worth examining as the number of women directors increases, but it would be a pity to subject any such investigations to a reductive label or limit them to women directors. Each film should be judged on its own merits and script. Films dealing with 'rite of passage', especially in contrast to the production of the previous decade, would be a worthwhile subject. New gender representations are examined in Marsh & Nair (2004) and Estrada (2005 and 2006). Other studies take genre as a starting point: Jordan (1995) on comedies, Kowalsky examines the production and distribution of 'S' film from 1977 to 1982 (2004), and can be complemented by Stock (1992, 1998). Various collections of articles like Talens & Zunzunegui (1998), P. Evans (1999), *Bulletin of Hispanic Studies* for 1999 and Mira (2005), all offer contributions on individual films, some of them under a generic title like 'Gender', 'Popular Cinema', etc., and there are numerous articles, some of which have been indicated in the text above. Homosexuality has received much attention, with among others Smith (1992, 1997), Deosthale (1992), Tropiano (1997), Perriam (1999a), Fouz Hernández & Perriam (2000) and Merlero (2004) all contributing to a growing body of work. One will need to keep in view the new periodical *Studies in Hispanic Cinemas*.

9

A Democratic Spain and Socialist Cinema
(1982–1989)

Political perspective

On 28 September 1982, on a full agenda of reforms and the shirt-tails of an anti-NATO debate, the Partido Socialista Obrero Español [PSOE/Spanish Socialist Workers' Party] won the third elections of the restored democracy with a landslide victory, and Felipe González stepped into office in December. Society was officially changing, as demonstrated for instance by the creation in 1983 of the Instituto de la Mujer [Institute for Women's Affairs] to support women against gender discrimination. Initially part of the Ministry of Culture and Education, now under the umbrella of the Ministry of Employment and Social Affairs, it was a very different socialist reply to the Sección Femenina of the Dictatorship. ETA assassinations remained a major problem and, in December 1983, the Grupos Antiterroristas de Liberación [GAL/Anti-Terrorist Liberation Squads], an organisation beyond the law, declared that it would combat ETA by the same underground means; arrests one year later revealed that the group was linked to the government. In June 1986, Felipe González won his second term of office, again with an absolute majority even though unemployment now stood at 20%. Spain had finally been accepted into the EC in 1985, became a full member in 1986, and joined NATO in 1987. In October 1989, the PSOE won its third term of office but with its smallest majority.

From DGC to ICAA

In spite of some excellent films made during the Transition, together with the arrival of new directors and new trends, cinema was still losing many spectators. The loss was explained by the increased hours of television broadcasting, and both the sales and hire of films on video (Hopewell, 1991: 113–22). The decline of cinema audiences provoked much discussion in the national press and film magazines. In December 1982, Javier Solana, the new Minister for

Culture, appointed Pilar Miró as director of the DGC. This move followed
the commitment made by the PSOE at the First Democratic Conference on
Spanish Cinema in December 1978 and was a response to repeated requests
from the industry, who felt better guidance was necessary to recover a healthy
national industry. Pilar Miró was the first film professional to be appointed to
the post and was backed by the professional friends who had been the dissident *auteurs* of the Dictatorship. Her time in office started with confidence
as Spain received its first Oscar in April 1983 with José Luis Garci's *Volver a
empezar* [1982 *Begin the Beguine*].[1] That same year the autonomous regions
started broadcasting their own television channels: the Basque in January
1983, Catalonia a year later, and Galician television in July 1985, which
would have an impact on film production (Jordan, in Graham & Labanyi,
1995: 361–9). Miró reformed the DGC, which was renamed the Instituto de
la Cinematografía y de las Artes Audiovisuales [ICAA/Institute for Film and
Audiovisual Arts] in 1984; she tightened up co-production regulations and
broadly strengthened the recently established links with television as well
as reorganised funding mechanism and priorities to enable 'quality cinema'.
Based on the conviction that Spanish Cinema could compete commercially
with Hollywood and other international productions, if financial resources
were available, she increased funding for individual films by restricting
the number of eligible films. This implied ignoring low-budget genre films
(the *cine de barrio* as produced by José Luis Dibildos, José Frade, Pedro
Masó and others) in favour of more serious and 'high-brow' narratives, as
well as encouraging films for children and supporting experimental cinema.
There was an intellectual and political choice in favour of the adaptations
of serious literary works, especially if these transmitted a democratic and
socialist Spanish heritage. She succeeded in improving the visual quality
of Spanish films, now known as the Miró look, to enable them to compete
against Hollywood productions by reintroducing advance funding. This
funding was modelled on the French 'avances sur recettes': advance credits
only refunded if subsequent box-office returns allowed it and could cover in
excess of 50% of the proposed budget. These were decided by two appointed
committees on the basis of script submission. The 'S' classification, which
restricted the distribution of too many films that were in fact not excessively
violent and/or sexually provocative, was replaced with a stricter 'X' certificate, and fewer theatres were issued licences to project the more explicit
films. She also reinstated the 'salas de arte y ensayos', theatres for art house

---

[1]   In this decade Garci wrote, directed and produced four other films, *El crack* [1981
The Crack] and its sequel in 1983, *Sesión continua* [1984 *Double Feature* – nominated for
the Oscars, but no award], and *Asignatura aprobada* [1987 *Course Completed* – two awards,
including the Goya for best director]. The last two dealt very differently but personally with the
problem of writing for screen and stage.

and experimental films. All these measures were considered very controversial and soon became known pejoratively as the 'Ley Miró' ['Miro Law', officially 'Decretos'], especially when box-office returns for the subsidised films did not match expectations (Triana Toribio, 2003: 110–19, 130). Miró herself claimed that the 'only flaw was that projects whose presentation of reality was too critical or raised any kind of moral problems in too harsh a manner were excluded' from funding (1990: 44).[2] However, 'the new legislation radically transformed the general technical level of film production, the quality of sets and costumes, the overall "look" of Spanish films, as well as improving the level of salaries and the duration of shooting schedules' (Jordan & Morgan, 2000: 183; and 1998: 1–3). The ICAA was nonetheless accused of being just as arbitrary as the previous censorship office and after being criticised of favouritism Miró handed in her notice in 1986. She then became head of RTVE, from which she resigned in 1988, this time accused of misappropriation of funds.

In 1986, Fernando Méndez Leite, another professional from the film industry,[3] was appointed as director of the ICAA, basically following the Miró priorities, which continued to be perceived as easy handouts for some. The national quota protection had to be revised when Spain was fully integrated in the EC as all European films were included as part of the screening quotas against other foreign films, basically US films. In an attempt to redress the declining number of films made, Méndez Leite spread the funding thinner and further but was forced to resign in 1988 because the funding policies were not working. Unacceptable debts were being accrued, cinema audiences were still falling and expensive production budgets were not matched by the expected box-office returns (Jordan & Morgan, 2000: 183, 180–4). Before leaving, Méndez Leite oversaw the creation of the Academia de las Artes y Ciencias Cinematográficas de España in 1986. Run by film professionals, it promotes Spanish Cinema and has distributed its own prizes since 1987: the Goyas (Triana Toribio, 2003: 116). The first awards went to Fernando Fernán Gómez whose *El viaje a ninguna parte* [1986, *Voyage to Nowhere*] won best film, best script and best director, and these would not be his last awards.

Introducing the literary heritage

Wanting to recover the past and prepare for the future, whether consciously or not, the ICAA rewarded and promoted a re-reading of history and literary

---

[2] In *Out of the Past* (1986; 225–32, 240–2), written during the 'Miró' years, Hopewell evaluated the situation with pessimism, confirmed in his 1991 article; but Spanish Cinema once again survived.

[3] He is not to be confused with his father, the film historian who also signed himself Fernando Méndez Leite.

works from a socialist perspective, selecting authors that were critical of the values of Franco's dictatorship (Faulkner, 2004a: 11–14). As Triana Toribio suggests, the basic strategy was the same as in the 1940s, but without the help of the censors, since the Francoist myths needed to be replaced by new ideologies (2003: 116–17). Betancor's *Valentina* [1982], Camus's *La colmena* [1982] and Chávarri's *Bearn* [1983] were all mentioned in the previous chapter. Vicente Aranda directed Luis Martín Santos's evocation of the post-war hardships of the 1940s in *Tiempo de silencio* [1986 *Time of Silence* – Goya for Victoria Abril] (Faulkner, 2004a: 33–46). Subsequently Aranda adapted Jesús Fernández Santos's novel *Los jinetes del alba* [1990 *Riders of the Dawn*], a Civil War narrative with a personal Republican perspective, into a five-part series for television. A harsher and more concentrated perspective on the war was taken up by Francesc Betriu's adaptation of Ramón Sender's *Réquiem por un campesino español* [1985 **Requiem for a Spanish Farmhand* – one award] a film narrated in five flashbacks through the memories of the parish priest [Antonio Ferrandis] while he is attending to the funeral of Paco [Antonio Banderas (Perriam, 2003: 44–69)], who has just been executed by rebel Nationalists, thus offering another personal history. Mario Camus adapted Miguel Delibes's *Los santos inocentes* [1984 *The Holy Innocents*], which won six awards including joint best actor in Cannes for Paco Rabal and Alfredo Landa. The film deals with social issues, presenting the abuse of power and exploitation of labourers by their master on a remote estate in Extremadura, where the poor are shown with all their suffering and dirty fingernails. Set in the mid-1960s, Hans Burmann's cinematography presents a desolate and timeless world of serfdom that indicts the insensitive landowners (Triana Toribio, 2003: 122–9; Carrera, 2005: 179–87). Antonio Giménez Rico uses social and sexual politics in his adaptation of Felipe Trigo's novel *Jarrapellejos* [1988 – Goya for best screenplay] to expose a similar abuse of authority and corruption of justice. Set in the rural Spain of 1912, it also has the effect of suggesting the situation has improved for modern-day Spaniards. Pilar Miró's *Werther* [1986 – four awards], a project conceived before she accepted her post at the DGC, was co-scripted with Camus and freely transposed Goethe's narrative blended with Massenet's opera to the present-day Cantabrian coast. But the production that really captured foreign viewers, despite being an incomplete work owing to producer Elías Querejeta's interruption of the filming, which was taking too long and costing too much, was Víctor Erice's second film *El sur* [1983 *The South* – three awards], based on a novella by Adelaida García Morales. Estrella, only heard in voice-overs, recalls her adolescence [Icíar Bollaín at fifteen] in 1957 and her childhood in 1949 [Sonsoles Aranguren at eight] focusing on her strong relationship with her introverted father [Omero Antonutti] in an attempt to understand his fascination for the South, with the subtext that he is one of those silenced Republicans exiled in a bleak valley of la Rioja (Evans & Fiddian, 1987: 127–

35; Martin-Márquez, 1995: 130–6). Other adaptations were more contemporary, such as Antonio Giménez Rico's direction of another Delibes novel *El disputado voto del señor Cayo* [1986 *Mr Cayo's Disputed Vote*], with Paco Rabal as the old village mayor with an electoral roll of three. It is a taut film exploring the politics and morality of canvassing that presents the 1977 election campaign as remembered in 1986.

Classical theatre was not a frequent source of inspiration, but a few plays were adapted for the screen, like Valle Inclán's *Luces de Bohemia* [1985 *Bohemian Nights*] scripted by Mario Camus and directed by Miguel Ángel Díez, or *Divinas palabras* [1986 *Divine Words* – four Goyas] directed by José Luis García Sánchez; but neither adaptation did justice to its original. Camus adapted García Lorca's *La casa de Bernarda Alba* [1987 *The House of Bernarda Alba*[4] – Goya for best production design], which Smith contrasts with Almodóvar's *Entre tinieblas* (1996: 17–36). Antonio Buero Vallejo's play *Un soñador para un pueblo* [1958 *A Dreamer for the People*] was very freely adapted for the decade by Josefina Molina in a sumptuous costume drama, *Esquilache* [1988 – two Goyas]. It introduced audiences to Carlos III's Italian minister, the Marqués de Esquilache [Fernando Fernán Gómez], and his programme of reforms and enlightenment by focusing on the reactionary riots of 1766, filmed and released at a time when Spain was being reformed and finding its way as a new partner in the EC.

More remote historical episodes were also tackled, and most of them were not politically innocent as they reflected the preoccupations when they were filmed in the 1980s (Jordan & Morgan, 1998: 53–4). Manuel Picazo's adaptation of Jesús Fernández Santos's novel *Extramuros* [1985 *Beyond the Walls* – five awards] is set in the sixteenth century with a conspiracy to simulate stigmata in order to raise donations for a convent fallen on hard times, complicated by the love between two of the nuns, played by Mercedes Sampietro and Carmen Maura, who both received acting awards, and with Aurora Bautista as the Prioress (Barbara Morris, 1991: 81–93). Carlos Saura, in an attempt to examine historical identities, anticipating the five hundred-year celebrations of 1992 and perhaps even in response to Werner Herzog's *Aguirre, der Zorn Gottes* [1972 *Aguirre: The Wrath of God*], filmed *El Dorado* [1988]. Following Aguirre's failed expedition down the Amazon to find a land and cities of gold, the film focuses on ambition, greed, violence and intolerance. It was the most expensive Spanish production to date, but failed at the box-office (D'Lugo, 1991: 230–4). Saura followed this with the ambitious *La noche oscura* [1989 *The Dark Night*], which interprets the writings of the mystic and lonely reforming monk Juan de Yepes [Juan Diego], now

---

4   In 1991 TV director Stuart Burge filmed an English version of the play, with Glenda Jackson as Bernarda Alba and Joan Plowright as Poncia. In Camus's adaptation these parts are played by Irene Gutiérrez Caba and Florinda Chico respectively, with Ana Belén as Adela.

known as Saint John of the Cross.[5] In 1984, Josefina Molina also directed the television mini-series *Teresa de Jesús*, starring Concha Velasco, which was then cut for release in theatres. Javier Aguirre adapted *La monja alférez* [1987 *The Lieutenant Nun*] based on De Quincey's novel dramatising the legend of Catalina de Erauso, played by Esperanza Roy. Jaime Camino made a personal and complex film, *Luces y sombras* [1988 *Lights and Shadows*], which presents a journey into the past as a child enters into the world of Felipe IV and Velázquez through the painting of 'Las Meninas'.

The above and the following were clearly made with an eye to capturing European spectators with Spanish subject matter, as examples of universal themes. After the destructive reviews of *Dulces horas* [1981], Saura accepted an offer from Jean-Claude Carrière, Buñuel's screenwriter for all the late French films, to direct *Antonieta* [1982]. Based on a novel by Andrés Henestrosa, it was a co-production with France and Mexico, thus breaking with Querejeta who had produced all his previous films; he did, however, keep Teo Escamilla as cinematographer and Pablo G. del Amo for the editing. *Antonieta* is another exploration of European and American identities with a psychologist Anna [Hanna Schygulla] in present-day Paris researching the reason(s) for the public suicide of Antonieta Rivas Mercado [Isabel Adjani], an influential Mexican art patroness who promoted European ideas as models for her native land, and who shot herself in Notre Dame Cathedral in 1931. The film involved much self-indulgent travelling and location shooting when the psychologist's investigation moves to Mexico to fill in the background. Gonzalo Suárez directed on his own playful script, *Remando al viento* [1988 *Rowing in the Wind* – six Goyas, and a San Sebastián Silver Shell], a film that explores the relationships between Byron [Hugh Grant] and the Shelleys, Mary [Lizzy McInnerny] and Percy [Valentine Pelka], and Claire Clairmont [Elizabeth Hurley]. Suárez then indulged himself even more with *Don Juan en los infiernos* [1991 *Don Juan in Hell* – Goya and Sant Jordi for Fernando Guillén in the title role], a bold visual adaptation of this European myth, starring Charo López as a mature Doña Elvira. It is a creationist interpretation of Molière's rationalist and atheist Dom Juan, with his valet Esganarel [Mario Pardo], which draws more on the Surrealist tradition, filmed with very dark cinematography by Carlos Suárez.[6] Thirteen months earlier Antonio Mercero had released *Don Juan mi querido fantasma* [1990 *Don Juan My Dear Ghost*], a riotous comedy directed at the home audience with

---

[5] A number of references to St John of the Cross's work are already present in *Ana y los lobos* [1973] and *Mamá cumple cien años* [1979].

[6] The character of Don Juan, according to his probable creator the Mercederian monk Tirso de Molina, is the man who betrays all, including himself. He has intrigued directors as early as the first recorded reels by the Baños brothers, dated 1908 (p. 17), as well as other playwrights and composers.

an awareness of Spanish traditions, as Don Juan is allowed out of purgatory on November first and given the opportunity to redeem himself with one good deed. The film exploits its Sevilian setting with plenty of flamenco as Don Juan is mistaken for the actor who plays his character in the traditional production of Zorrilla's play.

Remembering the Dictatorship

Reassessing the past continued with scripts specifically written to examine the Civil War, the post-war years, and Franco himself, thus opening previously forbidden closets (Jordan & Morgan, 1998: 23–6). In 1987, Bardem made *Lorca, muerte de un poeta* [*Lorca, the Death of a Poet*] for television. It is a documentary based on Ian Gibson's recently published research, and was originally broadcast in six episodes. Jaime Camino, born a month prior to the 1936 uprising, was interested in the moments just before the war and in 1984 had also made a television drama based on García Lorca, *El balcón abierto* [*The Open Balcony*]. In 1986 he filmed *Dragon Rapide* [three awards], which took its name from the De Havilland DH-89 that the industrialist Juan March[7] hired in the UK to get General Franco from the Canaries to his troops in Tetuan, ready for the rebellion. The film was made as a biopic covering the two weeks that led up to 18 July 1936, and is punctuated by references to Pablo Casals rehearsing Beethoven's Ninth in Barcelona (D'Lugo, 2002: 163–4). Jaime Chávarri's *Las bicicletas son para el verano* [1984 *Bicycles are for the Summer* – four awards] based on the very successful play by actor-director Fernando Fernán Gómez, is another personal story of how an insignificant Madrid family survives the Civil War. Berlanga, born in 1921, had lived through the war and was enlisted when 18, three months before the Republican capitulation; subsequently, in an attempt to redeem his father, condemned to death as a Republican politician, he volunteered for the División Azul [Blue Division, the Spanish regiment Franco sent to Germany to support the Nazi effort]. His father's execution was commuted to a prison sentence from which he was released in 1952 and he died six months later. Although scripted with Rafael Azcona in 1956, the film *La vaquilla* [*The Heifer*] was not made until 1985. It was the first humorous satire made about the war, full of gags and yet forcefully stressing the absurdity of war. It is set during the summer on the Aragonese front, site of some of the bloodiest confrontations, at a moment when nothing much happens and both sets of

---

[7] Saura's *El jardín de las delicias* [1970 *The Garden of Delights*] establishes a number of parallels between its protagonist and the Catalan industrialist.

trenches are bored.[8] A more serious approach was José Antonio Zorrilla's second film *A los cuatro vientos* [1987 *To the Four Winds*], a biopic of Basque poet Estebán Lauaxeta, a Catholic and promoter of the Basque language and nation, shot at the age of 31 by Franco's soldiers in 1937.

In Aranda's second adaptation of a Juan Marsé novel, *Si te dicen que caí* [1989 **If They Tell You I Fell* – five awards including a Goya and Sant Jordi for Jorge Sanz as best actor] there is a consciously contradictory narrative set in Barcelona with time jumps (1970s, 1940s, the war, concluding with the 1980s) in which Victoria Abril plays three different women, all to question the accuracy of individual and collective memories, recalling the years of hunger through a brutal depiction of violence and sex (Deveny, 1999: 230–9). In contrast the post-war years were presented nostalgically in Fernando Trueba's romance *El año de las luces* [1986 *Year of Enlightment* – two awards including the Berlin Silver Bear] about first love as experienced in 1942 in a tuberculosis sanatorium,[9] from a script written with Azcona and starring Maribel Verdú opposite Jorge Sanz. Antonio Giménez Rico's *Catorce estaciones* [1991 *Fourteen Stations*] is a thriller set in 1949 beginning at the Quai d'Orsay, then still the Paris railway station for the south, for a journey to Madrid full of dark surprises and assassins. Antonio Mercero's *Espérame en el cielo* [1987 *Wait for Me in Heaven* – one award] is another brilliant comedy based on the (not too far-fetched) hypothesis that Franco had a double, which also delivered a shrewd deconstruction of the regime's propaganda machine and the NO-DOs (Mitchell, 2004: 174–7). Manuel Gutiérrez Aragón's *La mitad del cielo* [1986 *Half of Heaven* – seven awards including San Sebastián Gold Shell and Sant Jordi best film] chronicles in references to films some twenty years of Dictatorship through the life of Rosa [Ángela Molina], her grandmother [Margarita Lozano] and her daughter [Carolina Silva]. It also questions the price of urbanisation and consumerism that took place during those years in contrast to the rural life and other traditions (Bentley, 1996: 259–73). Fernando Fernán Gómez's *El viaje a ninguna parte* [1986 – eight awards including three Goyas and Sant Jordi best film] looks back at the period from an old people's home in 1973, as Carlos Galván [José Sacristán] relates the hardships endured, muddled with his personal illusions, as an actor in a third-rate itinerant theatre troupe.[10] Fernán Gómez further explored

---

[8]   The film also includes two songs from *La hija de Juan Simón* [1935 **Juan Simon's Daughter*] in homage to Buñuel (Nair, 2000: 97).

[9]   The sanatorium is a recurring icon in those films that metaphorically link the post-war years with the war itself, grounded in reality by the fact that tuberculosis was endemic in the 1940s. A powerful example is Agustí Villaronga's *El mar* [2000 *The Sea*].

[10]   The setting and period had already been explored by Bardem in *Cómicos* [1954 *Thespians*] and Camus's *Los farsantes* [1964 **Frauds*]. A similar theme of faulty memory with more drastic consequences of the destructive power of jealousy is explored in Antonio Drove's last film, *El túnel* [1987 *The Tunnel*], adapted from Ernesto Sábato's novel.

the problems of memory in *El mar y el tiempo* [1989 *Time and the Sea*] for which Rafaela Aparicio won the 1990 Goya for best actress and María Asquerino for best supporting actress, with eight more nominations as well as the Special Jury Prize at the San Sebastián International Film Festival. Set in the 1960s, the film addresses Republican Spain, the war and of course the collective memory of the present-day spectators by contrasting the personal memories of two brothers, one of whom has just returned to Madrid from exile in Argentina. Fernán Gómez followed this up with another satirical comedy, set in November 1975, *Mambrú se fue a la guerra* [1986 *Mambrú Went to War*[11] – Goya for Fernán Gómez as best actor] in which an ex-Republican drummer-boy has spent the thirty-six years of the Dictatorship living in hiding in his own house; these cases were known as 'topos' [moles]. When Franco dies he can at last come out but if he does his wife's war-widow's pension, just granted by the government, would have to be repaid (Hopewell, 1986: 70 and 236). After ten years of silence Basilio Martín Patino returned with *Los paraísos perdidos* [1985 *The Lost Paradise*], a nostalgic film looking at socialist Spain and Salamanca from the perspective of a returned exile [Charo López] completing her translation of Hölderlin, described by the critics of the time as more than a film, a poem. Basilio Martín Patino's *Madrid* [1987 – one award] was made in 1986, a year that marked fifty years since Franco had implacably imposed himself on Spanish society. Patino approached the theme through the story of a German director [Rüdiger Vogler], the outsider in the capital, sent to make a documentary about the Civil War who questions himself, his job, his vocation and his subject matter, which now clashes with the present socio-political reality and his own personal values (Vernon, 1995: 175–85; Kinder, 1997: 73–82). The previous year, 1985, was the tenth anniversary of the return of the monarchy and democracy, and the King's Christmas speech focused on reconciliation. This would also be the subject of José Luis Borau's first comedy *Tata mía* [1986 *Dear Nanny* – one award], which brought Imperio Argentina back to the screen. It confronts a rebellious Carmen Maura, who has just escaped from her convent, with an authoritarian Miguel Rellán as feuding siblings, and brings in Alfredo Landa as the well-meaning neighbour infantilised by the repressive education of the regime. The film ridicules the patriarchal values still experienced by many Spaniards while introducing a Nationalist general who was opposed to such a long, unnecessary and destructive war. It concludes with Teo [Alfredo Landa] finally growing up but with a precarious reconciliation between the siblings (Fiddian, 1988: 14–18). It is a film that, both allegorically through its narra-

---

[11] This is the first line of a popular song originally sung by Napoleon's soldiers; the reference is to the Duke of Malborough, and the British troops replied with the same tune: 'For he's a jolly good fellow …'.

tive and characters and with its background references, reflects the tensions
of its time.

Crime

In 1984, television commissioned established directors Aranda, Bardem,
Fons, Franco, Olea and Uribe to make a series of seven quality films dramatising true criminal cases that were broadcast as *La huella del crimen*. The
series was continued with another four commissions in 1990: Costa, Drove,
Franco and Moleón.[12] Pedro Costa stayed with crime in his version of *El
caso Almería* [1984 *The Almería Affair*] concerning the investigation of the
shooting of three presumed Etarras by the Civil Guard. Eloy de la Iglesia
pursued his socio-political cinema with *El pico* [1983 *The Shoot*], a pun
on two of the points of view contrasted by the film: the pointed Civil Guard
hat of the father and the heroin injections of his son. As in his 1982 film
Colegas, *El pico* examines problems springing from within the family, here in
the context of a grey Bilbao that is trying to make its Basque independence
count and thus raising a political debate that was also implicit in the casting.
It was followed by *El pico II* [1984], which focused on the son's relapse into
drug addiction and its consequences, with an even stronger indictment of the
corrupt power of the forces of authority (Smith, 1992; 151–9). Then came
de la Iglesia's *La estanquera de Vallecas* [1987 *The Vallecas Tobaconist*[13]],
based on the play of the same name by José Luis Alonso de Santos. This is
a well-worked-out narrative about a hold-up and siege by two incompetent
delinquents who are out of their depth and where the suspense gradually
dissolves into comedy.

In between *Tiempo de silencio* and *Si te dicen que caí*, Aranda made *El
Lute (camina o revienta)* [1987 *Lute (Walk On or Die)* – eleven awards].
Lute was the nickname given to the gypsy Eleuterio Sánchez Rodríguez, a
minor delinquent who was turned into a folk hero by the media in the 1960s
when he escaped from prisons and brutal racial harassment by the police.[14]
A sequel followed in 1988. Both films were thrillers based on Sánchez
Rodríguez's own account of events and starred Imanol Arias in the title role
(Perriam, 2003: 28–30; Jordan & Morgan, 1998: 26–7). In Roberto Bodegas's

---

[12] As with all films mentioned further details, and cross-references, can be found on the
IMDb, although the year of release cannot always be trusted and it is better to double-check
using *MCU.es*, which is unfortunately not as versatile.

[13] The *estanco* is a feature of Spanish urban life, a tiny shop licensed to sell tobacco and
postage stamps, as well as related products, and the *estanquera* is the lady who runs the shop
here in the Madrid district of Vallecas.

[14] There was also the Boney M musical hit.

Matar al Nani [1988 **Kill Nani*] there is a similar violent manhunt but set in contemporary socialist Spain, even more critical of repressive authorities and racial discrimination. After a break following a failed comedy, *Viva la Pepa* [1981 **Hurray for Pepa*], Carlos Balagué from Barcelona started scripting and directing his own crime films based on real cases, like *Adela* [1987] or *L'amor és estrany/El amor es extraño* [1989 **Love is Strange*]. He later invented his own plot for the thriller *Mal d'amors/Mal de amores* [1993 **Lovesickness*]. It is Christmas in Barcelona when Carmen [Ángela Molina] has just been released from prison and falls again for another pretentious and jealous sponger [Juanjo Puigcorbé] who only knows how to use stolen credit cards and to exploit women. Antonio Mercero's adaptation of Delibes's novel *El tesoro* [1990 **The Treasure*] is a tale of ignorance and greed as a group of archaeologists arrive at a village to conduct their excavations. All of the above are visually very different from previous crime-thrillers, whose style could still be found in, for instance, Francisco Lara Polop's *La mujer del juez* [1984 **The Judge's Wife*] in which the bored spouse leaves herself and her husband open to blackmail. The reactionary perspective of this film is manifested in its representation of women and, even more telling, the soundtrack, which is in this case by Gregorio García Segura, whose music, like that of other composer Antón García Abril, often seems set in the late 1960s.

Transnational cinema

A number of directors, some mentioned above, shot their films abroad and used foreign actors, in the repeated attempts to capture international markets.[15] Although in the making since 1980 and not his first attempt at international co-productions, Borau's *On the line/Río abajo* [1984 – one award] starred David Carradine smuggling illegals across the Río Grande and Victoria Abril who, as a proud Mexican prostitute, invites an examination of colonialist attitudes through sexual politics (Kinder, 1993: 364–85). The location shooting in Nuevo Laredo, Laredo and surrounding desert allows the landscape to become a powerful force. Juan Luis Cebrián collaborated on the adaptation of his novel for Mario Camus's *La Rusa* [1987 **The Russian Woman*]. Another thriller-melodrama, it combines the personal emotions of a politician betraying his beliefs and his family against a background of corruption and conspiracies in a European context, and thus reflects the disillusion of some with the now well-established PSOE (Estrada, 2006). After *Lola*

---

15 In *Blood Cinema*, Kinder's chapter 7 refers a number of times to Borau's article 'Without Weapons' which examines the ideological need to make international films to place Spain on the map, as Buñuel, Picasso and many others had done previously with their own achievements.

[1986], which continued to explore and exploit the filming conventions of thrillers with an initial credit sequence only explained by the closing credits, Bigas Luna made *Anguish/Angustia* [1987 – four awards including the Sant Jordi best film], a powerful horror-within-a-horror film. Although fascinating for its meta-filmic reflections it was a commercial disaster, perhaps for its blending of different narratives and teeming references to other horror films (Willis, 2002).[16] Ann Stock describes it as the story of a collector, with less methodology than William Wyller's *The Collector* [1965], but a film that collects images and ideas from many other films, especially Buñuel's initial sequence from *Un Chien andalou* [1929] (Stock, 1998: 171–87). Ricardo Franco's *Berlín Blues* [1988 – Goya for sound and seven other nominations] is a Carmen-type triangle with echoes of *The Blue Angel* [1931 *Der Blaue Engel*], with Lola [Julia Migenes] in her club, Professor Hössler [Keith Baxter], director of the East Berlin Philharmonic and his protégé the promising concert pianist David Zimmerman [José Coronado], with the Berlin Wall in between and a studied cinematography by Teo Escamilla. Fernando Trueba left his comedies to adapt a Christopher Frank novel, *Twisted Obsessions/The Mad Monkey/El sueño del mono loco* [1989 – six Goyas], set in Paris and released with an English soundtrack, where dark intrigues are being woven around a writer [Jeff Goldblum] contracted to script a film as he tries to resolve his emotional problems. The very dark cinematography by José Luis Alcaine progressively envelops the film, which begins as a film-within-a-film announcing that we will never see the film we are watching (Kinder, 1993: 417–22). Alcaine was also the cinematographer for Fernando Colomo's new departure into science-fiction fantasy, *El caballero del Dragón* [1985 *Star Knight* – two awards] set in the Middle Ages where the knight Klever [Harvey Keitel] goes off to rescue an abducted princess [Maria Lamor]; but the abductor is a flying-saucer, not a dragon! The cast also includes Klaus Kinski and Fernando Rey. The film has had a much better cult following as a video release than in cinemas. Colomo's delightful comedy *La línea del cielo* [1983 *Skyline*] is an ironic reminder that these international gambits were not quite ready, yet!

From thriller to psycho-horror

Using Bigas Lunas's *Anguish* as his example, Willis argues that both films and spectators were becoming more sophisticated, and as generic boundaries were being blurred and transgressed in some of the new releases so 'the traditional divide between popular forms and radical avant-garde practice is

---

16 Unfortunately, I have only viewed a dubbed Spanish version, which certainly dampened my pleasure as the dubbed voices do not match the characters' psychology.

broken down' (Willis, 2002: 80). This merging of popular and experimental is part of the discourse of *The Mad Monkey* as both fictional screenwriter [Goldblum] and producer [Daniel Ceccaldi] are located in the world of popular cinema but decide to make an 'art film'. This is also true for a number of films mentioned, although judging by the positive response of film critics and failure of these films at the box-office, in the 1980s spectators were still being educated. After the exploratory melodrama *Parranda* [1977 *Binge* – one award] and comedy *Reina Zanahoria* [1978 *The Carrot Queen*], Gonzalo Suárez was ready to direct *Epílogo* [1984 *Epilogue* – two awards including one at Cannes]. It is an intricate narrative between a younger admirer Ditirambo[17] [José Sacristán] confronting his mentor, the older writer Rocabruno [Paco Rabal] who has lost his motivation in a world dominated by television, as their relationship with the woman in between [Charo López] is traced through flashbacks-within-flashbacks. The film also includes intercalated episodes as the two writers stimulate each other's narrative imagination, and these are shown in a variety of visual styles using the techniques of television, where Suárez had worked during the cinema crisis of the Transition (de Ros, 1999b" 210–25). An equally puzzling post-modern narrative about writing is Basilio Martín Patino's *La seducción del caos* [1991 *The Seduction of Chaos*]. *Otra vuelta de tuerca* [1985 *Another Turn of the Screw*] is not just another version of Henry James's novel but one with a different motivation as Eloy de la Iglesia replaces the female governess with a male tutor (Hopewell, 1986: 221–2). From a script written with Ricardo Franco, Imanol Uribe continued his thrillers with *Adios pequeña* [1986 *Bilbao Blues*], and then moved on to horror with *La luna negra* [1990 *The Black Moon* – four awards]. Ricardo Franco's own thriller *El sueño de Tánger* [*The Dream of Tangiers*], with clear echoes of *Casablanca* [1943 Michael Curtiz], was made in 1987 but not released until 1991 because of the production company's financial problems, similar to those that befell Pilar Miró with *El perro del hortelano* [1996 *The Dog in the Manger*]; both films were completed thanks to the goodwill of their crews. An intriguing and disturbing examination of family relationships is Jaime Chávarri's *El río de oro* [1986 *The Golden River* – one award], told with a voice-over as a sort of summer rite of passage. Vicente Aranda's *Fanny Pelopaja* [1984 *Fanny Strawtop*] is a thriller about a Barcelona bank heist that has a psychological dimension as it explains the character of the strong female criminal, Estefanía Sánchez aka Fanny Pelopaja [Fanny Cottençon] with all her wigs, and the sadistic ex-policeman who tracks her down, 'el Gallego' [Bruno Cremer].[18] Lluís Josep Comerón's

---

[17] Ditirambo is also the name of Gonzalo Suárez's production company, and the title of his first short made in 1966, expanded into his first film in 1967.
[18] It was a co-production, and the version released in France was edited differently without consulting Aranda.

penultimate film, *Puzzle* [1986], was another tense Barcelona thriller that exploited parallel montage to convey the impact of the title. Antonio Gonzalo also continued to make thrillers such as *Terroristas* [1987 *Terrorists*], while Emilio Martínez Lázaro's *Lulú de noche* [1986 *Lulu by Night*] is set in the world of the theatre, motivated by the search for an actor to play Jack the Ripper.

Comedies

By far the most prolific director of this period was Mariano Ozores who continued with his popular comedies. From 1982 to 1989 he wrote 27 films, directing 21 of them and four more scripted by others. But there were many directors who used humour as a means to convey their satirical picture of Spain. Jaime de Armiñán turned his skills to comedy: *En septiembre* [1982 *In September*] takes up the old school reunion; *Stico* [1985 – Berlin Silver Bear and Sant Jordi for Fernán Gómez as best actor] explores the master–slave relationship; *La hora bruja* [1985 *The Witching Hour*] exploits the supernatural; and *Mi general* [1987 *My general* – three awards] brings together Franco's old guard in a Barcelona hotel for seminars on NATO and its armament capacity run by young officers; the old generals quickly find themselves out of their depth with the new technology and soon behave like overgrown schoolboys. Antonio Giménez Rico's *Soldadito español* [1988 *Little Spanish Soldier*] is an even more critical look at the army and the comedy turns very bitter. After ten years' silence Francisco Regueiro came back with *Padre nuestro* [1985 *Our Father* – six awards including Montreal Grand Prix des Amériques], a lively satire on the double standards of those in authority and family values. In the Vatican a cardinal [Fernando Rey] learns that his daughter [Victoria Abril], a prostitute, has a daughter, and against the Pope's advice his Eminence decides to sort things out back in Spain before he dies.[19] Two other religious satires approached the reactionary Palmarian Catholic Church: José María Zabalza's *La de Troya en el Palmar* [1984] and Javier Palmero's only film, *Manuel y Clemente* [1986]. The first title refers to the village of El Palmar de Troya in Andalusia, where the visions that inspired the sect were said to have taken place in 1968 and where their cathedral was built, and the second title refers to its founder Clemente Domíngez y Gómez, who proclaimed himself Pope Gregory VII in 1978, and Manuel Alonso Corral who organised the finances (Prout, 2000: 123–33).[20] Berlanga's *Moros*

---

[19] See Moreno for a socio-political contextualisation of the anticlericalism in this and other comedies (1988: 264–72); also Perriam (2007: 27–38).

[20] In 2001, and in a serious if nostalgic mode, Gutiérrez Aragón released *Visionarios* [*Visionaries*] set near San Sebastián just before the Civil War.

y cristianos [1987 *Moors and Christians* – Goya for Verónica Forqué] did not have the same satirical bite as his earlier comedies even though it followed the same formula of building up and then destroying high hopes. 'Moors and Christians' is the name of a small long-established family firm that makes 'turrón' [a traditional type of nougat] in Jijona, and Berlanga relates their tribulations when they decide to modernise and compete against the national corporations. After *Mala racha* [1985 **Unlucky Streak*] about a fifth-rate boxer, José Luis Cuerda turned to comedies set in the countryside, either the forest or village, with *El bosque animado* [1987 **The Enchanted Forest* – seven awards including five Goyas with best film], integrating an impressive cast headed by Alfredo Landa and a script by Azcona. Then with his own script Cuerda presented village life in *Amanece que no es poco* [1989 **It's Dawn and No Mean Feat*], introducing impossible zany characters led by Antonio Resines and Luis Ciges in strange situations, but the magic realism of the narrative is not devoid of social satire. Another approach to revisiting the past was José Luis García Sánchez's comedy *Hay que deshacer la casa* [1986 **Must undo the House* – Goya for Amparo Rivelles] where two very different sisters must settle their father's estate during the Holy Week festivities. In *El vuelo de la paloma* [1989 *The Flight of the Dove*] García Sánchez presents contemporary Madrid on strike the day a television crew arrives to make a film about Franco entering the city in 1939, fifty years before, and Paloma [Ana Belén], a working-class mother of four, dreams of escaping her reality. He had previously directed *Pasodoble* [1988 – Goya for best musical score], a riotous carnival as a Cordoba gypsy clan and its matriarch take over an upper-class mansion turned into a museum while the forces of order and tradition besiege the squatters. The credits are sung rather than printed as the film exploits character stereotypes to good effect to present 'an original attempt to interrogate critically the historical experience of the "transición" [...] Spanish society has changed in appearance not in fundamentals' (Roque Baldovinos, 1998: 255–63); the old values prevail. Another view of Andalusia, also from a northerner's perspective, was Gutiérrez Aragón's *Malaventura* [1988 *Misadventure*]. Filmed in the streets of Seville, it is an intrigue based on a failed relationship with touches of dreams and magic, but it was received with little enthusiasm. With a very different type of humour, dressed again in the cloak of a fable, he had previously made *Feroz* [1984 **Ferocious*] an allegory on human nature represented by the retraining of a young boy metamorphosed into a bear. After *Malaventura* Gutiérrez Aragón focused his energies on the five-episode television series *El Quijote de Miguel de Cervantes* [1991] with Fernando Rey, himself in his fourth filmed adaptation of the novel, and Alfredo Landa as his Sancho.[21]

---

[21] In 2002 Gutiérrez Aragón released *El caballero don Quijote* [*Don Quixote, Knight*

Comedies also continued to focus on sexual relationships and couples. Gutiérrez Aragón's *La noche más hermosa* [1984 *The Most Beautiful Night*], starring one who might not be who she says she is, Bibí Andersen, is a comedy set in a world of illusions, the television studio, during the filming of Molière's *Dom Juan* in the context of Cervantes with echoes of Calderón (Kercher, 1992: 25–30). Also dealing with muddled couples, misunderstandings and coincidences are Fernando Trueba's *Sal gorda* [1984 *Coarse Salt* – one award] and *Sé infiel y no mires con quién* [1985 *Be Wanton and Tread no Shame* – Sant Jordi for Carmen Maura], which benefited from the glossy look of its bigger budget derived from his previous success. Manuel Summers was still interested in young love and directed the personal comedy *Me hace falta un bigote* [1986 **I Need a Moustache*], which opens with a reference to his delightful 1963 *Del rosa al amarillo*. Summers plays the part of a screen-writer-director making a film about his memories and experiences of puppy love in the 1940s, another film about making a film. His next films were his last, two poor musicals about the adventures of Los Hombres G [The G Men], a popular boy band that included Summers's son. Meanwhile Colomo's very successful comedy *La vida alegre* [1987 **This Happy Life* – Goya and Sant Jordi for Verónica Forqué] nonetheless addresses serious contemporary issues from AIDS and sexually transmitted diseases to the difficulties faced by the professional woman [Verónica Forqué], in this case by her unfaithful husband with a masculinity crisis [Antonio Resines] (Fiddian, 1999: 242–53). He followed this with *Miss Caribe* [1988] where, to her surprise, Ana Belén inherits a restaurant and brothel on an old ship that she wants to transform into a school, and *Bajarse al moro* [1989 *Going South Shopping*] in which endearing characters are trying to survive by trafficking drugs from Morocco. In Martínez Lázaro's *El juego más divertido* [1988 *The Most Amazing Game*] two lovers [Victoria Abril and Antonio Valero] try to be alone together and never manage it even though the TV soaps they star in are constantly casting them as lovers.

Musicals

Musicals, which had been the favourite fare of the Franco years and which appeared to have been rejected by Spaniards in transition, with the exception of Saura's innovative achievements, started to make a comeback. Great care was taken to present the songs in a manner that is diegetically justified within the narrative, which was most easily achieved by inventing characters who

Errant – Goya for José Luis Alcaine], starring Juan Luis Galiardo as the knight and Carlos Iglesias as the squire, to carry on with the abbreviated adventures of the Second Part of Cervantes's masterpiece.

were professional singers. At first musicals reappeared in what seemed like a conscious revival of the popular music of the 1940s.[22] García Sánchez's *La corte de faraón* [1985 *The Court of the Pharaoh* – San Sebastián Silver Shell, and a special mention for all the actors] begins with a performance in the late 1940s of the *zarzuela* that is stopped by the visiting censors, and the company is arrested. At the overcrowded police station, still in their Egyptian stage costumes as they attempt to justify themselves and through flashbacks to the performance and rehearsals, García Sánchez and Rafael Azcona managed to include all the numbers of the original *zarzuela*.[23] Jaime Chávarri's *Las cosas del querer* [1989 *The Things of Love*] integrates 14 songs from the 1940s and earlier as the film relates the relationship of three artists and the double standards then surrounding homosexuality, which was more easily tolerated as part of a stage representation since it could be accepted as just a performance. Any parallel with singer Miguel Molina's experience and treatment by the authorities was denied with an intertitle, but the songs chosen tell a different story. The film was followed in 1995 by the sequel, *Las cosas del querer, segunda parte*, set in Buenos Aires where Miguel Molina exiled himself. The sequel was also directed by Chávarri and both films were produced by Luis Sanz (Perriam, 1999b: 254–69). In contrast with the small number of musicals made, many films now included well-chosen soundtracks and songs that supporedt the narratives they presented. This is very evident in Almodóvar's films, both in the non-diegetic soundtrack and even, occasionally, with his own diegetic performance.

Pedro Almodóvar (1949, Calzada de Calatrava, Ciudad Real)

If in the 1950s and 1960s, contrary to the powers that were, the international face of Spanish Cinema belonged to Bardem and Berlanga, and Saura established himself in the 1960s to dominate in the 1970s. In the 1980s it was Almodóvar who found himself in the limelight of international film festivals even though he started filming without the benefits of formal training or official funding (Triana Toribio, 2003: 132–42). *¿Qué he hecho yo para merecer esto!!* [1984 *What Have I Done to Deserve This?!* – five awards including the Sant Jordi], although full of humour and the unexpected, is nonetheless a perceptive view of Spain where in many quarters patriarchal values did not change with the new democracy. It presents the problems faced by Gloria

---

[22] Rikki Morgan suggests that the identity crisis and insecurities of the 1940s and the very different growing insecurities of the second Socialist mandate may partially account for these affinities (1995: 155–6), and that these films tap into the nostalgic appeal (Jordan & Morgan, 1998: 37–9).

[23] See, in chapter 4, the section introducing the musicals, pp. 105–8 and n. 31 in particular.

9a The excesses of Almodóvar in *¿Qué he hecho yo para merecer esto!!* (1984)

[Carmen Maura], who is, in alphabetical order, carer, cleaner, cook, mistress, mother, *planchadora*,[24] unpaid prostitute, waitress and wife. It also parodies many different film genres, which are stereotyped in each of the apartments presented in the film, all in a playful and iconoclastic manner that offers, nonetheless, strong parallels with Nieves Conde's *Surcos* [*Furrows* 1951] (Triana Toribio, 1999: 226–41; Richardson, 2002: 140–58). Its success in New York motivated the Ministry of Culture to fund Almodóvar's next films. *Matador* [1986 *Matador* – five awards], the only film in this paragraph not to include Carmen Maura, is a melodramatic thriller that exploits the world of bullfighting and high fashion. It begins with the sequence of a Jesús Franco horror film watched on video, where extraordinary characters, both larger and smaller than life, are searching for their own fulfilment through death, and Eros meets Thanatos (Keown, 1992: 345–53; P. Evans, 1993: 325–35). *La ley del deseo* [1987 *Law of Desire* – nine awards including the Berlin Teddy and San Francisco International Lesbian & Gay Film Festival], in which gender becomes a performance rather than a biological determinate, quickly became a cult film for gay audiences in the USA (Smith, 1992: 188–203). At this stage Almodóvar was still an extravagant showman when promoting his films and gathering wider audiences. He had, however, mastered the art of story-telling, blending classical Hollywood genre melodrama and thrillers filtered

---

24 One paid to iron clothes, except that Gloria is not paid.

through traditional Spanish popular cinema, referring directly or implicitly to other films, mixing the comic and the *noir*, including parodies of television news or advertising clips of his own invention and even his mother and brother in cameo parts. He surprised with every new release, new collections of strange characters in supporting roles, and increasing self-references. *Mujeres al borde de un ataque de nervios* [1988 *Women on the Verge of a Nervous Breakdown* – eighteen awards, including Goyas for the best film, screenplay, editing, best actress and supporting actress] was the film that definitely placed him on the international map, which he has not left yet. In *Mujeres...* Pepa, unlike Gloria [both played by Carmen Maura], power-dresses with no sexual hang-ups; she is, however, emotionally dependent on a philanderer [Fernando Guillén] who has left her, pregnant, but she grows out of her dependence and in the process helps her friends overcome their problems. It is a film that gloriously presents and celebrates female solidarity (Deleyto, 1995: 49–63; P. Evans, 1996; Gunn, 2000: 165–75).

New directors

New but not so young directors also made their first feature while cinemas were being closed down or converted into multiplexes. Manuel Iborra's first comedy, *Tres por cuatro* [*Three Times Four*] released in 1981, was followed by a darker film, *Caín* [1987 *Cain*], set in an anarchic primary school. His first major success was *El baile del pato* [1989 *The Dance of the Duck*], a comedy full of coincidences and visual gags where Carlos [Antonio Resines] and Bea [Verónica Forqué] have separated but keep bumping into each other in a Madrid full of strange friends. Miguel Hermoso's first comedy, *Truhanes* [1983 *Truants* – two awards], is a buddy film that creates an entertaining relationship between two most unlikely characters [Paco Rabal and Arturo Fernández], and pleased both public and critics, spawning a television series in 1994. He quickly followed this with *Marbella un golpe de cinco estrellas* [1985 *Marbella Hot Spot*], a sting located in the playground of the very rich as Rod Taylor and Britt Ekland plan some easy money with local help. Hermoso's next comedy, *Loco veneno* [*Mad Poison*], was released in 1989. José Luis Guerín's first film *Los motivos de Berta* [1985 *Bertha's Motives* – Sant Jordi for best film], which took him two years to make, was released in black and white through special art house theatres; set back in time in rural Castile, it is a meditation about a young girl who comes to terms with her reality, lies and a suicide. Felipe Vega also made his first film in black and white, *Mientras haya luz* [1988 *While there is Light* – San Sebastián best new director], about an archaeologist who returns to his roots and renews his friendship with his old professor. He followed this with the ironically titled *El mejor de los tiempos* [1989 *The Best of Times*], which describes drugs and working conditions in the hothouses of El Ejido. Julio Sánchez Valdés made a brief appearance with *De tripas corazón* [1985 *Pluck Up Your Courage*], which he followed with a *maquis* story set in the mountains, *Luna de lobos* [1987 *A Moon for Wolves*], and the comedy *La fuente de la edad* [1991 *The Fountain of Time*], before establishing himself in television. Also dealing with the Civil War, Manolo Matjí, who already had a number of important scripts to his name, directed his first feature, *La guerra de los locos* [1987 *The Madmen's War* – one award], which claims to be based on a true incident in August 1936 and powerfully demonstrates that the patients who escape from a mental institution are really not so very different from the violent Republicans or Nationalists that they meet on their escape to nowhere; the implication is that war is madness (Deveny, 1993: 108–15). With already considerable experience in various areas of the film industry José Luis Berlanga, son of Luis G[arcía] Berlanga, directed his first film, *Barrios altos* [1987 *High Districts*], a thriller made with humour set in Barcelona and starring Victoria Abril. Rafael Moleón filmed his first and much darker thriller *Bâton Rouge* [1988 – two awards], also starring Victoria Abril together with Carmen Maura and Antonio Banderas. Both films were co-scripted by Agustín Díaz Yanes with music by Bernardo Bonezzi. From Bilbao Ernesto del Río directed his first film *El amor de ahora* [1987 *Present Love*] about an Etarra's attempt to leave the organisation.

Some actors who had gathered much experience of the industry used it to direct films of their own. Félix Rotaeta made two thrillers, *El placer de matar* [1988 *The Pleasure of Killing* – one award] and *Chatarra* [1991 *Scrap Heap*] in which Carmen Maura is stalked by a very problematic detective [Mario Gas]. José Sacristán directed three: *Soldados de plomo* [1983 *Lead Soldiers* –one award], *Cara de acelga* [1987 *Silver-Beet Face* – Goya for Marisol Carcinero], and *Yo me bajo a la próxima ¿y usted?* [1992 *I Get Off at the Next Stop, What About You?*]. Ana Belén directed *Cómo ser mujer y no morir en el intento* [1991 *How to be a Woman and not Die in the Attempt* – one award] with Carmen Maura as a journalist mother of two having to survive with her third husband, an insensitive Antonio Resines.

Catalan regional funding

Although cinema blossomed in Barcelona and Valencia during the silent era, the Dictatorship put many restrictions in place, including the use of Catalan except for occasional exclamations in a Castilian script. In the 1960s Catalan was tolerated for humour or local colour. In spite of restrictions Catalan studios had always been productive, following their own modified priorities, producing many, though not exclusively, police dramas in the Iquino studios. From the mid-1960s there were progressive explorations of Catalan problems and identities, as far the censors would permit. The bolder narrative departures of the so-called Barcelona Film School were also political statements, but these were tolerated as experimental cinema with very little possibility of audience impact. The 1970s brought the more accessible esperpentic excesses of 'S' films, and Valencian directors differentiated themselves from Barcelona. Catalonia also had its own film prizes, the Premios Sant Jordi, awarded annually by a panel of film critics since 1984.[25] The Generalitat now provided additional funding for cinema, and the promotion of Catalan, which had survived as an urban language with more success than Basque or Galician, both essentially rural languages. But films in Catalan, with less than a potential ten million spectators, cannot generate enough revenue unless Castilian versions are also distributed throughout the peninsula and potentially in America. Many films made in Barcelona within the framework of Spanish productions and genres have already been mentioned, and it would have been counterproductive to isolate them, but a number dealt more specifically with local issues whether made in Catalan and dubbed into Castilian or *vice versa*.[26] These were often more adventurous and experimental than the Madrid productions. Ventura Pons, after his documentary on José Pérez Ocaña, made three comedies pursuing his cause on sexual differences in rural contexts with *El vicari d'Olot* [1981 *The Vicar of Olot*] and in the city, *La rossa del bar* [1986 *The Blonde at the Bar*], as well as *Puta misèria!* [1989 *Damned Despair!*], where everything goes wrong with an attempted abduction, the last two with his own scripts. Francesc Bellmunt continued his activities with *Pà d'àngel* [1984 *Angel Bread*], which delights in switching genres and concludes with horror and the absurd as an atheist socialist barrister has to deal with his daughter's secret baptism into Catholicism. He followed this with more satirical comedies: *Un parell d'ous* [1985 *A Pair of Eggs/Balls*] in which a millionaire seeks a bride, and the black comedy *La ràdio folla* [1986 *Crazy Radio*] involving an all-night radio show and bikers. Bellmunt then added two thrillers, the first anticipating the Olympic Games, *El complot dels anells* [1988 *The Conspiracy of the Rings* – one award] and with more humour the case of a boxer exploring Valencian prostitution, *Un negro con un saxo* [1989 *A Black Man with a Saxophone*]. Gonzalo Herralde directed an adaptation of Juan Marsé's *Últimas tardes con Teresa*

---

[25] According to *IMDb*, the first award was in 1957 for *Calle mayor*. There were awards in 1959, 1965, 1967, 1972, 1977 and 1979, but not in every category. See p. 138, n. 29, and Porter i Moix 1972:, 274).

[26] Spectators still preferred dubbed films, even if a lot of the characterisation is lost when given a different voice, especially when the dubbing voice is already familiar. Furthermore, Catalan films now often include other languages to enhance and contrast relationships, which are lost in a monolingual dubbed version; see, for example, Bigas Luna's *La teta i la lluna* [1994 *The Tit and the Moon*], Manuel Balaguer's *El far* [1998 *The Lighthouse*] or Ventura Pons's *Amor idiota* [2005 *Idiot Love*].

[1984 *Last Evenings with Teresa*], a story of the attraction of mutual opposites between a feisty and sensual *charnego*, an Andalusian migrant [Ángel Alcázar], who lives by his wits and theft in 1950s Barcelona, and the blonde but frigid daughter [Maribel Martín] of an affluent industrialist. Herralde went on to direct *Laura, del cielo llega la noche* [1987 *Laura, the Night Falls from the Sky*], also made in Castilian but subsequently dubbed, which critically presented the provincial Catalan bourgeoisie before the days of the Republic. Antoni Verdaguer, after a number of shorts and a 'S' classification for *Las calientes orgías de una virgen* [1983 *The Hot Orgies of a Virgin*], directed *L'escot* [1987 *The Neckline*]. Antonio Chavarrías's *Una ombra en el jardí/Una sombra en el jardín* [1989 *A Shadow in the Garden* – Sant Jordi for best first work] is the study of a new tenant [Mathieu Carrière] who becomes obsessed by the previous occupant. It was Chavarrías, better known as a producer, who backed Jesús Garay's first feature after the latter had been involved on the margins of cinema and in underground productions, including two 16mm films. Garay continued to examine obsessive characters in his fantasy thriller *Mes enllà de la passió/Pasión lejana* [1987 *Beyond the Passion* – one award], which focuses more on the image and soundtrack than the narrative. This was followed by *La banyera* [1989 *The Bathtub* – three awards including Brussels Golden Raven]. The very independent Raúl Contel made a number of shorts as well as the experimental features *L'home ronyó* [1983 *The Voyeur*], *Crits sords* [1984 *Silent Screams*] and *Gent de fang* [1990 *Mud People*; 1991 as *Gente de barro*]; he directed and scripted all three, filmed and edited all but the first, acted in the second and produced the last as well as taking charge of the mise-en-scène and sound. Agustí Villaronga's first feature was a disturbing horror film, *Tras el cristal* [1987 *In a Glass Cage*],[27] described as an excessive presentation of sadistic violence towards children made all the more brutal for its homoerotic motivation and its explicit references to the Nazi Holocaust in the credit sequence, where the characters are 'presented not as deviant individuals but as violent subjects who have been constructed by a perverted culture' (Kinder, 1993: 183–96). He followed this with a sci-fi journey to Africa, *El niño de la luna* [1989 *Moon Child* – Goyas for best original script, make-up and costumes, and Sant Jordi for best film], a fantasy adventure about a telekinetic child who escapes from a clandestine research centre that wants to harness para-normal powers. In a more conventional framework that nonetheless owes a lot to Buñuel, Jordi Cadena filmed *La senyora* [1987 *The Lady of the House*], set in the 1900s, about an arranged marriage to an older husband who needs an heir but has an obsession with hygiene. His next film was very different and personal, *És quan dormo que hi veig clar/Al dormir lo veo claro* [1988 *I See Clearly*

---

[27] It was banned in Australia, and the *IMDb* states that a UK rating was not even sought.

when I Sleep], a black and white meta-filmic homage to one of Catalonia's avant-garde poets J.V. Foix, who had died the year before. In 1991 he returned to more traditional narratives in *Els papers d'Aspern* [*The Aspern Papers*], a free adaptation of Henry James set in Mallorca. Cadena's mentor, better known as a producer and then as a politician, Pere Portabella, scripted and filmed *Pont de Varsòvia* [1990 *The Warsaw Bridge* – one award]. Pursuing the limits of representation and the spectators' capacity for accepting these limits, it is loosely based on the premise of investigating how the burnt corpse of a scuba-diver was found in a forest fire but developed all sorts of suggestions and echoes of his previous films (Torreiro, 1998: 303–18, 313). Also experimental was the once-exiled Manuel Cussó-Ferrer's *Entreacte* [1988 **Intermission*], based on the avant-garde poetry of Joan Brossa. Very different was Gerardo Gormezano's first film, *El vent de l'illa/El viento de la isla* [1988 **The Island Wind* – Sant Jordi for best first work], a lyrical costume drama set on eighteenth-century Menorca, which was under British control at the time, hence the English and Menorcan soundtrack, and for which the cinematography by Xavier Gil makes the best use of the landscape. Still rooted in his Valencian environment, Carles Mira, who died of leukaemia at 45 in 1993, carried on with his satirical romps, *Qué nos quiten lo bailao* [1983 **We Had it so Good!*], *Karnabal* [1985 misspelling of 'Carnival' – one award], *Daniya, jardí de l'harem* [1988 *Daniya, Garden of the Harem*], with a more coherent narrative opposing Moors and Christians in thirteenth-century Valencia, and *El rey del Mambo* [1989 **Mambo King*].

Basque regional funding

In the Basque Provinces, motivated by Imanol Uribe's previous and unexpected successes at the box-office as well as the realisation that cinema can be a powerful vehicle for prestige, the Basque Government started generous top-up funding for Basque films in October 1982. Up to 25% of the production budget could be awarded, provided the film involved a regional issue and used some Basque technicians and actors. Even if the market was too restricted for distribution, a version with a Euskera soundtrack was required as a condition for funding (Stone, 2002: 140–1, 145). Uribe produced his third film, *La muerte de Mikel* [1984 *Mikel's Death*], with Aiete Films, his own company funded by his previous successes and profits. The film is an ironic and sarcastic presentation of the hypocritical values of some Basque nationalists, which explains in flashbacks why Mikel is rejected by both his family and his political friends when he comes out of the closet with his political and sexual differences (D'Lugo, 1999: 194–209; Jo Evans, 1999: 101–9). Some films went back to the past to remind the region of its history while also making indirect comments on the present situation. Examples

9b The strength of traditions in Armendáriz's *Tasio* (1984)

include Alfonso Ungría's *La conquista de Albania* [1984 *The Albanian Conquest*], an epic about a Navarrese expedition in 1370, critical of military expansion, and Pedro Olea's *Akelarre* [1984 *Witches' Sabbath*] about sixteenth-century witch hunts (Stone, 2002: 142–4). Elías Querejeta backed Montxo Armendáriz's first film, *Tasio* [1984], which lyrically evokes four key moments in the long life of a mountain charcoal-burner, occasional poacher by necessity, who is unwilling to change with the times (Hopewell, 1986: 234–6). His subsequent film *27 horas* [1986 *27 Hours* – San Sebastián Silver Shell] examines the adolescent casualties of drug abuse, indiscriminate sex and mindless violence; it was also Maribel Verdú's first credited appearance on the big screen. Enrique Urbizu's first film was *Tu novia está loca* [1988 *Your Girlfriend is Crazy* – Sant Jordi for María Barranco]. With some of the same actors [María Barranco, Antonio Resines, Pepo Oliva, Álex Angulo] Urbizu then made *Todo por la pasta* [1991 *All for the Dough* – Goya for Kiti Manver], which is an ingenious thriller, led by Bernardo Bonezzi's music, where a number of parties are after the millions of a bingo hall hold-up, in a chase through Bilbao and its region that are only identifiable if you have been there. Ana Díez's *Ander eta Yul* [1989 *Ander and Yul*], about the relationship of two ex-seminarists reunited after one has become a drug dealer and the other an Etarra, won her the Goya for best new director in 1990, although her next film had to wait until 1997, *Todo está oscuro* [*All is Dark*], a 'whatodowithit' rather than 'whodunit' that starts in Bilbao and unfolds in Colombia, but again asking what is the point of violence.

Galician regional funding

Galicia, not as industrialised as the Basque Country or Catalonia, but just as proud of its traditions and reputation as a land of migration and the supernatural, did not have as much funding available for its own cinema, and even lower numbers of potential spectators. Films like *Divinas palabras* required a Galician setting, but there were a few local features as well, exploiting the Galician stereotypes. *Urxa* [1989] is a tale that begins with the twentieth century and exploits the stereotype of Galicia as the land of ghosts and magic, produced, written and directed by Carlos López Piñeiro and Alfredo García Pinal. *Sempre Xonxa/Siempre Xonxa* [1990 *A Woman Forever*] was Chano Piñeiro's only feature film after a number of successful shorts. Based on his own screenplay and in Galician, it charts a journey of economic migration and return to the village by exploring the relationship between Concha [Uxía Blanco] and two men [Miguel Insua and Xavier Lourido] with a narrative of disasters and illusions, with humour and magic realism. It starts in 1947 and then goes on to cover four different decades, each one seen through the lens of a different season of the year.

Balance sheet

During the decade numbers both of productions and spectatorship declined steadily, in Spain and throughout Europe.[28] This is starting from 1982 when 118 feature films and 28 co-productions are recorded for Spain, the highest number of films distributed for any year on Vincendeau's (1995) tables, which begin in 1945. Inevitably audiences were still falling, from 156 million in 1982 to 78.1 million in 1989. The 1988 figure of 69.6 million is the lowest on Vincendeau's tables, which begin in 1951 for Spain. Production fluctuated downwards to 43 features and 5 co-productions in 1989 and to a mere 47 films the following year, the same level of production as in the late 1940s and early 1950s. From 1983 to 1989 inclusive, the average is 50 features a year and 10 co-productions. A similar decline was being recorded in Italy and France, which became the cinephile nation of Europe. French production fell from 134 features and 31 co-productions and audiences recorded at 201.9 million in 1982, to 66 features and 70 co-productions with audiences of 120.9 million in 1989. UK production was much lower than Spain's in the same period, distributing 35 features in 1986 and 27 in 1989, and yet as from 1984, when spectatorship dropped to its nadir of 58.4 million, viewers then started

---

28 It is not wise to accept the figures provided as absolutes, because there are considerable discrepancies when other production tables are consulted. Nonetheless these figures taken from Vincendeau's tables (1995: 464–8) provide helpful, albeit relative, comparative figures.

coming back to the cinema, with 96 million recorded in 1989, overtaking Spanish figures the year before. Throughout the decade there was a steady increase in international film festivals, an excellent way to showcase national production and for individual towns to develop their tourist infrastructure.

Viewing and further general reading

Triana Toribio has an important contribution on the priorities of the period, starting with the Miró reforms (2003). Jordan & Morgan-Tamosumas, both in their *Contemporary Spanish Cinema* (1998) and *Contemporary Spanish Cultural Studies* (2000) present a more detailed description of the period than can be offered here. Graham & Labanyi's *Spanish Cultural Studies* (1995) and John Hooper's *The New Spaniards* (1995) expand on the social developments. Besas and Hopewell's extremely useful accounts only reach to just before their dates of publication (1985 and 1986 respectively). Faulkner (2004a) and Deveny's two books (1999, 1993) become very useful as they deal with literary adaptations and films on the Civil War that were important to the production of the period. Almodóvar's films have generated numerous studies including six monographs by Smith (2000), Allinson (2001), Edwards (2001), D'Lugo (2006) and Acevedo Muñoz (2007), with another forthcoming by Ann Davies, and a volume of essays edited by Vernon & Morris (1995), with a further monograph on *Women on the Verge...* from P. Evans (1996). D'Lugo's book on Saura takes us up to 1989 (1991), followed by Stone (2004). Stone covers Basque cinema, especially Uribe and Armendáriz. Perriam's *Stars and Masculinities* (2003) provides a different perspective on the films mentioned here as well as the persona his selected actors would develop. Martin-Márquez covers a number of films with her *Feminine Discourse* (1999a). P.J. Smith's *Law of Desire* (1992) covers some of Eloy de la Iglesia and Almodóvar, and so does Kinder's *Blood Cinema* (2003). Rikki Morgan-Tamosumas has a perceptive study on the revival of musicals and Barry Jordan an assessment of 1980s comedy, both in the same issue of the *Revista Canadiense de Estudios Hispánicos* (1995), which also includes other generic syntheses in Spanish. There is a similar special issue of the *Quarterly Review of Film and Video* (1991) and the *Bulletin of Hispanic Studies* (1999). The new journal *Studies in Hispanic Cinemas* should provide more studies in its new and future issues. Many DVDs of films from the period are being made and distributed, but mostly for the Spanish market without subtitles.

Although the films fostered by the Miró reforms were 'dignified and sober', they were also considered to be 'too visually and aurally pleasing' (Triana Toribio, 2003: 127). For some they were just pretty films but for others they constituted quality cinema, 'cine de calidad'. They could be studied in contrast to the evolution of popular films with their increasing doses of excesses, black humour and/or the absurd. In fact, many interesting and successful films have transcended genres, and would profit from closer examination with reference to hybridisation or fusion of genres. There are also the metamorphoses of certain actors as they moved from the VCE to very different films in the 1980s, and just as important are the repercussions of the technical standards promoted by the Miró reforms on popular cinema. So-called road-movies, buddy films and rites of passage, would all provide material for research. The appeal to nostalgia is more problematic and needing qualification, if the spectators' only knowledge of the past is that it repressed and denied freedoms. Gender issues become increasingly pertinent, and so do social issues. In view of subsequent trends addressing social issues it would be interesting to examine the new positioning of gypsies in film narratives and how tourists are replaced by immigrants when extras are used in crowd scenes. The impact of regional funding is another important aspect, whether to discuss, question or promote identities or just for locations and atmosphere. 'Co-production' is becoming an outdated term, and films are now more usefully examined as 'transnational', as producers seek European funding and/or have greater freedom of movement across the Atlantic, thus raising the question of identity at regional and national level.

10

New Departures (1989–1996)

Political perspective

In the national elections of October 1989 the PSOE narrowly won its third term of office while the Partido Popular [PP/People's Party], a reorganised Alianza Popular [AP/Popular Alliance], the ideological offspring of the Franco regime, made considerable gains. In spite of the scandals that had started to prejudice the PSOE, the government was still able to benefit from the events of 1992. This was a wonderful year for Spain's image as Seville hosted the world exhibition, Barcelona held the Olympic Games, Madrid was European City of Culture, and the fifth centenary of Columbus's arrival in the Caribbean was celebrated throughout Spain. In addition there were important exhibitions on Hispano-Arabic culture in Granada and Judeo-Spanish Culture in Toledo, as if in atonement for 1492, which was also the year of the Reconquest of Granada by the troops of Isabel the Catholic and the expulsion of Jewish families. On 4 December 1992 the first centenary of Franco's birth was also commemorated by some. When the PSOE lost its absolute majority in the Cortes in the 1993 elections they managed to remain in power, but a series of effective general strikes, too many corruption scandals involving financiers, politicians and the police, together with revelations of GAL's illegal operations, economic recession and a severe unemployment crisis foreshadowed their downfall. All these problems and abuses of power found their way into the plots of films and may have contributed to the subsequent debacle of the PSOE. In the circumstances it was not surprising that the PP, having experienced a necessary facelift under José María Aznar's leadership, won the 1996 elections with the backing of the Autonomies.

New appointments at the Ministry of Culture

In July 1988, Jorge Semprún was appointed Minister of Culture, replacing Javier Solana. A Republican exile and defender of euro-communism, despite having been expelled from the PCE in 1965, Semprún had lived in France since the end of the Civil War. He has published much, mostly in French, and written a number of screenplays, including three for Costa-Gavras (Hooper, 1995: 338–9). One of his first decisions, made under pressure from the cinema industry and new EC legislation, was to reduce government film subsidies and to set up measures to facilitate private funding. Miguel Marías, at that time director of the Filmoteca, was appointed director of the ICAA in December 1988 with the brief to dismantle the Miró reforms, but he only remained in office for one year. In January 1990, Marías was replaced by Enrique Balmaseda, not a film person but a civil servant and expert in European media legislation. Semprún himself was replaced as Minister of Culture in March 1990, and two more appointments followed in subsequent years, hardly the recipe for effective management. The already difficult funding situation worsened when RTVE rescinded its contract with the film industry because of its own financial crisis, attributable to the loss in advertising revenues caused by increased competition from the private television channels that had just been legalised in December 1988 (Jordan, in Graham & Labanyi, 1995: 361–9; Maxwell, 1997: 260–83). These problems were compounded by the closure of many theatres – there was a dramatic drop from 3109 in 1985 to 1802 in 1990,[1] and there were not as yet many multiplexes. In December 1991, actors from both the theatre and film industry went on strike to protest at the funding reductions. Then, in 1992, there was an imposed return to projection quotas in line with new EU legislation, set at one day of European screening for three days of non-European, i.e. US films. However by 1994, after the GATT [General Agreement on Tariffs and Trade] talks, it became clear that it was not possible to enforce the protectionist measures against US imports (Wayne, 2002: 12–13). There was a slight compensation as credits with low bank interest were enabled by Balsameda's successor, Juan Miguel Lamet, but while the heavy investment in high-budget productions resulted in visually attractive films, it yielded very low returns in the box-office. By 1994 there were only 1237 theatres, though the increase in multiplexes meant that this amounted to 2377 screens. A multiplex could project one Spanish film in its smallest theatre, while using the larger screens to show the more secure and better promoted USA blockbusters (Heredero & Santamarina, 2002: 123). Under Carmen Alborch, the new Minister of Culture appointed in 1993, the ICAA was forced to abandon its advanced credit allowances so that funding now had to be sought privately by the producers, who had to accept the associated risks and were more cautious. Funding was now replaced by subsidies based on actual box-office returns, and the industry was placed on a commercial footing determined by spectatorship and market response. To encourage new talents an exception was made for new directors making their

---

[1]   See Hooper (1995: 337–9), and Hopewell (1991: 113–22). In 2000, Ventura Pons directed the delightfully sentimental *Anita no perd el tren/Anita no pierde el tren* [*Anita Takes a Chance*] about the closure of a cinema.

first two features; this was a boon for producers, and new directors came to be supported at the rate of about fourteen a year in this period. Fortunately, new investors also emerged, like the media and publishing group PRISA, who own the daily *El País* and other newspapers as well as magazines, large publishing concerns, music distribution centres and over 400 radio stations on both sides of the Atlantic. In 1991, through its subsidiary Sogecable, responsible for cable-digital television, PRISA created the production company Sogetel, now Sogecine, and Sogepaq to distribute the films,[2] and also started investing in new productions. RTVE then followed suit by signing new contracts and investing more in film production. The television channels of the Autonomies also started to fund films that included some regional interest, and the independent channels (Antena 3, Canal Plus, Telecinco) did not want to be left behind. These films could be released in theatres with prompt broadcast on television, while others were budgeted only for television release. This provided needed contracts and support for many involved in the cinema industry. Funding could also be sought from the Brussels EU Media Plus programme and from Eurimage in Strasbourg if at least three countries were involved in the production (Besas, 1997: 241–59). The National Film School was also reopened in 1994 under the auspices of the Madrid Town Council, and the Filmoteca Española (known as the Filmoteca Nacional during the Dictatorship) was given its new building in the Calle Magdalena 10 (see p. 27, n. 2; Jordan & Morgan, 2000: 184–8). The disasters anticipated in 1991 (Hopewell, 1991: 113–22; Besas, 1997: 241–59) were averted and, on more commercial foundations, Spanish Cinema grew in talent and strength as the century came to a close.

The changing position of women

In parallel with the legal push for necessary gender equality and the consequent adjustments in gender relations, creating what has been identified as crises in masculinities (Morgan, 1995b: 113–27; P. Evans, 1995c and 1999b; Estrada, 2005 and 2006), more films were made featuring women protagonists. This was the case for a variety of genres as well as for the new directors to be identified below, often to make the point that sexism is still present in democratic Spain and was not eradicated with the Dictatorship (Gámez Fuentes, 1999: 15–32). These films enabled the recognition of women to confirm their talents in strong roles, either empowered or victimised. Interesting scripts were offered to actresses such as Núria Espert, Rosa Maria Sardà, Charo

---

[2]   In 1998 they became partners with Warner Brothers. They also have a share in *The Independent*. 'Soge …' is a contraction of 'Sociedad General'.

López, Carmen Maura, Marisa Paredes, Mercedes Sampietro, Ana Belén, Verónica Forqué, Assumpta Serna, Victoria Abril, Adriana Ozores, María Barranco, Emma Suárez, Ángela Molina, Mercè Pons, Ana Torrent, Ariadna Gil, Aitana Sánchez-Gijón, Maribel Verdú, Penélope Cruz and others (Peter Evans, in Gies, 1999: 271–4; Jordan & Morgan, 1998: 125–40; Stone, 2002: 183–205; Jordan & Allinson, 2005: 117–33).

Almodóvar was there to promote some of them with his own publicity campaigns, although by 1989 he had fallen out with Carmen Maura. Victoria Abril became his leading lady in *¡Átame!* [1990 *Tie Me Up!* – six awards, including Sant Jordi best film], which as the title suggests is also about Marina's relationship to Ricki [Antonio Banderas] even if the narrative is from his point of view (Morgan, 1995: 113–27). *Tacones lejanos* [1991 *High Heels* – nine awards] concerns a daughter–mother relationship portrayed by Victoria Abril and Marisa Paredes in what could be labelled a melodramatic psychological thriller (Shaw, 2000: 55–62). In *Kika* [1993 – five awards, including the Sant Jordi best film and Goya for best actress], Verónica Forqué is a professional make-up artist and eternal optimist who, among many tribulations, has to deal with a serial killer and his repressed son [Peter Coyote and Álex Casanovas], all pursued by an extravagant Victoria Abril in Jean Paul Gaultier designs and her TV reality show 'Lo peor del día' [The Worst of the Day] (Smith, 1996: 37–55). In *La flor de mi secreto* [1995 *The Flower of my Secret* – four awards], Marisa Paredes plays a best-selling writer of sentimental romances who is on the verge of a nervous breakdown (Prout, 2004: 43–62). With this film and *Carne trémula* [1997 *Live Flesh* – eight awards, including a best supporting actor Goya for José Sancho], the Spanish relocation of a Ruth Rendell novel, there is a change of gear and the emergence of a 'more sober, reflective Almodóvar' (Jordan & Morgan, 1998: 84; Marsh, 2004c: pp. 53–70), but he maintains his focus on women, even if they are more fragile in these last two films.[3] Whatever his critics may affirm in Spain, he retains his trump card of presenting an entertaining narrative melodrama, full of little jokes and self-references to his films or anticipating others.[4] Abroad he has achieved a much more important status, and the average foreign spectator thinks of him as the representative of 'Spanish Cinema', in spite of his very individual style.

In 1991, Josefina Molina made *Lo más natural* [*The Most Natural Thing* – Goya for José Nieto's music] with Charo López as a solicitor who reassesses

---

[3] Subsequent films like *Todo sobre mi madre* [1999 *All about my Mother*], even *Hable con ella* [2002 *Talk to her*], and now *Volver* [2006 *To Return*] further illustrate this point.

[4] Up to March 2007 Almodóvar has won 81 personal awards, but few Goyas, and these are very recent: in 2007 for best film and best screenplay for *Volver*, in 2000 for best film and best director for *Todo ...*, and previously in 1989 for best film and best screenplay for *Mujeres al borde...*

her circumstances when she resumes her career after her divorce and finds
an opportunity to get back at her ex-husband. Pilar Miró made three films in
this period, just before she died of a heart attack in 1997. In *El pájaro de la
felicidad* [1993 *The Bird of Happiness* – two awards, including a Goya for
cinematographer José Luis Alcaine] Mercedes Sampietro portrays a restorer
of old paintings who also reconsiders her situation, in this case after suffering
the trauma of rape (Morgan, 1994: 325–37; Martí Olivella, 1997: 215–38).
El perro del hortelano [1996 *The Dog in the Manger*] was a bold adaptation
of the seventeenth-century classic comedy by Lope de Vega that presents
another woman in authority, Diana, Condesa de Belflor played by Emma
Suárez. It was bold because adaptations of seventeenth-century drama are
not frequent on the Spanish screen,[5] but it won twelve awards, including six
Goyas for its cinematography, costumes and sets. Owing to financial difficulties it was not released until after *Tu nombre envenena mis sueños* [1996
Your Name Poisons My Dreams – three awards]. A non-linear elliptical narrative, with two different sets of voice-overs, it is set during the first twelve
years of the Dictatorship as an investigation and other complications reveal
that Emma Suárez is avenging the war-time assassination of her boyfriend
(Allinson, 1999: 33–45).

Vicente Aranda has made a number of films with strong female protagonists. The *noir* biopic, *Amantes* [1991 *Lovers* – eleven awards including
Goyas for best director and film] questions Paco's [Jorge Sanz] masculinity
as he is dominated by two constructions of womanhood portrayed by Maribel
Verdú and Victoria Abril. As in many films it 'excavates the past in order to
understand the present, a project made all the more melancholy in the 1990s
in the atmosphere of centrist policies, corruption and privilege that engulfed
the politics of socialist government on the brink of collapse' (P. Evans, 1999b:
94–5; D'Lugo, 1998: 289–300). Three years later, in *La pasión turca* [1994
Turkish Passion – winning two of the twelve Goyas for which it was nomi-
nated], it is Ana Belén who escapes the claustrophobic town of Ávila in her
attempt to fulfil her sexual desires with a bisexual lover in an exotic Istanbul.
Aranda's *Libertarias* [1996 *Freedomfighters*], like Ken Loach's *Land and
Freedom/Tierra y libertad* [1995], is a semi-fictionalised history of the 'mili-
tiawomen' who fought the Nationalists as part of the Durruti column during
the Civil War, an aspect of the war up to then little known in Spain. Through
the stereotyped polarities of virgin nun and prostitute (see p. 183 and n.35),
the portrayed struggle for a freer society gave Belén, Abril, Gil, Loles León
and Laura Maña strong and interesting parts (Archibald, 2004: 84–91). In
Actrius/Actrices [1997 *Actresses* – Goya for best adapted screenplay] Ventura

---

[5] In 2006, Manuel Iborra adapted another Lope de Vega classic *La dama boba* [*Lady
Dimwit* – winning four awards at the Málaga Festival], about two sisters who adapt differently
to the patriarchal society in which they live.

Pons presents a young Mercè Pons as a theatre student preparing to play the life of a superstar by interviewing former pupils and colleagues [Rosa Maria Sardà, Núria Espert and Anna Lizarán], from whom she gets three very different accounts. Pedro Olea's costume drama *El maestro de esgrima* [1992 *The Fencing Master* – nine awards including three Goyas] set back against the socio-political conflicts of 1868 Madrid that led to the abdication of the Monarchy, presents a lady, played by Assumpta Serna, who requests fencing lessons from a now-retired master [Omero Antonutti].

In the field of comedy Gonzalo Suárez directed the fantasy *La reina anónima* [1992 *The Anonymous Queen*] about a husband [Juanjo Puigcorbé] who constantly humiliates his wife [Carmen Maura], but during his absence she receives the visit of a strange but good neighbour [Marisa Paredes] and learns to deal with the situation on a sumptuous dream-set. Emilio Martínez Lázaro made *Amo tu cama rica* [1992 **I Love your Lovely Bed* – five awards] about a loser [Pere Ponce] with the gift of the gab who is overwhelmed by a 'femme fatale' [Ariadna Gil]. Fernando Colomo paired Ana Belén and Maria Barranco as two friends who meet up again in *Rosa, rosae* [1993], a comedy about relationships with the symmetry of a Calderón Madrid play. Enrique Urbizu made *Cómo ser infeliz y disfrutarlo* [1994 *How to be Miserable and Enjoy It*] as the sequel to Ana Belén's *Cómo ser mujer y no morir en el intento* [1991 *How to be a Woman and not Die in the Attempt*] to see how Carmen [Carmen Maura] deals with men now that she is a widow. Francesc Betriu directed *La duquesa roja* [1997 **The Red Duchess*] in which an impoverished left-wing aristocrat [Rosa Maria Sardà], relying on her title, takes up the cause of the humble against the developers.[6] It is a riotous and esperpentic comedy that allows Betriu to bring in many social issues. Between 1988 and 1994 television commissioned 13 films all starting with the title *La mujer de tu vida* [**The Woman in Your Life*] and a more specific descriptor. One of the best was *La mujer feliz* 1988 José Miguel Ganga, [**The Happy Woman*] in which Carmen Maura has her toy boy [Antonio Banderas] just where she wants him by making him believe he is wanted by the police for murder. But it was Fernando Trueba's *Belle époque* [1992 *The Age of Beauty*] that attracted international attention with the Best Foreign Film Oscar in 1994 and twenty-four other awards including nine Goyas. An escapist comedy, it looks back with nostalgia at a pre-Republican Spain that never existed, questioning masculinity through a young army deserter [Jorge Sanz] who becomes an object of desire for Gil, Verdú, Cruz and Miriam Díaz Aroca (Jordan, 1999a/b). Strong female roles were also seen in more erotic films, like José Juan

---

6   There is a playful reference here to the 21st Duchess of Medina-Sidonia, Luisa Isabel Álvarez de Toledo y Maura (d. 2008), the head of the first family, which in 1445 was granted its title in perpetuity. She was arrested for political activities in the 1960s and was subsequently known as the Red Duchess. But the film is a fiction.

Bigas Luna's *Las edades de Lulú* [1990 *The Ages of Lulu* – Goya for María Barranco] based on a novel by Almudena Grandes, exploring the bisexual Madrid underworld. Gerardo Herrero, better known as a producer, directed another of Grandes's novels, *Malena es un nombre de tango* [1996 *Malena is the Name of a Tango*] about the consequences of a rigid upbringing, under the three Fs,[7] on Ariadna Gil in contrast to her twin sister played by Marta Belaustegui.

Shifts in social issues

Social issues, particularly drugs, formed the backdrop for many films during this period. Homosexuality, which had been a strong concern in the 1970s, especially in the films of Eloy de la Iglesia, was decriminalised in 1979. It was now taken for granted as a personal choice of relationship, as in Colomo's *Alegre ma non troppo* [1994 *Cheerful, but not Too Much* – three awards, including the Paris special jury], which is a comedy of manners set in the world of the Spanish National Youth Orchestra, where a son [Pere Ponce] must find his independence in spite of his interfering mother [Rosa Maria Sardà]. In the thriller genre Ernesto del Río directed *Hotel y domicilio* [1995 *In Hotels and at Home*] about a lonely bereaved man [Santiago Ramos] who gets involved with a hustler [Jorge Sanz]. Pedro Olea's *Morirás en Chafarinas* [1995 *Zafarinas*; Spanish islands off the coast of North Africa] is a thriller that raises the question of homosexuality in the army. Jaime de Armiñán took a retrospective approach in *El palomo cojo* [1995 *The Lame Dove*], a rites-of-passage narrative set in Andalusia one summer in the 1950s, as a young boy [Miguel Ángel Muñoz, better known for his television work] discovers his sexuality in the confines of his rather dysfunctional right-wing family. The new directors, introduced below, also broached the subject, from both male and female perspective, and it was mostly celebrated.[8]

Unemployment and disaffected marginalised youth seem to go hand in hand with drugs, sex and violence, and were the subject of a number of films about the new generation that did not have to struggle for its freedoms. Montxo Armendáriz's *Historias del Kronen* [1995 *Stories from the Kronen*[9] – two awards, including Goya for best adapted screenplay] is an adaptation of the novel with the same name about a group of bored young men from affluent Madrid families, who have no ideals or ambitions, and are hooked on

---

[7] Faith, Fatherland, and Family: pp. 87–8, 166.

[8] In 2006 civil partnerships were legalised, coinciding with Gómez Pereira's comedy *Reinas* [2005, *Queens*], although both the title and the film focus more on the five grooms' mothers than on the gay couples about to make history.

[9] The Kronen is the name of the bar that serves as a meeting place, for music and alcohol, and starting point for drugs and sex.

performing antisocial dares; they are 'causeless rebels [who] exacerbate the urban and moral decay that has led to their disenchantment' (Stone, 2002: 145; Faulkner, 2004a: 67–72). *Tres días de libertad* [1996 *Three Days on Parole*], José Antonio de la Loma's last film, returned to the streets and the Barcelona underworld with a story of being sucked back into a violent past during three days out of jail. There is much more sympathy for Alfonso Ungría's protagonist Martín [Zoe Berritatúa] in *África* [1996], who tries to survive his environment, the San Blas district of Madrid, and his *machista* father [Imanol Arias], through his running to emulate his hero Abebe Bikila.[10] He is spurred on in his efforts by his blossoming relationship with África [Elena Anaya], a young neighbour.

Society was slow in recognising the arrival of immigrants from other nations, illegal or not, whether from Africa, Latin America, Eastern Europe or Asia, and it took cinema even longer to reflect this change. The first director to tackle the issue square-on in film was Armendáriz in *Las cartas de Alou* [1990 *Letters from Alou* – eight awards including two Goyas and the San Sebastián Golden Shell]. It provides a very effective commentary through its presentation of racist violence that is usually mental and spoken rather than physical and with its use of the soundtrack, as Alou [Mulie Jarju] searches for work in various regions of Spain before being deported back to Senegal. *La recerca de la felicitat* [1993 *The Search for Happiness*] was a smaller project from Albert Abril with less funding and filmed in Catalan, pairing the marginalised down-and-out [Oriol Tramvia] with a Senegalese migrant [Bakalilu Jaiteh]. In 1996, there were five films dealing directly with immigrants. One is Antonio Chavarrías's *Susanna* [1996 – one award], in which Eva Santoloria in the title role is attracted in turn by two different worlds, that of an ex-convict [Àlex Casanovas] and of a more respectable Moroccan [Said Amel] who works as a *halal* butcher. A very different, more violent and allegorical perspective was presented in Imanol Uribe's *Bwana* [1996 – six awards including best director and best cinematography for Aguirresarobe at San Sebastián]. The differences are only partly explained by the fact that the film was based on Ignacio del Moral's play *La mirada del hombre oscuro* [*The Gaze of the Dark Man*] (Santaolalla, 1999: 111–22). Saura's thriller *Taxi* [1996 – two awards for Ingrid Rubio as a newcomer], which features Madrid by many night sequences, also takes up the issue but from the perspective of the white man [Carlos Fuentes], who reflects the patriarchal, sexist, racist and violent values of Fascism, but thinks again thanks to a Platonic Lady [Ingrid Rubio] (Fraser, 2006: 15–33). Felipe Vega's *El techo del mundo* [1995 *The Roof of the World*] takes a Spanish emigrant [Santiago

---

[10] Abebe Bikila was the Ethopian long-distance runner who was completely unknown until he won the 1964 Tokyo marathon barefoot.

Ramos] working in Switzerland who, after an accident that turns him into an amnesiac and a racist, is brought back to Spain where he ironically becomes dependent on an immigrant [Mulie Jarju]. *Más allá del jardín* [1996 *Beyond the Garden* – three awards including two Goyas] is a critical melodrama directed by Pedro Olea that presents Concha Velasco seeking escape and redemption through her work with refugees in Rwanda, and shows another side of the migration question. Cecilia Bartolomé's *Lejos de África* [1996 **Far from Africa*] takes a very different approach. It is a fictionalisation of the director's upbringing in Equatorial Guinea in the late 1950s told through the friendship of two girls separated by race, glimpsed at seven, fifteen and twenty, and the local world during the Dictatorship. The next ten years will see many more films in different genres exploring these conflicts within present-day Spain, together with other important issues such as domestic violence, which in this period was only dealt with as part of thrillers and the horror genre rather than as a social issue warranting serious discussion.

Thrillers

1991 was the year of *The Silence of the Lambs* [Jonathan Demme], and with a taste for the success of the Hollywood serial killer the subject was taken up by a number of the new directors introduced at the end of this chapter. Spanish Cinema also provided its own thrillers, contract killers and psycho-paths. Pedro Costa, for instance, based the psychopath in his *Una casa en las afueras* [1995 *House Out of Town*] on a true case. Then two years later he dramatised another true case for television, *El crimen del cine Oriente* [1997 **The Case of the Oriente Cinema*]. In Gonzalo Suárez's *Mi nombre es Sombra* [1996 **My Name is Shadow*], set in Asturias, there is a very new take on Dr Jekyll. Two years earlier Suárez had released *El detective y la muerte* [1994 *The Detective and Death* –three awards], a dark and puzzling fable set in Poland, in the old mansion of a tycoon who apparently wants his wife murdered. Carlos Pérez Ferré's *Best Seller, el premio* [1996 **Best Seller, The Prize*] is another wife murder by contract. Vicente Aranda's *Intruso* [1993 *Intruder* – one award] confines the tension to the home, and the intruder is Victoria Abril's first husband, Imanol Arias, who comes back into her life when she thinks she is happy with Antonio Valero. In Mario Camus's *Adosados* [1996 *Suburbs* – two awards in Montreal] a lie about the death of a pet dog triggers all sorts of unforeseen circumstances for a seemingly contented family. Rafael Moleón made two thrillers in 1996, *Mirada líquida* [**Liquid Look*] set on a Balearic Isle where Ana [Laura Cepeda] is impatient to inherit from her grandmother [Pilar Bardem], whereas on the Basque coast it was *Cuestión de suerte* [*A Question of Luck*] in which an abandoned car, a bag full of jewels and a corpse could be the answer for Eduardo Noriega.

In a different tone Carlos Saura had used the world of street performers in *Los zancos* [1984 *The Stilts* – one award], and he set *¡Dispara!* [1993 *Shoot!*], a film that concludes with the elegance of a tragedy, in the apparent glitter of the circus world, to explore the consequences of a brutal rape. As is apparent from the films mentioned above, drugs frequently formed part of the setting of thrillers, as well as comedies. Drugs are, however, central to Javier Elorrieta's *Cautivos de la sombra* [1993 *Wild Boys*], which with a good pace, intriguing relationships and high doses of violence, nudity and sex, shows their destructive impact, even if the make-up and hairstyles are always perfect. Elorrieta followed this up with an old-fashioned sex comedy on his own script, *Demasiado caliente para ti* [1996 *Too Hot for You*], about a disillusioned saxophonist who leaves Madrid for Cuba, but which was not well received.

Barcelona thrillers were making good returns at the box-office. Antonio Chavarrías carried on making dark thrillers like *Manila* [1992 – the name of a night club] in which there is a choice to be made between the money or an erotic relationship at every twist and turn. Starring Àlex Casanovas, this was Laura Mañá's first credited appearance, before she started directing in 2000. Vázquez Montalbán's favourite detective, Pepe Carvalho, was still going strong with adaptations such as Manuel Esteban *Los mares del sur* [1992 *The South Seas*]. Rafael Alcázar's *El laberinto griego* [1993 *The Greek Labyrinth*] with a screenplay co-written with Vázquez Montalbán himself presents another private detective [Omero Antonutti] with his own family problems on the case of a missing illegal bisexual Greek in Barcelona on the eve of the Olympics, and takes an ironic excursion into Catalan contemporary art. Agustí Villaronga's *Le Passager clandestin/El pasajero clandestino* [1996 *The Clandestine Passenger*], based on a Georges Simenon novel about a cursed inheritance, was made with an international cast, in French and subsequently dubbed into Castilian and Catalan.

Given the recent political events in Spain political thrillers were high on the agenda. With funding from Europe for an international cast and crew, Pilar Miró directed *Beltenebros* [1991 *Prince of Shadows* – three Goyas and Berlin Silver Bear], starring Terence Stamp as Darman, and released in English with subtitles. A story of betrayals, it relates a political assassination in 1962, a contract that reminds Captain Darman of another all too similar contract that he also undertook in Madrid in 1946. One pleasure of the film is the way the cinematic memory of the protagonist from Antonio Muñoz Molina's novel is transferred to the screen by Miró and Aguirresarobe's cinematography (Rolph, 1995: 117–25).[11] Giménez Rico's mystery train journey set in

---

11 The Silver Bear was awarded for cinematography. In this tale of betrayal, 'Beltenebros' could be literally translated as 'Handsome Darkness of Night' but it is also the name chosen by Don Quixote in imitation of the Knight Amadís de Gaula, who called himself Beltene-

1947, *Catorce estaciones* [1991 *Fourteen Stations*], also involves Republicans and assassins. With ETA still very active, terrorism provided an obvious context for thrillers and violence. Mario Camus's *Sombras en una batalla* [1993 *Shadows in a Conflict* – five awards including Goya for best screenplay to Camus] is told in flashback and only with indirect references to GAL, ETA and Yoyes.[12] It is a thriller in which Ana [Carmen Maura] experiences the consequences of her violent past and terrorism. The year before Camus had made a suspense mystery, *Después del sueño* [1992 *After the Dream*], about a Republican [Vlacar Vodack] returning from the USSR after 36 years' exile to meet his nephew, played by Carmelo Gómez (Perriam, 2003: 70–92), but he never sees his nephew and the mystery he leaves behind must be investigated. The Basque conflict and a dark Bilbao were also used as background to explore the tensions and conflicts experienced by characters, as in Juan Miñón's *La Blanca Paloma* [1990 *The White Dove* – four awards], which pits old Domingo [Paco Rabal], an Andalusian whose bar is home for other migrants from the south, against Mario [Antonio Banderas] a young ETA sympathiser, as both are physically attracted to Domingo's daughter Rocío [Emma Suárez]. Imanol Uribe's *Días contados* [1994 *Running out of Time* – twenty-four awards including nine Goyas, three from San Sebastián and the Sant Jordi] is another tense thriller that reworks the *Carmen* story with the conflict set within the context of an ETA terrorist cell (Stone, 2002: 148–52; Peter Evans, in Gies, 1999: 276). A different take on ETA was José Luis García Sánchez's contract to direct *La noche más larga* [1991 *The Longest Night*], which dealt with the events that led to 27 September 1975 when five members of ETA and FRAP [Frente Revolucionario Antifacista y Patriótico/ Antifascist and Patriotic Revolutionary Front] were executed in spite of international protests and the withdrawal of ambassadors. These events are evoked through flashbacks as an ex-barrister and a retired soldier [Juan Echanove and Juan Diego] meet by chance on the night train to Barcelona, revealing during the journey that both have now abandoned their previous convictions, thus examining changing attitudes to political commitments.

---

bros when he was tricked into believing his Lady Oriana no longer loved him. The target of Darman/Beltenebros's second contract 'se hace llamar Andrade' [has himself called Andrade], coincidentally the pseudonym used by General Franco when he wrote the initial script outline for *Raza* (chapter 4, pp. 90–1), even if the author of the original novel, Muñoz Molina, based the character on the historical Julián Grimau.

[12] Yoyes was the name taken by María Dolores González Katarain, an Etarista who later renounced violence and after a period of exile in Mexico accepted Madrid's offer of social reinsertion but was gunned down by ETA when she returned to the Basque Country. In 1999 Helena Taberna made *Yoyes*, a biopic of her life, starring Ana Torrent.

Rites of passage

One type of comedy, which targeted young men, so familiar in the 1960s and with a different purpose in the 1970s, was the 'rites of passage' or 'coming of age', whether set in the past or in the present and usually during Summer. *Belle époque* and *El palomo cojo* are good examples already mentioned. Jaime Chávarri takes advantage of Gabino Diego's gawky physique in *Tierno verano de lujurias y azoteas* [1993 *Tender Summer of Lust on the Rooftops*], a romantic comedy that emphasises the power of language. Pablo [Gabino Diego] arrives from Russia and falls in love with Marisa Paredes, the mature cousin he has never met, who is rehearsing for a performance of *A Midsummer Night's Dream* in the *barrio* square; and Titania falls in love with Bottom. Emilio Martínez Lázaro directed *Los peores años de nuestra vida* [1994 *The Worst Years of Our Lives* – Goya for best sound] about two brothers [Gabino Diego and Jorge Sanz] who fall in love with the same girl [Ariadna Gil]. Gabino Diego was also the protagonist of Antonio del Real's *Los hombres ~~nunca~~ siempre mienten* [1995 *Men Always Lie*], in which his compulsive lying allows him to become a promising novelist. In García Sánchez's *El seductor* [1995 *The Seducer*], if the setting reflects the times, and the affluent family has moved from a flat to a suburban villa on the outskirts of Madrid, the situation recalls the 1960s comedies as fifteen-year-old Cosme [Antonio Hortelano] fails his end-of-year examinations and must spend the summer at home studying with a private tutor [Enrique San Francisco] to prepare for the September resits. While the rest of the family is by the seaside he avoids studying and develops a relationship with the married woman [María Barranco] who is alone in the neighbouring villa. Starting from a similar setting but with a very different conclusion was *La buena vida* [1996 *The Good Life* – three awards, including a Goya for Luis Cuenca as best supporting actor in the role of the grandfather]. It was the first film from director David Trueba, who already had a number of successful screenplays to his name, and young Fernando Ramallo. In a different mode Gutiérrez Aragón's *El rey del río* [1995 *The King of the River* – three awards] is not just an angling film but another parable about growing up without a father but strong like the salmon king of the title. *Como un relámpago* [1997 Miguel Hermoso, *Like a Bolt of Lightning* – six awards, including a Goya for Santiago Ramos] was Eloy Azorín's first film playing a teenager who lives comfortably with his divorced mother [Assumpta Serna], a successful solicitor, but decides to set off on his own to look for his father [Santiago Ramos] whom he finds in the Canaries. In *Nexo* [1993 Jordi Cadena, *Nexus*], set in Barcelona, it is a young woman, played by Silvia Munt, who comes to terms with her childhood trauma in Bulgaria. García Sánchez's *Tranvía a la Malvarrosa* [1997 *Tramway to Malvarrosa* – three awards] is a biographical rites-of-passage tale, based on Manuel Vincent's reminiscences about growing up with privileges in 1958 when Manuel, played by Liberto Rabal (Perriam, 2003: 185–8), goes to Valencia for his law studies. In 1998, new director Fernando León de Aranoa spun the summer rites of passage round in his own script and film, *Barrio* [*Neighbourhood* – eleven awards including Goyas for best screenplay and director, four from San Sebastián], as three underprivileged fourteen-year-olds spend another summer in the rundown and depleted streets of their Madrid neighbourhood (Marsh, 2003: 165–73).

Imanol Uribe had an excellent break away from his label of national Basque director by turning to something completely different, a historical comedy: *El rey pasmado* [1991 *The Dumbfounded King* – eight Goyas]. The premise is young King Felipe IV, excellently captured by the gormless Gabino Diego, who must produce an heir but needs to be sexually initiated and wants to see Anne Roussell, his French Queen, naked. It is also an examination of hypocrisy and a deconstruction of historical myths that exaggerates historical details with a great sense of humour (Deveny, 1995: 96–116). Better known as a screenwriter, Manolo Matjí was contracted to direct *Mar de luna* [1996 *The Sea Below the Moon* – one award], a father–son conflict [José Sancho and Santiago Alonso] and a medieval road journey to find the sea, with Emma Penella and Amparo Rivelles in rewarding supporting roles.

Comedies and satire

Social issues, whether taken lightly or to excess, also lead to reflection. Fernando Fernán Gómez, still a very active actor and director, directed and starred in *Fuera de juego* [1991 *Offsides*] about elderly men who still want to be counted in a society that places them in residential care. In *Todos a la cárcel* [1993 *Everyone off to Jail* –five awards including Goyas for best director and best film] Berlanga came back with a chaotic satire on political institutions, with a vast cast of well-known comedians playing former dissidents and present influential figures who are organised into a prison reunion with a night in jail to recall the good old days of political arrests under Franco. With Azcona as a co-writer, José Luis García Sánchez directed two satirical comedies that build on old genres and themes: *Suspiros de España (y Portugal)* [1995 *Sighs from/for Spain (and Portugal)*], a road movie about two monks [Juan Echanove and Juan Luis Galiardo] who leave the monastery and survive on the road as they seek an inheritance; and its sequel *Siempre hay un camino a la derecha* [1997 *There's Always a Path to the Right*], which begins as the two friends are about to commit suicide only to be interrupted by a reality show host [Javier Gurruchaga].[13] There is an appetite for comedies

---

[13] Both films recall titles of Franco cinema *Suspiros de España* [1939 Benito Perojo] and *Hay un camino a la derecha* [1953 Francisco Rovira Beleta].

and satires that move from excess and farce to the unbelievable, which were found entertaining when they hit the right note. These were known as the 'comedias disparatadas', ridiculous comedies, which at this time frequently take the climate of personal opportunism that characterised the last term of Felipe González's PSOE government as their starting point. Carlos Suárez set *Adios tiburón* [1996 *Good Bye Shark*] in the yuppie context of the Barcelona stock exchange. Joaquín Trincado's first film, *Sálvate si puedes* [1995 *Save Yourself if You Can*] is set in Bilbao, exposing the misappropriation of government and Brussels funding for personal gain. José Luis Cuerda's *Tocando fondo* [1993 *Hitting Rock Bottom*] took a similar look at society's loss of values and self-respect, as uncle and nephew [Antonio Resines and Jorge Sanz] try to survive the recession. In *Así en el cielo como en la tierra* [1995 *On Earth as it is in Heaven* – two awards] Cuerda changed modes and moved into the world of caricatures to take a broader look at human affairs from the perspective of Heaven, represented as a little village near Segovia, where God [Fernán Gómez] tries to send a second son to earth to see if the general situation cannot be improved. With ¡¡Oh cielos!! [1995 *Heavens Above!!*] Ricardo Franco takes a similar tack with a self-centred womaniser [Gran Wyoming] who is given a second chance to live provided that he uses his job as a television commercial producer to create a campaign promoting the traditional family values of the old regime; Jesús Bonilla, who played Jesus in Cuerda's *Así en el cielo* is now the guardian angel, and Rafaela Aparicio plays the one we infer is God as she sits on a throne recalling *Mamá cumple cien años* [1979 *Mama Turns 100*]. With *Makinavaja, el último choriso* [1992 *Makiknife, the Last of the Small-time Crooks*] based on Ramón Tosas's 'Ivá' cartoon strip, Carlos Suárez departs into the kind of creationist comedies that will become very popular in the following decade. Later, Manuel Esteban's *Historias de la puta mili* [1994 *Tales of the Stinking Military Service*] was also based on a popular Ramón Tosas cartoon strip following the incompetence of new recruits who finally subvert a NATO exercise, thereby playing on the current controversial issue of compulsory military conscription.[14]

Battle of the sexes

Couples and relationships were still and will continue to be very much a part of film narratives of all sorts of different modes. Felipe Vega's *Un paraguas para tres* [1992 *An Umbrella for Three*] is a gentle comedy about two separated professionals [Eulalia Ramón and Juanjo Puigcorbé] who keep meeting in Madrid and for whom difficulties arise as other friends get involved. Ernesto

---

[14] Conscientious objectors were recognised as from 1984, and general military conscription was suspended in 2001.

del Río's *No me compliques la vida* [1993 *Don't Complicate my Life*] is a bittersweet comedy about a broken marriage and the ensuing emotional repercussions. The success of *Belle époque* allowed Trueba to make a comedy in Florida, *Two Much* [1995], pairing Antonio Banderas with Melanie Griffith and including references to the Lincoln Brigade. The title is a pun on 'too much' as Banderas thinks he must invent himself a twin brother in order to resolve his problematic relationships with two sisters. Using a completely different register Fernán Gómez directed *Siete mil días juntos* [1994 *Long Life Together* – award for best director at Peñiscola], a satirical black comedy that is critical of marriage as an institution when there is no love or respect, as experienced by Pilar Bardem and José Sacristán who have been married for twenty years and are set on mutual destruction. He then directed *Pesadilla para un rico* [1996 *Nightmare for a Wealthy Man*], another black comedy also co-scripted with Luis Alcoriza about the consequences of a middle-aged husband's sexual adventures with another corpse to be disposed of as the narrative progresses. A third corpse that has to be furtively disposed of is central to Juan Manuel Chumilla's *Amores que matan* [1996 *Loves that Kill*]. Jaime Chávarri's *Gran slalom* [1996 *The Great Slalom*] is a screwball comedy from Azcona's pen, with an accumulation of misunderstandings at a ski resort that bewilder a *guardia civil* officer [Juanjo Puigcorbé] who ends up having to escape from the consequences of his blunders dressed in drag.

In Catalan Ventura Pons follows single girls searching for relationships, or maybe just sex, in three consecutive films, all scripted by Joan Barbero: *Què t'hi jugues, Mari Pili?* [1991 *What Do You Bet, Mari Pili?* – one award] in which three flatmates dare each other to sleep with the first men who ask them their names; *Aquesta nit o mai* [1992 *Tonight or Never*] about midsummer's night in Barcelona where not all the relationships are heterosexual; and *Rosita Please!* [1994], which was partly filmed in Bulgaria. On his own script Pons then directed *El perquè de tot plegat* [1995 *What It's All About* – four awards], fifteen episodes set in Barcelona illustrating specific qualities and reflecting with more depth on Catalan youth culture. Also in Catalan and both released in 1995 are Antoni Verdaguer's *Parella de tres/Una pareja de tres* [*A Couple of Three* – one award] pairing off Rosa Maria Sardà and Carmen Maura, and *Dones i homes/Mujeres y hombres* [*Women and Men*] made for television about a recently separated couple [Silvia Munt and Anton Pep Muñoz] trying to survive in a feminist environment.

Family comedies

The family, which was so important to Francoist cinema, still has a place in serious films but started to lose importance in the comic portfolio as paying spectators preferred to view on screen the 'battle of the sexes'. In *¡Por fin* *solos!* [1994 *Alone, at last!*] Antonio del Real examines a middle-aged couple [Alfredo Landa and María José Alfonso] with four children who should really all be independent, a plot that generated a television spin-off the following year. Felipe Vega followed *Un paraguas ...* with *Grandes ocasiones* [1997 *Special Occasions*] that examines the relationships between another couple [Rosa Maria Sardà and Andrés Pajares] and their three children during the five years after their divorce. Eugenio Martín made a brief comeback with his last film, *La sal de la vida* [1996 *The Salt of Life*], which concerns the trials of a widower [Patxi Andión] whose children do not approve of his attempts to find a permanent companion.

From comedies to identities

José Juan Bigas Luna made three films, all co-scripted with Cuca Canals, with José Luis Alcaine at the camera and soundtracks by Nicola Piovani. These films have been identified as Bigas Luna's Hispanic *machismo* trilogy (Jordan & Morgan, 1998: 78), or just Iberian trilogy (P. Evans, 2004a: 260). They are concerned with the self-image of the Iberian male, or rather its deconstruction, and raise questions of national stereotypes. They include plenty of humour, but are not really comedies. They present a lot of flesh and sexual activities, but transcend the erotic to engage with social issues like consumerism, the exploitation of sex and nationalism. They could also be considered rites-of- passage films, even though two end in disaster. *Jamón, Jamón* [1992 *A Tale of Ham and Passion* – four awards, including the Silver Lion in Venice] is set against a barren landscape on either side of the highway in Aragon where lorries only stop to visit the roadside brothels, and involves two very different young men [Javier Bardem and Jordi Mollà] wanting the same girl [Penélope Cruz, in her first credited appearance after some television work]. Presenting much humour and even more sex, it concludes with a tableau of destruction referring back visually to Goya and Buñuel (Deleyto, 1999b: 270–85). *Huevos de oro* [1993 *Golden Balls* – four awards] focuses on the rise and fall of property developer Benito, played by Javier Bardem (Perriam, 2003: 93–119), in three episodes located in Melilla, Benidorm and Miami. Vulgar Benito from humble beginnings takes any shortcut to erect his dream skyscraper, raping the Benidorm skyline. He exploits the women he meets on the way but ends up impotent. It is another indictment of the *macho ibérico,* the consumer exploitation of sex and the opportunism for which the government was itself criticised (Fouz Hernández, 1999: 47–62), with a strong visual presence of sex, of Salvador Dalí's work and using Julio Iglesias songs. *La teta i la lluna* [1994 *The Tit and the Moon* – two awards] is told from the perspective of young Tete [Biel Durán]. Jealous and feeling excluded by the arrival of a baby brother, he asks the moon to grant him a lactating breast of

10a Emblems/icon in Bigas Luna's *Jamón, Jamón* (1992)

his own. Tete's rather surrealist explanation of his limited environment leads him to question his father's [Abel Folk] chauvinistic Catalan nationalism, which is matched by a visiting *pétomane* [Gérard Darmon] and his variety show, and to embrace the dream of European multicultural tolerance, echoed by a multilingual soundtrack. Bigas Luna's next films have been identified as his Mediterranean Woman trilogy and 'the sort of obsessions and desires they supposedly engender' (Jordan & Morgan, 1998: 174). *Bámbola* [1996] was shot in Italy with Mina [Valeria Marini], known as Bámbola, a *pizzeria* owner surrounded by demanding and jealous males. *La Femme de chambre du Titanic* [1997 *The Chambermaid on the Titanic* – six awards including Goyas for best screenplay and costumes] is set in France and is a romantic narrative about the power of storytelling. *Volavérunt* [1999 – San Sebastián Silver Shell for Aitana Sánchez-Gijón] is a costume drama set in Goya's Spain of 1802 during the investigation into the death of the Duchess of Alba [Aitana Sánchez-Gijón].

In his third Juan Marsé adaptation, *El amante bilingüe* [1993 *The Bilingual Lover*], Vicente Aranda also examines Catalan identities in a mixture of tones and fantasy, through sexual and linguistic politics, as well as performance, as an affluent Catalan wife [Ornella Muti] seduces and humiliates her husband [Imanol Arias], a *charnego*, from southern Spain (P. Evans, 1995c: 107–16). Fernando Colomo returned to his exploration of Spanish identities and stereotypes found in his *La línea del cielo* [1983 *Skyline*] with *El efecto mariposa* [1995 *The Butterfly Effect*], but this time it is set in London as a young Spaniard [Coque Malla] goes to spend the summer with his madcap aunt [María Barranco] to improve his English. Part of the humour of this film is that stereotypes of characters and places are turned upside down or reversed in a multiracial London viewed from a Spanish perspective. The narrative is framed with references to the increasing scandals that were about to push Felipe González's government out of office.

Musicals

Rikki Morgan links the revival of musicals, which she associates with a need for comfort and nostalgia, with the sense of social insecurity experienced during this phase of the PSOE government (1995a: 155). Singer Isabel Pantoja starred in Luis Sanz 's *Yo soy ésa* [1990 *I'm the One*] and in Pedro Olea's *El día que nací yo* [1991 *The Day I was Born*]; both were very successful at the box-office and engaged with the CIFESA musicals, but neither presented a critical look at the past (Morgan, 1995: 156–9). The first is set in the present and uses the film-within-a-film device with strong echoes of Sara Montiel's *El último cuplé* [1957 Juan de Orduña, *The Last Torch Song*] and Pantoja's own experience. The second recalls the Florián Rey and Imperio Argentina films of the 1930s (chapter 3). Saura's re-engagement with flamenco also took on the *españoladas* in a personal way with *¡Ay Carmela!* [1990 – twenty-two awards, including thirteen Goyas], adapting the original play about the murder of a thespian on the 1938 Aragonese front. It blatantly reverses the polarities of the 1940s' war films and frames the story between two contrasting performances from the Republican repertoire and thus captures 'the significance of the *canción española* [Spanish song] in the thirties and forties: its capacity for popular reappropriation and reinterpretation as an expression of unfulfilled desires or even rebellion' (Morgan, 1995: 164). Saura then moved on to film the documentaries *Sevillanas* [1992 – one award] and *Flamenco* [1995] in which he 'explores gypsy culture, treating it not as a tourist trap synecdoche for the whole of Spain, but as an important, even key element in the cultural fabric of the south' (P. Evans, in Gies, 1999: 268). Josefina Molina's *La Lola se va a los puertos* [1993 *Lola Leaves for the Ports* – first made by Orduña in 1947, and with Argentine and Mexican remakes] is set against the 1929 Seville world exhibition, a reminder for 1992, with Rocío Jurado as the flamenco diva caught between the prosperous father [Paco Rabal] and his son [José Sancho].

With the greater care to include performances naturally into their narrative, a number of films with excellent soundtracks could be qualified as musicals. Manuel Iborra's *Orquesta Club Virginia* [1992 *Club Virginia Orchestra* – three awards, including Goya for best soundtrack] is a comic rites-of-passage tale for Jorge Sanz (Perriam, 2003: 144–71), a guitarist in his father's [Antonio Resines] band as they tour the Middle East in June 1967 and find themselves caught up in the Six-Day War. Antonio Giménez Rico's *Tres palabras* [1993 *Three Words*] is a psychological drama that begins in the present at the funeral of a bolero singer, María Galván [Maribel Verdú]. Her former lover and film director Alfredo Puente [played by Fernando Guillén and his son Fernando Guillén Cuervo] then recalls their relationship in the 1950s. Maribel Verdú sings eight boleros, one of which contains the three words referred to in the title, 'cómo me gustas' [How I like you]. There was also a children's fantasy, *El niño invisible* [1995 Rafael Moleón, *The Invisible Boy*], starring teenybopper band Bom Bom Chip in a time-travel adventure to twelfth-century Toledo. If the need for comfort and nostalgia fostered musicals, José Luis Garci's glossy *Canción de cuna* [1994 *Cradle Song/*Lullaby* – fourteen awards, including four Goyas, three in Montreal and the Sant Jordi audience award] certainly satiated this desire with this popular remake of nuns bringing up a foundling in a late nineteenth-century convent. Nuns also reappeared in Pedro Masó's old-fashioned August release,[15] *Hermana, ¿ pero qué has hecho?* [1995 *Sister, What Have You Done?*], in which it is hoped that the convent's financial problems might be resolved when Lina Morgan as Sor Angela decides to hold up a bank; the film also included Aurora Bautista as the mother superior.

Historical reflections

When he returned from exile in Mexico where he had made two films, Antxon Eceiza carried on making documentaries as well as scripting and directing his last two films. *Ke arteko egunak/Días de humo* [1990 *Days of Smoke* – San Sebastián prize] presents the political reflections of a Basque exile returning home after twenty years in Mexico. In *Felicidades, tovarish* [1995 *Congratulations, Tovarish*] Paco Rabal is a former film editor, disillusioned by the failure and loss of communist ideals after the fall of the Berlin Wall, who takes to the road with his granddaughter [Ruth Gabriel] with whom he shares his thoughts. Moving back in time, Francisco Regueiro's last film *Madregilda* [1993 *Mother Gilda* – Goya, San Sebastián and Sant Jordi for Juan Echanove, with three more awards] is an ingenious and entertaining fantasy for which the cinematography and mise-en-scène create an oneiric and grotesque world that is only just recognisable. Based on an original script written with Ángel Fernández Santos, it presents a distorted vision of General Franco as head of state.[16] Carlos Balagué's *Un assumpte intern/*

---

[15] August is the worst time for a film release in Madrid, as most spectators are away on holiday, and distributors aim for a September release and the return of audiences to the capital.

[16] The title refers to Rita Hayworth in Charles Vidor's 1946 *Gilda*, which caused an outcry in Spain and provoked many denunciations especially in the religious press (Vernon, 1997: 36–64). When it was finally released spectators did not believe she only took one glove off

Asunto interno [*An Internal Affair* – three awards] was made in 1995 but had distribution difficulties and was not released in Barcelona until December 1996 and in Madrid until October 1997, as it dealt with the last case of the execution of an army conscript in 1972 after a miscarriage of justice by court-martial. Jaime Camino returned to the Civil War with *El largo invierno* [1992 *The Long Winter of '39*], looking at the fall of Barcelona as from New Year's Eve 1939, but the voice-over that filters the narrative through memory is flawed by the fact that most of the events presented could not have been witnessed by the butler [Vittorio Gassman].[17] Based on Eduardo Mendoza's novels about the industrial and urban development of Barcelona at the end of the nineteenth and beginning of the twentieth centuries Antonio Drove directed *La verdad sobre el caso Savolta* [1980 *The Truth on the Savolta Affair*] and Mario Camus *La ciudad de los prodigios* [1999 *The City of Wonders*]. Antoni Verdaguer directed *La teranyina/La telaraña* [1990 *The Spider's Web* – one award], adapted from Jaume Cabré's novel, chronicling a family saga from the beginning of the twentieth century through to the Moroccan Wars and the Tragic Week in 1909. Verdaguer followed this with a 300-minute television adventure on the slave trade on which some Catalan fortunes were built; this was subsequently cut to 148 minutes for cinema release as *Havanera 1820* [1993 *Havana 1820* – two awards]. Gonzalo Herralde's *La febre de l'or/La fiebre del oro* [1993 *Gold Fever*] set in 1880 was another Barcelona family saga also made for television and then cut by half to 168 minutes for theatre release.

José Luis García Sánchez adapted *Tirano Banderas* [1994 *Banderas, the Tyrant* – seven awards, six of them Goyas including best screen adaptation for García Sánchez and Azcona] from Valle Inclán's novel about the demise of a fictional Latin American tyrant. Juan Miñón's *La leyenda de Balthasar el castrado* [1996 *The Legend of Balthasar the Castrato* – two awards, including the Goya for best costumes] explored the life of the castrato [Coque Malla] and the closing years of the Spanish kingdom of Naples at the end of the seventeenth century; its release was delayed because of the success of Gérard Corbiau's *Farinelli* [1995]. For the five hundred-year celebrations Spanish money was invested in both *Christopher Columbus: The Discovery* [1992 John Glen] and the more European *1492, Conquest of Paradise* [1992 Ridley Scott], but Spanish Cinema offered something low-key and much more ironic, José Luis Cuerda's *La marrana* [1992 *The Sow* – three awards, including a

---

when coming down those steps. Other Spanish films, *Beltenebros*, for example, also refer to this *cause célèbre*, and *Más que amor, frenesí* [1996 *Not Love, Just Frenzy*] includes a poster of the film in its mise-en-scène.

[17] There are other flaws in this film in spite of, or because of the pedigrees of the five writers who collaborated on the script: Jaime Camino, Román Gubern, Nicolás Bernheim, Juan Marsé and Manuel Gutiérrez Aragón.

Goya for Alfredo Landa as best actor].[18] A delightful medieval road-movie, it deflates the pretensions of the year's narrative as two down-and-outs [Landa and Resines] on the run meet and decide to stay together accompanied by a sow and an amusing dialogue, at a time when Spanish Jews are being exiled. They eventually reach Palos in order to embark as sailors with other criminals on a promising voyage to a new world out of reach of the law. Moving further back in time with *Tramontana* [1991 *The Strong Wind*], Carlos Pérez Ferré has a group of unlikely wretches on a journey in 1231 to settle in the newly reconquered territories of Valencia.

A totally different and much more recent social reality was revisited by Gerardo Herrero's *Territorio Comanche* [1997 *Comanche Territory* – one award] based on Arturo Pérez-Reverte's book recalling his experience as an RTVE war correspondent in Bosnia. The film explores the horrors of war, and the Balkan context in particular, a subject and location that Daniel Calparsoro would take up again in 2002 with *Guerreros* [*Warriors*].

Worthwhile curiosities

Some interesting films that are not so easy to classify are on the borderline between feature documentary and fiction, capturing aspects of reality in their own personal way. Antonio del Real made *El río que nos lleva* [1989 *The River that Takes Us*] about loggers on the Tagus with actor Alfredo Landa and a brief appearance from Fernando Fernán Gómez. Filmed on location in Ireland, José Luis Guerín's *Innisfree* [1991 – three awards including Sant Jordi] is a documentary, or meditation, on the relationship between the village and John Ford's *The Quiet Man* [1951] (Kinder, 1997: 82–7). He followed this with *Tren de sombras* [1998 *A Train of Shadows* – five awards], again more interested in cinema and its silent origins than in telling a story. Victor Erice's *El sol del membrillo* [1992 *The Dream of Light* – four awards, including two at Cannes] is a meditation on art and workmanship, and the impossibility of realism in art. The realist painter Antonio López's attempt one summer to capture on canvas the impossible, the sunlight on the quince tree in his garden, is contrasted with the redecorating being done in his house by Polish workmen, as other friends come to visit the artist (Morgan, 1995c: 35–45). In 1994, Ricardo Franco returned to Chávarri's 1976 *El desencanto* (p. 241) to talk with the three Panero brothers after their mother's death, interviews that were released as *Después de tantos años* [*After So Many Years*]. Manuel Cussó-Ferrer pursued his experimental cinema with *L'última frontera* [1992 *His Last Frontier*]. Made over two years, it is reflections based on the dram-

---

[18] The Fifth Centenary fund was only available from 1988 to 1993.

atisation of Walter Benjamin's ideas and his escape from Nazi Germany to Catalonia, culminating with his suicide in 1940; a collage of flashbacks and voice-over, part fiction, part documentary, part metaphor. Using many special effects Cussó-Ferrer later filmed Salvador Dalí's screenplay and Surrealist journey *Babaouo* [1998], in which Babaouo [Hugo de Campos] searches a war-torn landscape for his lost love.

New directors

The financing, production and distribution difficulties mentioned at the beginning of the chapter did not handicap new directors, who were the only filmmakers granted advance funding. This encouraged, or attracted, the support of established directors with their own production companies such as Almodóvar (El Deseo), Bigas Luna (Lola Films), Borau (El Imán), Colomo (Fernando Colomo Producciones Cinematógraficas), Cuerda (Producciones del Escorpión), García de Leániz and Bollaín (Producciones La Iguana), Uribe (Aiete-Ariana Films), Trueba (Fernando Trueba Producciones Cinemató-graficas), and of course Querejeta PC. Crisis or not (Besas, 1997: 241–59), many of the new talents born in the 1950s and later, with a variety of genres and fresh ideas, were able to attract new spectators who like themselves were born during the times of growing affluence, with a television in the house. The new directors, even if not so young, benefited from the standards and new look established by the Miró reforms and brought inventive approaches to narratives, stretching generic borders, or rather merging genres, to play with expectations and allusions to create surprises. These references were often very culturally specific and addressed to 'an audience that often sees popular films of the 1940s and 1950s shown on [Spanish] television, but leaves in the dark audiences who do not have access to such local references' (Triana Toribio, 2003: 153).[19] For instance, Jesús Mora's first film, *A tiro limpio* [1995 *Clean Shooting*], was a remake in a different location of a 1963 film about small-time robbers for which he managed to cast María Asquerino, the original protagonist, in a different role.

In the genre of comedy a very successful newcomer, who continues to be popular, was Manuel Gómez Pereira. Having gathered experience as an

---

[19] As explained in previous chapters, Spanish television was first broadcast in 1956, although it was not until 1970 that the whole peninsula could receive transmissions. The increasing availability of televisions in the 1970s and 1980s, which contributed to the loss of cinemagoers, also exposed younger generations to older films, through, for instance, the Saturday series of *Cine de barrio*, Fernando Méndez Leite's *La noche del cine español*, Octavi Martí's *Cine classics* or José Luis Garci's *¡Qué grande es el cine!*, which was an experience unavailable to their elders.

assistant director in the 1980s and, with three television series to his credit, he started on his variation of the 'battle of the sexes' comedies, eclectically reinventing with his friends varied Hollywood screwball coincidences by placing Spanish characters in surprising relationships and ingenious situations. He found box-office success first with *Salsa rosa* [1992 *Pink Sauce* – one award], in which two women [Verónica Forqué and Maribel Verdú] who have just become friends decide to seduce each other's husbands with complications that exceed *Così fan tutte*. His promising reputation was then confirmed by *Por qué lo llaman amor cuando quieren decir sexo?* [1993 *Why do they Call it Love when they Mean Sex?* – three awards, including a Goya for Rosa Maria Sardà as best supporting actress], and *Todos los hombres sois iguales* [1994 *All Men Are the Same*[20] – seven awards including Goyas for best script and best actress for Cristina Marcos]. The latter film presented 'amusing deconstructions of machismo that left no doubt as to how far Spain's transition from a patriarchal state had resulted in the emasculation of its previously dominant males' (Stone, 2002: 120). This success of 1994 was followed by a television series and enabled him to set up the company Bocaboca to produce and finance his next films. *Boca a boca* [1995 *Mouth to Mouth* – seven awards including Javier Bardem's Goya for best actor] presented a different challenge for a bespectacled Bardem interpreting an aspiring actor trying to make ends meet by working for an erotic phone line while trying to be cast as the stereotypical Latin lover. *El amor perjudica seriamente la salud* [1997 *Love Can Seriously Damage Your Health* – two awards] follows a pair of occasional lovers [Ana Belén and Juanjo Puigcorbé] who keep meeting up over a thirty-year period at key moments for Spanish cultural development. It begins in 1965 when the Beatles gave their first live concert in the Madrid bullring, although on this first occasion the young lovers are represented by Penélope Cruz and Gabino Diego, and as usual in these encounters she dominates the situation. Gómez Pereira co-scripted *Salsa*, *¿Por qué*, *Todos los hombres* and *El amor* with Joaquín Oristrell, Yolanda García Serrano and Juan Luis Iborra, and they all teamed up to write *¿De qué se ríen las mujeres?* [1997 *What Makes Women Laugh?*], which Oristrell directed. It is a comedy that follows the problems of three performing sisters, played by Verónica Forqué, Candela Peña and Adriana Ozores, during their summer season in Benidorm. The same year Yolanda García Serrano and Juan Luis Iborra paired off to write and direct *Amor de hombre* [*The Love of a Man*], which won awards at both the Austin and Miami Gay & Lesbian Festivals and was nominated for more prizes but slated by the critics. It is a comedy of manners about Esperanza [Loles León], a primary school teacher divorced from a violent

---

20   The title with the verb 'sois' personalises the statement 'All You Men ...', which is not reflected by the *IMDb* title.

husband, whose friends, all gay, rely on her to sort out their problems and relationships, but are unaware of her needs. Its conclusion values friendship over sex. Gómez Pereira, García Serrano, J.L. Iborra and Oristrell would go on to collaborate very successfully into the next century.

In 1994 Álvaro Fernández Armero directed *Todo es mentira* [*Life's a Bitch* – one award], another bittersweet comedy of manners about four couples' difficulties as they struggle to survive present-day expectations, and with a part for Fernando Colomo. He followed this with *Brujas* [1996 **Witches*], in which three women [Beatriz Carvajal, Ana Álvarez and Penélope Cruz] of different generations, backgrounds and experience spend twenty-four hours together after finding themselves on the streets, thus exploring with some humour what it is to be a woman. Fernando León de Aranoa's first film *Familia* [1996 *Family* – eleven awards, including Goya and Sant Jordi for best new director and best new film] took a very different look at the family, exploring the legacy and expectations of Francoist values and their representation on stage and screen in a film full of surprises.

Comedy was becoming more varied, excessive and surreal. Álvaro Sáenz de Heredia, son of José Luis, finally took off with his own crazy ridiculous comedies, the so-called *comedias disparatadas*. His first, *Freddy el croupier* [**Freddy the Croupier*], was released in 1982, and he went on to consolidate his reputation, with the spectators but not with critics, with *Aquí huele a muerto* [1990 **Here I Smell a Corpse*], a burlesque of the horror film, and *El robobo de la jojoya* [1992 **The Thetheft of the Jejewel*]. Both films were vehicles for the zany television comedians Josema Yuste and Millán Salcedo, known as Martes y Trece,[21] and were followed by *Chechu y familia* [1992 **Chechu and Family*] and *Una chica entre un millón* [1994 **A Girl in a Million*]. In 1996 he cast another television comedian, Chiquito de la Calzada, in a spoof western *Aquí llega Condemor* [**Here Comes Condemor*]. Rooted in another absurd situation, but dealing with more topical issues, was Argentine Enrique Gabriel's *Krapatchouk* [1992 – three awards], a Franco-Hispano-Belgian co-production, about two migrant workers from the Balkans who get stuck in Paris through no fault of their own. Made two years earlier but only released in 1998 came Gabriel's *¡En la puta calle!* [1998 *Hitting Bottom* –one award] again dealing with the difficulties of employment and migrant workers, but this time set in Madrid. An unemployed electrician and repressed racist northerner [Ramón Barea] learns to get on with a more tolerant and optimistic Caribbean immigrant [Luis Alberto García] (Santaolalla, 2003a:

---

[21] The pair had previously appeared in another tailor-made film, Javier Aguirre's *Martes y Trece, ni te cases ni embarques* [1982]. The title plays on the proverb 'On Tuesday the thirteenth, do not get wed or set out on a journey', which refers to the culturally unlucky day, which is Tuesday 13, not Friday 13 in Spain.

153–63). After *Eskorpión* [1988 *Skorpion*] Ernesto Tellería came back with *Menos que cero* [1996 *Below Zero*], which also explores xenophobia and violent racism against immigrants, with a Romanian [Roman Luknár] trying to survive in Bilbao.

The threesome of Alfonso Albacete, Miguel Bardem and David Menkes joined together, backed by Fernando Colomo Producciones Cinematogtáficas, to script and direct *Más que amor, frenesí* [1996 *Not Love, Just Frenzy*]. It is an extravagant story in which the erotic comedy merges with the erotetic thriller to present party-girl flatmates [Cayetana Guillén Cuervo, Ingrid Rubio and Beatriz Santiago] and all the men who flutter around them. Santiago Aguilar and Luis Guridi, who had made three shorts together under the name of La Cuadrilla, pursued their partnership with three satirical films full of very black humour: *Justino, un asesino de la tercera edad* [1994 *Justino, Senior Citizen Killer*], *Matías, juez de línea* [1996 *Mathias, The Linesman*] and *Atilano presidente* [1998 *Atilano for President*], which with much irony explore in turn the bullfighting, football and political stereotypes. *Justino* won the 1995 Goya for best new director[s] and best new actor for Saturnino García, who appeared in all three films, and was perfectly cast with his deadpan performances (Jordan & Morgan, 1998: 79–80). Álex de la Iglesia's first film, and the first non-Almodóvar film produced by El Deseo, was a grotesque black comedy adventure, *Acción mutante* [1993 *Mutant Action* – three Goyas], in which he pushes and blurs generic limits even further in a successful pastiche of successful Hollywood science-fiction blockbusters and other genres (Buse, 2004: 9–22). He followed this with the equally extravagant but better-integrated narrative, *El día de la bestia* [1995 *The Day of the Beast* – winning fifteen prizes including six Goyas] sending up with visceral laughter the conventions of apocalyptic horror films, in which a clumsy and insignificant priest [Álex Angulo] seeks out the Antichrist in the streets of Madrid with the help of a heavy metalhead [Santiago Segura]. These imaginative excesses and hybridisation of genres are kept up in his subsequent films with equally irreverent gusto (Allinson, 1997: 15–30; Rabalska, 1999: 91–111), replete with references to Spanish and Hollywood cinema (Triana Toribio, 2003: 1–2). In similar excessive mode but less successful was Óscar Aibar's first film, *Atolladero* [1995 *Tight Spot*], a low-budget futuristic western set in the USA in 2048.

Mariano Barroso is from Barcelona but directed his first full-length feature in Mexico, *Es que Inclán está loco* [1990 *It is just that Inclan is Mad*]. He returned to Spain and directed *Mi hermano del alma* [1994 *My Soul Brother* – Goya and Sant Jordi awards for best new director], a black comedy about two very different brothers [Juanjo Puigcorbé and Carlos Hipólito] who get back together with great complications. This was followed by the thriller *Éxtasis* [1996 *Ecstasy* – one award], co-scripted with Oristrell, which has echoes of *La vida es sueño*, the picaresque, and a brilliant Federico Luppi, as three disaffected friends [Javier Bardem, Daniel Guzmán and Leire Berrocal] invent different risky stratagems to make fast money, bringing about a father–son conflict and betrayals. Manuel Huerga is better known for his television work, but in 1996 he directed his first feature film, *Antártida* [1995 **Antarctica* – Goya for Aguirresarobe's cinematography], a road-movie with a lot of rock music; it leads to personal discoveries as Ariadna Gil and Carlos Fuentes try to stay ahead of defrauded drug dealers and confront the old Spain that has not changed. Eduardo Campoy, who had been producing films since 1984, started directing in 1990 with the thriller *A solas contigo* [**Alone With You*]. It presents a police investigation involving the Spanish Intelligence Service and a blind Victoria Abril as the witness, from a screenplay by Agustín Díaz Yanes who also scripted Campoy's next two films *Demasiado corazón* [1992 *Too Much Heart*] in which Manuel Bandera must distinguish between the twins [Victoria Abril], and *Al límite* [1997 *To the Limit*] in which two professional women [Lydia Bosch and Béatrice Dalle] collaborate to catch a serial killer. Agustín Díaz Yanes scripted and directed his first film, *Nadie hablará de nosotras cuando hayamos muerto* [1995 *Nobody Will Speak of Us When We're Dead* – picking up eight Goyas, two Sant Jordis and two more awards in San Sebastián], a thriller about an unlucky but strong woman, again played by Victoria Abril, who must learn to survive in the macho world that has made a victim of her (Bentley, 1999: 325–46; Gámez Fuentes, 1999: 15–32). After a number of prize-winning shorts Basque Juanma Bajo Ulloa wrote and directed *Alas de mariposa* [1991 *Butterfly Wings* – eight awards, including three Goyas and the San Sebastián Golden Shell], and *La madre muerta* [1993 *The Dead Mother* – twelve prizes including Montreal and the British Independent Film Awards for best picture]. These are two very tense and very different violent psychological thrillers, both focalising from a female perspective (Jo Evans, 2007: 173–84). In 1997, Bajo Ulloa made a completely different hybrid comedy-action-thriller, *Airbag*, using a large cast of stars, which Triana Toribio has dubbed the new 'vulgar comedy' (2003: 151–5, 155) as the three protagonists go from brothel to brothel on the road to Portugal searching for a lost engagement ring. It was a box-office success, but its great excesses did not appeal to critics, although it did win three awards including the Goyas for editing and special effects (Maule, 2002: 64–77). Also from the Basque Country and into self-scripted hybrid thrillers that present social comments about disaffected and consequently delinquent youth at a time when there was a recession and an unemployment crisis, is Daniel Calparsoro. His first surprise was *Salto al vacío* [1995 *Leap into the Void* – winning a special mention at the first European First Film Festival in Angers, and the best film award in Bogota]. Protagonised by Najwa Nimri sporting a shaved head for her first major role, the sets and dark cinematography are just as eloquent as the hard language and violence (Crumbaugh, 2001: 40–57). Calparsoro followed this with more social concerns in *Pasajes*

[1996 *Passages*[22]], which explores the same desperate marginal society and broken dreams with some of the same actors (Prout, 2000: 283–94), themes repeated again in *A ciegas* [1997 *Blinded*], which focuses on ETA violence and *machismo* from which Marrubi [Najwa Nimri again] is trying to escape. Ray Loriga's first film *La pistola de mi hermano* [1997 *My Brother's Gun* – one award], an adaptation of his own novel *Caído del cielo*, is a very wordy but hard road movie that travels through a Spain that appears to offer no values worth living for. Also taking the thriller into new territory was Alejandro Amenábar, who was only 23 when he wrote, directed and composed his own music[23] for his first film *Tesis* [1996 *Thesis* – thirteen awards including seven Goyas]. *Tesis* is both a thriller and a reflection on screen violence as explored through Ángela's PhD research thesis that investigates the subject and takes her where no one would want to be (Buckley, 2002: 12–25; Hill, 2003: 1–9). It starred Ana Torrent, Eduardo Noriega, and Fele Martínez in his first major role (Perriam, 2003: 180–5). According to Moreiras Menor, in these narratives 'due to the absence of an object, or of a driving desire, the subject of the nineties is represented in terms of annihilation rather than construction. Violence, sex, disease, addiction, terror and, above all, boredom, are the affects and drives that dominate this cultural experience' (2004: 141, 135–42). Some of these social concerns were given a straightforward and realistic treatment. Jesús Delgado is the Spanish director to have taken AIDS as a central topic with his drama *La niña de tus sueños* [1995 *The Child of Your Dreams* – one award], about a young HIV-positive girl [Laura Rico] who is sent for the summer to a children's camp.

There was also a much fresher perspective brought by a number of women, mostly directing their own scripts, whose careers took off during the 1990s. Azucena Rodríguez's prison film, *Entre rojas* [1995 *Reds Together* – two awards], is a fiction based on her personal experience when she was arrested as a supposed political activist in 1974 that focuses on the strong bonds forged during her incarceration. Rodríguez followed this immediately with a more conventional comedy *Puede ser divertido* [1995 *It could be Fun*] about the friendship between two women who at first only have two things in common: a divorce and a son. Isabel Coixet, also from Barcelona, made her first film in 1989. *Demasiado viejo para morir joven* [*Too Old to Die Young*] is about the relationships between people of her lost and vulnerable generation, but its very critical reception forced her to survive by making short commercials. It was seven years later and in Oregon, USA, since no

---

22 The title, as well as alluding to Gabi/Nimri's dream to escape her depressing limited surroundings by going to America, is the name of the port town on the coast of Guipuzcoa, the film's location.

23 With *Mar adentro* [2004 *The Sea Within*] he also took charge of the editing. He also enjoys making cameo appearances.

one in Spain wanted to finance her, that she made her next feature, *Cosas que nunca te dije* [1996 *Things I Never Told You* – six awards including Sant Jordi for best film], with Lili Taylor and Andrew McCarthy. Again focusing on characters in need of affection, it definitely benefits by being viewed with the original English soundtrack (Triana Toribio, 2006: 49–66).

Gracia Querejeta after a few documentaries also filmed her own script. Produced by her father Elías Querejeta, *Una estación de paso* [1992 *Whistle Stop* – Valladolid special jury prize], shows Antonio [Santiago Alonso] discovering his own family's secrets when he attempts to unravel those of another family. Her next two films, again produced by her father, were also co-scripted with him. *El último viaje de Robert Rylands* [1996 *Robert Rylands' Last Journey* – five awards] and *Cuando vuelvas a mi lado* [1999 *By My Side Again* – four awards including two in San Sebastián and special mention in Berlin] are both psychological dramas. The first, set in an Oxford college, is a confession filmed in English and the second is about the physical and emotional journey of three sisters who meet again to fulfil their mother's last wish.

Chus Gutiérrez did not have such an easy beginning, and her first film, *Sublet* [1992 *Realquiler* in Spanish – one award], produced by Fernando Trueba and starring Icíar Bollaín, was based on Gutiérrez's own experience in New York where she attended film school. Her second film, *Sexo oral* [1994 *Aural Sex*[24]], made on a tiny budget, is an ingeniously edited collection of some sixty personal reflections and revelations to the camera about a wide range of sexual experiences. She was then contracted to direct *Alma gitana* [1996 *Gypsy Soul*] based on a script that never really satisfied her despite being rewritten a number of times. Presenting another version of Romeo and Juliet with a great many twists and differences, the film is set in the context of contemporary Madrid and questions as many stereotypes as it presents (Nair, 1999: 173–88; Smith, 2000a: 166–74). With a more adequate budget she made *Insomnio* [1998 *Sleepless in Madrid* – one award] about three insomniacs united by circumstances and the violence exercised by social pressures. Starting with Erice's *El sur* [1983], Icíar Bollaín had a successful acting career and in 1996 she applied herself to directing with *Hola ¿estás sola?* [1996 *Hi, Are You Alone?* – six awards including the Valladolid and Sant Jordi best first film]. Creating her own variation on the road and buddy movie, she explores a multi-ethnic Spain as two girlfriends [Candela Peña and Silke (Hornillos/Klein)] escape a present Valladolid that restricts their movements because they are female and offers them no prospects. Mónica Laguna's gentle comedy about three losers who meet up accidentally in a hut in the hills of Navarre, *Tengo una casa* [1996 *I Have a Home*], was

---

[24] Spanish translates aural/oral as 'oral' and so the English translation loses the pun.

10b Female solidarity in Bollaín's *Hola ¿estás sola?* (1995)

followed much later with the atmospheric *Juego de Luna* [2001 *Luna's game* – best first film in Málaga]. Dunia Ayaso and Felix Sabroso co-scripted and directed the comedy of manners, *Perdona bonita, pero Lucas me quería a mí* [1997 *Excuse me Darling, but Lucas only Loved Me*], about three gay friends who were all in love with their new and recently murdered flatmate, which complicates the police investigation. Another madcap comedy followed, *El grito en el cielo* [1998 *Shout Out*] satirising reality television shows looking for contestants. Eva Lesmes started in television but in 1996 directed *Pon un hombre en tu vida* [**Put a Man in your Life*] in an ingenious plot to examine gender stereotypes and perspectives. After a swimming pool accident Cristina Marcos and Tony Cantó find that they have exchanged bodies and each agrees to fulfil the other's responsibilities as a football coach and a bride-to-be.

Not all Catalan directors focused on Catalan issues, but the very versatile Rosa Vergés, after a lengthy apprenticeship, finally started directing from her own scripts that are firmly rooted in Barcelona. Her first feature, *Boom Boom* [1990 *Heart Beat – three awards including Goya for best new director], was a romantic comedy with four people trying to sort out their ever-changing relationships (Kinder, 1993: 422–9). She followed this with *Souvenir* [1994], another comedy this time about an amnesiac Japanese tourist [Futoshi Kasagawa] who is besotted with an air hostess [Emma Suárez]. Martà Balletbò-Coll, after studying film at Columbia University, New York, returned to make the endearing *Costa Brava: Family Album* [1995 – San Francisco Lesbian & Gay Audience Award]. Practically a homemade movie, which she produced, wrote, directed and co-starred in, it was released on television before the cinema. It describes a tender relationship between two young women embarking on their professional lives against the cityscape of an architecturally phallic Barcelona. She followed this with *Cariño he enviado a los hombres a la luna* [1998 *Darling, I've Sent the Men to the Moon*]. Catalan would offer her only a limited release and she preferred to film her first two features in English rather than Castilian and, like her recent *Sévigné* [2004 – three awards], which uses both Catalan and Castilian, all her films to date explore female relationships. Before turning to producing and television Mar Targarona wrote and directed the black comedy *Mor, veda meva/Muere vida mía* [1996 *Die, My Darling*] relating how four of the many women a philanderer [Georges Corraface] has seduced decide to get their own back. There were also Barcelona thrillers such as José Luis Acosta's only film, *Gimlet* [1996; the title refers to Philip Marlowe's favourite cocktail] about an investigation to protect Ángela Molina from a persistent stalker and his video camera, or Xavier Ribera Perpinyá's *Tot Verí/Puro veneno* [1996 *Pure Poison*] misleading the police over a wife's body. These last two directors have only made one film, and so has Tricicle [Joan Gràcia, Paco Mir and Carles Sans], a mime group that has been together since 1979. Having made five shorts and numerous television appearances, in 1996 they wrote, directed and starred in their silent farce about restoring an hotel to its former glory, *Palace* [*Palace Hotel*].

From the Basque Country Daniel Calparsoro's first three films are all set on the Basque coast and protagonise Najwa Nimri, but only the third, *A ciegas*, focuses on a specifically Basque issue; his themes and soundtracks, however, transcend the location of these early films. Another new and reflective Basque director who quickly established himself on the regional, national and international circuits with numerous prizes and a very personal filmography was Julio Medem. His first film *Vacas* [1992 *Cows* – seven awards: Goyas for best new director, original score and special effects, as well as Sant Jordi, Montreal, Tokyo and Torino for best first work] benefited from regional funding, and yet his reconstruction of a feuding families saga in three time frames of Basque history is interpreted by Rob Stone as a complex critique of Basque chauvinism (2002: 161–7; Richardson, 2002: 178–89; Santaolalla, 1999a: 310–24). Medem followed *Vacas* with *La ardilla roja* [1993 *The Red Squirrel* – nine awards, including the Prix de la Jeunesse in Cannes and a Goya for best score], a search for personal identity within the Basque context, a 'hybrid thriller [… and] anti-macho parable' (Jo Evans, 2002: 147–62). Then came the even more opaque and hermetic *Tierra* [1996 *Earth* – seven awards including more Goyas for best score and special effects] an 'achievement not only to hold fast to his narrative enigmas but also to rework and untie those rapturous myths which, most particularly in the case of the Basque Country, bind land so violently to language and to nationality' (Smith, 1999: 11–25). In contrast, Arantxa Lazkano has only made one feature film to date, *Urte ilunak/Los años oscuros* [1993 *The Dark Years*]. It is based on personal memories and shows the Basque situation through the eyes of a young girl as she grows up without really understanding what she experiences; the film has four sections of different length entitled 1946, 1952, 1958 and 1965 (Martí Olivella, 1997: 215–38). During this period another newcomer Maite Ruiz de Austri directed three full-length animation features for children based on a Basque whaling ship, *La leyenda del viento del norte* [1992 *The Legend of the North Wind*], *Regreso del viento del norte* [1994 *The Return of the North Wind*] and the ecological *¡Qué vecinos tan animales!* [1998 *What Beastly Neighbours!*]; these last two won the Goya award for animation.

Although born in Madrid in 1944, Pedro Carvajal who had been screen-writing since 1972 starting with *Flor de santidad*], finally directed one of his own scripts with Fernando Bauluz, *Martes de Carnaval* [1991 *Mardi Gras Carnival* – one award for Fernando Guillén], about a fifty-year-old alco-holic novelist who keeps dreaming his adolescence in stereotypical Galicia. Carvajal followed this with *El baile de las ánimas* [1994 *The Dance of Souls*], set in 1948 and starring the Molina sisters. It is a tale of Gothic fantasy and supernatural that also recovers Galician traditions and in which women regain the upper hand. Neither was successful at the box-office, and his next film, *Sabor Latino* [1996 *Latin Flavour*], took a completely different angle. Filmed in Cuba, it was the first fruit of an agreement to make 12 co-productions in three years.

Other interesting films were directed by people who were better known in other areas of the industry. For instance, film critic José María Carreño made his first and only film in 1990, *Ovejas negras* [*Black Sheep*], a black comedy about education in the 1960s at the hands of the Jesuit fathers. Well-known actor Imanol Arias made an erotic thriller, *Un asunto privado* [1996 *A Private Matter*], in which Pastora Vega hires out a handsome but illegal Cuban [Jorge Perugorría] who mistakenly assumes he is being offered easy money. María Miró, miscellaneous crew in film and television but mostly press photog-rapher, made *Los baúles del retorno* [1995 *The Return Luggage*], starring Silvia Munt to chronicle through its plot how Spanish Sahara was handed over to Morocco. They, like Acosta, Lazkano, Ribera Perpinyá and many others not mentioned, have unfortunately only made one film to date mainly because of funding difficulties. Others, like Chus Gutiérrez, Balletbò-Coll or Isabel Coixet, have had to struggle hard to obtain the necessary funding to continue making films. There are also those who struck the right key and with a little bit of luck are now established with a national and international following, like Alejando Amenábar, Alex de la Iglesia, Icíar Bollaín, Manuel Gómez Pereira, Fernando León de Aranoa, etc.

Co-productions with Latin America

As well as European-funded films like Miró's *Beltenebros* [1991] or Scott's *1492, Conquest of Paradise* [1992], co-productions with Latin American countries had become a fact of life when films acquired soundtracks, the same language enabling many more potential viewers. Already in 1931 the first Hispanoamerican Film Conference had brought together 14 Spanish-speaking countries worried by Hollywood's patronising attitude and growing dominance. Although there had been many earlier collaborations, like Bardem's *Sonatas* [1959] or Fernando Palacios's *Marisol rumbo a Río* [1963], in the early 1990s a lot more exchanges were initiated between Spain and the Americas, generating more films than the European co-productions. Actors like Argentine Héctor Alterio, Federico Luppi and Cecilia Roth had also already made many films in Spain. Spanish producers only now started investing more seriously in Latin America, for instance financing *Danzón* [1992 María Novaro, *Dancer* – six awards] with Spanish television as a partner, or *Guantanamera* [1995 Tomás Gutiérrez Alea and Juan Carlos Tabio – six awards] produced by Gerardo Herrero with funding from Tornasol, Alta, Canal Plus and Spanish television, films that respectively flew the Mexican and Cuban flags. Directors and actors also crossed the Atlantic to make films as different as *Tirano Banderas* [1994 García Sánchez] or *Maité* [1995 Eneko Olasagasti & Carlos Zabala], both in Cuba, or *Todo está oscuro* [1997 Ana Díez] in Colombia, and in Puerto Rico Gerardo Herrero himself directed *Shortcut to Paradise/Desvío al paraíso* [1994], a hard film dealing with paedophilia starring Charles Dance and his victim Katrina Gibson. Latin American actors made very successful films in Spain, for instance Cuban Jorge Perugorría in *La sal de la vida* [1996 Eugenio Martín], *Cachito* [1996 Enrique Urbizu] and *Un asunto privado* [1996 Imanol Arias], or Argentine Adolfo Aristarain's *Martin (Hache)* [1997 *Martin (H)*[25] – seventeen awards] set in Madrid and Almería province with Argentine actors Luppi, Roth and Juan Diego Botto. This important trend and fluidity that flourished in the 1990s has been consolidated in the twenty-first century. Indeed, Rob Rix suggests that a new category, Spanish-language films, is now needed (1999: 113–28), as indicated by the pattern set by specialised Film Festivals. Although the Huelva Latin American Film Festival had been going since 1975, between 1989 and 1996 a number of new festivals dedicated to Spanish language films have appeared, which also bring to the festival locations new revenues from the visiting cinephiles and tourists. The Brazilian Gramado Ibero-American Film

---

[25] The H, pronounced 'hache' in Spanish, is short for 'hijo' [son], and is equivalent to Junior, as father and son have the same name (Martín), so the son is called Hache [Junior/ Jay].

Festival started in 1992, the Biarritz Latin American and Nantes Spanish Film Festivals were inaugurated in 1993, the Barcelona Butaca in 1995, the Miami Hispanic and Lima Latin American Festivals appeared in 1996, the Lleida Latin American and Los Angeles Latino International in 1997, and the Málaga Spanish Film Festival was established in 1998, to name but a few.

Figures rather than facts[26]

After the 48 features made in 1989, production increased to a peak of 91 films in 1996, with a dip in 1994 of only 44 releases. Co-productions increased from five in 1989 to 22 in 1995 and 25 and over during the following years. Within these limitations there was an average of around 14 new directors a year making their first film. The modest growth in productions was matched by a similar modest increase in spectators. More multiplexes were built so the overall number of screens rose although the actual number of theatres dropped; in 1991, there were 1314 cinemas housing 1806 screens, whereas in 1996 there were 1217 cinemas with 2377 screens. In 1991, only 12 cinemas had more than six screens, but by 1997 there were 79 cinemas with six to eight screens and 33 with more than eight. Over the years the average cost of productions had increased greatly from 24.3 million pesetas in 1980, to 96 million during the Miró incumbency, 135 million in 1990, and 207.4 million pesetas in 1996. As in the previous decade Italy released more films than France, Spain or the UK, although the UK now had more spectators than Italy or Spain. France continued to have the largest audiences.

Viewing and further general reading

Jordan & Morgan-Tamosumas (1998 and 2000), Graham & Labanyi (1995), Hooper (1995), Triana Toribio (2003) and Jordan & Allinson (2005) are all very useful, and with Internet addresses, as are Perriam (2003) and Stone (2002). Almodóvar is still the most discussed director with studies by Smith (2000), Allinson (2001), Edwards (2001), D'Lugo (2006) and Acevedo Muñoz (2007), and another book announced by Ann Davies. Stone has brought out a monograph on Saura and flamenco (2004) and Medem (2007), with a

---

26 See p. 279, n. 28, and the warning about the accuracy of figures. Here the figures are taken from Heredero & Santamarina (2002): p. 103 for productions, p. 101 for spectators, p. 123 for cinemas and multiplexes, and p. 91 for budgets and costs. Rob Rix's table for co-productions (1999: 116) has not been quoted because it may have been compiled with different criteria, but it is another possible comparison.

second announced by Jo Evans. Álex de la Iglesia has now a monograph on his films co-written by Buse, Triana Toribio & Willis (2007). Special issues of the *Revista Canadiense de Estudios Hispánicos* (1995), *Bulletin of Hispanic Studies* (1999), *Post Script: Essays in Film and the Humanities* (2002), *Cineaste* (2003), *Hispanic Research Journal* (2007) and from now on the new journal *Studies in Hispanic Cinemas* provide valuable studies. The *International Journal of Iberian Studies* covers socio-political and cultural issues often the subject of contemporary films. Both Manchester University Press and Grant & Cutler have announced new series of books dedicated to Spanish-language cinema. DVD releases are much easier to obtain, but not always with subtitles, and they do present the problem of authenticity since it is not always clear whether they present the director's original version or an adapted version with a different screen-ratio after broadcast on television.

Further research would involve the presence and recovery of the *cine de barrio* in current films, as well as the development of the *comedias disparatadas* into the excesses of vulgar comedies and *esperpentos,* with their use of grotesque, extravagant, absurd and often black humour (Triana Toribio, 2003: 151–5), all producing a creationist cinema that exploits the cinema as cinema and for which special effects are not only possible but necessary. This leads to the hybridisation of traditional genres, and the blending/fusion of the popular with high culture. Interesting themes would include the uses and contrasts of the city, districts (*barrio*), suburban developments with their villas, or *chalets* as they are called in Spain, and the village or countryside, as filmic spaces that convey themes and social issues. Worthwhile analyses would cover the representation and metaphorical use of violence, as well as changes in the presentations of the perpetrators of violence in different genres. With this last, the development of suspense-terror-horror-supernatural plots and films would also be worth examining. The same is true for social issues which have now taken their place among narratives, whether employment, ageing, domestic violence, or migrants, and the development of what has been termed a *cine social.* The increasing use of multiple protagonists with intertwined and/or crossing paths, with all the related narrative and focalising problems, warrants some research. Gender representations, the position of women in society, and changing masculinities are also important topics (Estrada, 2006); with this a study of buddy films and/or road-movie structures would also be interesting, especially since topographical displacements are more often than not accompanied by a psychological journey. Transnational cinema is another field of study, which complicates notions of both national and regional cinema as well as questions of identities, whether these are linked with European or Latin American co-productions, and with reference to the latter the term needs re-examining given the fluidity of these 'collaborations'. Also important to funding is the relationship between television and cinema, as well as the importance of film reception, which can be approached as the marketing and targeting of spectators by age groups at regional, national and international levels. The increasing number of bi/tri-lingual films released, reflecting the country's linguistic plurality, is now worth examining both in term of reception, regional identity and characterisation.

Coda: Into the Twenty-First Century

The political climate

By the time Spanish Cinema celebrated its first centenary in 1996, Spain
had enjoyed thirty years of democracy with no interruption except the big
hiccough in 1981 with the Tejero coup. Spain felt more secure even if its
socialist government was being angrily criticised for excesses and opportunism. Under the leadership of José María Aznar the PP won the 1996 election with the backing of the Autonomies, or rather the PSOE was defeated
in the wake of their political and financial scandals. The PP was re-elected
in 2000 and its representatives increased from 156 to 189 seats, giving them
an absolute majority in the Cortes.[1] The PP looked likely to win a third
mandate in the 2004 election, in spite of general protests against Spain's
military intervention in Iraq and other dissatisfactions with numerous issues
highlighted in ¡Hay motivo! [2004 *There's Good Cause! – BFI title]. Directors, actors and other film professionals collaborated to create this unique
socio-political statement during the 2004 electoral campaign. It consists of
32 shorts and an epilogue, with each segment lasting about three minutes
and focusing on a specific issue about which the director wanted to challenge
the PP. The subjects covered range from the employment crisis, rise in the
cost of living, education, domestic violence, paedophilia, old age pensioners,
immigration, discrimination against homosexuals, manipulation of information, the 'Prestige' oil pollution scandal, ETA, Guantanamo, the Iraq war,
to other issues that, in the opinion of the directors, the government was not
facing adequately.[2] The PP nonetheless were predicted in opinion polls to
win the elections, but it was the government's error of judgement on 11
March, when they blamed ETA for the Madrid train bombs, that alienated the
voters three days later. On 10 March 2004 it did not seem credible that José
Luis Rodríguez Zapatero's PSOE might form the next government, but on 14
March they were given a surprise victory winning 164 seats.

[1]   175 seats will allow an absolute majority.
[2]   The DVD was available on request and on the Internet. It was also shown on some
independent and regional television channels. It can still be seen on YouTube.

The cinematographic credits

In 1994 José María Otero was appointed director of the ICAA, and whereas cabinets changed and ministers of culture moved, Otero stayed in post. He was briefly followed by José Miguel Onaindia and then Manuel Pérez Estremera. The present incumbent, Fernando Lara was appointed in 2005. During its eight years of office the PP consolidated the later PSOE film policy 'set on the path of deregulation and commercial viability', cutting down on state subsidies and letting market forces take their course (Jordan & Allinson, 2005: 28–9). This was and continues to be difficult when competing against Hollywood companies who hold all the cards and, as part of bigger and diverse corporations, can recover the costs of many unsuccessful films with a few global blockbusters which, preceded by massive publicity campaigns, then generate even more revenues on post-release merchandising (Wayne, 2002: 5–7). There is now further competition from US independent films. The US majors also have the capital to 'poach' talent from elsewhere; in the case of Spain this has resulted in Hollywood's successful marketing of Antonio Banderas and Penélope Cruz. Fortunately, there have been new agreements in place with television companies like RTVE, Sogecable, Antena 3, Canal plus, Telefónica, Via Digital or FORTA, as well as the channels of the Autono-mies and other Spanish media conglomerates such as PRISA, which have provided much-needed investment, but not on a par with the US producers. On the positive side, once a television channel owns the rights to a film it can broadcast it promptly and subsequently on DVD, even without a previous theatre release, and some very good films have slipped by in this way, as also happened with Canal Plus in France or UK Channel Four films. Extra televi-sion programming can be generated by features like 'Así se hizo …' [The Making of …], which, broadcast before the film's release, act as publicity and can be followed by evening chat shows. All these can be included on the DVD release with other extras like trailers, interviews, out-takes and mistakes, although DVD sales can only recover a fraction of the original investment. In the case of PRISA more revenues can be generated by subsequently re-releasing the DVD as a bargain offer with the weekend supplements of their newspaper El País. Nonetheless distributors, wanting market forces to prevail, continue to argue for unrestricted rights to project what they feel will draw local spectators and generate profits, regardless of the impact on national productions. The present Minister of Culture, Carmen Calvo, has not yet in mid-2007 published the new laws regulating funding in Spain, although it looks as if the protectionist quotas of 25% European films will continue, and that television will be asked to invest some 5% of their revenues in the Spanish film industry. Meanwhile through its films and series, like the popular 'Cuéntame cómo pasó' [2001 and still going, Antonio Cano *'Tell me How it Happened'] television companies not only provide some opportunities for directors and work for crews, but also serve as outlets for excellent actors like Imanol Arias, Ana Duato, María Galiana, and many others in the case of 'Cuéntame'. Crisis upon crisis, and this now includes film piracy as emphasised on all recent DVD releases, Spanish Cinema survives with productive and entertaining features (Jordan & Allinson, 2005: 32–3).

Stocktaking at the first centenary

As Spanish Cinema was getting ready to celebrate its first centenary, numerous different polls and surveys were taken during 1995 and 1996 to identify the best Spanish films to this date. The views of the general public were gathered rather haphazardly from those who bothered to fill in question-naires or were stopped at random in the street. Box-office figures were also used, but rarely do these concur with the critics' views. However, one enlight-ening survey gathered the informed but mixed opinions of those who know the profession, as practised for film festival juries. This was done by the Sunday supplement of the newspaper *El Mundo*, published on 17 December 1995. The directors were Pedro Almodóvar, Juan Antonio Bardem, Juanma Bajo Ulloa, Mariano Barroso, Álvaro Fernández Armero, Ricardo Franco, José Luis Garci, Manuel Gómez Pereira, Alex de la Iglesia and Pilar Miró, reflecting a range of experience and tastes that mattered. The actors were María Asquerino, Imanol Arias, Javier Bardem, Juan Echanove, Saturnino García, Marisa Paredes, Paco Rabal, José Sacristán and Concha Velasco. The critics, kept to a minority, were Carlos Boyero and Fernando Méndez Leite.[3] This is not a very large panel, it has more male voices than females, but it is made up of informed professionals from different generations, and their mixed views summarised in the following table lead to reflection:

Best Spanish films of the first centenary (to 1996)

	Director	Title	Year	Votes
1	Luis Buñuel	*Viridiana*	1961	(21)
2	Luis G. Berlanga	*El verdugo*	1964	(20)
3	Mario Camus	*Los santos inocentes*	1984	(15)
4	Víctor Erice	*El espíritu de la colmena*	1973	(14)
5	Luis G. Berlanga	*Plácido*	1961	(12)
6	Luis G. Berlanga	*Bienvenido míster Marshall*	1953	(11)
	Carlos Saura	*La caza*	1965	(11)
	Víctor Erice	*El sur*	1983	(11)
	Pedro Almodóvar	*¿Qué he hecho yo para merecer esto!*	1984	(11)

[3] The table has been compiled from Cecilia Ballesteros's survey for *La Revista de El Mundo* (1995: 42–5). The year mentioned is that of the film's release. All these films have been mentioned in preceding chapters.

	Fernando Fernán Gómez	El viaje a ninguna parte	1986	(11)
11	Juan Antonio Bardem	Calle mayor	1956	(10)
12	Miguel Picazo	La tía Tula	1954	(9)
13	Luis Buñuel	Tristana	1970	(8)
	José Juan Bigas Luna	Bilbao	1978	(8)
15	J.A. Nieves Conde	Surcos	1961	(7)
	Juan Antonio Bardem	Muerte de un ciclista	1955	(7)
	Marco Ferreri	El cochecito	1960	(7)
	José María Forqué	Atraco a las tres	1962	(7)
	José Luis Borau	Furtivos	1975	(7)
20	Fernando Fernán Gómez	El extraño viaje	1964	(6)
	Vicente Aranda	Amantes	1991	(6)
	Fernando Trueba	Belle époque	1992	(6)
23	J. L. Sáenz de Heredia	Historias de la radio	1955	(5)
	Jaime de Armiñán	Mi querida señorita	1972	(5)
	Mario Camus	La colmena	1982	(5)
	Agustí Villaronga	Tras el cristal	1987	(5)
	Pedro Almodóvar	La ley del deseo	1987	(5)
	Agustín Díaz Yanes	Nadie hablará de nosotros cuando ...	1995	(5)
29	Florián Rey	La aldea maldita	1930	(4)
	Lorenzo Llobet Gràcia	La vida en sombras	1948	(4)
	Carlos Saura	Deprisa. deprisa	1984	(4)
	Ricardo Franco	Después de tantos años	1994	(4)
33	Fernando Fernán Gómez	La vida por delante	1958	(3)
	José Luis García Sánchez	Las truchas	1978	(3)
	Iván Zulueta	Arrebato	1980	(3)
	Carlos Saura	Bodas de sangre	1981	(3)
	José Antonio Salgot	Mater amatísima	1980	(3)
	Manuel Gutiérrez Aragón	Demonios en El Jardín	1982	(3)
	Montxo Armendáriz	Tasio	1984	(3)
	Francisco Reguiero	Padre nuestro	1985	(3)
	Pedro Almodóvar	Mujeres al borde de un ataque ...	1988	(3)
	Julio Medem	Vacas	1992	(3)
	Imanol Uribe	Días contados	1994	(3)
44	Basilio Martín Patino	Canciones para después ...	1971	(2)
	Jaime Chávarri	El desencanto	1976	(2)
	Manuel Gutiérrez Aragón	Maravillas	1981	(2)
	Gonzalo Suárez	Remando al viento	1988	(2)
	José Luis Cuerda	Amanece que no es poco	1989	(2)
	Fernando Trueba	El sueño del mono loco	1989	(2)
	Juanma Bajo Ulloa	Alas de mariposa	1991	(2)

A turn up for the books

Productions and spectatorship have slowly reconsolidated and cinema has been invigorated by a new generation of directors well versed in different cinemas and wanting to emulate, in their own way, what they enjoy on screen. Given the funding system, providing their producers the benefit of advanced credit funding, many first-time directors are still coming forward, but since few have made more than one or two features, they have not been identified in a separate paragraph, nor have directors who happen to be women. Their priority has been to screen a good story, to give a new twist to old genres either by pushing the limits or by blurring them, often referred to as the hybridisation of genres. The emphasis is now on imaginative narratives with less respect for authority and tradition and, following Almodóvar's example, which opened many doors, the borders between high and low art are now not always relevant. Spanish Cinema had also benefited from the technical standards promoted by the costly and abandoned Miró reforms. *Bala perdida* [2003 *Lost Bullet*] by new director Pau Martínez, for example, recovers the western by using the old *chorizo* film sets in Almería where an ageing David Carradine is acting in a B film. This becomes the hideaway for Juanjo Puigcorbé who, on parole from prison, has just abducted his own son [José María Gómez] and is being pursued by the henchmen of a corrupt judge, his father-in-law [Juli Mira] who thinks he is protecting his daughter. With humour, the father–son relationship shifts from the road-movie mode to a thriller to a *noir* tale of betrayal, and includes a film-within-a-film motif as Mercedes Sampietro, the director of the B movie, has to resolve her own problems. It may sound like a strange plot but it is a well-integrated narrative that merges and plays on the different genres, and includes lyrical moments while effortlessly justifying some flamenco.

The chameleons

In 1997, after his successful debut with *Tesis* [1996 *Thesis*], Alejandro Amenábar, released *Abre los ojos* [*Open Your Eyes* – five awards], a psychological thriller, with a memorable opening sequence and a complex plot, in which a rich boy [Eduardo Noriega] tries too late to find his happiness (Perriam, 2003: 174–80; 2004a: 209–21; Smith, 2004: 91–102). The latter was remade as *Vanilla Sky* [2001] with an English screenplay and direction by Cameron Crowe (Herbert, 2006: 28–38). Next came the transnational production *The Others/Los otros* [2001 – twenty-two awards, including eight Goyas], set in a big house on the Island of Jersey in 1945, in which Nicole Kidman finally accepts a supernatural fact that she first finds impossible to understand. In 2004, he made *Mar adentro* [*The Sea Within* – fifty-nine awards, including the Oscar for best foreign language film and fourteen Goyas], which is based on the true story of Ramón Sampedro [Javier Bardem], his writings, his relationships and his fight for the legal right to euthanasia.[4] The multi-talented Amenábar has so far co-scripted all his films with Mateo Gil, composed his own original music for them and also edited *Mar adentro*. To date his co-writer Mateo Gil has only made one film, a tense Satanic cyber-

---

4 In 2002 Roberto Bodegas had made a television film on the ship's mechanic, *Condenado a vivir* [**Condemned to Live*].

11a Mental loneliness in Amenábar's *Abre los ojos* (1997)

fiction, *Nadie conoce a nadie* [1999 *Nobody Knows Anybody* – Goya for best special effects], which pits the wits of Eduardo Noriega against Jordi Mollà in a variety of games, from chess to virtual role plays with real bombs.

Other directors who have now demonstrated a high degree of versatility in their careers include actresses/screenwriters/directors like Icíar Bollaín, discussed elsewhere in this chapter, and Laura Mañá. Mañá moves elegantly from acting to screenwriting to directing. In 2000, she wrote and directed the curious *Sexo por compasión* [*Compassionate Sex* – six awards, including Sant Jordi best first film] in which Elisabeth Margoni plays a friendly wife trapped in a man's world by her own naivety, innocence and kindness. Using a narrative style that includes extraordinary elements as if they were part of normal everyday reality, that is to say with the visual style of the *cine social* rather than the fantastic presented through creationist techniques, *Sexo por compasión* has an aura of 'magic realism'.[5] Mañá then went on to make a tense claustrophobic psycho-thriller, *Palabras encadenadas* [2002 *Killing Words* – seven awards], which constructs an extraordinary relationship between Goya Toledo and Darío Grandinetti. Then with *Morir en San Hilario* [2005 *To Die in San Hilario*] she returned to humour and magic realism in a little village, in the middle of a literal nowhere, that survives by conducting tailor-made funerals. A hired gun on the run [Lluis Homar] stumbles into the village and thinks he has at last found refuge until he realises that the locals

---

5   The archetypal example of magical realism, a label that comes from 1970s literary criticism, is Gabriel García Márquez's novel *Cien años de soledad* [1967 *A Hundred Years of Solitude*].

have mistaken him for their next client. It is an implicit meditation on life and death that from the twenty-first century bears comparison with Jorge Manrique's fifteenth-century poem on the death of his father.

Álex de la Iglesia is another director who is coming to be identified as an *auteur* (Triana Toribio, 2003: 158–63), but when in 1997 he released *Perdita Durango* [*Dance with the Devil* – six awards including two Goyas], cast and filmed in Mexico and the USA, he sidestepped his usual humour with a parody of excess, violence, much gore and sex [Rosie Pérez and Javier Bardem], in which the Satanic meets the mobsters. He then returned to his black comedies with *Muertos de risa* [1999 *Dying from Laughter* – Goyas for Santiago Segura and Gran Wyoming as best actors], which begins as a satire of television comedians, then takes on political history, to focus on the destructive impact of fame, envy and hate (Kercher, 2002: 50–63). *La comunidad* [2000 *Common Wealth*[6] – twenty awards including three Goyas and San Sebastián for Carmen Maura] is another black comedy about the consuming power of material greed, which delightfully echoes many other films, which range from the Spanish popular tradition to Hitchcock and *Star Wars,* revealing how close he is to Berlanga's view of human nature, even if he is more excessive. In *Ochocientas balas* [2002 *Eight Hundred Bullets* – three awards including a Goya for best special effects] Álex de Iglesia exploited the old western sets of Almería, with a boy [Luis Castro] who seeks his grandfather [Sancho Gracia, who actually acted in many *chorizo* westerns] to discover the past that his mother [Carmen Maura] is keeping secret. *Crimen ferpecto* [2004 *Ferpect Crime* – two awards] paired Guillermo Toledo and Mónica Cervera as employees of Spain's biggest department store in its main branch on the Puerta del Sol in Madrid, but called Yeyo in the film. It is another esperpentic black comedy, this time exposing through its excess consumerism, sexism, greed, ambition and betrayal.

Very different is Isabel Coixet who, after *Cosas que nunca te dije* [1996 *Things I Never Told You*], co-scripted and directed *A los que aman* [1998 [*To*] *Those Who Love*], a Hispano-French production, which continues to explore vulnerable relationships in the context of a sober costume drama set in nineteenth-century Galicia. She then went back to British Columbia to follow Sarah Polley living a young mother's last few months with her family and a terminal cancer in *My Life Without Me/Mi vida sin mí* [2003 – fourteen awards, with two Goyas and the Sant Jordi best film]. Her next feature, *The Secret Life of Words/La vida secreta de las palabras* [2005 – seventeen awards, including four Goyas and again the Sant Jordi best film], was also filmed in English and set on an oil rig with three lonely characters [Sarah Polley, Tim

---

[6]   The title could also be translated as *The Residents' Association* or *The Community*, given the strong presence of Madrid in the film, officially known as The Community of Madrid (Maroto Camino, 2005: 333–42).

Robbins and Javier Cámara] locked into their own personal memories too painful to be verbalised (Triana Toribio, 2006: 49–66). She then made the fragment 'Bastille' for *Paris, je t'aime* [2006 *Paris, I Love You*], one of the twenty sketches about love in different parts of the city.

Still very versatile is director Julio Medem who, after the intriguing *Tierra* [1996 *Earth*], scripted and filmed *Los amantes del círculo polar* [1998 *The Lovers of the Arctic Circle* – twelve awards including two Goyas]. A visually beautiful love story, it concludes after many separations under the Arctic midnight sun, with another puzzling plot until the story is reconstructed with the help of its circular flashbacks, memories of the Civil War and attempts at reconciliation.[7] *Lucía y el sexo* [2001 *Sex and Lucia* –eight awards including Goyas for Paz Vega as best new actress and for Alberto Iglesias's music] shows another love story with a very different use of flashbacks and locations, set on a bright Mediterranean island contrasted through time jumps with a dark Madrid (Smith, 2005: 239–46). Although Medem plays with the pornographic image, his concerns are more about writing and filming fiction than sex. His next feature was a bold and controversial documentary interrogating Basque identity, *La pelota vasca/Euskal pilota. Larrua harriaren kontra* [*The Basque Ball: Skin Against the Wall*] with moving images, some from his own films, for which he shot 150 hours of interviews edited to 110 minutes for its release in 2003.

Pedro Almodóvar continues to produce, write and direct interesting and engaging narratives, some more provocative than others, and others more reflective than some. In 1999 *Todo sobre mi madre* [*All About My Mother* – forty-eight awards, including the Oscar for best language film, Cannes, Golden Globe, San Sebastián, two BAFTAs and seven Goyas] took most audiences by storm. This was not only because Almodóvar left his Madrid settings for Barcelona to explore the theme of motherhood, but he incorporated many other reflections on performance, gender, integrity, female solidarity, tolerance, aids and organ transplants, with a moving soundtrack from Alberto Iglesias and performances from Cecilia Roth, Marisa Paredes, Penélope Cruz and Antonia San Juan (Allinson, 2005: 229–37). He opened his next film, *Hable con ella* [2002 *Talk to Her* – thirty-three awards, including the Oscar for best screenplay, Golden Globe, two BAFTAs and a Goya], with the closing curtains of *Todo...*, just as *Todo...* develops the question of organ transplants that was originally introduced in *La flor de mi secreto*.[8] A very sensitive film that challenges audience reception with its presentation of the

---

[7]   The two lovers are each played by three different actors at different ages: Ana by Najwa Nimri, Kristel Díaz and Sara Valiente; Otto by Fele Martínez, Hugo Oliviera and Peru Medem.

[8]   With his constant and discrete intertextual as well as self-references with the reworking of his ideas, Almodóvar rewards his loyal viewers (Kinder, 2004: 9–25)

gentle and devoted male nurse played by Javier Cámara, *Hable* ... shows that appearances are seldom what they seem (Smith, 2005b: 873–89). As an homage to the silent movies and the Cine Doré (p. 27) it also includes a black and white sequence entitled *El amante menguante* [*The Shrinking Lover*], which is in fact crucial to Cámara's characterisation and the film's narrative. In *La mala educación* [2004 *Bad Education* – eleven awards], the main surprise was that Almodóvar focused explicitly on men and the Franco years as he presented the consequences of sexual abuse by the priests in charge of education. It is Almodóvar's darkest film to date, which as a story questions narratology as, by the end of the film, the narrators cannot be trusted (Pingree, 2004: 4–15). In 2006, the year he was given a special exhibition at the Musée de la Cinémathèque in Paris, he kept up his surprises and returned with *Volver* [*To Return* – forty awards, including five Goyas, best film and actresses in Cannes, and San Sebastián best film]. It is a return to comedy and a linear narrative; a return to women's relationships and to some of his favourite actresses, Carmen Maura, Penélope Cruz, and Chus Lampreave, adding Blanca Portillo and Lola Dueñas; a return to La Mancha and the village as the narrative returns to an old feud; and if one speaks French there is the return of the mother as Almodóvar offers a supernatural story, and the tango 'Volver' that gives the film its title (Smith, 2006: 16–18). However, the plot motivator is a disturbing case of paedophilia that is not explored directly in the film.

Although veteran Carlos Saura was identified as the face of Spain at international film festivals in the late 1960s and 1970s through his bold and provocative cinema of opposition, he never achieved a sustained popular status within Spain. His dissident narratives and cinematography were far too elliptical and at times allegorical for general appeal, although they were appreciated by those who wanted an end to the Dictatorship and/or could also transcend the immediate political context to enjoy his cinema as both art and entertainment. He always remained productive although his varied filmography has received mixed and perhaps overcritical reactions, possibly because he had previously overshadowed other Spanish directors on the international circuit as Almodóvar has recently. Released in 1996, the thriller *Taxi* explores race relations and the increasing violence experienced in Spanish society. The following year he made *Pajarico* [1997 *Little Bird* – two awards for Saura in Montreal and Nantes] a coming-of-age story as young Manuel [Antonio Martínez] spends a week with each of his three uncles' families while his parents are settling their divorce. Saura then returned to the musical, or rather to his individual construction of the genre with a film about tangos in *Tango, no me dejes nunca* [1998 *Tango* – eight awards, including a Goya], again with the device of a director [Miguel Ángel Solá] wanting to make a film about the essence of a dance in order to capture and investigate the question of creation, performance and emotion. *Salomé* [2002 – one award in Montreal and a

Goya] was another excursion into the de- and re-construction of the 'musical' genre, this time fusing ballet and flamenco from rehearsals to performance in order to present Salome's love for John the Baptist and her revenge. In 2005, he celebrated Isaac Albeñiz's suite in his own *Iberia* [Goya for José Luis López-Linares's cinematography], using professional dancers and in a similar format to *Sevillanas* [1992] and *Flamenco* [1995], now followed by the 2007 *Fados* about Portuguese 'soul' music. There were, however, other explorations to broaden his filmography. *Goya en Burdeos* [1999 *Goya in Bordeaux* – eleven awards among which four Goyas, including cinematography for Vittorio Storaro, and a Sant Jordi for Saura] was a biopic of the painter, starring Paco Rabal, and José Coronado as the younger Goya. It is narrated in flashbacks from his exile, through memories and nightmares, with a mise-en-scène and lighting that combines cinematography with the best of an audacious stage production. Saura then had a lot of fun co-scripting with Agustín Sánchez Vidal the homage *Buñuel y la mesa del rey Salomón* [2001 *Buñuel and King Solomon's Table* – Goya for special effects], in which the ageing Buñuel [Gran Wyoming] is commissioned to make a film about his youth [Pere Arquillué] and adventures in 1930 Toledo with Lorca [Adriá Collado] and Dalí [Ernesto Alterio], while including intertextual references to many films. *El séptimo día* [2004 *The Seventh Day* – three awards, including Montreal for Saura] was built on a press cutting and explores the consuming hate, harboured within the confines of the village, the *pueblo*, which could lead to the slaughter that concludes any civil war.

Documentaries

There is a tradition of interesting feature-length documentaries made in Spain that can be punctuated by Buñuel's *Tierra sin pan* (*Las Hurdes*) [1933, pp. 52–3], Val del Omar's experiments, *Tríptico elemental de España* [1960, p. 151], Patino's *Canciones para después de una guerra* [1971 but released in 1976, p. 210], and all those that blossomed when censorship and the NO-DOs officially came to an end (p. 227), so Medem's *Pelota* is not unique. There are a number of examples, not forgetting the political *¡Hay motivo!* (p. 317), like Helena Taberna's *Extranjeras* [2003 *Foreign Women] presenting interviews and images that reveal much about being a woman and a migrant in Spain (I. Ballesteros, 2005: 3–14). José Luis Guerín's imaginative *En construcción* [2000 *Under Construction* – nine awards] is a brilliantly edited documentary that took three years to film with the help of six film students, and chronicles the changing face of the El Raval Barrio, as a new block of luxury flats is being built in the old red light district of Barcelona, changing life for some and providing work for others (Nair, 2004: 103–18; Loxham, 2006: 35–48). Mercedes Álvarez, who edited *En construcción* with Núria Esquerra during the same three years, made her own contribution in 2004 with *El cielo gira* [*The Sky is Spinning* – nine awards], a moving description of the consequences of rural depopulation that captures a millennium of history in the landscapes as viewed by the few remaining inhabitants of the village of Aldealseñor in the province of Soria and the painter Peio Azketa as he loses his sight. The Peruvian Javier Corcuera took a more global perspective with *La espalda del mundo* [2000 *The Back of the World* – two awards] presenting three individual cases of human suffering in Peru, Kurdistan and Texas, co-scripted with Fernando de León Aranoa and Elías Querejeta, who produced it, with Jordi Abusada at the camera. In 2004 he contributed together with Patricia Ferreira, Javier Fesser, Chus Gutiérrez and Pere Joan Ventura to *En el mundo a cada rato* [*Every Second in the World*], each presenting the case of a different child in various underprivileged corners of the planet. It was made to support UNICEF's defence of children's rights whereas *La espalda del mundo* commemorated the fifty years of the UN's Universal Declaration of Human Rights. Like Julio Medem's *La pelota vasca/Euskal pilota*, another controversial documentary was Eterio Ortega Santillana's *Perseguidos* [2004 *Pursued*], co-scripted with and produced by Elías Querejeta, necessarily using unknown actors since it is based on interviews of family men in the Basque Country who have officially been given new identities, and in some cases bodyguards, for their protection.

One of the prices paid for the relatively peaceful transition to democracy was the so-called 'pact of forgetting', not to dig up the past to uncover all the horrors that occurred during the Civil War and in its aftermath (chapter 8).[9] This position upheld by the PP has now been challenged by official organisations like the Asociación para la Recuperación de la Memoria [Association for the Recovery of Memories], founded in 2000, and echoed by a number of documentaries and docudramas that have been made to retrieve the facts, lest too much is forgotten after so many years. They frequently include the word 'memory' in their title. Ortega Santillana, again with Querejeta, made *Noticias de una guerra* [2006 *News of a War*] on the events that led up to the Civil War. The philosopher María Zambrano [Pilar Bardem], her life, education, appointment as assistant professor in 1931, her writings, subsequent exile and return to Spain in 1984 was the subject of José Luis García Sánchez's docudrama *María querida* [2004 *Dearest María* – one award for Pilar Bardem]. Cinematographer José Luis López Linares and Javier Rioyo made *Extranjeros de sí mismos* [2000 *Strangers to Themselves*] to collect personal statements on foreign involvement on both sides of the Civil War, and from those Spaniards who later went to fight on the Russian front as part of Franco's División Azul. In 2001, Jaime Camino, whose last film had been

---

[9]   This paragraph was contributed by Jennie Holmes when she proofread the chapter.

released in 1992, released *Los niños de Rusia* [*The Children of Russia*], based on moving interviews about those Republican children sent to the Soviet Union for their security during the war. In 2004, Alberto Porlan's *Las cajas españolas* [*The Spanish Crates*] retold through a docudrama how the civil servants of the Republic managed to save the state treasures from the Prado, and other museums, during and after the siege and bombing of Madrid. Corcuera made *La guerrilla de la memoria* [2002 *The Guerrilla of Memory*] about what was remembered and forgotten of the *maquís*. In *Rejas en la memoria* [2004 *Bars on the Memory*] Manuel Palacios examines the Dictatorship's concentration camps, while Pau Vergara's *Más allá de la alambrada* [2005 *Beyond the Barbed Wire*] deals with Spanish Republicans sent to the Nazi concentration camps around Mauthausen in Austria. In *El tren de la memoria* [2005 *The Memory Train*] Marta Arribas and Ana Pérez retrace Josefina Cembrero's journey to Germany as an illegal economic migrant. The year 2006, the seventieth anniversary of the start of the Civil War, which was commemorated by declaring it the'Año de la Memoria Histórica' ['Year of Historical Memory'], was also marked by a number of interesting documentary film projects. These included *Imagenes contra el olvido*[10] [*Images not to Forget*], a DVD pack of ten previously unreleased documentaries and *Entre el dictador i jo* [2006 Juan A. Barrero, Raúl Cuevas, Guillem López, Mònica Rovira, Sandra Ruesga and Elia Urquiza, *Entre el dictador y yo/Between the Dictator and I*] for which six directors born after Franco's death were asked to make a short film about what Franco means for them.[11]

Historical films

A different manifestation of the same need to know, and not to forget, is present in many fictional narratives based on the same events but focalised through the personal fictions of the characters on screen. José Luis Cuerda's *La lengua de las mariposas* [1999 *Butterfly's Tongue* – five awards including Goya for best screenplay and San Sebastián Golden Shell] takes a nostalgic look at a little Galician village just before the uprising of 1936 to show through the experience of a child [Manuel Lozano] how many assumed sides through circumstances rather than convictions. In *La hora de los valientes* [1998 *A Time for Defiance* – seven awards including a best supporting actress Goya for Ariadna Gil] director Antonio Mercero uses the personal experience of an odd-job employee at the Prado Museum [Gabino Diego] to show

---

[10] No reference in the *IMDb*, but there is a web link at www.imagenescontraelolvido.com.

[11] No reference in the *IMDb*, but there is also a web link at http://entreeldictadorijo.com/_eng/index.html.

part of the story subsequently told by *Las cajas españolas* (Mitchell, 2004: 178–82). David Trueba adapted Javier Cercas's novel *Soldados de Salamina* [2003 *Soldiers of Salamina* – twelve awards including best cinematography for Javier Aguirresarobe] to present a Civil War that is no longer so polarised, and which involves a journey of self-discovery as a young novelist [Ariadna Gil] tries to piece together how the historical Rafael Sánchez Mazas [Ramón Fontseré] was spared by an unknown Republican soldier at the end of the war (Hughes, 2007: 369–86). Mexican director Guillermo del Toro took the horror of the Civil War as a perfect context for a ghost story in *El espinazo del diablo* [2001 *The Devil's Backbone* – six awards] (Lázaro Reboll, 2007: 39–51). Then, in *El laberinto del fauno* [2006 *Pan's Labyrinth*[12] – three Oscars and fifty-eight other awards], he used the violence of the immediate post-war years and the hunt for the *maquis* hiding in forested mountain slopes to present an imaginative and savage fairy tale, complete with a princess [Ivana Baquero], a very wicked stepfather/sadistic fascist officer [Sergi López], a Saturnine monster and an ambivalent faun [Doug Jones]. The *maquis* also inspired Montxo Armendáriz's drama *Silencio roto* [2001 *Broken Silence* – seven awards]. Fernando Colomo chose the same period but in Madrid with *Los años bárbaros* [1998 *The Stolen Years* – one award] as two students are sent to a concentration camp for writing a graffito on a university building. Agustí Villaronga's *El mar* [2000 *The Sea* – two awards] is another private story of the post-war years as three childhood friends meet up in a tuberculosis sanatorium after their memory had repressed a shared bloody murder from the Civil War. Much closer to historical events is Manuel Huerga's biopic of the last anarchist known to be executed in Spain, on 2 March 1974, *Salvador* [2006 *Salvador (Puig Antich)* – fourteen awards, seven at the Barcelona Film Festival, Sant Jordi for best film and the Goya for best screenplay]. On a screenplay started in 1987 Montxo Armendáriz's *Secretos del corazón* [1997 *Secrets of the Heart* – seventeen awards including four Goyas, the Sant Jordi and Oscar nomination], set in an old dark house in a village in Navarre during the repressive sixties, follows a young boy's [Andoni Eburu] discovery of family secrets (Deveny, 2000: 144–54; Stone, 2002: 103–7). The struggles and sacrifices of the illegal economic migrant are taken up through the personal reminiscences of actor Carlos Iglesias who dramatised and directed his family's experience in Switzerland, fictionalised with a dose of nostalgia in *Un franco, 14 pesetas* [2006 *Crossing Borders*[13] – five awards including Goya for best new director].

These difficult times, frequently presented through personal and collective memories, were not the only historical periods providing a context for recent

---

[12] Del Toro was displeased that the film was distributed as *Pan's Labyrinth*, rather than *The Faun's Labyrinth*, but it avoided confusion with 'Fawn'.

[13] The title refers to the 1960 rate of exchange for the Swiss franc.

films. There were other excursions which, in some instances, still kept a critical political edge. Agustín Díaz Yanes made *Alatriste* [2006 – four awards
including three Goyas], a swashbuckling action film that combines a number
of Arturo Pérez Reverte's popular episodic stories set in the seventeenth
century, about the soldiers and mercenaries who fought in Felipe IV's imperial wars. In a variety of visual styles ranging from recent Hollywood bellic
narratives to westerns, Díaz Yanes's film implicitly gives the lie to the glory
of Francoist historical films of the 1940s and 1950s and points to the vanity
of military interventions in foreign lands. Vicente Aranda went back to the
daughter of the Catholic Monarchs, putting sex and nudity into the passion
of his *Juana la loca* [2001 *Madness of Joan* – thirteen awards including three
Goyas], which attempts to be more convincing for contemporary spectators
than Juan de Orduña's *Locura de amor* [1948 *The Mad Queen*], although it
still remains close to the romantic play of the same title written by Manuel
Tamayo y Baus, first performed in 1855 (Martín Pérez, 2004: 71–85). The
same mode and focus on action prevailed in Aranda's version of Mérimée's
Carmen [2003 – two awards, including a Goya for costumes], and his adaptation of the Catalan chivalresque tale of *Tirante el Blanco* [2006].

There were also gentler and saccharine visions of the past focusing on
emotions, such as José Luis Garci's recent films. *You're the one* [2000 –
thirteen awards, four Goyas including best cinematography for Raúl Pérez
Cubero, a Berlin Silver Bear and European Film award], for instance, is a
nostalgic melodrama filmed in black and white, set in 1947 and going back
in time. It was not his only film with a sentimental tone and soothing glossy
look. *Historia de un beso* [2002 *Story of a Kiss* – one award], *Tío Vivo c.1950*
[2004 *Merry-go-round circa 1950* – one Goya], or his two remakes, *El abuelo*
[1998 *The Grandfather* – nine awards including Goya for Fernando Fernán
Gómez and Oscar nomination] and *Ninette* [2005 – Goya for Gil Parondo's
production design] were all co-scripted with Horacio Valcárcel, filmed by
Pérez Cubero and edited by Miguel González Sinde. Fernando Colomo *Al
sur de Granada* [2003 *South from Granada* –Goya for Juan Bardem's musical
score] was a biographical imagining of British Hispanist Gerald Brenan's
[Matthew Goode] discovery of Spain in the summer of 1919. Very similar
in tone but not in content is *El viaje de Carol* [2002 Imanol Uribe, *Carol's
Journey* – Berlin Glass Bear] in which the Civil War is seen from the perspective of a twelve-year-old girl [Clara Lago] who arrives in Spain from the USA
in 1938 with her Spanish mother [María Barranco] to look for her father [Ben
Temple] fighting with the International Brigades. With greater melodrama,
set before the Civil War and beautifully echoed by the barren landscapes of
the Canary Islands, is Antonio José Betancor's tale of the repressed passion of
an exiled doctor [Carmelo Gómez] in *Mararía* [1998 –four awards including
Goya for Juan Ruiz's cinematography]. By this stage even the *movida* of

the 1980s had become subject to nostalgia in Chus Gutiérrez's *El Calentito* [2005, the title is the name of a club – six awards].

Social issues

Another recent trend close to the documentary has been films focusing on social issues, as advocated by Juan Antonio Bardem at the 1955 Salamanca talks, presented with realism in such a way as to be credible. To mark the difference social realism and neo-realism these new films have been labelled *cine social* [social cinema] (Triana Toribio, 2003: 155–8), which relates to John Orr's 'Neo-Bazinian Realism' (2004: 301–4). For instance, as a law on domestic violence was being debated in the Cortes, Icíar Bollaín co-scripted and directed *Te doy mis ojos* [2003 *Take My Eyes* – thirty-nine awards, including seven Goyas, San Sebastián and Sant Jordi for best film], a hard but pertinent conjugal drama about the problem, starring Laia Marull and Luis Tosar. It is a film that has the merit of taking on the unacceptable violent husband's motivation, unlike Silvia Quer's more melodramatic television film, *Sara* [2003], which is set in a more affluent social context and, although based on a true case, focuses on the exploited and victimised young wife [Laura Conejo]. In his first film, *Solas* [1999 *Alone* – thirty-five awards, five of them Goyas, and including Berlin, Brussels and Sant Jordi for best film], Benito Zambrano also examined the consequences of domestic violence on a mother [María Galiana] and a daughter [Ana Fernández], through their individual loneliness and relationship when they have to spend some time together after a long separation, while the father [Pedro de Osca] is in hospital. It is a film made all the more moving for its silences (Leonard, 2004: 222–36). Miguel Albaladejo also takes up the consequences of such violence in a more melodramatic mode with *Rencor* [2002 **Resentment* – Goya for Lolita Flores as best new actress], although the film is just as much a vehicle for the daughter of Lola Flores, Lolita, and where Jorge Perugorría is more important for his violent portrayal than his Cuban identity. Based on a true event, Jorge Algora for his first (television) film turned the case of a person missing as a consequence of domestic violence into a thriller, *Viure de mentides/Mintiendo a la vida* [2005 *Lying to Life*]. Back to the more sober style of the *cine social*, in his hard-hitting first feature *El Bola* [2000 *Pellet*[14] – eighteen awards, including four Goyas], Achero Mañas, who had been acting for twenty years, presented an individual case of violence within the family, as the father [Manuel Morón] brutalises his son [Juan José Ballesta] who eventually escapes his situation

---

[14] Bola [Pellet] is the nickname given to Juan José Ballesta's character because he uses two large marbles as a comforter.

through friendship with a schoolmate [Pablo Galán] and his family. Juan José Ballesta was also the protagonist of Antonio Mercero's sensitive *Planta 4ª* [2003 *The Fourth Floor* – six awards including Hamburg, Málaga and Montreal for the director] looking with humour rather than sentimentality at the drama of young teenagers on the trauma recovery ward of a hospital. Dionisio Pérez's *El regalo de Silvia* [2003 *Silvia's present*] examines in a more melodramatic mode the question of organ transplants. These are only a few examples.

After *Barrio* [1998] Fernando León de Aranoa explored unemployment in *Los lunes al sol* [2002 *Mondays in the Sun* – thirty-seven awards, including five Goyas for best film, best director, and for the actors Javier Bardem, Luis Tosar and José Ángel Egido]. His *Princesas* [2006 *Princesses*] focuses on the friendship between Candela Peña and Micaela Nevárez who have turned to prostitution to make a living, and where the relationship is complicated by the fact that the second is an immigrant without papers. José Antonio Quirós's first film also addressed forced redundancies in *Pídele cuentas al rey* [2000 *Get the King to Answer* – six awards], starring Antonio Resines and Ariadna Ozores, in a story based on the actual protest march of an Asturian family to Madrid to ask why Article 35 of the Constitution was being ignored,[15] and exploring social and racial tensions along the way. Javier Maqua's *Chevrolet* [1997 – three awards for Isabel Ordaz], preferred to observe the urban marginalised through the relationships created around an abandoned car. There were also comedies drawing attention to the unemployment problem, like Álex Calvo Sotelo's first film *Se buscan fulmontís* [1999 *Fullmonties Wanted* – one award], taking Peter Cattaneo's *The Full Monty* [1997] one step further in a Spanish context, or David Serrano's very successful *Días de fútbol* [2003 *Football Days* – three awards including Goya to Fernando Tejero as best new actor]. Although he usually directs for television, Jorge Coira's *O ano da carracha/El año de la garrapata* [2004 *The Year of the Tick*] is a meta-comedy with direct address to the camera and retakes with different lighting, offering a cynical look at unemployable Félix Gómez, who has taken nine years to complete his undergraduate degree and, with his lack of commitment, still scrounges off his parents and friends. Gerardo Herrero's *Las razones de mis amigos* [2000 *Friends Have Reasons* – one award] sets the narrative in the 1990s, another employment crisis when one needed friends.

Issues of immigration and ethnicity are taken up in a number of films, although migrants are now a regular presence in films, just as tourists were in the 1960s. Manuel Gutiérrez Aragón's *Cosas que dejé en La Habana* [1998 *Things I Left in Havana* – two awards] is about three sisters [Violeta

---

[15] Article 35 begins 'Todos los españoles tienen el deber de trabajar y el derecho al trabajo ...' [All Spaniards have the duty to work and the right to work ...] (http://www.constitucion.es/constitucion/).

Rodríguez, Isabel Santos and Broselandia Hernández] who arrive in Madrid in search of a better life but are exploited by their aunt [Daisy Granados] and fall prey to another Cuban [Jorge Perugorría]. In *Flores de otro mundo* [1999 *Flowers from Another World* – six awards] Icíar Bollaín takes three potential couples to merge the fate of illegal migrants from Latin America with that of local rural depopulation (Nair, 2002: 38–49; Santaolalla, 2004: 129–38). Llorenç Soler's *Said* [1999 – one award] concentrates on a personal interracial relationship [Moroccan Naoufal Lhafi and Catalan Nuria Prims] to examine the problems faced by migrant workers and cultural differences (Nair, 2004: 103–18; Loxham, 2006: 35–48); and Alberto Rodríguez addresses these issues with a certain humour in *El traje* [2002 *The Suit* – one award]. In *Poniente* [2002 *Setting Sun* – four awards] Chus Gutiérrez presents the illegal workers' problems with a collective perspective, as well as the more melodramatic point of view of the female protatogonist [Cuca Escribano] and two very different personal experiences of migration [Farid Fatmi and José Coronado] (I. Ballesteros, 2005: 3–14). Rather than using the more sober style of the *cine social*, television films tend, in the main, to present social issues as melodramas or thrillers, even though the screenplays are often based on real cases. Examples include Dacil Pérez de Guzmán's *El camino de Víctor* [2005 *Victor's Journey*], which presents the problem of the immigrant single-parent family as seen from the perspective of the bullied son [Sergio Barranco]. Sigfrid Monleón's *Sindrome laboral* [2005 *Industrial Syndrome* – one award] dramatises a true incident resulting from the illegal working conditions of the exploited workforce in sweatshops. On the other hand, Carlos Molinero's *Salvajes* [2001 *Savages* – Goya for best screenplay], Ramón Parrado's first film *Rapados* [2004 *Skinheads*], or Jacobo Rispa's *Diario de un skin* [2005 *Diary of a Skinhead*], like Saura's *Taxi*, all take on xenophobia from the perspective of the perpetrators of racially motivated violence. Ignacio Vilar's *Ilegal* [2003 *Illegal*] approaches the issue through two competing television reporters wanting a scoop on the illegal traffic of African migrants.

Also engaging with social concerns are films about the disaffected and rebels, often without a cause and more out of boredom. In line with Armendáriz's *Historias del Kronen* [1995 *Stories from the Kronen*], for instance, Salvador García Ruiz's *Mensaka* [1998 – four awards including Goya for best screenplay, adapted from another novel by José Ángel Mañas] presents seven young people of different social backgrounds trying to find their identity through rock and drugs. The visual style of these films is self-conscious in the sense that it draws attention to itself, a trait that John Orr identifies as 'Traductive Realism' (2004: 305–7) because the image disrupts normal perception and thus the spectator's expectations. Calparsoro's first three films are a good example of this style, and so is his *Asfalto* [2000 *The City*], which now places Najwa Nimri in Madrid and casts her alongside Juan

Diego Botto and Gustavo Salmerón. In *Leo* [2000 – six awards, including the Goya for best director] veteran José Luis Borau approached the marginalised and disaffected through the personal drama of abused Leo(nor) [Icíar Bollaín] who survives by collecting discarded packaging from the streets, and captures the total devotion of a security guard [Javier Batanero]. *La pistola de mi hermano* [1997 *My Brother's Gun* – one award], the only film Ray Loriga has directed to date with *Teresa* forthcoming in 2007, is a road movie that presents a disenfranchised youth, devoid of any commitment, reacting violently to the moment.[16] Cesc Gay's coming-of-age narrative *Krámpack* [2000 *Nico and Dani* – ten awards including Cannes, Chicago and Hamburg for best director] focuses, in more affluent surroundings, on four adolescents' summer of self-discoveries. He followed this with *En la ciudad* [2003 *In the City* – eight awards, including a Goya and the San Sebastián Golden Shell] about the daily lives and problematic relationships of older and economically independent but uncommitted friends in Barcelona.

Family

The family continues to be a popular subject as made manifest by the television series 'Cuéntame cómo pasó', which also builds on the collective memory, or the more recent summer offering 'Abuela de verano' [starting in 2005, *'Summer Grandma'] directed by Mar Targarona and starring Rosa Maria Sardà. The following examples give just a taste of the great variety of modes and situations presented. Scriptwriter and occasional director Álvaro del Amo made *Una preciosa puesta de sol* [2003 *A Beautiful Sunset*] in which three generations of women, grandmother [Marisa Paredes], mother [Ana Torrent] and granddaughter [Marta Larralde], come to know each other better in spite of family tensions, which they try to resolve during a visit to a country hotel. Gracia Querejeta's *Cuando vuelvas a mi lado* [1999 *By My Side Again* – four awards, including special mention and cinematography at San Sebastián] focuses on mother–daughter and sibling relationships, with many flashbacks as three very different sisters [Mercedes Sampietro, Adriana Ozores and Rosa Mariscal] are brought together to honour their mother's dying wishes. Querejeta followed this with *Héctor* [2004 – nine awards] about a sensitive adolescent [Nilo Mur] who goes to live with his aunt [Adriana Ozores] when his mother dies, and has to decide whether to move to Mexico with his estranged father [Damián Alcázar] when he first appears in his life. Eduard Cortés's television film *Amb el 10 a l'esquena/El*

---

[16] Ray Loriga is better known as the screenwriter of *Carne Trémula* [1997 Almodóvar, *Live Flesh*], *El séptimo día* [2004 Saura, *The Seventh Day*] and *Ausentes* [2005 Calparsoro, *The Absent*].

10 en la espalda [2004 **With a 10 on his Shirt*] uses basketball to examine
a father–son conflict as Biel [Biel Durán] tries to live up to the expectations of his father [Fernando Guillén Cuervo] when his older brother suffers
an accident. Family ties are examined in Salvador García Ruiz's *El otro
barrio* [2000 *The Other Side* – two awards, including San Sebastián best
new director] that presents two psychological journeys [Jorge Alcázar and
Àlex Casanovas] within the prejudices of a violent society. Octavi Masia's
first (television) film, *Las palabras de Vero* [2005 **Veronica's Words*] follows
a single mother [Silvia Munt] bringing up her two teenagers, one of whom
has Down's syndrome [Biel Durán and Pilar Andrés]. Xavier Bermúdez's
León y Olvido [2005 *Leon and Olvido* – eight awards], which also deals
with Down's but through a very different narrative. Ramón Costafreda's
Más que hermanos [2005 **More than Siblings*] was his first film and for
television on a screenplay by Rosa Castro, based on the real case of parents
who then discover that they are siblings. Patricia Ferreira's *Para que no me
olvides* [2005 **So That You Don't Forget Me* – four awards] explores the
question of bereavement through a grandfather [Fernán Gómez] with a trau-
matised memory from the Civil War, a possessive mother [Emma Vilarasau]
and a loving girlfriend [Marta Etura]. In Gerardo Herrero's *Heroína* [2005
**Heroin(e)* – three awards] the title refers to the drug itself and to the mother
[Adriana Ozores] who fights publicly to save her son, leading other mothers
to prosecute the powerful heroin pushers in 1988 Vigo. Another unusual plot
is Manolo Matjí's *Horas de luz* [2004 *Hours of Light* – two awards] about
the growing relationship between a prison nurse and single mother [Emma
Suárez] and a triple murderer [Alberto San Juan] with a life sentence.

Gentle humour was another way of approaching the family. Emilio
Martínez Lázaro's father–son road movie set in 1974, *Carreteras secundarias* [1997 *Backroads* – one award] features Fernando Ramallo, in his first
film, discovering that his father [Antonio Resines] is not only a penniless
confidence trickster on the run, but an incompetent one at that. In *Más Pena
que Gloria* [2001 *No Pain, no Gain* – one award] Victor García León looks at
a teenage crush [Biel Durán] within the context of the family. Silvia Munt's
thought-provoking television film *Las hijas de Mohamed* [2003 *Mohamed's
Daughters*] presents a gynaecologist's [Alicia Borrachero] well intentioned
but culturally insensitive attempts to help a migrant woman [Gabriela Flores]
rejected by her husband [Abdel Aziz El Mountassir] after giving birth to yet
another daughter.

In the black comedy mode Javier Maqua's *Carne de gallina* [2002 *Chicken
Skin*[17]] gathers all the extended family together for a wedding with delightful

---

[17] 'Goose pimples' is probably a more accurate translation

336 BERNARD P.E. BENTLEY

accents in a former mining community in Asturias or, set in Madrid, Javier Rebolledo's *Marujas asesinas* [2001 *Killer Housewives*] builds its plot on the revenge of a victimised wife [Neus Asensi] on her insensitive chauvinist husband [Antonio Resines]. A family situation is turned into a psycho-drama in Ricardo Franco's *La buena estrella* [1997 *Lucky Star* – eighteen awards including five Goyas] as a limping pregnant prostitute [Maribel Verdú] has found security and affection with a castrated butcher [Antonio Resines], when her former boyfriend [Jordi Mollà] comes to scrounge on their kindness and turns their lives into a nightmare. His last film, *Lágrimas negras* [1999 *Black Tears* – one award], completed by Fernando Bauluz after Ricardo Franco's death, used another triangular situation to explore an unusual fatal attraction, and so did Gerardo Vera in *Segunda piel* [1999 *Second Skin* – two awards]. At first viewing, Miguel Albaladejo's *Cachorro* [2004 *Bearcub* – four awards including Montreal and Toulouse for the director] may seem odd in a section on the family, but as Jennie Holmes argues it is a film about the gay set in the Chueca *barrio* of Madrid that challenges the spectator to reconsider what constitutes a family.[18] Family is also the subject of Juan Pinzás's film *Días de voda/Días de boda* [2002 *Wedding Days* – two awards], which received a Dogme 95 Certificate. Presented as a home-video wedding, albeit in an affluent middle-class context, it is an obvious situation for a Dogme Film with its unpleasant surprises as unwelcome guests arrive.[19]

Thrillers

Imanol Uribe directed two well-wrought but different thrillers, *Extraños* [1999 *Strangers*] and *Plenilunio* [2000 *Plenilune* – three awards], made all the more interesting as both include an inspector [Carmelo Gómez and Miguel Ángel Solá respectively] with family problems to resolve as they work on the case. Luis Marías, better known as a screenwriter, wrote and directed *X/Equis* [2002 *X*], about another detective [Antonio Resines] who wakes up with a hangover, unable to remember what happened the night before, and is then assigned a murder investigation where all the circumstantial evidence points to him. The film concludes with redemptive rain, cleansing him although what he will do with the new evidence is not revealed. In *El alquimista*

---

18 PhD thesis on the family in contemporary Spanish Cinema, in progress at the University of St Andrews.

19 Dogme is a Danish avant-garde cinema movement with a manifesto of ten commandments, affirmed in order to be broken, making an aesthetic out of low-budget filmmaking and thus generating self-publicity. But how can the spectator trust that the film has not been edited and contains no retakes? (Orr, 2004: 311–15).

impaciente [2002 *The Impatient Alchemist* – two awards] Patricia Ferreira presents an investigation headed by two *guardias civiles* [Ingrid Rubio and Roberto Enríquez]. Enrique Urbizu's *Caja 507* [2002 *Box 507* – nine awards, including two Goyas and the Sant Jordi best film] is another film involving a conspiracy, also casting Antonio Resines, this time as a father who, when justice is denied, attempts to get it on his own terms against a fraudulent international company. Urbizu followed this with *La vida mancha* [2003 *Life Marks* – three awards] in which José Coronado plays a mysterious older brother who returns to visit his younger brother Juan Sanz after a thirteen-year absence, but one is a compulsive gambler. Two other thrillers based on the luck of cards released in 2001 are Pablo Llorca's *La espalda de Dios* [*Behind God's Back*] and Mónica Laguna's *El juego de Luna* [*Luna's Game* – one award], which is an atmospheric thriller as a poker player's daughter, Luna [Ana Torrent], learns to surpass her father in a man's game. Juan Carlos Fresnadillo's *Intacto* [2001 *Intact* – eleven awards including Goyas for best new director, and best new actor for Leonardo Sbaraglia, as well as a Sant Jordi for best first work] is a Borgesian fable about luck, chance or fate, which also features veterans Eusebio Poncela and Max von Sydow in effective hyperreal sets. Gonzalo Tapia's *Lena* [2001] returned to natural settings to present another daughter–father relationship [Marta Larralde and Manuel Manquiña] caught up in the alcohol and drug traffic of the harbour town of Vigo in Galicia. In the television film *Mar rojo* [2004 *Red Sea*] directed by Enric Alberich, Julia [Maribel Verdú] finds one million euros in her car and is at first not sure as to what to do. After *Más que amor, frenesí* [1996 *Not Love, Just Frenzy*] Miguel Bardem went on his own to make a very different fantasy thriller, *La mujer más fea del mundo* [1999 *The Ugliest Woman in the World* – two awards], which can be viewed as an esperpentic fable still bending genres with a serial killer [Elia Galera] who develops a relationship with the detective [Roberto Álvarez] on the case (Parrondo Coppel, 2004: 119–34). Miguel Bardem also made the captivating thriller, *Incautos* [2004 *Swindled* – one award], in which Ernesto Alterio relates his experience as a con man, his successes and misadventures, until the master artist played by Federico Luppi, followed by Victoria Abril, come into his life for another final sting. It is a film that constantly surprises as the plots twists and turns at sharp angles. Another fantasy thriller was María Ripoll's *Utopía* [2003 – *Utopia*], superbly filmed by David Carretero and edited by Nacho Ruiz Capilla, in which Leonardo Sbaraglia is cursed with visions of the future, Najwa Nimri is abducted by a sect, and Théky Karyo is a blind retired policeman trying to rescue her. Moving to cyberthrillers, there is Eduard Cortés's television film *La caverna* [2000 *The Cave*].

Another new departure is the use of the *pueblo* [village] as a space for thrillers like Saura's *El séptimo día*, Pablo Llorca's *Todas hieren* [1998 *They All Wound* – one award]; Daniel Cebrián's first film, *Cascabel* [2000 *Sleigh-*

bell's Ankle Bracelet[20] – two awards in Toulouse], co-scripted with Ricardo
Franco and Manuel Matjí, about repressed secrets that lead to domestic
violence; Álvaro Fernández Armero's El arte de morir [2000 The Art of
Dying – one award]; Gutiérrez Aragón's La vita que te espera [2004 Your
next life – three awards]; or the recent La noche de los girasoles [2006 The
Night of the Sunflowers – five awards including a Sant Jordi for best first
work] directed by newcomer Jorge Sánchez Cabezudo. Another most unusual
hybrid film set in Catalan Port Vendres in France and dubbed into Castilian
is Marc Recha's Les mans buides/Las manos vacías [2003 Where is Madame
Catherine?], which grows into a thriller and where most of the information is
conveyed through the images of hand-held cameras, flashbacks and editing,
reflecting rural poverty and hardships. Recha's other films, Pau i el seu
germà/Pau y su hermano [2001 Pau and his Brother –two awards] and Dies
d'agost/Días de agosto [2006 August Days], although not thrillers are also
very personal, concerned with the countryside, and both explore personal
and Catalan identities. Galicia continues to be the setting for thrillers that
contain touches of magic and the supernatural, such as Manuel Palacios's La
rosa de piedra [1999 *The Stone Rose] or Eloy Lozano's Bellas durmientes
[2001 *Sleeping Beauties].

   There are also more 'classical' horror films, like David Pujol's La biblia
negra [2001 *The Black Bible], which is a Gothic horror exploiting the Galician setting and where it takes 17 minutes to reach the Dark Old House. With
many television thrillers to his name, Pedro Costa's Mis estimadas víctimas
[2004 *My Dear Victims] tells the story of a serial killer [Fernando Guillén
Cuervo] who blames it all on his mother and family. Carlos Gil's Schoolkiller
[2001 El vigilante] is terror Spanish-style with echoes of Elm Street happen-
ings and The Blair Witch Project [1999 Daniel Myrick & Eduardo Sánchez],
including Jacinto Molina, aka Paul Naschy, still acting and writing screenplays
(pp. 207–8). Molina/Naschy's last direction was La noche del ejecutor [1992
The Night of the Executioner], whereas his werewolf Waldemar Daninsky
returned in Licántropo [1996 Francisco Rodríguez Gordillo, Lycanthropus]
and Tomb of the Werewolf [2004 Fred Olen Ray], while Rojo sangre [2004
Christian Molina, *Red Blood] was his last, or latest, screenplay. He wrote
and acted in all these films, and is still acting just as Jesús Franco, the other
cult figure of the 1970s, continues to work, directing more than fifteen films
since 1996, including Snake Woman [2005]; all to the delight of their fans.

---

20 The protagonist [Irene Visedo] is nicknamed Cascabel because of the ankle-bracelet
with sleigh bells that her father makes her wear to know where she is.

Trusting the other and conspiracies

The question of trust, or rather the lack of trust, is one that comes up repeatedly as a reflection of contemporary society where mistrust and conspiracy theories prevail because of uncovered abuses in the personal, professional or institutional trust placed on individuals, companies and governments. This is very much in line with Chris Carter's television series 'The X Files' which started its Spanish broadcast in 1994 as 'Expediente X'. Mateo Gil's film and its title, *Nadie conoce a nadie*, discussed above, encapsulate this theme. Calparsoro's *Asfalto* is a thriller of passion and betrayal à la *Jules et Jim* [1962 François Truffaut], which also asks who can be trusted. Calparsoro went on to make *Guerreros* [2002 *Warriors*] to comment on war in general and the Kosovo conflict in particular. The same setting was used by Eduard Cortés in his television *Carta mortal* [2003 **Death Card*] to initiate his psycho-thriller. Calparsoro followed *Guerreros* with a very different psychological thriller *Ausentes* [2005 *The Absents* – one award] encapsulating the contemporary mother's condition and sense of isolation.

Ventura Pons, very productive as a producer/screenwriter/director usually in Catalan, adapted Sergi Belbel's 1991 play *Caricies* [1998 *Caresses* – one award] in which he interlocks eleven vignettes, usually connected by a family tie, about individuals being cruel to each other (Faulkner, 2004a: 72–8). The deceit is also present within the family, even if for the best albeit mistaken intentions, as demonstrated by Eduard Cortés's first non-television film *La vida de nadie* [2002 *Nobody's Life* – two awards in Valladolid and Toulouse]. In Antonio Hernández's thriller *En la ciudad sin límites* [2002 *The City of No Limits* – five awards, including the Goya for best screenplay and supporting actress for Geraldine Chaplin] it is the family who lie to the father [Fernán Gómez] dying of cancer in a Paris hospital, and they lie to each other as each wants to control the family pharmaceutical company. The grandson Victor [Leonardo Sbaraglia] does not know what to believe, and gradually realises that his grandfather is not so much a victim of senile dementia as of a betrayal during the early years of the Franco regime, when trusting anybody was dangerous for ex-Republicans. Hernández's next two films, *Oculto* [2005 *Hidden*] and *Los Borgia* [2006 *The Borgias*], also explore the theme of deceit but in two very different contexts. With a quite different cinematographic language and minimalist sets, Roger Gual and Julio Wallowits's first film explores duplicity in the workplace. *Smoking_Room* [2002 – eight awards] with excellent actors, follows the gradual betrayal of Eduard Fernández who campaigns for a special room when smoking is banned from the building by the US owners of their Spanish branch. Further corporate distrust is illustrated in Marcelo Piñeyro's *El método* [2005 *The Method* – ten awards, including two Goyas], a suspense co-scripted with Mateo Gil, in which seven applicants for an important executive post are locked into a room and, using the Grönholm method, are obliged to select the one successful candidate themselves. Pedro Costa's *Acosada* [2003 *Harassment*], Eduard Cortés's *Mónica* [2003] and Sonia Sánchez's *Mobbing* [2006], for example, follow the cases and attempted prosecution of sexual aggression in professional contexts. In her first (television) film, *Autopsia* [2002 *Autopsy*], Milagros Bará bases her narrative on an apparently true case that begins with the investigation of a boy's corpse, which leads to the uncovering of a paedophile ring protected by men in high places, and Miguel Ángel Vivas's *Reflejos* [2002 *Reflections*] is a psychological *noir* police thriller concerning a child serial killer. Gerardo Herrero's transnational thriller *El misterio Galíndez* [2003 *The Galíndez File*] begins in 1986 as a PhD thesis researches an exiled Basque academic who disappeared from his New York flat in 1956. The investigation leads to uncovering thirty years of CIA covert conspiracies. Patricia Ferreira's first film, *Sé quién eres* [2000 *I Know Who You Are* – six awards, including Goya for best score], uses the psychological thriller and a romance to deal with the hidden side of the Transition. Helena Taberna, on the other hand, made the biopic *Yoyes* [2000 – six awards, but none of which were from festivals in Spain]. Yoyes was the name given to María Dolores González Katarain [Ana Torrent], an Etarra who renounced ETA and its violence, and was consequently gunned down by her previous comrades. Miguel Courtois's thriller *El lobo* [2004 *Wolf* – two Goyas for the editing and special effects] presents the true case of a mole [Eduardo Noriega] planted in an ETA cell from 1973 to 1975, showing how violence only brings more violence and betrayals lead to worse betrayals.

This lack of trust is also present as a desperate need to trust, and at times to trust the most unexpected in order to find peace of mind or redemption. This was part of the surprise and success of Amenábar's *Los otros*, mentioned above, but this sort of committed trust in the abject had been previously explored in the thriller *Los sin nombre* [1999 *The Nameless* – fifteen awards] scripted and directed by Jaume Balagueró on Ramsey Campbell's novel (Willis, 2004: 246–7), and in Noberto López Amado's first film, *Nos miran* [2003 *They're Watching Us* – one award]. Both begin as police investigations of a missing person and conclude as a parable of the fallible father who either destroys his child [Karra Elejalde in the former] or sacrifices himself [Carmelo Gómez in the latter]. These films exploit the supernatural and occult, although the *IMDb* identifies them as 'Horror' (Willis, 2004: 237–49).

A taste of Spanish humour

Comedy is still the most popular genre for the Spanish public. It entertains and relaxes, offers possible escape, and it now comes in all sorts of formats and blends. There are still the old-fashioned types that benefit from the now not so 'new look', like Raúl Marchand's *Atraco a las tres ... y media* [2003 *Hold up at 15:00 ... :30*], which reworks José María Forqué's *Atraco a las tres* [1962], co-scripted with Pedro Masó who had also been one of the original screenwriters. This film includes many references to the comedies of the period, and manages to recast Manuel Alexandre, this time as the dismissed elderly bank manager, Don Felipe. Set at the end of 2002 as the peseta was about to be replaced by the euro, the bank is taken over by a German conglomerate led by Otto Burmann [Carlos Larrañaga]. The joke is that Burmann is an important name in Spanish Cinema: Hans Burmann is an appreciated cinematographer and has been behind the camera since 1965; his brother Wolfgang is an important set designer and art director; and their father Siegfried had been art director in Spanish films since 1938. Eva Lesmes used a similar plot motivator to create the comedy of *El palo* [2001 *The Hold-up*] but with four women of very different social backgrounds (see p. 166, n. 11). Berlanga's *París–Tombuctú* [1999 – three awards] also returns to old gags to examine the futility of master plans, as another impotent Michel Piccoli [*Tamaño natural*, 1974 but only released in Spain in 1977] returns to the fictional Calabuch [1956 *Calabuch*], now gone post-modern, discovered by tourists and the perfect site for international conferences, for the extraordinary millennium erection inspired by Concha Velasco. It is a visual testament that gathers many characters and situations from the whole of Berlanga's filmography.[21]

With these examples it is an easy step to other far-fetched and entertaining plots. In 1998, Miguel Albaladejo wrote and directed *La primera noche de mi vida* [*My First Night* – fourteen awards] as, on the eve of the millennium, eleven pairs of friends crisscross the periphery of Madrid and must change their plans as they meet each other, which he followed by *El cielo abierto* [2001 *Ten Days Without Love* – three awards] as Miguel [Sergi López] finds out his wife has left him the day his mother-in-law [María José Alonso] arrives for a hospital visit, and then complications begin. In *Sin noticias de Dios* [2001 *No News from God/Don't Tempt Me* – two awards] Agustín Díaz Yanes presents Victoria Abril and Penélope Cruz as angels from heaven and hell who compete with ironic humour for the soul of a boxer [Demián Bichir] (Perriam, 2007: 34–6). This leads to creationist comedies that exploit the special effects that cinema and digitalisation can offer, and which are appreciated and enjoyed as such,[22] examples of which can be found in the

---

[21] In 2002, he made a twelve-minute short *El sueño de la maestra* [*The Teacher's Dream*], which goes back to Eloisa, the teacher in *¡Bienvenido míster Marshall!* [1953].

[22] The label 'creationist' is used to describe one of the types of 'hyperrealism' identified by John Orr (2004: 307–11). The 'hyperrealism' he identifies with *Les Amants du Pont-neuf* [1991 Leos Carax, *The Lovers on the Bridge*] and which one would associate with *La ciudad sin límites*, also set in Paris, or *El método* and *Intruso*, is different from those films that exploit

parodies and pastiche that are also favourites. Esteban Ibarretxe's first film *Sólo se muere dos veces* [1997 *You Only Die Twice* – two awards] takes on James Bond with Indiana Jones action, in a post-modern celebration of the horror film (with echoes of Méliès, Frankenstein, Dorian Gray, Tommy Cooper's death on stage, and repeated quotations from *La vida es sueño, pero la muerte aún más*[23]). The whole imaginatively integrates many horror motifs through its protagonist, Gastón Pallín [Álex Angulo], who looks like Quasimodo and is attracted by an Esmeralda [Rosana Pastor], including a prosecution judge and his friend Tete [Juan Inciarte] who is here as versatile as Jim Carrey with reminiscences of Paul Naschy [aka Jacinto Molina]. Ibarretxe followed this up in 2000 with another spoof, *¡Sabotaje!* [*Sabotage!!*], a European co-production about the battle of Waterloo with Stephen Fry as Wellington and David Suchet as Napoleon. It is a film that connects with all the Napoleonic musicals of the 1950s and 1960s. These excesses are taken up by others and suited actor Karra Elejalde who co-scripted and directed *Año Mariano* [2000 *Holy Mary*] and *Torapia* [2004 *Therabull*], which in the space of a mental rehabilitation clinic attacks some fundamental holy cows, and bulls, of Castilian tradition. Javier Fesser had previously scripted and filmed *El milagro de P Tinto* [1998 *The Miracle of P. Tinto* – five awards including Goya for special effects and Sant Jordi for best first work], casting veteran Luis Ciges as a man who for fifty years has wanted, without success, to be the patriarch of a numerous family. In 2003, Fesser made the film of Francisco Ibáñez's popular cartoon characters *La gran aventura de Mortadelo y Filemón* [2003 *Mortadelo y Filemón: The Big Adventure* – five Goyas], slapstick and farce that is at times politically incorrect and subversive.

These lead to what Triana Toribia has labelled the 'vulgar comedies', which offended many critics but have been so successful at the box-office precisely because of their politically incorrect bad taste taken to extremes (2003: 151–5, 155). These are associated with actor Santiago Segura, who had started with horror shorts (Willis, 2004: 242–4) and then went on to make *Torrente, el brazo tonto de la ley* [1998 *The Stupid Arm of the Law* – five awards including Goya for best new director and for veteran Tony Leblanc's comeback as best supporting actor]. This film generated enough revenues for two sequels to date, *Misión en Marbella* [2001 *Mission in Marbella*] and *Torrente 3: El protector* [2005 *The Bodyguard*]. In these films Santiago Segura plays the antihero, Torrente, an incompetent dishonourably discharged policeman, coarse, unkempt and aggressively violent, described by Triana Toribio as a

---

special effects and digitalisation to delight in unexpected images, 'creationism' discussed here. Easthope refers to creationist films as formalist (1993: 2–8, 53–67).

[23] Calderón's *La vida es sueño* is the Spanish equivalent of *Hamlet* with an equally famous soliloquy at the end of its second act, which returns as a motif throughout the film, although the closing lines are here changed to 'Life is a dream, / but death is an even bigger dream'.

'*facha* (right-wing), racist, sexist, [who] supports the football team Atlético de Madrid: [...] those characteristics are unlikely to be shared by one person in real life' (2003: 151; see also 2005: 147–56; Lázaro Reboll, 2005: 219–27). According to Jordan & Allinson '*Torrente's* appeal was based on its hybridity, its attractive combination of classic American genre conventions with certain Spanish filmic traditions such as vicious black humour, surrealism, explicit violence and crude, grotesque, stereotypes' (2005: 31, 109–16). He was not the only one to exploit this type of vulgar humour and setting, which are probably best qualified as burlesques of given (hybrid) genres. There was, for instance, Albert Saguer's *Vivancos 3* [2002 *Dirty Vivancos III*], whose first two parts would depend on the box-office returns of this initial third part. Paco Mir's *Lo mejor que le puede pasar a un croisán* [2003 *The Best Thing that can happen to a Croissant*] – which is of course to butter it up and make it disappear – moves into the burlesque of the private investigator and the cyberthriller. Juan Muñoz, another actor-screenwriter-director, made *Ja me maaten* [2000 *Oh They're Kiiilling Me*], a *grand guignol* scatological farce about a happily dysfunctional Madrid gypsy family who get involved with terrorists. Jesús Bonilla, who has frequently worked with Segura, wrote and directed both himself and Segura in the comedy *El oro de Moscú* [2003 *Moscow Gold*], an extravagant treasure hunt for the Republican gold reserve.

Not all comedies are so offensive. Manuel Gómez Pereira, who in 1999 had made *Entre las piernas* [*Between Your Legs* – one award], a thriller about sexual obsessions starring Victoria Abril and Javier Bardem, seems more comfortable in the field of the screwball comedy through which he skilfully presents and manipulates relationships. After *Off Key* [2001] came *Cosas que hacen que la vida valga la pena* [2004 *Things that Make Life Worthwhile* – six awards] and *Reinas* [2005 *Queens*]. In *Cosas que hacen* ... Ana Belén stars as a meticulous divorced mother, devoted to her son and her statistics, who is given a second chance for romance when Eduard Fernández intrudes into her life creating complications in her very ordered timetable and for her friends. *Reinas*, released when civil partnerships were legalised in Spain, presents the chaotic wedding preparations for six young men but the protagonists are really the five mothers and one father. It is a celebration of the sumptuous-set screwball comedies that build on both stereotypes and the screen persona of the single parents, who all have their own problems: Veronica Forqué is an absent-minded nymphomaniac, Carmen Maura an hotel manager exploited by her husband, Mercedes Sampietro the judge who will perform the first ceremonies, Bettiana Blum the lively eternal optimist who loses her dog in an echo of Hawks's 1938 *Bringing Up Baby*, Marisa Paredes a widowed actress who has been directed by Almodóvar and here falls in love with her gardener Lluís Homar, who cannot at first accept his homosexual son. It also draws on the important American talent

of Bettiana Blum, Daniel Hendler and Jorge Perugorría, as well as on Fernando Valverde straight out of his television series *El comisario*. Joaquín
Oristrell, who co-scripted all these films, also directed his own films such
as *Novios* [1999 *Engaged*], a Madrid romantic comedy centred on a father–
son conflict, with the family restaurant and athletics in competition as well
as a number of women, and *Inconscientes* [2004 *Irresponsible*], a clever
Freudian comedy about two 'detectives' looking for a missing husband at
the height of the psychiatric revolution in 1913 Barcelona. Yolanda García
Serrano and Juan Luis Iborra, who also collaborate on Pereira and Oristrell
screenplays, scripted and directed their second film together in 2000. *KM 0*
[*Kilometre Zero* – five awards] is a comedy of manners with no protagonist but a changing focus on fourteen people with their blind dates, failed
meetings, chance encounters and how their lives start to intertwine from the
'kilómetro cero', which refers to the spot in Madrid's Puerta del Sol from
where all distances in Spain are measured. *KM 0* was very popular at gay film
festivals and so was *A mi madre le gustan las mujeres* [2002 *My Mother Likes
Women* – nine awards] co-scripted and directed by Inés París and Daniela
Féjerman. This first feature film presents another comedy of manners as three
daughters struggle to accept that their divorced mother should have a Czech
professional pianist as a lover who also happens to be a woman. Their next
collaboration, *Semen (una historia de amor)* [2005 *Semen (A Love Story)*],
starring Leticia Dolera and father–son tandem, Héctor and Ernesto Alterio,
moves into the delightful absurd as Ernesto Alterio is in love and wants to
be a father. Meanwhile veteran Eloy de la Iglesia made *Los novios búlgaros*
[2003 *Bulgarian Lovers* – one award], a comedy with a lot of mood and
genre swings, and an ambivalent title that first refers to the Bulgarian boys
that attract Daniel [Fernando Guillén Cuervo] and then to the fact that the
one he falls for [Dritan Biba] is engaged to Anita Sinkovic. Miguel Bardem's
two collaborators, Alfonso Albacete and David Menkes, at times described
as extreme Almodovarians (Jordan & Morgan, 1998: 84–5), stayed together
to pursue their exploration of emotional relationships. The extravagant drug-
fuelled *Atómica* [1998 *Atomic*] was followed by *Sobreviviré* [1999 *I Will
Survive*] in which a delicate romantic relationship rearranges gender orien-
tations (Perriam, 2004b: 151–63), *I Love You Baby* [2001] with its touches
of Boy George, and *Entre vivir y soñar* [2004 *Searching for Love*], starring
Carmen Maura looking at romance at forty.

   Isabel Gardela was a newcomer whose first feature, *Tomándote* [2000 *Tea
for Two*[24] – one award], is a romantic comedy that examines cultural differences through the relationship between an uninhibited sexually active Catalan

---

[24] The title could be literally translated as *Having You!* which sounds the same as 'Having
Tea' in Spanish.

[Núria Prims] and a florist's assistant, a disciplined Indian Muslim called Jalil [Zack Qureshi]. In 1996, Gardela had collaborated with four other Catalan directors for the feature *El domini del sentits* [*Domain of the Sense*] in which she took the sense of smell, Judith Colell took 'sight', Núria Olivé-Bellés 'touch', Teresa Pelegri 'taste', and María Ripoll 'hearing'. Ripoll then went off to London to direct *If Only/Lluvia en los zapatos* [1998 *The Man with Rain in his Shoes* – three awards] in which Glaswegian David Henshall is given a second chance with his girlfriend Lena Headley through the intervention of two Quixotic dustmen [Eusebio Lázaro and Gustavo Salmerón], and Penélope Cruz also gets involved.[25] Also in English but filmed in California Ripoll directed the family comedy *Tortilla Soup* [2001 – two awards] from a script that others had already rewritten a number of times. Another clash of culture and personalities is humorously exploited in Ventura Pons's bilingual comedy *Amor idiota* [2005 *Idiot Love*] in which the incompetent Pere-Lluc [Santi Millán], in a state of permanent masculinity crisis, falls in love with Sandra [Cayetana Guillén Cuervo], a successful professional from Madrid.

Musicals

The musical as a genre, so lively and popular in Spain since the days of silent cinema (chapter 1), has mutated in the last decade to the extent that it is now misleading to identify films as a musical without adding further generic descriptors. Genres have become permeable and many films mentioned above integrate important and interesting soundtracks into their narratives, both diegetically and non-diegetically. Almoldóvar's films have become the archetype of this hybridisation, from his own unforgetable rendition of 'La bien pagá' with friend McNamara in *¿Qué he hecho yo para merecer esto!!* [1984 *What Have I Done to Deserve This?!*] to his *Volver* [2006], which is the name of the tango that Penélope Cruz sings in the film.[26] In some cases narratives have been written to the cloth of popular singers, as in the case of Miguel Albaladejo's *Rencor*, a tale for Lolita Flores to settle an emotional debt, or for Valencian singer Bebe cast in José Luis Cuerda's family romance, *La educación de las hadas* [2006 *The Education of Fairies*]; in both cases the singer-actors won Goyas for their performance. In other cases the plots follow the aspiration of musician or performers. In *Alma gitana* [1996 **Gypsy Soul*] Chus Gutiérrez rewrote the received script about a Romeo and Juliet relationship to consider social issues by reworking stereotypes and including

---

[25] The original English version on DVD is essential. The dubbed version released in Madrid theatres completely destroys the characterisation, and the verbal humour of Rafa Russo's script does not work.

[26] To be accurate, she lipsynchs it to the voice of Estrella Morente.

diegetically both traditional and fusion flamenco tracks with the participation of the band Ketama, who have themselves contributed to a number of films. Jaime Chávarri's *Besos para todos* [2000 *Kisses for Everyone* – two awards including Goya for makeup] is a rites-of-passage narrative with initiations to sex and student strikes, set in 1965 Cádiz evoked through the popular hits of the time. Chema de la Peña, with songs penned by *cantautor* [one who performs his own songs] Joaquín Sabina, directed *Isi/Disi – Amor a lo bestia* [2004 **Isi/Disi, Incredible Love*[27]] to attract metal fans of AC/DC who also enjoy Santiago Segura's smutty scatological humour; it was very popular at the box-office to the despair of respected film critics. Actor Fernando Guillén Cuervo's *Los managers* [2006 **The Managers*] is a road-movie about two losers [Manuel Tallafé and Enrique Illén] who decide to become managers and make a fortune by 'discovering' two talented brothers [Paco León and Fran Perea]. In a very different key, Daniel Cebrían's *Cascabel* presents the aspirations of his female protagonists [Irene Visedo and Pilar Punzano] to become successful singers. Carles Pastor Moreno's *A ras de suelo* [2005 **Flush to the Ground*] intertwines the lives of four different women [Rosana Pastor, Irene Montalà, Cristina Plazas, Anna Ycobalzeta] who do not know each other and experience very different problems but are linked by Caldito's jazz performances in the Valencia bar that they all visit regularly. There are many occasions when a film just has a memorable soundtrack like Manuel Huerga's biopic *Salvador (Puig Antich)*, where the musical numbers convey the temporal setting, moods and aspirations, and for which Lluís Llach won three music awards.

There are of course exceptions. Emilio Martínez Lázaro's *El otro lado de la cama* [2002 *The Other Side of the Bed* – six awards, including a Goya for its soundtrack] is an 'in your face' musical, where the main characters are presented as three couples who are all unfaithful to their partners and sing their thoughts and emotions to the camera, accompanied on-screen by professional dancers in routines reminiscent of Eurovision contests.[28] The film was extremely successful with the spectators and generated a sequel. In *Los 2 lados de la cama* [2005 *The Two Sides of the Bed*] two of the girlfriends [Paz Vega and Natalia Verbeke] have moved on, and the boys [Ernesto Alterio, Guillermo Toledo and Alberto San Juan] have found new girls [Pilar Castro, Lucía Jiménez and Verónica Sánchez] who join María Esteve. In his black comedy *20 centimetros* [2005 *20 Centimetres* – five awards] Ramón Salazar includes the numbers in elaborate oneiric sequences as part of his extravagant

---

[27] The colloquialism 'a lo bestia' is a superlative qualifier, which describes the worst or the best, depending on intonation.

[28] The screenwriter, David Serrano, went on to write and direct *Días de fútbol* in 2003 with the same group of actors.

plot, whereas in *Piedras* [2002 *Stones* – six awards] the musical soundtrack is integrated in the dramas of five women trying to resolve their different personal crises. There are also the interesting variations and experiments made by Carlos Saura mentioned at the beginning of the chapter.

Cinema for minors

Films made in Spain for younger viewers have always found it more difficult to compete against the Hollywood producers with their global advertising and distribution resources. Nonetheless there are interesting examples. Rosa Vergés's third film *Tic Tac* [1997 *Tick Tock* – two awards] is a parable in which time takes on a new meaning as a young boy [Sergi Ruiz] is left behind at Christmas on a railway platform where the minutes tick backwards. Miguel Albaladejo's *Manolito Gafotas* [1999 *Manolito Four Eyes* – Berlin Kinderhilfswerk award] on a script adapted with Elvira Lindo, the author of the original popular stories, focuses on Manolito's usually absent father [Roberto Álvarez] who takes family and son [David Sánchez del Rey] on a summer journey to the seaside. A sequel, *Manolito Gafotas en ¡mola ser jefe!* [*Manolito Gafotas in Great to be the Leader!*], was made in 2001 directed by actor Joan Potau but with a different cast. This spawned a television series in 2004, in which Adriana Ozores, the mother in the original film, returned to play the part. Oscar Vega's *Raluy, una noche en el circo* [2000 *Raluy, a Night with the Circus*] is an allegory where a little girl [Olga Molina] joins a circus that is under threat from the competition of television.

There is also a thriving output of full-length animation films that have been very successful at the box-office. Some of these deal with traditional stories, like José Pozo's *El Cid: La leyenda* [2003 *El Cid: The Legend* – Goya for best animation], *Los reyes magos* [2003 Antonio Navarro, *The Three Wise Men*], the Hispano-Argentine co-production directed by Juan Pablo Buscarini, *Pérez, el ratoncito de tus sueños* [2006 *The Hairy Tooth Fairy* – Goya for best animation], or Ángel de la Cruz and Monolo Gómez's *El bosque animado* [2001 *The Living Forest* –five awards including Goyas for best animation and best song] and their *El sueño de una noche de San Juan* [2005 *Midsummer Dream* – Goya for best animation] based on Shakespeare's play. Directors from the Basque Country have been particularly productive, including Juan Bautista Berasategi's *Ahmed, el príncipe de la Alhambra* [1998 *Ahmed, the Alhambra Prince*] and *El embrujo del Sur* [2008 *The Spell of the South*], which were both based on Washington Irving; Juanjo Elordi's Christmas stories *Olentzero: un cuento de Navidad* [2002 *Olentzero: A Christmas Story*] followed after other animations by *Olentzero y el tronco mágico* [2005 *Olentzero and the Tree Trunk*], or Txabi Basterretxea and Joxan Muñoz's *La isla del cangrejo* [2000 *Crab Island* – Goya for best animation]. Ángel

Izquierdo's *Dragon Hill* [2002 *La colina del dragón* – Goya for best anima-
tion] was made for English-speaking audiences.

Metacinema, films about making films

As cinema reached its hundredth birthday, films about making films increased
and, although they have always been made, they now proliferate. The situation of the screenwriter with writer's block is one repeated in a number
of films, whether it is superficially through the comedy-romance of Miguel
Álvarez's *Mi casa es tu casa* [2003 **My Home is Your Home*], the complex
relationships sketched by Vicente Pérez Herrero's *Cien maneras de acabar
con el amor* [2005 **A Hundred Ways to Stop Loving*], or a delicate romance
in a very minor key like Cesc Gay's *Ficció* [2006 *Fiction* –five awards],
where the landscape becomes very important. David Trueba's black comedy
Obra maestra [2000 *Masterpiece*] concerns two idiots [Santiago Segura and
Pedro Carbonell] determined to make a musical with a star [Ariadna Gil].
Nicolás Muñoz was working in television when he made his first feature
comedy, *Rewind* [1999] in which Andrés [Daniel Guzmán] wants to video
key moments of his life, but discovers a strange rewind button on his camera.
Montxo Arméndariz's *Obaba* [2005 – three awards including one Goya]
presents Lurdes [Pilar López de Ayala] who has left the city to shoot her
graduating film on rural depopulation in a northern village, the fictional
Obaba, and discovers through her interviews all sorts of village secrets whose
relationships the spectator has to assemble in a wider jigsaw puzzle. There
have also been successful feature-length documentaries about the cinema,
like Carlos Benpar's *Cineastas contra magnates* [2006 **Film Makers vs
Tycoons* – two awards], and in Catalan his *Cineastes en acció* [2006 **Film
Makers in Action* – three awards] released two months later, both presenting
the directors' right to have their works distributed as conceived.

There are also historical perspectives and commentaries. From his own
screenplay Pablo Berger's comedy, *Torremolinos 73* [2003 – fourteen awards,
including Goya for best new director and best leading actor], recreates the
destape as Alfredo [Javier Cámara], an unemployed door-to-door salesman of
the *Illustrated Universal Encyclopaedia of the Spanish Civil War*, is offered
the possibility of making underground pornographic shorts with his wife
[Candela Peña]. The film appropriately received Danish collaboration from
Nimbus Film Productions, the Danish Film Institute and TV2 Denmark.[29]
Fernando Trueba's *La niña de tus ojos* [1998 *The Girl of Your Dreams* –thir-

---

[29] I am grateful to Belén Vidal for allowing me to read her forthcoming article on the film,
which not only recreates the early 1970s but also engages in an intertextual dialogue between
pornography, popular comedy and 'Art House' cinema.

11b The transnationalism of Coixet's *La vida secreta de las palabras* (2005)

teen awards, including seven Goyas and Sant Jordis for Penélope Cruz and Rosa Maria Sardà] set in 1938 is a musical comedy inspired by the invitations made to Florián Rey and Benito Perojo to film in the German UFA studios. Trueba followed this with *El embrujo de Shanghai* [2002 *The Shanghai Spell* – three Goyas], a period-piece mystery that fuses reality and film *noir* in 1948 Barcelona, with a first love as the *maquis* is still operational and cinema is the only escape for dreaming. José Luis García Sánchez's docudrama *María querida* [2004] is presented as the documentary that Lola [María Botto] fails to make about the philosopher María Zambrano [Pilar Bardem] when the latter has returned to Spain after her long exile. And of course films like Carlos Saura's *Tango, no me dejes nunca* or *Fades*, which explore the question of performance and artistic creation through the camera.

Transnational productions

In the search for funding, producers now seek support from both commercial and regional television channels, which frequently combine and share the investment in individual films. But this is often not enough and another important source of funding, which does not invalidate local funding, is the European Union. This requires the participation of at least three countries for a film to be eligible. Perhaps even more fluid and productive, given the potential market and projected audiences, is the collaboration between Spanish-speaking countries thus consolidating the presence of transnational funding, which took off in the late 1990s as introduced in the previous chapter. The majority of the films mentioned in this chapter were funded by these multiple sources, although this has only been occasionally flagged. The Spanish-language collaborations (rather than co-productions) happen in a variety of combinations, from Spanish funding of films made in Latin America with local crews and actors like Daniel Díaz Torres's Cuban comedy *Hacerse el sueco* [2005 *Playing Swede* – four awards], to a Spanish director or actor's involvement in a Latin American film, like *La puta y la ballena* [2004 Luis Puenzo, *The Whore and the Whale* – three awards], with a wonderful sound-track, or American nationals involved in a production in Spain as in the case of Adolfo Aristarain's *Martín (Hache)* [1997], or his *Roma* [2004 – ten awards], which toggles between present-day Madrid and memories of Buenos Aires in the 1960s, bringing together Juan Diego Botto and Adolfo Sacristán, who is the one recalling his mother, Roma, played by Susú Percoraro. Peruvian Francisco Lombardi directed *Tinta roja* [2000 *Red Ink* – seven awards] with 61% Spanish funding and Fele Martínez, to present the initiation of a crime reporter on a tabloid newspaper. Argentine Marcos Carnevale, who has written much for Spanish television, is a good example of this transnational permeability. His gender-bending comedy *Almejas y mejillones* [2000 *Clams and Mussels*], filmed in Buenos Aires and Santa Cruz de Tenerife, brings together Leticia Brédice, Jorge Sanz and Silke in a love triangle, while his *Elsa y Fred* [2005 *Elsa and Fred* – four awards] is a warm octogenarian romance that brings together in Madrid the Uruguayan China Zorilla and Manuel Alexandre, veteran of the 1960s *cine de barrio*, with an homage to Fellini's *La dolce vita* [1960 *The Sweet Life*]. Alberto Lecchi's *Nueces para el amor* [2000 *Nuts for Love* – eight awards] uses Buenos Aires and Madrid for locations, pairs off Gastón Pauls with Ariadna Gil over three decades of interrupted romance, with a political subtext and a delicate balance of colour photography with paler tones and black and white. On a much more sombre note and set in Madrid is Manane Rodríguez's *Los pasos perdidos* [2001 *The Lost Footsteps*] about the implications for the family of the Argentine dictatorship (1976–83) and the children of the 'disappeared'. Mexican Guillermo del Toro's 2001 *El espinazo del diablo* and his 2007 Oscar best foreign film nomination, which collected three other Oscars, *El laberinto del fauno* [2006], were narratives set during the Franco years. Privileged with special funding there are plenty of Hispano-Cuban co-productions, like Manuel Gutiérrez Aragón's *Cosas que dejé en La Habana* [1998 – two awards], or Fernando Colomo's comedy and musical romp through Cuba, *Cuarteto de La Habana* [1999 *Havana Quartet* – one award], which revels in the cultural differences with an international set of actors from Cuba [Mirta Ibarra, Laura Ramos, Daisy Granados], from Spain [Javier Cámara, José Sacristán, Pilar Castro, Lola Lemos, Javier Gurruchaga], and Argentina [Ernesto Alterio and María Esteve]. Benito Zambrano's *Habana Blues* [2005 **Havana Blues* – seven awards including two Goyas] presents a lively soundtrack as two friends dream of leaving Cuba for Spain with a recording contract. Ángel Peláez's television film *Siempre Habana* [2006 *Always Havana*] is a delightful comedy about keeping up appearances and building on stereotypes when an inheritance comes up. Not that it is all comedy, as in Rafael Montesinos's television film *De colores* [2003 *Full of Colours* – one award], which presents an intelligent melodrama on the exploitation of a Cuban migrant, or Francisco Rodríguez who took a departure from his usual horror films with *90 millas* [2005 *90 Miles*], a Spanish production filmed in and off the Canaries about a family of Cubans who try to sail the 90 miles across the Straits of Florida on a homemade raft. There are also those American actors like Cecilia Roth, the Alterios father and son, Darío Grandinetti, Federico Luppi, Leonardo Sbaraglia, Miguel Ángel Solá, or Cuban Jorge Perugorría, who have become part of the Spanish acting establishment.

Not even a provisional conclusion, as cinema continues

In 2007, there are still many uneasy and unresolved tensions between the Ministry of Culture, distributors and producers, as well as the directors, film crews and actors who want to be creative and earn a living. Yet in spite of funding difficulties and crises, and disparaging critics back home, Spanish directors are making some very interesting films that can hold their own in the global market. There are also many accomplished actors in their own right, increasingly attractive to international productions like Victoria Abril, Antonio Banderas, Javier Bardem, Penélope Cruz or Paz Vega. Although many films are not particularly successful, a varied and innovative cinema is being screened, whether as popcorn for entertainment or food for thought. Furthermore both popular and academic interest is growing exponentially as 'Spanish cinema has become popular' outside its own geographical borders (P. Evans, 2004: 250). The Manchester ¡Viva! Spanish Film Festival, which has been growing in influence since 1994, sends its films on tour to Ireland and throughout the UK, every year widening its reach, while the London Spanish Film Festival established itself in 2005, and for the more prosperous spectators the international film festivals dedicated to Spanish-language films have multiplied in the last ten years. International film festivals and foreign audiences are becoming increasingly interested as the recent Oscar nominations of *El laberinto del fauno* and for Penélope Cruz in *Volver* demonstrate. In 2007 Spanish Cinema can be optimistic and flourish, just as in the days of the silent reels and films, judging by the many copies viewed with foreign language intertitles, cinema was part of Spain's international exports (chapter 1).

Viewing and further general reading

Most of the books mentioned at the end of the previous chapter will still be useful for these last ten years, as more are being published and need to be written. *Sight & Sound* magazine reviews Spanish-language films when they are released in the UK. Jordan & Allinson (2005) and Stone (2002) provide useful websites and addresses at the end of their books, but since these are subject to changes it is perhaps less frustrating to initiate Internet searches (titles, directors, producers, etc.). The most useful page has been the International Movie Database (http://www.imdb.com/), which has greatly expanded over the time this book has been written and could provide useful information for those interested in reception theory. Also important, but less user-friendly, is the complementary Ministerio de Cultura, Cine y Audiovisuales, base de datos de películas calificadas (http://www.mcu.es/index.html), with its details of releases in Spain, on ticket sales and revenues. Both should be cross-checked, and both recommend official sites to visit. As well as the increasing availability of DVDs, a new webpage was launched on 27 March 2007, which allows the legal downloading of films for as little as one euro at www.filmotech.com.

The many gaps inevitably left in this chapter, and in the rest of the book, could suggest many new lines of future research. Expanding and refining the Index will also bring up further research topics. On the other hand, I would be grateful to receive comments and information about anything important that I have taken for granted and omitted.

FILMOGRAPHY BY DIRECTORS MENTIONED

The year given is that of the film's release. The English translation of the titles are taken from the *IMDb* to facilitate searches and cross-references so that the full filmography of each director can be accessed. When no English translation was available, my own is indicated by an asterisk.

Abad de Santillán, Diego: 1977 *Why Did We Lose The War?* / ¿*Por qué perdimos la guerra?* 241

Abadal, Baltasar: 1919 *Dream or Reality?* / ¿*Sueño o realidad?* 22

Abbadie d'Arrast-Soriano, Harry d': 1934 *The Miller's Mischievous Wife* / *It Happened in Spain* / *La traviesa molinera* 65, 125

Abril, Albert: 1993 *The Search for Happiness* / *La recerca de la felicitat* 289

Acosta, José Luis: 1996 *Gimlet* 311

Aguirre, Javier: 1965 *Candido's Jobs* / *Los oficios de Cándido* 189

——: 1968 *They who Play the Piano* / *Los que tocan el piano* 168

——: 1969 *Once a Year, Being a Hippy Is Not Harmful* / *Una vez al año, ser hippy no hace daño* 168

——: 1969 *Unmarried and Mother in Life* / *Soltera y madre en la vida* 168, 211 n. 21

——: 1970 *Waxing Leg and Waning Skirt* / *Pierna creciente, falda menguante* 209

——: 1972 *Father and Unmarried* / *Soltero y padre en la vida* 211

——: 1973 *I Will Be Born Again* / *Volveré a nacer* 163

——: 1974 *The Smiths's Most Unusual Pregnancy* / *El insólito embarazo de los Martínez* 201

——: 1975 *Oscillatory Vibrations* / *Vibraciones oscilatorias* 209

——: 1975 *Slightly Widowed* / *Ligeramente viuda* 209

——: 1980 *The Consensus* / *El consenso* 240

——: 1980 *Children's War* / *La guerra de los niños* 250

——: 1982 *A Dog's Life* / *Vida–Perra* 232

——: 1982 *Friday and Thirteenth, Don't Even Move!* / *Martes y Trece, ni te cases ni embarques* 305

——: 1987 *The Lieutenant Nun* / *La monja alférez* 260

Aibar, Oscar: 1995 *Tight Spot* / *Atolladero* 306

Albacete, Alfonso and Miguel Bardem and David Menkes: 1996 *Not Love, Just Frenzy* / *Más que amor, frenesí* 137 n. 28, 301 n. 16, 306, 337

Albacete, Alfonso and David Menkes: 1998 *Atomic* / *Atómica* 344

——: 1999 *I Will Survive* / *Sobreviviré* 344

——: 2001 *I Love You Baby* 344

——: 2004 *Searching for Love* / *Entre vivir y soñar* 344

Albaladejo, Miguel: 1998 *My First Night* / *La primera noche de mi vida* 341

——: 1999 *Manolito Four Eyes* / *Manolito Gafotas* 347

——: 2001 *Ten Days Without Love* / *El cielo abierto* 341

——: 2002 *Resentment* / Rencor*   331, 345

——: 2004 *Bearcub / Cachorro*   336

Alberich, Enric: 2004 *Red Sea* / Mar rojo*   337

Alcázar, Rafael: 1993 *The Greek Labyrinth / El laberinto griego*   291

Alcocer, Santos: 1965 *The Last Hours* / Las últimas horas*   170

Alexandre, Margarita and Rafael Torrecilla: 1954 *Jesus* / Cristo*   127 n. 12

——: 1954 *The Lost City* / La ciudad perdida*   124

——: 1956 *The Cat / La gata*   127

Alfonso, Raúl: 1947 *Heroes of 95* / Héroes del 95*   112

——: 1955 *The Moorish Queen* / La reina mora*   31, 126

Algora, Jorge: 2005 *Lying to Life / Viure de mentides / Mintiendo a la vida*   331

Almeida, Sebastián: 1960 *The Emigrant* / El emigrante*   142

Almodóvar, Pedro: 1980 *Pepi, Luci, Bom and Other Girls on the Heap / Pepi, Luci, Bom y otras chicas del montón*   251

——: 1982 *Labyrinth of Passions / Laberinto de pasiones*   228 n. 5, 251

——: 1983 *Dark Habits / Entre tinieblas*   251, 259

——: 1984 *What Have I Done to Deserve This?! / ¿Qué he hecho yo para merecer esto!!*   271–2, 319, 345

——: 1986 *Matador*   272

——: 1987 *Law of Desire / La ley del deseo*   272, 320

——: 1988 *Women on the Verge of a Nervous Breakdown / Mujeres al borde de un ataque de nervios*   273, 285 n. 4, 320

——: 1990 *Tie Me Up! / ¡Átame!*   163 n. 8, 285

——: 1991 *High Heels / Tacones lejanos*   285

——: 1993 *Kika*   285

——: 1995 *The Flower of my Secret / La flor de mi secreto*   285, 324

——: 1998 *Live Flesh / Carne trémula*   285, 334 n. 16

——: 1999 *All About My Mother / Todo sobre mi madre*   xiv, 285 n. 3, 324

——: 2002 *Talk to Her / Hable con ella*   xiv, 10 n. 19, 27, 285 n. 3, 324–5

——: 2002 *The Shrinking Lover* / El amante menguante*   10 n. 19, 325

——: 2004 *Bad Education / La mala educación*   325

——: 2006 *To Return / Volver*   285 n. 3, 325, 345, 351

Alonso, Luis: 1924 *Pitusin's Luck* / La buenaventura de Pitusín*   29

——: 1926 *The Mad Woman of the House* / La loca de casa*   84

Álvarez, Mercedes: 2004 *The Sky is Spinning* / El cielo gira*   327

Álvarez, Miguel: 2003 *My Home is Your Home* / Mi casa es tu casa*   348

Amadori, Luis: 1958 *The Flower Girl* / La violetera*   141, 153

——: 1958 *Where Are You Going Alfonso XII? / ¿Dónde vas Alfonso XII?*   141, 153

——: 1958 *A Girl from Valladolid / Una muchachita de Valladolid*   142

——: 1960 *My Last Tango / Mi último tango*   141

——: 1961 *A Sin of Love* / Pecado de amor*   141, 154

——: 1964 *Like Peas in a Pod* / Como dos gotas de agua*   162

——: 1968 *Cristina Guzmán*   96, 162

Amenábar, Alejandro: 1996 *Thesis / Tesis*   308, 321

——: 1997 *Open Your Eyes / Abre los ojos*   xv, 321

——: 2001 *The Others / Los otros*   321, 340

——: 2004 *The Sea Within / Mar adentro*   308 n. 23, 321

Amo, Álvaro del: 1980 *Two* / Dos*   252

——: 2003 *A Beautiful Sunset* / Una preciosa puesta de sol*   334

Amo, Antonio del: 1937 *Crossing the Ebro* / El paso del Ebro*   74

——: 1937 *The Path to Victory* / El camino de la victoria*   74

——: 1937 *Single Command* / Mando único*   74

——: 1948 *The Guest of the Mist* / El huésped de las tinieblas*   105

——: 1949 *Wings of Youth* / Alas de juventud*   113

——: 1949 *Ninety Minutes* / Noventa minutos*   113

——: 1951 *Day by Day / Día tras día*   131–2, 134

——: 1954 *The Fisher of Songs* / El pescador de coplas*   126

——: 1955 *Cursed Mountain / Sierra maldita*   127, 221

——: 1955 *The Sun Rises Every Day* / El sol sale todos los días*   144

——: 1956 *The Little Nightingale / El pequeño ruiseñor*   144

——: 1958 *The Nightingale Up High* / El ruiseñor de las cumbres*   144, 154

——: 1960 *The Little Colonel / El pequeño coronel*   144

——: 1961 *Beautiful Memory* / Bello recuerdo*   144

——: 1963 *Tommy's Secret* / El secreto de Tomy*   160

——: 1965 *Son of Jesse James / El hijo de Jesse James*   173

Amorós, Jordi 'Ja' *et al*: 1979 *Stories of Love and Massacre* / Historias de amor y de masacre*   252

——: 1990 *Sparks of the Catalan Sword* / Despertaferro*   252

Anglada, Eugeni: 1978 *Rage / La ràbia*   246

——: 1982 *Red Interior* / Interior Roig*   246

Anonymous: 1896 *Arrival of the Teruel Train at Segorbe* / Llegada de un tren de Teruel a Segorbe*   2

——: 1913 *The Bloody Inn* / La posada sangrienta*   19

——: 1920 *The Life and Death of Joselito* / La vida de Joselito y su muerte*   30

Aranda, Vicente: 1965 *Brilliant Future / Brillante Porvenir*   192

——: 1965/1967 *Left-Handed Fate / Fata Morgana*   192

——: 1969 *The Cruel Women – The Exquisite Corpse / Las crueles – El cadáver exquisito*   192, 212

——: 1972 *The Blood-Spattered Bride / La novia ensangrentada*   212

——: 1974 *Claire is the Price / Clara es el precio*   212

——: 1977 *Change of Sex / Cambio de sexo*   235

——: 1979 *Girl with the Golden Panties / La muchacha de las bragas de oro*   243, 247

——: 1982 *Murder in the Central Committee / Asesinato en el comité central*   247

——: 1984 *Fanny Strawtop / Fanny Pelopaja*   267

——: 1986 *Time of Silence / Tiempo de silencio*   196, 258, 264

——: 1987 *Lute (Walk On or Die)* / El Lute (camina o revienta)*   264

——: 1988 *Lute II: Free tomorrow* / El Lute II: Mañana seré libre*   264

——: 1989 *If They Tell You I Fell* / Si te dicen que caí*   262, 264

——: 1990 *Riders of the Dawn / Los jinetes del alba* (TV)   258

——: 1991 *Lovers / Amantes*   286, 320

——: 1993 *Intruder / Intruso*   290, 341 n. 22

——: 1993 *The Bilingual Lover / El amante bilingüe*   298

——: 1994 *Turkish Passion / La pasión turca*   286

——: 1996 *Freedomfighters / Libertarias*   286

——: 2001 *Madness of Joan / Juana la loca*   17 n. 26, 101 n. 37

——: 2003 *Carmen*   23, 330

——: 2006 *The Knight Tirante el Blanco* / Tirante el Blanco*   330

Arévalo, Carlos: 1940 *¡Harka!*   90, 92

——: 1942 *Red and Black* / Rojo y negro*   49, 86

Arias, Imanol: 1996 *A Private Matter* / Un asunto privado*   312–13

Aristarain, Adolfo: 1997 *Martin (H) / Martín (Hache)*   313, 350

——: 2004 *Roma*   350

Armendáriz, Montxo: 1984 *Tasio*　278, 320
——: 1986 *27 Hours / 27 horas*　278
——: 1990 *Letters from Alou / Las cartas de Alou*　289
——: 1995 *Stories from the Kronen / Historias del Kronen*　288–9, 333
——: 1997 *Secrets of the Heart / Secretos del corazón*　329
——: 2001 *Broken Silence / Silencio roto*　329
——: 2005 *Obaba*　348
Armiñán, Jaime de: 1969 *Carola by Day, Carola by Night* / Carola de día, Carola de noche*　219
——: 1970 *They Say Lola Doesn't Live Alone* / La Lola, dicen que no vive sola*　219
——: 1972 *My Dearest Señorita / Mi querida señorita*　138, 230 n. 8, 219, 231, 320
——: 1973 *A Chaste Spaniard* / Un casto varón español*　219
——: 1974 *The Love of Captain Brando / El amor del capitán Brando*　200 n. 2, 219–20
——: 1975 *Gosh, Dad* / Jo, papá*　219
——: 1977 *It's Never Too Late / Nunca es tarde*　232
——: 1978 *At the Service of Spanish Womanhood / Al servicio de la mujer española*　231
——: 1980 *The Nest / El nido*　232
——: 1982 *In September* / En septiembre*　268
——: 1985 *The Witching Hour / La hora bruja*　268
——: 1987 *My General / Mi general*　268
——: 1995 *The Lame Dove* / El palomo cojo*　288, 293
Arnold, Jack: 1957 USA, *The Incredible Shrinking Man*　10 n. 19
Arribas, Marta and Ana Pérez: 2005 *The Memory Train* / El tren de la memoria*　328
Arroyo, Luis: 1947 *Dulcinea*　104
Artigot, Raúl: 1984 *Low in Nicotine* / Bajo en nicotina*　234
Atienza, Juan G[arcía]: 1962 *The Dynamiters / Los dinamiteros*　148, 166, 196
Aured, Carlos: 1973 *The Return of Walpurgis / El retorno de Walpurgis*　207
Ayaso, Dunia and Felix Sabroso: 1997 *Excuse me Darling, but Lucas only Loved Me / Perdona bonita, pero Lucas me quería a mí*　310
——: 1998 *Shout Out / El grito en el cielo*　310
Azkona, Mauro: 1929 *The Basterretxe Inheritance* / El mayorazgo de Basterretxe*　34
Aznar, Adolfo and Joan Vilà Vilamala: 1936 *College Boarding House / La casa de la Troya*　32 n. 9, 66
Aznar, Adolfo: 1932 *Mendicity and Charity* / Mendicidad y caridad*　72
Aznar, Tomás: 1975 *The Book of Good Love / El libro de buen amor*　205
Bajo Ulloa, Juanma: 1991 *Butterfly Wings / Alas de mariposa*　307, 320
——: 1993 *The Dead Mother / La madre muerta*　307
——: 1997 *Airbag*　307
Balagué, Carlos: 1981 *Hurray for Pepa* / Viva la Pepa*　265
——: 1987 *Adela*　265
——: 1989 *Love is Strange* / L'amor és estrany / El amor es extraño*　265
——: 1993 *Lovesickness* / Mal d'amors / Mal de amores*　265
——: 1995/1996 *An Internal Affair* / Un assumpte intern / Asunto interno*　300–1
Balaguer, Manuel: 1998 *The Lighthouse* / El far*　275 n. 26
Balagueró, Jaume: 1999 *The Nameless / Los sin nombre*　340
Balañá, Pere: 1965 *The Last Saturday* / El último sábado*　169
Balcázar, Alfonso: 1960 *Where Are You Going so Sad?* / ¿Dónde vas triste de ti?*　141
Balcázar, Jaime J: 1969 *Doing it the Spanish Way* / Españolear*　201
Balletbò-Coll, Marta: 1995 *Costa Brava: Family Album*　310–11

——: 1998 *Darling, I've Sent the Men to the Moon* / *Cariño he enviado los hombres a la luna* 311

——: 2004 *Madame de Sévigné** / *Sévigné* 311

Ballester Bustos, Luis and Fumio Kurokawa: 1981 *Around the World with Willy Fog* / *La vuelta al mundo de Willy Fog* (TV) 252

Ballester Bustos, Luis and Shigeo Koshi: 1986 *Dogtanian and the Three Muskehounds* / *D'Artacan y los tres mosqueperros* (TV) 252

Baños, Ricard de: 1905 *Bohemians** / *Bohemios* 30

Baños, Ricard de and Albert Marro: 1908 *Don Juan Tenorio* 17, 260 n. 6

——: 1909 *The Mad Queen* / *Locura de amor* 17, 101 n. 37

——: 1910 *Don Juan de Serrallonga* / *Don Juan de Serrallonga, o los bandoleros de las Guillerías* 17

——: 1910 *Don Juan Tenorio,* remake 17

——: 1911 *King Peter the Cruel** / *Don Pedro el Cruel* 15–16

——: 1912 *The Lovers of Teruel** / *Los amantes de Teruel* 17

——: 1913 *The Power of Fate** / *La fuerza del destino* 17

——: 1914 *The Ill-Loved** / *La malquerida* 17, 27–8, 84

——: 1914 *In the Orange Grove** / *Entre naranjos* 17

——: 1916 *Blood and Sand* / *Sangre y arena* 17

Baños, Ricard de: 1918 *Strength and Nobility** / *Fuerza y nobleza* 22

——: 1918 *The Harlequins of Silk and Gold** / *Los arlequines de seda y oro* 24

——: 1919 *The White Gypsy Girl** / *La gitana blanca* 24

——: 1922 *Don Juan Tenorio,* 2nd remake 17

——: 1933 *The Locket** / *El relicario* 56, 201

Bará, Milagros: 2002 *Autopsy** / *Autopsia* 340

Barbéris, René: 1930 France, *Un Trou dans le mur* 52

Bardem, Juan Antonio: not released *Barajas, Trans-oceanic Airport* / *Barajas, aeropuerto transoceánico* 150

Bardem Juan Antonio and Luis G[arcía] Berlanga: 1951/1953 *That Happy Couple** / *Esa pareja feliz* 82, 102, 119, 133–4, 136, 144–5, 192 n. 43

Bardem, Juan Antonio: 1954 *Thespians** / *Cómicos* 137–8, 260 n. 10,

——: 1954 *Merry Christmas** / *Felices pascuas* 137

——: 1955 *Death of Cyclist* / *Muerte de un ciclista* 137–8, 142, 320

——: 1956 *Main Street* / *Calle Mayor* 69–70, 138, 180, 230 n. 8, 320

——: 1957 *Vengeance – The Harvesters** / *La venganza – Los segadores* 138

——: 1959 *Sonatas* 138–9, 151, 313

——: 1960 *At Five in the Afternoon* / *A las cinco de la tarde* 139, 142, 149, 180

——: 1962 *The Innocents** / *Los inocentes* 180

——: 1963 *Nothing Ever Happens* / *Nunca pasa nada* 177, 180

——: 1965 *The Mechanical Pianos** / *Los pianos mecánicos* 180

——: 1970 *Varieties* / *Variétés* 213

——: 1971 *The Mysterious Island of Dr Nemo* / *La isla misteriosa* 214

——: 1973 *The Corruption of Chris Miller** / *La corrupción de Chris Miller* 161–2, 213

——: 1975 *The Power of Desire** / *El poder del deseo* 162, 213–4

——: 1977 *The Long Weekend* / *El puente* 243

——: 1979 *Seven Days in January* / *Siete días de enero* 243

——: 1987 *Lorca, the Death of a Poet* / *Lorca, muerte de un poeta* 261

Bardem, Miguel: 1999 *The Ugliest Woman in the World* / *La mujer más fea del mundo* 337

——: 2004 *Swindled* / *Incautos* 337

Baroja, Pío and Julio Baroja: 1980 *Guipuzkoa*   241–2
Barroso, Mariano: 1990 *It is just that Inclan is Mad** / *Es que Inclán está loco*   306
——: 1994 *My Soul Brother* / *Mi hermano del alma*   306
——: 1996 *Ecstasy* / *Éxtasis*   306
Bartolomé, Cecilia: 1978 *Lets Go, Barbara** / *Vámonos, Bárbara*   230
——: 1996 *Far from Africa (Black Island)* / *Lejos de África* (*Black Island*)   230 n. 9, 290
Bartolomé, Cecilia and José Juan: 1981/1983 *And After...** / *Después de...*   241
Basterretxea, Néstor: 1964 *The Pelota Players** / *Pelotari*   170
——: 1968 *Mother Earth** / *Ama lur* / *Tierra Madre*   170
Basterretxea, Txabi and Joxan Muñoz: 2000 *Crab Island* / *La isla del cangrejo*   347–8
Bauer, James: 1936 *Don't Kill Me** / *No me mates*   70
Bautista, Emilio: 1929/ 1932 *The Cascorro Heroe** / *El héroe de Cascorro*   34, 46 n. 43
Bayarri, Jaime: 1976 *The Book of Good Love II* / *El libro de buen amor II*   205
Behrendt, Hans: 1934 *Doña Francisquita*   46 n. 43, 126
Belén, Ana: 1991 *How to be a Woman and not Die in the Attempt* / *Cómo ser mujer y no morir en el intento*   274, 287
Bell, Monta: 1926 USA, *The Torrent*   17
Bellmunt, Francesc: 1974 *Robin Hood Will Never Die** / *Robin Hood nunca muere*   222
——: 1975 *Rock from Canet** / *Canet Rock*   222
——: 1975 *The New Songs** / *La nova cançó*   222
——: 1978 *The Orgy* / *L'orgia*   222, 238
——: 1979 *Catalan Cuckold* / *Salut i força al canut* / *Cuernos a la catalana*   238
——: 1980 *The Stoned Recruits** / *La quinta del porro*   238
——: 1984 *Angel Bread* / *Pà d'àngel*   275
——: 1985 *A Pair of Eggs/Balls** / *Un parell d'ous*   275
——: 1986 *Crazy Radio** / *La ràdio folla*   275
——: 1988 *The Conspiracy of the Rings** / *El complot dels anells*   275
——: 1989 *A Black Man with a Saxophone** / *Un negro con un saxo*   275
Beltrán, José María: 1935 *Agrarian Reform** / *Reforma agraria*   73
——: 1935 *Sowing** / *Siembra*   73
——: 1937 *Guernika*   74
Ben Lyziad, Farida: 2005 *Juanita Narboni's Dirty Rotten Life** / *La vida perra de Juanita Narboni*   58 n. 14, 232 n. 11
Benavides, Alfonso: 1933/1935 *Madrid Gets Divorced** / *Madrid se divorcia*   70
Benpar, Carlos: 2006 *Film Makers vs Tycoons** / *Cineastas contra magnates*   348
——: 2006 *Film Makers in Action** / *Cineastes en acció*   348
Berasategi, Juan Bautista: 1998 *Ahmed, the Alhambra Prince** / *Ahmed, el príncipe de la Alhambra*   347
——: 2008 *The Spell of the South** / *El embrujo del Sur*   347
Berger, Pablo: 2003 *Torremolinos 73* / *Torremolinos 73*   209 n. 17, 348
Berlanga, José Luis: 1987 *High Districts** / *Barrios altos*   274
Berlanga, Luis G[arcía]: 1953 *Welcome Mr Marshall!* / *¡Bienvenido míster Marshall!*   133–6, 154, 319, 341 n. 21
——: 1954 *Boyfriend in Sight* / *Novio a la vista*   114, 135
——: 1956 *Calabuch*   135–6, 341
——: 1957 *Thursday Miracles** / *Los jueves, milagros*   136
——: 1961 *Plácido*   136–7, 177, 179, 319
——: 1964 *The Executioner** / *El verdugo*   179, 319

——: 1967 *The Piranhas / Las pirañas / La boutique* 179
——: 1970 *Long Live the Bride and Groom / Vivan los novios* 179–80, 214
——: 1974/1977 *Love Doll / Grandeur Nature / Tamaño natural* 180, 214, 219, 226, 341
——: 1978 *The National Shotgun / La escopeta nacional* 183 n. 34, 237
——: 1985 *The Heifer / La vaquilla* 261–2
——: 1987 *Moors and Christians / Moros y cristianos* 268–9
——: 1993 *Everyone off to Jail / Todos a la cárcel* 294
——: 1999 *Paris–Timbuktu / París–Tombuctú* 135 n. 24, 341
——: 2002 *The Teacher's Dream* / El sueño de la maestra* 134 n. 22, 341 n. 12
Bermejo, Alberto: 1981 *Neighbours* / Vecinos* 233–4
Bermúdez, Xavier: 2005 *Leon and Olvido / León y Olvido* 335
Berriatúa, Luciano: 1976/1979 *The Scrounger* / El buscón* 249
Bertolucci, Bernardo: 1972 France-Italy, *Last Tango in Paris* 200
Betancor, Antonio: 1982 *Valentina* 248–9, 258
——: 1983 *1919, Dawn Chronicle* / 1919, Crónica del alba* 248–9
——: 1998 *Mararía* 330
Betriu, Francesc: 1973 *The Lonely Heart / Corazón solitario* 221
——: 1975 *Spanish Fury / Furia española* 221, 238
——: 1977 *The Andalusian Widow* / La viuda andaluza* 250
——: 1980 *The Loyal Servants* / Los fieles sirvientes* 238
——: 1982 *Diamond Square* / La plaça del diamant / La plaza del diamant*e 248
——: 1985 *Requiem for a Spanish Farmhand* / Réquiem por un campesino español* 234, 258
——: 1997 *The Red Duchess* / La duquesa roja* 287
Biadiu, Ramon: 1934 *Don Quixote's Journey / La ruta de Don Quijote* 72–3
Bigas Luna, José Juan: 1976 *Tattoo / Tatuaje* 228–9
——: 1978 *Bilbao* 229, 320
——: 1979 *Poodle / Caniche* 229
——: 1981 *Reborn / Renacer* 247
——: 1986 *Lola* 265–6
——: 1987 *Anguish / Angustia* 266
——: 1990 *The Ages of Lulu / Las edades de Lulú* 287–8
——: 1992 *Ham Ham / Jamón, Jamón* 177 n. 29, 297
——: 1993 *Golden Balls / Huevos de oro* 297
——: 1994 *The Tit and the Moon / La teta i la lluna* 275 n. 26, 297–8
——: 1996 *Bámbola* 298
——: 1997 *The Chambermaid on the Titanic / La Femme de chambre du Titanic* 298
——: 1999 *Volavérunt* 298
Blackston, J. Stewart: 1907 USA, *The Haunted Hotel* 7
Blasco, Ricardo: 1961 *Guns against the Law* / Armas contra la ley* 148
——: 1962 *Autopsy of a Criminal / Autopsia de un criminal* 148
Blothner, Reinhardt: 1926 *The Four Robinsons* / Los cuatro Robinsones* 83 n. 8
Bodegas, Roberto: 1971 *Spaniards in Paris / Españolas en París* 163, 217
——: 1973 *Healthy Married Life / Vida conyugal sana* 217
——: 1974 *The New Spaniards / Los nuevos españoles* 217
——: 1975 *The Adulteress / La adúltera* 217
——: 1976 *Out on Parole / Libertad provisional* 217
——: 1988 *Kill Nani* / Matar al Nani* 264–5
——: 2002 *Condemned to Live* / Condenado a vivir* 321
Bollaín, Icíar: 1996 *Hi, Are You Alone? / Hola ¿estás sola?* 309

——: 1999 *Flowers from Another World / Flores de otro mundo* 333
——: 2003 *Take My Eyes / Te doy mis ojos* 331
Bollo, Joaquí: 1965 *Gipsy* / Gitana* 160
Bonilla, Jesús: 2003 *Moscow Gold / El oro de Moscú* 343
Borau, José Luis: 1960 *In the River* / En el río* 184
——: 1963 *Brandy* 185
——: 1964 *Double Edged Crime / Crimen de doble filo* 185
——: 1975 *B Must Die / Hay que matar a B* 185, 211–12, 219
——: 1975 *Poachers* / Furtivos* 182 n. 34, 185, 200 n. 2, 212, 320
——: 1979 *Sabina / La Sabina* 231–2
——: 1984 *On the Line / Río abajo* 265
——: 1986 *Dear Nanny / Tata mía* 263–4
——: 2000 *Leo* 184, 334
Borgnetto, Luigi: 1916 Italy, *Maciste Alpino* 10
Bosch, Juan: 1957 *Marked Paths* / Sendas marcadas* 148
——: 1959 *In Cold Blood / A sangre fría* 148
——: 1962 *Palma Bay / Bahía de Palma* 165
Bresson, Robert: 1951 France, *Le Journal d'un curé de campagne* 121
Buchs, José: 1921 *The Fair of the Dove / La verbena de la Paloma* 30–8, 59, 163
——: 1922 *The Moorish Queen* / La reina mora* 31, 126
——: 1922 *Carcelera, Prison Songs* / Carceleras* 31, 56
——: 1922 *Moroccan Soul* / Alma rifeña* 31, 38
——: 1923 *Doloretes* 31
——: 1924 *The Cleansing Stain* / Mancha que limpia* 31
——: 1924 *Diego Corrientes* 71
——: 1925 *The Grandfather* / El abuelo* 33, 47, 84 n. 11, 205
——: 1925 *The Convent Child* / El niño de las monjas* 59
——: 1926 *Pilar Guerra* 33 n. 15, 47
——: 1927 *The Count of Maravillas* / El conde de Maravillas* 33
——: 1929 *The Old King who Raged* / El rey que rabió* 83
——: 1931 *General Prim* / Prim* 36 n. 20, 52
——: 1931 *Isabel de Solís, Queen of Granada / Isabel de Solís, reina de Granada* 52
——: 1932 *Carcelera, Prison Song / Carceleras* (remake) 31, 56
——: 1935 *Mother Happiness* / Madre Alegría* 59
——: 1935 *The Convent Child* / El niño de las monjas* 59
——: 1936 *The Lightning Bolt* / El rayo* 66
——: 1939 *The Old King who Raged* / El rey que rabió* (remake) 83
——: 1942 *A Famous Gentleman* / Un caballero famoso* 106
Buchs, Julio: 1964 *The Wages of Crime / El salario del crimen* 170
Buñuel, Luis: 1928 *An Andalusian Dog / Un Chien andalou* 41–5, 47, 73, 151, 193
——: 1930 *The Age of Gold* / L'Âge d'or* 38, 42–5, 47, 49, 55, 60, 64, 151
——: 1933 *Land Without Bread / Tierra sin pan, Las Hurdes* 42, 52–3, 326
——: 1935 *Juan Simon's Daughter* / La hija de Juan Simón* see Sáenz de Heredia, José Luis
——: 1935 *The Embittered Don Quentin* / Don Quintín el amargao* see Marquina, Luis
——: 1937 *Sentry, Keep Watch!* / ¡Centinela alerta!* see Grémillon, Jean
——: 1950 Mexico, *The Forgotten Ones / The Young and the Damned / Los olvidados* 11, 130, 132
——: 1951 Mexico, *Daughter of Deceit / La hija del engaño* 34, 60
——: 1952 Mexico, *Mexican Bus Ride / Subida al cielo* 29

——: 1953 Mexico, *This Strange Passion / El* 184

——: 1958 Mexico, *Nazarín* 84, 151, 180

——: 1960 Mexico-USA, *The Young One* 151

——: 1961 (Spain)-Mexico, *Viridiana* 42, 90 n. 21, 134 n. 21, 151–2, 180, 192 n. 43, 194, 216, 226, 319

——: 1969 France, *The Milky Way / La Voie lactée* 42

——: 1970 France-Italy-Spain, *Tristana* 42, 84 n. 11, 172, 180–1, 196, 216, 320

——: 1977 France, *That Obscure Object of Desire / Cet Obscur Objet du désir* 42, 217, 226, 231

Buscarini, Juan Pablo: 2006 *The Hairy Tooth Fairy / Pérez, el ratoncito de tus sueños* 347

Cadena, Jordi: 1981 *Barcelona South* / Barcelona Sur* 247

——: 1987 *The Lady of the House* / La senyora* 276

——: 1988 *I See Clearly when I Sleep* / És quan dormo que hi veig clar / Al dormir lo veo claro* 276–7

——: 1991 *The Aspern Papers / Els papers d'Aspern* 277

——: 1993 *Nexus* / Nexo* 293

Calparsoro, Daniel: 1995 *Leap into the Void / Salto al vacío* 307

——: 1996 *Passages / Pasajes* 307–8

——: 1997 *Blinded / A ciegas* 308

——: 2000 *The City* / Asfalto* 333–4, 339

——: 2002 *Warriors / Guerreros* 302, 339

——: 2005 *The Absent / Ausentes* 334 n. 16, 339

Calvache, Antonio: 1940 *Boy* 37

Calvo Sotelo, Álex: 1999 *Fullmonties Wanted* / Se buscan fulmontis* 332

Camacho, Francisco: 1929 *Zalacaín, the Adventurer* / Zalacaín el aventurero* 34–5, 46 n. 43

——: 1936 *The Village Priest* / El cura de aldea* 59

Camino, Jaime: 1963/1969 *The Happy Sixties / Los felices sesenta* 191

——: 1967 *Tomorrow is Another Day / Mañana será otro día* 191

——: 1968 *Spain Again / España otra vez* 191

——: 1969 *A Winter in Mallorca / Un invierno en Mallorca* 191

——: 1973 *My Private Teacher / Mi profesora particular* 213

——: 1976 *Long Vacation of 36 / Las largas vacaciones del 36* 244

——: 1977/1978 *The Old Memory / La vieja memoria* 240–1

——: 1984 *The Open Balcony* / El balcón abierto* 261

——: 1986 *Dragon Rapide* 261

——: 1988 *Lights and Shadows / Luces y sombras* 260

——: 1992 *The Long Winter of 39 / El largo invierno* 301

——: 2001 *The Children of Russia / Los niños de Rusia* 328

Campo, Enrique del: 1940 *Battleship Baleares* / El crucero Baleares* 85

Campoy, Eduardo: 1990 *Alone with You* / A solas contigo* 307

——: 1992 *Too Much Heart / Demasiado corazón* 307

——: 1997 *To the Limit / Al límite* 307

Camus, Mario: 1964 *Frauds* / Los farsantes* 187, 262 n. 10

——: 1964 *Young Sánchez* 184

——: 1966 *With the East Wind / Con el viento solano* 184

——: 1966 *When You Are Not Here* / Cuando tú no estás* 163

——: 1967 *At Sunset* / Al ponerse el sol* 163

——: 1968 *Let Them Talk / Digan lo que digan* 163

——: 1969 *That Woman / Esa mujer* 184

——: 1970 *The Wind's Anger* / *La cólera del viento*   211
——: 1972 *The Legend of the Mayor of Zalamea** / *Leyenda del alcalde de Zalamea*   205, 211
——: 1975 *The Birds of Baden Baden* / *Los pájaros de Baden Baden*   211
——: 1975 *The Young Bride* / *La joven casada*   211
——: 1978 *The Days of the Past* / *Los días del pasado*   162, 245
——: 1980 *Fortunata and Jacinta** / *Fortunata y Jacinta*   248
——: 1982 *The Beehive* / *La colmena*   248, 258, 320
——: 1984 *The Holy Innocents* / *Los santos inocentes*   204, 227 n. 4, 248, 258, 319
——: 1987 *The House of Bernarda Alba* / *La casa de Bernarda Alba*   259
——: 1987 *The Russian Woman** / *La Rusa*   265
——: 1992 *After the Dream* / *Después del sueño*   292
——: 1993 *Shadows in a Conflict* / *Sombras en una batalla*   292
——: 1996 *Suburbs* / *Adosados*   290
——: 1998 *The Return of El Coyote* / *La vuelta de El Coyote*   173 n. 22
——: 1999 *The City of Wonders** / *La ciudad de los prodigios*   301
Canel, Fausto: 1982 *Power Game* / *Juego de poder*   247
Capra, Frank: 1934 USA, *It Happened One Night*   58
——: 1944 USA, *It's a Wonderful Life*   94
Carax, Leos: 1991 France, *Les Amants du Pont-neuf*   341 n. 22
Cardona, René: 1960 *Adventures of Joselito and Tom Thumb* / *Aventuras de Joselito en América*   144
Carné, Marcel: 1938 France, *Quai des brumes*   71–2
Carnevale, Marcos: 2000 *Clams and Mussels* / *Almejas y mejillones*   350
——: 2005 *Elsa and Fred* / *Elsa y Fred*   350
Carrasco, Agustín: 1925 *Bride to Be** / *Pepita Jiménez*   205
Carreño, José María: 1990 *Black Sheep** / *Ovejas negras*   312
Carreras, José: 1916 *Charlie II and his Family** / *Charlot II y su familia*   29
Carreras, Michael: 1962 *The Savage Guns* / *Tierra brutal*   173
Carruthers, Bob: 1995 UK, *The Bruce*   101 n. 38
Carter, Chris: 1993–2002 USA, *X Files* / *Expediente X* (TV)   339
Carvajal, Pedro and Fernando Bauluz: 1991 *Mardi Gras Carnival** / *Martes de Carnaval*   312
Carvajal, Pedro: 1994 *The Dance of Souls** / *El baile de las ánimas*   312
——: 1996 *Latin Flavour* / *Sabor Latino*   312
Castellví, José María: 1944 *The Man Who Makes Them Fall in Love** / *El hombre que se las enamora*   94
Catalán, Feliciano: 1954 *A Plot on the Stage** / *Intriga en el escenario*   130
Caton-Jones, Michael: 1995 USA, *Rob Roy*   33, 101–2
Cattaneo, Peter: 1997 UK, *The Full Monty*   332
Cebrián, Daniel: 2000 *Sleighbell, Ankle Bracelet** / *Cascabel*   337–8, 346
Ceret, Domènec: 1915 *Excentric Series** / *Serie excéntrica*   29
Chaplin, Charles: 1914 USA, *A Busy Day*   28
——: 1931 USA, *City Lights*   141 n. 36
Chávarri, Jaime: 1974 *School Trip* / *Los viajes escolares*   222
——: 1976 *The Disenchantment* / *El desencanto*   222, 241, 302, 320
——: 1977 *To an Unknown God* / *A un dios desconocido*   235
——: 1980 *Dedicated to...* / *Dedicatoria*   232
——: 1982 *Luis and Virginia** / *Luis y Virginia*   249
——: 1983 *Bearn or the Dolls' Room** / *Bearn o la sala de las muñecas*   249, 258
——: 1984 *Bicycles are for the Summer* / *Las bicicletas son para el verano*   261

——: 1986 *The Golden River / El río de oro* 267

——: 1989 *The Things of Love / Las cosas del querer* 217

——: 1993 *Tender Summer of Lust on the Rooftops / Tierno verano de lujurias y azoteas* 293

——: 1995 *The Things of Love, Part Two* / Las cosas del querer, segunda parte* 271

——: 1996 *The Great Slalom* / Gran slalom* 296

——: 2000 *Kisses for Everyone / Besos para todos* 346

Chavarrías, Antonio: 1989 *A Shadow in the Garden* / Una ombra en el jardí / Una sombra en el jardín* 276

——: 1992 *Club Manila* / Manila* 291

——: 1996 *Susanna* 289

Chomón, Segundo de: 1902 *Train Crash / Choque de trenes* 7

——: 1904 *The Park Dandies* / Los guapos del parque* 7

——: 1904 *Tom Thumb / Pulgarcito* 7

——: 1905 *Gulliver in the Land of the Giants / Gulliver en el país de los gigantes* 7

——: 1905 *The Electric Hotel / El hotel eléctrico* 7–9

——: 1908 *Chinese Games* / Les Kiriki / Juegos chinos* 9

——: 1908 *Metamorphoses* / Les Vêtements cascadeurs / Transformaciones* 9–10

——: 1908? *Circus Act* / Atracción de circo* 10

——: 1909 *Journey to Jupiter* / Viaje a Jupiter* 10

——: 1910 *Poor Valbuena* / El pobre Valbuena* 10

——: 1910 *Carcelera, Prison Songs* / Carceleras* 10, 31

——: 1911 *The Daydream / Soñar despierto* 10

——: 1911 *The Handful of Roses* / El puñado de rosas* 10

Chumilla, Juan Manuel: 1996 *Loves that Kill* / Amores que matan* 296

Cirici Pellicer, Alexandre: 1950 *Once upon a time* / Érase una vez* 98

Codina, Josep Maria and Joan Maria: 1911 *Lethal Love* / Amor que mata* 13–15, 23

Codina, Josep Maria: 1912 *The Orchard Idiot* / El tonto de la huerta* 13

——: 1915 *The Sign of the Tribe* / El signo de la tribu* 22

Coira, Jorge: 2004 *The Year of the Tick / O ano da carracha / El año de la garrapata* 332

Coixet, Isabel: 1989 *Too Old to Die Young* / Demasiado viejo para morir joven* 308

——: 1996 *Things I Never Told You / Cosas que nunca te dije* 309, 323

——: 1998 *Those Who Love / A los que aman* 323

——: 2003 *My Life Without Me / Mi vida sin mí* 323

——: 2005 *The Secret Life of Words / La vida secreta de las palabras* 323–4

Coll, Julio: 1956 *Never Too Late* / Nunca es demasiado tarde* 148

——: 1958 *The Fifth Precinct* / Distrito quinto* 148

——: 1959 *A Glass of Whisky / Un vaso de whisky* 148

——: 1962 *The Crows* / Los cuervos* 148

——: 1964 *Fire / Fuego* 171

——: 1966 *High Season for Spies / Comando de asesinos* 171

——: 1968 *The Narco Men / Persecución hasta Valencia* 171

——: 1971 *The Araucana* / La Araucana* 171–2

Colomo, Fernando: 1977 *Paper Tigers* / Tigres de papel* 233

——: 1978 *What is a Girl like You Doing in a Place like This? / ¿Qué hace una chica como tú en un sitio como éste?* 233

——: 1980 *The Black Hand / La mano negra* 233

——: 1982 *I'm having a Crisis* / ¡Estoy en crisis!* 233

——: 1983 *Skyline / La línea del cielo* 233, 266, 298

——: 1985 *Star Knight / El caballero del Dragón* 266

——: 1987 *This Happy Life* / La vida alegre*   270

——: 1988 *Miss Caribe*   270

——: 1989 *Going South Shopping / Bajarse al moro*   270

——: 1993 *Rosa, rosae*   287

——: 1994 *Cheerful, but not Too Much* / Alegre ma non troppo*   288

——: 1995 *The Butterfly Effect / El efecto mariposa*   298

——: 1998 *The Stolen Years/ Los años bárbaros*   82, 329

——: 1999 *Havana Quartet / Cuarteto de La Habana*   350

——: 2003 *South from Granada / Al sur de Granada*   330

Comas, Ramón: 1968 *The Singing Priest* / Padre Coplillas*   159

Comencini, Luigi: 1991 *The Miracle of Marcelino / Marcelino, pan y vino*   122

Comerón, Lluís Josep: 1986 *Puzzle*   267–8

Contel, Raúl: 1983 *The Voyeur* / L'home ronyó*   276

——: 1984 *Silent Screams* / Crits sords*   276

——: 1990–1991 *Mud People* / Gent de fang / Gente de barro*   276

Contrera Torres, Miguel: 1927 *The Locket / El relicario*   56, 201

Corbiau, Gérard: 1995 France-Italy, *Farinelli*   301

Corcuera, Javier: 2000 *The Back of the World / La espalda del mundo*   327

——: 2002 *The Guerrilla of Memory / La guerrilla de la memoria*   328

Cortés, Eduard: 2000 *The Cave* / La caverna*   337

——: 2002 *Nobody's Life / La vida de nadie*   339

——: 2003 *Death Card* / Carta mortal*   339

——: 2003 *Mónica*   340

——: 2004 *With a 10 on his Shirt* / Amb el 10 a l'esquena / El 10 en la espalda*   334–5

Cortesina, Helena: 1921 *The Flower of Spain or the Legend of a Bullfighter* / Flor de España o la leyenda de un torero*   30, 36 n. 20

Costa, Pedro: 1984 *The Almería Affair* / El caso Almería*   264

——: 1995 *House Out of Town / Una casa en las afueras*   290

——: 1997 *The Case of the Oriente Cinema / El crimen del cine Oriente*   290

——: 2003 *Harassment* / Acosada*   340

——: 2004 *My Dear Victims* / Mis estimadas víctimas*   338

Costafreda, Ramón: 2005 *More than Siblings* / Más que hermanos*   335

Courtois, Miguel: 2004 *Wolf / El lobo*   223, 340

Cromwell, John: 1937 USA, *The Prisoner of Zenda*   86

Cronenberg, David: 1986 UK-USA, *The Fly*   9 n. 17

Crosland, Alan: 1927 USA, *Jazz Singer*   50, 53 n. 8

Crowe, Cameron: 2001 USA *Vanilla Sky*   xv, 321

Cruz, Ángel de la and Manolo Gómez: 2001 *The Living Forest / El bosque animado*   347

——: 2005 *Midsummer Dream / El sueño de una noche de San Juan*   347

Cruz Delgado, Palomo: 1974 *Magic Adventure / Mágica aventura*   176, 252

——: 1978 *Don Quijote de la Mancha* (TV)   252

——: 1983 *Gulliver's Travels* / Los viajes de Gulliver* (TV)   252

——: 1987 *The Four Musicians of Bremen* / Los cuatro músicos de Bremen*   252

Cuadrilla, La [Santiago Aguilar and Luis Guridi]: 1994 *Justino, Senior Citizen Killer / Justino, un asesino de la tercera edad*   306

——: 1996 *Mathias, the Linesman* / Matías, juez de línea*   306

——: 1998 *Atilano for President / Atilano presidente*   306

Cuerda, José Luis: 1982 *Odd and Even* / Pares y nones*   234

——: 1985 *Unlucky Streak* / Mala racha*   269

——: 1987 *The Enchanted Forest** / *El bosque animado* 269
——: 1989 *It's Dawn and No Mean Feat** / *Amanece que no es poco* 269, 320
——: 1992 *The Sow** / *La marrana* 301–2
——: 1993 *Hitting Rock Bottom** / *Tocando fondo* 295
——: 1995 *On Earth as it is in Heaven** / *Así en el cielo como en la tierra* 295
——: 1999 *Butterfly's Tongue* / *La lengua de las mariposas* 328
——: 2006 *The Education of Fairies* / *La educación de las hadas* 345
Cuesta, Antonio and Ángel García Cardona: 1906 *The Village Blind Man** / *El ciego de la aldea* 11–14
Cuesta, Antonio: 1908 *The Little Shepherd from Torrent** / *El pastorcito de Torrent* 13
Cukor, George: 1936 USA, *Romeo and Juliet* 113
Curtiz, Michael: 1943 USA, *Casablanca* 267
Cussó-Ferrer, Manuel: 1988 *Intermission** / *Entreacte* 277
——: 1992 *His Last Frontier** / *L'última frontera* 302–3
——: 1998 *Babaouo* 42, 303
Cuyàs, Narciso: 1908 *Don Quixote* / *Don Quijote* 11
Dassin, Jules: 1955 France, *Du rififi chez les hommes* 171
Decoin, Henry and Luis María Delgado: 1951 *Love and Desire* / *El deseo y el amor* / *Le Désir et l'amour* 131–2
Delgado, Fernando: 1919 *The Rose Madonna** / *La Madona de las rosas* 27, 36 n. 20
——: 1924 *The Little Rascals** / *Los granujas* 29, 34, 36 n. 20
——: 1927 *The Mendez Women** / *Las de Méndez* 35, 36 n. 20
——: 1927 *The Terrible Experience** / *La terrible lección* 35, 36 n. 20
——: 1934 *Twelve Men and a Woman* / *Doce hombres y una mujer* 62
——: 1936 *Currito of the Cross* / *Currito de la Cruz* 30, 65, 107 n. 45
——: 1936/1939 *A Cheerful Disposition** / *El genio alegre* 72, 78
——: 1936 *Towards a New Spain** / *Hacia una nueva España* 78
——: 1936 *Bilbao for Spain** / *Bilbao para España* 78
——: 1937 *Santander for Spain** / *Santander para España* 78
——: 1937 *Asturias for Spain** / *Asturias para España* 78
——: 1937 *General Mola's Funeral** / *Entierro del General Mola* 78
——: 1937 *The Navarrese Brigades** / *Brigadas de Navarra* 78
——: 1940 *The Little Gipsy girl* / *La gitanilla* 84, 111 n. 51
——: 1942 *Fortunato* 93
——: 1942 *Our Homeland** / *La patria chica* 107
Delgado, Jesús: 1995 *The Child of Your Dreams** / *La niña de tus sueños* 308
Delgado, Luis María: 1962 *Different* / *Diferente* 162
——: 1972 *Handsome Heir Seeks a Bride** / *Guapo heredero busca esposa* 204
——: 1972 *When the Horn Sounds* / *Cuando el cuerno suena* 204
——: 1981 *Where Can My Son Be?** / *¿Dónde estará mi niño?* 249–50
——: 1982 *Circus Mad* / *Loca por el circo* 250
Delgrás, Gonzalo: 1939 *The Complete Idiot** / *La tonta del bote* 84, 168
——: 1942 *A Fixed-Price Husband** / *Un marido a precio fijo* 95
——: 1942 *Countess Maria** / *La condesa María* 34 n. 18, 95
——: 1943 *Cristina Guzmán* 96, 162
——: 1944 *The High Altar** / *Altar mayor* 96
——: 1957 *Juan Simón's Daughter* / *La hija de Juan Simón* 61, 142
——: 1958 *The Christ of the Lamps** / *El Cristo de los faroles* 142
——: 1960 *Chinitas's Café** / *Café de Chinitas* 142
Demicheli, Tulio: 1959 *A Girl Against Napoleon* / *Carmen la de Ronda* 141, 149
——: 1978 *Lend Her to Me for the Night** / *Préstamela esta noche* 249

DeMille, Cecil B: 1915 USA, *Carmen*   23
Demme, Jonathan: 1991 USA, *The Silence of the Lambs*   290
Diamante, Julio: 1962/1965 *We Who Did Not Go to War** / *Los que no fuimos a la guerra*   188
——: 1964 *Time for Loving** / *Tiempo de amor*   188–9
——: 1965 *The Art of Living* / *El arte de vivir*   189
——: 1974 *Sex or no Sex** / *Sex o no sex*   209
——: 1976 *Carmen* / *La Carmen*   209
Díaz Morales, José: 1948 *Loyola, the Soldier Saint* / *El capitán de Loyola*   103
——: 1963 *The Mischief-Maker** / *La revoltosa*   163
Díaz Torres, Daniel: 2005 *Playing Swede* / *Hacerse el sueco*   350
Díaz Yanes, Agustín: 1995 *Nobody Will Speak of Us When We're Dead* / *Nadie hablará de nosotras cuando hayamos muerto*   307, 320
——: 2001 *No News from God* / *Don't Tempt Me* / *Sin noticias de Dios*   341
——: 2006 *Captain Alatriste* / *Alatriste*   330
Dieterle, William: 1938 USA, *Blockade*   74
Díez, Ana: 1989 *Ander and Yul** / *Ander eta Yul*   277
——: 1997 *All is Dark** / *Todo está oscuro*   277, 313
Díez, Miguel Ángel: 1985 *Bohemian Nights* / *Luces de Bohemia*   259
Domínguez Rodiño, Enrique: 1939 *Moroccan Ballads** / *Romancero marroquí*   79
Doria, Juan: 1913 *Carmen*   23
Drossner, Charles: 1916 *The Life of Christopher Columbus** / *La vida de Cristóbal Colón*   23–4
Drove, Antonio: 1974 *Lolita's Toccata and Fugue** / *Tocata y fuga de Lolita*   200 n. 2, 218
——: 1974 *My Wife is Very Respectable, Given the Circumstances** / *Mi mujer es muy decente, dentro de lo que cabe*   218
——: 1980 *The Truth on the Savolta Affair* / *La verdad sobre el caso Savolta*   247, 301
——: 1987 *The Tunnel* / *El túnel*   262 n. 10
Dunning, George: 1968 UK-USA, *Yellow Submarine*   176
Durán, Carlos: 1968 *Each time that…** / *Cada vez que…*   193
——: 1970 *Liberxina 90* / *Liberxina 90*   193
Eceiza, Antxon: 1963/1967 *Next Autumn** / *El próximo otoño*   188, 247
——: 1967 *Last Meeting** / *Último encuentro*   188
——: 1967 *Lying in State** / *De cuerpo presente*   188
——: 1970 *Secret Intentions** / *Las secretas intenciones*   188
——: 1990 *Days of Smoke** / *Días de humo* / *Ke arteko egunak*   300
——: 1995 *Congratulations, Tovarish** / *Felicidades, tovarish*   300
Eguiluz, Enrique: 1967 *The Mark of the Wolfman* / *La marca del hombre lobo*   174–5, 207
Elejalde, Karra: 2000 *Holy Mary* / *Año Mariano*   342
——: 2004 *Therabull** / *Torapia*   342
Elías, Francisco: 1928 *Pitouto Suicide Manufacturer** / *Pitouto, fabricante de suicidios*   29
——: 1930 *The Mystery of the Puerta del Sol** / *El misterio de la Puerta del Sol*   53–5
—— and José María Castellví: 1930 *Cinopolis* / *Cinópolis*   51, 94
—— and Camille Lemoine: 1932 *Pax*   56
Elías, Francisco: 1933 *Boliche*   57
——: 1935 *Rataplán*   57
——: 1936/1939 *María de la O*   65
——: 1939 *Bohemians** / *Bohemios*   30 n. 7, 65

——: 1955 *Marta* 57
Elordi, Juanjo 2002 *Olentzero: A Christmas story* / Olentzero: un cuento de Navidad* 347
——: 2005 *Olentzero and the Magic Tree Trunk* / Olentzero y el tronco mágico* 347
Elorrieta, Javier: 1993 *Wild Boys / Cautivos de la sombra* 290
——: 1996 *Too Hot for You* / Demasiado caliente para ti* 290
Elorrieta, José María 1960 *The University Chorus* / Pasa la tuna* 142
——: 1961 *Cradle song / Canción de cuna* 122
Enright, Ray: 1939 USA, *Angels Wash their Faces* 121
Epstein, Jean: 1928 France, *La Chute de la maison Usher* 41
Erice, Víctor: 1973 *The Spirit of the Beehive / El espíritu de la colmena* 64, 82, 177 n. 29, 221–2, 224, 235, 319
——: 1983 *The South / El sur* 258, 309, 319
——: 1992 *The Dream of Light / El sol del membrillo* 302
Escobar, Luis: 1950 *The Honesty of the Keyhole* / La honradez de la cerradura* 109
Escrivá, Vicente: 1963 *A Girl from La Mancha / Dulcinea* 104, 171
——: 1971 *Even if Hormones Wear Silk* / Aunque la hormona viste seda* 204
——: 1972 *The Inquisitive One / La curiosa* 204
——: 1973 *Smut Starts at the Pyrenees / Lo verde empieza en los Pirineos* 201, 204
——: 1976 *The Lascivious Andalusian* / La lozana andaluza* 239
——: 1977 *Girls... To the Drawing Room!* / Niñas... ¡al salón!* 239
——: 1978 *Visanteta's Virgin / El virgo de Visanteta* 239
——: 1979 *Visanteta, Be Still* / Visanteta, esta-te queta* 239
Esteban, Cristina: 1994 *If Only, Val del Omar / Ojalá, Val del Omar* 73 n. 31
Esteban, Manuel: 1992 *The South Seas* / Los mares del sur* 291
——: 1994 *Tales of the Stinking Military Service / Historias de la puta mili* 295
Esterlich, Juan: 1976 *The Anchorite / El anacoreta* 238
Esteva Crewe, Jacinto and Joaquim Jordà: 1967 *Dante is not Only Severe* / Dante no es únicamente severo* 193
Esteva Crewe, Jacinto: 1968 *After the Flood / Después del diluvio* 193
——: 1970 *Metamorphosis* / Metamorfosis* 193
——: 1970/1972 *Far from the Trees / Lejos de los árboles* 193
Estívalis, José María: 1936 *Flesh for Beasts* / Carne de fieras* 72
Faidellá, Juan: 1935 *A Mistake of Youth* / Error de juventud* 70
Farrow, John: 1959 USA, *John Paul Jones* 172
Feliu, Jordi: 1976/1984 *Alice in Spanish Wonderland / Alicia en la España de las maravillas* 246
——: 1981 *We Are and Will Be* / Som i serem* 246
Fellini, Federico: 1961 Italy, *La dolce vita* 150, 350
——: 1963 Italy, *Otto e mezzo* 160
Fernán Gómez, Fernando: 1956 *The Evil Carabel* / El malvado Carabel* 62 n. 20
——: 1958 *Life Ahead / La vida por delante* 145, 177, 320
——: 1959 *Life around us / La vida alrededor* 145
——: 1960 *For Men Only* / Sólo para hombres* 177–8
——: 1961 *Don Mendo's Revenge* / La venganza de don Mendo* 178
——: 1963 *Life Goes On* / El mundo sigue* 178
——: 1964/1967 *Strange Journey / El extraño viaje* 177–9, 320
——: 1966 *For Adults, with Caution* / Mayores con reparos* 179
——: 1970 *Imperfect Crime* / Crimen imperfecto* 213
——: 1971 *How to Get Married in Seven Days* / Cómo casarse en siete días* 213
——: 1974 *I Saw Her First / Yo la vi primero* 213

——: 1975 *The Mistress / La querida*   213

——: 1977 *My Daughter Hildegart / Mi hija Hildegart*   231

——: 1977 *Witch, Nothing but a Witch* / Bruja, más que bruja*   250

——: 1979 *Five Forks / Cinco tenedores*   238

——: 1986 *Mambrú Went to War / Mambrú se fue a la guerra*   263

——: 1986 *Voyage to Nowhere / El viaje a ninguna parte*   257, 262, 320

——: 1989 *Time and the Sea* / El mar y el tiempo*   262–3

——: 1991 *Offsides / Fuera de juego*   294

——: 1994 *Long Life Together / Siete mil días juntos*   296

——: 1996 *Nightmare for a Wealthy Man* / Pesadilla para un rico*   296

—— and José Luis García Sánchez: 2001 *Lázaro de Tormes*   149

Fernández, Ramón: 1961 *My Love is called Margarita* / Margarita se llama mi amor*   142

——: 1964 *Line-up of Suspects* / Rueda de sospechosos*   170

——: 1968 *Sister Yeah-Yeah* / Sor Ye-Ye*   159

——: 1970 *Thou Shalt not Covet thy Fifth Floor Neighbour / No desearás al vecino del quinto*   203, 235

——: 1971 *We're Counting on You, Simon* / Simón contamos contigo*   204

——: 1971 *Christ of the Ocean / El Cristo del océano*   205 n. 14

——: 1971 *The Limping Devil* / El diablo cojuelo*   205

——: 1972 *My Wife's Boyfriends* / Los novios de mi mujer*   204

——: 1975 *The Adulterer* / El adúltero*   204

——: 1982 *The Great Big Fuss* / El gran mogollón*   240

Fernández Ardavín, César: 1952 *The Call of Africa* / La llamada de África*   128

——: 1954 *An Impossible Crime? / ¿Crimen imposible?*   129

——: 1957 *And She Chose Hell* / Y eligió el infierno*   123

——: 1959 *Lazarillo de Tormes*   149

——: 1969 *The Wanton of Spain / La Celestina*   171

——: 1977 *Doña Perfecta*   249

Fernández Ardavín, Eusebio: 1928 *The Rose of Madrid* / La rosa de Madrid*   35

——: 1933 *Water in the Ground / Agua en el suelo*   57

——: 1935 *Broken Lives / Vidas rotas*   57, 62–3

——: 1935 *She Who Is Well Paid* / La bien pagada*   57

——: 1937 *The Moorish Queen* / La reina mora*   31, 126

——: 1940 *The Strange Marchioness* / La marquesona*   84

——: 1940 *The Queen's Flower Girl* / La florista de la reina*   84, 92, 97, 100

——: 1943 *The Standard Bearer* / El abanderado*   99

——: 1946 *The Queen's Little Soldier* / El doncel de la reina*   100

——: 1953 *The Beauty from Cadiz* / La bella de Cádiz*   108

Fernández Armero, Álvaro: 1994 *Life, a Bitch / Todo es mentira*   305

——: 1996 *Witches* / Brujas*   305

——: 2000 *The Art of Dying / El arte de morir*   338

Fernández Cuenca, Carlos: 1927 *He's My Man!* / ¡Es mi hombre!*   46 n. 43, 69

——: 1942 *Tanger Mysteries* / Los misterios de Tánger*   108

Fernández Santos, Jesús: 1964 *To Move On* / Llegar a más*   169

Ferreira, Patricia: 2000 *I Know Who You Are / Sé quién eres*   340

——: 2002 *The Impatient Alchemist / El alquimista impaciente*   336–7

——: 2005 *So That You Don't Forget Me* / Para que no me olvides*   335

Ferrer, Mel: 1965 *Every Day is a Holiday / Cabriola*   161

Ferreri, Marco: 1959/1963 *The Lads* / Los chicos*   142

——: 1959 *The Tiny Flat* / El pisito*   146

——: 1960 *The Wheelchair / El cochecito* 146, 150, 194, 320
——: 1973 France-Italy, *La Grande Bouffe* 200
Fesser, Javier: 1998 *The Miracle of P. Tinto / El milagro de P. Tinto* 342
——: 2003 *Mortadelo and Filemón: The Big Adventure / La gran aventura de Mortadelo y Filemón* 176, 342
Feuillade, Louis: 1924 France, *Le Coffret de Toledo,* 36
——: started in 1913 France, *Fantômas* 22
——: 1924 France, *La Petite Andalouse* 36
Flaherty, Robert: 1920–22 France-USA, *Nanook of the North* 41
Fleming, Victor: 1939 USA, *Gone with the Wind* 91
Florey, Robert: 1929 USA, *The Hole in the Wall* 52
Fons, Angelino: 1967 *The Search / La busca* 188
——: 1970 *Fortunata and Jacinta / Fortunata y Jacinta* 84 n. 11, 172, 188, 248
——: 1969 *Singing to Life / Cantando a la vida* 188
——: 1971 *First Surrender / La primera entrega* 210
——: 1972 *Marianela* 84 n. 11, 162, 172, 188, 209
——: 1973 *Conjugal Separation* / Separación matrimonial* 210
——: 1974 *My Son is not what he Seems / Mi hijo no es lo que parece* 210
——: 1976 *The House* / La casa* 210
——: 1976 *Emilia... Road Stop and Inn* / Emilia... parada y fonda* 210
Font, Josep Lluis: 1965 *Family Life* / Vida de familia* 191
Ford, John: 1951 USA, *The Quiet Man* 302
Forn, Josep Maria: 1961 *The Private life of A. N. Other* / La vida privada de Fulano de tal* 145
——: 1965/1967 *Burnt Skin* / La piel quemada* 169, 191
——: 1969/1975 *The Response* / La respuesta* 169
——: 1979 *Companys, Calatonia on Trial / Companys, procés a Catalunya* 246
Forqué, José María and Pedro Lazaga: 1951 *Dark María Morena* / María Morena* 127
Forqué, José María: 1953 *The Devil Plays the Flute* / El diablo toca la flauta* 128
——: 1956 *Ambassadors in Hell* / Embajadores en el infierno* 123
——: 1957 *Whom God Forgives / Amanecer en Puerta Oscura* 128, 149
——: 1958 *Night and Dawn* / La noche y el alba* 124, 149
——: 1958 *A Violent Fate / Un hecho violento* 149
——: 1960 *091 Police On the Line / 091 Policía al habla* 148
——: 1960 *Maribel and the Strange Family / Maribel y la extraña familia* 145, 166
——: 1961 *You Could Be a Murderer* / Usted puede ser un asesino* 148
——: 1962 *Hold-Up at Three* / Atraco a las tres* 144 n. 41, 148, 166, 320, 341
——: 1962 *Accident 703* / Accidente 703* 170
——: 1964 *I am Seventeen* / Tengo diecisiete años* 162
——: 1964 *A Holiday for Yvette* / Vacaciones para Ivette* 166
——: 1967 *A Million in the Bin* / Un millón en la basura* 166
——: 1967 *Those who have to Serve / Las que tienen que servir* 166
——: 1976 *The Second Power / El segundo poder* 247
Forsyth, Bill: 1983 UK, *Local Hero* 135 n. 25
Fortuny, Juan and Armando Seville: 1942 *Legion of Heroes* / Legión de héroes* 92
Fortuny, Juan: 1955 *King of the Road* / El rey de la carretera* 142
Foy, Brian: 1929 USA, *Lights of New York* 50
Fraile, Alfredo: 1938 *Rebuilding Spain* / Reconstruyendo España* 78
Franco, Jesús: 1961 *Screams in the Night* / Gritos en la noche* 174
——: 1962 *Vampiresses 1930* / Vampiresas 1930* 167–8

——: 1963 *Death Whistles the Blues* * / *La muerte silba un blues*   170
——: 1964 *Trouble in the City* * / *Rififí en la ciudad*   170–1, 212
——: 1965 *Miss Death* * / *Miss Muerte*   174
——: 1969 *99 Women* / *99 Mujeres*   207
——: 1970 *Count Dracula* / *El conde Drácula*   207
——: 1971 *Vampyros Lesbos* / *Las vampiras*   207, 222
——: 1992 *Don Quixote* / *Don Quijote de Orson Welles*   172
——: 2005 *Snake Woman*   338
Franco, Ricardo: 1970 *The Annual Debacle* * / *El desastre de Annual*   220
——: 1975/1976 *Pascual Duarte*   220, 248
——: 1978 *The Remains from the Shipwreck* / *Los restos del naufragio*   229–30
——: 1987/1991 *The Dream of Tangiers* / *El sueño de Tánger*   267
——: 1988 *Berlín Blues*   266
——: 1994 *After so many years...* * / *Después de tantos años*   241, 302, 320
——: 1995 *Heavens Above!!* * / *¡¡Oh cielos!!*   295
——: 1997 *Lucky Star* / *La buena estrella*   336
——: 1999 *Black Tears* / *Lágrimas negras*   336
Fresnadillo, Juan Carlos: 2001 *Intact* / *Intacto*   337
Fulton, Keith and Louis Pepe: 2002 UK-USA, *Lost in La Mancha*   172 n. 20
Gabriel, Enrique: 1992 *Krapatchouk*   305
——: 1996/1998 *Hitting Bottom* / *¡En la puta calle!*   305
Ganga, José Miguel: 1988 *The Happy Woman* * / *La mujer feliz*   287
Garay, Jesús: 1987 *Beyond Passion* * / *Més enllà de la passió* / *Pasión lejana*   276
——: 1989 *The Bathtub* * / *La banyera*   276
Garci, José Luis: 1977 *Unfinished Business* / *Asignatura pendiente*   229
——: 1978 *Alone in the Dark* / *Solos en la madrugada*   229
——: 1979 *Green Pastures* / *Las verdes praderas*   229
——: 1981 *The Crack* / *El crack*   204, 247, 256 n. 1
——: 1982 *Begin the Beguine* / *Volver a empezar*   xiv, 243, 256
——: 1983 *The Crack II* / *El crack II*   247, 256 n. 1
——: 1984 *Double Feature* / *Sesión continua*   256 n. 1
——: 1987 *Course Completed* / *Asignatura aprobada*   256 n. 1
——: 1994 *Cradle song* / *Canción de cuna*   122, 300
——: 1998 *The Grandfather* / *El abuelo*   330
——: 2000 *You're the One*   330
——: 2002 *Story of a Kiss* / *Historia de un beso*   330
——: 2004 *Merry-go-round circa 1950* * / *Tío Vivo c1950*   330
——: 2005 *Ninette*   330
García, Gerardo: 1979 *With Much Love* / *Con mucho cariño*   235
Garcia Cardona, Àngel: 1910 *Benítez Wants to Be a Bullfighter* * / *Benítez quiere ser torero*   13, 29
García del Val, Ángel: 1981/1983 *Each Viewing Is... Corpses* * / *Cada ver es...*   241
García León, Victor: 2001 *No Pain, no Gain* / *Más pena que gloria*   335
García Maroto, Eduardo: 1936 *The Daughter of the Penitentiary* * / *La hija del penal*   59
——: 1939 *The Four Robinsons* * / *Los cuatro Robinsones*   83, 111 n. 51
——: 1943 *Canelita, Cinamon Stick* * / *Canelita en rama*   83, 114
——: 1955 *Three Were Three* / *Tres eran tres*   129
García Pelayo, Gonzalo: 1978 *Living in Seville* * / *Vivir en Sevilla*   242
——: 1979 *Exchanging Partners on the Beach* * / *Intercambio de parejas frente al mar*   242

——: 1982 *Rushes of Joy* / Corridas de alegría* 242
García Ruiz, Salvador: 1998 *Mensaka* 333
——: 2000 *The Other Side / El otro barrio* 335
García Sánchez, José Luis: 1972 *Ferocious Love* / El love feroz* 221
——: 1976 *And They Lived Happily Ever After / Colorín colorado* 234
——: 1978 *Trout / Las truchas* 238, 320
——: 1980 *Dolores Ibárruri, the Pasionaria* / Dolores* 241
——: 1985 *The Court of the Pharaoh / La corte de faraón* 97 n. 31, 271
——: 1986 *Divine Words / Divinas palabras* 259
——: 1986 *Must Undo the House* / Hay que deshacer la casa* 268
——: 1988 *Pasodoble* 268
——: 1989 *The Flight of the Dove / El vuelo de la paloma* 268
——: 1991 *The Longest Night / La noche más larga* 292
——: 1994 *Banderas, the Tyrant / Tirano Banderas* 301, 313
——: 1995 *The Seducer / El seductor* 293
——: 1995 *Sighs from/for Spain (and Portugal)* / Suspiros de España (y Portugal)* 294
——: 1997 *There's Always a Path to the Right* / Siempre hay un camino a la derecha* 294
——: 1997 *Tramway to Malvarrosa / Tranvía a la Malvarrosa* 293
——: 2004 *Dearest María* / María querida* 327, 349
García Serrano, Rafael: 1967 *Lost Eyes* / Los ojos perdidos* 170
García Serrano Yolanda and Juan Luis Iborra: 1997 *The Love of a Man / Amor de hombre* 304
——: 2000 *Kilometre Zero* / KM 0* 344
García Vega, Fernando: 1969 *Lola the Coalgirl* / Lola la piconera* 160
García Viñolas, Manuel: 1938 *POWs* / Prisioneros de guerra* 78
——: 1942 *Castilian Wedding* / Boda en Castilla* 86–7
——: 1945 *Inés de Castro* 100, 102
Gardela, Isabel: 2000 *Tea for Two / Tomándote* 344–5
Gargallo, Francisco: 1934 *Sister Angelica* / Sor Angélica* 58
Gasnier, Louis with Florián Rey: 1933 *Suburban Melody / Melodía de arrabal* 52
Gaspar i Serra, Josep: 1901 *The Barcelona Incidents* / Los sucesos de Barcelona* 5
——: 1920 *Joselito, or the Life and Death of a Bullfighter* / Joselito, o la vida y muerte de un matador* 29
Gay, Cesc: 2000 *Nico and Dani / Krámpack* 334
——: 2003 *In the City / En la ciudad* 334
——: 2006 *Fiction / Ficció* 348
Gelabert, Fructuós: 1897 *Brawl in a Café* / Riña en un café* 5–6
——: 1898 *Doña María Cristina and Don Alfonso's Visit to Barcelona* / Visita de Doña María Cristina y don Alfonso XIII a Barcelona* 4
——: 1899 *Colliding Liners* / Choque de dos transatlánticos* 6
——: 1901 *Visit of the British Fleet to Barcelona* / Visita de la escuadra inglesa a Barcelona* 4
——: 1902 *Procession of the Daughters of Mary* / Procesión de las hijas de María* 4
——: 1902 *Horses at the Barcelona Race Course* / Carreras de caballos en el hipódromo de Barcelona* 5
——: 1903 *Bicycle Races in the Park* / Carreras de bicicletas en el parque* 5
——: 1906 *Free Beer* / Cerveza gratis* 6
——: 1907 *Dandies at the Park Dairy* / Los guapos de la vaquería del parque* 6
——: 1907 *The Lowlands* / Terra Baixa* 6

——: 1908 *Barcelona in 1908* / Barcelona en 1908*   5
——: 1908 *The Tricked Guard* / Guardia burlado*   6
——: 1908 *The Rivals* / Los competidores*   6
——: 1908 *Dolores / La Dolores*   6–7, 83 n. 9
——: 1908 *Lethal Love* / Amor que mata*   13
——: 1909 *Guzmán, the Good* / Guzmán, el Bueno*   15
——: 1911 *Bad Blood* / Mala raza*   6
——: 1915 *Chopin's Nocturne / El nocturno de Chopin*   7
——: 1920 *The Goring and Death of Joselito* / Cogida y muerte de Joselito*   30
——: 1928 *The Lacemaker / La puntaire / La encajera*   7
——: (Filmoteca de España compilation) *Lost Frames* / Imágenes perdidas*   5
Genina, Augusto: 1940 *The Siege of the Alcazar* / Sin novedad en el Alcázar*   89–90
Gibson, Mel: 1995 USA, *Braveheart*   101–2
Gil, Carlos: 2001 *Schoolkiller / El vigilante*   338
Gil, Mateo: 1999 *Nobody Knows Anybody / Nadie conoce a nadie*   321–2, 339
Gil, Rafael: 1937 *Health* / Sanidad*   74
——: 1938 *Resistance from the East* / Resistencia en el Levante*   74
——: 1939 *Machine Guns* / Ametralladoras*   74
——: 1942 *The Man Who Wanted to Kill Himself* / El hombre que se quiso matar*   94, 202
——: 1943 *Traces of Light* / Huella de luz*   94
——: 1944 *The Nail / El clavo*   96–7
——: 1947 *The Holy Queen* / Reina santa*   100, 108, 132
——: 1947 *The Faith / La fe*   103
——: 1948 *Don Quixote / Don Quijote de la Mancha*   104
——: 1948 *Our Sea / Mare nostrum*   105
——: 1948 *The Sunless Street* / La calle sin sol*   109, 118 n. 3
——: 1948 *Just Any Woman* / Una mujer cualquiera*   109
——: 1951 *Our Lady of Fatima / La señora de Fátima*   120, 154
——: 1952 *From Madrid to Heaven* / De Madrid al cielo*   118
——: 1952 *The Song of Sister Maria / Sor Intrépida*   121
——: 1953 *I Was a Parish Priest / La guerra de Dios*   121, 154, 221
——: 1954 *Judas's Kiss / El beso de Judas*   121
——: 1954 *He Died Fifteen Years Ago* / Murió hace quince años*   122
——: 1955 *The Cock Crow* / El canto del gallo*   122–3
——: 1956 *A Communion Suit* / Un traje blanco*   121
——: 1958 *Luxury Cabin* / Camarote de lujo*   94
——: 1959 *College Boarding House / La casa de la Troya*   32 n. 9, 142
——: 1960 *Litri and His Shadow* / El Litri y su sombra*   142
——: 1965 *Currito of the Cross / Currito de la Cruz*   30, 107 n. 45, 163
——: 1965 *Pedrito de Andia's New Life* / La vida nueva de Pedrito de Andía*   160
——: 1966 *He's My Man!* / ¡Es mi hombre!*   69
——: 1966 *The Path of the Rocío Pilgrimage* / Camino del rocío*   164
——: 1967 *Another's Wife* / La mujer de otro*   164
——: 1968 *The Sailor with Golden Fists* / El marino de los puños de oro*   166
——: 1969 *Blood in the Bullring* / Sangre en el ruedo*   163
——: 1970 *The Man Who Wanted to Kill Himself* / El hombre que se quiso matar*   94, 202
——: 1970 *The Locket* / El relicario*   201
——: 1971 *The Green Envelope* / El sobre verde*   201
——: 1972 *Nothing Less than a Real Man* / Nada menos que todo un hombre*   205

——: 1973 *Doubt / La duda*   205
——: 1973 *The Guerilla* / La guerrilla*   205
——: 1974 *The King is the Best Mayor* / El mejor alcalde, el rey*   205
——: 1974 *Death's Newlyweds* / Novios de la muerte*   206
——: 1979 *Father Cami's Wedding* / La boda del señor cura*   239
——: 1980 *Spoilt Brats* / Hijos de papá*   97 n. 30, 234
——: 1980 *And in the Third Year, He Rose Again* / Y al tercer año, resucitó*   239
——: 1982 *From the Old Shirt to a New Jacket* / De camisa vieja a chaqueta nueva*   239
——: 1983 *The Autonothemselves* / Las autonosuyas*   239
——: 1984 *The Cheerful Colsada Girls* / Las alegres chicas de Colsada*   250
Gil, Telesforo: 1924 *Edurne, Dressmaker from Bilbao* / Edurne, modista bilbaína*   34
Giménez Caballero, Ernesto: 1930 *The Essence of the Fair* / Esencia de Verbena*   42, 53 n. 8
Giménez Rico, Antonio: 1966 *Sunday Morning* / Mañana de domingo*   210
——: 1967 *The Bone / El hueso*   210
——: 1971 *Are You My Father?*/ ¿Es usted mi padre?*   210
——: 1976 *Family Portrait / Retrato de familia*   66 n. 24, 210, 244
——: 1977 *On Love and Death* / Del amor y de la muerte*   247
——: 1983 *Dressed in Blue* / Vestida de azul*   242
——: 1986 *Mr Cayo's Contested Vote* / El disputado voto del Sr Cayo*   49, 259
——: 1988 *Jarrapellejos*   258
——: 1988 *Little Spanish Soldier* / Soldadito español*   268
——: 1991 *Fourteen Stations / Catorce estaciones*   262, 291–2
——: 1993 *Three Words* / Tres palabras*   299
——: 2003 *Hotel Danubio*   131 n. 16
Glen, John: 1992 *USA, Christopher Columbus: The Discovery*   301
Gómez, Enrique: 1948 *The Party Goes On* / La fiesta sigue*   107
——: 1951 *Sweet Name* / Dulce nombre*   149
——: 1952 *Persecution in Madrid* / Persecución en Madrid*   129
Gómez de la Serna, Ramón: 1929 *The Orator – The Hand* / El orador – La mano*   53 n. 8, 54
Gómez Hidalgo, Francisco: 1927 *The Mismatched Bride* / La malcasada*   35
Gómez Pereira, Manuel: 1992 *Pink Sauce / Salsa rosa*   304
——: 1993 *Why do They Call it Love when they Mean Sex? / ¿Por qué lo llaman amor cuando quieren decir sexo?*   304
——: 1994 *All Men Are the Same / Todos los hombres sois iguales*   304
——: 1995 *Mouth to Mouth / Boca a boca*   304
——: 1997 *Love Can Seriously Damage Your Health / El amor perjudica seriamente la salud*   304
——: 1999 *Between Your Legs / Entre las piernas*   343
——: 2001 *Off Key*   343
——: 2004 *Things that Make Life Worthwhile* / Cosas que hacen que la vida valga la pena*   343
——: 2006 *Queens / Reinas*   288 n. 8, 343–4
Gonzalo, Antonio: 1981 *Too Much for Galvez* / Demasiado para Gálvez*   247
——: 1987 *Terrorists* / Terroristas*   268
Gordon, Rafael: 1979 *Times of the Constitution / Tiempos de constitución*   240
Gormezano, Gerardo: 1988 *The Island Wind* / El vent de l'illa / El viento de la isla*   277
Graciani, Antonio: 1934 *He Who Disappeared / El desaparecido*   70

Grau, Jordi: 1963 *Summer Night / Noche de verano* 190
——: 1964 *The Rash One / El espontáneo* 190
——: 1967 *Actaeon* / Acteón* 190
——: 1968 *A Love Story / Una historia de amor* 190
——: 1969 *Story of a Girl Alone / Historia de una chica sola* 191
——: 1976 *Back of the Store / La trastienda* 200 n. 2, 211, 224, 226
——: 1981 *The Bruch Drum* / El timbaler del Bruc / La leyenda del Bruch* 100
Grémillon, Jean: 1934 *Our Lady of Sorrows* / La Dolorosa* 57
—— and Luis Buñuel: 1937 *Sentry, Keep Watch!* / ¡Centinela alerta!* 61, 70
Grieco, Sergio: 1964 *The Clover-Leaf Girl* / La chica del trébol* 162, 189 n. 41
Griffith, D. W.: 1915 USA, *Birth of a Nation* 22
——: 1916 USA, *Intolerance* 22
Gual, Adrià: 1914 *The Mayor of Zalamea* / El alcalde de Zalamea* 17
——: 1914 *The Little Gipsy girl / La gitanilla* 17, 84
——: 1914 *Mystery of Grief* / Misterio de dolor* 17
——: 1915 *Linito Becomes a Bullfighter* / Linito se hace torero* 29
——: 1917 *The Daughter of the Sea* / La hija del mar* 121
Gual, Roger and Julio Wallowits: 2002 *Smoking_Room* 339
Güell, Xavier: 1935 *Paradise Recovered / El paraíso recobrado* 64
Guerín, José Luis: 1985 *Bertha's Motives* / Los motivos de Berta* 273
——: 1991 *Innisfree* 302
——: 1998 *A Train of Shadows* / Tren de sombras* 302
——: 2000 *Under Construction* / En construcción* 326–7
Guerín Hill, Claudio: 1972 *The House of the Doves / La casa de las palomas* 208
——: 1973 *A Bell from Hell / La campana del infierno* 208
Guevara, Enrique: 1978 *A Wild Sex Extravaganza* / Una loca extravagancia sexy* 228
Guibourt, Edmundo: 1938 *Blood Wedding / Bodas de sangre* 18
Guillén Cuervo, Fernando: 2006 *The Managers* / Los managers* 346
Gutiérrez, Chus: 1992 *Sublet / Realquiler* 309
——: 1994 *Oral-Aural Sex* / Sexo oral* 309
——: 1996 *Gypsy Soul* / Alma gitana* 309, 345–6
——: 1998 *Sleepless in Madrid / Insomnio* 309
——: 2002 *Setting Sun* / Poniente* 333
——: 2005 *El Calentito Club* / El Calentito* 251, 330–1
Gutiérrez, Ricardo: 1937 *For Spain* / Arriba España* 78
——: 1937 *The Reconquest of the Fatherland* / La reconquista de la patria* 78
——: 1945 *The Secret of the Dead Woman* / El secreto de la mujer muerta* 108
Gutiérrez Alea, Tomás and Juan Carlos Tabio: 1995 *Guantanamera* 313
Gutiérrez Aragón, Manuel: 1973 *Speak, Little Dumb Girl / Habla mudita* 221
——: 1977 *Black Litter / Camada negra* 243
——: 1978 *Somnambulists / Sonámbulos* 243
——: 1979 *Heart of the Forest / El corazón del bosque* 81, 245
——: 1981 *Maravillas* 237, 320
——: 1982 *Demons in The Garden / Demonios en El Jardín* 82, 245, 320
——: 1984 *Ferocious* / Feroz* 269
——: 1984 *The Most Beautiful Night / La noche más hermosa* 270
——: 1986 *Half of Heaven / La mitad del cielo* 262
——: 1988 *Misadventure / Malaventura* 269
——: 1991 *Don Quixote / El Quijote de Miguel de Cervantes* 269
——: 1995 *The King of the River* / El rey del río* 293
——: 1998 *Things I Left in Havana / Cosas que dejé en La Habana* 332, 350

——: 2001 *Visionaries / Visionarios*   268
——: 2002 *Don Quixote, Knight Errant / El caballero don Quijote* (TV)   269 n. 21
Gutiérrez Maesso, José: 1954 *The Mayor of Zalamea / El alcalde de Zalamea*   149
Gutiérrez Santos, José María: 1978 *Long Live Hazaña / ¡Arriba Hazaña!*   245
——: 1982 *The Autonomicals / Los autonómicos*   240
Gúzman Merino, Antonio: 1944 *Macarena*   105
Harlan, Richard: 1933 *Hatred / Odio*   66
Hathaway, Henry: 1964 USA, *Circus World*   173
Hawks, Howard: 1938 USA, *Bringing Up Baby*   343
Herbier, Marcel: 1921 France, *El Dorado*   36
Hermoso, Miguel: 1983 *Truants* / Truhanes*   273
——: 1985 *Marbella Hot Spot / Marbella un golpe de cinco estrellas*   273
——: 1989 *Mad Poison / Loco veneno*   273
——: 1997 *Like a Bolt of Lightning* / Como un relámpago*   293
Hernández, Antonio: 2002 *The City of No Limits / En la ciudad sin límites*   183 n. 36,
   339, 341 n. 22
——: 2005 *Hidden / Oculto*   183 n. 36, 339
——: 2006 *The Borgias / Los Borgia*   339
Herralde, Gonzalo: 1977 *Race, The Spirit of Franco / Raza, el espíritu de Franco*   241
——: 1978 *The Murderer from Pedralbes* / El asesino de Pedralbes*   242
——: 1981 *Jet Lag / Vértigo en Manhattan*   232
——: 1984 *Last Evenings with Teresa* / Últimas tardes con Teresa*   275–6
——: 1987 *Laura, the Night Falls from the Sky* / Laura, del cielo llega la noche*   276
——: 1993 *Gold Fever* / La febre de l'or / La fiebre del oro*   301
Herrero, Gerardo: 1994 *Shortcut to Paradise / Desvío al paraíso*   313
——: 1996 *Malena is the Name of a Tango* / Malena es un nombre de tango*   288
——: 1997 *Comanche Territory / Territorio Comanche*   302
——: 2000 *Friends Have Reasons / Las razones de mis amigos*   332
——: 2003 *The Galíndez File / El misterio Galíndez*   340
——: 2005 *Heroin(e)* / Heroína*   335
Herzog, Werner: 1972 Germany, *Aguirre, der Zorn Gottes*   259
Hill, George: 1929 USA, *The Big House*   51
Hitchcock, Alfred: 1929 UK, *Blackmail*   55
——: 1940 USA, *Rebecca*   113
——: 1945 USA, *Spellbound* 42 n. 33
——: 1954 USA, *Rear Window*   67
——: 1958 USA, *Vertigo* 111
——: 1960 USA, *Psycho*   212
Hogan, James P.: 1937 USA, *The Last Train from Madrid*   74
Huerga, Manuel: 1995 *Antarctica* / Antártida*   307
——: 2006 *Salvador (Puig Antich) / Salvador*   329, 346
Ibáñez Serrador, Narciso 'Chicho': 1969 *The Finishing School / La residencia*   175
——: 1976 *Would You Kill a Child? / ¿Quién puede matar a un niño?*   175, 208–9
Ibarretxe, Esteban: 1997 *You Only Die Twice* / Sólo se muere dos veces*   342
——: 2000 *Sabotage!!* / ¡¡Sabotaje!!*   342
Iborra, Manuel: 1981 *Three Times Four* / Tres por cuatro*   273
——: 1987 *Cain / Caín*   273
——: 1989 *The Dance of the Duck* / El baile del pato*   273
——: 1992 *Club Virginia Orchestra / Orquesta Club Virginia*   299
——: 2006 *Lady Dimwit* / La dama boba*   286 n. 5
Iglesia, Alex de la: 1993 *Mutant Action / Acción mutante*   306

——: 1995 *The Day of the Beast / El día de la bestia*   306
——: 1997 *Dance with the Devil / Perdita Durango*   323
——: 1999 *Dying from Laughter / Muertos de risa*   323
——: 2000 *Common Wealth / La comunidad*   135 n. 22, 323
——: 2002 *Eight Hundred Bullets / Ochocientas balas*   323
——: 2004 *Ferpect Crime / Crimen ferpecto*   323
Iglesia, Eloy de la: 1969 *Something Bitter in Your Mouth* / Algo amargo en la boca*
   220
——: 1970 *Quadrilateral* / Cuadrilátero*   220
——: 1971 *Glass Ceiling / El techo de cristal*   220
——: 1972/1974 *Week of the Killer / Cannibal Man / La semana del asesino*   220
——: 1973 *No One Heard the Scream / Nadie oyó gritar*   220
——: 1973 *Murder in a Blue World / Una gota de sangre para morir amando*   220
——: 1975 *Forbiden Love Game / Juego de amor prohibido*   220, 235
——: 1976 *The Other Bedroom* / La otra alcoba*   236 n. 16
——: 1977 *The Creature / La criatura*   236 n. 16
——: 1977 *Hidden Pleasures / Los placeres ocultos*   235
——: 1978 *The Priest* / El sacerdote*   235
——: 1978 *Confessions of a Congressman / El diputado*   235
——: 1980 *Afraid to Go Out at Night* / Miedo a salir de noche*   235
——: 1980 *Young Knives / Navajeros*   235
——: 1981 *The Minister's Wife* / La mujer del ministro*   235
——: 1982 *Pals / Colegas*   235, 264
——: 1983 *The Shoot* / El pico*   264
——: 1984 *The Shoot II* / El pico II*   264
——: 1985 *Another Turn of the Screw* / Otra vuelta de tuerca*   267
——: 1987 *The Vallecas Tobacconist* / La estanquera de Vallecas*   264
——: 2003 *Bulgarian Lovers / Los novios búlgaros*   344
Iglesias, Carlos: 2006 *Crossing Borders / Un franco, 14 pesetas*   217 n. 30, 329
Ingram, Rex: 1921 USA, *The Four Horsemen of the Apocalypse*   17
Iquino, Ignacio F: 1935 *On the Margin of the Law* / Al margen de la ley* 70
——: 1937 *Diego Corrientes*   71
——: 1941 *Heart of Gold* / Alma de Dios*   93
——: 1942 *We Thieves Are Honourable* / Los ladrones somos gente honrada*   95, 145
——: 1943 *A Family Confusion* / Un enredo de familia*   95
——: 1944 *Men Without Honour / Hombres sin honor*   95
——: 1944 *A Shadow at the Window* / Una sombra en la ventana*   95
——: 1945 *Guilty!* / ¡Cupable!*   95
——: 1948 *The Bruch Drum* / El tambor del Bruch*   100
——: 1950 *The Vila Family* / La familia Vila*   95, 118 n. 3
——: 1950 *The Criminal Brigade* / Brigada criminal*   109, 148
——: 1950 *The Story of a Staircase* / Historia de una escalera*   149
——: 1951 *The Pelegrín System* / El sistema Pelegrín*   128
——: 1952 *The Judas / El Judas*   121
——: 1955 *Closed Exit / Camino cortado*   130
——: 1958 *The Convent Child* / El niño de las monjas*   59
——: 1959 *Bon Voyage, Pablo! / ¡Buen viaje, Pablo!*   148
——: 1964 *Joe Dexter / Oeste Nevada Joe*   173
——: 1967 *Five Dollars for Ringo / Cinco pistolas de Texas*   173
——: 1973 *Criminal Abortion* / Aborto criminal*   206
——: 1973 *Girls for Hire* / Chicas de alquiler*   206

——: 1976 *Matrimonial Fraud** / *Fraude matrimonial* 206
Isasi-Isasmendi, Antonio: 1957 *Blood Rhapsody** / *Rapsodia de sangre* 123
——: 1959 *Diego Corrientes* 71
——: 1961 *A Land for All** / *Tierra de todos* 124
——: 1963 *The Adventures of Scaramouche* / *La máscara de Scaramouche* 174 n. 24
——: 1965 *Istanbul 65* / *Estambul 65* 171
——: 1968 *Our Man in Las Vegas* / *Las Vegas, 500 millones* 171
——: 1972 *Summertime Killer* / *Un verano para matar* 206
——: 1977 *The Dog** / *El perro* 247
Ivens, Joris: 1937 USA, *Spanish Earth* 74
Izquierdo, Ángel: 2002 *Dragon Hill* / *La colina del dragón* 348
Jaeckin, Just: 1974 France, *Emmanuelle* 226 n. 2
Jaén, Antonio de: 1969 *Prisoner in the City** / *Prisionero en la ciudad* 160
Jara, José: 1975 *The Four Brides of Augusto Pérez** / *Las cuatro novias de Augusto Pérez* 205
Jimeno Correas, Eduardo: 1896 *Leaving the Midday Mass on the Feast of Our Lady of Zaragoza** / *Salida de misa de doce del Pilar de Zaragoza* 2
——: 1896 *Greetings** / *Saludos* 3
Joffé, Roland: 1986 UK, *The Mission* 103
Jordà, Joaquim: 1996 *A Body in the Woods* / *Un cos al bosc* 193
Jordi, Elena: 1918 *Thais* 30
Juran, Nathan: 1958 USA, *The Seventh Voyage of Simbad* 174 n. 24
Karmen, Roman and Esfir Shub: 1939 USSR, *Ispaniya* 74
Klimovsky, León: 1955 *The Cheeky Miller's Wife** / *La pícara molinera* 125
——: 1956 *Honeymoon* / *Viaje de novios* 145
——: 1960 *Peace Never Starts** / *La paz empieza nunca* 124
——: 1964 *Stopover in Tenerife** / *Escala en Tenerife* 163
——: 1966 *A Girl for Two** / *Una chica para dos* 156, 163
——: 1971 *Shadow of the Werewolf* / *La noche de Walpurgis* 207
——: 1972 *The House of Bitches** / *La casa de las Chivas* 206
——: 1972 *Dr Jeckyll and the Wolfman* / *Dr Jekyll y el hombre lobo* 207
——: 1979 *The Hut** / *La barraca* (TV) 248
Koster, Henry: 1953 USA, *The Robe* 127
Kramer, Stanley: 1957 USA, *The Pride and the Passion* 172
Kubrick, Stanley: 1971 UK, *Clockwork Orange* 200
Ladoire, Óscar: 1982 *Problems and Mishaps** / *A contratiempo* 234
Laguna, Mónica: 1996 *I Have a Home** / *Tengo una casa* 309–10
——: 2001 *Luna's Game* / *Juego de Luna* 310, 337
Lang, Fritz: 1927 Germany, *Metropolis* 41
Lapeyra, Mariano: 1935 *Love on Manoeuvres** / *Amor en maniobras* 70
Lara, Antonio de: 1951 *A Room for Three** / *Habitación para tres* 128
Lara Polop, Francisco: 1972 *Murder Mansion* / *La mansión de la tiniebla* 208
——: 1973 *Bait for an Adolescent** / *Cebo para una adolecente* 208
——: 1974 *Perversion** / *Perversión* 208
——: 1975 *Obsession* / *Obsesión* 208
——: 1975 *The Protected One** / *La protegida* 208
——: 1984 *The Judge's Wife** / *La mujer del juez* 265
Larraz, José Ramón: 1970 *Whirlpool* 208
——: 1974 *Emma, Dark Doors** / *Emma, puertas oscuras* 208
——: 1976 *The End of Innocence** / *El fin de la inocencia* 208
——: 1977 *Peeping Tom** / *Mirón* 228

——: 1978 *The Coming of Sin* / *La visita del vicio* 228
——: 1979 *Magic Ejaculations** / *Polvos mágicos* 228
——: 1979 *And Give Us Our Daily Sex* / *El periscopio* 228
Lazaga, Pedro: 1950/1952 *The Hounded Man** / *El hombre acosado* 109
——: 1954 *The Platoon** / *La patrulla* 123
——: 1955/1962 *Prisoners' Rope** / *Cuerda de preso* 109 n. 47
——: 1956 *The Infinite Front** / *Frente infinito* 123
——: 1957 *The Girls in Blue* / *Las muchachas de azul* 145
——: 1958 *Ana Says Yes** / *Ana dice que sí* 145
——: 1958 *Summer Moon** / *Luna de verano* 145
——: 1959 *The Proud Infantry* / *La fiel infantería* 123, 153, 207
——: 1959 *The Tricksters** / *Los tramposos* 146, 164, 202
——: 1960 *The Economically Handicapped** / *Los económicamente débiles* 146
——: 1962 *Friday and Thirteenth** / *Martes y trece* 156, 229 n. 7
——: 1965 *Two Mad Mad Girls** / *Dos chicas locas locas* 162
——: 1965 *Forward Position** / *Posición avanzada* 170
——: 1965 *The Murderer's Face** / *El rostro del asesino* 170
——: 1966 *Mission Over and Beyond** / *Operación Plus Ultra* 164
——: 1966 *The Naval Cadets* / *Los guardiamarinas* 166
——: 1966 *City Life is not for Me* / *La ciudad no es para mí* 168, 196
——: 1967 *What Shall We Do with the Children?** / *¿Qué hacemos con los hijos?* 164
——: 1967 *Sister Citroen** / *Sor Citroen* 166
——: 1968 *Tourism is a Great Invention** / *El turismo es un gran invento* 164
——: 1969 *The Other Guernica Tree** / *El otro árbol de Guernica* 170, 207
——: 1969 *The Secretaries** / *Las secretarias* 160
——: 1969 *Why do we Sin at Forty?* / *¿Por qué pecamos a los cuarenta?* 165, 203 n. 9
——: 1969 *Old Man Made in Spain* / *Abuelo made in Spain* 168–9
——: 1970 *Money is Afraid** / *El dinero tiene miedo* 165, 202
——: 1970 *The Cat's Seven Lives* / *Las siete vidas del gato* 166
——: 1970 *The Summer of 1970** / *Verano 70* 203
——: 1970 *The Abominable Marbella Man** / *El abominable hombre de la Costa del Sol* 203
——: 1971 *Educating Father** / *Hay que educar a papá* 201
——: 1971 *Come to Germany, Pepe* / *Vente a Alemania, Pepe* 204
——: 1972 *Get a Girl out West** / *Vente a ligar al oeste* 172, 204
——: 1972 *The Father of the Child** / *El padre de la criatura* 164, 201
——: 1973 *Granpa has a Plan** / *El abuelo tiene un plan* 168, 201
——: 1974 *Five Pillows for the Night** / *Cinco almohadas para una noche* 165
——: 1975 *Three Swedish Girls for three Rodríguez** / *Tres suecas para tres Rodríguez* 167 n. 14
——: 1975 *The Happy Divorcee** / *El alegre divorciado* 204
——: 1977 *I Feel as Young as a Lad** / *Estoy hecho un chaval* 239
——: 1978 *Vote for Gundisalvo* / *Vota a Gundisalvo* 239
——: 1978 *What a Pair of Twins!** / *Vaya par de gemelos* 239
Lazkano, Arantxa: 1993 *The Dark Years* / *Urte ilunak* / *Los años oscuros* 311–2
Lean, David 1945 UK, *Brief Encounter* 157 n. 3
——: 1965 USA, *Dr Zhivago* 183
Leblanc, Tony: 1961 *Poor García** / *El pobre García* 167
Lecchi, Alberto: 2000 *Nuts for Love* / *Nueces para el amor* 350
León de Aranoa, Fernando: 1996 *Family* / *Familia* 305

——: 1998 *Neighbourhood** / *Barrio*   294, 332
——: 2002 *Mondays in the Sun* / *Los lunes al sol*   332
——: 2006 *Princesses* / *Princesas*   332
Lesmes, Eva: 1996 *Put a Man in your Life** / *Pon un hombre en tu vida*   310
——: 2001 *The Hold-up** / *El palo*   166, 341
Lester, Richard: 1965 UK, *Help*   212
Loach, Ken: 1995 *Land and Freedom* / *Tierra y libertad*   286
Loma, José Antonio de la: 1974 *The Last Trip* / *El último viaje*   106
——: 1977 *Street Warriors* / *Perros callejeros*   237
——: 1979 *Street Warriors II* / *Perros callejeros II*   237
——: 1985 *I, The Vaquilla** / *Yo, el Vaquilla*   237
——: 1996 *Three Days on Parole** / *Tres días de libertad*   289
Lombardi, Francisco: 2000 *Red Ink* / *Tinta roja*   350
López Amado, Norberto: 2003 *They're Watching Us* / *Nos miran*   340
López Linares, José Luis and Javier Rioyo: 2000 *Strangers to Themselves* / *Extranjeros de sí mismos*   327–8
López Piñeiro, Carlos and Alfredo García Pinal: 1989 *Urxa*   279
López Rubio, José: 1940 *The Ill-Loved** / *La malquerida*   28, 84
——: 1941 *Pepe Conde*   105
——: 1944 *Eugenia de Montijo*   100
——: 1946 *Pepe Conde's Crime** / *El crimen de Pepe Conde*   105
——: 1948 *Alhucemas*   112
Lorente, Germán: 1970 *Coqueluche on the Costa** / *Coqueluche*   202
Loriga, Ray : 1997 *My Brother's Gun* / *La pistola de mi hermano*   308, 334
——: 2007 *Theresa: The Body of Christ* / *Teresa, el cuerpo de Cristo*   334
Lozano, Eloy: 2001 *Sleeping Beauties** / *Bellas durmientes*   338
Lucas, George: 1977 USA, *Star Wars*   323
Lucia, Luis: 1943 *Thirteen-Thirteen** / *El trece- trece*   108
——: 1945 *A Business Man** / *Un hombre de negocio*   98
——: 1947 *Two Stories for Two** / *Dos cuentos para dos*   95
——: 1947 *The Princess of the Ursinos* / *La princesa de los Ursinos*   100, 104
——: 1949 *Currito of the Cross* / *Currito de la Cruz*   30, 107
——: 1949 *The Duchess of Benameji* / *La duquesa de Benameji*   106
——: 1950 *From Woman to Woman* / *De mujer a mujer*   113
——: 1951 *Dream of Andalusia** / *El sueño de Andalucía*   108, 126
——: 1952 *Lola the Coalgirl** / *Lola la piconera*   101, 125
——: 1952 *On the Edge of the City** / *Cerca de la ciudad*   121, 132
——: 1952 *Sister San Sulpicio* / *La hermana San Sulpicio*   125
——: 1953 *Jeromín, the Emperor's Son** / *Jeromín*   122
——: 1953 *Airport** / *Aeropuerto*   129
——: 1954 *Dark and Bright* / *Morena Clara*   69, 126
——: 1954 *An Andalusian Gentleman** / *Un caballero andaluz*   125, 142, 154
——: 1955 *Sister Happiness** / *Hermana Alegría*   126
——: 1955 *That Voice is a Gold Mine** / *Esa voz es una mina*   126
——: 1959 *Father Damian's Molokai ** / *Molokai*   121, 153
——: 1960 *The King of the Vikings* / *Prince in Chains** / *El príncipe encadenado*   149
——: 1960 *A Ray of Light** / *Un rayo de luz*   161
——: 1961 *An Angel has Arrived** / *Ha llegado un ángel*   161
——: 1962 *Lottery** / *Tómbola*   161
——: 1962 *Song of Youth** / *Canción de juventud*   162
——: 1963 *Rocío, the Dewdrop of La Mancha** / *Rocío de la Mancha*   162

——: 1965 *Zampo and Me* / *Zampo y yo*   162, 217
——: 1967 *Marisol's Four Weddings** / *Las cuatro bodas de Marisol*   161
——: 1968 *Both Alone** / *Solos los dos*   161
——: 1971 *The River Bank** / *La orilla*   206
——: 1972 *Between Two Loves** / *Entre dos amores*   201
Lumière, Louis: 1895 France, *L'Arroseur arrosé*,   5
Lupo, Rino: 1926 *Carmiña, The Flower of Galicia** / *Carmiña, flor de Galicia*   33
Lladó, Juan: 1954 *The Louts** / *Los gamberros*   128–9
Llobet Gràcia, Lorenzo: 1948/1953 *A Life in Shadow** / *Vida en sombras*   3, 109 n. 47,
   112–14, 118 n. 3, 252, 320
Llorca, Pablo: 1998 *They All Wound** / *Todas hieren*   337
——: 2001 *Behind God's Back* / *La espalda de Dios*   337
Lluch, Miguel: 1960 *Anchor Button** / *Botón de ancla*   108, 163, 166
Lluch, Vicente: 1956 *The Wait** / *La espera*   123
MacDonald, David: 1949 UK, *Christopher Columbus*   117
Macián, Francisco: 1966 *The Dream Wizard** / *El mago de los sueños*   176
——: 1968 *Give me a Little Lo-o-o-ving* / *Dame un poco de amooor*   176
Mackendrick, Alexander: 1949 UK, *Whisky Galore*   135 n. 25
Madrid, Jesús Luis: 1966 *Ruthless Colt of the Gringo* / *La venganza de Clark Harrison*
   209
——: 1970 *The Motorway Vampire** / *El vampiro de la autopista*   209
——: 1975 *English Strip-tease** / *Striptease a la inglesa*   209
Maish, Herbert: 1939 Germany, *Andalusische Nächte*   80
Malraux, André and Boris Perskine: 1939/1945 *Days of Hope* / *Sierra de Teruel*   74,
   132 n. 19
Mamoulian, Rouben: 1935 USA, *Becky Sharp*   67
——: 1941 USA, *Blood and Sand*   17
Mann, Anthony: 1961 USA, *El Cid*   172
——: 1964 USA, *Fall of the Roman Empire*   172–3
Mantilla, Fernando: 1936 *July 1936** / *Julio 1936*   73
——: 1937 *United to Victory** / *Por la unidad hacia la victoria*   73
Manzanos, Eduardo: 1954 *Good News** / *Buenas noticias*   128
——: 1956 *A Fail in Communism** / *Suspenso en comunismo*   123
——: 1957 *The Airbeauties** / *Las aeroguapas*   145
Mañá, Laura: 2000 *Compassionate Sex* / *Sexo por compasión*   322
——: 2002 *Killing Words* / *Palabras encadenadas*   322
——: 2005 *Morir en San Hilario* / *To Die in San Hilario*   322–3
Mañas, Achero: 2000 *Pellet* / *El Bola*   331–2
Maqua, Javier: 1980 *You are mad Briones* / *Tú estás loco Briones*   234
——: 1997 *Chevrolet*   234, 332
——: 2002 *Chicken Skin* / *Carne de gallina*   335
Marchand, Raúl: 2003 *Hold up at 15:00... :30** / *Atraco a las tres... y media*   341
Marco, Fernando: 1917 *The Phenomenal Bull** / *El toro fenómeno*   24
Marías, Luis: 2002 *X** / *X* / *Equis*   336
Mariscal Ana: 1953 *Segundo López, Urban Adventure** / *Segundo López, un aventurero
   urbano*   131, 171
——: 1954 *Mass in Santiago** / *Misa en Santiago*   127 n. 12
——: 1957/1960 *They Fired with their Lives** / *Con la vida hicieron fuego*   124
——: 1963 *The Journey** / *El camino*   171
——: 1966 *The Splendour of Andalusia* / *Los duendes de Andalucía*   160
——: 1967 *Dressed as a Bride** / *Vestida de novia*   160

Marischka, Ernst: 1955, 1956, 1957 Austria, *Sissi*   141

Marquina, Luis and Luis Buñuel: 1935 *The Embittered Don Quentin* / Don Quintín el amargao*   34, 55, 60

Marquina, Luis: 1936 *The Dancer and the Worker / El bailarín y el trabajador*   70

——: 1940 *The Last Hussar* / El último húsar*   100

——: 1941 *Whirlwind / Torbellino*   107

——: 1942 *Hollyhock / Malvaloca*   34, 105

——: 1942 *Lives Entwined* / Vidas cruzadas*   94

——: 1948 *Doña María the Brave* / Doña María la brava*   100

——: 1949 *Filigrana*   106

——: 1951 *Captain Poison / El capitán Veneno*   101

——: 1953 *Such is Madrid* / Así es Madrid*   128

——: 1961 *The Ship Company Widow* / La viudita naviera*   126

——: 1968 *Tuset Street*   190–1

Marro, Albert: 1914 *Diego Corrientes*   71

——: 1916 *Barcelona and its Mysteries* / Barcelona y sus misterios*   22

——: 1917 *The Testament of Diego Rocafort* / El testamento de Diego Rocafort*   22

Marsillach, Adolfo: 1972 *Flower of Holiness / Flor de santidad*   205, 312

Martín, Eugenio: 1962 *Hypnosis / Hipnosis*   171

——: 1960 *Conqueror of Maracaibo / Los corsarios del Caribe*   174 n. 24

——: 1966 *The Bounty Killer / El precio de un hombre*   174

——: 1972 *Horror Express / Pánico en el transiberiano*   174

——: 1996 *The Salt of Life* / La sal de la vida*   297, 313

Martínez, Pau: 2003 *Lost Bullet / Bala perdida*   172, 321

Martínez Arboleya, Joaquín: 1937 *War for Peace* / La guerra por la paz*   78

——: 1937 *The Will* / Voluntad*   78

Martínez de Rivas, Ramón: 1932 *Chopin's Nocturne / El nocturno de Chopin*   7

Martínez-Lázaro, Emilio: 1978 *What Max Said / Las palabras de Max*   235

——: 1980 *Their Golden Years / Sus años dorados*   235

——: 1986 *Lulu by Night / Lulú de noche*   268

——: 1988 *The Most Amazing Game / El juego más divertido*   270

——: 1992 *I Love your Lovely Bed* / Amo tu cama rica*   287

——: 1994 *The Worst Years of Our Lives / Los peores años de nuestra vida*   293

——: 1997 *Backroads / Carreteras secundarias*   335

——: 2002 *The Other Side of the Bed / El otro lado de la cama*   346

——: 2005 *The Two Sides of the Bed / Los 2 lados de la cama*   346

Masia, Octavi: 2005 *Veronica's Words* / Las palabras de Vero*   335

Masó, Pedro: 1971 *The Ibericas FC* / Las Ibéricas FC*   166

——: 1972 *A Girl and a Gentleman* / Una chica y un señor*   203

——: 1972 *Premarital Experiment* / Experiencia prematrimonial*   218

——: 1974 *A Man Like All the Others* / Un hombre como los demás*   203

——: 1975 *The Adolescents / Las adolescentes*   203

——: 1979 *The Family's Fine, Thanks* / La familia bien, gracias*   167, 234, 240

——: 1979 *Honey / La miel*   203 n. 8, 240

——: 1980 *The Forthcoming Divorce* / El divorcio que viene*   240

——: 1981 *127 Million, Tax-Free* / 127 millones libres de impuestos*   240

——: 1995 *Sister, What Have You Done? / Hermana, ¿ pero qué has hecho?*   300

——: 1999 *The Family... Thirty Years on* / La familia... treinta años después*   234

Matjí, Manolo: 1987 *The Madmen's War* / La guerra de los locos*   274

——: 1996 *The Sea Below the Moon* / Mar de luna*   294

——: 2004 *Hours of Light* / Horas de luz*   335

Medeiros, Maria de: 2000 Portugal, *Capitães de Abril*   223 n. 33
Medem, Julio: 1992 *Cows / Vacas*   311, 320
——: 1993 *The Red Squirrel / La ardilla roja*   311
——: 1996 *Earth / Tierra*   311, 324
——: 1998 *The Lovers of the Arctic Circle / Los amantes del círculo polar*   324
——: 2001 *Sex and Lucia / Lucía y el sexo*   324
——: 2003 *The Basque Ball: Skin Against the Wall / Euskal pilota Larrua harriaren kontra / La pelota vasca*   324, 327
Melford, George: 1924 USA, *Tiger Love*   62
Méndez Leite, Fernando: 1980 *Man of Fashion / El hombre de moda*   229
Mercanton, Louis: 1931 France-USA, *Marions-nous*   52
Mercero, Antonio: 1972 *The Phone Box / La cabina*   221
——: 1974 *Blood Stains in a New Car / Una mancha de sangre en un coche nuevo*   221
——: 1977 *Daddy's War / La guerra de papá*   234
——: 1982 *The Next Station* / La próxima estación*   234
——: 1987 *Wait for Me in Heaven / Espérame en el cielo*   262
——: 1990 *The Treasure* / El tesoro*   265
——: 1990 *Don Juan My Dear Ghost / Don Juan mi querido fantasma*   260–1
——: 1998 *A Time for Defiance / La hora de los valientes*   328–9
——: 2003 *The Fourth Floor / Planta 4ª*   332
Merino, Fernando: 1968 *The Dynamite is Served* / La dinamita está servida*   165
——: 1968 *The Underdeveloped* / Los subdesarrollados*   165–6
——: 1971 *Thou Shalt Not Covet thy Neigbour's Wife* / No desearás la mujer de tu prójimo*   203
Micón, Sabino: 1928 *The History of a Five Peseta Coin* / Historia de un duro*   41
——: 1930 *The Joy that Passes* / La alegría que pasa*   52
Mignoni, Fernando: 1938 *Our Guilty Man* / Nuestro culpable*   70 n. 27, 72
Mihura, Jerónimo: 1947 *Confidences* / Confidencia*   96 n. 29
——: 1949 *In a Corner of Spain* / En un rincón de España*   96
——: 1949 *They Always Return at Dawn* / Siempre vuelven de madrugada*   96
Minnelli, Vicente: 1961 USA, *The Four Horsemen of the Apocalypse*   17
Miñón, Juan: 1990 *The White Dove / La Blanca Paloma*   292
——: 1996 *The Legend of Balthasar the Castrato / La leyenda de Balthasar el castrado*   301
Mir, Paco: 2003 *The Best Thing that can Happen to a Croissant* / Lo mejor que le puede pasar a un croisán*   343
Mira, Carles: 1978 *The Prodigious Life of Father Vincent / La portentosa vida del pare Vicent*   238–9
——: 1980 *Caution to the Wind / Con el culo al aire*   239
——: 1981 *Royal Jelly* / Jalea real*   239
——: 1983 *We Had it so Good!* / Qué nos quiten lo bailao*   277
——: 1985 *Karnivel* / Karnabal*   277
——: 1988 *Daniya, Garden of the Harem / Daniya, jardí de l'harem*   277
——: 1989 *Mambo King* / El rey del mambo*   277
Miravitlles, Jaume: 1936–38 *Spain Today / Espanya al dia / España al día / Nouvelles d'Espagne*   73
Miró, María: 1995 *The Return Luggage* / Los baúles del retorno*   312
Miró, Pilar: 1976 *The Request / La petición*   230
——: 1979/1981 *The Cuenca Crime / El crimen de Cuenca*   4 n. 6, 12, 226–7, 230

——: 1980 *Gary Cooper Who Art in Heaven* / *Gary Cooper, que estás en los cielos* 230

——: 1982 *Let Us Talk Tonight** / *Hablamos esta noche* 230

——: 1986 *Werther* 258

——: 1991 *Prince of Shadows* / *Beltenebros* 291, 301 n. 16, 313

——: 1993 *The Bird of Happiness* / *El pájaro de la felicidad* 4 n. 6, 286

——: 1996 *The Dog in the Manger* / *El perro del hortelano* 267, 286

——: 1996 *Your Name Poisons My Dreams* / *Tu nombre envenena mis sueños* 286

Moleón, Rafael: 1988 *Bâton Rouge* 274

——: 1995 *The Invisible Boy** / *El niño invisible* 300

——: 1996 *Liquid Look** / *Mirada líquida* 290

——: 1996 *A Question of Luck* / *Cuestión de suerte* 290

Molina, Christian: 2004 *Red Blood** / *Rojo sangre* 338

Molina, Jacinto aka Paul Naschy: 1976 *Inquisition* / *Inquisición* 207

——: 1980 *The Return of the Wolfman* / *El retorno del hombre lobo* 207

——: 1992 *The Night of the Executioner* / *La noche del ejecutor* 338

Molina, Josefina: 1973 *Vera, a Cruel Story* / *Vera, un cuento cruel* 221

——: 1981 *Evening Performance** / *Función de noche* 230

——: 1984 *Saint Theresa** / *Teresa de Jesús* (TV) 260

——: 1988 *The Esquilache Reforms** / *Esquilache* 259

——: 1991 *The Most Natural Thing* / *Lo más natural* 285–6

——: 1993 *Lola Leaves for the Ports** / *La Lola se va a los puertos* 106, 299

Molinero, Carlos: 2001 *Savages** / *Salvajes* 333

Momplet, Antonio: 1953 *The Daughter of the Sea** / *La hija del mar* 121

Monleón, Sigfrid: 2005 *Industrial Syndrome** / *Síndrome laboral* 333

Montagu, Ivor: 1936 UK, *Defence of Madrid* 74

Montesinos, Rafael: 2003 *Full of Colours** / *De colores* 351

Mora, Jesús: 1996 *Clean Shooting** / *A tiro limpio* 170 n. 19, 303

Moreno, Armando: 1964/1965 *María Rosa* / *María Rosa* 169, 191

Moreno, Arturo: 1945 *Don Chickpea of La Mancha* / *Garbancito de la Mancha* 97, 175

——: 1948 *Happy Holidays* / *Alegres vacaciones* 97

——: 1951 *The Dreams of Tay-Pi* / *Los sueños de Tay-Pi* 97

Moreno Alba, Rafael: 1971 *Women of Doom* / *Las melancólicas* 200

——: 1975 *Bride to Be* / *Pepita Jiménez* 205

——: 1979 *My Liaison with Ana** / *Mis relaciones con Ana* 235

——: 1981 *Joys and Shadows** / *Los gozos y las sombras* (TV) 248

Morera, Eduardo: 1942 *Old Tuxedo** / *Viejo Smoking* 86

Munt, Silvia: 2003 *Mohamed's Daughters* / *Las hijas de Mohamed* 335

Muñoz, Juan: 2000 *Oh They're Kiiilling Me** / *Ja me maaten* 343

Muñoz, Nicolás: 1999 *Rewind* 348

Mur Oti, Manuel: 1949 *A Man on the Road** / *Un hombre va por el camino* 113, 130–1

——: 1949/1951 *Black Sky* / *Cielo negro* 113

——: 1953 *Condemned** / *Condenados* 127

——: 1955 *Pride* / *Orgullo* 127

——: 1956 *Fedra, the Devil's Daughter* / *Fedra* 127

——: 1967 *Crazy Youth** / *Loca juventud* 160

Murnau, F. W.: 1925 Germany, *Tartüff* 41

Musidora aka Jeanne Roques: 1919 *Vicenta* 30

——: 1924 *Land of Bulls** / *Tierra de los toros* 30

——: 1924 *Sun and Shadow** / *Sol y sombra*   30

Myrick, Daniel & Eduardo Sánchez: 1999 USA, *The Blair Witch Project*   337

Naschy, Paul see Molina, Jacinto

Navarro, Agustín: 1970 *Lesson for a Rascal** / *Enseñar a un sinverguenza*   202

——: 2003 *The Three Wise Men* / *Los reyes magos*   347

Neville, Edgar: 1931 *I Want to be Taken to Hollywood** / *Yo quiero que me lleven a Hollywood*   52, 62

——: 1935 *The Evil Carabel** / *El malvado Carabel*   62

——: 1936 *Miss Trevélez* / *La señorita de Trevélez*   69–70, 138

——: 1938 *University City** / *Ciudad Universitaria*   78

——: 1938 *Spanish Youth** / *Juventudes de España*   78

——: 1939 *Let Free Men Live!** / *¡Vivan los hombres libres!*   78

——: 1939 *Santa Rogelia*   82

——: 1939 *The Madrid Front** / *Frente de Madrid*   82

——: 1941 *Madrid Carnival** / *Verbena*   86

——: 1944 *The Tower of the Seven Hunchbacks* / *La torre de los siete jorobados*   110–1

——: 1945 *Her Life on a Thread** / *La vida en un hilo*   111

——: 1945 *Carnival Sunday** / *Domingo de carnaval*   111

——: 1946 *The Embroiderer Street Murder** / *El crimen de la calle de Bordadores*   111

——: 1947 *Nothing* / *Nada*   111

——: 1947 *The Bullfighter's Suit** / *El traje de luces*   106–7

——: 1948 *The Marquis of Salamanca** / *El marqués de Salamanca*   97

——: 1948 *Mister Esteve** / *El señor Esteve*   97

——: 1950 *The Last Horse* / *El último caballo*   111–12, 118 n. 3

——: 1952 *Flamenco* / *Duende y misterio del flamenco*   126

——: 1959 *The Ball** / *El baile*   124

——: 1960 *My Street** / *Mi calle*   124

Niblo, Fred: 1922 USA, *Blood and Sand*   17

——: 1925 USA, *Ben Hur*   17

——: 1926 USA, *The Temptress*   17

Nieves Conde, José Antonio: 1946 *Path Unknown* / *Senda ignorada*   109

——: 1948 *Anxieties** / *Angustia*   109

——: 1949 *Night Arrival** / *Llegada de noche*   109

——: 1951 *Reckless* / *Balarrasa*   103, 120–1, 153

——: 1951 *Furrows* / *Surcos*   90 n. 21, 117–18, 130–1, 133, 155, 272, 320

——: 1955 *Goldfish** / *Los peces rojos*   118, 129

——: 1956 *We are All Needed* / *Todos somos necesarios*   147

——: 1958 *The Tenant* / *El inquilino*   147

——: 1963 *The Devil also Weeps** / *El diablo también llora*   170

——: 1964 *The Prehistoric Sound* / *El sonido de la muerte*   174

——: 1976 *Beyond Desire** / *Más allá del deseo*   206

Noriega, Manuel: 1922 *Heart of Gold** / *Alma de Dios*   93

Noriega, Manuel and Alejandro Pérez Lugín: 1925 *College Boarding House* / *La casa de la Troya*   32–3, 38, 66, 92 n. 22

Noriega, Manuel: 1925 *The Embittered Don Quentin** / *Don Quintín el amargao*   34, 60

——: 1925 *Madrid in the Year 2000** / *Madrid en el año 2000*   36 n. 20, 41

Nosseck, Max: 1934 *One Week of Happiness* / *Una semana de felicidad*   63

——: 1935 *A Big Guy* / *Poderoso Caballero*   63

——: 1935 *Eastern Adventure** / *Aventura oriental*   63
Novaro, María: 1992 *Dancer** / *Danzón*   313
Núñez, Iñaki: 1978 *Curfew** / *Toque de queda*   241
Nuñez, Ricardo: 1956 *Malagueña*   142
Olasagasti, Eneko and Carlos Zabala: 1995 *Maité*   313
Olavarría, Alejandro: 1924 *A Drama in Bilbao** / *Un drama en Bilbao*   34
Olea, Pedro: 1968 *Days of Faded Colour** / *Días de viejo color*   218
——: 1969 *In a Different World** / *En un mundo diferente*   218
——: 1971 *The Ancines Woods* / *El bosque del lobo*   218
——: 1972 *A House without Boundaries* / *La casa sin fronteras*   218–19
——: 1973 *It is not Good for Man to be Alone** / *No es bueno que el hombre esté solo*   219
——: 1974 *Tormento*   219
——: 1975 *One Two Three, Fire!** / *Pim, pam, pum ¡fuego!*   219
——: 1976 *La Corea*   219
——: 1978 *A Man called Autumn Flower* / *Un hombre llamado Flor de Otoño*   236, 247
——: 1984 *Witches' Sabbath** / *Akelarre*   278
——: 1991 *The Day I was Born** / *El día que nací yo*   299
——: 1992 *The Fencing Master* / *El maestro de esgrima*   287
——: 1995 *Zafarinas* / *Morirás en Chafarinas*   288
——: 1996 *Beyond the Garden* / *Más allá del jardín*   290
Olen Ray, Fred: 2003 USA, *Tomb of the Werewolf*   175, 208, 338
Oliver, Juan: 1920 *Death of Joselito** / *La muerte de Joselito*   30
Ontañón, Santiago: 1936 *The Carnations** / *Los claveles*   57
Ophüls, Max: 1955 France, *Lola Montès*   107
Orduña, Juan de: 1928 *A Film Adventure** / *Una aventura de cine*   105
——: 1940 *Granada Suite** / *Suite Granadina*   86
——: 1940 *Fair in Seville** / *Feria en Sevilla*   86
——: 1942 *Follow the Legion!!* / *¡¡A mí la legión!!*   92
——: 1943 *Delightfully Foolish** / *Deliciosamente tontos*   93–4
——: 1944 *Life Begins at Midnight** / *La vida empieza a medianoche*   94
——: 1944 *She, He and His Millions** / *Ella, él y sus millones*   94
——: 1946 *White Mission** / *Misión blanca*   103
——: 1947 *Spanish Serenade* / *Serenata española*   107
——: 1947 *Lola Leaves for the Ports** / *La Lola se va a los puertos*   106, 299
——: 1948 *The Mad Queen* / *Locura de amor*   17 n. 26, 101, 103–4, 330
——: 1950 *Agustina of Aragon* / *Agustina de Aragón*   99–101, 121 n. 3, 147 n. 44
——: 1950 *Trifles* / *Pequeñeces*   103–4, 121 n. 3
——: 1951 *The Lioness of Castile** / *La leona de Castilla*   101, 121 n. 3, 153
——: 1951 *Dawn of America** / *Alba de América*   117–18, 154
——: 1954 *Zalacaín, the Adventurer** / *Zalacaín el aventurero*   35, 149
——: 1954 *Reeds and Mud** / *Cañas y barro*   149
——: 1954 *Father Cigarette** / *El padre pitillo*   129
——: 1957 *Last Torch Song* / *El último cuplé*   141–2, 147, 153, 299
——: 1961 *Theresa* / *Teresa de Jesús*   122
——: !962 *Bohemians** / *Bohemios*   30 n. 7
——: 1965 *Rustic Chivalry* / *Aragonese Virtue* / *Nobleza baturra*   33
——: 1969 *The Mischief-Maker** / *La revoltosa*   163
——: 1970 *The Complete Idiot** / *La tonta del bote*   84, 168
——: 1972 *The Farmhouse** / *El caserío*   201

——: 1973 *You've Made Me Lose the Trial (My Mind)** / *Me has hecho perder el juicio* 201

Oristrell, Joaquín: 1997 *What Makes Women Laugh?* / *¿De qué se ríen las mujeres?* 304

——: 1999 *Engaged** / *Novios* 344

——: 2004 *Irresponsibles** / *Inconscientes* 344

Ortega Santillana, Eterio: 2004 *Pursued** / *Perseguidos* 327

——: 2006 *News of a War** / *Noticias de una guerra* 327

Ossorio, Amando de: 1971 *Night of the Blind Dead* / *La noche del terror ciego* 208

Ozores, Mariano: 1965 *To Die in Spain* / *Morir en España* 170

——: 1967 *Missión Cabaret** / *Operación cabaretera* 165

——: 1967 *Forty Degrees in the Shade** / *Cuarenta grados a la sombra* 167 n. 14

——: 1972 *Two Chorus Line Girls** / *Dos chicas de revistas* 168

——: 1973 *The Stray Sheep** / *La descariada* 201

——: 1973 *Madam Doctor** / *Señora Doctor* 202

——: 1973 *They Called Her the Godmother** / *La llamaban la madrina* 202

——: 1973 *A Nun and a Don Juan**/ *Una monja y un don Juan* 202

——: 1974 *The Hen-pecked Husband** / *El calzonazos* 201

——: 1978 *What the Skipper Says...** / *Donde hay patrón...* 249

——: 1982 *On the Floor!** / *¡Todos al suelo!* 240

——: 1982 *The Socialists are Coming!** / *¡Qué vienen los socialistas!* 240

Palacios, Fernando: 1959 *Valentine's Day* / *El día de los enamorados* 145

——: 1961 *Threesome from the Red Cross** / *Tres de la Cruz Roja* 146

——: 1962 *The Big Family* / *La gran familia* 144 n. 41, 167, 234

——: 1963 *Marisol Goes to Río** / *Marisol rumbo a Río* 161, 313

——: 1964 *Find That Girl* / *Búsqueme a esta chica* 161, 163

——: 1965 *The Family Plus One* / *La familia y uno más* 167, 234

——: 1965 *Whisky and Vodka** / *Whisky y Vodka* 162

Palacios, Manuel: 1999 *The Stone Rose** / *La rosa de piedra* 338

——: 2004 *Bars on the Memory** / *Rejas en la memoria* 328

Palmer, Russell: 1939 USA, *Defenders of the Faith* 79

Palmero, Javier: 1986 *Manuel and Clemente** / *Manuel y Clemente* 268

Pamplona, Clemente: 1958 *Duty Pharmacy** / *Farmacia de guardia* 147

Pangua, José Antonio: 1981 *The Chronicle of a Moment* / *Crónica de un instante* 233–4

Parellada, Juan: 1942 *Wings of Peace** / *Alas de paz* 86

París, Inés and Daniela Féjerman: 2002 *My Mother Likes Women* / *A mi madre le gustan las mujeres* 344

——: 2005 *Semen (A Love Story)** / *Semen (una historia de amor)* 344

Parrado, Ramón: 2004 *Skinheads** / *Rapados* 333

Pastor Moreno, Carles: 2005 *Flush with the Ground** / *A ras de suelo* 346

Pastrone, Giovanni: 1914 Italy, *Cabiria* 10

——: 1916 Italy, *La Guerra e il sogno di Momi* 10

Patino, Basilio Martín: 1967 *Nine Letters to Bertha* / *Nueve cartas a Berta* 187

——: 1969 *Love and Other Solitudes* / *Del amor y otras soledades* 187

——: 1971/1976 *Songs for after a War** / *Canciones para después de una guerra* 210, 216, 240, 320, 326

——: 1974/1977 *Francisco Franco, the Leader** / *Caudillo* 210, 240

——: 1974/1977 *Dearest Excecutioners* / *Queridísimos verdugos* 210, 240

——: 1985 *The Lost Paradise* / *Los paraísos perdidos* 263

——: 1987 *Madrid* 263

——: 1991 *The Seduction of Chaos* / La seducción del caos* 267
Paul, Robert W.: 1896 USA, *Tour through Spain and Portugal* 1 n. 1
Peláez, Ángel: 2006 *Always Havana* / Siempre Habana* 350–1
Pellegrini, Clauco: 1957 *Perhaps Tomorrow* / Tal vez mañana* 149
Peña, Chema de la: 2004 *Isi/Disi, Incredible Love* / Isi/Disi – Amor a lo bestia* 346
Pereyra, Miguel: 1936 *Naval Protection* / Asilo Naval* 78
——: 1936 *With the Brigades of Navarre* / Con las brigadas de Navarra* 78
——: 1937 *The Capture of Bilbao* / La toma de Bilbao* 78
Pérez, Dionisio: 2003 *Silvia's present* / El regalo de Silvia* 332
Pérez de Guzmán, Dacil: 2005 *Victor's Journey* / El camino de Victor* 333
Pérez Dolz, Francisco: 1963 *Clean Shooting* / A tiro limpio* 170, 303
Pérez Ferré, Carlos: 1991 *The Strong Wind* / Tramontana* 302
——: 1996 *Best Seller, The Prize* / Best Seller, el premio* 290
Pérez Herrero, Vicente: 2005 *A Hundred Ways to Stop Loving* / Cien maneras de acabar con el amor* 348
Pérez Lugín, Alejandro: 1925 *Currito of the Cross / Currito de la Cruz* 30, 36 n. 20, 65, 107 n. 45
Perla, Alejandro: 1952 *Don Juan Tenorio* 149
Perojo, Benito: 1914 *Mr Someone Falls in Love with Manon* / Fulano de Tal se enamora de Manón* 18, 29
——: 1915 *Clarita y Peladilla at a Football Match* / Clarita y Peladilla en el fútbol* 29
——: 1915 *Clarita y Peladilla go to the Bullfight* / Clarita y Peladilla van a los toros* 29
——: 1923 *For Ever* / Para toda la vida* 38
——: 1924 *Beyond Death* / Más allá de la muerte* 38
——: 1925 *Boy* 37–8
——: 1926 *Hollyhock / Malvaloca* 34, 37
——: 1927 *Countess Maria* / La condesa María* 34, 37, 95
——: 1927 *The Black Man with a White Soul* / El negro que tenía el alma blanca* 10, 37–8, 58
——: 1928 *Aimless Hearts* / Corazones sin rumbo / Herzen ohne Ziel* 37
——: 1929 *Wine Cellars / La bodega* 38, 51
——: 1930 *The Sevilian Spell* / El embrujo de Sevilla / L'ensorcellement de Séville* 50–1
——: 1930 *A Lucky Man* / Un hombre de suerte* 52
——: 1931 *Mother!* / Mamá* 51–2
——: 1932 *The Man Who Laughed at Love* / El hombre que se reía del amor* 56, 62
——: 1933 *Susana has a Secret / Susana tiene un secreto* 56
——: 1933 *A Prisoner has Escaped / Se ha fugado un preso* 56
——: 1934 *World Crisis / Crisis mundial* 57, 65
——: 1934 *The Black Man with a White Soul* / El negro que tenía el alma blanca* (remake) 58, 65
——: 1935 *He's My Man!* / ¡Es mi hombre!* 69
——: 1935 *The Road to Cairo* / Rumbo al Cairo* 59
——: 1935 *The Fair of the Dove / La verbena de la Paloma* 31, 59, 66–8, 163
——: 1936 *Our Natasha* / Nuestra Natacha* 71, 81
——: 1938 *The Barber of Seville / El barbero de Sevilla* 81, 111 n. 51
——: 1938 *Spanish Sighs* / Suspiros de España* 81, 294 n. 13,
——: 1939 *Mariquilla Terremoto* 81
——: 1940 *The Children of the Night* / Los hijos de la noche* 82

——: 1940 *The Last Carnival* / La última falla* 82
——: 1940 *Marianela* 84
——: 1941 *Reluctant Hero* / Héroe a la fuerza* 93
——: 1942 *Goyesques* / Goyescas* 106
——: 1947 *Song of Dolores / La copla de la Dolores* 7
——: 1949 *I'm not Mata Hari / Yo no soy la Mata-Hari* 114
——: 1950 *Blood in Castile* / Sangre en Castilla* 114
Pi, Rosario: 1936 *The Wildcat* / El gato montés* 62, 66, 127
——: 1937/1939 *Windmills / Molinos de viento* 62
Picazo, Miguel: 1964 *Aunt Tula* / La tía Tula* 138, 186, 230 n. 8, 320
——: 1967 *Obscure August Dreams / Oscuros sueños de agosto* 186
——: 1976 *The Clear Motives of Desire* / Los claros motivos del deseo* 249 n. 37
——: 1977 *The Man who Knew Love / El hombre que supo amar* 249
——: 1985 *Beyond the Walls / Extramuros* 186, 259
Pinzás, Juan: 2002 *Wedding Days* / Días de voda / Días de boda* 336
Piñeiro, Chano: 1990 *A Woman Forever / Sempre Xonxa / Siempre Xonxa* 279
Piñeyro, Marcelo: 2005 *The Method / El método* 339, 341 n. 22
Pons, Ventura: 1978 *Ocaña, An Intermittent Portrait / Ocaña, retrat intermitent* 234, 275
——: 1981 *The Vicar of Olot* / El vicari d'Olot* 275
——: 1986 *The Blonde at the Bar* / La rossa del bar* 275
——: 1989 *Damned Despair !* / Puta misèria!* 275
——: 1991 *What do you Bet, Mari Pili?* / Què t'hi jugues, Mari Pili? / El porqué de las cosas* 296
——: 1992 *Tonight or Never* / Aquesta nit o mai* 296
——: 1994 *Rosita, Please!* 296
——: 1995 *What It's All about / El perquè de tot plegat* 296
——: 1997 *Actresses / Actrius / Actrices* 286–7
——: 1998 *Caresses / Carícies* 339
——: 2000 *Anita Takes a Chance / Anita no perd el tren / Anita no pierde el tren* 283 n. 1
——: 2005 *Idiot Love / Amor idiota* 275 n. 26, 345
Pontecorvo, Gillo: 1980 *Operation Ogre / Operación Ogro* 198, 243
Porlan, Alberto: 2004 *The Spanish Crates* / Las cajas españolas* 328–9
Portabella, Pere: 1969 *Nocturne 29 / Nocturno 29* 194
——: 1970 *Trellis* / Umbracle* 194
——: 1977 *General Report...* / Informe general...* 242
——: 1990 *The Warsaw Bridge / Pont de Varsòvia* 277
Potau, Joan: 2001 *Manolito Gafotas in Great to be the Leader!* / Manolito Gafotas en ¡mola ser jefe!* 347
Pottier, Richard: 1952 France, *Imperial Violets* / Violetas Imperiales* 108
Pozo, José: 2003 *El Cid: The Legend / El Cid: La leyenda* 347
Pratt, Gilbert: 1922 USA, *Mud and Sand* 17
Promio, Alexandre: 1896 *Pupils Leaving the French Girls' School* / Salida de las alumnas del Colegio de San Luis de los franceses* 1
——: 1896 *Arrival of Bullfighters at the Ring* / Llegada de los toreros a la plaza* 2
——: 1897 *Sevillanas* 2
——: 1898 *Charge of the Queen's Lancers* / Carga de los lanceros de la Reina* 2
——: 1898 *Artillery Manoeuvres at Vicalvaro* / Maniobras de la artillería en Vicálvaro* 2
Puche, Pedro: 1937 *Low Districts* / Barrios bajos* 70–2, 109, 118 n. 3

Puenzo, Luis: 2004 *The Whore and the Whale* / *La puta y la ballena*   350
Puga, Ricardo: 1918 *Vested Interests** / *Los intereses creados*   27, 31
Pujol, David: 2001 *The Black Bible** / *La biblia negra*   338
Quadreny, Ramón: 1942 *Blood in the Snow** / *Sangre en la nieve*   108
——: 1943 *The Girl with the Cat** / *La chica del gato*   94
——: 1944 *An Operetta Girl** / *Una chica de opereta*   94
Quer, Silvia: 2003 *Sara*   331
Querejeta, Gracia: 1992 *Whistle Stop* / *Una estación de paso*   309
——: 1996 *Robert Rylands' Last Journey* / *El último viaje de Robert Rylands*   309
——: 1999 *By My Side Again* / *Cuando vuelvas a mi lado*   309, 334
——: 2004 *Héctor*   334
Quevedo, Nino: 1970 *Goya, a Story of Solitude** / *Goya, historia de una soledad*   220
Quintana, Ricardo: 1940 *Basque Pelota** / *Jai-Alai*   61
Quirós, José Antonio: 2000 *Get the King to Answer** / *Pídele cuentas al rey*   332
Ramírez, Pedro L: 1955 *Recruit with a child** / *Recluta con niño*   144
——: 1956 *We Thieves Are Honourable** / *Los ladrones somos gente honrada*   145–6
——: 1957 *KO Miguel* / *El tigre de Chamberí*   146
——: 1963 *The Guerrillas** / *Los guerrilleros*   160
Ray, Man: 1928 France, *L'Étoile de mer*   41
Ray, Nicholas: 1961 USA, *King of Kings*   172
——: 1963 USA, *55 Days at Peking*   172
Real, Antonio del: 1980 *The Powerful Influence of the Moon** / *El poderoso influjo de la luna*   234
——: 1982 *Looking for Pete** / *Buscando a Perico*   234
——: 1989 *The River that Takes Us** / *El río que nos lleva*   302
——: 1994 *Alone, at last!* / *¡Por fin solos!*   297
——: 1995 *Men Always Lie* / *Los hombres ~~nunca~~ siempre mienten*   293
Rebolledo, Javier: 2001 *Killer Housewives* / *Marujas asesinas*   336
Recha, Marc: 2001 *Pau and his Brother* / *Pau i el seu germà* / *Pau y su hermano*   338
——: 2003 *Where is Madame Catherine?* / *Les mans buides* / *Las manos vacías*   338
——: 2006 *August Days* / *Dies d'agost* / *Días de agosto*   338
Regueiro, Francisco: 1963 *The Good Love* / *El buen amor*   186
——: 1965 *Lover** / *Amador*   186, 188
——: 1967 *Smashing Up* / *Si volvemos a vernos*   186
——: 1969 *I Poison Myself with Blues** / *Me enveneno de azules*   186
——: 1972 *Love Letter from a Murderer** / *Carta de amor de un asesino*   209
——: 1975 *Sleep, Sleep my Love** / *Duerme, duerme mi amor*   209
——: 1975 *Blanca's Weddings** / *Las bodas de Blanca*   209
——: 1985 *Our Father* / *Padre nuestro*   186, 268, 320
——: 1993 *Mother Gilda** / *Madregilda*   90 n. 21, 300
Reig, Joaquín: 1938 *Heroic Spain** / *España heroica* / *Helden in Spanien*   79
Renais, Alain: 1959 France, *Hiroshima mon amour*   74
Renoir, Jean: 1924 France, *La Fille de l'eau*   41
Rey, Florián: 1924 *The Mischief-Maker** / *La revoltosa*   29, 33, 163
——: 1924 *The Bullfighter's Medal** / *La medalla del torero*   29
——: 1925 *Lazarillo de Tormes* / *El Lazarillo de Tormes*   29, 149 n. 47
——: 1927 *Sister San Sulpicio* / *La hermana San Sulpicio*   37, 59, 125
——: 1927 *The Village priest** / *El cura de aldea*   59
——: 1928 *The Virgin Mary's Carnations** / *Los claveles de la Virgen*   37
——: 1929 *Agustina de Aragón*   101
——: 1930 *Pitouto Farm-Hand** / *Pitouto, mozo de granja*   29

——: 1930 *Pitouto with His Little Heart* / Pitouto tiene su corazoncito* 29
——: 1930 *The Cursed Village / La aldea maldita* 38–40, 47, 83, 118, 230 n. 8; 320
——: 1930 *Football, Love and Bullfighting* / Fútbol, amor y toros* 60
——: 1931 *Nothing but the Truth / La pura verdad* 52
——: 1931 *Her Wedding Night / Su noche de bodas* 52
——: 1931 *Laughter's the Best Remedy* / Lo mejor es reír* 52
——: 1933 *Suburban Melody / Melodía de arrabal* 52
——: 1933 *The Sierra of Ronda* / Sierra de Ronda* 56
——: 1934 *Sister San Sulpicio / La hermana San Sulpicio* (remake) 37, 59, 63
——: 1934 *Mother's Boyfriend* / El novio de mamá* 57
——: 1935 *Rustic Chivalry / Aragonese Virtue / Nobleza baturra* 33, 63, 66–7, 146 n. 42
——: 1936 *Dark and Bright / Morena Clara* 63, 66, 69, 93, 126
——: 1938 *Carmen / Carmen, la de Triana* 80, 106, 114
——: 1939 *The Song of Aixa / La canción de Aixa* 80, 93
——: 1940 *Dolores / La Dolores* 7, 83–4, 111 n. 51
——: 1941 *Stowaway on Board!* / ¡Polizón a bordo!* 84
——: 1942 *The Cursed Village / La aldea maldita* (remake) 38–40, 47, 83, 118
——: 1943 *Osoria* 84
——: 1943 *Idols* / Ídolos* 106
——: 1948 *A Toast for Manolete* / Brindis a Manolete* 107
——: 1948 *Soledad, the Cicada* / La Cigarra* 108
——: 1950 *Tales of the Alhambra* / Cuentos de la Alhambra* 105
——: 1954 *The Girl with the Jar / La moza del cántaro* 149
Ribas, Antonio: 1976 *The Burned City / La ciutat cremada / La ciudad quemada* 5, 246
——: 1983–1984 *Victory* / Victòria!* 246
Ribera Perpinyá, Xavier: 1996 *Pure Poison* / Tot Verí / Puro veneno* 311
Río, Ernesto del: 1987 *Present Love* / El amor de ahora* 274
——: 1993 *Don't Complicate my Life* / No me compliques la vida* 295–6
——: 1995 *In Hotels and at Home* / Hotel y domicilio* 288
Ripoll, María: 1998 *If Only / The Man with Rain in his Shoes / Lluvia en los zapatos* 345
——: 2001 *Tortilla Soup* 345
——: 2003 *Utopia* / Utopía* 337
Rispa, Jacobo: 2005 *Diary of a Skinhead* / Diario de un skin* 333
Robbins, Jerome and Robert Wise: 1961 USA, *West Side Story* 160
Rodríguez, Alberto: 2002 *The Suit / El traje* 333
Rodríguez, Azucena: 1995 *Red Together* / Entre rojas* 308
——: 1995 *It could be Fun* / Puede ser divertido* 308
Rodríguez, Francisco: 2005 *90 Miles* / 90 millas* 351
Rodríguez, Manane: 2001 *The Lost Steps* / Los pasos perdidos* 350
Rodríguez Gordillo, Francisco: 1996 *Lycanthropus: The Moonlight Murders / Licántropo* 208, 338
Roques, Jeanne see Musidora
Roldán, Fernando: 1931 *Fermín Galán* 6 n. 20, 54
——: 1933 *In the Mire* / Sobre el cieno* 70
——: 1936 *Luis Candelas* 72
Román, Antonio: 1935 *A Hymn to Migration* / Canto a la emigración* 73
——: 1935 *The Enchanted City* / La ciudad encantada* 73
——: 1940 *Merida* 86

——: 1940 *From the Alhambra to the Albaicín* / De la Alhambra al Albaicín*   86
——: 1940 *The Man and his Cart* / El hombre y el carro*   86
——: 1941 *The Squadron / Escuadrilla*   91, 96
——: 1942 *Marriage in Hell* / Boda en el infierno*   96
——: 1943 *The House of Rain* / La casa de la lluvia*   96
——: 1943 *Intrigue* / Intriga*   96
——: 1944 *Lola Montes*   107
——: 1945 *Last Stand in the Philippines* / Los últimos de Filipinas*   92, 96, 114
——: 1947 *The Sheepwell* / Fuenteovejuna*   104
——: 1949 *A Love Bewitched* / El amor brujo*   160, 250–1
——: 1952 *Last Day* / Último día*   130
——: 1955 *The Taming of the Shrew / La fierecilla domada*   149
——: 1957 *Dawn* / Madrugada*   149
——: 1958 *Peace Bombs* / Bombas para la paz*   123, 135
——: 1958 *Bugles of Fear / Los clarines del miedo*   142
——: 1966/1968 *Savage Gringo / Ringo de Nebraska*   173
——: 1969 *The Gypsy's Inn* / El mesón del gitano*   160
Romero Marchent, Joaquín: 1956/1959 *The Two Nobodies* / Fulano y Mengano*   145
——: 1955 *The Coyote / El Coyote*   173
——: 1956 *The Judgement of the Coyote / La justicia del Coyote*   173
——: 1962 *Zorro the Avenger / La venganza del Zorro*   173
——: 1962 *The Shadow of Zorro / L'ombra di Zorro / La sombra del Zorro*   173
——: 1963 *Gunfight at High Noon / El sabor de la venganza*   173
——: 1964 *Hour of Death / Antes llega la muerte*   173
Romero Marchent, Rafael: 1966 *Sharp-Shooting Twin Sisters / Dos pistolas gemelas*
    162
——: 1982 *All Is Possible in Granada* / Todo es posible en Granada*   129, 162, 250
Ronconori, Mario: 1926 *Valencian Rose* / Rosa de Levante*   33 n. 15
Rossen, Robert: 1955 USA, *Alexander the Great*   172
Rossif, Frédéric: 1963 France, *Mourir à Madrid*   170
Rotaeta, Félix: 1988 *The Pleasure of Killing / El placer de matar*   274
——: 1991 *Scrap Heap* / Chatarra*   274
Roussel, Henri: 1924 and 1932 France, *Violettes impériales*   141
Rovira Beleta, Francisco: 1950 *Blood Moon* / Luna de sangre*   149
——: 1953 *There is a Path to the Right / Hay un camino a la derecha*   294 n. 13
——: 1954 *Eleven Pairs of Boots* / Once pares de botas*   128
——: 1956 *The Andalusia Express* / El expreso de Andalucía*   70, 148
——: 1961 *The Robbers / Los atracadores*   148
——: 1962 *The Tarantos* / Los Tarantos*   160
——: 1967 *A Love Bewitched* / El amor brujo*   160, 250–1
——: 1973 *Roses and Green Pepper / No encontré rosas para mi madre*   214 n. 26
Ruiz Castillo, Arturo: 1936 *War in the Fields* / Guerra en el campo*   78
——: 1938 *War in the Snow* / Guerra en la nieve*   78
——: 1941 *Gardens of Spain* / Jardines de España*   86
——: 1944 *Wine and other Beverages* / Vino y otras bebidas*   86
——: 1947 *The Preoccupations of Shanti Andía* / Las inquietudes de Shanti Andía*
    103
——: 1949 *The Godless Swamp / La manigua sin Dios*   103
——: 1949 *The Sanctuary Does Not Surrender / El santuario no se rinde*   112
——: 1951 *Catherine of England* / Catalina de Inglaterra*   101
——: 1952 *The Black Lagoon* / La laguna negra*   149

——: 1953 *Two Paths** / *Dos caminos*   124, 147 n. 44

——: 1955 *Aces looking for Peace** / *Los ases buscan la paz*   128 n. 15, 147 n. 44

Ruiz de Austri, Maite: 1992 *The Legend of the North Wind** / *La leyenda del viento del norte*
312

——: 1994 *The Return of the North Wind** / *Regreso del viento del norte*   312

——: 1998 *What Beastly Neighbours!** / *¡Qué vecinos tan animales!*   312

Ruiz Vergara, Fernando: 1980 *Our Lady of the Rocío** / *Rocío*   42

Russell, Ken: 1971 UK, *The Devils*   200

Sacristán, José: 1983 *Lead Soldiers** / *Soldados de plomo*   274

——: 1987 *Silver-Beet Face* / *Cara de acelga*   274

——: 1992 *I Get Off at the Next Stop, What About You?* / *Yo me bajo a la próxima ¿y usted?*   274

Sáenz de Heredia, Álvaro: 1982 *Freddy the Croupier** / *Freddy el croupier*   305

——: 1990 *Here I Smell a Corpse** / *Aquí huele a muerto*   305

——: 1992 *The Thetheft of the Jejewel** / *El robobo de la jojoya*   305

——: 1992 *Chechu and Family** / *Chechu y familia*   305

——: 1994 *A Girl in a Million** / *Una chica entre un millón*   305

——: 1996 *Here Comes Condemor** / *Aquí llega Condemor*   305

Sáenz de Heredia, José Luis: 1934 *Patricio Looked at a Star* / *Patricio miró a una estrella*   61

Sáenz de Heredia and Luis Buñuel: 1935 *Juan Simon's Daughter** / *La hija de Juan Simón*   55, 61, 135, 146 n. 42, 262 n. 8

——: 1936 *Who Loves Me?** / *¿Quién me quiere a mí?*   61

Sáenz de Heredia, José Luis: 1941 *Don't You Look at Me** / *A mí no me mire usted*   90

——: 1941 *Race* / *Raza*   81, 87–8, 90–1, 100, 111 n. 51, 114, 123

——: 1943 *The Scandal* / *El escándalo*   96

——: 1945 *Bamboo** / *Bambú*   92

——: 1945 *Fate Apologises** / *El destino se disculpa*   111

——: 1947 *Mariona Rebull*   97

——: 1948 *The Harvest is Rich* / *La mies es mucha*   103, 121 n. 8

——: 1948 *The Waters Run Black** / *Las aguas bajan negras*   105, 118 n. 3

——: 1950 *Don Juan*   104

——: 1951 *The Spirit of a Race* / *Espíritu de una raza* (remake)   91, 123

——: 1952 *Eyes Leave Prints** / *Los ojos dejan huellas*   129

——: 1954 *All is Possible in Granada* / *Todo es posible en Granada*   129

——: 1955 *Radio Stories** / *Historias de la radio*   129, 153, 320

——: 1960 *The Reprieve* / *El indulto*   149

——: 1962 *The Mustard Grain** / *El grano de mostaza*   129

——: 1963 *The Fair of the Dove* / *La verbena de la Paloma*   31, 68, 163

——: 1964 *Franco, The Man** / *Franco: ese hombre*   170

——: 1965 *Television Stories** / *Historias de la televisión*   129

——: 1967 *But What Sort of a Country are we Living in?** / *Pero ¿en qué país vivimos?*   159

——: 1968 *Almost Public Relations** / *Relaciones casi públicas*   159

——: 1969 *A Skirt at Court** / *Juicio de faldas*   159

——: 1970 *Mr Goesby Thebook** / *Don Erre que erre*   201

——: 1970 *The Decent One** / *La decente*   202

——: 1970 *What a Fuss of a Nativity!** / *¡Se armó el belén!*   202

——: 1971 *You Owe Me a Body** / *Me debes un muerto*   159

——: 1974 *When the Children Arrive from Marseilles* / Cuando los niños vienen de Marsella* 201

Saguer, Albert: 2002 *Dirty Vivancos III / Vivancos 3* 343

Salaberry, Enrique: 1959 *Vargas's Inn / Venta de Vargas* 140–1

Salazar, Ramón: 2005 *20 Centimetres / 20 centimetros* 346–7

——: 2002 *Stones / Piedras* 347

Salgot, Josep Antón: 1980 *Mother Dearly Beloved / Mater amatísima* 231, 320

Salvador, Julio: 1950 *P O Box 1001* / Apartado de correos 1001* 109, 118 n. 3

——: 1958 *Now We Have a Car* / Ya tenemos coche* 146

Salvia, Rafael: 1953 *Flight 971* / Vuelo 971* 122

——: 1954 *Manolo, Urban Policeman* / Manolo, guardia urbano* 145

——: 1958 *The Red Cross Girls / Las chicas de la Cruz Roja* 145, 153

Sánchez, Sonia: 2006 *Mobbing* 340

Sánchez Cabezudo, Jorge: 2006 *The Night of the Sunflowers / La noche de los girasoles* 338

Sánchez Valdés, Julio: 1985 *Pluck Up Your Courage* / De tripas corazón* 274

——: 1987 *A Moon for Wolves* / Luna de lobos* 274

——: 1991 *The Fountain of Time* / La fuente de la edad* 274

Santillán, Antonio: 1955 *The Glass Eye / El ojo de cristal* 148

——: 1963 *Twisted Path* / Senda torcida* 170

Santos, Mateo: 1936 *Report on the Revolutionary Movement in Barcelona* / Reportaje del movimiento revolucionario en Barcelona* 73

——: 1936 *Barcelona Working for the Front Lines* / Barcelona trabaja para el frente* 73

Santugini, José: 1936 *A Woman in Danger / Una mujer en peligro* 70

Sanz, Luis: 1990 *I'm the One / Yo soy ésa* 299

Saraceni, Julio: 1979 *Alejandra, My Love* / Alejandra mon amour* 249

Saslavsky, Luis: 1962 *The Balcony Beneath the Moon* / El balcón de la luna* 125

Sau Olite, Antonio: 1937 *Dawn of Hope* / Aurora de esperanza* 71, 118 n. 3

Saura, Carlos: 1959/1961 *The Delinquents / Los golfos* 131, 142, 150, 182, 190, 194, 237

——: 1963 *Lament for a Bandit* / Llanto por un bandido* 182

——: 1966 *The Hunt / La caza* 170 n. 17, 182–3, 188, 319

——: 1967 *Peppermint Frappé / Peppermint frappé* 183, 188, 216, 231 n. 10

——: 1968 *Stress is Three / Stress es tres tres* 183

——: 1969 *Honeycomb / La madriguera* 184

——: 1970 *The Garden of Delights / El jardín de las delicias* 81, 214–5, 245, 261 n. 7

——: 1973 *Anna and the Wolves / Ana y los lobos* 88, 116 n. 1, 146 n. 42, 215, 222, 231, 260 n. 5

——: 1974 *Cousin Angelica / La prima Angélica* 200, 215–6, 231 n. 10, 245

——: 1976 *Raise Ravens / Cría cuervos* 183, 216–17, 230 n. 8, 231 n. 10

——: 1977 *Elisa, My Life / Elisa, vida mía* 230

——: 1978 *Blindfolded Eyes / Los ojos vendados* 243

——: 1979 *Mama Turns a Hundred / Mamá cumple cien años* 146 n. 42, 230, 260 n. 5, 295

——: 1981 *Blood Wedding / Bodas de sangre* 162, 250, 320

——: 1980 *Fast, Fast / Deprisa, deprisa* 237, 320

——: 1982 *Sweet Hours / Dulces horas* 182, 246, 260

——: 1982 *Antonieta* 260

——: 1983 *Carmen* 162, 250

——: 1984 *The Stilts / Los zancos* 291

——: 1986 *A Love Bewitched / El amor brujo*   160, 250–1
——: 1988 *El Dorado*   259
——: 1989 *The Dark Night / La noche oscura*   259–60
——: 1990 *¡Ay Carmela!*   299
——: 1992 *Sevillanas*   251, 299, 326
——: 1993 *Shoot! / ¡Dispara!*   291
——: 1995 *Flamenco*   299, 326
——: 1996 *Taxi*   289, 325, 333
——: 1997 *Little Bird / Pajarico*   325
——: 1998 *Tango / Tango, no me dejes nunca*   251, 325, 349
——: 1999 *Goya in Bordeaux / Goya en Burdeos*   326
——: 2001 *Buñuel and King Solomon's Table / Buñuel y la mesa del rey Salomón*   326
——: 2002 *Salomé*   251, 325–6
——: 2004 *The Seventh Day / El séptimo día*   326, 334 n. 16, 337
——: 2005 *Iberia*   251, 326
——: 2007 *Fados*   326, 349
Schertzinger, Victor: 1929 USA, *Nothing but the Truth*   52
Scott, Ridley: 1992 UK-France-Spain, *1492, Conquest of Paradise*   301
Segura, Santiago: 1998 *Torrente, the Stupid Arm of the Law / Torrente, el brazo tonto de la ley*   167 n. 14, 342–3
——: 2001 *Mission in Marbella / Misión en Marbella*   342
——: 2005 *The Bodyguard* / Torrente 3: El protector*   342
Sellier, Louis Joseph: 1897 *Gas Factory* / Fábrica de gas*   3
——: 1897 *Mina Square* / Plaza de Mina*   3
Sennett, Mack: 1924 USA, *Bull and Sand*   17
Serrano, David: 2003 *Football Days / Días de fútbol*   332, 346
Serrano de Osma, Carlos: 1947 *Abel Sánchez*   104, 109 n. 47
——: 1947 *The Black Siren / La sirena negra*   105, 109 n. 47
——: 1947 *The Spell* / Embrujo*   107–9
——: 1951 *Facing the Sea* / Rostro al mar*   124
——: 1952 *The Evil Forest / Parsifal*   122
——: 1960 *The Red Rose* / La rosa roja*   140
Setó, Javier: 1952 *Forbidden Trade* / Mercado prohibido*   129
——: 1956 *Blond Arrow / Saeta rubia*   128 n. 15
——: 1959 *Bread, Love and Andalusia / Pan, amor y Andalucía*   142
——: 1964 *The Scandal / El escándalo*   96
Sher, Jack: 1960 UK-USA, *The Worlds of Gulliver*   174 n. 24
Sherman, George: 1964 *The New Cinderella / La nueva Cenicienta*   161
Sica, Vittorio de: 1948 Italy, *Ladri di biciclette*   130
Sobrevila, Nemesio: 1927 *To the Madrid Hollywood* / Al Hollywood madrileño*   41, 46 n. 43
——: 1928 *Absolute Spanish* / Lo más español*   42
——: 1929 *The Sixth Sense* / El sexto sentido*   42, 47, 252
——: 1938 *Happy Swallows* / Elai-Alai*   74
Sol(lín), Mauricio: 1938 *Women at War* / La mujer y la guerra*   74
Soler, Llorenç: 1999 *Saïd*   333
Sota, Pedro de la: 1979 *Sabino Arana, the Basque* / Sabino Arana*   243
Suárez, Carlos: 1992 *Makiknife, the Last of the Small-time Crooks* / Makinavaja, el último choriso*   295
——: 1996 *Good Bye Shark* / Adios tiburón*   295
Suárez, Gonzalo: 1967/1969 *Ditirambo / Ditirambo*   193

——: 1969 *The Strange Case of Dr Faustus** / *El extraño caso del Dr Fausto*   193
——: 1971 *Morbidness – Perversion** / *Morbo*   212
——: 1974 *House of the Damned* / *La loba y la paloma*   200 n. 2, 213
——: 1974 *The Regent's Wife* / *La Regenta*   205, 213
——: 1976 *Beatriz*   213
——: 1977 *Binge* / *Parranda*   267
——: 1978 *The Carrot Queen* / *Reina Zanahoria*   267
——: 1984 *Epilogue** / *Epílogo*   267
——: 1988 *Rowing in the Wind* / *Remando al viento*   260, 320
——: 1991 *Don Juan in Hell* / *Don Juan en los infiernos*   260
——: 1992 *The Anonymous Queen* / *La reina anónima*   287
——: 1994 *The Detective and Death* / *El detective y la muerte*   290
——: 1996 *My Name is Shadow** / *Mi nombre es Sombra*   290
Suárez, Julio: 2000 *At Full Gallop* / *A galope tendido*   174
Suárez de Lezo, Luis: 1951 *Service at Sea** / *Servicio en la mar*   62, 124
Summers, Manuel: 1963 *From Pink... to Yellow* / *Del rosa... al amarillo*   185, 270
——: 1964 *The Girl in Mourning* / *La niña de luto*   185
——: 1966 *Snakes and Ladders* / *El juego de la oca*   185
——: 1966 *Broken Toys* / *Juguetes rotos*   185
——: 1968 *We Are Not Made of Stone* / *No somos de piedra*   185
——: 1969 *Why Does Your Husband Deceive You?* / *¿Por qué te engaña tu marido?*   185
——: 1970 *Urtain, King of the Mountains* / *Urtain, el rey de la selva*   185
——: 1971 *Goodbye Stork, Goodbye* / *Adios cigüeña, adios*   210
——: 1973 *The Baby is Ours** / *El niño es nuestro*   210
——: 1975 *I'm a Woman Already* / *¡Ya soy mujer!*   210
——: 1977 *My First Sin* / *Mi primer pecado – Mi primera experienca*   242
——: 1982 *Everybody's Good** / *To er mundo é güeno*   242
——: 1982 *Everybody's... Better** / *To er mundo é... mejó*   242
——: 1985 *Everybody's Too Much** / *To er mundo é demasiao*   242
——: 1986 *I Need a Moustache** / *Me hace falta un bigote*   270
——: 1987 *Let the Flesh Suffer!* / *Sufre Mamón*   270
——: 1988 *Let your Hair down** / *Suéltate el pelo*   270
Taberna, Helena: 1999 *Yoyes*   292 n. 12, 340
——: 2003 *Foreign Women** / *Extranjeras*   326
Tapia, Gonzalo: 2001 *Lena*   337
Targarona, Mar: 1996 *Die, My Darling* / *Mor, veda meva* / *Muere vida mía*   311
Taurog, Norman: 1938 USA, *Boys' Town*   121
Távora, Pilar: 1983 *Lullabies of Thorns** / *Nanas de espinas*   230
——: 1988 *Yerma*   230
Tellería, Ernesto: 1988 *Skorpion** / *Eskorpión*   306
——: 1996 *Below Zero** / *Menos que cero*   306
Thomas, Gerald: 1953 UK, *Carry on Sergeant*   165 n. 10
——: 1992 UK, *Carry on Columbus*   165 n. 10
Thous Orts, Maximiliano: 1924 *Dolores* / *La Dolores*   7, 83 n. 9
Togores i Muntades, Josep de: 1917 *The Vagrant** / *El Golfo*   18, 21–3
Toro, Guillermo del: 2001 *The Devil's Backbone* / *El espinazo del diablo*   329, 350
——: 2006 *Pan's Labyrinth* / *El laberinto del fauno*   329, 350–1
Torrado, Ramón: 1948 *Anchor Button** / *Botón de ancla*   108, 201
——: 1951 *The Threesome of the Air** / *La trinca del aire*   108
——: 1951 *The Girl at the Inn* / *La niña de la venta*   125

——: 1952 *Estrella, the Star of the Sierra Morena** / *La estrella de Sierra Morena* 125

——: 1954 *Hollyhock / Malvaloca*   34, 125

——: 1958 *María de la O*   65, 140

——: 1961 *Brother Broom** / *Fray Escoba*   121, 154

——: 1964 *Black Angel of the Mississippi / Bienvenido padre Murray*   173

——: 1965 *Shoot to Kill / Los cuatreros*   173

——: 1965 *My Song is for You** / *Mi canción es para ti*   159

——: 1966 *A Kiss in the Harbour / Un beso en el puerto*   159

——: 1966 *Father Manolo** / *El padre Manolo*   159

——: 1969 *Love at Top Speed** / *Amor a todo gas*   160

——: 1971 *In a New World** / *En un mundo nuevo*   201

——: 1971 *The Rebel Mountain** / *La montaña rebelde*   206

——: 1974 *Gentlemen with Anchor Buttons** / *Los caballeros del botón de ancla*   108, 201

Torre, Claudio de la: 1942 *The White Dove / La blanca paloma*   105

——: 1943 *The Wetland Mystery** / *Misterio en la marisma*   96

Tricicle [Joan Gràcia, Paco Mir and Carles Sans]: 1996 *Palace Hotel** / *Palace*   311

Trincado, Joaquín: 1995 *Save Yourself if You Can** / *Sálvate si puedes*   295

Trueba, David: 1996 *The Good Life / La buena vida*   293

——: 2000 *Masterpiece / Obra maestra*   348

——: 2003 *Soldiers of Salamina / Soldados de Salamina*   160, 329

Trueba, Fernando: 1980 *First Work / Ópera prima*   233

——: 1982 *While the Body Lasts** / *Mientras el cuerpo aguante*   242

——: 1984 *Coarse Salt / Sal gorda*   270

——: 1985 *Be Wanton and Tread no Shame / Sé infiel y no mires con quién*   270

——: 1986 *Year of Enlightment / El año de las luces*   262

——: 1989 *Twisted Obsessions / The Mad Monkey / El sueño del mono loco*   266–7, 320

——: 1992 *The Age of Beauty / Belle époque*   xiv, 287, 293, 296, 320

——: 1995 *Two Much*   296

——: 1998 *The Girl of Your Dreams / La niña de tus ojos*   80, 348–9

——: 2002 *The Shanghai Spell / El embrujo de Shanghai*   88, 349

Truffaut, François: 1962 France, *Jules et Jim*   334

Turtle, Frank: 1931 USA, *Her Wedding Night*   52

Ulargui, Saturnino: 1929 *Spanish Eyes / La canción del día*   50

Ungría, Alfonso: 1971 *The Man in Hiding / El hombre oculto*   220

——: 1974 *Gone to the Mountain** / *Tirarse al monte*   220

——: 1976 *Gulliver*   244 n. 31

——: 1978 *Soldiers** / *Soldados*   244

——: 1980 *Cervantes* (TV)   244 n. 31

——: 1984 *The Albanian Conquest** / *La conquista de Albania*   278

——: 1996 *Africa / África*   289

Urbizu, Enrique: 1988 *Your Girlfriend is Crazy / Tu novia está loca*   278

——: 1991 *All for the Dough** / *Todo por la pasta*   278

——: 1994 *How to be Miserable and Enjoy It / Cómo ser infeliz y disfrutarlo*   287

——: 1996 *Cachito*   313

——: 2002 *Box 507 / Caja 507*   337

——: 2003 *Life Marks / La vida mancha*   337

Uribe, Imanol: 1979 *The Burgos Trial / El proceso de Burgos*   241–2

——: 1981 *Escape from Segovia / La fuga de Segovia*   242

——: 1984 *Mikel's Death / La muerte de Mikel* 277
——: 1986 *Bilbao Blues / Adios pequeña* 267
——: 1990 *The Crime on the Andalusia Express* / El crimen del expreso de Andalucía* 70
——: 1990 *The Black Moon / La luna negra* 267
——: 1991 *The Dumbfounded King / El rey pasmado* 294
——: 1994 *Running out of Time / Días contados* 292, 320
——: 1996 *Bwana* 289
——: 1999 *Strangers* / Extraños* 336
——: 2000 *Plenilune / Plenilunio* 336
——: 2002 *Carol's Journey / El viaje de Carol* 330
Vajda, Ladislao: 1943 *A Palace for Sale / Se vende un palacio* 94
——: 1947 *The Neighbourhood* / Barrio* 109
——: 1951 *Spanish Serenade* / Ronda española* 87
——: 1953 *Doña Francisquita* 126
——: 1953 *Meat for the Gallows* / Carne de horca* 127, 182
——: 1954 *The Adventurer of Seville / Aventuras del barbero de Sevilla* 127
——: 1955 *The Miracle of Marcelino / Marcelino, pan y vino* 122, 142, 153, 205 n. 14
——: 1956 *My Uncle Jacinto* / Mi tío Jacinto* 142
——: 1956 *Bullfighting Afternoon* / Tarde de toros* 142–3, 153
——: 1957 *An Angel over Brooklyn / Un ángel pasó por Brooklyn* 143
——: 1959 *It Happened in Broad Daylight / El cebo* 148
——: 1960 *Maria, Registered in Bilbao* / María, matrícula de Bilbao* 148 n. 46
Val del Omar, José: 1937 *Swimming* / Natación* 73 n. 31
——: 1937 *Gymnastics* / Gimnasia* 73 n. 31
——: 1960 *Fire in Castille* / Fuego en Castilla* 73 n. 31
——: 1960 *Elemental Triptych of Spain* / Tríptico elemental de España* 73, 151, 326
Vara Cuervo, Rafael: 1966–71 *Mortadelo & Filemón, Private Investigations* / Mortadelo y Filemón, agencia de información* (TV) 176
Varda, Agnès: 1961 France, *Cléo de 5 à 7* 177 n. 28
Various: 1964–82 *Tales to Keep you Awake* / Historias para no dormir* (TV) 175
——: 1988,1990 *The Prints of Crime* / La huella del crimen* (TV) 264
——: 1988–94 *The Woman in Your Life* / La mujer de tu vida* (TV) 287
——: 1996 *Domain of the Sense / El domini del sentits* 346
——: 1999 *The Detective Inspector / El comisario* (TV) 344
——: 2001 *Tell me How it Happened* / Cuéntame cómo pasó* (TV) 167 n. 14, 318–9, 334
——: 2004 *Every Second in the World* / En el mundo a cada rato* 327
——: 2004 *Manolito Gafotas* (TV) 347
——: 2004 *There's Good Cause!* / ¡Hay motivo!* 317, 326
——: 2005 *Summer Grandma* / Abuela de verano* (TV) 334
——: 2006 *Images not to Forget* / Imágenes contra el olvido* 328
——: 2006 *Paris, I Love You / Paris, je t'aime* 324
——: 2006 *Between the Dictator and I / Entre el dictador i jo / Entre el dictador y yo* 328
Vega, Felipe: 1988 *While There is Light* / Mientras haya luz* 273
——: 1989 *The Best of Times* / El mejor de los tiempos* 273–4
——: 1992 *An Umbrella for Three / Un paraguas para tres* 295, 297
——: 1995 *The Roof of the World* / El techo del mundo* 289
——: 1997 *Special Occasions* / Grandes ocasiones* 297
——: 2000 *Raluy, a Night with the Circus* / Raluy, una noche en el circo* 347

Velo, Carlos: 1935 *City and Country* / Ciudad y campo*   73
——: 1935 *Phillip II and the Escorial Palace* / Felipe II y El Escorial*   73
——: 1935 *Tuna Fishing* / Almadrabas*   73
——: 1935 *Galicia and Compostela* / Galicia y Compostela*   73
——: 1936 *Saudade*   73
Vera, Gerardo: 1992 *A Woman in the Rain / Una mujer bajo la lluvia*   111 n. 49
——: 1996 *The Wanton of Spain / La Celestina*   171
——: 1999 *Second Skin / Segunda piel*   336
Verdaguer, Antoni: 1983 *The Hot Orgies of a Virgin* / Las calientes orgìas de una virgen*   276
——: 1987 *The Neckline* / L'escot* 276
——: 1990 *The Spider's Web* / La teranyina / La telaraña*   301
——: 1993 *Havana 1820* / Havanera 1820*   301
——: 1995 *A Couple of Three* / Parella de tres / Una pareja de tres*   296
——: 1995 *Women and Men* / Dones i homes / Mujeres y hombres*   296
Vergara, Pau: 2005 *Beyond the Barbed Wire* / Más allá de la alambrada*   328
Vergés, Rosa: 1990 *Heart Beat* / Boom Boom*   310
——: 1994 *Souvenir*   310
——: 1997 *Tick Tock* / Tic Tac*   347
Vidor, Charles: 1946 USA, *Gilda*   300 n. 16
Vidor, King: 1959 USA, *Solomon and Sheba*   172
Vilà Vilamala, Joan: 1925 *Rustic Chivalry / Aragonese Virtue / Nobleza baturra*   33
——: 1932 *How the Spanish Republic was Born / Cómo nació la República española*   72
Viladomat, Domingo and Mariano del Pombo: 1951 *Close to Heaven* / Cerca del cielo*   123, 147 n. 44
Viladomat, Domingo: 1961 *Mischievous Dog* / Perro golfo*   145
Vilar, Ignacio: 2003 *Illegal / Ilegal*   333
Villaronga, Agustí: 1987 *In a Glass Cage / Tras el cristal*   276, 320
——: 1989 *Moon Child / El niño de la luna*   276
——: 1996 *The Clandestine Passenger* / Le Passager clandestin / El pasajero clandestino*   291
——: 2000 *The Sea / El mar*   89, 262 n. 9, 329
Villatoro, Ángel: 1936 *The Defence of Madrid / Defensa de Madrid*   73
Viota, Paulino: 1977 *Tooth and Nail* / Con uñas y dientes*   247
——: 1984 *Hand to Hand* / Cuerpo a cuerpo*   247
Visconti, Luchino: 1960 Italy, *Rocco e i suoi fratelli*   184
Vivas, Miguel Ángel: 2002 *Reflections* / Reflejos*   340
Von Sternberg, Josef: 1929 Germany, *Der blaue Engel*   55, 266
——: 1935 USA, *The Devil is a woman*   64
Von Stroheim, Erich: 1923 USA, *Greed*   41
Wallace, Richard: 1929 USA, *Innocents of Paris*   50
Walsh, Raoul: 1915 USA, *Carmen*   23
Welles, Orson: 1942 USA *The Magnificent Ambersons*   111
——: 1955 France-Spain-Switzerland, *Confidential Report / Mister Arkadin*   172
——: 1966 France-Spain-Switzerland, *Chimes at Midnight / Campanadas a medianoche*   172
Whale, James: 1931 USA, *Frankenstein*   222
Wilson, Elsie Jane: 1918 USA, *Beauty in Chains*   84
Wood, Sam: 1930 USA, *Way for a Sailor*   51
Wyler, William: 1965 UK-USA, *The Collector*   266

Xaudaró, Joaquin and Ricardo García López: 1932 *The Rat First** / *El rata primero* 63
——: 1933 *Juan Simón's Girl* / *La novia de Juan Simón* 63
Yagüe, Jesús: 1977 *Facing the Sun that Warms You Best* / *Cara al sol que más calienta* 238
Young, Terence: 1954 *That Lady* / *La princesa de Éboli* 120
Zabalza, José María: 1965 *Three Dollars of Lead* / *Las malditas pistolas de Dallas* 174
——: 1970 *The Arizona Rebels** / *Los rebeldes de Arizona* 174
——: 1972 *The Fury of the Wolfman* / *La furia del hombre lobo* 207
——: 1984 *The Trojan in the Palmar** / *La de Troya en el Palmar* 268
Zacarías, Miguel: 1957 Mexico-Spain, *Maricruz* 126
Zambrano, Benito: 1999 *Alone* / *Solas* 331
——: 2005 *Havana Blues** / *Habana Blues* 350
Zorrilla, José Antonio: 1983 *The Deal** / *El arreglo* 247
——: 1987 *To the Four Winds* / *A los cuatro vientos* 262
Zulueta, Iván: 1969 *What's the Time Mr Wolf?** / *Un, dos, tres, al escondite inglés* 212, 222
——: 1980 *Rapture* / *Arrebato* 251–2, 320
——: 1989 *Eyelids** / *Párpados* 252

FILMOGRAPHY OF TITLES MENTIONED

The English translation of the titles are taken from the *IMDb* to facilitate searches and cross-references. When no translation was available, my own is indicated by an asterisk. The year given is that of the film's release, and in the case of a delay, usually due to censorship, the release date is the second.

With the titles, CH follows C, L is followed LL, and N by Ñ.

2 lados de la cama, Los / The Two Sides of the Bed 2005, Emilio Martínez Lázaro   346
20 centimetros / 20 Centimetres 2005, Ramón Salazar   346–7
27 horas / 27 Hours 1986, Montxo Armendáriz   278
55 Days at Peking 1963 USA, Nicholas Ray   172
90 millas / 90 Miles* 2005, Francisco Rodríguez   351
091 Policía al habla / 091 Police On Line 1960, José María Forqué   148
99 Mujeres / 99 Women 1969, Jesús Franco   207
127 millones libres de impuestos / 127 Million Tax-Free* 1981, Pedro Masó   240
1492, Conquest of Paradise 1992 UK-France-Spain, Ridley Scott   301
1919, Crónica del alba / 1919, Dawn Chronicle* 1983, Antonio Betancor   248–9
A ciegas / Blinded 1997, Daniel Calparsoro   308
A contratiempo / Problems and Mishaps* 1982, Óscar Ladoire   234
A galope tendido / At Full Gallop 2000, Julio Suárez   174
A las cinco de la tarde / At Five in the Afternoon 1960, Juan Antonio Bardem   139, 142, 149, 180
A los cuatro vientos / To the Four Winds 1987, José Antonio Zorrilla   262
A los que aman / Those Who Love 1998, Isabel Coixet   323
¡¡A mí la legión!! / Follow the Legion!! 1942, Juan de Orduña   92
A mi madre le gustan las mujeres / My Mother Likes Women 2002, Inés París and Daniela Féjerman   344
A mí no me mire usted / Don't You Look at Me* 1941, José Luis Sáenz de Heredia   90
A ras de suelo / Flush with the Ground* 2005, Carles Pastor Moreno   346
A sangre fría / In Cold Blood 1959, Juan Bosch   148
A solas contigo / Alone with You* 1990, Eduardo Campoy   307
A tiro limpio / Clean Shooting* 1963, Francisco Pérez Dolz   170, 303
——— 1996, Jesús Mora   170 n. 19, 303
A un dios desconocido / To an Unknown God 1977, Jaime Chávarri   235
abanderado, El / The Standard Bearer* 1943, Eusebio Fernández Ardavín   99
Abel Sánchez 1947, Carlos Serrano de Osma   104, 109 n. 47
abominable hombre de la Costa del Sol, El / The Abominable Marbella Man* 1970, Pedro Lazaga   203
Aborto criminal / Criminal Abortion* 1973, Ignacio F. Iquino   206
Abre los ojos / Open Your Eyes 1997, Alejandro Amenábar   xv, 321
Abuela de verano (TV) / *Summer Grandma** 2005, Various   334

Abuelo made in Spain / Old Man Made in Spain 1969, Pedro Lazaga   168–9
abuelo tiene un plan, El / Granpa has a Plan* 1973, Pedro Lazaga   168, 201
abuelo, El / The Grandfather* 1925, José Buchs   33, 47, 84, n. 11, 205
—— 1998, José Luis Garci   330
Accidente 703 / Accident 703* 1962, José María Forqué   170
Acción mutante / Mutant Action 1993, Alex de la Iglesia   306
Acosada / Harassment* 2003, Pedro Costa   340
Acteón / Actaeon 1967, Jordi Grau   190
Actrices / Actrius / Actresses 1997, Ventura Pons   286–7
Adela 1987, Carlos Balagué   265
Adios cigüeña, adios / Goodbye Stork, Goodbye 1971, Manuel Summers   210
Adios pequeña / Bilbao Blues 1986, Imanol Uribe   267
Adios tiburón / Good Bye Shark* 1996, Carlos Suárez   295
adolescentes, Las / The Adolescents 1975, Pedro Masó   203
Adosados / Suburbs 1996, Mario Camus   290
adúltera, La / The Adulteress 1975, Roberto Bodegas   217
adúltero, El / The Adulterer* 1975, Ramón Fernández   204
aeroguapas, Las / The Airbeauties* 1957, Eduardo Manzanos   145
Aeropuerto / Airport* 1953, Luis Lucia   129
África / Africa 1996, Alfonso Ungría   289
Âge d'or, L' / Age of Gold* 1930, Luis Buñuel   38, 42–5, 47, 49, 55, 60, 64, 151
Agua en el suelo / Water in the Ground 1933, Eusebio Fernández Ardavín   57
aguas bajan negras, Las / The Waters Run Black* 1948, José Luis Sáenz de
    Heredia   105, 118 n. 3
Aguirre, der Zorn Gottes 1972 Germany, Werner Herzog   259
Agustina de Aragón / 1929, Florián Rey   101
—— 1950, Juan de Orduña   99–101, 121 n. 3, 147 n. 44
Ahmed, el príncipe de la Alhambra / Ahmed, the Alhambra Prince* 1998, Juan Bautista
    Berasategi   347
Airbag 1997, Juanma Bajo Ulloa   307
Akelarre / Witches' Sabbath* 1984, Pedro Olea   278
Al Hollywood madrileño / To the Madrid Hollywood* 1927, Nemesio Sobrevila   41, 46
    n. 43
Al límite / To the Limit 1997, Eduardo Campoy   307
Al margen de la ley / On the Margin of the Law* 1935, Ignacio F. Iquino   70
Al ponerse el sol / At Sunset* 1967, Mario Camus   163
Al servicio de la mujer española / At the Service of Spanish Womanhood 1978, Jaime de
    Armiñán   231
Al sur de Granada / South from Granada 2003, Fernando Colomo   330
Alas de juventud / Wings of Youth* 1949, Antonio del Amo   113
Alas de mariposa / Butterfly Wings 1991, Juanma Bajo Ulloa   307, 320
Alas de paz / Wings of Peace* 1942, Juan Parellada   86
Alatriste / Captain Alatriste 2006, Agustín Díaz Yanes   330
Alba de América / Dawn of America* 1951, Juan de Orduña   117–18, 154
alcalde de Zalamea, El / The Mayor of Zalamea* 1914, Adrià Gual   17
—— 1954, José Gutiérrez Maesso   149
aldea maldita, La / The Cursed Village 1930 and 1942, Florián Rey   38–40, 47, 83,
    118, 230 n. 8, 320
alegre divorciado, El / The Happy Divorcee* 1975, Pedro Lazaga   204
Alegre ma non troppo / Cheerful, but not Too Much* 1994, Fernando Colomo   288
alegres chicas de Colsada, Las / The Cheerful Colsada Girls* 1984, Rafael Gil   250

Alegres vacaciones / Happy Holidays 1948, Arturo Moreno   97

alegría que pasa, La / The Joy that Passes* 1930, Sabino Micón   52

Alejandra mon amour / Alejandra, My Love* 1979, Julio Saraceni   249

Alexander the Great 1955 USA, Robert Rossen   172

Algo amargo en la boca / Something Bitter in Your Mouth* 1969, Eloy de la Iglesia   220

Alhucemas 1948, José López Rubio   112

Alicia en la España de las maravillas / Alice in Spanish Wonderland 1976/1984, Jordi Feliu   246

Alma de Dios / Heart of Gold* 1922, Manuel Noriega   93

—— 1941, Ignacio F. Iquino   93

Alma gitana / Gypsy Soul* 1996, Chus Gutiérrez   309, 345–6

Alma rifeña / Moroccan Soul* 1922, José Buchs   31, 38

Almadrabas / Tuna Fishing* 1935, Carlos Velo   73

Almejas y mejillones / Clams and Mussels 2000, Marcos Carnevale   350

alquimista impaciente, El / The Impatient Alchemist 2002, Patricia Ferreira   336–7

Altar mayor / The High Altar* 1944, Gonzalo Delgrás   96

Ama lur / Tierra Madre / Mother Earth* 1968, Néstor Basterretxea   170

Amador / Lover* 1965, Francisco Regueiro   186, 188

Amanece que no es poco / It's Dawn and No Mean Feat* 1989, José Luis Cuerda   269, 320

Amanecer en Puerta Oscura / Whom God Forgives 1957, José María Forqué   128, 149

amante bilingüe, El / The Bilingual Lover 1993, Vicente Aranda   298

amante menguante, El / The Shrinking Lover* 2002, Pedro Almodóvar   10 n. 19, 325

Amantes / Lovers 1991, Vicente Aranda   286, 320

amantes de Teruel, Los / The Lovers of Teruel* 1912, Ricard de Baños and Albert Marro   17

amantes del círculo polar, Los / The Lovers of the Arctic Circle 1998, Julio Medem   324

Amants du Pont-neuf, Les 1991 France, Leos Carax   341 n. 22

Amb el 10 a l'esquena / El 10 en la espalda / With a 10 on his Shirt* 2004, Eduard Cortés   334–5

Ametralladoras / Machine Guns* 1939, Rafael Gil   74

Amo tu cama rica / I Love your Lovely Bed* 1992, Emilio Martínez Lázaro   287

Amor a todo gas / Love at Top Speed* 1969, Ramón Torrado   160

amor brujo, El / A Love Bewitched 1949, Antonio Román   160, 250–1

—— 1967, Francisco Rovira Beleta   160, 250–1

—— 1986, Carlos Saura   160, 250–1

amor de ahora, El / Present Love* 1987, Ernesto del Río   274

Amor de hombre / The Love of a Man 1997, Yolanda García Serrano Yolanda and Juan Luis Iborra   304

amor del capitán Brando, El / The Love of Captain Brando 1974, Jaime de Armiñán   200 n. 2, 219–20

Amor en maniobras / Love on Manoeuvres* 1935, Mariano Lapeyra   70

amor és estrany, L' / El amor es extraño / Love is Strange* 1989, Carlos Balagué   265

Amor idiota / Idiot Love 2005, Ventura Pons   275 n. 26, 345

amor perjudica seriamente la salud, El / Love Can Seriously Damage Your Health 1997, Manuel Gómez Pereira   304

Amor que mata / Lethal Love* 1908, Fructuós Gelabert   13

—— 1911, Josep Maria Codina and Joan Maria Codina   13–15, 23

Amores que matan / Loves that Kill* 1996, Juan Manuel Chumilla   296

Ana dice que sí / Ana Says Yes* 1958, Pedro Lazaga   145

Ana y los lobos / Anna and the Wolves 1973, Carlos Saura   88, 116 n. 1, 146 n. 42, 215, 222, 231, 260 n. 5

anacoreta, El / The Anchorite 1976, Juan Esterlich   238

Andalusische Nächte 1939 Germany, Herbert Maish   80

Ander eta Yul / Ander and Yul* 1989, Ana Díez   277

ángel pasó por Brooklyn, Un / An Angel over Brooklyn 1957, Ladislao Vajda   143

Angels Wash their Faces 1939 USA, Ray Enright   121

Angustia / Anxieties* 1948, José Antonio Nieves Conde   109

Angustia / Anguish 1987, José Juan Bigas Luna   266

Anita no pierde el tren / Anita no perd el tren / Anita Takes a Chance 2000, Ventura Pons   283 n. 1

ano da carracha, O / El año de la garrapata / The Year of the Tick 2004, Jorge Coira   332

Antártida / Antarctica* 1995, Manuel Huerga   307

Antes llega la muerte / Hour of Death 1964, Joaquín Romero Marchent   173

Antonieta 1982, Carlos Saura   260

año de las luces, El / Year of Enlightment 1986, Fernando Trueba   262

Año Mariano / Holy Mary 2000, Karra Elejalde   342

años bárbaros, Los / The Stolen Years/ 1998, Fernando Colomo   82, 329

Apartado de correos 1001 / P O Box 1001* 1950, Julio Salvador   109, 118 n. 3

Aquesta nit o mai / Tonight or Never* 1992, Ventura Pons   296

Aquí huele a muerto / Here I Smell a Corpse* 1990, Álvaro Sáenz de Heredia   305

Aquí llega Condemor / Here Comes Condemor* 1996, Álvaro Sáenz de Heredia   305

Araucana, La / The Araucana* 1971, Julio Coll   171–2

ardilla roja, La / The Red Squirrel 1993, Julio Medem   311

arlequines de seda y oro, Los / The Harlequins of Silk and Gold* 1918, Ricard de Baños   24

Armas contra la ley / Guns against the Law* 1961, Ricardo Blasco   148

Arrebato / Rapture 1980, Iván Zulueta   251–2, 320

arreglo, El / The Deal* 1983, José Antonio Zorrilla   247

Arriba España / For Spain* 1937, Ricardo Gutiérrez   78

¡Arriba Hazaña! / Long Live Hazaña 1978, José María Gutiérrez Santos   245

Arroseur arrosé, L' 1895 France, Louis Lumière   5

arte de morir, El / The Art of Dying 2000, Álvaro Fernández Armero   338

arte de vivir, El / The Art of Living 1965, Julio Diamante   189

ases buscan la paz, Los / Aces looking for Peace* 1955, Arturo Ruiz Castillo   128 n. 15, 147 n. 44

Asesinato en el comité central / Murder in the Central Committee 1982, Vicente Aranda   247

asesino de Pedralbes, El / The Pedralbes Murderer* 1978, Gonzalo Herralde   242

Asfalto / The City* 2000, Daniel Calparsoro   333–4, 339

Así en el cielo como en la tierra / On Earth as it is in Heaven* 1995, José Luis Cuerda   295

Así es Madrid / Such is Madrid* 1953, Luis Marquina   128

Asignatura aprobada / Course Completed 1987, José Luis Garci   256 n. 1

Asignatura pendiente / Unfinished Business 1977, José Luis Garci   229

Asilo Naval / Naval Protection* 1936, Miguel Pereyra   78

assumpte intern, Un / Asunto interno / An Internal Affair* 1995/1996, Carlos Balagué   300–1

Asturias para España / Asturias for Spain* 1937, Fernando Delgado   78 *asunto privado, Un / A Private Matter** 1996, Imanol Arias   312–13

¡Átame! / Tie Me Up! 1990, Pedro Almodóvar   163 n. 8, 285

Atilano presidente / Atilano for President 1998, La Cuadrilla [Santiago Aguilar and Luis Guridi]   306

Atolladero / Tight Spot 1995, Oscar Aibar   306

Atómica / Atomic* 1998, Alfonso Albacete and David Menkes   344

atracadores, Los / The Robbers 1961, Francisco Rovira Beleta   148

Atracción de circo / Circus Act*, Segundo de Chomón   10

Atraco a las tres / Hold-Up at Three* 1962, José María Forqué   144 n. 41, 148, 166, 320, 341

Atraco a las tres... y media / Hold up at 15:00... :30* 2003, Raúl Marchand   341

Aunque la hormona viste seda / Even if Hormones Wear Silk* 1971,Vicente Escrivá   204

Aurora de esperanza / Dawn of Hope* 1937, Antonio Sau Olite   71, 118 n. 3

Ausentes / The Absent 2005, Daniel Calparsoro   334 n. 16, 339

autonómicos, Los / The Autonomicals 1982, José María Gutiérrez Santos   240

autonosuyas, Las / The Autonothemselves* 1983, Rafael Gil   239

Autopsia / Autopsy* 2002, Milagros Bará   340

Autopsia de un criminal / Autopsy of a Criminal 1962, Ricardo Blasco   148

aventura de cine, Una / A Film Adventure* 1928, Juan de Orduña   105

Aventura oriental / Eastern Adventure* 1935, Max Nosseck   63

Aventuras de Joselito en América / Adventures of Joselito and Tom Thumb 1960, René Cardona   144

Aventuras del barbero de Sevilla / The Adventurer of Seville 1954, Ladislao Vajda   127

¡Ay Carmela! 1990, Carlos Saura   299

Babaouo 1998, Manuel Cussó-Ferrer   42, 303

Bahía de Palma / Palma Bay 1962, Juan Bosch   165

bailarín y el trabajador, El / The Dancer and the Worker 1936, Luis Marquina   70

baile de las ánimas, El / The Dance of Souls* 1994, Pedro Carvajal   312

baile del pato, El / The Dance of the Duck* 1989, Manuel Iborra   273

baile, El / The Ball* 1959, Edgar Neville   124

Bajarse al moro / Going South Shopping 1989, Fernando Colomo   270

Bajo en nicotina / Low in Nicotine* 1984, Raúl Artigot   234

Bala perdida / Lost Bullet 2003, Pau Martínez   172, 321

Balarrasa / Reckless 1951, José Antonio Nieves Conde   103, 120–1, 153

balcón abierto, El / The Open Balcony* 1984, Jaime Camino   261

balcón de la luna, El / The Balcony Beneath the Moon* 1962, Luis Saslavsky   125

Bámbola 1996, José Juan Bigas Luna   298

Bambú / Bamboo* 1945, José Luis Sáenz de Heredia   92

banyera, La / The Bathtub* 1989, Jesús Garay   276

Barajas, aeropuerto transoceánico / Barajas, Trans-oceanic Airport (not released), Juan Antonio Bardem   150

barbero de Sevilla, El / The Barber of Seville 1938, Benito Perojo   81, 111 n. 51

Barcelona en 1908 / Barcelona in 1908* 1908, Fructuós Gelabert   5

Barcelona Sur / Barcelona South* 1981, Jordi Cadena   247

Barcelona trabaja para el frente / Barcelona Working for the Front Lines* 1936, Mateo Santos   73

Barcelona y sus misterios / Barcelona and its Mysteries* 1916, Albert Marro   22

barraca, La (TV) */ The Hut** 1979, León Klimovsky   248

Barrio / The Neighbourhood* 1947, Ladislao Vajda   109

Barrio / Neighbourhood* 1998, Fernando León de Aranoa   294, 332

Barrios altos / High Districts* 1987, José Luis Berlanga   274
Barrios bajos / Low Districts* 1937, Pedro Puche   70–2, 109, 118 n. 3
Bâton Rouge 1988, Rafael Moleón   274
baúles del retorno, Los / The Return Luggage* 1995, María Miró   312
Bearn o la sala de las muñecas / Bearn or the Dolls' Room* 1983, Jaime Chávarri
   249, 258
Beatriz 1976, Gonzalo Suárez   213
Beauty in Chains 1918 USA, Elsie Jane Wilson   84
Becky Sharp 1935 USA, Rouben Mamoulian   67
Beltenebros / Prince of Shadows 1991, Pilar Miró   291, 301 n. 16, 313
bella de Cádiz, La / The Beauty from Cadiz* 1953, Eusebio Fernández Ardavín   108
Bellas durmientes / Sleeping Beauties* 2001, Eloy Lozano   338
Belle époque / The Age of Beauty 1992, Fernando Trueba   xiv, 287, 293, 296, 320
Bello recuerdo / Beautiful Memory* 1961, Antonio del Amo   144
Ben Hur 1925 USA, Fred Niblo   17
Benítez quiere ser torero / Benítez Wants to Be a Bullfighter* 1910, Àngel Garcia Cardona
   13, 29
Berlín Blues 1988, Ricardo Franco   266
beso de Judas, El / Judas's Kiss 1954, Rafael Gil   121
beso en el puerto, Un / A Kiss in the Harbour 1966, Ramón Torrado   159
Besos para todos / Kisses for Everyone 2000, Jaime Chávarri   346
Best Seller, el premio / Best Seller, The Prize* 1996, Carlos Pérez Ferré   290
biblia negra, La / The Black Bible* 2001, David Pujol   338
bicicletas son para el verano, Las / Bicycles are for the Summer 1984, Jaime Chávarri
   261
bien pagada, La / She Who Is Well Paid* 1935, Eusebio Fernández Ardavín   57
¡Bienvenido míster Marshall! / Welcome Mr Marshall! 1953, Luis G[arcía]
   Berlanga   133–6, 154, 319, 341 n. 21
Bienvenido padre Murray / Black Angel of the Mississippi 1964, Ramón Torrado   173
Big House, The 1929 USA, George Hill   51
Bilbao 1978, José Juan Bigas Luna   229, 320
Bilbao para España / Bilbao for Spain* 1936, Fernando Delgado   78
Birth of a Nation 1915 USA, D. W. Griffith   22
Blair Witch Project, The 1999 USA, Daniel Myrick and Eduardo Sánchez   337
blanca paloma, La / The White Dove 1942, Claudio de la Torre   105
Blanca Paloma, La / The White Dove 1990, Juan Miñón   292
Blackmail 1929 UK, Alfred Hitchcock   55
Blockade 1938 USA, William Dieterle   74
blaue Engel, Der 1929 Germany, Josef Von Sternberg   55, 266
Blood and Sand 1922 USA, Fred Niblo   17
—— 1941 USA, Rouben Mamoulian   17
Boca a boca / Mouth to Mouth 1995, Manuel Gómez Pereira   304
boda del señor cura, La / Father Cami's Wedding* 1979, Rafael Gil   239
Boda en Castilla / Castilian Wedding* 1942, Manuel García Viñolas   86–7
Boda en el infierno / Marriage in Hell* 1942, Antonio Román   96
bodas de Blanca, Las / Blanca's Weddings* 1975, Francisco Regueiro   209
Bodas de sangre / Blood Wedding 1938, Edmundo Guibourt   18
—— 1981 Saura, Carlos   162, 250, 320
bodega, La, Wine Cellars 1929, Benito Perojo   38, 51
Bohemios / Bohemians* 1905, Ricard de Baños   30
—— 1939, Francisco Elías   30 n. 7, 65

—— 1962, Juan de Orduña   30 n. 7
Boliche 1933, Francisco Elías   57
Bombas para la paz / *Peace Bombs** 1958, Antonio Román   123, 135
Boom Boom / *Heart Beat** 1990, Rosa Vergés   310
Borgia, Los / *The Borgias* 2006, Antonio Hernández   339
bosque animado, El / *The Enchanted Forest** 1987, José Luis Cuerda   269
bosque animado, El / *The Living Forest* 2001, Ángel de la Cruz and Manolo Gómez   347
bosque del lobo, El / *The Ancines Woods* 1971, Pedro Olea   218
Botón de ancla / *Anchor Button** 1948, Ramón Torrado   108, 201
—— 1960 Miguel Lluch   108, 163, 166
Boy 1925, Benito Perojo   37–8
—— 1940, Antonio Calvache   37
Boys' Town 1938 USA, Norman Taurog   121
Brandy 1963, José Luis Borau   185
Braveheart 1995 USA, Mel Gibson   101–2
Brief Encounter 1945 UK, David Lean   157 n. 3
Brigada criminal / *The Criminal Brigade** 1950, Ignacio F. Iquino   109, 148
Brigadas de Navarra / *The Navarrese Brigades** 1937, Fernando Delgado   78
Brillante Porvenir / *Brilliant Future* 1965, Vicente Aranda   192
Brindis a Manolete / *A Toast for Manolete** 1948, Florián Rey   107
Bringing Up Baby 1938 USA, Howard Hawks   343
Bruce, The 1995 UK, Bob Carruthers   101 n. .38
Bruja, más que bruja / *Witch, Nothing but a Witch** 1977, Fernando Fernán Gómez   250
Brujas / *Witches** 1996, Álvaro Fernández Armero   305
buen amor, El / *The Good Love* 1963, Francisco Regueiro   186
¡Buen viaje, Pablo! / *Bon Voyage, Pablo!* 1959, Ignacio F. Iquino   148
buena estrella, La / *Lucky Star* 1997, Ricardo Franco   336
buena vida, La / *The Good Life* 1996, David Trueba   293
Buenas noticias / *Good News** 1954, Eduardo Manzanos   128
buenaventura de Pitusín, La / *Pitusin's Luck** 1924, Luis Alonso   29
Bull and Sand 1924 USA, Mack Sennett   17
Buñuel y la mesa del rey Salomón / *Buñuel and King Solomon's Table* 2001, Carlos Saura   326
busca, La / *The Search* 1967, Angelino Fons   188
Buscando a Perico / *Looking for Pete** 1982, Antonio del Real   234
buscón, El / *The Scrounger** 1976/1979, Luciano Berriatúa   249
Búsqueme a esta chica / *Find That Girl* 1964, Fernando Palacios   161, 163
Busy Day, A 1914 USA, Charles Chaplin   28
Bwana 1996, Imanol Uribe   289
caballero andaluz, Un / *An Andalusian Gentleman** 1954, Luis Lucia   125, 142, 154
caballero del Dragón, El / *Star Knight* 1985, Fernando Colomo   266
caballero don Quijote, El (TV) / *Don Quixote, Knight Errant* 2002, Manuel Gutiérrez Aragón   269 n. 21
caballero famoso, Un / *A Famous Gentleman** 1942, José Buchs   106
caballeros del botón de ancla, Los / *Gentlemen with Anchor Buttons** 1974, Ramón Torrado   108, 201
cabina, La / *The Phone Box* 1972, Antonio Mercero   221
Cabiria 1914 Italy, Giovanni Pastrone   10
Cabriola / *Every Day is a Holiday* 1965, Mel Ferrer   161

Cachito 1996, Enrique Urbizu 313

Cachorro / Bearcub 2004, Miguel Albaladejo 336

Cada ver es... / Each Viewing Is...Corpses* 1981/1983, Ángel García del Val 241

Cada vez que... / Each time that...* 1968, Carlos Durán 193

Café de Chinitas / Chinitas's Café* 1960, Gonzalo Delgrás 142

Caín / Cain 1987, Manuel Iborra 273

Caja 507 / Box 507 2002, Enrique Urbizu 337

cajas españolas, Las / The Spanish Crates* 2004, Alberto Porlan 328–9

Calabuch 1956, Luis G[arcía] Berlanga 135–6, 341

El Calentito / El Calentito Club* 2005, Chus Gutiérrez 251, 330–1

calientes orgías de una virgen, Las / The Hot Orgies of a Virgin* 1983, Antoni Verdaguer 276

calzonazos, El / The Hen-pecked Husband* 1974, Mariano Ozores 201

Calle Mayor / Main Street 1956, Juan Antonio Bardem 69–70, 138, 180, 230 n. 8, 320

calle sin sol, La / The Sunless Street* 1948, Rafael Gil 109, 118 n. 3

Camada negra / Black Litter 1977, Manuel Gutiérrez Aragón 243

Camarote de lujo / Luxury Cabin* 1958, Rafael Gil 94

Cambio de sexo / Change of Sex 1977, Vicente Aranda 235

camino, El / The Journey* 1963, Ana Mariscal 171

Camino cortado / Closed Exit 1955, Ignacio F. Iquino 130

camino de la victoria, El / The Path to Victory* 1937, Antonio del Amo 74

camino de Victor, El / Victor's Journey* 2005, Dacil Pérez de Guzmán 333

Camino del rocío / The Path of the Rocío Pilgrimage* 1966, Rafael Gil 164

campana del infierno, La / A Bell from Hell 1973, Claudio Guerín Hill 208

Campanadas a medianoche / Chimes at Midnight 1966 France-Spain-Switzerland, Orson Welles 172

canción de Aixa, La / The Song of Aixa 1939, Florián Rey 80, 93

Canción de cuna / Cradle song 1961, José María Eliorreta 122

—— 1994, José Luis Garci 122, 300

Canción de juventud / Song of Youth* 1962, Luis Lucia 162

canción del día, La / Spanish Eyes 1929, Saturnino Ulargui 50

Canciones para después de una guerra / Songs for after a War* 1971/1976, Basilio Martín Patino 210, 216, 240, 320, 326

Canelita en rama / Canelita, Cinamon Stick* 1943, Eduardo García Maroto 83, 114

Canet Rock / Rock from Canet* 1975, Francesc Bellmunt 222

Caniche / Poodle 1979, José Juan Bigas Luna 229

Cantando a la vida / Singing to Life 1969, Angelino Fons 188

Canto a la emigración / A Hymn to Migration* 1935, Antonio Román 73

canto del gallo, El / The Cock Crow* 1955, Rafael Gil 122–3

Cañas y barro / Reeds and Mud* 1954, Juan de Orduña 149

Capitães de Abril 2000 Portugal, Maria de Medeiros 223 n. 33

capitán de Loyola, El / Loyola, the Soldier Saint 1948, José Díaz Morales 103

capitán Veneno, El / Captain Poison 1951, Luis Marquina 101

Cara al sol que más calienta / Facing the Sun that Warms You Best 1977, Jesús Yagüe 238

Cara de acelga / Silver-Beet Face 1987, José Sacristán 274

Carceleras / Carcelera, Prison Songs* 1910, Segundo de Chomón 10, 31

—— 1922 and 1932, José Buchs 31, 56

Carga de los lanceros de la Reina / Charge of the Queen's Lancers* 1898, Alexandre Promio 2

Carícies / Caresses 1998, Ventura Pons 339

Cariño he enviado los hombres a la luna / Darling, I've Sent the Men to the Moon 1998, Marta Balletbò-Coll   311

Carmen 1913, Juan Doria   23

—— 1915 USA, Cecil B. DeMille   23

—— 1915 USA, Raoul Walsh   23

—— 1983, Carlos Saura   xvii, 162, 250

—— 2003, Vicente Aranda   23 n. 36, 330

Carmen, La / Carmen 1976, Julio Diamante   209

Carmen la de Ronda / A Girl Against Napoleon 1959, Tulio Demicheli   141, 149

Carmen, la de Triana / Carmen 1938, Florián Rey   80, 106, 114

Carmiña, flor de Galicia / Carmiña, The Flower of Galicia* 1926, Rino Lupo   33

Carne de fieras / Flesh for Beasts* 1936, José María Estívalis   72

Carne de gallina / Chicken Skin 2002, Javier Maqua   335

Carne de horca / Meat for the Gallows* 1953, Ladislao Vajda   127, 182

Carne trémula / Live Flesh 1998, Pedro Almodóvar   xv n. 3, 285, 334 n. 16

Carola de día, Carola de noche / Carola by Day, Carola by Night* 1969, Jaime de Armiñán   219

Carreras de bicicletas en el parque / Bicycle Races in the Park* 1903, Fructuós Gelabert   5

Carreras de caballos en el hipódromo de Barcelona / Horses at the Barcelona Race Course* 1902, Fructuós Gelabert   5

Carreteras secundarias / Backroads 1997, Emilio Martínez Lázaro   335

Carry on Columbus 1992 UK, Gerald Thomas   165 n. 10

Carry on Sergeant 1958 UK, Gerald Thomas   165 n. 10

Carta de amor de un asesino / Love Letter from a Murderer* 1972, Francisco Regueiro   209

Carta mortal / Death Card* 2003, Eduard Cortés   339

cartas de Alou, Las / Letters from Alou 1990, Montxo Armendáriz   289

casa, La / The House* 1976, Angelino Fons   210

casa de Bernarda Alba, La / The House of Bernarda Alba 1987, Mario Camus   259

casa de la lluvia, La / The House of Rain* 1943, Antonio Román   96

casa de la Troya, La / College Boarding House 1925, Manuel Noriega and Alejandro Pérez Lugín   32–3, 38, 66, 92 n. 22

—— 1936, Adolfo Aznar and Joan Vilà Vilamala   32 n. 9, 66

—— 1959, Rafael Gil   32 n. 9, 142

casa de las Chivas, La / The House of Bitches* 1972, León Klimovsky   206

casa de las palomas, La / The House of the Doves 1972, Claudio Guerín Hill   208

casa en las afueras, Una / House Out of Town 1995, Pedro Costa   290

casa sin fronteras, La / A House without Boundaries 1972, Pedro Olea   218–19

Casablanca 1943 USA, Michael Curtiz   267

Cascabel / Sleighbell, Ankle Bracelet* 2000, Daniel Cebrián   337–8, 346

caserío, El / The Farmhouse* 1972, Juan de Orduña   201

caso Almería, El / The Almería Affair* 1984, Pedro Costa   264

casto varón español, Un / A Chaste Spaniard* 1973, Jaime de Armiñán   219

Catalina de Inglaterra / Catherine of England* 1951, Arturo Ruiz Castillo   101

Catorce estaciones / Fourteen Stations 1991, Antonio Giménez Rico   262, 291–2

Caudillo / Francisco Franco, the Leader* 1974/1977, Basilio Martín Patino   210, 240

Cautivos de la sombra / Wild Boys 1993, Javier Elorrieta   290

caverna, La / The Cave* 2000, Eduard Cortés   337

caza, La / The Hunt 1966, Carlos Saura   170 n. 17, 182–3, 188, 319

cebo, El / It Happened in Broad Daylight 1959, Ladislao Vajda   148

Cebo para una adolecente / Bait for an Adolescent* 1973, Francisco Lara Polop 208

Celestina, La / The Wanton of Spain 1969, César Fernández Ardavín 171

—— 1996, Gerardo Vera 171

¡Centinela alerta! / Sentry, Keep Watch!* 1937, Jean Grémillon with Luis Buñuel 61, 70

Cerca de la ciudad / On the Edge of the City* 1952, Luis Lucia 121, 132

Cerca del cielo / Close to Heaven* 1951, Domingo Viladomat and Mariano del Pombo 123, 147 n. 44

Cervantes (TV) 1980, Alfonso Ungría 244 n. 31

Cerveza gratis / Free Beer* 1906, Fructuós Gelabert 6

Cet Obscur Objet du désir / That Obscure Object of Desire 1977 France, Luis Buñuel 42, 217, 226, 231

ciego de la aldea, El / The Village Blind Man* 1906, Antonio Cuesta and Ángel García Cardona 11–14

cielo abierto, El / Ten Days Without Love 2001, Miguel Albaladejo 341

cielo gira, El / The Sky is Spinning* 2004, Mercedes Álvarez 327

Cielo negro / Black Sky 1949/1951, Manuel Mur Oti 113

Cien maneras de acabar con el amor/ A Hundred Ways to Stop Loving* 2005, Vicente Pérez Herrero 348

Cinco almohadas para una noche / Five Pillows for the Night* 1974, Pedro Lazaga 165

Cinco pistolas de Texas / Five Dollars for Ringo 1967, Ignacio F. Iquino 173

Cinco tenedores / Five Forks 1979, Fernando Fernán Gómez 238

Cineastas contra magnates / Film Makers vs Tycoons* 2006, Carlos Benpar 348

Cineastes en acció / Film Makers in Action* 2006, Carlos Benpar 348

Cinópolis / Cinopolis 1930, Francisco Elías and José María Castellví 51, 94

Circus World 1964 USA, Henry Hathaway 173

City Lights 1931 USA, Charles Chaplin, 141 n. 36

ciudad de los prodigios, La / The City of Wonders* 1999, Mario Camus 301

ciudad encantada, La / The Enchanted City* 1935, Antonio Román 73

ciudad no es para mí, La / City Life is not for Me 1966, Pedro Lazaga 168, 196

ciudad perdida, La / The Lost City* 1954, Margarita Alexandre and Rafael Torrecilla 124

ciudad quemada, La / La ciutat cremada / The Burned City 1976, Antonio Ribas 5, 246

Ciudad Universitaria / University City* 1938, Edgar Neville 78

Ciudad y campo / City and Country* 1935, Carlos Velo 73

Clara es el precio / Claire is the Price 1974, Vicente Aranda 212

clarines del miedo, Los / Bugles of Fear 1958, Antonio Román 142

Clarita y Peladilla en el fútbol / Clarita y Peladilla at a Football Match* 1915, Benito Perojo 29

Clarita y Peladilla van a los toros / Clarita y Peladilla go to the Bullfight* 1915, Benito Perojo 29

claros motivos del deseo, Los / The Clear Motives of Desire* 1976, Miguel Picazo 249 n. 37

claveles, Los / The Carnations* 1936, Santiago Ontañón 57

claveles de la Virgen, Los / The Virgin Mary's Carnations* 1928, Florián Rey 37

clavo, El / The Nail 1944, Rafael Gil 96–7

Cléo de 5 à 7 1961 France, Agnès Varda 177 n. 28

Clockwork Orange 1971 UK, Stanley Kubrick 200

cochecito, El / The Wheelchair 1960, Marco Ferreri 146, 150, 194, 320

Coffret de Toledo, Le 1924 France, Louis Feuillade   36
Cogida y muerte de Joselito / The Goring and Death of Joselito* 1920, Fructuós Gelabert 30
Colegas / Pals 1982, Eloy de la Iglesia   235, 264
cólera del viento, La / The Wind's Anger 1970, Mario Camus   211
colina del dragón, La / Dragon Hill 2002, Ángel Izquierdo   348
Collector, The 1965 UK-USA, William Wyler   266
colmena, La / The Beehive 1982, Mario Camus   248, 258, 320
Colorín colorado / And They Lived Happily Ever After 1976, José Luis García Sánchez 234
comisario, El (TV) */ The Detective Inspector* 1999, Various   344
Comando de asesinos / High Season for Spies 1966, Julio Coll   171
Cómicos / Thespians* 1954, Juan Antonio Bardem   137–8, 260 n. 10,
Cómo casarse en siete días / How to Get Married in Seven Days* 1971, Fernando Fernán Gómez   213
Como dos gotas de agua / Like Peas in a Pod* 1964, Luis Amadori   162
Cómo nació la República española / How the Spanish Republic was Born 1932, Joan Vilà Vilamala   72
Cómo ser infeliz y disfrutarlo / How to be Miserable and Enjoy It 1994, Enrique Urbizu 287
Cómo ser mujer y no morir en el intento / How to be a Woman and not Die in the Attempt 1991, Ana Belén   274, 287
Como un relámpago / Like a Bolt of Lightning* 1997, Miguel Hermoso   293
Companys, procés a Catalunya / Companys, Calatonia on Trial 1979, Josep Maria Forn 246
competidores, Los / The Rivals* 1908, Fructuós Gelabert   6
complot dels anells, El / The Conspiracy of the Rings* 1988, Francesc Bellmunt   275
comunidad, La / Common Wealth 2000, Alex de la Iglesia   135 n. 22, 323
Con el culo al aire / Caution to the Wind 1980, Carles Mira   239
Con el viento solano / With the East Wind 1966, Mario Camus   184
Con la vida hicieron fuego / They Fired with their Lives* 1957/1960, Ana Mariscal 124
Con las brigadas de Navarra / With the Brigades of Navarre* 1936, Miguel Pereyra 78
Con mucho cariño / With Much Love 1979, Gerardo García   235
Con uñas y dientes / Tooth and Nail* 1977, Paulino Viota   247
conde de Maravillas, El / The Count of Maravillas* 1927, José Buchs   33
conde Drácula, El / Count Dracula 1970, Jesús Franco   207
Condenado a vivir / Condemned to Live* 2002, Roberto Bodegas   321
Condenados / Condemned* 1953, Manuel Mur Oti   127
condesa María , La / Countess Maria* 1927, Benito Perojo   34, 37, 95
—— 1942, Gonzalo Delgrás   34 n. 18, 95
Confidencia / Confidences* 1947, Jerónimo Mihura   96 n. 29
conquista de Albania, La / The Albanian Conquest* 1984, Alfonso Ungría   278
Consenso, El / The Consensus* 1980, Javier Aguirre   240
copla de la Dolores, La / Song of Dolores 1947, Benito Perojo   7
Coqueluche / Coqueluche on the Costa* 1970, Germán Lorente   202
corazón del bosque, El / Heart of the Forest 1979, Manuel Gutiérrez Aragón   81, 245
Corazón solitario / The Lonely Heart 1973, Francesc Betriu   221
Corazones sin rumbo / Herzen ohne Ziel / Aimless Hearts* 1928, Benito Perojo   37
Corridas de alegría / Rushes of Joy* 1982, Gonzalo García Pelayo   242

corrupción de Chris Miller, La / The Corruption of Chris Miller* 1973, Juan Antonio
    Bardem   161–2, 213
corsarios del Caribe, Los / Conqueror of Maracaibo 1960, Eugenio Martín   174 n. 24
corte de faraón, La / The Court of the Pharaoh 1985, José Luis García Sánchez   97
    n. 31, 271
cos al bosc, Un / A Body in the Woods 1996, Joaquim Jordà   193
cosas del querer, Las / The Things of Love 1989, Jaime Chávarri   217
cosas del querer, segunda parte, Las / The Things of Love, Part Two* 1995, Jaime
    Chávarri   271
Cosas que dejé en La Habana / Things I Left in Havana 1998, Manuel Gutiérrez
    Aragón   332, 350
Cosas que hacen que la vida valga la pena / Things that Make Life Worthwhile* 2004,
    Manuel Gómez Pereira   343
Cosas que nunca te dije / Things I Never Told You 1996, Isabel Coixet   309, 323
Costa Brava: Family Album 1995, Marta Balletbò-Coll   310–1
crack, El / The Crack 1981, José Luis Garci   204, 247, 256 n. 1
crack II, El / The Crack II 1983, José Luis Garci   247, 256 n. 1
Cría cuervos / Raise Ravens 1976, Carlos Saura   183, 216–17, 230 n. 8, 231 n. 10
criatura, La / The Creature 1977, Eloy de la Iglesia   236 n. 16
crimen de Cuenca, El / The Cuenca Crime 1979/1981, Pilar Miró   4 n. 6, 11, 226–7,
    230
Crimen de doble filo / Double Edged Crime 1964, José Luis Borau   185
crimen de la calle de Bordadores, El / The Embroiderer Street Murder* 1946, Edgar
    Neville   111
crimen de Pepe Conde, El / Pepe Conde's Crime* 1946, José López Rubio   105
crimen del cine Oriente, El / The Case of the Oriente Cinema 1997, Pedro Costa   290
crimen del expreso de Andalucía, El / The Crime on the Andalusia Express* 1990,
    Imanol Uribe   70
Crimen ferpecto / Ferpect Crime 2004, Álex de la Iglesia   323
Crimen imperfecto / Imperfect Crime* 1970, Fernando Fernán Gómez   213
¿Crimen imposible? / An Impossible Crime? 1954, César Fernández Ardavín   129
Crisis mundial / World Crisis 1934, Benito Perojo   57, 65
Cristina Guzmán 1943, Gonzalo Delgrás   96, 162
—— 1968, Luis Amadori   96, 162
Cristo / Jesus* 1954, Margarita Alexandre and Rafael Torrecilla   127 n. 12
Cristo de los faroles, El / The Christ of the Lamps* 1958, Gonzalo Delgrás   142
Cristo del océano, El / Christ of the Ocean 1971, Ramón Fernández   205 n. 14
Crits sords / Silent Screams* 1984, Raúl Contel   276
Crónica de un instante / The Chronicle of a Moment 1981, José Antonio Pangua   233–
    4
crucero Baleares, El / Battleship Baleares* 1940, Enrique del Campo   85
crueles, Las – El cadáver exquisito / The Cruel Women – The Exquisite Corpse 1969,
    Vicente Aranda   192, 212
Cuadrilátero / Quadrilateral* 1970, Eloy de la Iglesia   220
Cuando el cuerno suena / When the Horn Sounds 1972, Luis María Delgado   204
Cuando los niños vienen de Marsella / When the Children Arrive from Marseilles*
    1974, José Luis Sáenz de Heredia   201
Cuando tú no estás / When You Are Not Here* 1966, Mario Camus   163
Cuando vuelvas a mi lado / By My Side Again 1999, Gracia Querejeta   309, 334
Cuarenta grados a la sombra / Forty Degrees in the Shade* 1967, Mariano
    Ozores   167 n. 14

Cuarteto de La Habana / Havana Quartet 1999, Fernando Colomo   350
cuatreros, Los / Shoot to Kill 1965, Ramón Torrado   173
cuatro bodas de Marisol, Las / Marisol's Four Weddings* 1967, Luis Lucia   161
cuatro músicos de Bremen, Los / The Four Musicians of Bremen* 1987, Palomo Cruz
    Delgado   252
cuatro novias de Augusto Pérez, Las / The Four Brides of Augusto Pérez* 1975, José
    Jara   205
cuatro Robinsones, Los / The Four Robinsons* 1926, Reinhardt Blothner   83 n. 8
—— 1939, Eduardo García Maroto   83, 111 n. 51
Cuéntame cómo pasó (TV) / *Tell me How it Happened** 2001, Various   167 n. 14,
    318–19, 334
Cuentos de la Alhambra / Tales of the Alhambra* 1950, Florián Rey   105
Cuerda de preso / Prisoners' Rope* 1955/1962, Pedro Lazaga   109 n. 47
Cuerpo a cuerpo / Hand to Hand* 1984, Paulino Viota   247
cuervos, Los / The Crows* 1962, Julio Coll   148
Cuestión de suerte / A Question of Luck 1996, Rafael Moleón   290
¡Cupable! / Guilty!* 1945, Ignacio F. Iquino   95
cura de aldea, El / The Village priest* 1927, Florián Rey   59
—— 1936, Francisco Camacho   59
curiosa, La / The Inquisitive One 1972, Vicente Escrivá   204
Currito de la Cruz / Currito of the Cross 1925, Alejandro Pérez Lugín   30, 36 n. 20,
    65, 107 n. 45
—— 1936, Fernando Delgado   30, 65, 107 n. 45
—— 1949, Luis Lucia   30, 107
—— 1965, Rafael Gil   30, 107 n. 45, 163
Charlot II y su familia / Charlie II and his Family* 1916, José Carreras   29
Chatarra / Scrap Heap* 1991, Félix Rotaeta   274
Chechu y familia / Chechu and Family* 1992, Álvaro Sáenz de Heredia   305
Chevrolet 1997, Javier Maqua   234, 332
chica de opereta, Una / An Operetta Girl* 1944, Ramón Quadreny   94
chica del gato, La / The Girl with the Cat* 1943, Ramón Quadreny   94
chica del trébol, La / The Clover-Leaf Girl* 1964, Sergio Grieco   162, 189 n. 41
chica entre un millón, Una / A Girl in a Million* 1994, Álvaro Sáenz de Heredia   305
chica para dos, Una / A Girl for Two* 1966, León Klimovsky   156, 163
chica y un señor, Una / A Girl and a Gentleman* 1972, Pedro Masó   203
Chicas de alquiler / Girls for Hire* 1973, Ignacio F. Iquino   206
chicas de la Cruz Roja, Las / The Red Cross Girls 1958, Rafael Salvia   145, 153
chicos, Los / The Lads* 1959/1963, Marco Ferreri   142
Chien andalou, Un / An Andalusian Dog 1928, Luis Buñuel   41–5, 47, 73, 151, 193
Choque de dos transatlánticos / Colliding Liners* 1899, Fructuós Gelabert   6
Choque de trenes / Train Crash 1902, Segundo de Chomón   7
Christopher Columbus 1949 UK, David MacDonald   117
Christopher Columbus: The Discovery 1992 USA, John Glen   301
Chute de la maison Usher, La 1928 France, Jean Epstein   41
D'Artacan y los tres mosqueperros (TV) / *Dogtanian and the Three Muskehounds* 1986,
    Luis Ballester Bustos and Shigeo Koshi   252
dama boba, La / Lady Dimwit* 2006, Manuel Iborra   286 n. 5
Dame un poco de amooor / Give me a Little Lo-o-o-ving 1968, Francisco Macián   176
Daniya, jardí de l'harem / Daniya, Garden of the Harem 1988, Carles Mira   277
Dante no es únicamente severo / Dante is not Only Severe* 1967, Jacinto Esteva Crewe
    and Joaquim Jordà   193

Danzón / Dancer* 1992, María Novaro   313

De camisa vieja a chaqueta nueva / From the Old Shirt to a New Jacket* 1982, Rafael Gil   239

De colores / Full of Colours* 2003, Rafael Montesinos   351

De cuerpo presente / Lying in State* 1967, Antxon Eceiza   188

De la Alhambra al Albaicín / From the Alhambra to the Albaicín* 1940, Antonio Román   86

De Madrid al cielo / From Madrid to Heaven* 1952, Rafael Gil   118

De mujer a mujer / From Woman to Woman 1950, Luis Lucia   113

¿De qué se ríen las mujeres? / What Makes Women Laugh? 1997, Joaquín Oristrell   304

De tripas corazón / Pluck Up Your Courage* 1985, Julio Sánchez Valdés   274

de Troya en el Palmar, La / The Trojan in the Palmar* 1984, José María Zabalza   268

decente, La / The Decent One* 1970, José Luis Sáenz de Heredia   202

Dedicatoria / Dedicated to ... 1980, Jaime Chávarri   232

Defence of Madrid 1936 UK, Ivor Montagu   74

Defenders of the Faith 1939 USA, Russell Palmer   79

Defensa de Madrid / The Defence of Madrid 1936, Ángel Villatoro   73

Del amor y de la muerte / On Love and Death* 1977, Antonio Giménez Rico   247

Del amor y otras soledades / Love and Other Solitudes 1969, Basilio Martín Patino   187

Del rosa... al amarillo / From Pink... to Yellow 1963, Manuel Summers   185, 270

Deliciosamente tontos / Delightfully Foolish* 1943, Juan de Orduña   93–4

Demasiado caliente para ti / Too Hot for You* 1996, Javier Elorrieta   290

Demasiado corazón / Too Much Heart 1992, Eduardo Campoy   307

Demasiado para Gálvez / Too Much for Galvez* 1981, Antonio Gonzalo   247

Demasiado viejo para morir joven / Too Old to Die Young* 1989, Isabel Coixet   308

Demonios en El Jardín / Demons in The Garden 1982, Manuel Gutiérrez Aragón   82, 245, 320

Deprisa, deprisa / Fast, Fast 1980, Carlos Saura   237, 320

desaparecido, El / He Who Disappeared 1934, Antonio Graciani   70

desastre de Annual, El / The Annual Debacle* 1970, Ricardo Franco   220

descariada, La / The Stray Sheep* 1973, Mariano Ozores   201

desencanto, El / The Disenchantment 1976, Jaime Chávarri   222, 241, 302, 320

deseo y el amor, El / Le Désir et l'amour / Love and Desire 1951, Henry Decoin and Luis María Delgado   131–2

Despertaferro / Sparks of the Catalan Sword* 1990, Jordi 'Ja' Amorós   252

Después de... / And After...* 1981/1983, Cecilia and José Juan Bartolomé   241

Después de tantos años / After so many years...* 1994, Ricardo Franco   241, 302, 320

Después del diluvio / After the Flood 1968, Jacinto Esteva Crewe   193

Después del sueño / After the Dream 1992, Mario Camus   292

destino se disculpa, El / Fate Apologises* 1945, José Luis Sáenz de Heredia   111

Desvío al paraíso / Shortcut to Paradise 1994, Gerardo Herrero   313

detective y la muerte, El / The Detective and Death 1994, Gonzalo Suárez   290

Devil is a woman, The 1935 USA, Josef Von Sternberg   64

Devils, The 1971 UK, Ken Russell   200

día de la bestia, El / The Day of the Beast 1995, Alex de la Iglesia   306

día de los enamorados, El / Valentine's Day 1959, Fernando Palacios   145

día que nací yo, El / The Day I was Born* 1991, Pedro Olea   299

Día tras día / Day by Day 1951, Antonio del Amo   131–2, 134

diablo cojuelo, El / The Limping Devil* 1971, Ramón Fernández   205 *diablo también llora, El / The Devil also Weeps** 1963, José Antonio Nieves Conde 170

*diablo toca la flauta, El / The Devil Plays the Flute** 1953, José María Forqué 128

*Diario de un skin / Diary of a Skinhead** 2005, Jacobo Rispa 333

Días contados / Running out of Time 1994, Imanol Uribe 292, 320

Días de agosto / Dies d'agost / August Days 2006, Marc Recha 338

Días de fútbol / Football Days 2003, David Serrano 332, 346

*Días de humo / Ke arteko egunak / Days of Smoke** 1990, Antxon Eceiza 300

*Días de viejo color / Days of Faded Colour** 1968, Pedro Olea 218

*Días de voda / Días de boda / Wedding Days** 2002, Juan Pinzás 336

días del pasado, Los / The Days of the Past 1978, Mario Camus 162, 245

Diego Corrientes 1914, Albert Marro 71

—— 1924, José Buchs 71

—— 1937, Ignacio F. Iquino 71

—— 1959, Antonio Isasi-Isasmendi 71

Diferente / Different 1962, Luis María Delgado 162

Digan lo que digan / Let Them Talk 1968, Mario Camus 163

*dinamita está servida, La / The Dynamite is Served** 1968, Fernando Merino 165

dinamiteros, Los / The Dynamiters 1962, Juan G[arcía] Atienza 148, 166, 196

*dinero tiene miedo, El / Money is Afraid** 1970, Pedro Lazaga 165, 202

diputado, El / Confessions of a Congressman 1978, Eloy de la Iglesia 235

¡Dispara! / Shoot! 1993, Carlos Saura 291

*disputado voto del Sr Cayo, El / Mr Cayo's Contested Vote** 1986, Antonio Giménez Rico 49, 259

*Distrito quinto / The Fifth Precinct** 1958, Julio Coll 148

Ditirambo 1967/1969, Gonzalo Suárez 193

Divinas palabras / Divine Words 1986, José Luis García Sánchez 259

*divorcio que viene, El / The Forthcoming Divorce** 1980, Pedro Masó 240

Doce hombres y una mujer / Twelve Men and a Woman 1934, Fernando Delgado 62

dolce vita, La 1961 Italy, Federico Fellini 150, 350

*Dolores / Dolores Ibárruri, the Pasionaria** 1980, José Luis García Sánchez 241

Doloretes 1923, José Buchs 31

*Dolorosa, La / Our Lady of Sorrows** 1934, Jean Grémillon 57

*Domingo de carnaval / Carnival Sunday** 1945, Edgar Neville 111

domini del sentits, El / Domain of the Sense 1996, Various 346

*Don Erre que erre / Mr Goesby Thebook** 1970, José Luis Sáenz de Heredia 201

Don Juan 1950, José Luis Sáenz de Heredia 104

Don Juan de Serrallonga, o los bandoleros de las Guillerías / Don Juan de Serrallonga 1910, Ricard de Baños and Albert Marro 17

Don Juan en los infiernos / Don Juan in Hell 1991, Gonzalo Suárez 260

Don Juan mi querido fantasma / Don Juan My Dear Ghost 1990, Antonio Mercero 260–1

Don Juan Tenorio 1908, 1910 and 1922 Ricard de Baños and Albert Marro 17, 260 n. 6

—— 1952, Alejandro Perla 149

*Don Pedro el Cruel / King Peter the Cruel** 1911, Ricard de Baños and Albert Marro 15–16

*Don Quijote / Don Quixote** 1908, Narciso Cuyàs 11

Don Quijote de la Mancha / Don Quixote 1948, Rafael Gil 104

Don Quijote de la Mancha (TV) 1978, Palomo Cruz Delgado 252

Don Quijote de Orson Welles / Don Quixote 1992, Jesús Franco 172

Don Quintín el amargao / The Embittered Don Quentin* 1925, Manuel Noriega 34, 60
—— 1935, Luis Marquina with Luis Buñuel 34, 55, 60
doncel de la reina, El / The Queen's Little Soldier* 1946, Eusebio Fernández Ardavín 100
Dónde estará mi niño? / Where Can My Son Be?* 1981, Luis María Delgado 249–50
Donde hay patrón... / What the Skipper Says...* 1978, Mariano Ozores 249
¿Dónde vas Alfonso XII? / Where Are You Going Alfonso XII? 1958, Luis Amadori 141, 153
¿Dónde vas triste de ti? / Where Are You Going so Sad?* 1960, Alfonso Balcázar 141
Doña Francisquita 1934, Hans Behrendt 46 n. 43, 126
—— 1953, Ladislao Vajda 126
Doña María la brava / Doña María the Brave* 1948, Luis Marquina 100
Doña Perfecta 1977, César Fernández Ardavín 249
Dorado, El 1921 France, Marcel L'Herbier 36
Dorado, El 1988, Carlos Saura 259
Dos / Two* 1980, Álvaro del Amo 252
Dos caminos / Two Paths* 1953, Arturo Ruiz Castillo 124, 147 n. 44
Dos cuentos para dos / Two Stories for Two* 1947, Luis Lucia 95
Dos chicas de revistas / Two Chorus Line Girls* 1972, Mariano Ozores 168
Dos chicas locas locas / Two Mad Mad Girls* 1965, Pedro Lazaga 162
Dos pistolas gemelas / Sharp-Shooting Twin Sisters 1966, Rafael Romero Marchent 162
Dr Jekyll y el hombre lobo / Dr Jeckyll and the Wolfman 1972, León Klimovsky 207
Dr Zhivago 1965 USA, David Lean 183
Dragon Rapide 1986, Jaime Camino 261
drama en Bilbao, Un / A Drama in Bilbao* 1924, Alejandro Olavarría 34
Du rififi chez les hommes 1955 France, Jules Dassin 171
duda, La / Doubt 1973, Rafael Gil 205
Duende y misterio del flamenco / Flamenco 1952, Edgar Neville 126
duendes de Andalucía, Los / The Splendour of Andalusia 1966, Ana Mariscal 160
Duerme, duerme mi amor / Sleep, Sleep my Love* 1975, Francisco Regueiro 209
Dulce nombre / Sweet Name* 1951, Enrique Gómez 149
Dulces horas / Sweet Hours 1982, Carlos Saura 182, 246, 260
Dulcinea 1947, Luis Arroyo 104
Dulcinea / A Girl from La Mancha 1963, Vicente Escrivá 104, 171
duquesa de Benamejí, La / The Duchess of Benameji 1949, Luis Lucia 106
duquesa roja, La / The Red Duchess* 1997, Francesc Betriu 287
económicamente débiles, Los / The Economically Handicapped* 1960, Pedro Lazaga 146
edades de Lulú, Las / The Ages of Lulu 1990, José Juan Bigas Luna 287–8
educación de las hadas, La / The Education of Fairies 2006, José Luis Cuerda 345
Edurne, modista bilbaína / Edurne, Dressmaker from Bilbao* 1924, Telesforo Gil 34
efecto mariposa, El / The Butterfly Effect 1995, Fernando Colomo 298
El / This Strange Passion 1953 Mexico, Luis Buñuel 184
El Bola / Pellet 2000, Achero Mañas 331–2
El Cid 1961 USA, Anthony Mann 172
El Cid: La leyenda / El Cid: The Legend 2003, José Pozo 347
El Coyote / The Coyote 1955, Joaquín Romero Marchent 173
El Litri y su sombra / Litri and His Shadow* 1960, Rafael Gil 142
El Lute (camina o revienta) / Lute (Walk On or Die)* 1987, Vicente Aranda 264
El Lute II: Mañana seré libre / Lute II: Free tomorrow* 1988, Vicente Aranda 264

Elai-Alai / Happy Swallows* 1938, Nemesio Sobrevila   74
Elisa, vida mía / Elisa, My Life 1977, Carlos Saura   230
Elsa y Fred / Elsa and Fred 2005, Marcos Carnevale   350
Ella, él y sus millones / She, He and His Millions* 1944, Juan de Orduña   94
Embajadores en el infierno / Ambassadors in Hell* 1956, José María Forqué   123
Embrujo / The Spell* 1947, Carlos Serrano de Osma   107–9
embrujo de Sevilla, El / L'ensorcellement de Séville / The Sevilian Spell* 1930, Benito Perojo   50–1
embrujo de Shanghai, El / The Shanghai Spell 2002, Fernando Trueba   88, 349
embrujo del Sur, El / The Spell of the South* 2008, Juan Bautista Berasategi   347
emigrante, El / The Emigrant* 1960, Sebastián Almeida   142
Emilia... parada y fonda / Emilia... Road Stop and Inn* 1976, Angelino Fons   210
Emma, puertas oscuras / Emma, Dark Doors* 1974, José Ramón Larraz   208
Emmanuelle 1974 France, Just Jaeckin   226 n. 2
En construcción / Under Construction* 2000, José Luis Guerín   326–7
En el mundo a cada rato / Every Second in the World* 2004, Various   327
En el río / In the River* 1960, José Luis Borau   184
En la ciudad / In the City 2003, Cesc Gay   334
En la ciudad sin límites / The City of No Limits 2002, Antonio Hernández   183 n. 36, 339, 341 n. 22
En la puta calle! / Hitting Bottom 1996/1998, Enrique Gabriel   305
En septiembre / In September* 1982, Jaime de Armiñán   268
En un mundo diferente / In a Different World* 1969, Pedro Olea   218
En un mundo nuevo / In a New World* 1971, Ramón Torrado   201
En un rincón de España / In a Corner of Spain* 1949, Jerónimo Mihura   96
enredo de familia, Un / A Family Confusion* 1943, Ignacio F. Iquino   95
Enseñar a un sinverguenza / Lesson for a Rascal* 1970, Agustín Navarro   202
Entierro del General Mola / General Mola's Funeral* 1937, Fernando Delgado   78
Entre dos amores / Between Two Loves* 1972, Luis Lucia   201
Entre el dictador i jo / Entre el dictador y yo / Between the Dictator and I 2006, Various   328
Entre las piernas / Between Your Legs 1999, Manuel Gómez Pereira   343
Entre naranjos / In the Orange Grove* 1914, Ricard de Baños and Albert Marro   17
Entre rojas / Red Together* 1995, Azucena Rodríguez   308
Entre tinieblas / Dark Habits 1983, Pedro Almodóvar   251, 259
Entre vivir y soñar / Searching for Love 2004, Alfonso Albacete and David Menkes   344
Entreacte / Intermission* 1988, Manuel Cussó-Ferrer   277
Epílogo / Epilogue* 1984, Gonzalo Suárez   267
Érase una vez / Once upon a time* 1950, Alexandre Cirici Pellicer   98
Error de juventud / A Mistake of Youth* 1935, Juan Faidellá   70
¡Es mi hombre! / He's My Man!* 1927, Carlos Fernández Cuenca   46 n. 43, 69
—— 1935, Benito Perojo   69
—— 1966, Rafael Gil   69
És quan dormo que hi veig clar / Al dormir lo veo claro / I See Clearly when I Sleep* 1988, Jordi Cadena   276–7
Es que Inclán está loco / It is just that Inclan is Mad* 1990, Mariano Barroso   306
¿Es usted mi padre? / Are You My Father?* 1971, Antonio Giménez Rico   210
Esa mujer / That Woman 1969, Mario Camus   184
Esa pareja feliz / That Happy Couple* 1951/1953, Juan Antonio Bardem and Luis G[arcía] Berlanga   82, 102, 119, 133–4, 136, 144–5, 192 n. 43

Esa voz es una mina / That Voice is a Gold Mine 1955, Luis Lucia 126
Escala en Tenerife / Stopover in Tenerife 1964, León Klimovsky 163
escándalo, El / The Scandal 1943, José Luis Sáenz de Heredia 96
—— 1964, Javier Setó 96
escopeta nacional, La / The National Shotgun 1978, Luis G[arcía] Berlanga 183 n. 34,
237
escot, L' / The Neckline 1987, Antoni Verdaguer 276
Escuadrilla / The Squadron 1941, Antonio Román 91, 96
Esencia de Verbena / The Essence of the Fair 1930, Ernesto Giménez Caballero 42,
53 n. 8
Eskorpión / Skorpion 1988, Ernesto Tellería 306
espalda de Dios, La / Behind God's Back 2001, Pablo Llorca 337
espalda del mundo, La / The Back of the World 2000, Javier Corcuera 327
Espanya al dia / España al día / Nouvelles d'Espagne / Spain Today 1936–38, Jaume
Miravitlles 73
España heroica / Helden in Spanien / Heroic Spain 1938, Joaquín Reig 79
España otra vez / Spain Again 1968, Jaime Camino 191
Españolas en París / Spaniards in Paris 1971, Roberto Bodegas 163, 217
Españolear / Doing it the Spanish Way 1969, Jaime J. Balcázar 201
espera, La / The Wait 1956, Vicente Lluch 123
Espérame en el cielo / Wait for Me in Heaven 1987, Antonio Mercero 262
espinazo del diablo, El / The Devil's Backbone 2001, Guillermo del Toro 329, 350
espíritu de la colmena, El / The Spirit of the Beehive 1973, Víctor Erice 64, 82, 177
n. 29, 221–2, 224, 235, 319
Espíritu de una raza / The Spirit of a Race 1951, José Luis Sáenz de Heredia 91, 123
espontáneo, El / The Rash One 1964, Jordi Grau 190
Esquilache / The Esquilache Reforms 1988, Josefina Molina 259
estación de paso, Una / Whistle Stop 1992, Gracia Querejeta 309
Estambul 65 / Istanbul 65 1965, Antonio Isasi-Isasmendi 171
estanquera de Vallecas, La / The Vallecas Tobacconist 1987, Eloy de la Iglesia 264
¡Estoy en crisis! / I'm having a Crisis 1982, Fernando Colomo 233
Estoy hecho un chaval / I Feel as Young as a Lad 1977, Pedro Lazaga 239
estrella de Sierra Morena, La / Estrella, the Star of the Sierra Morena 1952, Ramón
Torrado 125
Étoile de mer, L' 1928 France, Man Ray 41
Eugenia de Montijo 1944, José López Rubio 100
Experiencia prematrimonial / Premarital Experiment 1972, Pedro Masó 218
expreso de Andalucía, El / The Andalusia Express 1956, Francisco Rovira Beleta 70,
148
Éxtasis / Ecstasy 1996, Mariano Barroso 306
Extramuros / Beyond the Walls 1985, Miguel Picazo 186, 259
Extranjeras / Foreign Women 2003, Helena Taberna 326
Extranjeros de sí mismos / Strangers to Themselves 2000, José Luis López Linares and
Javier Rioyo 327–8
extraño caso del Dr Fausto, El / The Strange Case of Dr Faustus 1969, Gonzalo
Suárez 193
extraño viaje, El / Strange Journey 1964/1967, Fernando Fernán Gómez 177–9, 320
Extraños / Strangers 1999, Imanol Uribe 336
Fábrica de gas / Gas Factory 1897, Louis Joseph Sellier 3
Fados 2007, Carlos Saura 326, 349
Fall of the Roman Empire 1964 USA, Anthony Mann 172–3

Familia / Family 1996, Fernando León de Aranoa   305
familia bien, gracias, La / The Family's Fine, Thanks* 1979, Pedro Masó   167, 234, 240
familia y uno más, La / The Family Plus One 1965, Fernando Palacios   167, 234
familia... treinta años después, La / The Family... Thirty Years on* 1999, Pedro Masó   234
familia Vila, La / The Vila Family* 1950, Ignacio F. Iquino   95, 118 n. 3
Fanny Pelopaja / Fanny Strawtop 1984, Vicente Aranda   267
Fantômas started in 1913 France, Louis Feuillade   22
far, El / The Lighthouse* 1998, Manuel Balaguer   275 n. 26
Farinelli 1995 France-Italy, Gérard Corbiau   301
Farmacia de guardia / Duty Pharmacy* 1958, Clemente Pamplona   147
farsantes, Los / Frauds* 1964, Mario Camus   187, 262 n. 10
Fata Morgana / Left-Handed Fate 1965/1967, Vicente Aranda   192
fe, La / The Faith 1947, Rafael Gil   103
febre de l'or, La / La fiebre del oro / Gold Fever* 1993, Gonzalo Herralde   301
Fedra / Fedra, The Devil's Daughter 1956, Manuel Mur Oti   127
Felices pascuas / Merry Christmas* 1954, Juan Antonio Bardem   137
felices sesenta, Los / The Happy Sixties 1963/1969, Jaime Camino   191
Felicidades, tovarish / Congratulations, Tovarish* 1995, Antxon Eceiza   300
Felipe II y El Escorial / Phillip II and the Escorial Palace* 1935, Carlos Velo   73
Femme de chambre du Titanic, La / The Chambermaid on the Titanic 1997, José Juan Bigas Luna   298
Feria en Sevilla / Fair in Seville* 1940, Juan de Orduña   86
Fermín Galán 1931, Fernando Roldán   36 n. 20, 54
Feroz / Ferocious* 1984, Manuel Gutiérrez Aragón   269
Ficció / Fiction 2006, Cesc Gay   348
fiel infantería, La / The Proud Infantry 1959, Pedro Lazaga   123, 153, 207
fieles sirvientes, Los / The Loyal Servants* 1980, Francesc Betriu   238
fierecilla domada, La / The Taming of the Shrew 1955, Antonio Román   149
fiesta sigue, La / The Party Goes On* 1948, Enrique Gómez   107
Filigrana 1949, Luis Marquina   106
Fille de l'eau, La 1924 France, Jean Renoir   41
fin de la inocencia, El / The End of Innocence* 1976, José Ramón Larraz   228
Flamenco 1995, Carlos Saura   299, 326
Flor de España o la leyenda de un torero / The Flower of Spain or the Legend of a Bullfighter* 1921, Helena Cortesina   30, 36 n. 20
flor de mi secreto, La / The Flower of my Secret 1995, Pedro Almodóvar   285, 324
Flor de santidad / Flower of Holiness 1972, Adolfo Marsillach   205, 312
Flores de otro mundo / Flowers from Another World 1999, Icíar Bollaín   333
florista de la reina, La / The Queen's Flower Girl* 1940, Eusebio Fernández Ardavín   84, 92, 97, 100
Fly, The 1986 UK-USA, David Cronenberg   9 n. 17
Fortunata y Jacinta / Fortunata and Jacinta 1970, Angelino Fons   84 n. 11, 172, 188, 248
—— 1980, Mario Camus   248
Fortunato 1942, Fernando Delgado   93
Four Horsemen of the Apocalypse, The 1921 USA, Rex Ingram   17
—— 1961 USA, Vicente Minnelli   17
Franco: ese hombre / Franco, The Man* 1964, José Luis Sáenz de Heredia   170
Frankenstein 1931 USA, James Whale   222

Fraude matrimonial / Matrimonial Fraud* 1976, Ignacio F. Iquino   206
Fray Escoba / Brother Broom* 1961, Ramón Torrado   121, 154
Freddy el croupier / Freddy the Croupier* 1982, Álvaro Sáenz de Heredia   305
Frente de Madrid / The Madrid Front* 1939, Edgar Neville   82
Frente infinito / The Infinite Front* 1956, Pedro Lazaga   123
Fuego / Fire 1964, Julio Coll   171
Fuego en Castilla / Fire in Castille* 1960, José Val del Omar   73 n. 31
fuente de la edad, La / The Fountain of Time* 1991, Julio Sánchez Valdés   274
Fuenteovejuna / The Sheepwell* 1947, Antonio Román   104
Fuera de juego / Offsides 1991, Fernando Fernán Gómez   294
fuerza del destino, La / The Power of Fate* 1913, Ricard de Baños and Albert Marro   17
Fuerza y nobleza / Strength and Nobility* 1918, Ricard de Baños   22
fuga de Segovia, La / Escape from Segovia 1981, Imanol Uribe   242
Fulano de Tal se enamora de Manón / Mr Someone Falls in Love with Manon* 1914, Benito Perojo   18, 29
Fulano y Mengano / The Two Nobodies* 1956/1959, Joaquín Romero Marchent   145
Full Monty, The 1997 UK, Peter Cattaneo   332
Función de noche / Evening Performance* 1981, Josefina Molina   230
furia del hombre lobo, La / The Fury of the Wolfman 1972, José María Zabalza   207
Furia española / Spanish Fury 1975, Francesc Betriu   221, 238
Furtivos / Poachers* 1975, José Luis Borau   182 n. 34, 185, 200 n. 2, 212, 320
Fútbol, amor y toros / Football, Love and Bullfighting* 1930, Florián Rey   60
Galicia y Compostela / Galicia and Compostela* 1935, Carlos Velo   73
gamberros, Los / The Louts* 1954, Juan Lladó   128–9
Garbancito de la Mancha / Don Chickpea of La Mancha 1945, Arturo Moreno   97, 175
Gary Cooper, que estás en los cielos / Gary Cooper Who Art in Heaven 1980, Pilar Miró   230
gata, La / The Cat 1956, Margarita Alexandre and Rafael Torrecilla   127
gato montés, El / The Wildcat* 1936, Rosario Pi   62, 66, 127
genio alegre, El / A Cheerful Disposition* 1936/1939, Fernando Delgado   72, 78
Gent de fang / Gente de barro / Mud People* 1990–1991, Raúl Contel   276
Gilda 1946 USA, Charles Vidor   300 n. 16
Gimlet 1996, José Luis Acosta   311
Gimnasia / Gymnastics* 1937, José Val del Omar   73 n. 31
Gitana / Gipsy* 1965, Joaquín Bollo   160
gitana blanca, La / The White Gypsy Girl* 1919, Ricard de Baños   24
gitanilla, La / The Little Gipsy girl 1914, Adrià Gual   17, 84
——— 1940, Fernando Delgado   84, 111 n. 51
golfo, El / The Vagrant* 1917, Josep de Togores i Muntades   18, 21–3
golfos, Los / The Delinquents 1959/1961, Carlos Saura   131, 142, 150, 182, 190, 194, 237
Gone with the Wind 1939 USA, Victor Fleming   91
gota de sangre para morir amando, Una / Murder in a Blue World 1973, Eloy de la Iglesia   220
Goya en Burdeos / Goya in Bordeaux 1999, Carlos Saura   326
Goya, historia de una soledad / Goya, a Story of Solitude* 1970, Nino Quevedo   220
Goyescas / Goyesques* 1942, Benito Perojo   106
gozos y las sombras, Los (TV) */ Joys and Shadows** 1981, Rafael Moreno Alba   248

gran aventura de Mortadelo y Filemón, La / Mortadelo and Filemón: The Big Adventure 2003, Javier Fesser 176, 342

gran familia, La / The Big Family 1962, Fernando Palacios 144 n. 41, 167, 234

gran mogollón, El / The Great Big Fuss* 1982, Ramón Fernández 240

Gran slalom / The Great Slalom* 1996, Jaime Chávarri 296

Grande Bouffe, La 1973 France-Italy, Marco Ferreri 200

Grandes ocasiones / Special Occasions* 1997, Felipe Vega 297

grano de mostaza, El / The Mustard Grain* 1962, José Luis Sáenz de Heredia 129

granujas, Los / The Little Rascals* 1924, Fernando Delgado 29, 34, 36 n. 20

Greed 1923 USA, Erich Von Stroheim 41

grito en el cielo, El / Shout Out 1998, Dunia Ayaso and Felix Sabroso 310

Gritos en la noche / Screams in the Night* 1961, Jesús Franco 174

Guantanamera 1995, Tomás Gutiérrez Alea and Juan Carlos Tabio 313

Guapo heredero busca esposa / Handsome Heir Seeks a Bride* 1972, Luis María Delgado 204

guapos de la vaquería del parque, Los / Dandies at the Park Dairy* 1907, Fructuós Gelabert 6

guapos del parque, Los / The Park Dandies* 1904, Segundo de Chomón 7

Guardia burlado / The Tricked Guard* 1908, Fructuós Gelabert 6

guardiamarinas, Los / The Naval Cadets 1966, Pedro Lazaga 166

Guernika 1937, José María Beltrán 74

guerra de Dios, La / I Was a Parish Priest 1953, Rafael Gil 121, 154, 221

guerra de los locos, La / The Madmen's War* 1987, Manolo Matjí 274

guerra de los niños, La / Children's War 1980, Javier Aguirre 250

guerra de papá, La / Daddy's War 1977, Antonio Mercero 234

Guerra e il sogno di Momi, La 1916 Italy, Giovanni Pastrone 10

Guerra en el campo / War in the Fields* 1936, Arturo Ruiz Castillo 78

Guerra en la nieve / War in the Snow* 1938, Arturo Ruiz Castillo 78

guerra por la paz, La / War for Peace* 1937, Joaquín Martínez Arboleya 78

Guerreros / Warriors 2002, Daniel Calparsoro 302, 339

guerrilla, La / The Guerilla* 1973, Rafael Gil 205

guerrilla de la memoria, La / The Guerrilla of Memory 2002, Javier Corcuera 328

guerrilleros, Los / The Guerrillas* 1963, Pedro L. Rámirez 160

Guipuzkoa / 1980, Pío and Julio Baroja 241–2

Gulliver 1976, Alfonso Ungría 244 n. 31

Gulliver en el país de los gigantes / Gulliver in the Land of the Giants 1905, Segundo de Chomón 7

Guzmán, el Bueno / Guzmán, the Good* 1909, Fructuós Gelabert 15

Ha llegado un ángel / An Angel has Arrived* 1961, Luis Lucia 161

Habana Blues / Havana Blues* 2005, Benito Zambrano 350

Habitación para tres / A Room for Three* 1951, Antonio de Lara 128

Habla mudita / Speak, Little Dumb Girl 1973, Manuel Gutiérrez Aragón 221

Hablamos esta noche / Let Us Talk Tonight* 1982, Pilar Miró 230

Hable con ella / Talk to Her 2002, Pedro Almodóvar xiv–xv, 10 n. 19, 27, 285 n. 3, 324–5

Hacerse el sueco / Playing Swede 2005, Daniel Díaz Torres 350

Hacia una nueva España / Towards a New Spain* 1936, Fernando Delgado 78

¡Harka! / Harka! 1940, Carlos Arévalo 90, 92

Haunted Hotel, The 1907 USA, J. Stewart Blackston 7

Havanera 1820 / Havana 1820* 1993, Antoni Verdaguer 301

¡Hay motivo! / There's Good Cause!* 2004, Various 317, 326

Hay que deshacer la casa / Must Undo the House* 1986, José Luis García Sánchez 268

Hay que educar a papá / Educating Father* 1971, Pedro Lazaga 201

Hay que matar a B / B Must Die 1975, José Luis Borau 185, 211–12, 219

Hay un camino a la derecha / There is a Path to the Right 1953, Francisco Rovira Beleta 294 n. 13

hecho violento, Un / A Violent Fate 1958, José María Forqué 149

Héctor 2004, Gracia Querejeta 334

Help 1965 UK, Richard Lester 212

Her Wedding Night 1931 USA, Frank Turtle 52

Hermana Alegría / Sister Happiness* 1955, Luis Lucia 126

Hermana, ¿pero qué has hecho? / Sister, What Have You Done? 1995, Pedro Masó 300

hermana San Sulpicio, La / Sister San Sulpicio 1927 and 1934, Florián Rey 37, 59, 63, 125

—— 1952, Luis Lucia 125

Héroe a la fuerza / Reluctant Hero* 1941, Benito Perojo 93

Héroe de Cascorro, El / The Cascorro Heroe* 1929/1932, Emilio Bautista 34, 46 n. 43

Héroes del 95 / Heroes of 95* 1947, Raúl Alfonso 112

Heroína / Heroin(e)* 2005, Gerardo Herrero 335

hija de Juan Simón, La / Juan Simon's Daughter* 1935 José Luis Sáenz de Heredia with Luis Buñuel 55, 61, 135, 146 n. 42, 262 n. 8

—— 1957, Gonzalo Delgrás 61, 142

hija del engaño, La / Daughter of Deceit 1951 Mexico, Luis Buñuel 34, 60

hija del mar, La / The Daughter of the Sea* 1917, Adrià Gual 121

—— 1953, Antonio Momplet 121

hija del penal, La / The Daughter of the Penitentiary* 1936, Eduardo García Maroto 59

hijas de Mohamed, Las / Mohamed's Daughters 2003, Silvia Munt 335

hijo de Jesse James, El / Son of Jesse James 1965, Antonio del Amo 173

hijos de la noche, Los / The Children of the Night* 1940, Benito Perojo 82

Hijos de papá / Spoilt Brats* 1980, Rafael Gil 97 n. 30, 234

Hipnosis / Hypnosis 1962, Eugenio Martín 171

Hiroshima mon amour 1959 France, Alain Renais 74

historia de amor, Una / A Love Story 1968, Jordi Grau 190

Historia de un beso / Story of a Kiss 2002, José Luis Garci 330

Historia de un duro / The History of a Five Peseta Coin* 1928, Sabino Micón 41

Historia de una chica sola / Story of a Girl Alone 1969, Jordi Grau 191

Historia de una escalera / The Story of a Staircase* 1950, Ignacio F. Iquino 149

Historias de amor y de masacre / Stories of Love and Massacre* 1979, Jordi 'Ja' Amorós *et al.* 252

Historias de la puta mili / Tales of the Stinking Military Service 1994, Manuel Esteban 295

Historias de la radio / Radio Stories* 1955, José Luis Sáenz de Heredia 129, 153, 320

Historias de la televisión / Television Stories* 1965, José Luis Sáenz de Heredia 129

Historias del Kronen / Stories from the Kronen 1995, Montxo Armendáriz 288–9, 333

Historias para no dormir (TV) */ Tales to Keep You Awake** 1964–82, Various 175

Hola ¿estás sola? / Hi, Are You Alone? 1996, Icíar Bollaín 309

Hole in the Wall, The 1929 USA, Robert Florey 52

hombre acosado, El / The Hounded Man* 1950/1952, Pedro Lazaga 109

hombre como los demás, Un / A Man Like All the Others* 1974, Pedro Masó 203

hombre de moda, El / Man of Fashion 1980, Fernando Méndez Leite 229

hombre de negocio, Un / A Business Man* 1945, Luis Lucia   98
hombre de suerte, Un / A Lucky Man* 1930, Benito Perojo   52
hombre llamado Flor de Otoño, Un / A Man called Autumn Flower 1978, Pedro Olea
   236, 247
hombre oculto, El / The Man in Hiding 1971, Alfonso Ungría   220
hombre que se las enamora, El / The Man Who Makes Them Fall In Love* 1944, José
   María Castellví   94
hombre que se quiso matar, El / The Man Who Wanted to Kill Himself* 1942 and 1970,
   Rafael Gil   94, 202
hombre que se reía del amor, El / The Man Who Laughed at Love* 1932, Benito Perojo
   56, 62
hombre que supo amar, El / The Man who Knew Love 1977, Miguel Picazo   249
hombre va por el camino, Un / A Man on the Road* 1949, Manuel Mur Oti   113,
   130–1
hombre y el carro, El / The Man and his Cart* 1940, Antonio Román   86
hombres ~~nunca~~ siempre mienten, Los / Men Always Lie 1995, Antonio del Real   293
Hombres sin honor / Men Without Honour 1944, Ignacio F. Iquino   95
home ronyó, L' / The Voyeur* 1983, Raúl Contel   276
honradez de la cerradura, La / The Honesty of the Keyhole* 1950, Luis Escobar   109
hora bruja, La / The Witching Hour 1985, Jaime de Armiñán   268
hora de los valientes, La / A Time for Defiance 1998, Antonio Mercero   328–9
Horas de luz / Hours of Light* 2004, Manolo Matjí   335
Hotel Danubio 2003, Antonio Giménez Rico   131 n. 16
hotel eléctrico, El / The Electric Hotel 1905, Segundo de Chomón   7–9
Hotel y domicilio / In Hotels and at Home* 1995, Ernesto del Río   288
Huella de luz / Traces of Light* 1943, Rafael Gil   94
huella del crimen, La (TV) */ The Prints of Crime** 1988 and 1990, Various   264
hueso, El / The Bone 1967, Antonio Giménez Rico   210
huésped de las tinieblas, El / The Guest of the Mist* 1948, Antonio del Amo   105
Huevos de oro / Golden Balls 1993, José Juan Bigas Luna   297
I Love You Baby 2001, Alfonso Albacete and David Menkes   344
Iberia 2005, Carlos Saura   251, 326
Ibéricas FC, Las / The Ibericas FC* 1971, Pedro Masó   166
Ídolos / Idols* 1943, Florián Rey   106
Ilegal / Illegal 2003, Ignacio Vilar   333
Imágenes contra el olvido / Images not to Forget* 2006, Various   328
Imágenes perdidas / Lost Frames* compilation, Fructuós Gelabert   5
Incautos / Swindled 2004, Miguel Bardem   337
Inconscientes / Irresponsibles* 2004, Joaquín Oristrell   344
Incredible Shrinking Man, The 1957 USA, Jack Arnold   10 n. 19
indulto, El / The Reprieve 1960, José Luis Sáenz de Heredia   149
Inés de Castro 1945, Manuel García Viñolas   100, 102
Informe general... / General Report...* 1977, Pere Portabella   242
Innisfree 1991, José Luis Guerín   302
Innocents of Paris 1929 USA, Richard Wallace   50
inocentes, Los / The Innocents* 1962, Juan Antonio Bardem   180
inquietudes de Shanti Andía, Las / The Preoccupations of Shanti Andia* 1947, Arturo
   Ruiz Castillo   103
inquilino, El / The Tenant 1958, José Antonio Nieves Conde   147
Inquisición / Inquisition 1976, Jacinto Molina aka Paul Naschy   207

insólito embarazo de los Martínez, El / The Smiths's Most Unusual Pregnancy* 1974, Javier Aguirre 201

Insomnio / Sleepless in Madrid 1998, Chus Gutiérrez 309

Intacto / Intact 2001, Juan Carlos Fresnadillo 337

Intercambio de parejas frente al mar / Exchanging Partners on the Beach* 1979, Gonzalo García Pelayo 242

intereses creados, Los / Vested Interests* 1918, Ricardo Puga 27, 31

Interior Roig / Red Interior* 1982, Eugeni Anglada 246

Intolerance 1916 USA, D. W. Griffith 22

Intriga / Intrigue* 1943, Antonio Román 96

Intriga en el escenario / Plot on the Stage* 1954, Feliciano Catalán 130

Intruso / Intruder 1993, Vicente Aranda 290, 341 n. 22

invierno en Mallorca, Un / A Winter in Mallorca 1969, Jaime Camino 191

Isabel de Solís, reina de Granada / Isabel de Solís, Queen of Granada 1931, José Buchs 52

Isi/Disi – Amor a lo bestia / Isi/Disi, Incredible Love* 2004, Chema de la Peña 346

isla del cangrejo, La / Crab Island 2000, Txabi Basterretxea and Joxan Muñoz 347–8

isla misteriosa, La / The Mysterious Island of Dr Nemo 1971, Juan Antonio Bardem 214

Ispaniya 1939 USSR, Roman Karmen and Esfir Shub 74

It Happened One Night 1934 USA, Frank Capra 58

It's a Wonderful Life 1944 USA, Frank Capra 94

Ja me maaten / Oh They're Kiiilling Me* 2000, Juan Muñoz 343

Jai-Alai / Basque Pelota* 1940, Ricardo Quintana 61

Jalea real / Royal Jelly* 1981, Carles Mira 239

Jamón, Jamón / Ham Ham 1992, José Juan Bigas Luna 177 n. 29, 297

jardín de las delicias, El / The Garden of Delights 1970, Carlos Saura 81, 214–15, 245, 261 n. 7

Jardines de España / Gardens of Spain* 1941, Arturo Ruiz Castillo 86

Jarrapellejos 1988, Antonio Giménez Rico 258

Jazz Singer, The 1927 USA, Alan Crosland 50, 53 n. 8

Jeromín / Jeromín, the Emperor's Son* 1953, Luis Lucia 122

jinetes del alba, Los (TV*) / Riders of the Dawn* 1990, Vicente Aranda 258

Jo, papá / Gosh, Dad* 1975, Jaime de Armiñán 219

John Paul Jones 1959 USA, John Farrow 172

Joselito, o la vida y muerte de un matador / Joselito, or the Life and Death of a Bullfighter* 1920, Josep Gaspar i Serra 29

Journal d'un curé de campagne, Le 1951 France, Robert Bresson 121

joven casada, La / The Young Bride 1975, Mario Camus 211

Juana la loca / Madness of Joan 2001, Vicente Aranda 17 n. 26, 101 n. 37

Judas, El / The Judas 1952, Ignacio F. Iquino 121

Juego de amor prohibido / Forbiden Love Game 1975, Eloy de la Iglesia 220, 235

juego de la oca, El / Snakes and Ladders 1966, Manuel Summers 185

Juego de Luna / Luna's Game 2001, Mónica Laguna 310, 337

Juego de poder / Power Game 1982, Fausto Canel 247

juego más divertido, El / The Most Amazing Game 1988, Emilio Martínez Lázaro 270

jueves, milagros, Los / Thursday Miracles* 1957, Luis G[arcía] Berlanga 136

Juguetes rotos / Broken Toys 1966, Manuel Summers 185

Juicio de faldas / A Skirt at Court* 1969, José Luis Sáenz de Heredia 159

Jules et Jim 1962 France, François Truffaut 334

Julio 1936 / July 1936* 1936, Fernando Mantilla 73

justicia del Coyote, La / The Judgement of the Coyote 1956, Joaquín Romero Marchent
173

Justino, un asesino de la tercera edad / Justino, Senior Citizen Killer 1994, La Cuadrilla
[Santiago Aguilar and Luis Guridi] 306

Juventudes de España / Spanish Youth* 1938, Edgar Neville 78

Karnabal / Karnivel* 1985, Carles Mira 277

Kika 1993, Pedro Almodóvar xv n. 3, 285

King of Kings 1961 USA, Nicholas Ray 172

Kiriki, Les / Juegos chinos / Chinese Games* 1908, Segundo de Chomón 9

KM 0 / Kilometre Zero* 2000, Yolanda García Serrano and Juan Luis Iborra 344

Krámpack / Nico and Dani 2000, Cesc Gay 334

Krapatchouk 1992, Enrique Gabriel 305

La Cigarra / Soledad, the Cicada* 1948, Florián Rey 108

La Corea 1976, Pedro Olea 219

La Dolores / Dolores 1908, Fructuós Gelabert 6–7, 89 n. 9

—— 1924, Maximiliano Thous Orts 7, 83 n. 9

—— 1940, Florián Rey 7, 83–4, 111 n. 51

La llamaban la madrina / They Called Her the Godmother* 1973, Mariano Ozores
202

La Lola, dicen que no vive sola, / They Say Lola Doesn't Live Alone* 1970, Jaime de
Armiñán 219

Laberinto de pasiones / Labyrinth of Passions 1982, Pedro Almodóvar 228 n. 5, 251

laberinto del fauno, El / Pan's Labyrinth 2006, Guillermo del Toro 329, 350–1

laberinto griego, El / The Greek Labyrinth 1993, Rafael Alcázar 291

Ladri di biciclette 1948 Italy, Vittorio de Sica 130

ladrones somos gente honrada, Los / We Thieves Are Honourable* 1942, Ignacio F. Iquino
95, 145

—— 1956, Pedro L. Ramírez 95, 145–6

Lágrimas negras / Black Tears 1999, Ricardo Franco 336

laguna negra, La / The Black Lagoon* 1952, Arturo Ruiz Castillo 149

largas vacaciones del 36, Las / Long Vacation of 36 1976, Jaime Camino 244

largo invierno, El / The Long Winter of 39 1992, Jaime Camino 301

Las de Méndez / The Mendez Women* 1927, Fernando Delgado 35, 36 n. 20

Las Vegas, 500 millones / Our Man in Las Vegas 1968, Antonio Isasi-Isasmendi 171

Last Tango in Paris 1972 France-Italy, Bernardo Bertolucci 200

Last Train from Madrid, The 1937 USA, James P. Hogan 74

Laura, del cielo llega la noche / Laura, the Night Falls from the Sky* 1987, Gonzalo
Herralde 276

Lazarillo de Tormes, El / Lazarillo de Tormes 1925, Florián Rey 29, 149 n. 47

—— 1959, César Fernández Ardavín 149

—— 2001, Fernando Fernán Gómez and José Luis García Sánchez 149

Legión de héroes / Legion of Heroes* 1942, Juan Fortuny and Armando Seville 92

Lejos de África (Black Island) / Far from Africa (Black Island) 1996, Cecilia Bartolomé
230 n. 9, 290

Lejos de los árboles / Far from the Trees 1970/1972, Jacinto Esteva Crewe 193

Lena 2001, Gonzalo Tapia 337

lengua de las mariposas, La / Butterfly's Tongue 1999, José Luis Cuerda 328

Leo 2000, José Luis Borau 184, 334

León y Olvido / Leon and Olvido 2005, Xavier Bermúdez 335

leona de Castilla, La / The Lioness of Castile* 1951, Juan de Orduña 101, 121 n. 3,
153

ley del deseo, La / Law of Desire 1987, Pedro Almodóvar   272, 320

leyenda de Balthasar el castrado, La / The Legend of Balthasar the Castrato 1996, Juan Miñón   301

Leyenda del alcalde de Zalamea, La / The Legend of the Mayor of Zalamea* 1972, Mario Camus   205, 211

leyenda del viento del norte, La / The Legend of the North Wind* 1992, Maite Ruiz de Austri   312

Libertad provisional / Out on Parole 1976, Roberto Bodegas   217

Libertarias / Freedomfighters 1996, Vicente Aranda   286

Liberxina 90 / Liberxina 90 1970, Carlos Durán   193

libro de buen amor, El / The Book of Good Love 1975, Tomás Aznar   205

libro de buen amor II, El / The Book of Good Love II 1976, Jaime Bayarri   205

Licántropo / Lycanthropus: The Moonlight Murders 1996, Francisco Rodríguez Gordillo   208, 338

Ligeramente viuda / Slightly Widowed* 1975, Javier Aguirre   209

Lights of New York 1929 USA, Brian Foy   50

línea del cielo, La / Skyline 1983, Fernando Colomo   233, 266, 298

Linito se hace torero / Linito Becomes a Bullfighter* 1915, Adrià Gual   29

Lo más español / Absolute Spanish* 1928, Nemesio Sobrevila   42

Lo más natural / The Most Natural Thing 1991, Josefina Molina   285–6

Lo mejor es reír / Laughter's the Best Remedy* 1931, Forián Rey 52

Lo mejor que le puede pasar a un croisán / The Best Thing that can Happen to a Croissant* 2003, Paco Mir   343

Lo verde empieza en los Pireneos / Smut Starts at the Pyrenees 1973, Vicente Escrivá   201, 204

loba y la paloma, La / House of the Damned 1974, Gonzalo Suárez   200 n. 2, 213

lobo, El / Wolf 2004, Miguel Courtois   223, 340

loca de casa, La / The Mad Woman of the House* 1926, Luis Alonso   84

loca extravagancia sexy, Una / A Wild Sex Extravaganza* 1978, Enrique Guevara   228

Loca juventud / Crazy Youth* 1967, Manuel Mur Oti   160

Loca por el circo / Circus Mad 1982, Luis María Delgado   250

Local Hero 1983 UK, Bill Forsyth   135 n. 25

Loco veneno / Mad Poison 1989, Miguel Hermoso   273

Locura de amor / The Mad Queen 1909, Ricard de Baños and Albert Marro   17, 101 n. 37

—— 1948, Juan de Orduña   17 n. 26, 101, 103–4, 330

Lola 1986, José Juan Bigas Luna   265–6

Lola la piconera / Lola the Coalgirl* 1952, Luis Lucia   101, 125

—— 1969, Fernando García Vega   160

Lola Montes 1944, Antonio Román 107

Lola Montès 1955 France, Max Ophüls   107

Lola se va a los puertos, La / Lola Leaves for the Ports* 1947, Juan de Orduña   106, 299

—— 1993, Josefina Molina   106, 299

Lorca, muerte de un poeta / Lorca, the Death of a Poet 1987, Juan Antonio Bardem   261

Los que no fuimos a la guerra / We Who Did Not Go to War* 1962/1965, Julio Diamante   188

Los que tocan el piano / They who Play the Piano 1968 Aguirre, Javier   168

Los sin nombre / The Nameless 1999, Jaume Balagueró   340

Lost in La Mancha 2002 UK-USA, Keith Fulton and Louis Pepe   172 n. 20

*love feroz, El / Ferocious Love** 1972, José Luis García Sánchez   221
*lozana andaluza, La / The Lascivious Andalusian** 1976, Vicente Escrivá   239
Luces de Bohemia / Bohemian Nights 1985, Miguel Ángel Díez   259
Luces y sombras / Lights and Shadows 1988, Jaime Camino   260
Lucía y el sexo / Sex and Lucia 2001, Julio Medem   324
Luis Candelas 1936, Fernando Roldán   72
*Luis y Virginia / Luis and Virginia** 1982, Jaime Chávarri   249
Lulú de noche / Lulu by Night 1986, Emilio Martínez Lázaro   268
*Luna de lobos / A Moon for Wolves** 1987, Julio Sánchez Valdés   274
*Luna de sangre / Blood Moon** 1950, Francisco Rovira Beleta   149
*Luna de verano / Summer Moon** 1958, Pedro Lazaga   145
luna negra, La / The Black Moon 1990, Imanol Uribe   267
lunes al sol, Los / Mondays in the Sun 2002, Fernando León de Aranoa   332
*llamada de África, La / The Call of Africa** 1952, César Fernández Ardavín   128
*Llanto por un bandido / Lament for a Bandit** 1963, Carlos Saura   182
*Llegada de los toreros a la plaza / Arrival of Bullfighters at the Ring** 1896, Alexandre
    Promio   2
*Llegada de noche / Night Arrival** 1949, José Antonio Nieves Conde   109
*Llegada de un tren de Teruel a Segorbe / Arrival of the Teruel Train at Segorbe** 1896,
    Anonymous   2
*Llegar a más / To Move On** 1964, Jesús Fernández Santos   169
Lluvia en los zapatos / If Only / The Man with Rain in his Shoes 1998, María Ripoll
    345
Macarena 1944, Antonio Gúzman Merino   105
Maciste Alpino 1916 Italy, Luigi Borgnetto   10
*Madona de las rosas, La / The Rose Madonna** 1919, Fernando Delgado   27, 36 n. 20
*Madre Alegría / Mother Happiness** 1935, José Buchs   59
madre muerta, La / The Dead Mother 1993, Juanma Bajo Ulloa   307
*Madregilda / Mother Gilda** 1993, Francisco Regueiro   90 n. 21, 300
Madrid 1987, Basilio Martín Patino   263
*Madrid en el año 2000 / Madrid in the Year 2000** 1925, Manuel Noriega   36 n. 20, 41
*Madrid se divorcia / Madrid Gets Divorced** 1933/1935, Alfonso Benavides   70
madriguera, La / Honeycomb 1969, Carlos Saura   184
*Madrugada / Dawn** 1957, Antonio Román   149
maestro de esgrima, El / The Fencing Master 1992, Pedro   287
Mágica aventura / Magic Adventure 1974, Palomo Cruz Delgado   176, 252
Magnificent Ambersons, The 1942 USA, Orson Welles   111
*mago de los sueños, El / The Dream Wizard** 1966, Francisco Macián   176
Maité 1995, Eneko Olasagasti and Carlos Zabala   313
*Makinavaja, el último choriso / Makiknife, the Last of the Small-time Crooks** 1992,
    Carlos Suárez   295
*Mal d'amors / Mal de amores / Lovesickness** 1993, Carlos Balagué   265
mala educación, La / Bad Education 2004, Pedro Almodóvar   xv n. 3, 325
*Mala racha / Unlucky Streak** 1985, José Luis Cuerda   269
*Mala raza / Bad Blood** 1911, Fructuós Gelabert   6
Malagueña 1956, Ricardo Nuñez   142
Malaventura / Misadventure 1988, Manuel Gutiérrez Aragón   269
*malcasada, La / The Mismatched Bride** 1927, Francisco Gómez Hidalgo   35
malditas pistolas de Dallas, Las / Three Dollars of Lead 1965, José María Zabalza   174
*Malena es un nombre de tango / Malena is the Name of a Tango** 1996, Gerardo
    Herrero   288

malquerida, La / The Ill-Loved* 1914, Ricard de Baños and Albert Marro 17, 27–8, 84
—— 1940, José López Rubio 28, 84
malvado Carabel, El / The Evil Carabel* 1935, Edgar Neville 62
—— 1956 Fernando Fernán Gómez 62
Malvaloca / Hollyhock 1926, Benito Perojo 34, 37
—— 1942, Luis Marquina 34, 105
—— 1954, Ramón Torrado 34, 125
Mamá / Mother!* 1931, Benito Perojo 51–2
Mamá cumple cien años / Mama Turns a Hundred 1979, Carlos Saura 146 n. 42, 230, 260 n. 5, 295
Mambrú se fue a la guerra / Mambrú Went to War 1986, Fernando Fernán Gómez 263
managers, Los / The Managers* 2006, Fernando Guillén Cuervo 346
mancha de sangre en un coche nuevo, Una / Blood Stains in a New Car 1974, Antonio Mercero 221
Mancha que limpia / The Cleansing Stain* 1924, José Buchs 31
Mando único / Single Command* 1937, Antonio del Amo 74
manigua sin Dios, La / The Godless Swamp 1949, Arturo Ruiz Castillo 103
Manila / Club Manila* 1992, Antonio Chavarrías 291
Maniobras de la artillería en Vicálvaro / Artillery Manoeuvres at Vicalvaro* 1898, Alexandre Promio 2
mano negra, La / The Black Hand 1980, Fernando Colomo 233
Manolito Gafotas / Manolito Four Eyes 1999, Miguel Albaladejo 347
Manolito Gafotas (TV) / 2004, Various 347
Manolito Gafotas en ¡mola ser jefe! / Manolito Gafotas in Great to be the Leader!* 2001, Joan Potau 347
Manolo, guardia urbano / Manolo, Urban Policeman* 1954, Rafael Salvia 145
mans buides, Les / Las manos vacías / Where is Madame Catherine? 2003, Marc Recha 338
mansión de la tiniebla, La / Murder Mansion 1972, Francisco Lara Polop 208
Manuel y Clemente / Manuel and Clemente* 1986, Javier Palmero 268
Mañana de domingo / Sunday Morning* 1966, Antonio Giménez Rico 210
Mañana será otro día / Tomorrow is Another Day 1967, Jaime Camino 191
mar, El / The Sea 2000, Agustí Villaronga 89, 262 n. 9, 329
Mar adentro / The Sea Within 2004, Alejandro Amenábar 308 n. 23, 321
Mar de luna / The Sea Below the Moon* 1996, Manolo Matjí 294
Mar rojo / Red Sea* 2004, Enric Alberich 337
mar y el tiempo, El / Time and the Sea* 1989, Fernando Fernán Gómez 262–3
Mararía 1998, Antonio Betancor 330
Maravillas 1981, Manuel Gutiérrez Aragón 237, 320
Marbella un golpe de cinco estrellas / Marbella Hot Spot 1985, Miguel Hermoso 273
marca del hombre lobo, La / The Mark of the Wolfman 1967, Enrique Eguiluz 174–5, 207
Marcelino, pan y vino / The Miracle of Marcelino 1955, Ladislao Vajda 122, 142, 153, 205 n. 14
—— Luigi Comencini 122
Mare nostrum / Our Sea 1948, Rafael Gil 105
mares del sur, Los / The South Seas* 1992, Manuel Esteban 291
Margarita se llama mi amor / My Love is called Margarita* 1961, Ramón Fernández 142
María de la O 1936/1939, Francisco Elías 65
—— 1958, Ramón Torrado 65, 140

María Morena / Dark María Morena* 1951, José María Forqué and Pedro Lazaga   127
María querida / Dearest María* 2004, José Luis García Sánchez   327, 349
María Rosa 1964/1965, Armando Moreno   169, 191
María, matrícula de Bilbao / Maria, Registered in Bilbao* 1960, Ladislao Vajda   148
   n. 46
Marianela 1940, Benito Perojo   84
—— 1972, Angelino Fons   84 n. 11, 162, 172, 188, 209
Maribel y la extraña familia / Maribel and the Strange Family 1960, José María
   Forqué   145, 166
Maricruz 1957 Mexico-Spain, Miguel Zacarías   126
marido a precio fijo, Un / A Fixed-Price Husband* 1942, Gonzalo Delgrás   95
marino de los puños de oro, El / The Sailor with Golden Fists* 1968, Rafael Gil   166
Mariona Rebull 1947, José Luis Sáenz de Heredia   97
Marions-nous 1931 France-USA, Louis Mercanton   52
Mariquilla Terremoto 1939, Benito Perojo   81
Marisol rumbo a Río / Marisol Goes to Río* 1963, Fernando Palacios   161, 313
marqués de Salamanca, El / The Marquis of Salamanca* 1948, Edgar Neville   97
marquesona, La / The Strange Marchioness* 1940, Eusebio Fernández Ardavín   84
marrana, La / The Sow* 1992, José Luis Cuerda   301–2
Marta 1955, Francisco Elías   57
Martes de Carnaval / Mardi Gras Carnival* 1991, Pedro Carvajal and Fernando Bauluz
   312
Martes y trece / Friday and Thirteenth* 1962, Pedro Lazaga   156, 229 n. 7
Martes y Trece, ni te cases ni embarques / Friday and Thirteenth, Don't Even Move!*
   1982, Javier Aguirre   305
Martín (Hache) / Martin (H) 1997, Adolfo Aristarain   313, 350
Marujas asesinas / Killer Housewives 2001, Javier Rebolledo   336
Más allá de la alambrada / Beyond the Barbed Wire* 2005, Pau Vergara   328
Más allá de la muerte/ Beyond Death* 1924, Benito Perojo   38
Más allá del deseo / Beyond Desire* 1976, José Antonio Nieves Conde   206
Más allá del jardín / Beyond the Garden 1996, Pedro Olea   290
Más pena que gloria / No Pain, no Gain 2001, Victor García León   335
Más que amor, frenesí / Not Love, Just Frenzy 1996, Alfonso Albacete, Miguel Bardem
   and David Menkes   137 n. 28, 301 n. 16, 306, 337
Más que hermanos / More than Siblings* 2005, Ramón Costafreda   335
máscara de Scaramouche, La / The Adventures of Scaramouche 1963, Antonio Isasi-
   Isasmendi   174 n. 24
Matador 1986, Pedro Almodóvar   272
Matar al Nani / Kill Nani* 1988, Roberto Bodegas   264–5
Mater amatísima / Mother Dearly Beloved 1980, Josep Antón Salgot   231, 320
Matías, juez de línea / Mathias, the Linesman* 1996, La Cuadrilla [Santiago Aguilar
   and Luis Guridi]   306
mayorazgo de Basterretxe, El / The Basterretxe Inheritance* 1929, Mauro Azkona   34
Mayores con reparos / For Adults, with Caution* 1966, Fernando Fernán Gómez   179
Me debes un muerto / You Owe Me a Body* 1971, José Luis Sáenz de Heredia   159
Me enveneno de azules / I Poison Myself with Blues* 1969, Francisco Regueiro   186
Me hace falta un bigote / I Need a Moustache* 1986, Manuel Summers   270
Me has hecho perder el juicio / You've Made Me Lose the Trial (My Mind)* 1973, Juan
   de Orduña   201
medalla del torero, La / The Bullfighter's Medal* 1924, Florián Rey   29
mejor alcalde el rey, El / The King is the Best Mayor* 1974, Rafael Gil   205

mejor de los tiempo, El / The Best of Times* 1989, Felipe Vega   273–4
melancólicas, Las / Women of Doom 1971, Rafael Moreno Alba   200
Melodía de arrabal / Suburban Melody 1933, Louis Gasnier with Florián Rey   52
Mendicidad y caridad / Mendicity and Charity* 1932, Adolfo Aznar   72
Menos que cero / Below Zero* 1996, Ernesto Tellería   306
Mensaka 1998, Salvador García Ruiz   333
Mercado prohibido / Forbidden Trade* 1952, Javier Setó   129
Merida 1940, Antonio Román   86
mesón del gitano, El / The Gypsy's Inn* 1969, Antonio Román   160
Metamorfosis / Metamorphosis* 1970, Jacinto Esteva Crewe   193
método, El / The Method 2005, Marcelo Piñeyro   339, 341 n. 22
Metropolis 1927 Germany, Fritz Lang   41
Mi calle / My Street* 1960, Edgar Neville   124
Mi canción es para ti / My Song is for You* 1965, Ramón Torrado   159
Mi casa es tu casa / My Home is Your Home* 2003, Miguel Álvarez   348
Mi general / My General 1987, Jaime de Armiñán   268
Mi hermano del alma / My Soul Brother 1994, Mariano Barroso   306
Mi hija Hildegart / My Daughter Hildegart 1977, Fernando Fernán Gómez   231
Mi hijo no es lo que parece / My Son is not what he Seems 1974, Angelino Fons   210
*Mi mujer es muy decente, dentro de lo que cabe / My Wife is Very Respectable, Given
    the Circumstances** 1974, Antonio Drove   218
Mi nombre es Sombra / My Name is Shadow* 1996, Gonzalo Suárez   290
Mi primera experiencia – Mi primer pecado / My First Sin 1977, Manuel Summers
    242
Mi profesora particicular / My Private Teacher 1973, Jaime Camino   213
Mi querida señorita / My Dearest Señorita 1972, Jaime de Armiñán   138, 230 n. 8,
    219, 231, 320
Mi tío Jacinto / My Uncle Jacinto* 1956, Ladislao Vajda   142
Mi último tango / My Last Tango 1960, Luis Amadori   141
Mi vida sin mí / My Life Without Me 2003, Isabel Coixet   323
Miedo a salir de noche / Afraid to Go Out at Night* 1980, Eloy de la Iglesia   235
miel, La / Honey 1979, Pedro Masó   203 n. 8, 240
Mientras el cuerpo aguante / While the Body Lasts* 1982, Fernando Trueba   242
Mientras haya luz / While There is Light* 1988, Felipe Vega   273
mies es mucha, La / The Harvest is Rich 1948, José Luis Sáenz de Heredia   103, 121
    n. 8
milagro de P. Tinto, El / The Miracle of P. Tinto 1998, Javier Fesser   342
millón en la basura, Un / A Million in the Bin* 1967, José María Forqué   166
Mirada líquida / Liquid Look* 1996, Rafael Moleón   290
Mirón / Peeping Tom* 1977, José Ramón Larraz   228
Mis estimadas víctimas / My Dear Victims* 2004, Pedro Costa   338
Mis relaciones con Ana / My Liaison with Ana* 1979, Rafael Moreno Alba   235
Misa en Santiago / Mass in Santiago* 1954, Ana Mariscal   127 n. 12
Misión blanca / White Mission* 1946, Juan de Orduña   103
Misión en Marbella / Mission in Marbella 2001, Santiago Segura   342
Miss Caribe 1988, Fernando Colomo   270
Miss Muerte / Miss Death* 1965, Jesús Franco   174
Mission, The 1986 UK, Roland Joffé   103
Mister Arkadin / Confidential Report 1955 France-Spain-Switzerland, Orson Welles
    172
Misterio de dolor / Mystery of Grief* 1914, Adrià Gual   17

*misterio de la Puerta del Sol, El / The Mystery of the Puerta del Sol** 1930, Francisco Elías 53–5

*Misterio en la marisma / The Wetland Mystery** 1943, Claudio de la Torre 96

misterio Galíndez, El / The Galíndez File 2003, Gerardo Herrero 340

*misterios de Tánger, Los / Tanger Mysteries** 1942, Carlos Fernández Cuenca 108

mitad del cielo, La / Half of Heaven 1986, Manuel Gutiérrez Aragón 262

Mobbing 2006, Sonia Sánchez 340

Molinos de viento / Windmills 1937/1939, Rosario Pi 62

Molokai / Father Damian's Molokai * 1959, Luis Lucia 121, 153

Mónica 2003, Eduard Cortés 340

monja alférez, La / The Lieutenant Nun 1987, Javier Aguirre 260

*monja y un don Juan, Una / A Nun and a Don Juan** 1973, Mariano Ozores 202

*montaña rebelde, La / The Rebel Mountain** 1971, Ramón Torrado 206

Mor, veda meva / Muere vida mía / Die, My Darling 1996, Mar Targarona 311

*Morbo / Morbidness – Perversion** 1971, Gonzalo Suárez 212

Morena Clara / Dark and Bright 1936, Florián Rey 63, 66, 69, 93, 126

—— 1954, Luis Lucia 69, 126

Morir en España / To Die in Spain 1965, Mariano Ozores 170

Morir en San Hilario / To Die in San Hilario 2005, Laura Mañá 322–3

Morirás en Chafarinas / Zafarinas 1995, Pedro Olea 288

Moros y cristianos / Moors and Christians 1987, Luis G[arcía] Berlanga 268–9

Mortadelo y Filemón, agencia de información (TV) */ Mortadelo & Filemón, Private Investigations** 1966–71, Rafael Vara Cuervo 176

*motivos de Berta, Los / Bertha's Motives** 1985, José Luis Guerín 273

Mourir à Madrid 1963 France, Frédéric Rossif 170

moza del cántaro, La / The Girl with the Jar 1954, Florián Rey 149

muchacha de las bragas de oro, La / Girl with the Golden Panties 1979, Vicente Aranda 243, 247

muchachas de azul, Las / The Girls in Blue 1957, Pedro Lazaga 145

muchachita de Valladolid, Una / A Girl from Valladolid 1958, Luis Amadori 142

Mud and Sand 1922 USA, Gilbert Pratt 17

*muerte de Joselito, La / Death of Joselito** 1920, Juan Oliver 30

muerte de Mikel, La / Mikel's Death 1984, Imanol Uribe 277

Muerte de un ciclista / Death of Cyclist 1955, Juan Antonio Bardem 137–8, 142, 320

*muerte silba un blues, La / Death Whistles the Blues** 1963, Jesús Franco 170

Muertos de risa / Dying from Laughter 1999, Alex de la Iglesia 323

mujer bajo la lluvia, Una / A Woman in the Rain 1992, Gerardo Vera 111 n. 49

*mujer cualquiera, Una / Just Any Woman** 1948, Rafael Gil 109

*mujer de otro, La / Another's Wife** 1967, Rafael Gil 164

mujer de tu vida, La (TV) */ The Woman in Your Life** 1988–94, Various 287

*mujer del juez, La / The Judge's Wife** 1984, Fancisco Lara Polop 265

*mujer del ministro, La / The Minister's Wife** 1981, Eloy de la Iglesia 235

mujer en peligro, Una / A Woman in Danger 1936, José Santugini 70

*mujer feliz, La / The Happy Woman** 1988, José Miguel Ganga 287

mujer más fea del mundo, La / The Ugliest Woman in the World 1999, Miguel Bardem 337

*mujer y la guerra, La / Women at War** 1938, Mauricio Sol(lín) 74

Mujeres al borde de un ataque de nervios / Women on the Verge of a Nervous Breakdown 1988, Pedro Almodóvar 273, 285 n. 4, 320

*Mujeres y hombres / Dones i homes / Women and Men** 1995, Antoni Verdaguer 296

*mundo sigue, El / Life Goes On** 1963, Fernando Fernán Gómez 178

Murió hace quince años / He Died Fifteen Years Ago* 1954, Rafael Gil   122

Nada / Nothing 1947, Edgar Neville   111

Nada menos que todo un hombre / Nothing Less than a Real Man* 1972, Rafael Gil   205

Nadie conoce a nadie / Nobody Knows Anybody 1999, Mateo Gil   321–2, 339

Nadie hablará de nosotras cuando hayamos muerto / Nobody Will Speak of Us When We're Dead 1995, Agustín Díaz Yanes   307, 320

Nadie oyó gritar / No One Heard the Scream 1973, Eloy de la Iglesia   220

Nanas de espinas / Lullabies of Thorns* 1983, Pilar Távora   230

Nanook of the North 1920–22 France-USA, Robert Flaherty   41

Natación / Swimming* 1937, José Val del Omar   73 n. 31

Navajeros / Young Knives 1980, Eloy de la Iglesia   235

Nazarín 1958 Mexico, Luis Buñuel   84, 151, 180

negro con un saxo, Un / A Black Man with a Saxophone* 1989, Francesc Bellmunt   275

negro que tenía el alma blanca, El / The Black Man with a White Soul* 1927 and 1934, Benito Perojo   10, 37–8, 58, 65

Nexo / Nexus* 1993, Jordi Cadena   293

Nido, El / The Nest 1980 Armiñán, Jaime de   232

Ninette 2005, José Luis Garci   330

niña de la venta, La / The Girl at the Inn 1951, Ramón Torrado   125

niña de luto, La / The Girl in Mourning 1964, Manuel Summers   185

niña de tus ojos, La / The Girl of Your Dreams 1998, Fernando Trueba   80, 348–9

niña de tus sueños, La / The Child of Your Dreams* 1995, Jesús Delgado   308

Niñas... ¡al salón! / Girls... To the Drawing Room!* 1977, Vicente Escrivá   239

niño de la luna, El / Moon Child 1989, Agustí Villaronga   276

niño de las monjas, El / The Convent Child* 1925 and 1935, José Buchs   59

—— 1958, Ignacio F. Iquino   59

niño es nuestro, El / The Baby is Ours* 1973, Manuel Summers   210

niño invisible, El / The Invisible Boy* 1995, Rafael Moleón   300

niños de Rusia, Los / The Children of Russia 2001, Jaime Camino   328

No desearás al vecino del quinto / Thou Shalt not Covet thy Fifth Floor Neighbour 1970, Ramón Fernández   203, 235

No desearás la mujer de tu prójimo / Thou Shalt Not Covet thy Neigbour's Wife* 1971, Fernando Merino   203

No encontré rosas para mi madre / Roses and Green Pepper 1973, Francisco Rovira Beleta   214 n. 26

No es bueno que el hombre esté solo / It is not Good for Man to be Alone* 1973, Pedro Olea   219

No me compliques la vida / Don't Complicate my Life* 1993, Ernesto del Río   295–6

No me mates / Don't Kill Me* 1936, James Bauer   70

No somos de piedra / We Are Not Made of Stone 1968, Manuel Summers   185

Nobleza baturra / Rustic Chivalry / Aragonese Virtue 1925, Joan Vilà Vilamala   33

—— 1935, Florián Rey   33, 63, 66–7, 146 n. 42

—— 1965, Juan de Orduña   33

Nocturno 29 / Nocturne 29 1969, Pere Portabella   194

nocturno de Chopin, El / Chopin's Nocturne 1915, Fructuós Gelabert   7

—— 1932, Ramón Martínez de Rivas   7

noche de los girasoles, La / The Night of the Sunflowers 2006, Jorge Sánchez Cabezudo   338

Noche de verano / Summer Night 1963, Jordi Grau   190

noche de Walpurgis, La / Shadow of the Werewolf 1971, León Klimovsky   207

noche del ejecutor, La/ The Night of the Executioner 1992, Jacinto Molina   338

noche del terror ciego, La / Night of the Blind Dead 1971, Amando de Ossorio   208

noche más hermosa, La / The Most Beautiful Night 1984, Manuel Gutiérrez Aragón   270

noche más larga, La / The Longest Night 1991, José Luis García Sánchez   292

noche oscura, La / The Dark Night 1989, Carlos Saura   259–60

noche y el alba, La / Night and Dawn* 1958, José María Forqué   124, 149

Nos miran / They're Watching Us 2003, Norberto López Amado   340

Nothing but the Truth 1929 USA, Victor Schertzinger   52

Noticias de una guerra / News of a War* 2006, Eterio Ortega Santillana   327

nova cançó, La / The New Songs* 1975, Francesc Bellmunt   222

Noventa minutos / Ninety Minutes* 1949, Antonio del Amo   113

novia de Juan Simón, La / Juan Simón's Girl 1933, Joaquin Xaudaró and Ricardo García López   63

novia ensangrentada, La / The Blood-Spattered Bride 1972, Vicente Aranda   192, 212

Novio a la vista / Boyfriend in Sight 1954, Luis G[arcía] Berlanga   114, 135

novio de mamá, El / Mother's Boyfriend* 1934, Florián Rey   57

Novios / Engaged* 1999, Joaquín Oristrell   344

novios búlgaros, Los / Bulgarian Lovers 2003, Eloy de la Iglesia   344

Novios de la muerte / Death's Newlyweds* 1974, Rafael Gil   206

novios de mi mujer, Los / My Wife's Boyfriends* 1972, Ramón Fernández   204

Nueces para el amor / Nuts for Love 2000, Alberto Lecchi   350

Nuestra Natacha / Our Natasha* 1936, Benito Perojo   71, 81

Nuestro culpable / Our Guilty Man* 1938, Fernando Mignoni   70 n. 27, 72

nueva Cenicienta, La / The New Cinderella 1964, George Sherman   161

Nueve cartas a Berta / Nine Letters to Bertha 1967, Basilio Martín Patino   187

nuevos españoles, Los / The New Spaniards 1974, Roberto Bodegas   217

Nunca es demasiado tarde / Never Too Late* 1956, Julio Coll   148

Nunca es tarde / It's Never Too Late 1977, Jaime de Armiñán   232

Nunca pasa nada / Nothing Ever Happens 1963, Juan Antonio Bardem   177, 180

Obaba 2005, Montxo Arméndariz   348

Obra maestra / Masterpiece 2000, David Trueba   348

Obsesión / Obsession 1975, Francisco Lara Polop   208

Ocaña, retrat intermitent / Ocaña, An Intermittent Portrait 1978, Ventura Pons   234, 275

Oculto / Hidden 2005, Antonio Hernández   183 n. 36, 339

Ochocientas balas / Eight Hundred Bullets 2002, Álex de la Iglesia   323

Odio / Hatred 1933, Richard Harlan   66

Oeste Nevada Joe / Joe Dexter 1964, Ignacio F. Iquino   173

Off Key 2001, Manuel Gómez Pereira   343

oficios de Cándido, Los / Candido's Jobs* 1965, Javier Aguirre   189

¡¡Oh cielos!! / Heavens Above!!* 1995, Ricardo Franco   295

Ojalá, Val del Omar / If Only, Val del Omar 1994, Cristina Esteban   73 n. 31

ojo de cristal, El / The Glass Eye 1955, Antonio Santillán   148

ojos dejan huellas, Los / Eyes Leave Prints* 1952, José Luis Sáenz de Heredia   129

ojos perdidos, Los / Lost Eyes* 1967, Rafael García Serrano   170

ojos vendados, Los / Blindfolded Eyes 1978, Carlos Saura   243

Olentzero: un cuento de Navidad / Olentzero: A Christmas Story* 2002, Juanjo Elordi   347

Olentzero y el tronco mágico / Olentzero and the Magic Tree Trunk* 2005, Juanjo Elordi   347

olvidados, Los / The Forgotten Ones 1950 Mexico, Luis Buñuel   11, 130, 132
ombra en el jardí, Una / Una sombra en el jardín / A Shadow in the Garden* 1989, Antonio Chavarrías   276
Once pares de botas / Eleven Pairs of Boots* 1954, Francisco Rovira Beleta   128
Ópera prima / First Work 1980, Fernando Trueba   233
Operación cabaretera / Missión Cabaret* 1967, Mariano Ozores   165
Operación Ogro / Operation Ogre 1980, Gillo Pontecorvo   198, 243
Operación Plus Ultra / Mission Over and Beyond* 1966, Pedro Lazaga   164
orador, El – La mano / The Orator – The Hand* 1929, Ramón Gómez de la Serna   53 n. 8, 54
orgía, L' / The Orgy 1978, Francesc Bellmunt   222, 238
Orgullo / Pride 1955, Manuel Mur Oti   127
orilla, La / The River Bank* 1971, Luis Lucia   206
oro de Moscú, El / Moscow Gold 2003, Jesús Bonilla   343
Orquesta Club Virginia / Club Virginia Orchestra 1992, Manuel Iborra   299
Oscuros sueños de agosto / Obscure August Dreams 1967, Miguel Picazo   186
Osoria 1943, Florián Rey   84
otra alcoba, La / The Other Bedroom* 1976, Eloy de la Iglesia   236 n. 16
Otra vuelta de tuerca / Another Turn of the Screw* 1985, Eloy de la Iglesia   267
otro árbol de Guernica, El / The Other Guernica Tree* 1969, Pedro Lazaga   170, 207
otro barrio, El / The Other Side 2000, Salvador García Ruiz   335
otro lado de la cama, El / The Other Side of the Bed 2002, Emilio Martínez Lázaro   346
Otros, Los / The Others 2001, Alejandro Amenábar   321, 340
Otto e mezzo 1963 Italy, Federico Fellini   160
Ovejas negras / Black Sheep* 1990, José María Carreño   312
Pà d'àngel / Angel Bread 1984, Francesc Bellmunt   275
Padre Coplillas / The Singing Priest* 1968, Ramón Comas   159
padre de la criatura, El / The Father of the Child* 1972, Pedro Lazaga   164, 201
padre Manolo, El / Father Manolo* 1966, Ramón Torrado   159
Padre nuestro / Our Father 1985, Francisco Regueiro   186, 268, 320
padre pitillo, El / Father Cigarette* 1954, Juan de Orduña   129
Pajarico / Little Bird 1997, Carlos Saura   325
pájaro de la felicidad, El / The Bird of Happiness 1993, Pilar Miró   4 n. 6, 286
pájaros de Baden Baden, Los / The Birds of Baden Baden 1975, Mario Camus   211
palabras de Max, Las / What Max Said 1978, Emilio Martínez-Lázaro   235
palabras de Vero, Las / Veronica's Words* 2005, Octavi Masia   335
Palabras encadenadas / Killing Words 2002, Laura Mañá   322
Palace / Palace Hotel* 1996, Tricicle [Joan Gràcia, Paco Mir and Carles Sans]   311
palo, El / The Hold-up* 2001, Eva Lesmes   166, 341
palomo cojo, El / The Lame Dove* 1995, Jaime de Armiñán   288, 293
Pan, amor y Andalucía / Bread, Love and Andalusia 1959, Javier Setó   142
Pánico en el transiberiano / Horror Express 1972, Eugenio Martín   174
papers d'Aspern, Els / The Aspern Papers 1991, Jordi Cadena   277
Para que no me olvides / So That You Don't Forget Me* 2005, Patricia Ferreira   335
Para toda la vida / For Ever* 1923, Benito Perojo   38
paraguas para tres, Un / An Umbrella for Three 1992, Felipe Vega   295, 297
paraíso recobrado, El / Paradise Recovered 1935, Xavier Güell   64
paraísos perdidos, Los / The Lost Paradise 1985, Basilio Martín Patino   263
parell d'ous, Un / A Pair of Eggs/Balls* 1985, Francesc Bellmunt   275
Parella de tres / Una pareja de tres / A Couple of Three* 1995, Antoni Verdaguer   296

*Pares y nones / Odd and Even** 1982, José Luis Cuerda   234

Paris, je t'aime / Paris, I Love You 2006, Various   324

París–Tombuctú / Paris–Timbuktu 1999, Luis G[arcía] Berlanga   135 n. 24, 341

*Párpados / Eyelids** 1989, Iván Zulueta   252

Parranda / Binge 1977, Gonzalo Suárez   267

Parsifal / The Evil Forest 1952, Carlos Serrano de Osma   122

*Pasa la tuna / The University Chorus** 1960, José María Elorrieta   142

*pasajero clandestino, El / Le Passager clandestin / The Clandestine Passenger** 1996,
    Agustí Villaronga   291

Pasajes / Passages 1996, Daniel Calparsoro   307–8

Pascual Duarte 1975/1976, Ricardo Franco   220, 248

*Pasión lejana / Més enllà de la passió / Beyond the Passion** 1987, Jesús Garay   276

pasión turca, La / Turkish Passion 1994, Vicente Aranda   286

*paso del Ebro, El / Crossing the Ebro** 1937, Antonio del Amo   74

Pasodoble 1988, José Luis García Sánchez   268

*pasos perdidos, Los / The Lost Steps** 2001, Manane Rodríguez   350

*pastorcito de Torrent, El / The Little Shepherd from Torrent** 1908, Antonio Cuesta   13

*patria chica, La / Our Homeland** 1942, Fernando Delgado   107

Patricio miró a una estrella / Patricio Looked at a Star 1934, José Luis Sáenz de
    Heredia   61

*patrulla, La / The Platoon** 1954, Pedro Lazaga   123

Pau i el seu germà Pau y su hermano / Pau and his Brother 2001, Marc Recha   338

Pax 1932, Francisco Elías and Camille Lemoine   56

*paz empieza nunca, La / Peace Never Starts** 1960, León Klimovsky   124

*Pecado de amor / A Sin of Love** 1961, Luis Amadori   141, 154

*peces rojos, Los / Goldfish** 1955, José Antonio Nieves Conde   118, 129

*pelota vasca, La / Euskal pilota Larrua harriaren kontra / The Basque Ball: Skin
    Against the Wall* 2003, Julio Medem   324, 327

*Pelotari / The Pelota Players** 1964, Néstor Basterretxea   170

peores años de nuestra vida, Los / The Worst Years of Our Lives 1994, Emilio Martínez
    Lázaro   293

Pepe Conde 1941, José López Rubio   105

*Pepi, Luci, Bom y otras chicas del montón / Pepi, Luci, Bom and Other Girls on the
    Heap* 1980, Pedro Almodóvar   251

Pepita Jiménez / Bride to Be 1925, Agustín Carrasco   205

———— 1975, Rafael Moreno Alba   205

Peppermint frappé / Peppermint Frappé 1967, Carlos Saura   183, 188, 216, 231 n. 10

Pequeñeces / Trifles 1950, Juan de Orduña   103–4, 121 n. 3

pequeño coronel, El / The Little Colonel 1960, Antonio del Amo   144

pequeño ruiseñor, El / The Little Nightingale 1956, Antonio del Amo   144

Perdita Durango / Dance with the Devil 1997, Alex de la Iglesia   323

*Perdona bonita, pero Lucas me quería a mí / Excuse me Darling, but Lucas only Loved
    Me* 1997, Dunia Ayaso and Felix Sabroso   310

Pérez, el ratoncito de tus sueños / The Hairy Tooth Fairy 2006, Juan Pablo Buscarini
    347

periscopio, El / And Give Us Our Daily Sex 1979, José Ramón Larraz   228

*Pero ¿en qué país vivimos? / But What Sort of a Country are we Living in?** 1967, José
    Luis Sáenz de Heredia   159

perquè de tot plegat, El / What It's All about 1995, Ventura Pons   296

*perro, El / The Dog** 1977, Antonio Isasi-Isasmendi   247

perro del hortelano, El / The Dog in the Manger 1996, Pilar Miró   267, 286

Perro golfo / Mischievous Dog* 1961, Domingo Viladomat   145
Perros callejeros / Street Warriors 1977, José Antonio de la Loma   237
Perros callejeros II / Street Warriors II 1979, José Antonio de la Loma   237
Persecución en Madrid / Persecution in Madrid* 1952, Enrique Gómez   129
Persecución hasta Valencia / The Narco Men 1968, Julio Coll   171
Perseguidos / Pursued* 2004, Eterio Ortega Santillana   327
Perversión / Perversion* 1974, Francisco Lara Polop   208
Pesadilla para un rico / Nightmare for a Wealthy Man* 1996, Fernando Fernán Gómez   296
pescador de coplas, El / The Fisher of Songs* 1954, Antonio del Amo   126
petición, La / The Request 1976, Pilar Miró   230
Petite Andalouse, La 1924 France, Louis Feuillade   36
pianos mecánicos, Los / The Mechanical Pianos* 1965, Juan Antonio Bardem   180
pícara molinera, La / The Cheeky Miller's Wife* 1955, León Klimovsky   125
pico, El / The Shoot* 1983, Eloy de la Iglesia   264
pico II, El / The Shoot II* 1984, Eloy de la Iglesia   264
Pídele cuentas al rey / Get the King to Answer* 2000, José Antonio Quirós   332
Piedras / Stones 2002, Ramón Salazar   347
piel quemada, La / Burnt Skin* 1965/1967, Josep Maria Forn   169, 191
Pierna creciente, falda menguante / Waxing Leg and Waning Skirt* 1970, Javier Aguirre   209
Pilar Guerra 1926, José Buchs   33 n. 15, 47
Pim, pam, pum ¡fuego! / One Two Three, Fire!* 1975, Pedro Olea   219
pirañas, Las/ La boutique / The Piranhas 1967, Luis G[arcía] Berlanga   179
pisito, El / The Tiny Flat* 1959, Marco Ferreri   146
pistola de mi hermano, La / My Brother's Gun 1997, Ray Loriga   308, 334
Pitouto, fabricante de suicidios / Pitouto Suicide Manufacturer* 1928, Francisco Elías   29
Pitouto, mozo de granja / Pitouto Farm-Hand* 1930, Florián Rey   29
Pitouto tiene su corazoncito / Pitouto with His Little Heart* 1930, Florián Rey   29
plaça del diamant, La / La plaza del diamante / Diamond Square* 1982, Francesc Betriu   248
placer de matar, El / The Pleasure of Killing 1988, Félix Rotaeta   274
placeres ocultos, Los / Hidden Pleasures 1977, Eloy de la Iglesia   235
Plácido 1961, Luis G[arcía] Berlanga   136–7, 177, 179, 319
Planta 4ª / The Fourth Floor 2003, Antonio Mercero   332
Plaza de Mina / Mina Square* 1897, Louis Joseph Sellier   3
Plenilunio / Plenilune 2000, Imanol Uribe   336
pobre García, El / Poor García* 1961, Tony Leblanc   167
pobre Valbuena, El / Poor Valbuena* 1910, Segundo de Chomón   10
poder del deseo, El / The Power of Desire* 1975, Juan Antonio Bardem   162, 213–14
Poderoso Caballero / A Big Guy 1935, Max Nosseck   63
poderoso influjo de la luna, El / The Powerful Influence of the Moon* 1980, Antonio del Real   234
Polizón a bordo! / Stowaway on Board!* 1941, Florián Rey   84
Polvos mágicos / Magic Ejaculations* 1979, José Ramón Larraz   228
Pon un hombre en tu vida / Put a Man in your Life* 1996, Eva Lesmes   310
Poniente / Setting Sun* 2002, Chus Gutiérrez   333
Pont de Varsòvia / The Warsaw Bridge 1990, Pere Portabella   277
¡Por fin solos! / Alone, at last! 1994, Antonio del Real   297
Por la unidad hacia la victoria / United to Victory* 1937, Fernando Mantilla   73

¿Por qué lo llaman amor cuando quieren decir sexo? / Why do they Call it Love when they Mean Sex? 1993, Manuel Gómez Pereira   304

¿Por qué pecamos a los cuarenta? / Why do we Sin at Forty? 1969, Pedro Lazaga   165, 203 n. 9

¿Por qué perdimos la guerra? / Why Did We Lose The War?* 1977, Diego Abad de Santillán   241

¿Por qué te engaña tu marido? / Why Does Your Husband Deceive You? 1969, Manuel Summers   185

portentosa vida del pare Vicent, La / The Prodigious life of Father Vincent 1978, Carles Mira   238–9

posada sangrienta, La / The Bloody Inn* 1913, Anonymous   19

Posición avanzada / Forward Position* 1965, Pedro Lazaga   170

precio de un hombre, El / The Bounty Killer 1966, Eugenio Martín   174

preciosa puesta de sol, Una / A Beautiful Sunset* 2003, Álvaro del Amo   334

Préstamela esta noche / Lend Her to Me for the Night* 1978, Tulio Demicheli   249

Pride and the Passion, The 1957 USA, Stanley Kramer   172

Prim / General Prim* 1931, José Buchs   36 n. 20, 52

prima Angélica, La / Cousin Angelica 1974, Carlos Saura   200, 215–6, 231 n. 10, 245

primera entrega, La / First Surrender 1971, Angelino Fons   210

primera noche de mi vida, La / My First Night 1998, Miguel Albaladejo   341

princesa de Éboli, La / That Lady 1954, Terence Young   120

princesa de los Ursinos, La The Princess of the Ursinos 1947, Luis Lucia   100, 104

Princesas / Princesses 2006, Fernando León de Aranoa   332

príncipe encadenado, El / The King of the Vikings / The Prince in Chains* 1960, Luis Lucia   149

Prisionero en la ciudad / Prisoner in the City* 1969, Antonio de Jaén   160

Prisioneros de guerra / POWs* 1938, Manuel García Viñolas   78

Prisoner of Zenda, The 1937 USA, John Cromwell   86

Procesión de las hijas de María / Procession of the Daughters of Mary* 1902, Fructuós Gelabert   4

proceso de Burgos, El / The Burgos Trial 1979, Imanol Uribe   241–2

protegida, La / The Protected One* 1975, Francisco Lara Polop   208

próxima estación, La / The Next Station* 1982, Antonio Mercero   234

próximo otoño, El / Next Autumn* 1963/1967, Antxon Eceiza   188, 247

Psycho 1960 USA, Alfred Hitchcock   212

Puede ser divertido / It could be Fun* 1995, Azucena Rodríguez   308

puente, El / The Long Weekend 1977, Juan Antonio Bardem   243

Pulgarcito / Tom Thumb 1904, Segundo de Chomón   7

puntaire, La / La encajera / The Lacemaker 1928, Fructuós Gelabert   7

puñado de rosas, El / The Handful of Roses* 1911, Segundo de Chomón   10

pura verdad, La / Nothing but the Truth 1931, Florián Rey   52

Puta misèria! / Damned Despair!* 1989, Ventura Pons   275

puta y la ballena, La / The Whore and the Whale 2004, Luis Puenzo   350

Puzzle 1986, Lluís Josep Comerón   267–8

Quai des brumes 1938 France, Marcel Carné   71–2

¿Qué hace una chica como tú en un sitio como éste? / What is a Girl like You Doing in a Place like This? 1978, Fernando Colomo   233

¿Qué hacemos con los hijos? / What Shall We Do with the Children?* 1967, Pedro Lazaga   164

¿Qué he hecho yo para merecer esto!! / What Have I Done to Deserve This?! 1984, Pedro Almodóvar   271–2, 319, 345

Qué nos quiten lo bailao / We Had it so Good!* 1983, Carles Mira   277
Què t'hi jugues, Mari Pili? / What do you Bet, Mari Pili* 1991, Ventura Pons   296
que tienen que servir, Las / Those who have to Serve 1967, José María Forqué   166
¡Qué vecinos tan animales! / What Beastly Neighbours!* 1998, Maite Ruiz de Austri   312
¡Qué vienen los socialistas! / The Socialists are Coming!* 1982, Mariano Ozores   240
querida, La / The Mistress 1975, Fernando Fernán Gómez   213
Queridísimos verdugos / Dearest Excecutioners 1974/1977, Basilio Martín Patino   210, 240
¿Quién me quiere a mí? / Who Loves Me?* 1936, José Luis Sáenz de Heredia with Luis Buñuel   61
¿Quién puede matar a un niño? / Would You Kill a Child? 1976, Narciso Ibáñez Serrador 'Chicho'   175, 208–9
Quiet Man, The 1951 USA, John Ford   302
Quijote de Miguel de Cervantes, El / Don Quixote 1991, Manuel Gutiérrez Aragón   269
quinta del porro, La / The Stoned Recruits* 1980, Francesc Bellmunt   238
ràbia, La / Rage 1978, Eugeni Anglada   246
ràdio folla, La / Crazy Radio* 1986, Francesc Bellmunt   275
Raluy, una noche en el circo / Raluy, a Night with the Circus* 2000, Oscar Vega   347
Rapados / Skinheads* 2004, Ramón Parrado   333
Rapsodia de sangre / Blood Rhapsody* 1957, Antonio Isasi-Isasmendi   123
rata primero, El / The Rat First* 1932, Joaquin Xaudaró and Ricardo García López   63
Rataplán 1935, Francisco Elías   57
rayo, El / The Lightning Bolt* 1936, José Buchs   66
rayo de luz, Un / A Ray of Light* 1960, Luis Lucia   161
Raza / Race 1941, José Luis Sáenz de Heredia   xv, 81, 87–8, 90–1, 100, 111 n. 51, 114, 123
Raza, el espíritu de Franco / Race, The Spirit of Franco 1977, Gonzalo Herralde   241
razones de mis amigos, Las / Friends Have Reasons 2000, Gerardo Herrero   332
Realquiler / Sublet 1992, Chus Gutiérrez   309
Rear Window 1954 USA, Alfred Hitchcock   67
Rebecca 1940 USA, Alfred Hitchcock   113
rebeldes de Arizona, Los / The Arizona Rebels* 1970, José María Zabalza   174
recerca de la felicitat, La / The Search for Happiness* 1993, Albert Abril   289
Recluta con niño / Recruit with a child* 1955, Pedro L. Ramírez   144
reconquista de la patria, La / The Reconquest of the Fatherland* 1937, Ricardo Gutiérrez   78
Reconstruyendo España / Rebuilding Spain* 1938, Alfredo Fraile   78
Reflejos / Reflections* 2002, Miguel Ángel Vivas   340
Reforma agraria / Agrarian Reform* 1935, José María Beltrán   73
regalo de Silvia, El / Silvia's present* 2003, Dionisio Pérez   332
Regenta, La / The Regent's Wife 1974, Gonzalo Suárez   205, 213
Regreso del viento del norte / The Return of the North Wind* 1994, Maite Ruiz de Austri   312
reina anónima, La / The Anonymous Queen 1992, Gonzalo Suárez   287
reina mora, La / The Moorish Queen* 1922, José Buchs   31, 126
——— 1937, Eusebio Fernández Ardavín   31, 126
——— 1955, Raúl Alfonso   31, 126
Reina santa / The Holy Queen* 1947, Rafael Gil   100, 108, 132
Reina Zanahoria, La / The Carrot Queen 1978, Gonzalo Suárez   267

Reinas / Queens 2006, Manuel Gómez Pereira   288 n. 8, 343–4

Rejas en la memoria / Bars on the Memory* 2004, Manuel Palacios   328

Relaciones casi públicas / Almost Public Relations* 1968, José Luis Sáenz de Heredia   159

relicario, El / The Locket* 1927, Miguel Contrera Torres   56, 201

—— 1933, Ricard de Baños   56, 201

—— 1970, Rafael Gil   201

Remando al viento / Rowing in the Wind 1988, Gonzalo Suárez   260, 320

Renacer / Reborn 1981, José Juan Bigas Luna   247

Rencor / Resentment* 2002, Miguel Albaladejo   331, 345

Reportaje del movimiento revolucionario en Barcelona / Report on the Revolutionary Movement in Barcelona* 1936, Mateo Santos   73

Réquiem por un campesino español / Requiem for a Spanish Farmhand* 1985, Francesc Betriu   234, 258

Residencia, La / The Finishing School 1969, Narciso Ibáñez Serrador 'Chicho'   175

Resistencia en el Levante / Resistance from the East* 1938, Rafael Gil   74

respuesta, La / The Response* 1969/ 1975, Josep Maria Forn   169

restos del naufragio, Los / The Remains from the Shipwreck 1978, Ricardo Franco   229–30

retorno de Walpurgis, El / The Return of Walpurgis 1973, Carlos Aured   207

retorno del hombre lobo, El / The Return of the Wolfman 1980, Jacinto Molina   207

Retrato de familia / Family Portrait 1976, Antonio Giménez Rico   66 n. 24, 210, 244

revoltosa, La / The Mischief-Maker* 1924, Florián Rey   29, 33, 163

—— 1963, José Díaz Morales   163

—— 1969, Juan de Orduña   163

Rewind 1999, Nicolás Muñoz   348

rey de la carretera, El / King of the Road* 1955, Juan Fortuny   142

rey del mambo, El / Mambo King* 1989, Carles Mira   277

rey del río, El / The King of the River* 1995, Manuel Gutiérrez Aragón   293

rey pasmado, El / The Dumbfounded King 1991, Imanol Uribe   294

rey que rabió, El / The Old King who Raged* 1929 and 1939, José Buchs   83

reyes magos, Los / The Three Wise Men 2003, Antonio Navarro   347

Rififí en la ciudad / Trouble in the City* 1964, Jesús Franco   170–1, 212

Ringo de Nebraska / Savage Gringo 1966/1968, Antonio Román   173

Riña en un café / Brawl in a Café* 1897, Fructuós Gelabert   5–6

Río abajo / On the Line 1984, José Luis Borau   265

río de oro, El / The Golden River 1986, Jaime Chávarri   267

río que nos lleva, El / The River that Takes Us* 1989, Antonio del Real   302

Rob Roy 1995 USA, Michael Caton-Jones   33, 101–2

Robe, The 1953 USA, Henry Koster   127

Robin Hood nunca muere / Robin Hood Will Never Die* 1974, Francesc Bellmunt   222

robobo de la jojoya, El / The Thetheft of the Jejewel* 1992, Álvaro Sáenz de Heredia   305

Rocco e i suoi fratelli 1960 Italy, Luchino Visconti   184

Rocío / Our Lady of the Rocío* 1980, Fernando Ruiz Vergara   242

Rocío de la Mancha / Rocío, the Dewdrop of La Mancha* 1963, Luis Lucia   162

Rojo sangre / Red Blood* 2004, Christian Molina   338

Rojo y negro / Red and Black* 1942, Carlos Arévalo   49, 86

Roma 2004, Adolfo Aristarain   350

Romancero marroquí / Moroccan Ballads* 1939, Enrique Domínguez Rodiño   79

Romeo and Juliet 1936 USA, George Cukor   113

Ronda española / Spanish Serrenade* 1951, Ladislao Vajda 87
Rosa de Levante / Valencian Rose* 1926, Mario Ronconori 33 n. 15
rosa de Madrid, La / The Rose of Madrid* 1928, Eusebio Fernández Ardavín 35
rosa de piedra, La / The Stone Rose* 1999, Manuel Palacios 338
rosa roja, La / The Red Rose* 1960, Carlos Serrano de Osma 140
Rosa, rosae 1993, Fernando Colomo 287
Rosita, Please! / 1994, Ventura Pons 296
rossa del bar, La / The Blonde at the Bar* 1986, Ventura Pons 275
Rostro al mar / Facing the Sea* 1951, Carlos Serrano de Osma 124
rostro del asesino, El / The Murderer's Face* 1965, Pedro Lazaga 170
Rueda de sospechosos / Line-up of Suspects* 1964, Ramón Fernández 170
ruiseñor de las cumbres, El / The Nightingale Up High* 1958, Antonio del Amo 144, 154
Rumbo al Cairo / The Road to Cairo* 1935, Benito Perojo 59
Rusa, La / The Russian Woman* 1987, Mario Camus 265
ruta de Don Quijote, La / Don Quixote's Journey 1934, Ramon Biadiu 72–3
Sabina, La / Sabina 1979, José Luis Borau 231–2
Sabino Arana / Sabino Arana, the Basque* 1979, Pedro de la Sota 243
sabor de la venganza, El / Gunfight at High Noon 1963, Joaquín Romero Marchent 173
Sabor Latino / Latin Flavour 1996, Pedro Carvajal 312
¡Sabotaje! / Sabotage!!* 2000, Esteban Ibarretxe 342
sacerdote, El / The Priest* 1978, Eloy de la Iglesia 235
Saeta rubia / Blond Arrow 1956, Javier Setó 128 n. 15
Saïd 1999, Llorenç Soler 333
sal de la vida, La / The Salt of Life* 1996, Eugenio Martín 297, 313
Sal gorda / Coarse Salt 1984, Fernando Trueba 270
salario del crimen, El / The Wages of Crime 1964, Julio Buchs 170
Salida de las alumnas del Colegio de San Luis de los franceses / Pupils Leaving the French Girls' School* 1896, Alexandre Promio 1
Salida de misa de doce del Pilar de Zaragoza / Leaving the Midday Mass on the Feast of Our Lady of Zaragoza* 1896, Eduardo Jimeno Correas 2
Salomé 2002, Carlos Saura 251, 325–6
Salsa rosa / Pink Sauce 1992, Manuel Gómez Pereira 304
Salto al vacío / Leap into the Void 1995, Daniel Calparsoro 307
Saludos / Greetings* 1896, Eduardo Jimeno Correas 3
Salut i força al canut / Cuernos a la catalana / Catalan Cuckold 1979, Francesc Bellmunt 238
Salvador / Salvador (Puig Antich) 2006, Manuel Huerga 329, 346
Salvajes / Savages* 2001, Carlos Molinero 333
Sálvate si puedes / Save Yourself if You Can* 1995, Joaquín Trincado 295
Sangre en Castilla / Blood in Castile* 1950, Benito Perojo 114
Sangre en el ruedo / Blood in the Bullring* 1969, Rafael Gil 163
Sangre en la nieve / Blood in the Snow* 1942, Ramón Quadreny 108
Sangre y arena / Blood and Sand 1916, Ricard de Baños and Albert Marro 17
Sanidad / Health* 1937, Rafael Gil 74
Santa Rogelia 1939, Edgar Neville 82
Santander para España / Santander for Spain* 1937, Fernando Delgado 78
santos inocentes, Los / The Holy Innocents 1984, Mario Camus 204, 227 n. 4, 248, 258, 319

santuario no se rinde, El / The Sanctuary Does Not Surrender 1949, Arturo Ruiz Castillo
    112
Sara 2003, Silvia Quer   331
Saudade 1936, Carlos Velo   73
*¡Se armó el belén! / What a Fuss of a Nativity!** 1970, José Luis Sáenz de Heredia
    202
*Se buscan fulmontís / Fullmonties Wanted** 1999, Álex Calvo Sotelo   332
Se ha fugado un preso / A Prisoner has Escaped 1933, Benito Perojo   56
Sé infiel y no mires con quién / Be Wanton and Tread no Shame 1985, Fernando Trueba
    270
Sé quién eres / I Know Who You Are 2000, Patricia Ferreira   340
Se vende un palacio / A Palace for Sale 1943, Ladislao Vajda   94
*secretarias, Las / The Secretaries** 1969, Pedro Lazaga   160
*secretas intenciones, Las / Secret Intentions** 1970, Antxon Eceiza   188
*secreto de la mujer muerta / The Secret of the Dead Woman** 1945, Ricardo Gutiérrez
    108
*secreto de Tomy, El / Tommy's Secret** 1963, Antonio del Amo   160
Secretos del corazón / Secrets of the Heart 1997, Montxo Armendáriz   329
*seducción del caos, La / The Seduction of Chaos** 1991, Basilio Martín Patino   267
seductor, El / The Seducer 1995, José Luis García Sánchez   293
Segunda piel / Second Skin 1999, Gerardo Vera   336
*Segundo López, un aventurero urbano / Segundo López, Urban Adventure** 1953, Ana
    Mariscal   131, 171
segundo poder, El / The Second Power 1976, José María Forqué   247
semana de felicidad, Una / One Week of Happiness 1934, Max Nosseck   63
semana del asesino, La / Week of the Killer / Cannibal Man 1972/1974, Eloy de la Iglesia
    220
*Semen (una historia de amor) / *Semen (A Love Story)* 2005, Inés París and Daniela
    Féjerman   344
Senda ignorada / Path Unknown 1946, José Antonio Nieves Conde   109
*Senda torcida / Twisted Path** 1963, Antonio Santillán   170
*Sendas marcadas / Marked Paths** 1957, Juan Bosch   148
*senyora, La / The Lady of the House** 1987, Jordi Cadena   276
*señor Esteve, El / Mister Esteve** 1948, Edgar Neville   97
señora de Fátima, La / Our Lady of Fatima 1951, Rafael Gil   120, 154
*Señora Doctor / Madam Doctor** 1973, Mariano Ozores   202
señorita de Trevélez, La / Miss Trevélez 1936, Edgar Neville   69–70, 138
*Separación matrimonial / Conjugal Separation** 1973, Angelino Fons   210
séptimo día, El / The Seventh Day 2004, Carlos Saura   326, 334 n. 16, 337
Serenata española / Spanish Serenade 1947, Juan de Orduña   107
*Serie excéntrica / Excentric Series** 1915, Domènec Ceret   29
*Servicio en la mar / Service at Sea** 1951, Luis Suárez de Lezo   62, 124
Sesión continua / Double Feature 1984, José Luis Garci   256 n. 1
Seventh Voyage of Simbad, The 1958 USA, Nathan Juran   174 n. 24
*Sévigné / Madame de Sévigné** 2004, Marta Balletbò-Coll   311
Sevillanas 1897, Alexandre Promio   2
——— 1992, Carlos Saura   251, 299, 326
*Sex o no sex / Sex or no Sex** 1974, Julio Diamante   209
*Sexo oral / Oral-Aural Sex** 1994, Chus Gutiérrez   309
Sexo por compasión / Compassionate Sex 2000, Laura Mañá   322
*sexto sentido, El / The Sixth Sense** 1929, Nemesio Sobrevila   42, 47, 252

Si te dicen que caí / If They Tell You I Fell* 1989, Vicente Aranda   262, 264
Si volvemos a vernos / Smashing Up 1967, Francisco Regueiro   186
Siembra / Sowing* 1935, José María Beltrán   73
Siempre Habana / Always Havana* 2006, Ángel Peláez   350–1
Siempre hay un camino a la derecha / There's Always a Path to the Right* 1997, José
   Luis García Sánchez   294
Siempre vuelven de madrugada / They Always Return at Dawn* 1949, Jerónimo Mihura
   96
Siempre Xonxa / Sempre Xonxa / A Woman Forever 1990, Chano Piñeiro   279
Sierra de Ronda / The Sierra of Ronda* 1933, Florián Rey   56
Sierra de Teruel / Days of Hope 1939/1945, André Malraux and Boris Perskine   74,
   132 n. 19
Sierra maldita / Cursed Mountain 1955, Antonio del Amo   127, 221
Siete días de enero / Seven Days in January 1979, Juan Antonio Bardem   243
Siete mil días juntos / Long Life Together 1994, Fernando Fernán Gómez   296
siete vidas del gato, Las / The Cat's Seven Lives 1970, Pedro Lazaga   166
signo de la tribu, El / The Sign of the Tribe* 1915, Josep Maria Codina   22
Silence of the Lambs, The 1991 USA, Jonathan Demme   290
Silencio roto / Broken Silence 2001, Montxo Armendáriz   329
Simón contamos contigo / We're Counting on You, Simon* 1971, Ramón Fernández
   204
Sin noticias de Dios / No News from God / Don't Tempt Me 2001, Agustín Díaz Yanes
   341
Sin novedad en el Alcázar / The Siege of the Alcazar* 1940, Augusto Genina   89–90
Sindrome laboral / Industrial Syndrome* 2005, Sigfrid Monleón   333
sirena negra, La / The Black Siren 1947, Carlos Serrano de Osma   105, 109 n. 47
Sissi 1955, 1956 and 1957 Austria, Ernst Marischka   141
sistema Pelegrín, El / The Pelegrín System* 1951, Ignacio F. Iquino   128
Smoking_Room 2002, Roger Gual and Julio Wallowits   339
Snake Woman 2005, Jesús Franco   338
Sobre el cieno / In the Mire* 1933, Fernando Roldán   70
sobre verde, El / The Green Envelope* 1971, Rafael Gil   201
Sobreviviré / I Will Survive 1999, Alfonso Albacete and David Menkes   344
sol del membrillo, El / The Dream of Light 1992, Victor Erice   302
sol sale todos los días, El / The Sun Rises Every Day* 1955, Antonio del Amo   144
Sol y sombre / Sun and Shadow* 1924, Musidora [Jeanne Roques]   30
Solas / Alone 1999, Benito Zambrano   331
Soldadito español / Little Spanish Soldier* 1988, Antonio Giménez Rico   268
Soldados / Soldiers* 1978, Alfonso Ungría   244
Soldados de plomo / Lead Soldiers* 1983, José Sacristán   274
Soldados de Salamina / Soldiers of Salamina 2003, David Trueba   160, 329
Sólo para hombres / For Men Only* 1960, Fernando Fernán Gómez   177–8
Sólo se muere dos veces / You Only Die Twice* 1997, Esteban Ibarretxe   342
Solomon and Sheba 1959 USA, King Vidor   172
Solos en la madrugada / Alone in the Dark 1978, José Luis Garci   229
Solos los dos / Both Alone* 1968, Luis Lucia   161
Soltera y madre en la vida / Unmarried and Mother in Life 1969, Javier Aguirre   168,
   211 n. 21
Soltero y padre en la vida / Father and Unmarried 1972, Javier Aguirre   211
Som i serem / We Are and Will Be* 1981, Jordi Feliu   246

sombra del Zorro, La / The Shadow of Zorro / L'ombra di Zorro 1962, Joaquín Romero Marchent   173
sombra en la ventana, Una / A Shadow at the Window* 1944, Ignacio F. Iquino   95
Sombras en una batalla / Shadows in a Conflict 1993, Mario Camus   292
Sonámbulos / Somnambulists 1978, Manuel Gutiérrez Aragón   243
Sonatas 1959, Juan Antonio Bardem   138–9, 151, 313
Soñar despierto / The Daydream 1911, Segundo de Chomón   10
sonido de la muerte, El / The Prehistoric Sound 1964, José Antonio Nieves Conde   174
Sor Angélica / Sister Angelica* 1934, Francisco Gargallo   58
Sor Citroen / Sister Citroen* 1967, Pedro Lazaga   166
Sor Intrépida / The Song of Sister Maria 1952, Rafael Gil   121
Sor Ye-Ye / Sister Yeah-Yeah* 1968, Ramón Fernández   159
Souvenir 1994, Rosa Vergés   310
Spanish Earth 1937 USA, Joris Ivens   74
Spellbound 1945 USA, Alfred Hitchcock   42 n. 33
Star Wars 1977 USA, George Lucas   323
Stress es tres tres / Stress is Three 1968, Carlos Saura   183
Striptease a la inglesa / English Strip-tease* 1975, Jesús Luis Madrid   209
Su noche de bodas / Her Wedding Night 1931, Florián Rey   52
subdesarrollados, Los / The Underdeveloped* 1968, Fernando Merino   165–6
Subida al cielo / Mexican Bus Ride 1952 Mexico, Luis Buñuel   29
Suburban Melody / Melodía de arrabal 1933, Louis Gasnier with Florián Rey 52
sucesos de Barcelona, Los / The Barcelona Incidents* 1901, Josep Gaspar i Serra   5
Suéltate el pelo / Let your Hair down* 1988, Manuel Summers   270
sueño de Andalucía, El / Dream of Andalusia* 1951, Luis Lucia   108, 126
sueño de la maestra, El / The Teacher's Dream* 2002, Luis G[arcía] Berlanga   134 n. 22, 341 n. 12
sueño de Tánger, El / The Dream of Tangiers 1987/1991, Ricardo Franco   267
sueño de una noche de San Juan, El / Midsummer Dream 2005, Ángel de la Cruz and Manolo Gómez   347
sueño del mono loco, El / Twisted Obsessions / The Mad Monkey 1989, Fernando Trueba   266–7, 320
¿Sueño o realidad? / Dream or Reality?* 1919, Baltasar Abadal   22
sueños de Tay-Pi, Los / The Dreams of Tay-Pi 1951, Arturo Moreno   97
Sufre Mamón / Let the Flesh Suffer! 1987, Manuel Summers   270
Suite Granadina / Granada Suite* 1940, Juan de Orduña   86
sur, El / The South 1983, Víctor Erice   258, 309, 319
Surcos / Furrows 1951, José Antonio Nieves Conde   90 n. 21, 117–18, 130–1, 133, 155, 272, 320
Sus años dorados / Their Golden Years 1980, Emilio Martínez-Lázaro   235
Susana tiene un secreto / Susana has a Secret 1933, Benito Perojo   56
Susanna 1996, Antonio Chavarrías   289
Suspenso en comunismo / A Fail in Communism* 1956, Eduardo Manzanos   123
Suspiros de España / Spanish Sighs* 1938, Benito Perojo   81, 294 n. 13
Suspiros de España (y Portugal) / Sighs from/for Spain (and Portugal)* 1995, José Luis García Sánchez   294
Tacones lejanos / High Heels 1991, Pedro Almodóvar   285
Tal vez mañana / Perhaps Tomorrow* 1957, Clauco Pellegrini   149
Tamaño natural / Love Doll / Grandeur Nature 1974/1977, Luis G[arcía] Berlanga   180, 214, 219, 226, 341
tambor del Bruch, El / The Bruch Drum* 1948, Ignacio F. Iquino   100

Tango, no me dejes nunca / Tango 1998, Carlos Saura   251, 325, 349

Tarantos, Los/ The Tarantos* 1962, Francisco Rovira Beleta   160

Tarde de toros / Bullfighting Afternoon* 1956, Ladislao Vajda   142–3, 153

Tartüff 1925 Germany, F. W. Murnau   41

Tasio 1984, Montxo Armendáriz   278, 320

Tata mía / Dear Nanny 1986, José Luis Borau   263–4

Tatuaje / Tattoo 1976, José Juan Bigas Luna   228–9

Taxi 1996, Carlos Saura   289, 325, 333

Te doy mis ojos / Take My Eyes 2003, Icíar Bollaín   331

techo de cristal, El / Glass Ceiling 1971, Eloy de la Iglesia   220

techo del mundo, El / The Roof of the World* 1995, Felipe Vega   289

Temptress, The 1926 USA, Fred Niblo   17

Tengo diecisiete años / I am Seventeen* 1964 Forqué, José María   162

Tengo una casa / I Have a Home* 1996, Mónica Laguna   309–10

teranyina, La / La telaraña / The Spider's Web* 1990, Antoni Verdaguer   301

Teresa de Jesús / Saint Theresa 1961, Juan de Orduña   122

Teresa de Jesús (TV) / *Saint Theresa** 1984, Josefina Molina   260

Teresa, el cuerpo de Cristo / Theresa: The Body of Christ 2007, Ray Loriga   334

Terra Baixa / The Lowlands* 1907, Fructuós Gelabert   6

terrible lección, La / The Terrible Experience* 1927, Fernando Delgado   35, 36 n. 20

Territorio Comanche / Comanche Territory 1997, Gerardo Herrero   302

Terroristas / Terrorists* 1987, Antonio Gonzalo   268

Tesis / Thesis 1996, Alejandro Amenábar   308, 321

tesoro, El / The Treasure* 1990, Antonio Mercero   265

testamento de Diego Rocafort, El / The Testament of Diego Rocafort* 1917, Albert Marro   22

teta i la lluna, La / The Tit and the Moon 1994, José Juan Bigas Luna   275 n. 26, 297–8

Thais 1918, Elena Jordi   30 n. 5

tía Tula, La / Aunt Tula* 1964, Miguel Picazo   138, 186, 230 n. 8, 320

Tic Tac / Tick Tock* 1997, Rosa Vergés   347

Tiempo de amor / Time for Loving* 1964, Julio Diamante   188–9

Tiempo de silencio / Time of Silence 1986, Vicente Aranda   196, 258, 264

Tiempos de constitución / Times of the Constitution 1979, Rafael Gordon   240

Tierno verano de lujurias y azoteas / Tender Summer of Lust on the Rooftops 1993, Jaime Chávarri   293

Tierra / Earth 1996, Julio Medem   311, 324

Tierra brutal / The Savage Guns 1962, Michael Carreras   173

Tierra de los toros / Land of Bulls* 1924, Musidora [Jeanne Roques]   30

Tierra de todos / A Land for All* 1961, Antonio Isasi-Isasmendi   124

Tierra sin pan, Las Hurdes / Land Without Bread 1933, Luis Buñuel   42, 52–3, 326

Tierra y libertad / Land and Freedom 1995, Ken Loach   286

Tiger Love 1924 USA, George Melford   62

tigre de Chamberí, El / KO Miguel 1957, Pedro L Ramírez   146

Tigres de papel / Paper Tigers* 1977, Fernando Colomo   233

timbaler del Bruc, El / La leyenda del Bruch / The Bruch Drum* 1981, Jordi Grau   100

Tinta roja / Red Ink 2000, Francisco Lombardi   350

Tío Vivo c1950 / Merry-go-round circa 1950* 2004, José Luis Garci   330

Tirano Banderas / Banderas, the Tyrant 1994, José Luis García Sánchez   301, 313

Tirante el Blanco / The Knight Tirante el Blanco* 2006, Vicente Aranda   330

Tirarse al monte / Gone to the Mountain* 1974, Alfonso Ungría   220

To er mundo é demasiao / Everybody's Too Much* 1985, Manuel Summers   242

To er mundo é güeno / Everybody's Good* 1982, Manuel Summers   242

To er mundo é... mejó / Everybody's... Better* 1982, Manuel Summers   242

Tocando fondo / Hitting Rock Bottom* 1993, José Luis Cuerda   295

Tocata y fuga de Lolita / Lolita's Toccata and Fugue* 1974, Antonio Drove   200 n. 2, 218

Todas hieren / They All Wound* 1998, Pablo Llorca   337

Todo es mentira / Life, a Bitch 1994, Álvaro Fernández Armero   305

Todo es posible en Granada / All is Possible in Granada 1954, José Luis Sáenz de Heredia   129

—— 1982, Rafael Romero Marchent   129, 162, 250

Todo está oscuro / All is Dark* 1997, Ana Díez   277, 313

Todo por la pasta / All for the Dough* 1991, Enrique Urbizu   278

Todo sobre mi madre / All About My Mother 1999, Pedro Almodóvar   xiv, 285 n. 3, 324

Todos a la cárcel / Everyone off to Jail 1993, Luis G[arcía] Berlanga   294

Todos al suelo! / On the Floor!* 1982, Mariano Ozores   240

Todos los hombres sois iguales / All Men Are the Same 1994, Manuel Gómez Pereira   304

Todos somos necesarios / We are All Needed 1956, José Antonio Nieves Conde   147

toma de Bilbao, La / The Capture of Bilbao* 1937, Miguel Pereyra   78

Tomándote / Tea for Two 2000, Isabel Gardela   344–5

Tomb of the Werewolf 2003 USA, Fred Olen Ray   175, 208, 338

Tómbola / Lottery* 1962, Luis Lucia   161

tonta del bote, La / The Complete Idiot* 1939, Gonzalo Delgrás   84, 168

—— 1970, Juan de Orduña   84, 168

tonto de la huerta, El / The Orchard Idiot* 1912, Josep Maria Codina   13

Toque de queda / Curfew* 1978, Iñaki Núñez   241

Torapia / Therabull* 2004, Karra Elejalde   342

Torbellino / Whirlwind 1941, Luis Marquina   107

Tormento 1974, Pedro Olea   219

toro fenómeno, El / The Phenomenal Bull* 1917, Fernando Marco   24

torre de los siete jorobados, La / The Tower of the Seven Hunchbacks 1944, Edgar Neville   110–1

Torremolinos 73 / Torremolinos 73 2003, Pablo Berger   209 n. 17, 348

Torrent, The 1926 USA, Monta Bell   17

Torrente 3: El protector / The Bodyguard* 2005, Santiago Segura   342

Torrente, el brazo tonto de la ley / Torrente, the Stupid Arm of the Law 1998, Santiago Segura   167 n. 14, 342–3

Tortilla Soup 2001, María Ripoll   345

Tot verí / Puro veneno / Pure Poison* 1996, Xavier Ribera Perpinyá   311

Tour through Spain and Portugal 1896 USA, Robert W. Paul   1 n. 1

traje, El / The Suit 2002, Alberto Rodríguez   333

traje blanco, Un / A Communion Suit* 1956, Rafael Gil   121

traje de luces, El / The Bullfighter's Suit* 1947, Edgar Neville   106–7

Tramontana / The Strong Wind* 1991, Carlos Pérez Ferré   302

tramposos, Los / The Tricksters* 1959, Pedro Lazaga   146, 164, 202

Tranvía a la Malvarrosa / Tramway to Malvarrosa 1997, José Luis García Sánchez   293

Tras el cristal / In a Glass Cage 1987, Agustí Villaronga   276, 320

trastienda, La / Back of the Store 1976, Jordi Grau   200 n. 2, 211, 224, 226

traviesa molinera, La / The Miller's Mischievous Wife* / *It Happened in Spain* 1934, Harry d'Abbadie d'Arrast-Soriano   65, 125 *trece- trece, El / Thirteen-Thirteen** 1943, Luis Lucia   108

tren de la memoria, El / The Memory Train* 2005, Marta Arribas and Ana Pérez   328

Tren de sombras / A Train of Shadows* 1998, José Luis Guerín   302

Tres de la Cruz Roja / Threesome from the Red Cross* 1961, Fernando Palacios   146

Tres días de libertad / Three Days on Parole* 1996, José Antonio de la Loma   289

Tres eran tres / Three Were Three 1955, Eduardo García Maroto   129

Tres palabras / Three Words* 1993, Antonio Giménez Rico   299

Tres por cuatro / Three Times Four* 1981, Manuel Iborra   273

Tres suecas para tres Rodríguez / Three Swedish Girls for three Rodríguez* 1975, Pedro Lazaga   167 n. 14

trinca del aire, La / The Threesome of the Air* 1951, Ramón Torrado   108

Tríptico elemental de España / Elemental Triptych of Spain* 1960, José Val del Omar   73, 151, 326

Tristana 1970, Luis Buñuel   42, 84 n. 11, 172, 180–1, 196, 216, 320

Trou dans le mur, Un 1930 France, René Barbéris   52

truchas, Las / Trout 1978, José Luis García Sánchez   238, 320

Truhanes / Truants* 1983, Miguel Hermoso   273

Tú estás loco Briones / You are mad Briones 1980, Javier Maqua   234

Tu nombre envenena mis sueños / Your Name Poisons My Dreams 1996, Pilar Miró   286

Tu novia está loca / Your Girlfriend is Crazy 1988, Enrique Urbizu   278

túnel, El / The Tunnel 1987, Antonio Drove   262 n. 10

turismo es un gran invento, El / Tourism is a Great Invention* 1968, Pedro Lazaga   164

Tuset Street 1968, Luis Marquina   190–1

Two Much 1995, Fernando Trueba   296

última falla, La / The Last Carnival* 1940, Benito Perojo   82

última frontera, L' / His Last Frontier* 1992, Manuel Cussó-Ferrer   302–3

últimas horas, Las / The Last Hours* 1965, Santos Alcocer   170

Últimas tardes con Teresa / Last Evenings with Teresa* 1984, Gonzalo Herralde   275–6

último caballo, El / The Last Horse 1950, Edgar Neville   111–12, 118 n. 3

último cuplé, El / Last Torch Song 1957, Juan de Orduña   141–2, 147, 153, 299

Último día / Last Day* 1952, Antonio Román   130

Último encuentro / Last Meeting* 1967, Antxon Eceiza   188

último húsar, El / The Last Hussar* 1940, Luis Marquina   100

último sábado, El / The Last Saturday* 1965, Pere Balañá   169

último viaje, El / The Last Trip 1974, José Antonio de la Loma   106

último viaje de Robert Rylands, El / Robert Rylands' Last Journey 1996, Gracia Quere-jeta   309

últimos de Filipinas, Los / Last Stand in the Philippines* 1945, Antonio Román   92, 96, 114

Umbracle / Trellis* 1970, Pere Portabella   194

Un franco, 14 pesetas / Crossing Borders 2006, Carlos Iglesias   217 n. 30, 329

Un, dos, tres, al escondite inglés / What's the Time Mr Wolf?* 1969, Iván Zulueta   212, 222

Una vez al año, ser hippy no hace daño / Once a Year, Being a Hippy Is Not Harmful* 1969, Javier Aguirre   168

Urtain, el rey de la selva / Urtain, King of the Mountains 1970, Manuel Summers   185

Urte ilunak / Los años oscuros / The Dark Years 1993, Arantxa Lazkano   311–12

Urxa 1989, Carlos López Piñeiro and Alfredo García Pinal   279

Usted puede ser un asesino / You Could Be a Murderer* 1961, José María Forqué   148

Utopía / Utopia* 2003, María Ripoll   337

Vacaciones para Ivette / A Holiday for Yvette* 1964, José María Forqué   166
Vacas / Cows 1992, Julio Medem   311, 320
Valentina 1982, Antonio Betancor   248–9, 258
Vámonos, Bárbara / Lets Go, Barbara* 1978, Cecilia Bartolomé   230
vampiras, Las / Vampyros Lesbos 1971, Jesús Franco   207, 222
Vampiresas 1930 / Vampiresses 1930* 1962, Jesús Franco   167–8
vampiro de la autopista, El / The Motorway Vampire* 1970, Jesús Luis Madrid   209
Vanilla Sky 2001 USA, Cameron Crowe   xv, 321
vaquilla, La / The Heifer 1985, Luis G[arcía] Berlanga   261–2
Variétés / Varieties 1970, Juan Antonio Bardem   213
vaso de whisky, Un / A Glass of Whisky 1959, Julio Coll   148
Vaya par de gemelos / What a Pair of Twins!* 1978, Pedro Lazaga   239
Vecinos / Neighbours* 1981, Alberto Bermejo   233–4
venganza, La – Los segadores / Vengeance –The Harvesters* 1957, Juan Antonio Bardem   138
venganza de Clark Harrison, La / Ruthless Colt of the Gringo 1966, Jesús Luis Madrid   209
venganza de don Mendo, La / Don Mendo's Revenge* 1961, Fernando Fernán Gómez   178
venganza del Zorro, La / Zorro the Avenger 1962, Joaquín Romero Marchent   173
vent de l'illa, El / El viento de la isla / The Island Wind* 1988, Gerardo Gormezano   277
Venta de Vargas / Vargas's Inn 1959, Enrique Salaberry   140–1
Vente a Alemania, Pepe / Come to Germany, Pepe 1971, Pedro Lazaga   204
Vente a ligar al oeste / Get a Girl out West* 1972, Pedro Lazaga   172, 204
Vera, un cuento cruel / Vera, a Cruel Story 1973, Josefina Molina   221
Verano 70 / The Summer of 1970* 1970, Pedro Lazaga   203
verano para matar, Un / Summertime Killer 1972, Antonio Isasi-Isasmendi   206
Verbena / Madrid Carnival* 1941, Edgar Neville   86
verbena de la Paloma, La / The Fair of the Dove 1921, José Buchs   30–8, 59, 163
—— 1935, Benito Perojo   31, 59, 66–8, 163
—— 1963, José Luis Sáenz de Heredia   31, 68, 163
verdad sobre el caso Savolta, La / The Truth on the Savolta Affair 1980, Antonio Drove   247, 301
verdes praderas, Las / Green Pastures 1979, José Luis Garci   229
verdugo, El / The Executioner* 1964, Luis G[arcía] Berlanga   179, 319
Vertigo 1958 USA, Alfred Hitchcock   111
Vértigo en Manhattan / Jet Lag 1981, Gerardo Herralde   232
Vestida de azul / Dressed in Blue* 1983, Antonio Giménez Rico   242
Vestida de novia / Dressed as a Bride* 1967, Ana Mariscal   160
Vêtements cascadeurs, Les / Transformaciones / Metamorphoses* 1908, Segundo de Chomón   9–10
Viaje a Jupiter / Journey to Jupiter* 1909, Segundo de Chomón   10
viaje a ninguna parte, El / Voyage to Nowhere 1986, Fernando Fernán Gómez   257, 262, 320
viaje de Carol, El / Carol's Journey 2002, Imanol Uribe   330
Viaje de novios / Honeymoon 1956, León Klimovsky   145
viajes de Gulliver, Los (TV) / Gulliver's Travels* 1983, Palomo Cruz Delgado   252
viajes escolares, Los / School Trip 1974, Jaime Chávarri   222
Vibraciones oscilatorias / Oscillatory Vibrations* 1975, Javier Aguirre   209
vicari d'Olot, El / The Vicar of Olot* 1981, Ventura Pons   275

Vicenta 1919, Musidora [Jeanne Roques]   30

Victòria! / Victory* 1983–1984, Antoni Ribas   246

vida alegre, La / This Happy Life* 1987, Fernando Colomo   270

vida alrededor, La / Life Around Us 1959, Fernando Fernán Gómez   145

Vida conyugal sana / Healthy Married Life 1973, Roberto Bodegas   217

vida de Cristóbal Colón, La / The Life of Christopher Columbus* 1916, Charles
    Drossner   23–4

Vida de familia / Family Life* 1965, Josep Lluis Font   191

vida de Joselito y su muerte, La / The Life and Death of Joselito* 1920, Anonymous
    30

vida de nadie, La / Nobody's Life 2002, Eduard Cortés   339

vida empieza a medianoche, La / Life Begins at Midnight* 1944, Juan de Orduña   94

Vida en sombras / A Life in Shadow* 1948/1953, Lorenzo Llobet Gràcia   3, 109 n. 47,
    112–14, 118 n. 3, 252, 320

vida en un hilo, La / Her Life on a Thread* 1945, Edgar Neville   111

vida mancha, La / Life Marks 2003, Enrique Urbizu   337

vida nueva de Pedrito de Andía, La / Pedrito de Andia's New Life* 1965, Rafael Gil
    160

Vida–Perra / A Dog's Life* 1982, Javier Aguirre   232

vida perra de Juanita Narboni, La / Juanita Narboni's Dirty Rotten Life* 2005, Farida
    Ben Lyziad   58 n. 14, 232 n. 11

vida por delante, La / Life Ahead 1958 Fernando Fernán Gómez   145, 177, 320

vida privada de Fulano de tal, La / The Private life of A N Other* 1961, Josep Maria
    Forn   145

vida secreta de las palabras, La / The Secret Life of Words 2005, Isabel Coixet   323–4

Vidas cruzadas / Lives Entwined* 1942, Luis Marquina   94

Vidas rotas / Broken Lives 1935, Eusebio Fernández Ardavín   57, 62–3

vieja memoria, La / The Old Memory 1977/1978, Jaime Camino   240–1

Viejo Smoking / Old Tuxedo* 1942, Eduardo Morera   86

vigilante, El / Schoolkiller 2001, Carlos Gil   338

Vino y otras bebidas / Wine and other Beverages* 1944, Arturo Ruiz Castillo   86

Violetas Imperiales / Imperial Violets* 1952 France, Richard Pottier   108

violetera, La / The Flower Girl* 1958, Luis Amadori   141, 153

Violettes impériales 1924 and 1932 France, Henri Roussel   141

virgo de Visanteta, El / Visanteta's Virgin 1978, Vicente Escrivá   239

Viridiana 1961 (Spain)-Mexico, Luis Buñuel   xvii, 42, 90 n. 21, 134 n. 21, 151–2, 180,
    192 n. 43, 194, 216, 226, 319

Visanteta, esta-te queta / Visanteta, Be Still* 1979, Vicente Escrivá   239

Visionarios / Visionaries 2001, Manuel Gutiérrez Aragón   268

*Visita de Doña María Cristina y don Alfonso XIII a Barcelona / Doña María Cristina
    and Don Alfonso's visit to Barcelona** 1898, Fructuós Gelabert   4

Visita de la escuadra inglesa a Barcelona / Visit of the British Fleet to Barcelona*
    1901, Fructuós Gelabert   4

visita del vicio, La / The Coming of Sin 1978, José Ramón Larraz   228

viuda andaluza, La / The Andalusian Widow* 1977, Francesc Betriu   250

viudita naviera, La / The Ship Company Widow* 1961, Luis Marquina   126

Viure de mentides / Mintiendo a la vida / Lying to Life 2005, Jorge Algora   331

Viva la Pepa / Hurray for Pepa* 1981, Carlos Balagué   265

¡Vivan los hombres libres! / Let Free Men Live!* 1939, Edgar Neville   78

Vivan los novios / Long Live the Bride and Groom 1970, Luis G[arcía] Berlanga   179–
    80, 214

Vivancos 3 / Dirty Vivancos III 2002, Albert Saguer   343
Vivir en Sevilla / Living in Seville* 1978, Gonzalo García Pelayo   242
Voie lactée, La / The Milky Way 1969 France, Luis Buñuel   42
Volavérunt 1999, José Juan Bigas Luna   298
Voluntad / The Will* 1937, Joaquín Martínez Arboleya   78
Volver / To Return 2006, Pedro Almodóvar   xv n. 3, 285 n. 3, 325, 345, 351
Volver a empezar / Begin the Beguine 1982, José Luis Garci   xiv, 243, 256
Volveré a nacer / I Will Be Born Again* 1973, Javier Aguirre   163
Vota a Gundisalvo / Vote for Gundisalvo 1978, Pedro Lazaga   239
Vuelo 971 / Flight 971* 1953, Rafael Salvia   122
vuelo de la paloma, El / The Flight of the Dove 1989, José Luis García Sánchez   268
vuelta al mundo de Willy Fog, La (TV) */ Around the World with Willy Fog* 1981, Luis
    Ballester Bustos and Fumio Kurokawa   252
vuelta de El Coyote, La / The Return of El Coyote 1998, Mario Camus   173 n. 22
Way for a Sailor 1930 USA, Sam Wood   51
Werther 1986, Pilar Miró   258
West Side Story 1961 USA, Jerome Robbins and Robert Wise   160
Whirlpool 1970, José Ramón Larraz   208
Whisky Galore 1949 UK, Alexander Mackendrick   135 n. 25
Whisky y Vodka / Whisky and Vodka* 1965, Fernando Palacios   162
Worlds of Gulliver, The 1960 UK-USA, Jack Sher   174 n. 24
X Equis / X* 2002, Luis Marías   336
X Files / Expediente X (TV) 1993–2002 USA, Chris Carter   339
Y al tercer año, resucitó / And in the Third Year, He Rose Again* 1980, Rafael Gil   239
Y eligió el infierno / And She Chose Hell* 1957, César Fernández Ardavín   123
Ya soy mujer! / I'm a Woman Already 1975, Manuel Summers   210
Ya tenemos coche / Now We Have a Car* 1958, Julio Salvador   146
Yellow Submarine 1968 UK-USA, George Dunning   176
Yerma / 1988, Pilar Távora   230
Yo la vi primero / I Saw Her First 1974, Fernando Fernán Gómez   213
Yo me bajo a la próxima ¿y usted? / I Get Off at the Next Stop, What About You? 1992,
    José Sacristán   274
Yo no soy la Mata-Hari / I'm not Mata Hari 1949, Benito Perojo   114
Yo quiero que me lleven a Hollywood / I Want to be Taken to Hollywood* 1931, Edgar
    Neville   52, 62
Yo soy ésa / I'm the One 1990, Luis Sanz   299
Yo, el Vaquilla / I, The Vaquilla* 1985, José Antonio de la Loma   237
You're the One / 2000, José Luis Garci   330
Young One, The 1960 Mexico-USA, Luis Buñuel   151
Young Sánchez 1964, Mario Camus   184
Yoyes 1999, Helena Taberna   292 n. 12, 340
Zalacaín el aventurero / Zalacaín, the Adventurer* 1929, Francisco Camacho   34–5, 46
    n. 43
—— 1954 Orduña, Juan de   35, 149
Zampo y yo / Zampo and Me 1965, Luis Lucia   162, 217
Zancos, Los / The Stilts 1984, Carlos Saura   291

BIBLIOGRAPHY

Very few texts not in English have been included in this selection, but references to research in Spanish, and other languages, can be found in the bibliographies of all the texts included. In Spain each individual will tend to have one name, followed by a patronymic and matronymic, which is the format followed here, although there are many exceptions among artists.

Acevedo Muñoz, Ernesto R. 2007. *Pedro Almodóvar*. London: BFI, World Directors

Alderson, David, and Linda Anderson. 2000. *Territories of Desire in Queer Culture*: *Refiguring Contemporary Boundaries*. Manchester: Manchester University Press

Allinson, Mark. 1997. 'Not matadors, not natural born killers: Violence in three films by young Spanish directors'. *Bulletin of Hispanic Studies* (Liverpool) 74/4, pp. 315–30

——. 1999. 'Pilar Miró's last two films: History, adaptation and genre'. *Spanish Cinema Calling the Shots*. Ed. Rob Rix and Roberto Rodríguez Saona. Leeds: Trinity and All Saints College, pp. 33–45

——. 2001. *A Spanish Labyrinth. The Films of Pedro Almodóvar*. London and New York: IB Tauris

——. 2003. 'Is the auteur dead? The case of Juanma Bajo Ulloa'. *International Journal of Iberian Studies* 15/3, pp. 143–51

——. 2003 rpt. 'Alaska: Star of stage and screen and optimistic punk'. *Constructing Identity in Twentieth Century Spain: Theoretical Debates and Cultural Practice*. Ed. Jo Labanyi. Oxford: Oxford University Press, pp. 222–36

——. 2005. '*Calle mayor / Main Street*'; '*Todo sobre mi madre / All About My Mother*'. *24 Frames: The Cinema of Spain and Portugal*. Ed Alberto Mira. London and New York: Wallflower Press, pp. 79–87, 229–37

Amago, Samuel. 2007. 'Todo sobre Barcelona: Refiguring Spanish identities in recent European cinema'. *Hispanic Research Journal* 8/1, pp. 11–25

Anon. 1981. '*Bienvenido, mr Marshall*: la secuencia no rodada'. *Contracampo* 24, pp. 23–5

Aranda, Francisco. 1975. *Luis Buñuel: A Critical Biography*, translated by David Robinson. London: Secker & Warburg. Original, *Luis Buñuel: biográfica crítica* (Barcelona: Lumen, 1969)

Archibald, David. 2004. 'Reframing the past: Representations of the Spanish Civil War in popular Spanish cinema'. *Spanish Popular Cinema*. Ed. Antonio

Lázaro Reboll and Andrew Willis. Manchester: Manchester University Press, pp. 76–91

Arocena, Carmen. 1996. *Victor Erice*. Madrid: Cátedra, Signo e imagen 26

Arroyo, José. 1992. '*La ley del deseo*: A gay seduction'. *Popular European Cinema*. Ed. Richard Dyer and Ginette Vincendeau. London and New York: Routledge, pp. 31–46

Aub, Max. 1985. *Conversaciones con Buñuel*. Ed. Federico Álvarez. Madrid: Aguilar

Ávila, Alejandro. 1997. *La historia del doblaje cinematográfico*. Barcelona: CIMS, Comunicación Global

Ballesteros, Cecilia. 1995. 'Cintas de Oro'. *Revista de El Mundo* 17 December, pp. 42–5

Ballesteros, Isolina. 2001. *Cine (ins)urgente: Textos fílmicos y contextos culturales de la España posfranquista*. Madrid: Fundamentos, Colección Arte

——. 2005. 'Embracing the other: The feminization of Spanish "immigration cinema"'. *Studies in Hispanic Cinemas* 2/1, pp. 5–14

Baxter, John. 1994. *Buñuel*. London: Fourth Estate

Beckwith, Stacy N. 1998. 'Seeing beyond the delicate: Luis García-Berlanga's *Novio a la vista*'. *Modes of Representation in Spanish Cinema*. Ed. Jenaro Talens and Santos Zunzunegui. Minneapolis and London: University of Minneapolis Press, pp. 113–27

Benavent, Francisco María. 2000. *Cine español de los noventa. Diccionario de películas, directores y temático*. Bilbao: Mensajero

Bentley, Bernard P.E. 1995a. 'The film as text'. *Forum for Modern Language Studies* 31/1, pp. 1–7

——. 1995b. 'The credit sequence of *La mitad del cielo* (1986)'. *Forum for Modern Language Studies* 31/3, pp. 259–73

——. 1999. 'The eroteticism of *Nadie hablará de nosotras cuando hayamos muerto* (Díaz Yanes, 1995)'. *Spanish Cinema. The Auteurist Tradition*. Ed. Peter W. Evans. Oxford: University Press, pp. 325–46

——. 2004. '*Fuenteovejuna* en 1947: la hipoteca del presente'. *Memoria de la palabra. Actas del VI Congreso de la Asociación Internacional del Siglo de Oro*, vol. I. Ed. María Luisa Lobato and Francisco Domínguez Matito. Madrid: Iberoamericana and Vervuert, pp. 331–6

Besas, Peter. 1985. *Behind the Spanish Lens: Spanish Cinema under Fascism and Democracy*. Denver, CO: Arden Press

——. 1997. 'The financial structure of Spanish Cinema'. *Refiguring Spain. Cinema/Media/Representation*. Ed. Marsha Kinder. Durham, NC and London: Duke University Press, pp. 241–59

Bonaddio, Federico. 2004. 'Dressing as foreigners: Historical and musical dramas of the early Franco period'. *Spanish Popular Cinema*. Ed. Antonio Lázaro Reboll and Andrew Willis. Manchester: Manchester University Press, pp 24–39

Bonet Mojica, Lluís. 1996a. 'Pantallas de la posguerra, imagen de una frustración'. *Historia y Vida* Extra 83, pp. 44–55

——. 1996b. 'El éxodo republicano'. *Historia y Vida* Extra 83, pp. 56–7

Borau, José Luis. 1983. 'Without weapons'. *Quarterly Review of Film Studies* 8/2, pp. 85–90

Bordwell, David, and Kristin Thompson. 1990. *Film Art. An Introduction.* New York: McGraw-Hill, 3rd rev. edn with subsequent reprints and revised editions

Bosch, Aurora, and María Fernanda del Rincón. 1998. 'Franco and Hollywood, 1939–56'. *New Left Review* 232, pp. 112–27

Buckley, Christina A. 2000. 'Commercial is no longer a dirty word for Spanish cinema'. *Cine-Lit 2000: Essays on Hispanic Film and Fiction.* Ed. George Cabello-Castellet, Jaume Martí-Olivella, and Guy H. Wood. Portland & Corvallis, OR: Portland and Oregon State Universities and Reed College, pp. 201–6

——. 2002. 'Alejandro Amenábar's *Tesis*: Art, commerce and renewal in Spanish Cinema'. *Post Script: Essays in Film and the Humanities* 21/2, pp. 1–15

Buñuel, Luis, and Jean-Claude Carrière. 1987. *My Last Breath*, translated by Abigail Israel. Glasgow: Collins, Fontana Flamingo, 3rd impression. Original *Mon Dernier Soupir* (Paris: Laffont, 1982)

Buse, Peter, Nuria Triana Toribio, and Andrew Willis. 2004. 'Esto no es un juego, es *Acción mutante* (1997): The provocations of Álex de la Iglesia'. *Journal of Iberian and Latin American Studies* 10/1, pp. 9–22

——. 2007. *Álex de la Iglesia.* Manchester: Manchester University Press, Spanish and Latin American Film Makers

Cabello-Castellet, George, Jaume Martí-Olivella, and Guy H. Wood (eds). 1992. *Cine-Lit: Essays on Peninsular Film and Fiction.* Portland & Corvallis, OR: Portland and Oregon State Universities and Reed College

Cañeque, Carlos, and Maite Grau. 1993. *¡Bienvenido Mr Berlanga!* Barcelona: Destino, Destino libro 341

Caparrós Lera, José María. 1981. *Arte y política en el cine de la República (1931–1939).* Barcelona: Ediciones 7½

——. 1983. *El cine español bajo el régimen de Franco (1936–1975).* Barcelona: EU, Universitat de Barcelona

——. 1986. 'The Spanish cinema industry in the Spanish Civil War, 1936–1939'. *Film and History* 16/2, pp. 35–46

——. 1992. *El cine español de la democracia. De la muerte de Franco al 'cambio' socialista (1975–1989).* Barcelona: Anthropos

——. 1999. *El cine de nuestros días (1994–1998).* Madrid: Rialp

——. 2006. *La pantalla popular. El cine español durante el gobierno de la derecha (1996–2003).* Madrid: Akal

Caparrós Lera, José María, and Rafael de España. 1987. *The Spanish Cinema. An Historical Approach*, translated by Carl J. Mora. Barcelona: Film Historia

Carranque de Ríos, Andrés. 1997. *Cinematógrafo.* Madrid: Viamonte. First published 1936

Carrera, Elena. 2005. '*Los santos inocentes / The Holy Innocents*'. *24 Frames: The Cinema of Spain and Portugal.* Ed. Alberto Mira. London and New York: Wallflower Press, pp. 179–87

Carroll, Noël. 1988. *Mystifying Movies: Fads and Fallacies in Contemporary Film Theory*. New York: Columbia University Press

Cerón Gómez, Juan Francisco. 1998. *El cine de Juan Antonio Bardem*. Universidad de Murcia

Christie, Ian. 1994. *The Last Machine: Early Cinema and the Birth of the Modern World*. London: British Film Institute and British Broadcasting Corporation Educational Developments

Clemens, Valdine. 1999. *The Return of the Repressed: Gothic Horror from* The Castle of Otranto *to* Alien. New York: SUNY Press

Coira Nieto, José Antonio. 1999. *Antonio Román. Director de cine*. Santiago de Compostela: Xunta de Galicia

Colmena, Enrique. 1996. *Vicente Aranda*. Madrid: Cátedra, Signo e imagen 27

Company-Ramón, Juan Miguel. 1998. 'The Brigadier's Crusade: Florián Rey's *Carmen la de Triana*'. *Modes of Representation in Spanish Cinema*. Ed. Jenaro Talens and Santos Zunzunegui. Minneapolis and London: University of Minneapolis Press, pp. 73–80

Corrigan, Timothy. 1997. *A Short Guide to Writing About Film*. London and New York; Longman, with subsequent reprints and revised editions

Crumbaugh, Justin. 2001. 'An aesthetics of industrial ruins in Bilbao: Daniel Calparsoro's *Leap into the Void* (*Salto al vacío*) and Frank Ghery's Guggenheim Museum Bilbao'. *International Journal of Iberian Studies* 14/1, pp. 40–57

——. 2002. 'Spain is different: Touring late-Francoist cinema with Manolo Escobar'. *Hispanic Research Journal* 3/3, pp. 261–76

Cueto, Roberto (ed.). 1998. *Los desarraigados en el cine español*. Gijón: Festival Internacional de Gijón

Dapena, Gerard. 2002. '*Solas*: Andalusian mothers in a global context'. *Post Script: Essays in Film and the Humanities* 21/2, pp. 26–37

——. 2004. '*La corona negra*: The international face of Francoist cinema'. *Studies in Hispanic Cinemas* 1/2, pp. 119–26

Davies, Alan. 2003. 'Male sexuality and Basque separatism in two films by Imanol Uribe'. *Hispanic Research Journal* 4/2, pp. 121–32

Davies, Ann. 2004. 'The Spanish *femme fatale* and the cinematic negotiation of Spanishness'. *Studies in Hispanic Cinemas* 1/1, pp. 5–16

De Stefano, George. 1986. 'Post-Franco frankness'. *Film Comments* 22/3, pp. 58–60

Deleyto, Celestino. 1994. 'Rewriting Spain: Metafiction and intertextuality in Saura's *Carmen*'. *Journal of Hispanic Research* 2/2, pp. 238–47

——.1995. 'Postmodernism and parody in Almodóvar's *Mujeres al borde de un ataque de nervios*'. *Forum for Modern Language Studies* 31/1, pp. 1–7

——. 1999a. 'Women and other monsters: Frankenstein and the role of the mother in *El espíritu de la colmena*'. *Bulletin of Hispanic Studies* (Glasgow) 76/1, pp. 39–51

——. 1999b. 'Motherland: Space, femininity, and Spanishness in *Jamón Jamón* (Bigas Luna, 1992)'. *Spanish Cinema. The Auteurist Tradition*. Ed. Peter W. Evans. Oxford: University Press, pp. 270–86

Delgado, Maria. 1999. 'Saura's *Los golfos* (1959; released 1962): Heralding a New Cinema 1960s'. *Spanish Cinema. The Auteurist Tradition*. Ed. Peter W. Evans. Oxford: University Press, pp. 38–54

Deosthale, Duleep C. 1992. 'Sex, society and oppression in post-Franco cinema: The homosexual statement in Iglesia's *El diputado*'. *Cine-Lit: Essays on Peninsular Film and Fiction*. Ed. George Cabello-Castellet, Jaume Martí-Olivella and Guy H. Wood. Portland & Corvallis, OR: Portland and Oregon State Universities and Reed College, pp. 10–18

Deveny, Thomas G. 1993, *Cain on Screen: Contemporary Spanish Cinema*. Lanham, MD: Scarecrow Press

——. 1995. 'The libidinous gaze: Screen adaptation of *Crónica del rey pasmado*'. *Cine-Lit II: Essays on Hispanic Film and Fiction*. Ed. George Cabello-Castellet, Jaume Martí-Olivella and Guy H. Wood. Portland & Corvallis, OR: Portland and Oregon State Universities and Reed College, pp. 96–105

——. 1999. *Contemporary Spanish Film from Fiction*. Lanham, MD: Scarecrow Press

——. 2000. 'Child's play: Juvenile meta-acting in Spanish cinema'. *Cine-Lit 2000: Essays on Hispanic Film and Fiction*. Ed. George Cabello-Castellet, Jaume Martí-Olivella and Guy H. Wood. Portland & Corvallis, OR: Portland and Oregon State Universities and Reed College, pp. 144–54

Dickinson, Robert. 1991. 'The unbearable weight of winning: Garci's trilogy of melancholy and the foreign language Oscar'. *Spectator* 11/2, pp. 6–15

Diez Puertas, Emeterio. 2003. *Historia social del cine en España*. Madrid: Fundamentos

D'Lugo, Marvin. 1991. *The Films of Carlos Saura: The Practice of Seeing*. Princeton: University Press

——. 1995. 'Almodóvar's city of desires'. *Quarterly Review of Films and Videos* 13/4, pp. 47–65

——. 1997a. *Guide to the Cinema of Spain*. Westport, CT and London: Greenwood Press

——. 1997b. '*La teta i la lluna*: The form of transnational cinema in Spain'. *Refiguring Spain. Cinema/Media/Representation*. Ed. Marsha Kinder. Durham, NC and London: Duke University Press, pp. 196–214

——. 1998. 'Vicente Aranda's *Amantes*: History as cultural style in Spanish Cinema'. *Modes of Representation in Spanish Cinema*. Ed. Jenaro Talens and Santos Zunzunegui. Minneapolis and London: University of Minneapolis Press, pp. 289–300

——. 1999. 'Re-imagining the community: Imanol Uribe's *La muerte de Mikel* (1983) and the cinema of transition'. *Spanish Cinema. The Auteurist Tradition*. Oxford: University Press, pp. 194–209

——. 2002a. 'Catalan cinema: Historical experience and cinematic practice'. *The European Cinema Reader*. Ed. Catherine Fowler. London and New York: Routledge, pp. 163–73. A full version can be found in *Quarterly Review of Film and Video* 13/4 (1991), pp. 131–46

——. 2002b. 'The geopolitical aesthetic in recent Spanish cinema'. *Post Script: Essays in Film and the Humanities* 21/2, pp. 79–90

——. 2006. *Pedro Almodóvar*. Urbana and Chicago: University of Illinois Press, Contemporary Film Directors

Doanne, Mary Ann. 1987. *The Desire to Desire: The Woman's Film of the 1940s*. Bloomington: Indiana University Press

Donapetry, María. 1998. *La otra mirada. La mujer y el cine en la cultura española*. New Orleans: University Press of the South, Iberian Studies 17

Dongan, Christine. 1984. '*Tristana*: une transcription allégorique de la deuxième République espagnole, Tristana et le discours libertaire'. *Les Cahiers de la Cinémathèque* 38/39, pp. 168–76

Drummond, Phillip. 1977. 'Textual space in *Un Chien andalou*'. *Screen* 18/3, pp. 55–119

Easthope, Antony (ed.). 1993. *Contemporary Film Theory*. London and New York: Longman, Critical Readers

Edwards, Gwynne. 1982. *The Discreet Art of Luis Buñuel. A Reading of his Films*. London and Boston: Marion Boyars

——. 1988. *Indecent Exposure (Buñuel, Saura, Erice, Almodóvar)*. London and New York: Boyars

——. 1992. 'Saura's *Bodas de sangre*: Play into film'. *Bulletin of Hispanic Studies in Honour of Geoffrey Ribbans*, pp. 275–82

——. 1997. 'The persistence of memory: Carlos Saura's *La caza* and *La prima Angélica*'. *Journal of Iberian and Latin American Studies* 3/2, pp. 191–203

——. 2001. *Almodóvar: Labyrinths of Passions*. London: Peter Owen

——. 2005. *A Companion to Luis Buñuel*. London: Támesis

Ehrlich, Linda C. (ed.). 2000. *An Open Window: The Cinema of Victor Erice*. Lanham, MD: Scarecrow Press

Eidsvik, Charles. 1981. 'Dark laughter, Buñuel's *Tristana* (1970) from the novel by Benito Pérez Galdós'. *Modern European Filmakers and the Art of Adaptation*. Ed. Andrew Horton and Joan Magretta. New York: Frederick Ungar, pp. 173–87

España, Rafael de. 1986. 'Images of the Spanish Civil War in the Spanish feature films'. *Historical Journal of Film, Radio and Television* 6/2, pp. 223–36

Estrada, Isabel. 2005. 'Political and gender transitions in José Luis Garci's *Solos en la madrugada* (1978)'. *Studies in Hispanic Cinemas* 1/3, pp. 137–50

——. 2006. 'Transitional masculinities in a labyrinth of solitude: Replacing patriarchy in Spanish Films (1977–1987)'. *Bulletin of Spanish Studies* 83/2, pp. 265–80

Evans, Jo. 1999. 'Imanol Uribe's *La muerte de Mikel*: Policing the gaze / mind the gap'. *Bulletin of Hispanic Studies* (Glasgow) 76/1, pp. 101–9

——. 2002 "*La ardilla roja*: The compulsive nostalgia of popular love songs'. *Cultura Popular: Studies in Spanish and Latin American Popular Culture*. Ed. Shelley Godsland and Anne M. White. Bern: Peter Lang, pp. 147–62

——. 2005a. 'Pudovkin and the censors: Juan Antonio Bardem's *Muerte de un ciclista*'. *Hispanic Research Journal* 8/3, pp. 253–65

——. 2005b. '*Piedras* and the fetish: "Don't look now"'. *Studies in Hispanic Cinemas* 2/2, pp. 69–82

———. 2007. '*La madre muerta* (*The Dead Mother*, 1993) and *Tierra* (*Earth*, 1995): Basque identity, or just the other?' *New Cinemas* 4/3, pp. 173–84

Evans, Peter W. 1993. 'Almodóvar's *Matador*: Genre, subjectivity and desire'. *Bulletin of Hispanic Studies* 70/3, pp. 325–35

———. 1995a. *The Films of Luis Buñuel. Subjectivity and Desire*. Oxford: Clarendon Press, Oxford Hispanic Studies

———. 1995b. 'Buñuel and *Tristana*: Who is doing what to whom?' *Carnal Knowledge. Essays on the Flesh, Sex and Sexuality in Hispanic Letters and Film (Symposium – Pittsburgh April 1991)*. Ed. Pamela Bacarisse, pp. 91–8

———. 1995c. 'Doubling up: Masculinity and the vicissitudes of instinct in *El amante bilingüe* (1993)'. *Revista Canadiense de Estudios Hispánicos* 20/1, pp. 107–16

———. 1996. *Women on the Verge of a Nervous Breakdown*. London: BFI

———. 1997. *From Golden Age to Silver Screen: The* Comedia *on Film (Papers in Spanish Theatre 5)*. London: Queen Mary and Westfield College

——— (ed.). 1999. *Spanish Cinema. The Auteurist Tradition*. Oxford: University Press

———. 1999a. 'Furtivos (Borau, 1975): My mother, my lover'. *Spanish Cinema. The Auteurist Tradition*. Ed. Peter W. Evans. Oxford: University Press, pp. 115–27

———. 1999b. 'The Dame in the Kimono: *Amantes*, Spanish *noir* and the *femme fatale*'. *Bulletin of Hispanic Studies* (Glasgow) 76/1, pp. 93–100

———. 2000. 'Cheaper by the dozen: *La gran familia*, Francoism and Spanish family comedy'. *100 years of European Cinema. Entertainment or Ideology?* Ed. Diana Holmes and Alison Smith. Manchester and New York: Manchester University Press, pp. 77–88

———. 2003 rpt. 'Victoria Abril: The sex which is not one'. *Constructing Identity in Twentieth Century Spain: Theoretical Debates and Cultural Practice*. Ed. Jo Labanyi. Oxford: Oxford University Press, pp. 128–37

———. 2004a. 'Contemporary Spanish cinema'. *European Cinema*. Ed. Elizabeth Ezra. Oxford and New York: Oxford University Press, pp. 250–64

———. 2004b. 'Marisol: The Spanish Cinderella'. *Spanish Popular Cinema*. Ed. Antonio Lázaro Reboll and Andrew Willis. Manchester: Manchester University Press, pp. 129–41

———. 2005. '*Viridiana*'. *24 Frames: The Cinema of Spain and Portugal*. Ed. Alberto Mira. London and New York: Wallflower Press, pp. 99–107

Evans, Peter W. and Robin Fiddian. 1987. 'Victor Erice's *El sur*: A narrative of star-cross'd lovers'. *Bulletin of Hispanic Studies* 64/2, pp. 127–35

Evans, Peter W. and Isabel Santaolalla (eds). 2004. *Luis Buñuel: New Readings*. London: BFI

Everett, Wendy (ed.). 2005. 2nd edn. *European Identity in Cinema*. Bristol: Intellect Books

Fanés, Félix. 1982. *CIFESA, la antorcha de los éxitos*. Valencia: Institución Alfonso El Magnánimo

———. 1989. *El cas CIFESA: vint anys de cine espanyol (1931–1951)*. Valencia: Filmoteca de la Generalitat Valenciana

Faulkner, Sally. 2004a. *Literary Adaptations in Spanish Cinema*. London: Támesis

——. 2004b. 'The question of authenticity: Camus's film adaptation of Cela's *La colmena*'. *Studies in Hispanic Cinemas* 1/1, pp. 17–25

——. 2006. *A Cinema of Contradiction. Spanish Film in the 1960s*. Edinburgh: Edinburgh University Press

Fernández Mellado, Rafael, and Fernando Alonso Barahona (eds). 1997. *Rafael Gil, director de cine*. Madrid: Centro Cultural del Conde Duque and Comunidad de Madrid

Ferrán, Ofelia, and Kathleen Glenn (eds). 2002. *Women's Narrative and Film in 20th Century Spain*. London and New York: Routledge

Fiddian, Robin W. 1988. 'Carrying Spanish films to Newcastle: José Luis Borau and *Tata mía*'. *Vida Hispánica* 37/Autumn, pp. 14–18

——. 1989. 'The roles and representation of women in two films by José Luis Borau'. *Essays on Hispanic Themes in Honour of Edward C. Riley*. Ed. Jennifer Lowe and Philip Swanson. Edinburgh: Department of Hispanic Studies, pp. 289–314

——. 1995. 'The cook, the restaurateur, his wife, her lover, etc., in *Cinco tenedores* by Fernando Fernán Gómez'. *Revista Canadiense de Estudios Hispánicos* 20/1, pp. 93–106

——. 1999a. '*La vida alegre* (Colomo, 1986)'. *Spanish Cinema. The Auteurist Tradition*. Ed. Peter W. Evans. Oxford: University Press, pp. 242–53

——. 1999b. 'The state of the art: An interview with José Luis Borau'. *Bulletin of Hispanic Studies* (Glasgow), 76/1, pp. 1–10

Fiddian, Robin W. and Peter W. Evans. 1988. *Challenges to Authority: Fiction and Film in Contemporary Spain*. London: Támesis

Fisher, Lucy. 1998. 'Modernity and Postmodernity: *High Heels* and *Imitation of Life*'. *Play it Again Sam: Retakes on Remakes*. Ed. Andrew Horton and Stuart Y. McDougal. Berkeley: University of California Press

Flesler, Daniela. 2004. 'New racism, intercultural romance, and the immigration question in contemporary Spanish cinema'. *Studies in Hispanic Cinemas* 1/2, pp. 103–17

Forbes, Jill, and Sarah Street (eds). 2000. *European Cinema. An Introduction*. Basingstocke: Palgrave

Fouz Hernández, Santiago. 1999, 'All that glitters is not gold: Reading Javier Bardem's body in Bigas Luna's *Golden Balls*'. *Spanish Cinema Calling the Shots*. Ed. Rob Rix and Roberto Rodríguez Saona. Leeds: Trinity and All Saints College, pp. 47–62

——. 2000 '¿*Generación X?* Spanish urban youth culture at the end of the century in Maña's/Armendáriz's *Historias del Kronen*'. *Romance Quaterly* 18/1, 83–98

Fouz Hernández, Santiago, and Chris Perriam. 2000. 'Beyond Almodóvar: Homosexuality in Spanish Cinema of the 1990s'. *Territories of Desire in Queer Culture: Refiguring Contemporary Boundaries*. Ed. David Alderson and Linda Anderson. Manchester: Manchester University Press, pp. 96–111

Fraser, Benjamin. 2006. 'The space in the film and the film in the space: Madrid's

Retiro Park and Carlos Saura's *Taxi*'. *Studies in Hispanic Cinemas* 3/1, pp. 15–33

Fuentes, Victor. 2004. 'The constant exile in Buñuel'. *Luis Buñuel: New Readings*. Ed. Peter W. Evans and Isabel Santaolalla. London: BFI, pp. 159–72

Gabilondo, Joseba. 2003 rpt. 'Uncanny identity: Violence, gaze, and desire in contemporary Basque cinema'. *Constructing Identity in Twentieth Century Spain: Theoretical Debates and Cultural Practice*. Ed. Jo Labanyi. Oxford: Oxford University Press, pp. 262–79

Galt, Rosalind. 2007. 'Missed encounters: Reading, *catalanitat*, the Barcelona School'. *Screen* 48/2, pp. 193–210

Gámez Fuentes, María José. 1999. 'A female quest for matrilineage and resistance in 1990's Spain: *Nadie hablará de nosotras cuando hayamos muerto*'. *Spanish Cinema Calling the Shots*. Ed. Rob Rix and Roberto Rodríguez Saona. Leeds: Trinity and All Saints College, pp. 15–32

——. 2000. 'Never one without the other: Empowering readings of the mother–daughter relationship in contemporary Spain'. *Mothers and Daughters: Connection, Empowerment, and Transformation*. Ed. Andrea O'Reilly and Sharon Abbey. Lanham, MD: Rowman & Littlefield, pp. 47–59

——. 2003. 'Women in Spanish Cinema: "Raiders of the Missing Mother"?' *Cineaste* 29/1, pp. 38–43

García Escudero, José María. 1954. *La historia en cien palabras del cine español y otros escritos sobre cine*. Salamanca: Publicaciones del cine-club del S.E.U. de Salamanca, cuaderno 1, p. 11

——. 1962. *Cine español*. Madrid: Rialp

García Fernández, Emilio C. 1985. *Historia ilustrada del cine español*. Madrid: Planeta

——. 2002. *El cine español entre 1896 y 1939. Historia, industria, filmografía y documentos*. Barcelona: Ariel

García Soza, Gladis, and Anne M. White. 2002. 'Spellbound: Resisting the power of popular myth in Erice's *El espíritu de la colmena*'. *Cultura Popular: Studies in Spanish and Latin American Popular Culture*. Ed. Shelley Godsland and Anne M. White. Bern: Peter Lang, pp. 163–74

Garland, David. 1991. 'A ms-take in the making? Transexualism post-Franco, post modern, post-haste?' *Quarterly Review of Film and Video* 13/4, pp. 95–102

Garlinger, Patrick Paul. 2004. 'All about Agrado, or the sincerity of camp in Almodóvar's *Todo sobre mi madre*'. *Journal of Hispanic Cultural Studies* 5/1, pp. 117–34

Gies, David T. (ed.). 1999. *The Cambridge Companion to Spanish Culture*. Cambridge: Cambridge University Press

Ginger, Andrew. 2007. 'Space, time, desire on the Atlantic in three Spanish films of the 1920s'. *Hispanic Research Journal* 8/1, pp. 69–78

Girelli, Elisabetta. 2006. 'The power of the masquerade: *Mujeres al borde de un ataque de nervios* and the construction of femininity'. *Hispanic Research Journal* 7/3, pp. 251–8

Godsland, Shelley, and Anne M. White (eds). 2002. *Cultura Popular: Studies in Spanish and Latin American Popular Culture*. Bern: Peter Lang

Gómez, Asunción. 2002. 'La representación de la mujer en el cine español de los años 40 y 50: del cine bélico al neorrealismo'. *Bulletin of Spanish Studies* 79/5, pp. 575–89

Gómez de la Serna, Ramón. 1995. *Cinelandia*. Madrid: Valdemar, Autores Españoles. First published 1923

Gómez Rufo, Antonio. 1990. *Berlanga. Contra el poder y la gloria. Escenas de una vida*. Madrid: Temas de Hoy 15

Gómez Sierra, Esther. 2004. ' "Palace of Seeds" from an experience of local cinemas in post-war Madrid to a suggested approach to film audiences'. *Spanish Popular Cinema*. Ed. Antonio Lázaro Reboll and Andrew Willis. Manchester and New York: Manchester University Press, pp. 92–112

González Ballesteros, Teodoro. 1981. *Aspectos jurídicos de la censura cinematográfica en España con especial referencia al periodo 1936–1977*. Madrid: Universidad Complutense

González Medina, José Luis. 1997. 'E. G. Maroto's *Canelita en rama* (1943): The politics of carnival, Facism and National(ist) vertebration in a postwar Spanish film'. *Journal of Iberian and Latin American Studies* 3/1, pp. 15–29

González Requena, Jesús. 1998. '*Vida en sombras*: The *recusado*'s shadow in Spanish postwar cinema'. *Modes of Representation in Spanish Cinema*. Ed. Jenaro Talens and Santos Zunzunegui. Minneapolis and London: University of Minneapolis Press, pp. 83–103

Gorostiza, Jorge. 1997. *Directores artísticos del cine español*. Madrid, Cátedra and Filmoteca Española, Serie mayor

Graham, Helen, and Jo Labanyi (eds). 1995. *Spanish Cultural Studies: An Introduction. The Struggle for Modernity*. Oxford: Oxford University Press

Gubern, Román. 1994. *Benito Perojo. Pionerismo y supervivencia*. Madrid: Filmoteca Española

——. 1995. 'The Civil War: Inquest or excorcism?' *Quarterly Review of Film and Video* 13/4, pp. 103–12

——. 1998. 'Benito Perojo's *La verbena de la Paloma*'. *Modes of Representation in Spanish Cinema*. Ed. Jenaro Talens and Santos Zunzunegui. Minneapolis and London: University of Minneapolis Press, pp. 49–57

——. 1999. *Proyector de luna. La generación del '27 y el cine*. Barcelona: Anagrama, Colección Argumentos

Gubern, Román, José Enrique Monterde, Julio Pérez Perucha, Esteve Riambau, and Casimiro Torreiro. 1995. *Historia del cine español*. Madrid: Cátedra, Signo e imagen 40

Gunn, Elizabeth. 2000. 'The verge of Almodóvar's Spain: A space for subversive humour'. *Cine-Lit 2000: Essays on Hispanic Film and Fiction*. Ed. George Cabello-Castellet, Jaume Martí-Olivella, and Guy H. Wood. Portland & Corvallis, OR: Portland and Oregon State Universities and Reed College, pp. 165–75

Gutiérez Albilla, Julián Daniel. 2004. 'Between the phobic object and the dissident subject: Abjection and vampirism in Luis Buñuel's *Viridiana*'. *Gender and Spanish Cinema.* Ed. Steven Marsh and Parvati Nair. New York and Oxford: Berg, pp. 13–31

Hammond, Paul. 1997. *L'Âge d'or.* London: British Film Institute, BFI Film Classics

——. 2004. 'Lost and found: Buñuel, *L'Âge d'or* and Surrealism'. *Luis Buñuel: New Readings.* Ed. Peter W. Evans and Isabel Santaolalla. London: BFI, pp. 13–26

Harvard, Robert G. 1983. 'Luis Buñuel: Objects and phantoms'. *Luis Buñuel: A Symposium.* Ed. Margaret A. Rees. Leeds: Trinity and All Saints, pp. 59–88

Hawkins, Joan. 2000. *Cutting Edge. Art Horror and the Horrific Avant-garde.* Minneapolis and London: University of Minnesota Press

Herbert, Daniel. 2006. '*Sky*'s the limit: Transnationality and identity in *Abre los ojos* and *Vanilla Sky*'. *Film Quarterly* 60/1, pp. 28–38

Heredero, Carlos F. 1993. *Las huellas del tiempo: Cine español 1951–61.* Valencia: Filmoteca de la Generalitat Valenciana and Filmoteca Española

——. 2003. 'New creators of the millennium: Transforming the directing scene in Spain', translated by Dennis and Joan West. *Cineaste* 29/1, pp. 32–6

Heredero, Carlos F. and Antonio Santamarina. 2002. *Semillas de futuro: Cine español 1990–2001.* Barcelona: Sociedad Estatal España Nuevo Milenio

Hernández-Les, Juan, and Manuel Hidalgo. 1981. *El último austro-húngaro: conversaciones con Berlanga.* Barcelona: Anagrama

Higginbotham, Virginia. 1988. *Spanish Film under Franco.* Austin: University of Texas Press

——. 1998. *The Spirit of the Beehive / El espíritu de la colmena.* Trowbridge: Flicks Books, Cineteck

Hill, Matt. 2003. 'Whose postmodern horror? Alejandro Amenábar's *Tesis* (1996)'. *Kinoeye* 3/5, pp. 1–9

Hjort, Mette, and Scott Mackenzie (eds). 2000. *Cinema and Nation.* London and New York: Routledge

Holder, John D. 1998. '*Pata negra*: Goya's cudgel motif in two contemporary Spanish films'. *Donaire* 10 (April), pp. 31–6

Holguin, Antonio. 1994. *Pedro Almodóvar.* Madrid: Cátedra, Signo e imagen 20

Holmes, Diana, and Alison Smith (eds). 2000. *100 years of European Cinema. Entertainment or Ideology?* Manchester and New York: Manchester University Press

Hooper, John. 1987. *The Spaniards. A Portrait of New Spain.* London: Penguin. First published Viking, 1986

——. 1995. *The New Spaniards.* London: Penguin

Hopewell, John. 1986. *Out of the Past: Spanish Cinema after Franco.* London: British Film Institute

——. 1989. *El cine español después de Franco 1973–1988.* Madrid: El Arquero

——. 1991. 'Art and a lack of money: The crises of the Spanish film industry, 1977–1990'. *Quarterly Review of Film Studies* 13/4, pp. 113–22

——. 1999. '*El corazón del bosque* (Gutiérrez Aragón, 1979): Mist, myth, and history'. *Spanish Cinema. The Auteurist Tradition*. Ed. Peter W. Evans. Oxford: University Press, pp. 164–75

Hughes, Arthur. 2007. 'Between history and memory: Creating a new subjectivity in David Trueba's film *Soldados de Salamina*'. *Bulletin of Spanish Studies* 84/3, pp. 369–86

Ibarz, Mercè. 2004. 'A serious experiment: *Land Without Bread*, 1933'. *Luis Buñuel: New Readings*. Ed. Peter W. Evans and Isabel Santaolalla. London: BFI, pp. 27–42

IMDb (Internet Movie Database). http://www.moviedatabase.com/ or http://www.imdb.com/

Insdorf, Annette. 1983. '"Soñar con tus ojos": Carlos Saura's melodic cinema'. *Quarterly Review of Film Studies* 8/2, pp. 49–53

Jancovich, Mark, and Antonio Lázaro Reboll *et al.* (eds). 2003. *Defining Cult Movies: The Cultural Politics of Oppositional Taste*. Manchester: Manchester University Press

Jordan, Barry. 1990. *Writing and Politics in Franco's Spain*. London and New York: Routledge

——. 1991. 'Culture and opposition in Franco's Spain: The reception of Italian Neo-realist cinema in the 1950s'. *European History Quarterly* 21/2, pp 209–38

——. 1995. 'Genre cinema in Spain in the 1970s: The case of comedy'. *Revista Canadiense de Estudios Hispánicos* 20/1, pp. 127–41

——. 1999a. 'Refiguring the past in the post-Franco fiction film: Fernando Trueba's *Belle Époque*'. *Bulletin of Hispanic Studies* (Glasgow) 76/1, pp. 139–56

——. 1999b. 'Promiscuity, pleasure and girl power: Fernando Trueba's *Belle Époque* (1992)'. *Spanish Cinema. The Auteurist Tradition*. Ed. Peter W. Evans. Oxford: University Press, pp. 286–309

——. 2003a. 'Revisiting the *comedia sexy ibérica: No desearás al vecino del quinto* (Ramón Fernández, 1971)'. *International Journal of Iberian Studies* 15/3, pp. 167–86

——. 2003b. 'Spain's new cinema of the 1990s: Santiago Segura and the Torrente phenomenon'. *New Cinemas* 1/3, pp. 167–78

——. 2005. 'Late-Francoist popular comedy and the "reactionary" film text'. *Studies in Hispanic Cinemas* 2/2, pp. 83–104

Jordan, Barry, and Mark Allinson. 2005. *Spanish Cinema: A Student's Guide*. London: Hodder Arnold

Jordan, Barry, and Rikki Morgan-Tamosunas. 1998. *Contemporary Spanish Cinema*. Manchester: Manchester University Press

——. 2000. *Contemporary Spanish Cultural Studies*. London: Arnold

Kenworthy, Patricia. 1992. 'A political *Pascual Duarte*'. *Cine-Lit: Essays on Peninsular Film and Fiction*. Ed. George Cabello-Castellet, Jaume Martí-Olivella, and Guy H. Wood. Portland & Corvallis, OR: Portland and Oregon State Universities and Reed College, pp. 55–9

Keown, Dominic. 1992. 'Ethics and aesthetics in Almodóvar's *Matador*'. *Bulletin of Hispanic Studies in Honour of Geoffrey Ribbans*, pp. 345–53

——. 1999. 'Feminism, politics and psychosis in Fernán Gómez's *Mi hija Hilde-*

gart (1977)'. *Spanish Cinema. The Auteurist Tradition.* Ed. Peter W. Evans. Oxford: University Press, pp. 147–63

———. 2005. 'The critique of reification: A subversive current within the cinema of contemporary Spain'. *European Identity in Cinema.* Ed. Wendy Everett. Bristol: Intellect Books, pp. 67–78

Kercher, Dona M. 1992. 'Cervantes on film: Exemplary tales and *La noche más hermosa*'. *Cine-Lit: Essays on Peninsular Film and Fiction.* Ed. George Cabello-Castellet, Jaume Martí-Olivella, and Guy H. Wood. Portland & Corvallis, OR: Portland and Oregon State Universities and Reed College, pp. 25–30

———. 1995. 'The "magical episodes" of the *Quijote* on film: Gutiérrez Aragón's *Maravillas*'. *Cine-Lit II: Essays on Hispanic Film and Fiction.* Ed. George Cabello-Castellet, Jaume Martí-Olivella, and Guy H. Wood. Portland & Corvallis, OR: Portland and Oregon State Universities and Reed College, pp. 86–95

———. 2002. 'Hitting the mark from television to film: Violence, timing, and the comedy team in Alex de la Iglesia's *Muertos de risa* (1999)'. *Post Script: Essays in Film and the Humanities* 21/2, pp. 50–63

Kinder, Marsha. 1983. 'Children of Franco in the New Spanish Cinema'. *Quarterly Review for Film Studies* 8/2, pp. 57–76

———. 1992. 'Micro and macro regionalism in *Vida en sombras* and beyond'. *Cine-Lit: Essays on Peninsular Film and Fiction.* Ed. George Cabello-Castellet, Jaume Martí-Olivella, and Guy H. Wood. Portland & Corvallis, OR: Portland and Oregon State Universities and Reed College, pp. 86–95

———. 1993. *Blood Cinema. The Reconstruction of National Identity in Spain.* Berkeley: University of California Press

——— (ed.). 1997. *Refiguring Spain. Cinema/Media/Representation.* Durham, NC and London: Duke University Press

———. 1999. 'Sex change and cultural transformation in Aranda and Abril's *Cambio de sexo* (1977)'. *Spanish Cinema. The Auteurist Tradition.* Ed. Peter W. Evans. Oxford: University Press, pp. 128–46

———. 2004–5. 'Reinventing the motherland: Almodóvar's brain-dead trilogy'. *Film Quarterly* 58/3, pp. 9–25

Kirkham, Pat, and Janet Thumin (eds) 1995. *Me Jane: Masculinity, Movies, and Women.* London: Lawrence & Wishart

Kovács, Katherine S. 1981. 'Loss and recuperation in the garden of delights'. *Cine-tracts* 4/2 and 3, pp. 45–54

———. 2001. 'The plain in Spain: Geography and national identity in Spanish cinema'. *Quarterly Review of Film and Video* 13/4, pp. 17–46

Kowalsky, Daniel. 2004. 'Rated S: Softcore pornography and the Spanish transition to democracy'. *Spanish Popular Cinema.* Ed. Antonio Lázaro Reboll and Andrew Willis. Manchester: Manchester University Press, pp 188–208

Labanyi, Jo. 1995. 'Masculinity and the family in crisis: Reading Unamuno through *film noir* (Serrano de Osma's adaptation of *Abel Sánchez*)'. *Romance Studies* 26, pp. 7–21

———. 1997. 'Race, gender and disavowal in Spanish cinema of the early Franco period: The missionary film and the folkloric musical'. *Screen* 38/3, pp. 215–31

——. 1999. 'Fetichism and the problem of sexual difference in Buñuel's *Tristana* (1970)'. *Spanish Cinema. The Auteurist Tradition*. Ed. Peter W. Evans. Oxford: University Press, pp. 76–92

——. 2000a. 'Feminizing the nation: Women, subordination and subversion in post-Civil War Spanish cinema'. *Heroines without Heroes. Reconstructing Female and National Identities in European Cinema, 1945–51*. Ed. Ulrike Sieglohr. London and New York: Cassell, pp. 162–82

——. 2000b. 'Misgeneration, nation formation and cross-racial identifications in the early Francoist folkloric film musical'. *Hybridity and its Discontents: Politics, Science, Culture*. Ed. Avtar Brah and Annie Coombes. London and New York: Routledge

—— (ed.). 2003 rpt. *Constructing Identity in Contemporary Spain: Theoretical Debates and Cultural Practice*. Oxford: Oxford University Press

——. 2004. 'Costume, identity and spectator pleasure in historical films of the early Franco period'. *Gender and Spanish Cinema*. Ed. Steven Marsh and Parvati Nair. New York and Oxford: Berg, pp. 33–51

Larraz, Emmanuel. 1986. *Le Cinéma espagnol des origines à nos jours*. Paris: Éditions du Cerf, 7 Art

Larrea, Carlota. 2001. 'Spanish film within the UK and Irish HE system: A survey of teaching'. *Vida Hispánica* 23/Spring, pp. 23–8

Lázaro Reboll, Antonio. 2002 'Exploitation in the cinema of Klimovsky and Franco'. *Cultura Popular: Studies in Spanish and Latin American Popular Culture*. Ed. Shelley Godsland and Anne M. White. Bern: Peter Lang, pp. 83–96

——. 2004. 'Screening "Chicho": The horror ventures of Narciso Ibáñez Serrador'. *Spanish Popular Cinema*. Ed. Antonio Lázaro Reboll and Andrew Willis. Manchester: Manchester University Press, pp. 152–69

——. 2005. '*La noche de Walpurgis / Shadow of the Werewolf*'; '*Torrente: el brazo tonto de la ley / Torrente the Dumb Arm of the Law* and *Torrente 2: misión en Marbella / Torrente 2: Mission in Marbella*'. *24 Frames: The Cinema of Spain and Portugal*. Ed. Alberto Mira. London and New York: Wallflower Press, pp. 129–36, 219–27

——. 2007. 'The transnational reception of *El espinazo del diablo* (Guillermo del Toro 2001)'. *Hispanic Research Journal* 8/1, pp. 39–51

Lázaro Reboll, Antonio, and Andrew Willis (eds). 2004. *Spanish Popular Cinema*. Manchester and New York: Manchester University Press

Lee, Laurie. 1974. *As I Walked Out One Midsummer's Morning*. Harmondsworth: Penguin. First published André Deutsch, 1969

Leonard, Candyce. 2004. '*Solas* and the unbearable condition of loneliness in the late 1990s'. *Spanish Popular Cinema*. Ed. Antonio Lázaro Reboll and Andrew Willis. Manchester: Manchester University Press, pp. 222–36

Lev, Leora. 2001. 'Returns of the repressed: Memory, oblivion and abjection in Spanish cinema'. *Revista de Estudios Hispánicos* 35, pp. 165–78

Llinás, Francisco. 1997. *Ladislao Vajda. El húngaro errante*. Valladolid: 42 Semana Internacional de Cine
—— 1998. 'Redundancy and Passion: Juan de Orduña at Cifesa'. *Modes of Representation in Spanish Cinema*. Ed. Jenaro Talens and Santos Zunzunegui. Minneapolis and London: University of Minneapolis Press, pp. 104–12
Louis, Anja. 1999. 'Carmen de Burgos and the question of divorce'. *Journal of Iberian and Latin American Studies* 5/1, pp. 49–63
Loxham, Abigail. 2006. 'Barcelona under construction: The democratic potential of touch and vision in city cinema in *En construcción* (2001)'. *Studies in Hispanic Cinemas* 3/1, pp. 35–48
Macdonald, Alice. 1998. 'Performing gender and nation in *¡Ay Carmela!*' *Journal of Iberian and Latin American Studies* 4/1, pp. 47–59
McDermott, Annella. 2000 *'Viridiana'; 'Carmen'. European Cinema: An Introduction*. Ed. Jill Forbes and Sarah Street. Basingstoke and New York: Palgrave, pp. 108–19, 133–42
Mandrell, James. 1995. 'Sense and sensibility, or latent heterosexuality and *Labyrinth of Passions'. Post-Franco, Postmodern: The Films of Pedro Almodóvar*. Ed. Kathleen M. Vernon and Barbara Morris. Westport, CT and London: Greenwood, pp. 41–57
Maroto Camino, Mercedes. 2005. *'Madrid me mata*: Killing the husband in Alex de la Iglesia's *La comunidad* (2000) and Pedro Almodóvar's *¿Qué he hecho yo para merecer esto!!* (1984)'. *Forum for Modern Language Studies* 41/3, pp. 333–42
Marsh, Steven. 1999. 'Enemies of the *Patria*: Fools, cranks and tricksters in the film comedies of Jéronimo Mihura'. *Journal of Iberian and Latin American Studies* 5/1, pp. 65–75
——. 2003. 'Tracks, traces and common places: Fernando León de Aranoa's *Barrio* (1998) and the layered landscape of everyday life in contemporary Madrid'. *New Cinemas* 1/3, pp. 165–73
——. 2004a. 'City, *costumbrismo* and stereotypes: Populist discourse and popular culture in Edgar Neville's *El crimen de la calle de Bordadores* (1946)'. *Studies in Hispanic Cinemas* 1/1, pp. 27–41
——. 2004b. 'Populism, the national-popular and the politics of Luis García Berlanga'. *Spanish Popular Cinema*. Ed. Antonio Lázaro Reboll and Andrew Willis. Manchester: Manchester University Press, pp. 113–28
——. 2004c. 'Gender and the city of Madrid in *Carne trémula'. Gender and Spanish Cinema*. Ed. Steven Marsh and Parvati Nair. New York and Oxford: Berg, pp. 53–70
——. 2004d. 'Villar del Río revisited: The chronotope of Berlanga's *¡Bienvenido Mister Marshall!' Bulletin of Hispanic Studies* (Liverpool) 81/1, pp. 25–41
——. 2006. *Popular Spanish Film under Franco. Comedy and the Weakening of the State*. Basingstoke and New York: Palgrave Macmillan
Marsh, Steven, and Parvati Nair. 2004. *Gender and Spanish Cinema*. New York and Oxford: Berg
Martí-Olivella, Jaume. 1995. 'Toward a new transcultural dialogue in Spanish

Film'. *Spain Today: Essays on Literature Culture, Society*. Ed. José Colmeiro *et al.* Hanover, NH: Dartmouth College, pp. 47–66

——. 1997. 'Regendering Spain's political bodies: Nationality and gender in the films of Pilar Miró and Arantxa Lazcano'. *Refiguring Spain. Cinema/Media/ Representation*. Ed. Marsha Kinder. Durham, NC and London: Duke University Press, pp. 215–38

——. 2003. *Basque Cinema: An Introduction*. Reno, NV: University of Nevada Centre for Basque Studies

Martín Cabrera, Luis. 2002. 'Postcolonial memories and racial violence in *Flores de otro mundo*'. *Journal of Spanish Cultural Studies* 3/1, pp. 43–55

Martin-Márquez, Susan L. 1995. 'Desire and narrative agency in *El sur*'. *Cine-Lit II: Essays on Hispanic Film and Fiction*. Ed. George Cabello-Castellet, Jaume Martí-Olivella, and Guy H. Wood. Portland & Corvallis, OR: Portland and Oregon State Universities and Reed College, pp. 130–6

——. 1999a. *Feminist Discourse and Spanish Cinema. Sight Unseen*. Oxford: University Press

——. 1999b. 'Culture and acculturation in Manuel Summers's *Del rosa... al amarillo* (1963)'. *Spanish Cinema. The Auteurist Tradition*. Ed. Peter W. Evans. Oxford: University Press, pp. 325–46

——. 2002. 'A world of difference in home making: The films of Icíar Bollaín'. *Women's Narrative and Film in 20th Century Spain*. Ed. Ofelia Ferrán and Kathleen Glenn. London and New York: Routledge, pp. 256–72

——. 2004. 'Pedro Almódovar's martenal transplants: From *Matador* to *All About my Mother*'. *Bulletin of Hispanic Studies* (Liverpool) 81/3, pp. 497–509

Martín Pérez, Celia. 2004. 'Madness, queenship and womanhood in Orduña's *Locura de amor* (1948) and Aranda's *Juana la loca* (2001)'. *Gender and Spanish Cinema*. Ed. Steven Marsh and Parvati Nair. New York and Oxford: Berg, pp. 71–85

Maule, Rosanna. 2002. 'Juanma Ullua's *Airbag* and the politics of Spanish regional autorship'. *Post Script: Essays in Film and the Humanities* 21/2, pp. 64–77

Maxwell, Richard. 1997. 'Spatial eruptions, global grids: Regionalist TV in Spain and dialectics of identity politics'. *Refiguring Spain. Cinema/Media/Represen-tation*. Ed. Marsha Kinder. Durham, NC and London: Duke University Press, pp. 260–83

MCU.ES (Ministerio de Cultura, base de datos de películas) http://www.mcu. es/cine/index.html

Medina de la Viña, Elena. 2000. *Cine negro y policíaco español de los años cincuenta*. Barcelona: Laertes

Melero Salvador, Alejandro. 2004. 'New sexual politics in the cinema of the transition to democracy: de la Iglesia's *El diputado* (1978)'. *Gender and Spanish Cinema*. Ed. Steven Marsh and Parvati Nair. New York and Oxford: Berg, pp. 87–102

Mellen, Joan. 1978. *The World of Luis Buñuel: Essays in Criticism*. New York: Oxford University Press

Membrez, Nancy J. 1989. ' "Llévame al cine, mama": The cinematograph in Spain 1896–1920'. *Romance Languages Annual* 1 (1991), pp. 540–7

Méndez Leite, Fernando. 1965. *Historia del cine español*, 2 vols. Madrid: Rialp

Miles, Robert J. 2007. 'Víctor Erice as fugitive'. *Bulletin of Spanish Studies* 84/1, pp. 57–78

Miller, Beth. 1983. 'From mistress to murderess: The metamorphosis of Buñuel's Tristana'. *Women in Hispanic Literature: Icons and Fallen Idols*. Ed. Beth Miller. Berkeley: University of California, pp. 340–59

Mínguez Arranz, Noberto. 2002. *Spanish Film and the Postwar Novel: Reading and Watching Narrative Texts*. Westport, CT: Praeger

Mira, Alberto. 1999. 'Al cine por razón de Estado: estética y política en *Alba de América*'. *Bulletin of Hispanic Studies* (Glasgow) 76/1, pp. 123–38

——. 2004. 'Spectacular metaphors: The rhetoric of historical representation in Cifesa epics'. *Spanish Popular Cinema*. Ed. Antonio Lázaro Reboll and Andrew Willis. Manchester: Manchester University Press, pp. 60–75

—— (ed.). 2005. *24 Frames: The Cinema of Spain and Portugal*. London and New York: Wallflower Press

Miró, Pilar. 1990. 'Ten years of Spanish Cinema', translated by Alma Amell. *Literature, the Arts, and Democracy. Spain in the Eighties*. Ed. Samuel Amell. London and Toronto: Associated University Press, pp. 38–46

Mitchell, Philip. 2004. 'Re-appraising Antonio Mercero: film authorship and the *intuición popular*'. *Spanish Popular Cinema*. Ed. Antonio Lázaro Reboll and Andrew Willis. Manchester: Manchester University Press, pp. 169–87

Moix, Terenci. 1993. *Suspiros de España. La copla y el cine de nuestro recuerdo*. Barcelona: Plaza y Janes

Molina Foix, Vicente. 1977. *New Cinema in Spain*. London: British Film Institute

——. 2003. *Manuel Gutiérrez Aragón*. Madrid: Cátedra, Signo e imagen 60

Monaco, James. 1981. *How to Read a Film. The Art, Technology, Language, History, and Theory of Film and Media*. Oxford and New York: University Press, rev. edn with subsequent reprints and revised editions

Monegal, Antonio. 1994. *Viaje a la luna. Federico García Lorca*. Valencia: Generalitat and Filmoteca, Pre-textos

——. 1998. 'Images of war: The hunting metaphor'. *Modes of Representation in Spanish Cinema*. Ed. Jenaro Talens and Santos Zunzunegui. Minneapolis and London: University of Minneapolis Press, pp. 203–15

Monterde, José Enrique. 1989. 'El cine histórico durante la transición política'. *Escritos sobre el cine español: 1973–1987*. Ed. Vicente Benet. Valencia: Filmóteca de la Generalitat, pp. 45–63

Moreiras Menor, Cristina. 2000. 'Spectacle, trauma and violence in contemporary Spain'. *Contemporary Spanish Cultural Studies*. Ed. Barry Jordan and Rikki Morgan-Tamosunas. London: Arnold, pp. 135–42

Moreno, Andrés. 1998. 'A search for identity: Francisco Regueiro's *Padre nuestro*'. *Modes of Representation in Spanish Cinema*. Ed. Jenaro Talens and

Santos Zunzunegui. Minneapolis and London: University of Minneapolis Press, pp. 264–72

Morgan, Rikki. 1994–5. 'Woman and isolation in Pilar Miró's *El pájaro de la felicidad* (1993)'. *Journal of Hispanic Research* 3, pp. 325–37

——. 1995a. 'Nostalgia and the contemporary Spanish musical film'. *Revista Canadiense de Estudios Hispánicos* 20/1, pp. 151–66

——. 1995b. 'Pedro Almodóvar's *Tie me up! Tie me down!*: The mechanism of masculinity'. Ed. Pat Kirkham and Janet Thumin, *Me Jane: Masculinity, movies, and women*. London: Lawrence & Wishart, pp. 113–27

——. 1995c. 'Realism and the creative process in Víctor Erice's *El sol de membrillo*'. *Journal of Iberian and Latin American Studies* 1/1, pp. 35–45

——. 1999. 'Narrative, desire and critical discourse in Pedro Almodóvar's *Carne trémula* (1997)'. *Journal of Iberian and Latin-American Studies* 8/2, pp. 185–99

——. 1999. 'Female subjectivity in *Gary Cooper que estás en los cielos* (Miró, 1980)'. *Spanish Cinema. The Auteurist Tradition*. Ed. Peter W. Evans. Oxford: University Press, pp. 176–93

——. 2000. 'Ideological testimony in Joris Iven's *The Spanish Earth, 1937*'. *International Journal of Iberian Studies* 13/1, pp. 45–54

Morris, Barbara. 1991. 'Fetish or wound: Discourses on the female body in Miguel Picazo's *Extramuros*'. *Revista de Estudios Hispánicos* 25/1, pp. 81–93

Morris, Cyril B. 1980. *This Loving Darkness. The Cinema and Spanish Writers 1920–1936*. Oxford: Oxford University Press for the University of Hull

Mortimore, Roger. 1975. 'Buñuel, Sáenz de Heredia and Filmófono'. *Sight and Sound* 44/Summer, pp. 180–2

Mulvey, Laura. 1989. *Visual and Other Pleasures*. Basingstoke: Macmillan, Language, Discourse, Society

Nair, Parvati. 1999. 'Between being and becoming: An ethnographic examination of border crossing in *Alma gitana* (Chus Gutiérrez 1995)'. *Journal of Iberian and Latin American Studies* 5/2, pp. 173–88

——. 2000. 'Displacing the hero: Masculine ambivalence in the cinema of Luis García Berlanga'. *100 years of European Cinema. Entertainment or Ideology?* Ed. Diana Holmes and Alison Smith. Manchester and New York: Manchester University Press, pp. 89–99

——. 2002. 'In modernity's wake: Transculturality, deterritorialization and the question of community in Icíar Bollaín's *Flores de otro mundo* (*Flowers from Another World*)'. *Post Script: Essays in Film and the Humanities* 21/2, pp. 38–49

——. 2004. 'Borderline men: Gender, place and power in representations of Moroccans in recent Spanish cinema'. *Gender and Spanish Cinema*. Ed. Steven Marsh and Parvati Nair. New York and Oxford: Berg, pp. 103–18

Oficina Informativa Española/Diplomatic Information Office. 1950. *The Spanish Cinema*. Madrid: Oficina Informativa Española. First published 1949

Oms, Marcel. 1985. *Don Luis Buñuel*. Paris: Cerf, 7 Art

Orr, John. 2004. 'New directions in European cinema'. *European Cinema*. Ed.

Elizabeth Ezra. Oxford and New York: Oxford University Press, pp. 299–317

Ostherr, Kirsten. 1992. 'Margins of vision: Azaría and Nieves in *Los santos inocentes*'. *Cine-Lit: Essays on Peninsular Film and Fiction*. Ed. George Cabello-Castellet, Jaume Martí-Olivella, and Guy H. Wood. Portland & Corvallis, OR: Portland and Oregon State Universities and Reed College, pp. 60–7

Parrondo Coppel, Eva. 2004. 'A psychoanalysis of *La mujer más fea del mundo* (1999)'. *Gender and Spanish Cinema*. Ed. Steven Marsh and Parvati Nair. New York and Oxford: Berg, pp. 119–34

Paun de García, Susan. 1992. '*Los santos inocentes*: Novel to film. A sharper image of evil'. *Cine-Lit: Essays on Peninsular Film and Fiction*. Ed. George Cabello-Castellet, Jaume Martí-Olivella, and Guy H. Wood. Portland & Corvallis, OR: Portland and Oregon State Universities and Reed College, pp. 68–74

Pavlovic, Tatjana. 1992. '*¡Bienvenido, Mr Marshall!* and the renewal of Spanish Cinema'. *Cine-Lit: Essays on Peninsular Film and Fiction*. Ed. George Cabello-Castellet, Jaume Martí-Olivella, and Guy H. Wood. Portland & Corvallis, OR: Portland and Oregon State Universities and Reed College, pp. 169–74

——. 2003. *Despotic Bodies and Transgressive Bodies: Spanish Culture from Francisco Franco to Jesús Franco*. New York: SUNY Press

——. 2004. 'Gender and Spanish horror film'. *Gender and Spanish Cinema*. Ed. Steven Marsh and Parvati Nair. New York and Oxford: Berg, pp. 135–50

Penn, Sheldon. 2005. 'From *L'Age d'or* to *El día de la bestia*: Between the ideal and the unspeakable'. *Journal of Iberian and Latin American Studies* 11/1, pp. 25–38

Pereira, Oscar. 1998. 'Pastiche and deformation of history in José Luis Garcí's *Asignatura pendiente*'. *Modes of Representation in Spanish Cinema*. Ed. Jenaro Talens and Santos Zunzunegui. Minneapolis and London: University of Minneapolis Press, pp. 158–70

Pérez Bowie, José Antonio. 1996. *Materiales para un sueño. En torno a la recepción del cine en España. 1896–1936*. Salamanca: Librería Cervantes

Pérez Millán, Juan Antonio. 2003. 'Women are also the future: Women directors in recent Spanish cinema', translated by Dennis and Joan West. *Cineaste* 29/1, pp. 50–5

Pérez Perucha, Julio (ed.). 1982. *El cinema de Edgar Neville*. Valladolid: 27 Semana Internacional de Cine

——. 1992. *Cine español. Algunos jalones significativos (1896–1936)*. Madrid: Films 210

—— (ed.). 1997. *Antología crítica del cine español 1906–1995. Flor en la sombra*. Madrid: Cátedra & Filmoteca Española, Serie mayor

Perriam, Chris. 1999a. '*A un dios desconocido*: Resurrecting a queer identity under Lorca's spell'. *Bulletin of Hispanic Studies* (Glagow) 76/1, pp. 77–91

——. 1999b. '*Las cosas del querer* (Chávarri, 1989)'. *Spanish Cinema. The Auteurist Tradition*. Ed. Peter W. Evans. Oxford: University Press, pp. 255–69

——. 2003. *Stars and Masculinities in Spanish Cinema*. Oxford: University Press

——. 2004a. 'Alejandro Amenábar's *Abre los ojos/Open Your Eyes* (1997)'. *Spanish Popular Cinema*. Ed. Antonio Lázaro Reboll and Andrew Willis. Manchester: Manchester University Press, pp. 209–21

——. 2004b. 'Heterosociality in *Segunda piel* (Gerardo Vera, 2000) and *Sobreviviré* (Alfonso Albacete and David Menkes, 1999): Strong women or same old story'. *Gender and Spanish Cinema*. Ed. Steven Marsh and Parvati Nair. New York and Oxford: Berg, pp. 151–64

——. 2005a. '*El último cuplé / Last Torch Song*'. *24 Frames: The Cinema of Spain and Portugal*. Ed. Alberto Mira. London and New York: Wallflower Press, pp. 89–96

——. 2005b. 'Two transnational stars: Antonio Banderas and Penélope Cruz'. *Studies in Hispanic Cinemas* 2/1, pp. 29–45

——. 2007. 'Victoria Abril in transnational context'. *Hispanic Research Journal* 8/1, pp. 27–38

Pineda Novo, Daniel. 1991. *Las folklóricas y el cine*. Huelva: Festival de Cine Iberoamericano

Pingree, Geoff. 2004. 'Pedro Almodóvar and the new politics of Spain'. *Cineaste* 30/1, pp. 4–15

Pohl, Burkhard, and Jörg Türschmann (eds). 2007. *Miradas* glocales: *Cine español en el cambio de milenio*. Madrid and Frankfurt am Main: Iberoamericana and Vervuert

Porter i Moix, Miquel. 1992. *Història del cinema a Catalunya 1895–1990*. Barcelona: Generalitat de Catalunya

Powrie, Phil, and Chris Perriam (dirs.). *The Carmen Project*, http:www.ncl.ac.uk/crif/Carmen.htm

Pozo Arenas, Santiago. 1984. *La industria del cine en España. Legislación y aspectos económicos (1896–1970)*. Barcelona: EU, Universitat de Barcelona

Prado, José María. 2005. 'Llaves para un centenario'. Ed. Antonio Santamarina. *Filmoteca Española. Cincuenta años de historia (1953–2003)*. Madrid: Ministerio de Cultura, Filmoteca Española, pp. 9–18

Preston, Paul. 1993. *Franco. A Biography*. Glasgow: HarperCollins

Prout, Ryan. 1999. 'Kicking the habit? Cinema, gender, and the ethics of care in Almodóvar's *Entre tinieblas*'. *Bulletin of Hispanic Studies* (Glagow) 76/1, pp. 53–66

——. 2000. 'Sects and secularity: Another cinema, another Spain'; 'Femme foetal: the triple terror of the young Basque woman in *Pasages*'. *Contemporary Spanish Cultural Studies*. Ed. Barry Jordan and Rikki Morgan-Tamosunas. London: Arnold, pp. 123–33, 283–94

——. 2004. 'All about Spain: Transplant and identity in *La flor de mi secreto* and *Todo sobre mi madre*'. *Studies in Hispanic Cinemas* 1/1, pp. 43–62

——. 2005. '*Marcelino pan y vino / The Miracle of Marcelino*', '*El Diputado / Confessions of a Congressman*'. *24 Frames: The Cinema of Spain and Portugal*. Ed. Alberto Mira. London and New York: Wallflower Press, pp. 71–7, 159–67

Rabalska, Carmen. 1999, 'A dark desire for the grotesque'. *Spanish Cinema Calling the Shots*. Ed. Rob Rix and Roberto Rodríguez Saona. Leeds: Trinity and All Saints College, pp. 91–111

——. 2000. 'A canon of disability: Deformity, illness and transgression in Spanish cinema'. *International Journal of Iberian Studies* 13/1, pp. 25–33

Riambau, Esteve. 2003. 'Public money and private business (or how to survive Hollywood's imperialism): Film production in Spain (1984–2002)', translated by Richard Keenan. *Cineaste* 29/1, pp. 56–61

Richardson, Nathan E. 2002. *Postmodern* Paletos. *Immigration, Democracy, and Globalization in Spanish Narrative and Film, 1950–2000*. Lewisburg and London: Bucknell University Press and Associated University Presses

Riley, Edward C. 1984. 'The story of Ana in *El espíritu de la colmena*'. *Bulletin of Hispanic Studies* 61/4, pp. 491–7

Rix, Rob and Roberto Rodríguez Saona (eds). 1999. *Spanish Cinema Calling the Shots*. Leeds: Trinity and All Saints College

Roberts, Stephen. 1999. 'In search of a new Spanish Realism: Bardem's *Calle mayor* (1956)'. *Spanish Cinema. The Auteurist Tradition*. Ed. Peter W. Evans. Oxford: University Press, pp. 19–37

Robertson, Sandra. 2000. 'Life is virtual dream: Aménabar reading Calderón'. *Cine-Lit 2000: Essays on Hispanic Film and Fiction*. Ed. George Cabello-Castellet, Jaume Martí-Olivella, and Guy H. Wood. Portland & Corvallis, OR: Portland and Oregon State Universities and Reed College, pp. 115–25

Rodríguez, José Luis. 2004. 'Contamination and transformation: A Kristevan reading of Luis Buñuel's *Viridiana*'. *Studies in Hispanic Cinemas* 1/3, pp. 169–80

Rodríguez, Juan. Accessed 25/07/05. 'La aportación del exilio republicano español al cine mexicano', http://clio.rediris.es/exilio/cinejuan.htm, 13pp.

Rodríguez, Pilar. 1997. 'Dark memories, tragic lives: Representations of the Basque nation in three contemporary films'. *Anuario de Cine y Literatura en Español* 2, pp. 129–44

Rolph, Wendy. 1995. 'Desire the dark: *Beltenebros* goes to the movies'. *Revista Canadiense de Estudios Hispánicos* 20/1, pp. 117–25

——. 1999. '¡*Bienvenido Mr Marshall!* (Berlanga 1952)'. *Spanish Cinema. The Auteurist Tradition*. Ed. Peter W. Evans. Oxford: University Press, pp. 8–18

Roque Baldovinos, Roberto. 1998. 'Sexual revolution against the State? José Luis García Sánchez's *Pasodoble*'. *Modes of Representation in Spanish Cinema*. Ed. Jenaro Talens and Santos Zunzunegui. Minneapolis and London: University of Minneapolis Press, pp. 255–63

Ros, Xon de. 1995. 'Víctor Erice's "voluntad de estilo" in *El espíritu de la colmena* (1973)'. *Forum for Modern Language Studies* 31/1, pp. 74–83

——. 1999a. 'Innocence lost: Sound and silence in *El espíritu de la colmena*'. *Bulletin of Hispanic Studies* (Glagow) 76/1, pp. 27–37

——. 1999b. '*Epílogo* (Suárez, 1984)'. *Spanish Cinema. The Auteurist Tradition*. Ed. Peter W. Evans. Oxford: University Press, pp. 210–25

Sala Noguer, Ramón. 1993. *El cine en la España republicana durante la guerra civil (1936–1939)*. Bilbao: Mensajero

Sánchez, Antonio. 1997. 'Women immune to a nervous breakdown: The representation of women in Julio Medem's film'. *Journal of Iberian and Latin American Studies* 3/2, pp. 147–61
——. 2000. 'Postmodernism and the contemporary Spanish avant-garde'. *Contemporary Spanish Cultural Studies*. Ed. Barry Jordan and Rikki Morgan-Tamosunas. London: Arnold, pp. 101–10
Sánchez Biosca, Vicente. 2005. '*Arrebato / Rapture*'. *24 Frames: The Cinema of Spain and Portugal*. Ed. Alberto Mira. London and New York: Wallflower Press, pp. 169–77
Sánchez Noriega, José Luis. 1998. *Mario Camus*. Madrid: Cátedra, Signo e imagen 40
Sánchez Vidal, Agustín. 1984. *Luis Buñuel, Obra cinematográfica*. Madrid: Ediciones JC
——. 1988. *El cine de Carlos Saura*. Zaragoza: Caja de Ahorros de la Inmaculada
——. 1991. *El cine de Florián Rey*. Zaragoza: Caja de Ahorros de la Inmaculada
——. 2005. '*La aldea maldita / The Cursed Village*'. *24 Frames: The Cinema of Spain and Portugal*. Ed. Alberto Mira. London and New York: Wallflower Press, pp. 13–21
Santamarina, Antonio. 2005. *Filmoteca Española. Cincuenta años de historia (1953–2003)*. Madrid: Ministerio de Cultura, Filmoteca Española
Santaolalla, Isabel. 1999a. 'Julio Medem's *Vacas* (1991): Historicizing the forest'. *Spanish Cinema. The Auteurist Tradition*. Ed. Peter W. Evans. Oxford: University Press, pp. 310–24
——. 1999b. 'Close encounters: Racial otherness in Imanol Uribe's *Bwana*'. *Bulletin of Hispanic Studies* (Glasgow) 76/1, pp. 113–24
——. 2003a. 'Behold the man! Masculinity and ethnicity in *Bwana* (1996) and *En la puta calle* (1998)'. *European Cinema: Inside Out. Images of the Self and the Other in Postcolonial European Cinema*. Ed. Guido Rings and Rikki Morgan. Heidelberg: Universitätsverlag C. Winter, pp 129–38
——. 2003b. 'The representation of ethnicity and "race" in contemporary Spanish cinema'. *Cineaste* 29/1, pp. 44–50
——. 2003 rpt. 'Ethnic and racial / configurations in contemporary Spanish culture'. *Constructing Identity in Twentieth Century Spain: Theoretical Debates and Cultural Practice*. Ed. Jo Labanyi. Oxford: Oxford University Press, pp. 55–71
——. 2004. 'The "Road that turning always …". Replacing the familiar and the unfamiliar in Icíar Bollaín's *Flowers from Another World* (1999)'. *Studies in European Cinema* 1/2, pp. 129–38
——. 2005a. '*Los últimos de Filipinas / Last Stand in the Philippines*'. *24 Frames: The Cinema of Spain and Portugal*. Ed. Alberto Mira. London and New York: Wallflower Press, pp. 50–9
——. 2005b. *Los 'Otros': etnicidad y 'raza' en el cine español contemporáneo*. Zaragoza and Madrid: Prensas Universitarias de Zaragoza and Ocho y Medio

Santoro, Patricia. 1996. *Novel into Film: The Case of* La familia de Pascual Duarte and *Los santos inocentes*. Newark: University of Delaware Press

Schaefer, Claudia. 2003. *Bored to Distraction: Cinema of Excess in End-of-the-century Mexico and Spain*. Albany: State University of New York Press

Schwartz, Ronald. 1991. *The Great Spanish Films: 1950–1990*. Metuchen, NJ and London: Scarecrow

Seguin, Jean-Claude. 1994. *Histoire du cinéma espagnol*. Paris: Nathan, Université 128. Translated by José Manuel Revuelta, *Historia del cine español* (Madrid: Acento, 1995)

Shaw, Deborah. 2000. 'Men in high heels: The feminine man and performances of feminity in *Tacones lejanos* by Pedro Almodóvar'. *Journal of Iberian and Latin American Studies* 6/1, pp. 55–62

Sieglohr, Ulrike. 2000. *Heroines with Heroes. Reconstructing Female and National Identities in European Cinema, 1945–51*. London and New York: Cassell

Smith, Paul Julian. 1992. *Laws of Desire. Questions of Homosexuality in Spanish Writing and Film 1960–1990*. Oxford: Clarendon Press

———. 1994. *Desire Unlimited. The Cinema of Pedro Almodóvar*. London and New York: Verso. 2002 Second updated edition includes reviews published in *Sight and Sound*.

———. 1995. '*Pepi, Luci, Bom* and *Dark Habits*: Lesbian comedy, lesbian tragedy'. *Post-Franco, Postmodern: The Films of Pedro Almodóvar*. Ed. Kathleen M. Vernon and Barbara Morris. Westport, CT and London: Greenwood, pp. 25–40

———. 1996. *Vision Machines. Cinema, Literature and Sexuality in Spain and Cuba, 1983–93*. London and New York: Verso

———. 1997 'Pornography, masculinity, homosexuality: Almodóvar's *Matador* and *La ley del deseo*'. *Refiguring Spain. Cinema/Media/Representation.* Ed. Marsha Kinder. Durham, NC and London: Duke University Press, pp. 178–95

———. 'Homosexuality, regionalism and mass culture: Eloy de la Iglesia's cinema of the transition'. *Modes of Representation in Spanish Cinema*. Ed. Jenaro Talens and Santos Zunzunegui. Minneapolis and London: University of Minneapolis Press, pp. 216–15

———. 1999a. 'Between metaphysics and scienticism: Rehistoricising Víctor Erice's *El espíriru de la colmena* (1973)'. *Spanish Cinema. The Auteurist Tradition*. Ed. Peter W. Evans. Oxford: University Press, pp. 93–114

———. 1999b. 'Between heaven and earth: Grounding Julio Medem's *Tierra*'. *Bulletin of Hispanic Studies* (Glasgow) 76/1, pp. 11–25

———. 1999c. 'The representation of the gypsies in contemporary Spanish cinema'. *Spanish Cinema Calling the Shots*. Ed. Rob Rix and Roberto Rodríguez Saona. Leeds: Trinity and All Saints College, pp. 65–90

———. 2000a. *The Moderns. Time, Space, and Subjectivity in Contemporary Spanish Culture*. Oxford and New York: Oxford University Press

———. 2000b. 'Only connect' [on Almodóvar's *Hable con ella*]. *Sight and Sound* 12/7, pp. 24–7

——. 2003. *Contemporary Spanish Culture: TV, Fashion, Art, and Film*. Malden, MA: Polity Press

——. 2004. 'High anxiety: *Abre los ojos/Vanilla Sky*'. *Journal of Romance Studies* 4/1, pp. 91–102

——. 2005a. '*Lucía y el sexo / Sex and Lucía*'. *24 Frames: The Cinema of Spain and Portugal*. Ed. Alberto Mira. London and New York: Wallflower Press, pp. 239–46

——. 2005b. '*All About My Mother* (1999): Narrative, themes and technique'. *Film Analysis: A Norton Reader*. Ed. Jeffrey Geiger and R.L. Rutsky. New York: Norton, pp. 873–89

——. 2006a. *Television in Spain: From Franco to Almodóvar*. London: Támesis

——. 2006b. 'Women, windmills, and wedge heels' [on Almodóvar's *Volver*]. *Sight and Sound* 16/6, pp. 16–18

Sorlin, Pierre. 1991. *European Cinemas European Societies 1939–1990*. London and New York: Routledge, Studies in Film, Television and the Media

Stock, Ann Marie. 1992. 'Deconstructing cinematographic conventions and reconsidering pornography in Bigas Luna's *Bilbao*'. *Cine-Lit: Essays on Peninsular Film and Fiction*. Ed. George Cabello-Castellet, Jaume Martí-Castellet and Guy H. Wood. Portland & Corvallis, OR: Portland and Oregon State Universities and Reed College, pp. 10–18

——. 1998. 'Eyeing our collections: Selecting images, juxtaposing fragments, and exposing conventions in the films of Bigas Luna'. *Modes of Representation in Spanish Cinema*. Ed. Jenaro Talens and Santos Zunzunegui. Minneapolis and London: University of Minneapolis Press, pp. 171–87

Stone, Rob. 2002. *Spanish Cinema*. Harlow: Longman, Pearson Education, Inside Film

——. 2004a. *The Flamenco Tradition in the Works of Federico García Lorca and Carlos Saura*. London and New York: Edwin Mellen Press

——. 2004b. '¡Victoria? a modern Magdalene'. *Gender and Spanish Cinema*. Ed. Steven Marsh and Parvati Nair. New York and Oxford: Berg, pp. 165–82

——. 2007. *Julio Medem*. Manchester: Manchester University Press, Spanish and Latin American Film Makers

Strauss, Frederic (ed.). 1995. *Almodóvar on Almodóvar*, translated by Yves Balgneres. London: Faber & Faber

Talens, Jenaro. 1993. *The Branded Eye: Buñuel's Un Chien andalou*, translated by Giulia Colaizzi. Minneapolis: University of Minnesota Press, Original *El ojo tachado. Lectura de Un Chien andalou de Luis Buñuel* (Madrid: Cátedra [Signo e imagen 3], 1986)

Talens, Jenaro, and Santos Zunzunegui (eds). 1998. *Modes of Representation in Spanish Cinema*. Minneapolis and London: University of Minneapolis Press

Thompson, Kristin, and David Bordwell. 2003. *Film History. An Introduction*. Boston: McGraw Hill. 2nd edn

Thompson, Stith. 1955–8. *Motif-Index of Folk-Literature*. Copenhagen: Roskilde & Bagger

Tjersland, Todd. 2003. 'Cinema of the doomed: The tragic horror of Paul

Naschy'. *Fear Without Frontiers: Horror Cinema Across the Globe.* Ed. Steven Schneider. London: Fab Press, pp. 69–80

Tohill, Cathal, and Pete Tombs. 1994. *Immoral Tales: European Sex and Horror Movies, 1956–1984.* New York: St Martin's Griffin

Tolentino, Roland B. 1997 'Nations, nationalisms, and *Los últimos de Filipinas*: An imperialist desire for colonialist nostalgia'. *Refiguring Spain. Cinema/ Media/ Representation.* Ed. Marsha Kinder. Durham, NC and London: Duke University Press, pp. 133–53

Torreiro, Casimiro. 1998. 'Aimez-vous la représentation? Notes on the cinema of Pere Portabella and on *Informe General*'. *Modes of Representation in Spanish Cinema.* Ed. Jenaro Talens and Santos Zunzunegui. Minneapolis and London: University of Minneapolis Press, pp. 303–18

Torres, Augusto M. (ed.). 1986. *Spanish Cinema 1896–1983,* translated by E. Nelson Modlin III. Madrid: Ministerio de Cultura, Instituto del Cine

Triana Toribio, Núria. 1996. 'Almodóvar's melodramatic mise-en-scène: Madrid as a setting for melodrama'. *Bulletin of Hispanic Studies* (Liverpool) 73/2, pp. 179–89

——. 1998. 'In memorian. Pilar Miró (1940–1997)'. *Film History* 10, pp. 231–40

——. 1999. '*¿Qué he hecho yo para merecer esto?* (Almodóvar, 1984)'. *Spanish Cinema. The Auteurist Tradition.* Ed. Peter W. Evans. Oxford: University Press, pp. 226–41

——. 2000a. 'Ana Mariscal: Franco's disavowed star'. *Heroines with Heroes. Reconstructing Female and National Identities in European Cinema, 1945–51.* Ed. Ulrike Sieglohr. London and New York: Cassell, pp. 184–95

——. 2000b. 'A punk called Pedro: *la movida* in the films of Pedro Almodóvar'. *Contemporary Spanish Cultural Studies.* Ed. Barry Jordan and Rikki Morgan-Tamosunas. London: Arnold, pp. 274–82

——. 2002–3. 'Transitions that count: Josefina Molina'. *International Journal of Iberian Studies* 15/2, pp. 84–90

——. 2003. *Spanish National Cinema.* Routledge, National Cinema Series

——. 2005. 'Santiago Segura: Just when you thought that Spanish masculinities were getting better'. *Hispanic Research Journal* 5/2, pp. 147–56

——. 2006. 'Anyplace North America: On the transnational road with Isabel Coixet'. *Studies in Hispanic Cinemas* 3/1, pp. 49–66

Tropiano, Stephen. 1997, 'Out of the cinematic closet: Homosexuality in the films of Eloy de la Iglesia'. *Refiguring Spain. Cinema/Media/Representation.* Ed. Marsha Kinder. Durham, NC and London: Duke University Press, pp. 157–77

Vernon, Kathleen M. 1986. 'Re-viewing the Spanish Civil War: Franco's film *Raza*'. *Film and History* 16/2, pp. 26–34

——. 1989. '*La politique des auteurs*: Narrative point of view in *Pascual Duarte*'. *Hispania* 72/1, pp. 87–96

——. 1995. 'Crossing city limits: Fiction, documentary, history in Basilio Martín Patino's *Madrid*'. *Cine-Lit II: Essays on Hispanic Film and Fiction.* Ed. George Cabello-Castellet, Jaume Martí-Olivella, and Guy H. Wood. Portland

& Corvallis, OR: Portland and Oregon State Universities and Reed College, pp. 174–85

———. 1997. 'Reading Hollywood in/and Spanish cinema: From trade wars to transculturation'. *Refiguring Spain. Cinema/Media/Representation*. Ed. Marsha Kinder. Durham, NC and London: Duke University Press, pp. 36–64

———. 1999. 'Culture and cinema to 1975'. *The Cambridge Companion to Spanish Culture*. Ed. David T. Gies. Cambridge: Cambridge University Press

———. 2004. 'Theatricality, melodrama and stardom in *El último cuplé*'. *Gender and Spanish Cinema*. Ed. Steven Marsh and Parvati Nair. New York and Oxford: Berg, pp. 183–99

Vernon, Kathleen M. and Barbara Morris (eds). 1995. *Post-Franco, Postmodern: The Films of Pedro Almodóvar*. Westport, CT and London: Greenwood

Via Rivera, Marian. 2004. 'A journey into the labyrinth: Intertextual readings of Borges and Cortázar in Julio Medem's *Los amantes del círculo polar* (1998)'. *Journal of Iberian and Latin American Studies* 10/2, pp. 205–12

Vidal, Nuria. 1988. *The Films of Pedro Almodóvar*, translated by Linda Moor and Victoria Hughes. Madrid: Ministerio de Cultura, Instituto del Cine

Vilarós, Teresa. 1998. 'Mother country, fatherland: The uncanny Spain of Manuel Gutiérrez Aragón'. *Modes of Representation in Spanish Cinema*. Ed. Jenaro Talens and Santos Zunzunegui. Minneapolis and London: University of Minneapolis Press, pp. 188–202

Vincendeau, Ginette (ed.). 1995. *Encyclopedia of European Cinema*. London: British Film Institute

Walker, Lesley Heins. 1998. 'What did I do to deserve this? The "Mother" in the films of Pedro Almodóvar'. *Modes of Representation in Spanish Cinema*. Ed. Jenaro Talens and Santos Zunzunegui. Minneapolis and London: University of Minneapolis Press, pp. 273–88

Wayne, Mike. 2002. *The Politics of Contemporary European Cinema*. Bristol: Intellect Books

White, Anne M. 1999. '*Manchas negras, manchas blancas*: Looking again at Julio Medem's *Vacas*'. *Spanish Cinema Calling the Shots*. Ed. Rob Rix and Roberto Rodríguez Saona. Leeds: Trinity and All Saints College, pp. 1–14

———. 2003. 'Seeing double? The remaking of Alejandro Amenábar's *Abre los ojos* as Cameron Crowe's *Vanilla Sky*'. *International Journal of Iberian Studies* 15/3, pp. 187–97

Williams, Linda. 1992. *Figures of Desire: A Theory and Analysis of Surrealist Film*. Berkeley: University of California Press, originally published in 1981

Willis, Andrew. 2002. '*Angustia* and the self-reflexive horror film'. *Cultura Popular: Studies in Spanish and Latin American Popular Culture*. Ed. Shelley Godsland and Anne M. White. Bern: Peter Lang, pp. 72–82

———. 2003. 'Spanish horror and the flight from "art" cinema'. *Defining Cult Movies: The Cultural Politics of Oppositional Taste*. Ed. Mark Jancovich, Antonio Lázaro Reboll *et al*. Manchester: Manchester University Press, pp. 71–83

———. 2004. 'From the margins to the mainstream: Trends in recent Spanish horror cinema'. *Spanish Popular Cinema.* Ed. Antonio Lázaro Reboll and Andrew Willis. Manchester: Manchester University Press, pp. 237–49

Woods, Eva. 2004a. 'From rags to riches: The ideology of stardom in folkloric musical comedy films of the late 1930s and 1940s'. *Spanish Popular Cinema.* Ed. Antonio Lázaro Reboll and Andrew Willis. Manchester: Manchester University Press, pp. 40–59

——. 2004b. 'Radio Free *folklóricas*: Cultural, gender and spatial hierarchies in *Torbellino* (1941)'. *Gender and Spanish Cinema.* Ed. Steven Marsh and Parvati Nair. New York and Oxford: Berg, pp. 201–18

Wright, Sarah. 2005. 'Dropping the mask: Theatricality and absorption in Sáenz de Heredia's *Don Juan*'. *Screen* 46/4, pp. 415–31

Zecchi, Barbara. 2005. 'All about mothers: Pronatalist discourses in contemporary Spanish cinema'. *West Chester University College Literature* 32/1, pp. 146–64

Zunzunegui, Santos. 1985. 'La producción fílmica en el País Vasco: 1936–1939'. *Revista de Occidente* 53, pp. 23–31

INDEX OF NAMES AND SUBJECTS

Individuals have been identified by profession, and public figures and events are indexed only if they are represented in a film. Awards are indexed only when they appear outside brackets in the text.

AACC [Academia de las Artes y Ciencias Cinematográficas] *see under* film organisations
Abad de Santillán, Diego (director)   241
Abadal, Baltasar (cinematographer)   3, 22
Abbadie d'Arrast-Soriano, Harry d' (director)   65, 125
Abril, Albert (director)   289
Abril, Victoria (actor)   231, 236, 247, 249, 262, 265, 268, 270, 274, 285–6, 290, 307, 337, 341, 343, 351
Abusada, Jordi (cinematographer)   327
Academia de las Artes y Ciencias Cinematográficas [Spanish Film Academy] *see under* film organisation, AACC
Acero, Ricardo (actor)   106
Acosta, José Luis (director)   311–12
Acustic *see under* dubbing
Adjani, Isabel (actor)   260
ageing   218, 221, 229–30, 262, 294, 297, 315, 317, 327, 349–50
Aguilar, Santiago *see* La Cuadrilla
Aguirre, Javier (director)   163, 168, 189, 201, 209, 211, 228, 232, 240, 250, 260, 305
Aguirresarobe, Javier (cinematographer)   289, 291, 307, 329
Aibar, Oscar (director)   306
AIDS   270, 308, 324
Air Force *see under* military
Alarcón, Pedro de (author)   96, 101
Alaria, Alfredo (dancer)   163
Alatriste, Gustavo (producer)   151–2
Alba, Tota (actor)   178

Albacete, Alfonso (director/screenwriter)   137 n. 28, 301 n. 16, 306, 337, 344
Albaladejo, Miguel (director)   331, 336, 341, 345, 347
Albéñiz, Isaac (composer)   107, 326
Alberich, Enric (director)   337
Alberti, Rafael (poet)   xiii, xv, 43 n. 35, 44 n. 37, 74
Alborch, Carmen (minister of culture)   283
Alcaine, José Luis (cinematographer)   266, 269 n. 21, 286, 297
Alcázar, Ángel (actor)   276
Alcázar, Damián (actor)   335
Alcázar, Jorge (actor)   335
Alcázar, Rafael (director)   291
Alcocer, Santos (producer/screenwriter/ director)   170
Alcocer, Teresa (editor)   196
Alcoriza, Luis (screenwriter/actor)   296
Alejandro, Julio (screenwriter)   151, 180
Alexandre, Margarita (director/ producer)   124, 127, 155
Alexandre, Manuel (actor)   167, 341, 350
Alfonso XII   141, 153
Alfonso XIII   4, 19 n. 32, 31, 49
Alfonso, María José (actor)   185, 297
Alfonso, Raúl (director)   31, 112, 126
Algora, Francisco (actor)   240, 249
Algora, Jorge (director)   331
Algueró, Augusto (composer)   218
Almeida, Sebastián (director)   142
Almodóvar, Pedro (director/screenwriter/ producer)   xiv–xv, 10 n. 19, 27 n. 2, 163 n. 7, 228 n. 5, 251, 254, 259,

271–3, 280, 285, 303, 314, 319–21, 324–5, 334 n. 16, 343–5, 351
Alonso, Luis (director)   29, 84
Alonso, Mercedes (editor)   196
Alonso, Rafael (actor)   204
Alonso, Santiago (actor)   294
Alonso de Santos, José Luis (playwright)   264
Alterio, Ernesto (actor)   326, 337, 344, 346, 350–1
Alterio, Héctor (actor)   216, 232, 234, 313, 344, 351
Álvarez, Ana (actor)   305
Álvarez, Mercedes (editor/director)   327
Álvarez, Miguel (director)   348
Álvarez, Roberto (actor)   337, 347
Álvarez Quintero, Serafín and Joaquín (playwrights)   34, 57, 93, 107
Álvaro, Primitivo (production manager)   189
Amadori, Luis (director)   96, 141–2, 153–4, 162
Amaya, Carmen (dancer/actor)   61, 65, 160
Amel, Said (actor)   289
Amenábar, Alejandro (director/ screenwriter/composer)   xv, 308, 312, 321, 340
Amich i Bert, Josep (director)   24
Amo, Álvaro del (director/screenwriter)   252, 334
Amo, Antonio del (director)   74, 105, 113–4, 126–7, 131–2, 134, 144, 154, 160, 173, 220–1
Amo, Pablo G[arcía] (editor)   189, 260
Amorós, Jordi 'Ja' (comics' author)   252
Andalusia, locations   38, 65–6, 69, 81, 93–5, 105–8, 140, 231, 242, 268, 288
   Almería   172, 313, 321, 323
   Cadiz   126, 346
   Cordoba   72, 269
   Costa del Sol   161
   Granada   36, 56
   Huelva   242
   Malaga   34
   Marbella   203, 249, 273, 342
   Murcia   274
   Ronda   24, 56, 80, 141
   Seville   34, 36, 50, 59, 80, 142, 231, 242, 260, 269, 299

Andersen, Bibí [Bibiana/Manuela Fernández Chica] (actor)   236, 270
Andersen, Hans Christian (author)   176, 252
Andión, Patxi (actor)   297
Andrés, Ángel (actor)   167
Andrés, Pilar (actor)   335
Andreu, Simón (actor)   206, 235 n. 15
Angelillo [Ángel Sampedro Montero] (singer/actor)   58, 61–2, 86
Anglada, Darius (actor)   246
Anglada, Eugeni (director)   246
Angulo, Álex (actor)   278, 306, 342
animation   xvi, 10, 24, 60, 63, 97–8, 175–6, 252, 312, 347–8
animation for adults   252
Animatograph   1
Antonutti, Omero (actor)   258, 287, 291
Aparicio, Rafaela (actor)   146, 161 n. 6, 164, 166–7, 178, 231, 263, 295
'apertura' see under Franco Regime
Aragon, locations   31, 33–34, 57, 66–7, 83–4, 261, 297, 299
   Zaragoza   2–3, 6–7, 101
Araguren, Sonsoles (actor)   258
Arana, Sabino (politician)   243
Aranda, Vicente (director)   17 n. 26, 23 n. 36, 55, 74, 101 n. 37, 192–3, 196, 212, 235, 243, 247, 258, 262, 264, 267, 286, 290, 298, 320, 330, 341 n. 22
Araña, Beatriz de (actor)   112
Arévalo, Carlos (director)   49, 86, 90, 92
Argamasilla, Joaquín (DNC director)   118–20
Argentina, Imperio [Magdalena Nile del Río] (actor)   37–8, 51–2, 58–9, 66, 69, 80, 83, 93, 106, 108, 141, 184, 263, 299
Arias, Imanol (actor)   111 n. 49, 249, 264, 289–90, 298, 312–13, 319
Arias Navarro, Carlos (government president)   198–9, 225
Arias Salgado, Gabriel (minister)   157
Aristarain, Adolfo (director)   313, 350
armed forces see under military
Armendáriz, Montxo   278, 280, 288–9, 320, 329, 333, 348
Armiñán, Jaime de (director/screenwriter)   138, 200 n. 2, 219–20, 230–2, 268, 288, 293, 320

Arniches, Carlos (playwright)   34, 57, 60–1, 69, 138
Arnold, Jack (director)   10 n. 19
Arnoul, Françoise (actor)   132 n. 18
Arquillé, Pere (actor)   326
Arribas, Marta (director)   328
Arroyo, Luis (director)   104
Arte y cinematografía see under magazines
Artigot, Raúl (cinematographer/ director)   234
Asensi, Neus (actor)   336
Asins Arbó, Manuel (composer)   137
Asquerino, María (actor)   263, 303, 319
Asquerino, Mariano (actor)   100
Asturias, locations   96, 129, 290, 336
Atienza, Juan G[arcía] (director)   148, 166, 196
Aub, Max (author)   45, 74, 244
August releases   300
Aured, Carlos (director)   207, 228
auteur cinema   181, 194, 209, 217, 254, 256, 323
autonomous regions   226, 240–2, 256, 274–9, 281–2
avant-garde *see* experimental cinema
awards/prizes   157, 182, *see also* Festivals
   CEC [Círculo de Escritores Cinematofráficos/Screenwriters' Circle]   153 n. 49
   Fotógramas de Plata   153 n. 49
   Goyas   257, 263, 278, 285–7
   IE [de interés especial]   157, 199
   IM [de interés militar]   85
   IN [de interés nacional]   85, 118, 120, 153 n. 49
   Oscars   xiv, 136, 160, 243, 250, 256, 287, 321, 324, 329, 350–1
   PNC [premio nacional de cinematografía]   85, 96, 113, 153 n. 49, 157 n. 3, 181
   Sant Jordi   138 n. 29, 186 n. 39, 275
   Sindicato Nacional del Espectáculo   85
Ayaso, Dunia (director)   310
Azcona, Rafael (screenwriter)   137, 145, 179, 184, 190, 200, 214, 216, 231, 237, 240, 261–2, 269, 271, 294, 296, 301
Azketa, Peio (painter)   327

Azkona, Mauro (director)   34
Aznar, Adolfo (director)   32 n. 9, 66, 72
Aznar, Tomás (director)   205
Azorín [José Martínez Ruiz] (author)   205
Azorín, Eloy (actor)   293

Baena, Juan Julio de (cinematographer)   150
Baez 'El Litri', Miguel (bullfighter)   142
Baeza, Elsa (actor)   187
Bajo Ulloa, Juanma (director)   307, 319–20
Baker, Stanley (actor)   205
Balagué, Carlos   265, 300–1
Balaguer, Manuel (director)   275 n. 26
Balagueró, Jaume (director)   340
Balañá, Pere (director)   169
Balcázar, Alfonso (director)   141, 173, 228
Balcázar, Jaime J. (director)   173, 201
Balearic Islands, locations   59, 209, 290, 324
   Mallorca   191, 249, 277
   Menorca   277
Balet, Ramón (producer)   97
ballads   11, 16, 127
Ballesta, Juan José (actor)   331–2
Ballester Bustos, Luis (animation)   252
Balletbò-Coll, Marta (director/ screenwriter/actor)   310–12
Balmaseda, Enrique (ICAA director)   283
Bandera, Manuel (actor)   307
Banderas, Antonio (actor)   xv, 111 n. 49, 258, 274, 285, 287, 292, 296, 318, 351
bandits *see* bandoleros
bandoleros   17, 23, 31, 56, 62, 71–2, 105–6, 125, 127–8, 140, 144, 182
Baños, Ramon (director/cinematographer/ screenwriter)   5, 16–17, 22, 24
Baños, Ricard (director/screenwriter)   5, 15–17, 22–4, 27–8, 30, 47, 56, 84, 101 n. 37, 201, 260 n. 6
Bará, Milagros (director)   340
Baquero, Ivana (actor)   329
Barbéris, René (director)   52
Barbero, Joan (screenwriter)   296
Barcelona School   191–4, 196
Bardem, Carlos (actor)   137 n. 28

Bardem, Javier (actor)   137 n. 28, 297,
    304, 307, 319, 321, 323, 332, 343, 351
Bardem, Juan (composer)   330
Bardem, Juan Antonio (director)   69–70,
    82, 102, 119, 132–3, 135, 137–40,
    142, 144–5, 149–51, 154–5, 161–2,
    176–7, 180, 192 n. 43, 196, 208,
    213–14, 230 n. 8, 243, 260 n. 10, 261,
    264, 271, 313, 319–20, 331
Bardem, Miguel (director/screenwriter)
    137 n. 28, 306, 337, 344
Bardem, Mónica (actor)   137 n. 28
Bardem, Pilar (actor)   137 n. 28, 213,
    290, 296, 327, 349
Bardem, Rafael (actor)   137
Barea, Ramón (actor)   305
Baroja, Julio (director)   241–2
Baroja, Pío (author)   34–5, 42, 104, 149,
    188, 241–2
barraca [fair booth] see under screens
Barranco, María (actor)   278, 285,
    287–8, 293, 298, 330
Barranco, Sergio (actor)   333
Barreto, Marino (singer)   58
barrio cinema see under comedy, popular
barrio cinemas see under screens
Barroso, Mariano (director/screenwriter)
    306, 319
Bartolomé, Cecilia (director)   230, 241,
    290
Bartolomé, José Juan (director)   241
Basehart, Richard (actor)   173
Basque Country
    Carlist War see war films
    cinema   33–4, 61–2, 170, 226, 262,
        264, 275, 277–8, 280, 300, 307–8,
        311–12, 347–8
    identities   33–4, 61–2, 88–9, 169–70,
        226, 241, 243, 256, 262, 264,
        277–8, 281, 292, 294, 300, 308,
        311–12, 324, 327, 340
    language   61–2, 88–9, 170, 226, 262,
        264, 275, 277, 311–12, 324, 327
    nationalists   120, 140, 157, 198,
        222–3, 226, 241, 243, 262, 264,
        277, 292, 311–12, 324, 327, 340
Basque Country, locations   21, 34, 61–2,
    74, 160, 258, 277–8, 290, 292, 307–9,
    324, 329
    Bilbao   21, 78, 219, 264, 274, 292,
        295, 306, 311–12

    Pamplona   36, 211
    San Sebastián   268
Basterretxea, Néstor (director)   170
Basterretxea, Txabi (animation)   347–8
Batanero, Javier (actor)   334
Baty, Gaston (playwright)   104, 171
Bauer, James (director)   70
Bauluz, Fernando (director)   312, 336
Bautista, Aurora (actor)   17 n. 26, 101,
    103, 122, 127, 138, 186, 259, 300
Bautista, Emilio (director)   34, 46 n. 43
Baxter, Keith (actor)   213, 266
Bayarri, Jaime (director)   205
Beatles (band)   176, 193, 304
Beaumarchais, Pierre-Augustin Caron de
    (playwright)   81
Bebe [María Nieves Rebolledo Vila]
    (singer/actor)   345
Bécquer, Florencia (actor)   83
Bécquer, Gustavo Adolfo (poet)   105
Beethoven, Ludwig van (composer)   217,
    261
Behrendt, Hans (director) 46 n. 43, 126
Belaustegui, Marta (actor)   288
Belén, Ana (actor)   162–3, 200 n. 2, 213,
    217, 219, 245, 259 n. 4, 269–70, 274,
    285–7, 304, 343
Bell, Monta (director)   17
Bellmunt, Francesc (director)   222, 238,
    275
Beltrán, José María (cinematographer)
    60, 73–4
Ben Lyziad, Farida (director)   58 n. 14,
    232 n. 11
Benavente, Jacinto (playwright)   17,
    27–8, 31, 37–8, 57, 70, 109
Benavides, Alfonso (director)   70
Benjamin, Walter (author)   303
Benpar, Carlos (director)   348
Berasategi, Juan Bautista (animation)
    347
Berger, Pablo (director)   209 n. 17, 348
Bergman, Ingmar (director)   184 n. 37
Berkeley, Busby (director)   76
Berlanga, José Luis (director)   274
Berlanga, Luis G[arcía] (director)   xiv,
    82, 114, 123, 128–9, 133–7, 140 n. 32,
    150, 154, 174, 176–80, 183 n. 34, 196,
    214, 219, 226, 237, 261–2, 268–9,
    271, 294, 319, 323, 341
Bermejo, Alberto (director)   233–4

Bermúdez, Xavier (director) 335
Bernard, Raymond (director) 108
Berriatúa, Luciano (director) 249
Berrocal, Leire (actor) 307
Bertolucci, Bernardo (director) 200
Bessie, Alvah (screenwriter) 191
Betancor, Antonio (director) 248–9, 258, 330
Betriu, Francesc (director/screenwriter) 221, 234, 238, 248, 250, 258, 287
Biadiu, Ramon (director) 72–3
Biba, Dritan (actor) 344
Bigas Luna, José Juan (director/screenwriter/producer) 177 n. 29, 228–9, 231, 247, 265–6, 275 n. 26, 287–8, 297–98, 303, 320
Birkin, Jane (actor) 203 n. 8
Bizet, Georges (composer) see Carmen
black market/trafficking 95, 108–9, 112, 118, 135, 219, 245
    ration books 82, 112, 116, 119
Blackston, J. Stuart (photographer) 7
Blair, Betsy (actor) 138
Blanche, Francis (actor/screenwriter) 200
Blanco, Enrique (producer/director) 36, 41
Blanco, Uxía (actor) 279
Blasco, Carlos (screenwriter) 104
Blasco, Ricardo (director) 148
Blasco Ibáñez, Vicente (author) 13, 17, 38, 105, 149, 248
Blay, José María (producer) 97
Blothner, Renhardt (director) 83 n. 8
Blue Division see under military
Blum, Bettiana (actor) 343–4
Bódalo, José (actor) 234
Bodegas, Roberto (director) 163, 217, 264–5, 321 n. 4
Bodin, Richard (journalist) 45 n. 39
Bofill, Ricardo (director) 193
Bogart, Humphrey (actor) 98
Bolas, Xan das (actor) 167
bolero see under songs
Bollaín, Icíar (actor/director/producer) 258, 303, 309, 312, 322, 331, 333–4
Bollo, Joaquí (director) 160
Bollywood cinema 108
Bond, James 007 (character) 165, 171
Bonezzi, Bernardo (composer) 274
Bonilla, Jesús (actor/director) 295, 343

booth see under screens
Borau, José Luis (director/producer) 2 n. 3, 182 n. 34, 184–5, 189, 194, 200 n. 2, 211–12, 219, 224, 231–2, 263–5, 303, 320, 334
Borcosque, Carlos (director) 51
Borges, Jorge Luis (author) 337
Borgnetto, Luigi (director) 10
Borrachero, Alicia (actor) 335
Bosch, Juan (director) 148, 165, 228
Bosch, Lydia (actor) 307
Bosè, Lucia (actor) 138, 187
Botto, Juan Diego (actor) 247, 313, 333–4, 350
Botto, María (actor) 349
Bouquet, Carole (actor) 231
Bourgeois, Émile (producer/director) 23
Boy George [George Alan O'Dowd] (singer) 344
boxing 146, 166, 184–5, 193, 269, 275, 341
Brahms, Johannes (composer) 53
Brava, Mario (director) 173
Bravo, Estanislao (photographer) 3
Brédice, Leticia (actor) 350
Brenan, Gerald (Hispanist) 330
Bresson, Robert (director) 121
Breton, André (author) 44
Briski, Norman (actor) 244
British Board of Censors see under censorship
British Cinematograph Act see under protectionism
Bronston, Samuel (producer) 172–3
Brooks, Mel (director/producer) 129
Brossa, Joan (poet) 277
Brú, María (actor) 69
Bruno, Sonia (actor) 164
Buchs [Echandía], José (director) 28, 30–8, 47, 52, 56, 59, 66, 71, 83, 84 n. 11, 106, 113, 126, 163, 205
Buchs, Julio (director) 170
buddy films 145–6, 264, 273, 281, 294–5, 301–2, 308–9, 315
budgets see under protectionism
Buero Vallejo, Antonio (playwright) 149, 182, 259
bullfighting see toros
Buñuel, Luis (director) xiv, xvii, 3, 7, 11, 19–20, 24–9, 34, 38, 41–7, 49, 51–3, 55, 58, 60–1, 64, 73–5, 84, 90

n. 21, 96, 110 n. 48, 130, 132, 134 n.
21, 151–2, 155, 172, 180–4, 192–4,
196, 214, 216–17, 223–4, 226, 231,
254, 266, 276, 297, 319–20, 326
Burge, Stuart (TV director)   259 n. 4
Burgos, Carmen de (author)   36
Burgos trials, December 1970   198,
241–2
Burmann, Hans (cinematographer)   258,
341
Burmann, Sigfrido (decorator)   111, 341
Burmann, Wolfgang (decorator)   341
Buscarini, Juan Pablo (animation)   347

Caballinas Gallas, Pío (minister)   199–
200
Cabré, Jaume (author)   301
Cadena, Jordi (director)   247, 276–7, 293
Cahiers du Cinéma see under magazines
Calderón de la Barca, Pedro (playwright)
17, 149, 183, 205, 211, 270, 287, 306,
342
Calle, José (actor)   66
Callejo, María Luz (actor)   35
Calparsoro, Daniel (director)   302,
307–8, 311, 333–4, 339
Calvache, Antonio (director)   37
Calvo, Armando (actor)   94, 96
Calvo, Carmen (minister of culture)   318
Calvo, Juan (actor)   104
Calvo, Pablito (actor)   122, 143
Calvo Sotelo, Álex (director)   332
Camacho, Francisco (director)   34–5, 46
n. 43, 59
Cámara, Javier (actor)   324–5, 348, 350
Cámara Española de Cinematografía 1915
[Spanish Film Council]   36
Camino, Jaime (director)   191, 194, 213,
240–1, 244, 260–1, 301, 328
Campbell, Ramsey (author)   340
Campo, Enrique del (director)   85
Campos, Hugo de (actor)   302
Campos, Susana (actor)   145
Campoy, Eduardo (director)   307
Camus, Mario (director/screenwriter)
163, 173 n. 22, 182, 184, 187, 189,
204–5, 207 n. 16, 211, 227 n. 4, 245,
248, 258–9, 262 n. 10, 265, 290, 292,
301, 319–20
Canada, location   323
Canales, Susana (actor)   113

Canary Islands, locations   3, 170 n. 19,
330, 350–1
Canals, Cuca (screenwriter)   297
Canel, Fausto (director)   247
Cano, Antonio (director)   318–9
Caño 'El Pireo', Manuel (bullfighter)
163
Cantó, Tony (actor)   310
Cantudo, María José (actor)   200 n. 2
Capra, Frank (director)   58, 76, 94
Capucine [Germaine Lefebvre]   192
Caracol, Manolo [Manuel Ortega Juárez]
(singer)   107
Carax, Leos (director)   341 n. 22
Carbonell, Pedro (actor)   348
carceleras [prison songs] *see under* song
Carcinero, Marisol (actor)   274
Cardona, René (director)   144
Carlist wars *see under* war films
Carmen   23–4, 80, 106, 141, 162, 250,
266, 292, 330
Carné, Marcel (director)   71–2, 76
Carnevale, Marcos (director)   350
Carol, Martine (actor)   107, 132 n. 18
Carradine, David (actor)   265, 321
Carranque de Ríos, Andrés (actor/author)
46 n. 43, 57, 107
Carrasco, Agustín (director)   205
Carrasco, Joaquim (actor)   17
Carreño, José María (director/critic)   312
Carreras, José (director)   29
Carreras, Michael (director)   173
Carrero Blanco, Luis (admiral,
government president)   194, 198, 225,
243
Carretero, David (cinematographer)   337
Carrey, Jim (actor)   342
Carrière, Jean Claude (screenwriter)   26,
174, 214, 260
Carrière, Mathieu (actor)   276
Carrillo, Mari (actor)   84, 164
Carroll, Lewis (author)   246
Carruthers, Bob (director)   101 n. .38
Carry On films   165 n. 10
Carter, Chris (director)   339
cartoons *see* animation
Carvajal, Beatriz (actor)   305
Carvajal, Pedro (screenwriter/director)
312
Carvalho, Pepe (fictional detective) *see
under* Vázquez Montalbán, Manuel

Casal, Antonio (actor) 94, 108
Casals, Pablo (musician) 261
Casanova, Vicente (producer) 58, 73, 78, 80, 99, *see also* CIFESA
Casanovas, Àlex (actor) 285, 289, 291, 335
Cases, Guillermo (composer) 141
Casona, Alejandro (playwright) 71
Cassen [Casto Sendra] (actor) 167, 221
Castellví, José María (director) 51, 94
Castile-León/Mancha, locations 38, 40, 59, 134, 138, 180, 325
   Cuenca 150, 183, 226
   Salamanca 187, 263
   Soria 327
   Toledo 89–90, 180, 185–6, 300, 326, 331
Castresana, Luis de (author) 170
Castro, Estrellita (actor) 81, 107
Castro, Luis (actor) 323
Castro, Pilar (actor) 346, 350
Castro, Rosa (screenwriter) 335
Castro, Rosalía de (poet) 33
Catala, Muriel (actor) 213
Catalán, Feliciano (director) 130
Catalan identities 88–9, 95, 121, 169, 190–4, 222, 226, 229, 246, 252, 256, 275–6, 281, 291, 296–8, 301, 330, 338, 345
   cinema 1, 4–13, 15–18, 21–23, 190–4, 212–13, 274–7, 296
   Generalitat 246
   language 88–9, 102, 115, 121, 191, 222, 242, 246, 274–5, 277, 289, 296, 310–11, 338–9, 345
   Tragic Week (July 1909) 5, 17, 246, 301
Catalonia, locations
   Barcelona 4–5, 22, 37, 70, 73, 97, 109, 147–8, 160, 221, 236, 244, 247–8, 262, 265, 267–8, 274, 289, 293, 295–6, 301, 310–11, 324, 326, 334, 344–5, 349
   Costa Brava 96, 180, 191
   Lloret de Mar 169
   Sitges 179
Caton-Jones, Michael (director) 33, 101 n. 38
Cattaneo, Peter (director) 332
CEA [Cinematografica Española Americana] *see* studios

Cebrián, Daniel (director) 337–8, 346
Cebrián, Juan Luis (author) 265
Cebrián, Ramón (actor) 58
Ceccaldi, Daniel (actor) 267
Cela, Camilo José (author) 220, 248
censorship
   examples of cuts 53, 56, 58, 82–7, 103, 106, 109–14, 118, 121–9, 146–51, 158, 170–1, 178–89, 192–4, 203, 210–11, 216–21, 244, 271
   legislation
      Alfonso XIII 19–20, 34–35
      Democracy 64, 157, 226, 240
      Dictatorship 64, 85–9, 98, 119, 154, 157–87, 181–2, 199–200, 206, 224, 226, 326
      Republic 64, 157
   organisations
      British Board of Censors 20
      Comisión de Censura Cinematográfica [Film Censorship Commission] 77
      JSCC 77–8, 98
      JSOC 98, 117, 119, 131, 157
      National Board of Censorship (USA) 20
   outmanoeuvered 133, 217, 171, 182, 224
      allegory/symbolism 137–39, 150, 176, 180–1, 213–7, 221, 325
      historical displacement 84, 93, 96–7, 102–3, 106, 121, 138, 180, 182, 208, 213
      horror 208–9, 212, 224
      humour 133–7, 176–80
      geographical displacement 171, 180, 206, 208, 211–12
      uncensored viewing 158, 200, 204
Cepeda, Laura (actor) 290
Cercas, Javier (author) 160 n. 5
Ceret, Domènec (director) 29
Cernuda, Luis (poet) 65
Cervantes, Miguel de 11, 17, 24, 46 n. 44, 73, 104, 171–2, 174, 183, 252, 269–70, 345, *see also Don Quijote*
Cervera, Mónica (actor) 323
Chabrol, Claude (director) 192
Chaplin, Charles (actor/director/producer) 13, 28–9, 40, 76, 86, 141 n. 36, 158

Chaplin, Geraldine (actor)   183–4, 215–6, 339
Charlot see Chaplin, Charles
Charmatín see under studios
Chávarri, Jaime (director/ screenwriter)   212, 217, 222, 232, 235, 241, 249, 258, 261, 267, 271, 293, 296, 302, 320, 346
Chavarrías, Antonio (producer/director)   276, 289, 291
Chevalier, Maurice (singer/actor)   50
Chico, Florinda (actor)   167, 204, 259 n. 4
child actors   29, 34, 37, 121–2, 143–4, 171, 196, 203 n. 6, 215, 219, 222, 231, 249, 288, 297–8, 323, 328–9, 331–4, 347
children's cinema   158, 162, 210, 250, 256, 260, 300, 347–8, see also animation
Chiquito de la Calzada [Gregorio Sánchez Fernández] (comedian)   305
Chomón y Ruiz, Segundo de (photographer/director)   7–10, 15 n. 22, 18, 25, 30–1, 38
Chopin, Frédéric (composer)   191
chorizo see under westerns
Christie, Madeleine (actor)   232
Chronophone see under sound systems
Chumilla, Juan Manuel (director)   296
church
    Catholic values   18, 40, 49, 64, 83, 85, 87–9, 91, 102–4, 109, 115–17, 120–23, 137, 149, 152–3, 180, 205, 213, 268, 275
    classification of films   64, 131, 133, 152, 163, 300 n. 16
    clergy   57, 59, 66, 95, 102–3, 119–22, 139, 206, 219, 239, 250, 258, 268, 325, see also comedy
    disestablishment movement   157, 198, 226
    hagiographies   103, 119, 121–2, 238–39, 249, 259–60
    nuns   4, 37, 58–9, 121–2, 151–2, 186, 206, 259, 300, see also comedy
    on screen   3–4, 195 n. 45
Ciencias de la Imagen Visual y Auditiva [Visual and Audio Image Studies] see under film schools, CIVA
CIFESA [Compañía Industrial Film

Española, Sociedad Anónima] see under production companies
Ciges, Luis (actor)   167, 269, 342
Cine, El see under magazines
cine cruzada see under war films
cine de arte y ensayo see screens
cine de curas see under church, clergy
cine de levita see under costume drama
Cine Doré see under screens
cine social see under realism
Cineclub Español (Madrid) see under screens
Cineclub Zaragoza see under screens
Cinefotocolor see under colour processing
cinema/screens/theatres see under screens
Cinema Nôvo   191
Cinema Universitario see under magazines
Cinemacoloris see under colour processing
Cinematograph   1
Cinespaña see under newsreels
circus   10, 72, 162, 173, 250, 291, 347
Cirici Pellicer, Alexandre (director)   98
Ciudad Lineal see under studios
CIVA [Ciencias de la Imagen Visual y Auditiva] see under film schools
Civil Guards see under military
civil partnerships   288 n. 8, 343
civil war on screen see under war films
Clair, René (director)   76
Clarín [Leopoldo Alas] (author)   205, 213
Clark, Ken (actor)   173
Classification Board   226
clergy films [cine de curas] see under church
Closas, Alberto (actor)   138, 149, 164, 167, 234
Codina, Joan Maria (director/ cinematographer)   13, 22–3
Codina, Josep Maria (director/ cinematographer)   13, 22–3
Coello, Vicente (screenwriter/ producer)   164, 166
Cofiño, Adolfo (decorator)   169
Coira, Jorge (director)   332
Coixet, Isabel (director/ screenwriter)   308–9, 312, 323–4
Cold War see under war films
Colell, Judith (director)   345

Coliseum, Barcelona *see under* screens
Coll, Julio (screenwriter/director) 148, 171–2
Collado, Adrià (actor) 326
Collinson, Peter (director) 197
Coloma, Luis S.J. (author) 103
Colomé, Antoñita (actor) 57–8
Colomo, Fernando (director/screenwriter/producer) 81–2, 233, 239, 266, 270, 287–8, 298, 303, 305, 330
colour processing 10, 67, 71, 123, 125, 127, 152, 181, 186, 200
   Cinefotocolor 96, 125
   Cinemacoloris 10
Columbus, Christopher *see under* historical films, Catholic Monarchs
Comas, Ramón (director) 159
Comédie Française 23
comedy 5–6, 13, 15, 28–9, 56, 69–70, 93–95, 128–9, 155, 223, 254, 268, 273–4, 280, 287, 291–8, 303–6, 310, 322, 325, 332, 335, 340–6, 350–1
   black humour 146, 178–9, 186, 209, 217, 221, 237, 275, 281, 296, 306, 311–12, 315, 323, 335–6, 342–346, 348
   clergy 125–6, 129, 136, 159, 163, 201–3, 294, 306
   comedias de chicas 145
   comedias rosas 128
   creationist 110–11, 295, 260, 295, 315, 322, 341–3
   crime *see* crime spoofs
   esperpento 146 n. 43, 155, 237–9, 275, 287, 300, 306, 315, 323, 337, 342–3
   Hollywood 28–9, 51–2, 128–9, 156, 272, 343
   Iberian sex comedies 202–4, 214, 217, 297
   landismo 203–4
   Madrid comedies (madrileñas) 229, 232–4
   nuns 59, 63, 125–6, 159, 166, 184, 202, 239, 251, 300
   popular/barrio 124–9, 140–7, 155, 158–69, 177, 196, 200–4, 217, 238, 254, 256, 273, 281, 303, 315, 323
   ridiculous (disparatadas) 287, 295, 305–6, 310–11, 315
   sainetes 28, 30, 34, 60

screwball 296, 304, 343
vulgar/bad taste 307, 315, 342–3
white telephone 93–4
Comencini, Luigi (director) 122
Comerón, Lluís Josep (director) 267–8
Comisión de Censura Cinematográfica [Film Censorship Commission] *see under* censorship
commentator 20, 42
communism 71, 86, 91, 95, 121–4, 152, 155, 179, 300, 308
   PCE 137, 139, 225, 241, 243, 247
Companys, Lluis (politician) 246
concentration camps 81–2, 248–9, 328–9, 249
Conejo, Laura (actor) 331
conferences/talks 36, 54, 57, 130, 139, 193, 227, 256, 341
conscription/recruits *see under* military
conspiracies 171, 211, 247, 259, 265, 291–2, 301, 337, 339–40
consumerism 133, 156, 164–8, 177, 183, 196, 224, 238, 262, 297, 323
Contel, Raúl (screenwriter/director) 276
Contrera Torres, Miguel (director) 56, 201
co-productions 37, 100, 108, 119–20, 126, 132 n. 18, 138, 142, 144, 149, 152, 156, 171–5, 180, 182, 194–5, 204, 206–8, 212, 223, 243, 247, 252–3, 256, 260, 279–80, 305, 312, 314, 323, 342, 347–8
   different versions 119, 126, 146, 175, 197, 200, 267 n. 18
   Latin American *see under* Latin America
   subsidies 157–8, 194, 312
Corbiau, Gérard (director) 301
Corcuera, Javier (director) 327–8
Coronado, José (actor) 266, 326, 333, 337
Cortés, Dolores (actor) 67
Cortés, Eduard (director) 334–5, 337, 339–40
Cortesina, Angélica (actor) 30
Cortesina, Helena (director/actor) 30, 36 n. 20
Cortesina, Ofelia (actor) 30
cortijo *see* folkloric films
Costa, Pedro (director) 264, 290, 338, 340

Costa-Gravas, Constantin (director)   283
Costafreda, Ramón (director)   335
costumbrismo [local colour]   28, 31, 107
costume drama   96–7, 99–102, 106,
    126–8, 139–42, 230, 248–9, 267–9,
    277, 287, 298, 323, 349
Cottençon, Fanny (actor)   267
Courtois, Miguel (director)   223, 340
Coyote, Peter (actor)   285
creationism   7, 9, 15, 110–11, 260, 295,
    315, see also realism
Cremer, Bruno (actor)   267
Crespi, Agustin (TV director)   154
crime   11–13, 19–20, 70, 95–6, 103,
    108–11, 115, 117–18, 127, 129–30,
    147–9, 155, 170–1, 185, 196, 209–13,
    216–17, 226–8, 264–5, 267, 273, 274,
    289, 303
crime spoofs   57, 95, 110–11, 148, 155,
    165–6, 196, 202, 213, 233, 247, 264,
    274, 300, 305, 341–3
Cromwell, John (director)   86
Cronenberg, David (director)   9 n. 17
Crosland, Alan (director)   50
Crowe, Cameron (director)   xv, 321
Cruz, Ángel de la (animation)   347
Cruz, Julio de la (actor)   231
Cruz, Penelope (actor)   xv, 285, 287,
    297, 304–5, 318, 324–5, 341, 345,
    349, 351
Cruz Delgado, Palomo (animation)   176,
    252
Cuadrado, Luis (cinematographer)   189,
    216
Cuadrilla, La [Santiago Aguilar and Luis
    Guridi] (directors)   306
Cuban war see under war films
Cuenca, Luis (actor)   293
Cuerda, José Luis (director)   234, 269,
    295, 301–3, 320, 328, 345
Cuesta, Antonio (director)   11–14
Cukor, George (director)   113
cuplé see under songs
Curtiz, Michael (director)   267
Cushing, Peter (actor)   174
Cussó-Ferrer, Manuel (director)   42, 277,
    302–3
Cuyàs, Narciso (director)   11

Dalí, Salvador (painter)   42–4, 73, 151,
    297, 303, 326

Dalle, Beatriz (actor)   307
Dalton, Timothy (actor)   249
dance   47, 61, 87, 103, 124–26
    ballet   325–6
    flamenco   2, 9, 23–4, 59, 61, 65, 67,
        80, 101, 105–8, 111, 126, 136 n.
        26, 138, 140–1, 159–61, 184, 201,
        250–1, 261, 269, 299, 314, 321,
        326, 346
    jota   33, 65
    sardana   95
    tango   108, 141, 350
    tarantella   141
Dance, Charles (actor)   313
Darmon, Gérard (actor)   297
Darmstaedler, Erich (producer)   62
Dassin, Jules (director)   171
Davenport, Nigel (actor)   213
Decoin, Henry (director)   131–2
Delegación/Departamento Nacional
    de Cinematografía [National Film
    Department] see under government,
    DNC
Delgado [Valverde], Fernando
    (director)   27–30, 34–6, 62, 65, 72,
    78, 84, 93, 107 n. 45, 107, 111 n. 51,
    113
Delgado, J E (cinematographer)   50
Delgado, Jesús (director)   308
Delgado, Luis María (director)   131–2,
    162, 204, 228, 249–50
Delgrás, Gonzalo (director)   34 n. 18, 61,
    84, 95–6, 142, 162, 168
Delibes, Miguel (author)   171, 227 n. 4,
    230, 244, 248, 258–9, 265
Delicado, Francisco (author)   250
delinquents/disaffected   121, 132, 142–3,
    150, 184, 188, 233, 236–7, 264–5,
    278, 288–89, 307–8, 333–4
Demicheli, Tulio (director)   141, 149,
    228, 249
DeMille, Cecil B (director)   23
Demme, Jonathan (director)   290
Deneuve, Catherine (actor)   180–1
'destape' see under sex on screen
detectives/inspectors   108–11, 115,
    129–30, 148, 170–1, 193, 247, 267,
    274, 290–1, 311, 342–4
DGC [Director General de
    Cinematografía] see under government
DGCPE [Dirección/Director General de

Cultura Popular y Espectáculos] *see under* government
Diamante, Julio (director) 188–9, 209
Díaz, Rogelia (DGCPE) 199
Díaz Aroca, Miriam (actor) 287
Díaz Gimeno, Rosita (actor) 58, 72, 86
Díaz Morales, José (director) 103, 163
Díaz Torres, Daniel (director) 350
Díaz Yanes, Agustín (director/screenwriter) 274, 307, 320, 330, 341
Dicenta, Daniel (actor) 230
dictatorship *see* Franco regime
Diego, Gabino (actor) 293–4, 304
Diego, Juan (actor) 259, 292
Dieterle, William (director) 74
Díez, Ana (director) 277, 313
Díez, Miguel Ángel (director) 259
Dilbidos, José Luis (screenwriter/producer) 145, 164, 168, 217–18, 229, 256
Dirección General de Cultura Popular y Espectáculos [Popular Culture and Performance Department] *see under* government, DGCPE
Director General de Cinematografía [Managing Director of Cinema] *see under* government, DGC
dissidents *see under* Francoist values
División Azul [Blue Division] *see under* military
divorce *see under* family
DNC [Delegación/Departamento/Dirección Nacional de Cinematografía] *see under* government
documentaries xvi, 2, 4, 16–17, 30–31, 42, 45, 72–4, 78–9, 82, 86–7, 90, 114, 126, 151, 169–70, 210–11, 222, 230, 236, 240–2, 261, 263, 299, 302–3, 309, 317, 324, 326–8, 348
Dogme 95 336
Dolera, Leticia (actor) 344
Domínguez Rodiño, Enrique (director) 79
Don Juan on screen 17, 56, 104, 149, 260–1, 270
Don Quijote/Quixote on screen 11, 73, 104, 171–2, 174, 252, 269, 291 n. 11
Dorado, Conchita (actor) 35
Doria, Giovanni [Juan] (director) 23
Dos Passos, John (author) 74

Drossner, Charles J. (producer/director) 23–4
Drove, Antonio (director/screenwriter) 200 n. 2, 212, 218, 247, 262 n. 10, 264, 301
drugs 109, 129, 171, 206, 221, 236–8, 251–2, 264, 270, 272, 274, 278, 288–9, 291, 307–8, 333, 335, 337, 344
Duato, Ana (actor) 319
dubbing companies
  Acustic 58
  Fono España 58
  MGM 58
  Trilla-La Riva 58
  Warner 60
dubbing from Catalan 238, 246, 275, 338
dubbing to Spanish 51–2, 54, 86, 88–9, 91, 98, 119, 123, 147, 158, 218, 275, 291
Dueñas, Lola (actor) 325
Dunn, Michael (actor) 213
Dunning, George (director) 176
Dúo Dinámico [Ramón Arcusa and Manuel de la Calva] (singers) 108, 161, 163, 201 n. 3
Durán, Biel (actor) 297, 335
Durán, Carlos (director) 193
Durán, Rafael (actor) 84, 94–6, 103, 111
Dúrcal, Rocío [María de los Ángeles de las Heras Ortiz] (actor/singer) 161 n. 6, 188, 207 n. 16, 218
Duverger, Albert (cinematographer) 38
DVDs/videos 253, 255, 272, 318–19, 328

Eburu, Andoni (actor) 329
Eceiza, Antxon (director) 188–9, 209, 247, 300
ECESA [Estudios Cinema Español, Sociedad Anónima] *see under* production companies
Echanove, Juan (actor) 292, 294, 300, 319
Echegaray, José (playwright) 6
Eckland, Britt (actor) 273
Edison, Thomas (inventor) 1
editing *see* montage
education 3–4, 6, 35–6, 53, 71–2, 77, 98–9, 221, 231, 233, 245, 312, 317, 325, 327

film   xiii–xvii, 20, 64, 99, 266–7
misiones pedagógicas   72
Egido, José Ángel (actor)   332
Eguiluz, Enrique (director)   174–5, 207
Eisenstein, Sergei (director)   76
Elejalde, Karra (actor/director)   340, 342
Elías, Francisco (director)   29, 30 n. 7,
    47, 51, 53, 56–7, 65, 72, 75, 94
Elordi, Juanjo (animation)   347
Elorrieta, Javier (director)   290
Elorrieta, José María (director)   122, 142
Elstree Studios see under studios
Elviro, Pedro see Pitouto
Enright, Ray (director)   121
Enríquez, Roberto (actor)   337
EOC [Escuela Oficial de Cine] see film
    schools
Epstein, Jean (director)   41
Erice, Victor (director)   64, 82, 177 n.
    29, 221–2, 224, 235, 258, 302, 309,
    319
Ernst, Max (painter)   45 n. 40
Escamilla, Teo (cinematographer)   189,
    216, 260, 266
Escapism see under spectatorship
Escobar, Luis (director)   109, 238
Escobar, Manolo (singer/actor)   159–60,
    201, 249
Escribano, Cuca (actor)   333
Escrivá, Vicente (screenwriter/director)
    104, 121, 171, 201, 204, 228, 239
Escudero, Vicente (dancer)   184
Escuela Oficial de Cine [Official Film
    School] see under film schools, EOC
espagnolades/españoladas see folkloric
    films
Espantaleón, Juan (actor)   66, 104
Espanya al dia see under newsreels
esperpento see under comedy
Espert, Núria (actor)   169, 284, 287
Espina, Concha (author)   36, 62, 96, 149
Esquerra, Núria (editor)   327
Esteban, Cristina (director)   73 n. 31
Esteban, Manuel (director)   291, 295
Esterlich, Juan (director)   178, 238
Esteva Crewe, Jacinto (director)   193
Esteve, María (actor)   346, 350
Estívalis, José María, aka Guerra, Armand
    (director)   72
Estrada, Carlos (actor)   192

ETA [Euskadi ta Askatasuna] see under
    Basque Country and terrorism
Etura, Marta (actor)   335
European film legislation   283, 349
European funding   281, 283–4, 291, 295,
    313, 342, 349
Euskadi ta Askatasuna [Basque Land and
    Liberty] see under Basque Country
    and terrorism
exiles   18, 58, 72, 81, 86, 96, 122, 124,
    127, 129, 187, 209, 219, 243, 263,
    271, 273, 277, 292, 300, 326–8, 349
experimental cinema   30, 40–5, 47,
    60, 112–13, 151, 181, 189–94, 196,
    211–12, 232, 251, 256–7, 266–7,
    275–7, 302–3
explicador/picotero see commentator
exports (films) see under production facts
Extremadura, location   258

Fs, three see under Francoist values
Faidella, Juan (director)   70
Fairbanks Jr, Douglas (actor)   86
Falla, Manuel de (composer)   250
Faltoyano, Fiorella (actress)   229
family   14, 39–40, 45, 51 n. 2, 66 n. 24,
    69, 87–8, 111, 115–16, 118, 145, 155,
    167–9, 178, 186, 196, 201, 210–12,
    215, 224, 226, 231–2, 236–7, 241,
    264–5, 267–9, 277, 288, 290, 293,
    295–7, 301, 305, 309, 311, 323, 329,
    331–2, 334–6, 338–40, 342, 345, 350
    alternate   11–14, 142, 145, 150, 161,
        237, 288–9, 294, 306–8, 331–3
    conflict   105, 112, 124–5, 127, 138,
        155, 164, 210, 214–15, 222, 234–7,
        234–5
    divorce   35, 49, 61, 70, 96, 109, 187,
        204, 210, 218, 226, 229–30, 233,
        240, 250, 286, 293, 296–7, 308,
        325, 343, 345
    father-daughter   61, 142, 168, 218,
        231, 258, 268, 275, 321, 337–8
    father-son   15, 148, 236, 264, 289,
        294, 299, 307, 321, 335, 344, 347
    incest   52, 212, 232, 243, 334–5
    mother-daughter   13–15, 216, 221–2,
        230–1, 247, 285, 309, 324–5, 331,
        334–5, 344
    mother-son   34, 179, 203 n. 8, 214,

231, 272, 288, 293, 308, 333, 338, 343
mothers 34, 40, 51, 58, 61, 88, 95, 105, 118, 274, 288, 324, 335, 339
patriarchal 87–8, 105–6, 118, 138, 164, 180–1, 184, 186, 196, 226, 231–5, 249, 263–4, 271–2, 342
single parent 34, 61, 105, 203, 231, 240, 308, 333, 335, 343
violence 213, 290, 315, 317, 331, 334–5, 338
Farrow, John (director) 172
Farrucini Cinema see screens
Fatmi, Farid (actor) 333
Féjerman, Daniela (director) 344
Feliu, Jordi (director) 246
Félix, María (actor) 109
Fellini, Federico (director) 150, 160, 350
Ferdinand of Aragon see under historical films, Catholic Monarchs
Fernán Caballero [Cecilia Böhl de Faber] (author) 149
Fernán Gómez, Fernando (actor/director/ screenwriter) 62 n. 20, 69, 94, 101, 103, 108, 111–12, 120, 123, 126, 133, 145, 149, 154, 158, 171, 176–9, 213, 215, 219, 222, 230–1, 237–8, 246, 250, 252, 257, 259, 261–3, 268, 295–6, 302, 320, 335, 339
Fernández, Ana (actor) 331
Fernández, Arturo (actor) 164–5, 201, 218, 273
Fernández, Eduard (actor) 339, 343
Fernández, Nani (actor) 92, 112
Fernández, Ramón (director) 142, 154, 159, 170, 203–5, 228, 235, 240
Fernández Ardavín, César (director) 123, 128–9, 149, 171, 249
Fernández Ardavín, Eusebio (director) 31, 35, 57, 62–3, 84, 92, 97, 99–100, 108, 126
Fernández Armero, Álvaro (director) 305, 319, 338
Fernández Cuenca, Carlos (director/ screenwriter) 46 n. 43, 69, 108
Fernández Flórez, Wenceslao (author) 105, 188
Fernández Santos, Ángel (author) 300
Fernández Santos, Jesús (author/ director) 169, 258
Ferrandis, Antonio (actor) 220, 252, 258

Ferreira, Patricia (director) 327, 335–7, 340
Ferrer, Mel (director) 161
Ferreri, Marco (director) 142, 146, 150, 154, 194, 200, 237, 320
Fesser, Javier (director) 176, 327, 342
festivals, films xiv–xv, 119, 153–4, 181, 184 n. 37, 214, 271–3, 280, 313–14, 319, 325, 351
Amsterdam 252
Angers 307
Barcelona Butaca 314
Berlin 149, 180, 236, 252
Biarritz 314
Cannes 112, 133–4, 137, 150–1, 180, 186, 248, 250, 252, 258
FIPRESCI 150
Gramado 313–14
Huelva 313
Lima 314
Lisbon 252
Lleida 314
London Spanish Film 351
Los Angeles 314
Malaga 314
Manchester ¡Viva! Spanish Film 351
Miami 314
Montreal 251–2
Moscow 250
Nantes 314
San Sebastián 119, 221, 263
Sitges 175, 193
Valencia 252
Valladolid 119, 153 n. 49
Venice 56, 83–4, 90, 179, 188
Feuillade, Louis (director) 22, 36
Feyder, Jacques (director) 24
film clubs see under screens
Film España see under newsreels
film history (Spain) xvi–xvii, 2 n. 4, 7 n. 14, 18, 25–7, 46–7, 112–13, 130, 139, 302–3 n. 19, 319
Film Ideal see under magazines
film organisations
   AACC 257
   ICAA 256–7, 283, 318
   ICC 242
film schools
   CIVA 194, 199, 284
   EOC 158, 171, 181, 185, 191, 194,

201, 211–12, 217–18, 221–2, 230, 243
IIEC   98, 130, 132–4, 137, 139, 149, 158, 174, 182, 184, 188–9
film-within-film *see* metacinema
Filmoteca Española   xiv, 2, 13, 24, 26–7, 37, 47, 63, 75, 283–4
Filmoteca Nacional   xiv, 119, 158, 199
Finch, John (actor)   247
Flaherty, Robert (director)   41
flamenco *see under* dance
fleapit cinemas *see under* screens, barrio *and* comedy, popular
Fleming, Victor (director)   91
Flores, Gabriela (actor)   335
Flores, Lola (singer/actor)   69, 107, 125–7, 140, 331
Flores, Lolita (singer)   331, 345
Flores González, Josefa, aka Marisol (singer/actor)   160–3, 184–5, 195, 213, 218–19, 245
Florey, Robert (director)   52
Flotats, José María (actor)   219
Foix i Mas, Josep Vicenç (poet)   277
folclóricas *see* folkloric films
Folk, Abel (actor)   298
folkloric films   6, 23, 36, 47, 56–7, 59, 65–6, 69, 75, 81, 83, 87, 105–8, 114–15, 124–27, 139, 140–1, 154–5, 250, 299
   cortijo   65–6, 127, 244
   historical   101, 106–7, 125
   señorito   66, 244
Fono España *see under* dubbing
Fons, Angelino (director/screenwriter)   84 n. 11, 162, 172, 182, 188–9, 209–10, 224, 248, 264
Font, Josep Lluis (director)   191
Fontseré, Ramón (actor)   329
football films   29, 60, 128, 136 n. 26, 146, 166, 221, 306, 310, 332, 346 n. 28
Ford, John (director)   302
Forn, Josep Maria (director)   145, 169, 191, 246
Forqué, José María (director)   123–4, 127–8, 144–5, 148–9, 162, 166, 170, 219, 247, 285, 304, 320, 341
Forqué, Verónica (actor)   233, 240, 269–70, 273, 343
Forsyth, Bill (director)   135 n. 25

Fortuny, Juan (director)   92, 142
Fosco, Piero *see* Pastrone, Giovanni
Fotogramas see under magazines
Fox Movietone camera   50
Foy, Brian (director)   50
Frade, José (producer)   256
Fraga Iribarne, Manuel (minister)   157, 194
Fraile, Alfredo (cinematographer)   78
France, Anatole (author)   205 n. 14
Francis, Eve (actor)   36
Francis, Mari (actor)   164
Franco, Jesús (director/producer/screenwriter/composer/actor)   167–8, 170–2, 174, 178, 207–8, 212, 220, 222, 228, 272, 338
Franco, Ricardo (director/screenwriter)   220, 229–30, 241, 248, 264, 266–7, 295, 302, 319–20, 336, 338
Franco Bahamonde, Francisco (Generalísimo)   35, 90, 170, 177, 210, 222, 225, 239, 241–2, 250, 261–2, 269, 291 n. 11, 300
Franco regime
   dissidents/opposition   82, 132–40, 146, 150–2, 154–5, 176, 181–94, 207–18, 256
   Fs, three   77, 87–89, 103, 116, 119, 132, 144, 215, 288, 325
   legislation, marriage   226
   opening out
      cinematographically/'destape' *see* sex
      politically/'apertura'   157, 198, 200, 216–17, 223
   reconciliation   82, 89, 87, 112, 123–4, 169, 182, 225, 263, 324, 329
   values   xiv, 49–50, 77, 80–1, 85, 87–93, 101–5, 112, 115, 117, 122–24, 140, 144, 146, 155, 157, 161, 164, 180, 201–2, 205, 220, 222, 226, 305, 307
Frank, Christopher (author)   266
Free Cinema   191
Fresnadillo, Juan Carlos (director)   337
Fresno, Maruchi (actor)   100
Fry, Stephen (actor)   342
Fuentes, Carlos (actor)   289, 307
Fuentes, Mariola (actor)   232 n. 11
funding for films *see* protectionism

Gabriel, Enrique (director) 305
Gabriel, Ruth (actor) 300
Gaceta Literaria, La see under
magazines
Gadé, Analía (actor) 145, 177, 179
Gades, Antonio (dancer) 160, 184, 245,
250–1
GAL [Grupos Antiterroristas de
Liberación] 255, 282, 292, 340, *see
also* terrorism
Galán, Pablo (actor) 332
Galdós *see* Pérez Galdós, Benito
Galera, Elia (actor) 337
Galiana, Manuel (actor) 231
Galiana, María (actor) 319, 331
Galiardo, José Luis (actor) 269 n. 21,
294
Galicia
cinema 3, 73, 86, 96, 279, 332
identities 32–3, 73, 88–9, 96, 226,
234, 256, 279, 281, 312
language 88–9, 279
locations 32–3, 66, 73, 84, 96, 108,
218, 269, 312, 323, 328, 332, 336,
338
Corunna 3
Santiago de Compostela 32–3,
331
Vigo 337
Galvé, Elisa (actor) 137–8
gambling 148, 305, 322, 337
Gamboa, Jaime (actor) 219
Gance, Abel (director) 10, 110 n. 48
Ganga, José Miguel (director) 287
Garay, Jesús (director) 276
Garbo, Greta (actor) 17
Garcés, Isabel (actor) 161, 167
Garci, José Luis (director/screenwriter)
xiv, 122, 204, 229, 243, 247, 256, 300,
319, 330
García, Gerardo (director) 235
García, Luis Alberto (actor) 305
García, Sara (actor) 166
García, Saturnino (actor) 306, 319
García Abril, Antón (composer) 169,
207 n. 16, 265
García Berlanga, Luis *see* Berlanga, Luis
G[arcía]
García Cardona, Àngel (director) 3,
11–14
Garcia Cardona, Àngel (director) 13, 29

García de Leániz, Santiago (producer) *see*
La Iguana
García del Val, Ángel (director) 241
García Escudero, José María (DNC
director) 117–18, 139–40, 155,
157–8, 181–2, 189, 194–5, 199, 206,
209, 227
García Galisteo, María del Carmen *see*
Carmen Sevilla
García León, Victor (director) 335
García López, Ricardo, aka K-Hito
(animation) 63
García Lorca, Federico (author) 18,
42–3, 78, 136 n. 26, 230, 236, 250,
259, 261, 326
García Maroto, Eduardo (director) 59–
60, 78, 83, 111 n. 51, 114, 129, 172
García Márquez, Gabriel (author) 322
n. 5
García Morales, Adelaida (author) 258
García Pelayo, Gonzalo (director) 242
García Pinal, Alfredo (screenwriter/
director) 279
García Ruiz, Salvador (director) 333,
335
García Sánchez, José Luis (director) 97
n. 31, 149, 220–1, 234, 238, 241, 259,
268, 271, 292–4, 301, 313, 320, 327,
349
García Segura, Gregorio (composer)
265
García Serrano, Rafael (author/
screenwriter/director) 170
García Serrano, Yolanda (screenwriter/
director) 304–5, 344
García Vega, Fernando (director) 160
García Viñolas, Manuel Augusto (director/
propaganda office) 77–8, 85–7, 100,
102
Gardel, Carlos (singer/actor) 52, 86
Gardela, Isabel (director) 344–5
Gargallo, Francisco (director) 58
Gärtner, Heinrich *see* Guerner, Enrique
Gas, Mario (actor) 274
Gasnier, Louis (director) 52
Gaspar i Serra, Josep
(cinematographer) 5, 29, 35
Gassman, Vitorio (actor) 301
Gaultier, Jean Paul (costumes) 285
Gay, Cesc (director) 334, 348

Gelabert i Badiella, Fructuós
    (photographer)   4–7, 10, 13, 15–6, 18,
    25, 30, 83 n. 9, 89–90
gender relationships *see* masculinities *and*
    women
General Agreement on Tariffs and Trade
    see under protectionism, GATT
Generation of '27   41
Generation of '98   4, 35
Genina, Augusto (director)   89–90
genres, blurring/hybridity   93, 108,
    115, 125, 129–31, 137, 192, 229–30,
    247, 251, 266–7, 273, 275, 281, 303,
    306–7, 311, 315, 320–1, 337–8, 342–3,
    345–7
Gibson, Katrina (actor)   313
Gibson, Mel (director)   101–2
Gijón, Salvador (animation)   176
Gil, Ariadna (actor)   285–8, 293, 307,
    329, 348, 350
Gil, Carlos (director)   338
Gil, Mateo (screenwriter/director)   xv,
    321–2, 339
Gil, Miguelito (actor)   121, 144
Gil, Rafael (director)   30 n. 4, 32 n. 9,
    69, 74, 94, 96–7, 100, 103–5, 107–9,
    114, 118, 120–3, 132, 142, 154, 160,
    163–4, 166, 201–2, 205–6, 221, 234,
    239, 250
Gil, Telesforo (director)   34
Gil, Xavier (cinematographer)   277
Gilliam, Terry (animation/screenwriter/
    director/actor)   137, 172 n. 20
Giménez Caballero, Ernesto   37, 40–2,
    44–5, 53 n. 8
Giménez Rico, Antonio (director)   49, 66
    n. 24, 131 n. 16, 210, 242, 244, 247,
    258–9, 262, 268, 291–2, 299
Gimpera, Teresa (actor)   164, 192, 234
Glen, John (director)   301
Godard, Jean-Luc (director)   184 n. 37,
    193
Godoy, Agustín (actor)   57
Goethe, Johann Wolfgang von   258
Goldberger, Guillermo/Willy
    (cinematographer)   62
Goldberger, Isodoro/Issy
    (cinematographer)   96
Goldblum, Jeff (actor)   266
Gómez, Carmelo (actor)   292, 330, 336,
    340

Gómez, Enrique (director)   107, 129, 149
Gómez, Félix (actor)   332
Gómez, José Luis (actor)   232, 248
Gómez 'Gallito', José (bullfighter)   30
Gómez, José María (actor)   321
Gómez, Manolo (animation)   347
Gómez, Paloma (actor)   249
Gómez Bur, Manolo (actor)   146, 165,
    167–8
Gómez de la Serna, Ramón (author)   19,
    41–3, 46 n. 43, 50, 54
Gómez Hidalgo, Francisco (director)   35
Gómez Pereira, Manuel (director/
    screenwriter/producer)   288 n. 8,
    303–5, 312, 319, 343–4
Góngora y Argote, Luis de (poet)   41
González, Cesáreo (producer)   68, 84
González, Felipe (government
    president)   255, 286, 294–5, 297, 299
González Katarain, María Dolores *see*
    Yoyes
Gónzalez Perojo, Benito *see* Perojo Benito
González Sinde, Miguel (editor)   330
Gonzalo, Antonio (director)   247, 268
Gonzalo, Eloy (soldier)   37
Goode, Matthew (actor)   330
Gordon, Rafael (director)   240
Gormezano, Gerardo (director)   277
government and cinema *see also*
    censorship
    DGC   227, 255–6
    DGCPE   194, 199
    DNC   77, 85, 98, 117
    MIT   116–7, 152, 157, 179, 199
    Press and Propaganda Office   77,
        86–7, 262
Goya, Francisco de (painter)   106, 182,
    220, 297–8, 326
Goyanes, Manuel J. (producer)   161
Goyas *see under* awards
Goytisolo, José Agustín (author)   217
Gràcia, Paco (director/comedian)   311
Gracia, Sancho (actor)   323
Graciani, Antonio (director)   70
Gran Wyoming [José Miguel Monzón]
    (actor)   295, 323, 326
Granados, Daisy (actor)   332, 350
Granados, Enrique (composer)   106
Grandes, Almudeña (author)   288
Grandinetti, Darío (actor)   322, 351
Grant, Hugh (actor)   260

Grau, Jordi (director)   100, 190–1, 200 n.
    2, 211, 224, 226
Grémillon, Jean (director)   57, 61, 70
Grieco, Sergio (director) 162, 189 n. 41
Griffith D. W. (director)   22
Griffith, Melanie (actor)   296
Grupos Antiterroristas de Liberación
    [Anti-Terrorist Liberation Squads] *see*
    under GAL
Gual, Adrià (playwright/director)   7,
    17–18, 29, 84, 121
Gual, Roger (director)   339
Gubern (critic/screenwriter/director)   192
Güell, Xavier (director)   64
Guerín, José Luis (director)   273, 302,
    326–7
Guerín Hill, Claudio (director)   208
Guerner, Enrique (cinematographer)   62–
    3
Guerra, Armand *see* Estívalis, José María
Guerra, Señora M. (actor)   15
Guerrero, María (actor)   84
Guevara, Enrique (director)   228
Guibourt, Edmundo (director)   18
Guillén, Fernando (actor)   260, 273, 300,
    312
Guillén Cuervo, Cayetana (actor)   306,
    345
Guillén Cuervo, Fernando (actor/
    screenwriter/director)   300, 335, 338,
    344, 346
Guimerà, Àngel (playwright)   6, 121, 169
Guridi, Luis *see* La Cuadrilla
Gurruchaga, Javier (actor)   294, 350
Gutiérrez, Chus (director)   251, 309, 312,
    327, 330–1, 333, 345–6
Gutiérrez, Lydia (actor)   34
Gutiérrez, Ricardo (director)   78, 108
Gutiérrez Alea, Tomás (director)   127,
    313
Gutiérrez Aragón, Manuel (director/
    screenwriter)   81–2, 182, 212, 221,
    237, 243, 245, 262, 268–70, 293, 320,
    332, 350
Gutiérrez Caba, Emilio (actor)   187
Gutiérrez Caba, Irene (actor)   259 n. 4
Gutiérrez Caba, Julia (actor)   165
Gutiérrez Maesso, José (director)   149–
    50
Gutiérrez Santos, José María (director)
    240, 245

Guzmán, Daniel (actor)   307, 348
Gúzman Merino, Antonio (director)   105
Gwenn, Edmund (actor)   135
gypsies   17, 24, 62, 65, 69, 84, 93, 101,
    105–8, 124–7, 140–1, 160, 184, 224,
    250–1, 264–5, 269, 281, 299, 309,
    342, *see also* race/ethnicity

Habay, Andrea (actor)   23
Halévy, Ludovic (composer) *see Carmen*
Harlan, Richard (director)   66
Hathaway, Henry (director)   173
Hawks, Howard (director)   343
Hayworth, Rita (actor)   300 n. 16
Headley, Lena (actor)   345
Hebrew heritage   21, 110–11, 237, 282,
    302, 326
Hemingway, Ernest (author)   74
Hendler, Daniel (actor)   344
Henestrosa, Andrés (author)   260
Henshall, David (actor)   345
Herbier, Marcel L' (director)   36, 110
    n. 48
Hermoso, Miguel (director)   273, 293
Hernán, Josita (actor)   84, 94
Hernández, Antonio (director)   183 n. 36,
    339, 341 n. 22
Hernández, Broselandia (actor)   337
Herralde, Gonzalo (director)   232, 241–2,
    275–6, 301
Herrera, Lola (actor)   230, 234
Herrero, Gerardo (producer/director)
    288, 302, 313, 332, 335, 340,
Herzog, Werner (director)   259
HFP [Hispano-Film-Produktion] *see under*
    production companies
Hill, George (director)   51
Hipólito, Carlos (actor)   306
Hispanoamerican Film Conference,
    October 1931   54, 57, 313
historical films   15–17, 23–4, 52, 54, 56,
    90–91, 99–102, 117, 133 n. 20
    Catholic Monarchs [Isabel and
       Fernando]   79, 101, 104, 117, 171,
       173, 282, 301–2, 330
    Civil War *see under* war films *and*
       memory: recovery
    eighteenth century   106, 220, 259,
       298
    historical displacement *see under*
       censorship

Middle Ages 15–17, 100–1, 238–9, 247–8, 252, 266, 277–8, 294, 300–2, 330, 347
Napoleonic 10, 99–101, 182, 205, 342
Post-War Years 219–22, 246, 258, 262–3, 271
sixteenth/seventeenth century 17, 73, 100–1, 120–2, 171–2, 186, 205, 239, 247, 259–61, 278, 294, 301, 330, 339
Transition 225, 232, 239–40, 244, 248–9, 255–6, 259, 269, 340
apathy/'pasotismo' 232–3, 240–242, 247
Hitchcock, Alfred (director) 40, 42 n. 33, 55, 67, 111, 113, 181, 183, 212, 323
Hogan, James P. (director) 74
Hollywood
competition xv, 22, 25–26, 28, 36, 51–2, 58, 74–7, 109, 147, 199, 256, 313, 318, 348
influence 29, 51, 59, 62, 102, 109, 111, 113, 128–9, 137, 148, 155, 161, 168, 170, 229, 246–7, 272, 290, 304, 330, see also under comedies
Homar, Lluís (actor) 322, 343
homosexuality 92, 163, 203, 210, 226, 232, 235–6, 251, 254, 267, 271–2, 276–7, 288, 296, 304–5, 309–10, 317, 324–5, 336, 343–5
Hopper, Denis (actor) 247
Hortelano, Antonio (actor) 293
horror/terror 157–8, 171, 174–5, 181, 195–7, 207–9, 211–12, 215, 218, 220, 224, 228, 251, 266–7, 276, 290, 305–6, 329, 340, 351
horrotica 196, 200, 207–8, 228
hospital/sanatorium 262, 274, 324–5, 329, 331–2, 339, 341–2
housing problems 117–18, 133, 146–7, 156, 179, 287
Huerga, Manuel (director) 307, 329, 346
Huerta, Ángel (cinematographer) 11
hunting 182, 237–8
Hurley, Elizabeth (actor) 260
Hurtado, Alfredo see Pitusín
Hussey, Olivia (actor) 206
hybrid genre see under genres

Ibáñez, Francisco (comics' author) 176, 342
Ibáñez, Paco (singer) 217
Ibáñez Serrador, Narciso 'Chicho' (director) 175, 208–9
Ibar, José Manuel 'Urtain' (boxer) 185
Ibarra, Marta (actor) 350
Ibarretxe, Esteban (director) 342
Ibárruri 'La Pasionaria', Dolores (politician) 241
Iborra, Juan Luis (screenwriter/director) 304–5, 344
Iborra, Manuel (director) 273, 286 n. 5, 299
ICAA [Instituto de la Cinematografía y de las Artes Audiovisuales] see under film organisations
Icaza, Carmen de (author) 96
ICC [Institut del Cinema Català] see under film organisations
Iglesia, Alex de la (director) 135 n. 22, 306, 312, 315, 319, 323
Iglesia, Eloy de la (screenwriter/director) 220, 235–6, 264, 267, 280, 288, 344
Iglesias, Alberto (composer) 324
Iglesias, Carlos (actor/director) 217 n. 30, 269 n. 21, 329
Iglesias, Julio (singer) 297
IIEC [Instituto de Investigaciones y Experiencias Cinematográficas] see film schools
Illén, Enrique (actor) 346
illiteracy see education
IM [de interés militar / of Military Significance] 85
IN [de interés nacional / of National Significance] 85
Inciarte, Juan (actor) 342
Ingram, Rex (director) 17
Institut del Cinema Català [Catalan Film Institute] see under film organisations, ICC
Instituto de Investigaciones y Experiencias Cinematográficas [Cinema Research and Experiments Institute] see film schools, IIEC
Instituto de la Cinematografía y de las Artes Audiovisuales [Institute for Film and Audiovisual Arts] see under film organisations, ICAA

Instituto de la Mujer [Institute for
    Women's Affair]   255
Insua, Miguel (actor)   279
interés militar, de *see* IM
interés nacional, de *see* IN
International Brigades *see under* military
intertitles   6–7, 10, 13–17, 20–2, 24, 29,
    32–3, 38–40, 43–4, 54–55, 118, 249,
    271
Iquino, Ignacio F[errés] (director/
    producer)   59 n. 15, 70–1, 93, 95–6,
    100, 109, 114–15, 118 n. 3, 121, 124,
    128–30, 145, 148–9, 154, 173, 184,
    190, 206, 228, 274
Iranzo, Antonio (actor)   169
Irving, Washington (author)   105, 347
Isabel of Castile *see under* historical
    films, Catholic Monarchs
Isasi-Isasmendi, Antonio (director)   71,
    123–4, 171, 174 n. 24, 206, 247
Isbert, José (actor)   93, 134, 145–6,
    166–7
Isbert, María (actor)   167
Italian Cinema Week, 1951 and 1953   130
Ivens, Joris (director)   74
Izquierdo, Ángel (animation)   348

Jackson, Glenda (actor)   259 n. 4
Jaeckin, Just (director)   226 n. 2
Jaén, Antonio de (director)   160
Jaiteh, Bakalilu (actor)   289
James, Henry (author)   267, 277
Jara, José (director)   205
Jarju, Mulie (actor)   290
Jiménez, Lucía (actor)   346
Jiménez Fernández, José *see* Joselito
Jimeno Correas, Eduardo (photographer)
    2–3
Joffé, Roland (director)   103
Joinville Studios *see under* studios
Jones, Doug (actor)   329
Jordà, Joaquim (screenwriter/director)
    193
Jordi, Elena (director)   30 n. 4
Joselito [José Jiménez Fernández] (singer/
    actor)   143–4, 160
jota *see under* dance
Jovè, Angel (actor)   229
JSCC [Junta Superior de Censura
    Cinematográfica] *see under* censorship,
    organisations

JSOC [Junta Superior de Orientación
    Cinematográfica] *see under* censorship,
    organisations
Juan Carlos I   198, 210, 225, 243
Judaism *see* Hebrew heritage
Junta Superior de Censura
    Cinematográfica [Supreme Board of
    Film Censorship] *see under* censorship,
    organisations, JSCC
Junta Superior de Orientación
    Cinematográfica [Supreme Board for
    Film Guidance] *see under* censorship,
    organisations, JSOC
Jurado, Rocío [María del Rocío
    Mohedano] (actor/singer)   160, 213,
    299
Juran, Nathan (director)   174 n. 24

Karina [María Isabel Llaudés Santiago]
    (singer/actor)   201
Karmen, Roman (director)   74
Karyo, Théky (actor)   337
Kasagawa, Futoshi (actor)   301
Keaton, Buster (actor/director)   28
Keitel, Harvey (actor)   266
Ketama (band)   346
Keystone comedy   13, *see also* Sennett,
    Mack
K-Hito *see* García López, Ricardo
Kidman, Nicole (actor)   321
Kinetoscope   1
Kinski, Klaus (actor)   207, 266
Klimovsky, León (director)   124–5, 145,
    156, 163, 206–7, 213, 248
Koshi, Shigeo (animation)   252
Koster, Henry (director)   127
Kramer, Stanley (director)   172
Kubrick, Stanley (director)   200
Kurokawak Fumio (animation)   252

Laboratories   25, 34 n. 16, 63, 71, 78
    Riera   98
Ladoire, Óscar (actor/director)   233–4
Ladrón de Guevara, María Fernanda
    (actor)   94 n. 24
Laforet, Carmen (author)   111
Lago, Claro (actor)   330
Laguna, Mónica (director)   309–10, 337
Lajarrige, Bernard (actor)   137
Lajos, Julia (actor)   69, 94 n. 25
Lamarque, Libertad (singer/actor)   144

Lamet, Juan Miguel (ICAA director)
283
Lamor, Maria (actor) 266
Lampreave, Chus (actor) 325
Landa, Alfredo (actor) 165–6, 168,
172, 185, 203–5, 229, 234, 239, 243,
247, 258, 263, 269, 297, 302, *see also*
comedy, landismo
Lang, Fritz (director) 41
Lapeyra, Mariano (director) 70
Lara, Antonio de (director) 128
Lara, Fernando (ICAA director) 318
Lara Polop, Francisco (director) 208,
265
Larralde, Marta (actor) 334, 337
Larraz, José Ramón (director) 208, 228
Larrañaga, Carlos (actor) 179, 341
Larrañaga, Pedro (actor) 35, 38, 40
Larruquert, Fernando (director) 170
Latin America
collaborations 29, 32 n. 9, 36, 51, 54,
57, 71, 126, 151–2, 312–14, 350
locations
Argentina 18, 179, 271, 322, 350
Brazil 161, 313
Colombia 277, 313
Cuba 301, 312–13, 350–1
Mexico 35, 126, 138, 204, 260,
306–7, 313, 323
Peru 350
Puerto Rico 313
Lauaxeta, Esteban (poet) 262
Laurel, Stan (director/actor) 17
Laurence, L. L. (producer) 45
Laydu, Claude (actor) 121
Lazaga, Pedro (director/screenwriter)
104, 107, 109, 114, 123, 127, 145–6,
153–4, 156, 160, 162, 164–70, 172,
196, 201–4, 207 n. 16, 229 n. 7,
238–9
Lazarillo de Tormes 11, 13, 29, 149
Lázaro, Eusebio (actor) 345
Lazkano, Arantxa (director) 311–12
Lean, David (director) 157 n. 3, 183
Leblanc, Tony (actor) 146, 165, 167–8,
202
Lecchi, Alberto (director) 350
Lee, Christopher (actor) 174, 194, 207
Lee, Laurie (author) 63–4
legion/ary *see under* military
legislation for cinema 19–20, 36, 54,

64, 77, 85–9, 98, 119, 318, *see also*
Europe
Leitão de Barros, José (director) 100
Lejárraga y García, María (playwright)
51 n. 4
Lemoine, Camille (director) 56
Lemos, Lola (actor) 350
León, Loles (actor) 286, 304–5
León, Paco (actor) 346
León de Aranoa, Fernando (director/
screenwriter) 294, 305, 312, 327, 332
Leone, Sergio (director) 173
Leonís, Charito (actor) 67
Lesmes, Eva (director) 166, 310, 341
Lester, Richard (director) 193, 212
Lezana, Sara (actor) 160
Lhafi, Naoufal (actor) 333
Ligero, Miguel (actor) 52, 57, 59, 67–9,
81, 93, 105, 108, 163
Lindo, Elvira (author) 347
Liotti, Daniele (actor) 17 n. 26
literary adaptations 6, 11, 15–18, 46,
104–5, 115, 138, 148–9, 171–2, 188,
196, 205, 224, 238, 248–9, 253–4,
256–9, 280
Lizarán, Anna (actor) 287
Lladó, Juan (director) 128–9
Llarch, Lluís (composer) 346
Llobet Gràcia, Lorenzo (director) 3, 109
n. 47, 112–14, 118 n. 3, 252, 320
Llorca, Pablo (director) 337
Lloyd, Harold (actor) 28
Lluch, Miguel (director) 108, 163, 166
Lluch, Vicente (director) 123
Loach, Ken (director) 286
Loma, José Antonio de la (director) 106,
237, 289
Lombardi, Francisco (director) 350
Lope de Vega [Félix Lope de Vega y
Carpio] (author) 102 n. 39, 104, 126,
149, 205, 211, 286
López, Antonio (painter) 302
López, Charo (actor) 213, 246, 260, 263,
267, 284–5
López, Sergi (actor) 329, 341
López Amado, Norberto (director) 340
López de Alaya, Pilar (actor) 17 n. 26,
348
López García, Victoriano (IIEC director)
98
López Heredia, Irene (actor) 21

López Linares, José Luis
  (cinematographer/director/producer)
  326–8
López Piñeiro, Carlos (screenwriter/
  director) 279
López Rubio, José (director) 28, 84,
  100, 105, 112
López Vázquez, José Luis (actor) 138,
  146, 156, 165, 167, 183, 203–4,
  214–16, 218–19, 221, 234, 238
Lorente, Germán (director) 202
Loriga, Ray (director) 308, 334
Los Bravos (band) 176
Los Brincos (band) 218
Los Gritos (band) 169
Los Hombres G (band) 270
Lourido, Xavier (actor) 279
Lozano, Eloy (director) 338
Lozano, Manuel (actor) 328
Lozano, Margarita (actor) 262
Lubitsch, Ernst (director) 76, 93
Lucas, George (director) 323
Lucia, Luis (director) 30 n. 4, 69, 95,
  98, 100–1, 104, 106–8, 113–14, 121–2,
  125–6, 129, 132, 142, 149, 153–4,
  161–2, 201, 206, 217
Luknár, Roman (actor) 306
Lumière, Louis and Auguste
  (photographers) 1–2, 5, 15 n. 22
Luna, Manuel (actor) 66, 69, 80, 106,
  125
Lupo, Rino (director) 33
Luppi, Federico (actor) 306, 313, 337,
  351

McCarthy, Andrew (actor) 309
MacDonald, David (director) 117
McInnerny, Lizzy (actor) 260
Mackendrick, Alexander (director) 135
  n. 25
McNamara, Fabio/Fanny (singer/
  composer/actor) 345
Machado, Antonio (poet) 46, 106, 149
Machado, Manuel (poet) 46, 106
Madrid, locations 1–2, 18, 28, 30, 41–2,
  53, 61, 67, 73–4, 86, 90, 93, 96, 100,
  109–12, 118, 132, 143, 148, 150,
  163, 190, 219, 233–4, 236, 248, 261,
  263–4, 269, 273, 287, 289, 293–5,
  305, 309, 313, 323–4, 328–9, 333–6,
  341–4, 350

Madrid, Jesús Luis (director) 174, 209
magazines, film
  Arte y Cinematografía 20
  Cahiers du Cinéma 181
  Cine, El 20
  Cinema Universitario 131
  Film Ideal 182
  Fotogramas 37, 192
  Gaceta Literaria, La 35, 37, 41
  Mirador 41
  Mundo Cinematográfico 20
  Novela Cinematográfica del Hogar,
    La 46
  Novela Semanal Cinematográfica,
    La 46
  Nuestro Cine 64, 181, 193
  Objetivo 131, 139–40
  Pantalla, La 36–7
  Popular Films 37
  Primer Plano 85, 89, 93, 99
  Sight & Sound xv, 352
magic realism 269, 279, 322
Maish, Herbert (director) 80
Making of … / Así se hizo 318
Maldern, Karl (actor) 206
Malla, Coque (singer/actor) 298, 301
Mallorquí, José (comics' author) 173
Malraux, André (author) 74, 132 n. 19
Mamoulian, Rouben (director) 17, 67
Mañá, Laura (director/screenwriter/actor)
  286, 291, 322–3
Mañas, Achero (actor/director) 331–2
Mañas, Alfredo (playwright) 160
Mañas, José Ángel (author) 333
Mann, Anthony (director) 172–3
Manquiña, Manuel (actor) 337
Manrique, Jorge (poet) 323
Mantilla, Fernando (director) 73
Manuel, Víctor (actor) 213
Manver, Kiti (actor) 221, 233, 278
Manzanos, Eduardo (director) 123, 128,
  145
Maqua, Javier (director) 234, 332, 335
maquis see under military
March, Juan (industrialist) 215, 261
Marchand, Corrine (actor) 177
Marchand, Raúl (director) 341
Marco, Fernando (distributor) 24
Marcos, Cristina (actor) 237, 304, 310
Margoni, Elisabeth (actor) 322
Mariano, Luis (singer/actor) 108, 126–7

Marías, Luis (screenwriter/director) 336
Marías, Miguel (ICAA director) 283
Marín, Guillermo (actor) 111
Marini, Valeria (actor) 298
Mariscal, Ana (actor/director/producer)
    69, 84, 94, 100, 104, 113–14, 124, 127
    n. 12, 131, 155, 160, 171
Mariscal, Rosa (actor) 334
Marischka, Ernst (director) 141
Marisol see Flores González, Josefa
Maristany, Josep Maria (cinematographer)
    23
Márquez López, Francisca see Meller,
    Raquel
Marquina, Luis (director) 34, 55, 60, 70,
    94, 100–1, 105–6, 107, 114, 126, 128,
    190–1
Marro, Albert (director/producer) 15–17,
    22, 71, 260 n. 6
Marsé, Juan (author) 243, 262, 298
Marsillach, Adolfo (actor/director) 123–
    4, 132, 205, 312
Martín, Eugenio (director) 171, 174,
    297, 313
Martín, Maribel (actor) 276
Martín, Rafael (actor) 160
Martín Gaite, Carmen (author) 210
Martínez, Antonio (director) 220
Martínez, Fele (actor) 308, 324, 350
Martínez, Julia (actor) 137
Martínez, Pau (director) 172, 321
Martínez Arboleya, Joaquín (director)
    78
Martínez de Rivas, Ramón (director) 7
Martínez del Castillo, Antonio see Rey,
    Florián
Martínez-Lázaro, Emilio (director) 235,
    268, 270, 287, 293, 335, 346
Martínez Palomo 'Palomeque', Joaquín
    (bullfighter) 29
Martínez Sierra, Gregorio (playwright)
    51
Martínez Soria, Paco (actor) 166, 168–9,
    201, 204, 239
Marull, Laia (actor) 331
Marx Brothers comedies 128
Masia, Octavi (director) 335
Masó, Pedro (producer/screenwriter/
    director) 145, 164, 166–9, 203, 218,
    234, 240, 256, 300, 341
Massenet, Jules (composer) 258

Massiel [María Félix de los Ángeles
    Santamaría Espinosa] (singer) 160,
    188
Mata, Pedro (author) 56
Mateldi, Godofredo (director) 23
Mateo Salcedo 'Miguelín', Miguel
    (bullfighter) 201
Mateos, Julián (actor) 184
Mathieu, Jeanne (actor) 8
Matjí, Manolo (screenwriter/director)
    274, 294, 335
Maura, Carmen (actor) 233, 259, 263,
    270, 272–4, 285, 287, 292, 296, 323,
    325, 343–4
Mayo, Alfredo (actor) 84, 92, 94, 99,
    105–6, 109, 112, 183, 241
Meca, Ramón (actor) 39
Medeiros, Maria de (actor/director/
    screenwriter) 223
Medem, Julio (director) 311, 314, 320,
    324, 326–7
Meilhac, Henri (composer) see Carmen
Mejías, José Antonio (actor) 171
Melford, George (director) 62
Méliès, Georges (photographer) 1, 7, 9,
    15 n. 22, 342
Meller, Raquel [Francisca Márquez
    López] (singer/actor) 24–5, 71, 141
melodrama 6, 11–15, 18, 21–3, 32–5,
    37–8, 57, 59–62, 84, 95–7, 100–3,
    113–14, 121, 178, 186, 206, 211, 272,
    285, 330, 331, 333
    rural 11–13, 17–18, 38–40, 96,
        127–8, 138
memory 184, 210, 214–16, 219–20, 231,
    243, 245–6, 258, 262–3, 301, 324,
    335, 348
    uncensored recovery 240–1, 244–6,
        254, 261–4, 274, 280, 286, 291–2,
        300–1, 308, 311–12, 324, 327–9,
        330, 339, 349
men
    machismo 192, 197, 208, 236, 243,
        287, 289, 295, 297–8, 304, 307–8,
        311, 322–3, 331, 336, 338, 340,
        342–3
    masculinities 40, 60–1, 87–8, 90–2,
        106, 148 n. 46, 182–3, 196, 203,
        229, 231–2, 244, 270, 274, 280,
        284–7, 293, 297–8, 304, 315,

324–5, 331, 340–2, 345, *see also* comedies
paleto 144–5, 168–9, 203–4
patriarchy 38–40, 66–7, 83, 95, 105–6, 186, 230, 289, 304, 331
pícaro 144–5, 202, 335, 343, 346
Menéndez, Juanjo (actor) 145, 167, 203
Menéndez Leite, Fernando (director/critic/ director ICAA) 229, 319
Mendoza, Eduardo (author) 247, 301
Menkes, David (director) 306, 344
Mercanton, Louis (director) 52
Mercero, Antonio (director/ screenwriter) 147 n. 45, 221, 234, 260–2, 265, 328–9, 332
Mérimée, Prosper (author) 23 n. 36, 250, 330, *see also Carmen*
Merino, Aitor (actor) 174
Merino, Fernando (director) 165–6, 203
Merino, Francisco (actor) 237
Merino, [Mary del] Carmen (actor) 59
Merino, Ricardo (actor) 80
Merlo, Ismael (actor) 106
metacinema 42, 51, 105, 108, 126, 147, 191, 222, 250–2, 263, 266, 270, 299, 321, 332, 348–9
MGM [Metro-Goldwyn-Mayer] *see under* production companies
Micón, Sabino Antonio (director) 41, 52
Migenes, Julia (actor) 266
Mignoni, Fernando (director) 70 n. 27, 72
migration/migrants *see also* exiles
legislation 118
from Spain 73, 94, 142, 156, 169, 204, 217, 231, 289–90, 315, 317, 328–9, 333
to Spain 62–3, 94, 96, 115, 125, 141, 191, 281, 289–90, 293, 302, 305–6, 309, 312, 315, 317, 326, 332–3, 335, 344–5, 351
within Spain 38–40, 73, 84, 117–18, 164, 169–70, 179, 276, 292, 298, 315, 327, 330
Mihura, Jerónimo (director) 96
Mihura, Miguel (screenwriter) 60, 82–3, 96, 123, 133, 177
Mikaela [Woods] (actor) 168
Miles, Sarah (actor) 205
military on screen 2, 70, 101, 261–3, 268, 288

Air Force 91, 96, 108
División Azul [Blue Division] 95, 123, 261, 328
Guardia Civil [Civil Guards] 12, 64, 109 n. 47, 112, 226–7, 264–5, 296, 337
International Brigades 79, 112, 191, 296, 327, 330
Legion/ary 92, 103, 120, 206
maquis/guerillas 81, 106, 124, 162, 220, 244–5, 274, 328, 329, 349
North African troops 79, 81, 90
recruits, conscription 61, 70, 111–12, 144, 238, 295, 301
Republican soldiers 73–4, 79, 86, 89–90, 112, 124
Millán, Santi (actor) 345
Millán Astray, José (general/minister) 35, 77, 300
Miller, Arthur (playwright) 217
Mills, Juliet (actor) 247
Ministerio de Información y Turismo [Ministry of Information and Tourism] *see under* government, MIT
Minnelli, Vicente (director) 17
Miñón, Juan (director) 292, 301
Mir, Paco (director/comedian) 311, 343
Mira, Carles (director) 238–9, 277
Mira, Juli (actor) 321
Mirador (Barcelona) *see* screens
Miralles, Alfredo (screenwriter) 59
Miranda, Soledad [Soledad Rendón Bueno] (actor) 163, 207
Miravitlles, Jaume (author) 73
Miró, María (director) 312
Miró, Pilar (director/screenwriter/DGC and ICAA director) 4 n. 6, 12, 185, 207 n. 16, 226–7, 230, 235, 254, 258, 267, 286, 291, 301 n. 16, 313–14, 319
Miró look 256–7, 280, 303, 330, 340
Miró reforms 253, 256–7, 280–1, 283, 321
Misiones Pedagógicas *see under* education
Mistral, Jorge (actor) 103, 108, 125, 127
MIT [Ministerio de Información y Turismo] *see under* government
Mitchum, Christopher (actor) 206
Modot, Gaston (actor) 38
Moleón, Rafael (director) 264, 274, 290, 300, 338
Molière (playwright) 260, 270

Molina, Ángela (actor)   111 n. 49, 231,
  245, 262, 265, 285, 311–12
Molina, Antonio (actor/singer)   126, 142
Molina, Jacinto aka Naschy, Paul   172
  n. 20, 174–5, 207–8, 338, 342
Molina, Josefina (director)   106, 221,
  230, 254, 259–60, 285–6, 299
Molina, Miguel/Miky (actor)   237, 249
Molina, Miguel (singer)   271
Molina, Mónica (actor)   312
Molina, Olga (actor)   347
Molina, Paulina (actor)   233
Molinero, Carlos (director)   333
Mollà, Jordi (actor)   297, 322, 336
Momplet, Antonio (director)   121
Moncloa pact   225, 232, 243, 327
Monleón, Sigfrid (director)   333
montage   4, 7, 9–10, 16–17, 21, 33–5,
  37, 40, 42 n. 31, 53–4, 59, 67, 70,
  79–80, 132, 138, 148, 150–1, 159,
  169, 185, 187–8, 191, 210, 240–1,
  268, 307, 326, 338
Montagu, Ivor (filmmaker)   73–4
Montalà, Irene (actor)   346
Montenegro, Conchita (actor)   96, 106–7
Montes, Conchita (actor)   96, 111
Montesinos, Rafael (director)   351
Montherlant, Henry de (playwright)   100
Montiel, Sara [María Antonia Abad]
  (actor)   101, 103–4, 141, 155, 165,
  184, 190, 213, 299
Montllor, Ovidi (actor)   239
Mora, Jesús (director)   170 n. 19, 303
Moral, Ignacio del (playwright)   289
Morales, Gracita (actor)   165–7, 202
Morales, María Luz (journalist)   48
Morán, Manolo (actor)   96, 104, 134,
  144–5, 167
More, Will (actor)   252
Moreno, Antoñita (actor)   126
Moreno, Armando (director)   169, 191
Moreno, Arturo (director)   97, 175
Moreno, María (actor)   29
Moreno Alba, Rafael (director)   200,
  205, 235, 248
Morente, Estrela (singer)   345 n. 26
Morera, Eduardo (director)   86
Morgan, Lina [María de los Ángeles
  López Segovia] (actor)   166–8, 202,
  300
Moro, José Luis (animation)   176

Morocco, location   10, 24, 31, 80, 90
Morocco see under war films
Moróm, Manuel (actor)   331
Mountassir, Abdel Aziz El (actor)   355
movida   251–2, 330–1
Mozart, Wolfgang Amadeus (composer)
  304
M-Technofantasy   176
Multiplexes see under screens
Mundo Cinematográfico see under
  magazines
Muñoz, Amparo (actor)   200 n. 2, 208,
  212, 218
Muñoz, Anton Pep (actor)   296
Muñoz, Joxan (animation)   347
Muñoz, Juan (actor/screenwriter/director)
  343
Muñoz, Miguel Ángel (actor)   288
Muñoz, Nicolás (director)   348
Muñoz, Pilar (actor)   61
Muñoz Fontán, José (DNC director)   152
Muñoz Molina, Antonio (author)   296
Muñoz Seca, Pedro (playwright)   57
Muñoz Suay, Ricardo (author)   139, 192
Munt, Silvia (actor/director)   234, 238
  n. 24, 248, 293, 296, 312, 335
Mur, Nilo (actor)   334
Mur Oti, Manuel (screenwriter/director)
  113–14, 127, 130–1, 160
Murià, Magí (director)   18
Murnau, F. W. (director)   41
musicals   28, 30–1, 56–9, 62, 65, 69–70,
  72, 75, 80, 82, 84, 92–5, 101, 105–8,
  114, 124–27, 140–4, 156, 159–64,
  167–8, 188, 212–13, 218–19, 249–50,
  270, 280, 299–300, 325–6, 345–7, 348,
  see also songs
  Napoleon(ic)   99–101, 114, 125,
    140–1, 160, 263, 270–1, 342
  zarzuela   10, 28, 30–1, 57, 62, 65–8,
    83, 126–7, 163, 201, 250, 271
Musidora, aka Roques, Jeanne (director/
  actor)   30
Muti, Ornella (actor)   218, 298
Mutua de Defensa Cinematográfica
  [Association for the Protection of
  Cimema]   18
Myrick, Daniel (director)   337

Naschy, Paul see Molina, Jacinto

National Board of Censorship (USA) *see* censorship
National Catholicism 79, 90, 99, 113, 120, 157, 182, 209, *see also* church
Navarro, Agustín (animation) 202, 347
Navarro, María Esperanza (actor) 140
navy 4, 62, 85–6, 108, 124, 166, 201
NCE *see* Nuevo Cine Español
Neorealism, neo-realism *see under* realism
Nevárez, Micaela (actor) 332
Neville, Edgar (director/screenwriter) 51–2, 59, 62, 65, 69–70, 75, 78–9, 82, 86, 97, 106–7, 110–12, 114, 118 n. 3, 124, 126, 135, 138, 154, 237
New Spanish Cinema *see* Nuevo Cine Español
newsreels 2, 4, 13, 16, 28, 36, 242
  Cinespaña 72
  Espanya al dia 73
  Film España 72
  Nationalist 77–9
  NO-DO 86, 132 n. 18, 227, 240, 262, 326
  Noticiario Español 72, 78
  Republican 72–74
Niblo, Fred (director) 17
Nieto, José (actor) 95–96, 172–3
Nieto, José (composer) 285
Nieva, Petra de (editor) 169, 196
Nieves Conde, José Antonio (director) 90 n. 21, 103, 109, 114, 117–18, 120–1, 129–31, 133, 147, 153–5, 170, 174, 206, 272, 320
Nile del Río, Magdalena *see* Argentina, Imperio
Nimri, Najwa (actor) 307–8, 311, 324, 333, 337
Noailles, Charles de (Vicomte) 44
NO-DO [Noticiarios y Documentales] *see under* newsreels
Noriega, Eduardo (actor) 290, 308, 321–2, 340
Noriega, Manuel (director) 32–4, 36 n. 20, 38, 41, 60, 66, 92–3
Nosseck, Max (producer/director) 63
Noticiario Español *see under* newsreels
Noticiarios y Documentales *see under* newsreels, NO-DO
Nouvelle Vague 177 n. 28, 181, 191
Nouvelles d'Espagne see under newsreels, *Espanya al dia*

Novaro, María (director) 313
Novela Cinematográfica del Hogar, La see under magazines
Novela Semanal Cinematográfica, La see under magazines
nudity 48, 64, 72, 86, 165, 199–200, 205, 228, 242, 291, 297, 330
Nuevo Cine Español [NCE/New Spanish Cinema] 158–9, 176, 181–90, 195–6, 209–12
Núñez, Iñaki (director) 241
Núñez, Ricardo (actor) 57, 59
Núñez, Ricardo (director) 142

Objetivo see under magazines
Ocaña, José Pérez (personality) 236
occult/supernatural 268–9, 279, 306, 312, 321, 323, 325, 329, 338–40
Ochoa, Margarita de (editor) 70 n. 27, 76, 138, 196
Olasagasti, Eneko (director) 313
Olavarría, Alejandro (director) 34 n. 16
Olea, Pedro (director) 218–9, 236, 247, 264, 278, 287–8, 290, 299
Olen Ray, Fred (director) 175
Oliva, Pepe (actor) 278
Olivé-Bellés, Núria (director) 345
Oliver, Juan (director) 29
Oliver, Juan Luis (editor) 193
Olózaga, José (actor) 21
Onaindia, José Miguel (ICAA director) 318
Ontañón, Santiago (director) 57
Ontañón, Sara (editor) 70, 72, 76, 92, 103, 112, 126, 147, 196
Ophüls, Max (director) 107
Opus Dei 99, 103, 140, 190, 211, 219, 238
Orano, Alessio (actor) 218
Ordaz, Isabel (actor) 332
Orduña, Juan de (director/actor) 17 n. 26, 30 n. 7, 33, 35, 37, 66, 84, 86, 91–4, 99–101, 103–4, 105–7, 114–15, 117–18, 121–2, 129, 141–2, 147, 149, 153–4, 163, 168, 201, 299, 330
Orduña, Pepita (editor) 134
Orellana, Carlos (director) 32 n. 9
organ transplants 324, 332
Oristrell, Joaquín (screenwriter/director) 304–6, 344
Orphea Films *see under* studios

Ortega Santillana, Eterio (director) 327
Osca, Paco de (actor) 331
Oscars see under awards
Ossorio, Amando de (director) 208
Otero, José María (ICAA director) 318
Ovid (poet) 193
O'Wisiedo, Mayra (actor) 109
Ozores, Adriana (actor) 202 n. 6, 285,
    332, 334–5, 347
Ozores, Antonio (actor) 146, 167, 202
    n. 6
Ozores, Emma (actor) 202 n. 6
Ozores, José Luis (actor) 146, 202 n. 6
Ozores, Mariano (actor) 202 n. 6
Ozores, Mariano (director) 165, 167–
    168, 170, 201–2, 240, 249, 268

Pablo, Luis de (composer) 189
Pacheco, Godofredo (cinematographer)
    171
Pacheco, Mari-Tere (actor) 61
Pàdua Tramullas, Antoni (photographer)
    3, 11
paedophilia 276, 312–13, 317, 325, 340
Pajares, Andrés (actor) 297
Palacios, Fernando (director) 144–6,
    161–3, 167, 234, 313
Palacios, Manuel (director) 328, 338
Palacio Valdés. Armando (author) 105
Paleto see under men
Palmer, Lilli (actor) 175
Palmer, Russell (director) 79
Palmero, Javier (director) 268
Palomo Linares, Sebastián (bullfighter)
    161
Pamplona, Clemente (screenwriter/
    director) 147
Panero, Leopoldo (poet) and family 222,
    241, 302
Pangua, José Antonio (director) 233–4
Pantalla, La see under magazines
Pantoja, Isabel (singer) 299
Parchís (band) 250
Parda, Mario (actor) 260
Pardo Bazán, Emilia (author) 105, 149
Paredes, María (editor) 72
Paredes, Marisa (actor) 146, 233, 285,
    287, 293, 319, 324, 334, 343
Parellada, Juan (director) 86
Parera, Valentín (actor) 37, 51
París, Inés (director) 344

Paris, location 40, 43, 51–2, 96, 108,
    163, 168, 180, 217, 260, 262, 266,
    305, 324, 339
parody 17, 24, 41–2, 52–3, 57, 61–2,
    92, 102, 123, 126, 128–9, 133–4, 148,
    165–6, 250, 252, 272–3, 323, 342
Parondo, Gil (designer) 330
Parra, Vicente (actor) 141, 163, 220
Parrado, Ramón (director) 333
Pastor, Rosana 342, 346
Pastor, Víctor (actor) 38
Pastor Moreno, Carles (director) 346
Pastrone, Giovanni, aka Fosco, Piero
    (director) 10
Patino, Basilio Martín (director/
    screenwriter) 139, 187, 189, 195,
    210, 216, 220, 240, 263, 267, 320, 326
Paul, Robert W. (photographer) 1
Pauls, Gastón (actor) 350
Peck, Gregory (actor) 42 n. 33
Peladilla (character) 29
Peláez, Ángel (director) 350–1
Pelegri, Teresa (director) 345
Pelka, Valentine (actor) 260
Pellegrini, Clauco (director) 149
Peña, Candela (actor) 309, 332, 348
Peña, Chema de la (director) 346
Peña, Julio (dancer/actor) 65, 107, 112
Peña, Luis (actor/editor) 32, 90, 92–3,
    96
Penella, Emma (actor) 188, 213, 294
Penella, Manuel (composer) 62
Percoraro, Susú (actor) 350
Perea, Fran (actor) 346
Peret [Pedro Pubill Calaf] (singer) 160
Pereyra, Miguel (director) 78
Pérez, Ana (directors) 328
Pérez, Dionisio (director) 332
Pérez, Rosie (actor) 323
Pérez Bueno, Artemio (actor) 21
Pérez Cubero, Raul (cinematographer)
    330
Pérez de Guzmán, Dacil (director) 333
Pérez Dolz, Francisco (director) 170,
    303
Pérez Estremera, Manuel (ICAA director)
    318
Pérez Ferré, Carlos (director) 290, 302
Pérez Galdós, Benito (author) 33, 84,
    162, 172, 180, 188, 205, 209–10, 219,
    248–9

Pérez Herrero, Vicente (director) 348
Pérez Lugín, Alejandro (author/director)
  30, 32–3, 36 n. 20, 38, 65–6, 92 n. 22,
  105, 107 n. 45
Pérez Reverte, Arturo (author) 302, 330
Perkins, Millie (actor) 171
Perla, Alejandro (director) 149
Perojo, Benito (director/producer) 7, 10,
  18, 28–29, 31, 34, 37–8, 50–2, 56–60,
  62, 65–9, 71–2, 75–6, 81–2, 84, 89,
  93, 95, 105–6, 110 n. 48, 111 n. 51,
  113–14, 127, 135, 141, 162–3, 294
  n. 13, 349
Perrault, Charles (author) 176, 252
Perrin, Jacques (actor) 188
Perugorría, Jorge (actor) 312–13, 331–2,
  344, 351
Peskine, Boris (director) 74
Philippines see under war films
Phonofilm see under sound systems
Photophon RCA see under sound systems
Pi, Rosario (director/producer) 52, 56,
  62, 66, 76, 127
Picazo, Miguel (director) 138, 186, 189,
  230 n. 8, 249, 259, 320
Piccoli, Michel (actor) 135 n. 24, 214,
  341
picotero/explicador see commentator
Pidgeon, Walter (actor) 111 n. 50
Pili and Mili [Emilia and Pilar Bayona
  Sarriá] (actors) 162
Pina, Silvia (actor) 151
Piñeiro, Chano (director) 279
Piñeyro, Marcelo (director) 339, 341
  n. 22
Pino, Rosario (actor) 52
Pinzás, Juan (director) 336
Piovani, Nicola (composer) 297
Piquer, Conchita (actor) 37, 83, 106
Pisacane, Carlo (actor) 166
Pisano, Isabel (actor) 229
Pitouto, aka Elviro, Pedro (actor) 29, 33
Pitusín aka Hurtado, Alfredo (actor) 29,
  34, 37
Plazas, Cristina (actor) 346
Pleasance, Donald (actor) 213
Plowright, Joan (actor) 259 n. 4
PNC [Premios Nacionales de
  Cinematógrafía/National Film Awards]
  see under awards
Pochet, Arthur (cinematographer) 56

Pocino, Benito (actor) 176
Politti, Luis (actor) 245
Pollatschick, Géza (producer) 62
Polley, Sarah (actor) 323
Pombo, Mariano del (director) 123, 147
  n. 44
Pomés, Isabel de (actor) 94, 99, 112
Ponce, Pere (actor) 287–8
Poncela, Eusebio (actor) 252, 337
Pons, Mercè (actor) 285–6
Pons, Ventura (director) 234, 275, 283
  n. 1, 286–7, 296, 339, 345
Ponte, María Luisa (actor) 248
Pontecorvo, Gillo (director) 198, 243
popular cinema xvi, 46–8, 60–1, 93–6,
  105–8, 155, 157, 189, 195, 224, 268,
  323, see also under comedy, popular
Popular Films see under magazines
Porlan, Alberto (director) 328–9
Portabella, Pere (producer/director) 150–
  1, 193–4, 242, 277
Portas, Rafael (director) 30 n. 7
Portillo, Blanca (actor) 325
post-synchronisation see under sound
Potau, Joan (actor/director) 347
Pottier, Richard (director) 108
Pozo, José (animation) 347
Prada, José María (actor) 132, 215
Pradera, María Dolores (singer/actor)
  108, 112
Pratt, Gilbert (director) 17
Premios Nacionales de Cinematógrafía
  see under awards, PNC
press 1, 20, 24 n. 14, 35, 45, 47, 51,
  57, 60, 75–6, 111, 128, 131, 150, 152,
  163, 180, 210, 212, 223, 252, 255,
  300, 326
Prévert, Pierre (poet) 45 n. 40
Primer Plano see under magazines
Primo de Rivera, Miguel (general/
  dictator) 27, 34–35, 47, 248
Prims, Núria (actor) 333, 345
PRISA [Promotora de Información
  Sociedad Anónima] 284, 318
prison(ers) 31, 56, 59–60, 109 n. 47,
  207, 241–2, 264, 289, 294, 298, 308,
  328, 335
prizes see awards
production companies, Spanish
  Agata Films 217
  Aiete 277, 303

Alta   313
Altamira   132–4
Argos Films   29
Aspa Films   103, 121 n. 8
Atlántida   31
Barcinógrafo   17–18
Benito Perojo   162–3
Bocaboca   304
Boreal Films   18
Bosco Films   131
Cantabría Cine   31
CEA   57–8, 92
Chapalo Films   18, 103
CIFESA   57–60, 66, 70, 73, 75, 78,
   80, 83–4, 93, 95, 97–102, 104, 106,
   117, 122, 141, 299
Condal Films   18, 22
Cuesta Films   11, 13, 18
Deseo, El   303, 306
Dessy Films   18, 21
Diana Exclusivas   52, 56, 59
Diorama   11, 18
Ditirambo   267
ECESA   58
Emisora Films   95, 125, 148
Escorpión, el   303
Estela Films   98
Estudios Castilla   176
Estudios Moros   97, 175–6
Falcó Films   11, 18
Fernando Colomo P.C.   303, 306
Fernando Trueba   303, 309
Film Española   31
Filmófono   60–2, 96, 132 n. 19
Films 59   150–1, 194
Films Barcelona   18
Films Cinématographiques   23
Fox Film   51
Goya Films   33
Hispano Films   16, 18, 22
Iberia Films   18
Ibérica Films   63
IFI(SA)   95, 121, 148, 274
Iguana, La   303
Imán, El   185, 212, 303
Inca Films   62
Iris Films   18
Itala Film   10
Laya Films   73, 86
Lola Films   303
Macaya y Marro   18

Macián Films   176
Madrid-Cines   27
Madrid Films   36, 41
Nickel Odeon   247
Patria Films   18, 29, 31
Producciones Iquino   148, 274
Querejeta P.C.   182, 188–9, 214, 234,
   303, 327
Royal Films   17, 18, 24
Salamandra, La   233
Segre Films   18
Star Films   56, 62
Studio Films   18, 28
Suevia Films   83–4, 98–9, 108, 126,
   247
Tibidabo Films   13, 18
Tibidabo Films SA   191
Tornasol   313
Troya Films   32
UNINCI   134, 151–2, 180, 189
production companies, foreign   172–3
   Columbia Pictures   58
   Disney   60, 97–98, 175, 228
   Gaumont   11, 17, 36, 51
   HFP   79–82, 91, 349
   Lumière Frères   1–2, 5
   Méliès   7, 9, 11
   MGM   34, 45, 58, 121
   Paramount   52, 58
   Pathé Films   6–7, 10–11, 25
   Samuel Bronston Productions   172
   Twentieth-Century Fox   173
   Warner Brothers   58, 60, 284
production facts and tables   xiv
   1897–1917   18, 22–5
   1918–1931   27–9, 36–7
   1931–1939   50–4, 63–4, 70–2
   1939–1951   80–4, 88, 98–99, 101–2,
      113–14
   1951–1961   119–20, 139–40, 152–54
   1961–1969   157–9, 194–5, 164–5,
      168–9, 181–2, 191–2, 194–5
   1969–1976   199–201, 209, 218,
      222–4
   1976–1982   226–8, 253, 267
   1982–1989   255–8, 274–5, 279–80
   1989–1996   282–5, 303, 308, 312–14
   1996–2006   317–21, 345, 349–50,
      351
   exports   xiv, 2, 5–6, 8, 13, 22–5,
      30, 38, 40, 51, 65, 70, 80, 107,

119, 158, 189, 200 n. 2, 217, 247, 252, 260, 265–6, 280, 298, 308–9, 349–51
Promio, Alexandre (photographer) 1–2, 5, 23
Promotora de Información Sociedad Anónima [Information Promotion Limited] see PRISA
prostitution 35, 70, 118, 186, 219, 229, 265, 268, 270, 272, 286, 297, 307, 332, 336
protectionism
   box-office controls 158, 227, 283
   British Cinematograph Act 37
   budgets 21, 23, 29, 33–4, 112, 117, 141, 147–8, 154, 161, 165–6, 174, 182, 194, 197, 204, 208, 224, 232, 251–2, 256, 259, 283, 314
   funding/subsidies 23, 25, 28, 21, 36, 85, 88, 117, 119, 157, 181, 192, 194, 199, 253, 256–7, 267, 283, 303, 312, 315, 318, 320, 349, 351
   GATT 283
   imports (films) 1–2, 11, 22, 24–5, 36–7, 54, 58, 71, 74–5, 88, 97–8, 113, 119, 133, 158, 161, 170, 175, 181, 199, 227, 257, 283, 318, see also Hollywood
   quotas 36–7, 88, 119, 181, 227, 257, 283, 318
provincial values 161, 164, 167–9, 177–9, 183–8, 196, 201–2, 212, 219, 240, 272
Puche, Pedro (director) 70–2, 109, 118 n. 3
Puchol, Luisa (actor) 202 n. 6
pueblo see rural settings and under melodrama
Puenzo, Luis (director) 350
Puga, Ricardo (director) 27, 31
Puigcorbé, Juanjo (actor) 238 n. 24, 265, 287, 295–6, 304, 306, 321
Pujol, David (director) 338
Punzano, Pilar (actor) 346

Quadreny, Ramón (director) 94, 108, 193
Quer, Silvia (director) 331
Querejeta, Elías (producer/screenwriter) 182, 189, 194, 196, 214, 216–17, 221, 241, 248, 258, 260, 278, 327

Querejeta, Gracia (director/screenwriter) 309, 334
Quevedo, Nino (director) 220
Quincey, Thomas de (author) 260
Quinn, Anthony (actor) 249
Quintana, Ricardo (director) 61–2
Quintero brothers see Álvarez Quintero, Serafín and Joaquín
Quintillá, Elvira (actor) 133–4
Quirós, José Antonio (director) 332
quotas see protectionism
Qureshi, Zack (actor) 345

Rabal, Liberto (actor) 294
Rabal, Paco [Francisco] (actor) 109, 122–3, 128, 138, 148, 152, 163–4, 169, 182, 186, 219–20, 258, 267, 273, 292, 299–300, 319, 326
race/ethnicity (tension) 38, 62, 105–6, 151, 160, 184, 186, 208, 264–5, 289–90, 305–6, 309, 325, 332–3, 342–3
radio 27, 60
radio on screen 107, 129, 133, 201, 229, 275
Radio Television Española [RTVE] see under television
Raimon [Pelegero Sanchis] (singer) 191
Ramallo, Fernando (actor) 293, 335
Ramírez, Pedro L. (director) 95, 144–6, 160
Ramón, Eulalia (actor) 295
Ramos, Laura (actor) 350
Ramos, Santiago (actor) 288, 293
Randall, Mónica (actor) 221
Raphael [Rafael Martos Sánchez] (singer) 163, 184
ration books see under black market
Ray, Man (photographer/painter) 41
Ray, Nicholas (director) 172
Real, Antonio del (director) 234, 293, 297, 302
realism 17, 118, 331, see also creationism
   cine social 315, 322
   neo-realism 118, 121, 130–3, 139, 150, 154–5, 331
   social realism 331
Rebolledo, Javier (director) 336
Recha, Marc (director) 338
Recuperación de la Memoria 225, 327–8, see also memory

reels 1–16, 23, 28, 29
Regueiro, Francisco (director) 90 n. 21,
 186, 188–9, 209, 268, 300, 320
Reig, Alberto (JSOC director) 86, 132,
 see also NO-DO
Reig, Joaquín (director) 79, 86, see also
 government, press
Reina, Juanita (actor) 101, 104–7, 125
Rellán, Miguel (actor) 263
Remacha, Fernando (composer) 60
remembering see memory
Renais, Alain (director) 74
Renault, Edouard (cinematographer) 24,
 74
Renault, René (sound engineer) 56, 74
Rendell, Ruth (author) 285
Renoir, Jean (director) 41
Residencia de Estudiantes (Madrid) 28,
 43
Resines, Antonio (actor) 233–4, 269–70,
 273–4, 278, 295, 299, 302, 332, 335–7
Rey, Fernando (actor) 17 n. 26, 71,
 92, 100–1, 104, 122, 134, 152, 162,
 172–3, 181, 205, 231, 247, 249, 266,
 268–9
Rey, Florián (director) 7, 28–30, 33, 37–
 40, 47, 52, 56, 58–60, 63, 66–7, 69,
 75–6, 80, 83–4, 93, 101, 105–8, 111
 n. 51, 113–14, 118, 125–6, 146 n. 42,
 149, 163, 230 n. 8, 299, 320, 349
Rey, Pedro del (editor) 150, 170, 185
Rey, Roberto (actor) 52, 67, 81
Ribas, Antonio (director) 5, 246
Ribera Perpinyá, Xavier (director) 311
Rico, Laura (actor) 308
Rico, Paquita (actor) 125–6, 141, 153,
 173
Ridruejo, Dioniso (propaganda office)
 82
Riera see under laboratories
Río, Ernesto del (director) 274, 288,
 295–6
riots in/out of cinemas see under
 spectatorship
Rioyo, Javier (director) 327–8
Ripoll, María (director) 337, 345
Rispa, Jacobo (director) 333
rites of passage 28, 142–3, 150, 166–7,
 216–17, 236–7, 246, 248–9, 263–4,
 267, 280, 287–8, 293–4, 297–9, 307–9,

321, 325, 329–30, 334, 346, 350, see
 also summer narratives
Rivelles, Amparo (actor) 95–6, 100,
 103–6, 113, 269, 294
Rivelles, Rafael (actor) 56, 80, 93–5,
 106
road movies 142, 230, 243, 247, 281,
 294, 300–2, 307–8 , 309, 315, 321,
 332, 334–6
Robbins, Jerome and Robert Wise
 (directors) 160
Robbins, Tim (actor) 323–4
Robinson, Edward G. (actor) 134
Robles, Margarita (actor) 95
Robles Piquer, Carlos (DGCPE) 194,
 199
Rodoreda, Mercè (author) 248
Rodrigo, Raquel (actor) 67, 81
Rodríguez, Alberto (director) 333
Rodríguez, Azucena (director) 308
Rodríguez, Francisco (director) 351
Rodríguez, Manane (director) 350
Rodríguez, Miguel Ángel (actor) 144
Rodríguez, Violeta (actor) 333
Rodríguez Gordillo, Francisco
 (director) 208, 338
Rodríguez Marín, Francisco (academic)
 46
Roesset, Julio (director) 29
Rojas, Manuel (cinematographer) 169
Roldán, Fernando (director) 6 n. 20, 54,
 70, 72
Román, Antonio (director) 73, 86, 91–2,
 96, 104, 107, 114, 123, 130, 135, 142,
 149, 160, 173, 250–1
Romero Marchent, Ana María (editor)
 196
Romero Marchent, Joaquín (director)
 145, 173
Romero Marchent, Rafael (director) 129,
 162, 250
Ronconori, Mario (director) 33 n. 15
Roques, Jeanne see Musidora
Rosinski, Johanna (editor) 80
Rossen, Robert (director) 172
Rossif, Frédéric (director) 170
Rotaeta, Félix (actor/director) 274
Roth, Cecilia (actor) 313, 324, 351
Rousby, Erwin (photographer) 1
Roussel, Anne (actor) 294

Roussel, Henri (director) 141
Rovira, Juan (actor) 23
Rovira Beleta, Francisco (director) 70,
    128, 148–9, 160, 214 n. 26, 250–1,
    294 n. 13
Roy, Esperanza (actor) 232, 260
RTVE [Radio Televisión Española] *see
    under* televisión
Rubio, Ingrid (actor) 289, 306, 337
Ruiz, Juan [Arcipreste de Hita] (poet)
    205
Ruiz, Juan (cinematographer) 330
Ruiz, Sergi (actor) 347
Ruiz Capilla, Nacho (editor) 337
Ruiz Castillo, Arturo (director) 78, 86,
    101, 103, 112, 124, 128 n. 15, 147
    n. 44, 149
Ruiz de Austri, Maite (director) 312
Ruiz Vergara, Fernando (director) 42
rural settings, pueblo 11–13, 39–40, 134,
    144, 171, 196, 220–1, 224, 231–2,
    239–40, 246, 249, 258–9, 262, 265,
    273, 275, 315, 322, 325–7, 329, 333,
    337–8, 348
rural values (post-dictatorship) *see*
    provincial values
Russell, Ken (director) 200
Russo, Rafa (screenwriter) 345

Sabina, Joaquín (singer/composer) 346
Sabroso, Félix (director) 310
Sacristán, José (actor) 167–8, 202, 204,
    218, 229, 233, 236, 262, 267, 274,
    296, 319, 350
Sáenz de Heredia, Álvaro (director) 305
Sáenz de Heredia, Ángel (producer) 18
Sáenz de Heredia, José Luis
    (director) 31, 55, 61, 68, 81, 87–8,
    90–3, 96–7, 100, 103–5, 111, 114,
    118 n. 3, 121 n. 8, 123, 129, 135, 146
    n. 42, 149, 153, 163, 159, 170, 201–2,
    262 n. 8, 305, 320
Sáez, Elena (screenwriter) 189
Saguer, Albert (director) 343
sainete *see under* comedy
Salaberry, Enrique (director) 140–1
Salamanca Talks, 1955 139, 158, 331
Salazar, Ramón (director) 346–7
Salcedo, Millán [Martes y Trece] (actor)
    305
Salgado, Rosa (editor) 196

Salgado, Rosa María (actor) 104
Salgot, Josep Antón (director) 231, 320
Salmerón, Gustavo (actor) 334, 345
Salvador, Julio (director) 109, 118 n. 3,
    146
Salvia, Rafael (director) 122, 145, 153
Sampedro, Matilde (actor) 137
Sampedro Montero, Ángel *see* Angelillo
Sampietro, Mercedes (actor) 230, 259,
    285–6, 321, 334, 343
Samuelson, George (director) 50
San Francisco, Enrique (actor) 293
San Juan, Alberto (actor) 335, 346
San Juan, Antonia (actor) 324
Sánchez, Alicia (actor) 200 n. 2
Sánchez, Eduardo (director) 337
Sánchez, Verónica (actor) 346
Sánchez Bella, Alfredo (minister) 179,
    194, 199–200
Sánchez Cabezudo, Jorge (director) 338
Sánchez del Rey, David (actor) 346
Sánchez Ferlosio, Chicho (singer) 242
Sánchez-Gijón, Aitana (actor) 285, 298
Sánchez Mazas, Rafael (author) 160,
    329
Sánchez Rodríguez, Eleuterio (author)
    264
Sánchez Valdés, Julio (director) 274
Sánchez Vidal, Agustín (screenwriter/
    critic) 326
Sanchiz, Perfiria (actor) 69
Sancho, José (actor) 285, 294, 299
Sand, George (author) 191
Sans, Carles (comedian/director) 311
Sant Jordi *see under* awards
Santaolalla, Marta (actor) 94
Santiago, Alonso (actor) 309
Santiago, Beatriz (actor) 306
Santillán, Antonio (director) 148, 170
Santoloria, Eva (actor) 289
Santos, Isabel (actor) 333
Santos, Mateo (director) 73
Santugini, José (director) 70
Sanz, Jorge (actor) 203 n. 6, 249, 262,
    286–8, 293, 295, 299, 350
Sanz, Juan (actor) 337
Sanz, Luis (producer/director) 271, 299
Saraceni, Julio (director) 249
Sardà, Rosa Maria (actor) 284, 287–8,
    296–7, 304, 334, 349
sardana *see under* dance

Sarka, Raymond de (actor) 37
Saslavsky, Luis (director) 125
Sastre, Alfonso (playwright) 128, 139, 149, 180
satire 50, 53, 56–7, 65, 111, 123, 128–9, 133, 186, 196, 210, 217, 237–40, 243, 252, 261, 268–9, 277, 294–9, 305–6, 323
Sau Olite, Antonio (director) 71, 118 n. 3
Saura, Carlos (director) xiv, xvii, 81, 88, 116 n. 1, 131, 142, 146, 150–2, 154, 156, 160, 162, 170 n. 17, 182–4, 188–90, 194, 196, 200, 209, 214–17, 222–3, 230–1, 237, 243, 245–6, 250–1, 254, 259–61, 270–1, 280, 289, 291, 295, 299, 314, 319–20, 325–6, 333–4, 337, 347, 349
Sazatornil 'Saza', José (actor) 167–8, 202
Sbaraglia, Leonardo (actor) 337, 339, 351
Schertzinger, Victor (director) 52
Schild[knecht], Pierre (decorator) 38, 110 n. 48
Schneider, Romy (actor) 141
school syllabus xiii, 64
Schygulla, Hanna (actor) 260
science fiction 10, 192, 218, 266, 276, 300, 306, 322
screens/theatres/cinemas 19–20, 27, 50, 63, 75, 119, 152, 199, 253, 256, 273, 283–4, 314
    Barcelona Coliseum 50
    barraca/fair booth 7, 19, 64
    barrio cinemas/neighbourhood/ fleapits 105–6, 124–9, 144–6, 159, 201, 281, 283
    Cine Callao 34
    Cine Doré 27, 325
    Farrucini Cinema 19
    multiplexes 273, 283, 314
    open air xiii, 63–4
    Real Cinema Madrid 50
    Studio 28 44
    Ursulines 44
screens, special theatres 44, 60, 140, 192, 228, 273
    Cineclub (Madrid) 40–41, 50–1, 119
    Cineclub (Salamanca) 139
    Cineclub (Zaragoza) 44, 119

Film clubs 98, 140, 158
    Mirador (Barcelona) 41, 44
    salas de arte y ensayo 44, 158, 181, 194, 256
screenwriting 126, 256 n. 1, 266–7, 270, 326, 348
Seberg, Jean (actor) 162
Sección Femenina 88 n. 16, 255
Segura, Santiago (actor/screenwriter/ director) 167 n. 14, 306, 323, 342–3, 346, 348
Sellier, Joseph Louis (photographer) 3
Semprún, Jorge (author/minister of culture) 134 n. 21, 282
Sender, Ramón (author) 248, 258
Seneca (author) 127
Senillosa, Antoni de (director) 193
Sennett, Mack (director/producer) 13, 17, 28
señorito see under folkloric films
serial films 22
Serna, Assumpta (actor) 238 n. 24, 285, 287, 293
Serrano, David (director) 332, 346 n. 28
Serrano de Osma, Carlos (director) 104–5, 107–9, 122, 124, 140
Servais, Jean (actor) 171
Setó, Javier (director) 96, 128–9, 142
Sevilla, Carmen [María del Carmen García Galisteo] (actor) 106, 108, 125–6, 132 n. 18, 133, 142, 149, 164, 200–1, 213,
Sevilla, Lolita (actor) 133
Sevilla Studios, Madrid see under studios
Seville, Armando (director) 92
sex on screen
    'destape' 200, 202–5, 211, 213, 217, 223, 228, 242, 348
    education 188–9, 202, 210–11, 217, 219–20, 230–1, 233 , 236, 278, 309
    erotic 119–20, 206, 208–9, 212, 228, 230, 239, 287–8, 297, 306, 312
    pornography 35, 48, 207–9, 214, 228–9, 235, 247, 323–4, 348
    repression 127, 164–5, 168–9, 181, 189, 195, 197, 203–4, 206–8, 214, 218–19, 221, 224, 228, 230, 235, 285, 288, 330
    'S' films 226, 228–9, 241, 253–4, 256, 275–6, 348
    STD 35, 270

violence   35, 127, 151, 186, 276,
   286–7, 291, 304–5, 307, 315, 317,
   323–5, 340
   X rating   253, 256
Shakespearian plots   95, 149, 160, 293,
   309, 345, 347
Sher, Jack (director)   174 n. 24
Shub, Esfir (director)   74
Sica, Vittorio de (director)   130
Sight & Sound see under magazines
Silberman, Serge (producer)   174
Silke [Hornillos/Klein] (actor)   309, 350
Silva, Carolina (actor)   262
Silva, Margarita (actor)   23
Simenon, Georges (author)   109, 291
Sindicato Nacional del Espectáculo
   [National Performers' Guild]   85
Sinkovic, Anita (actor)   344
Sitges Film School Week, 1967   193–4
smuggling see under black market
Sobrevila, Nemesio (director)   41–2,
   46–7, 61, 74, 252
Sociedad Española de Dibujos Animados
   [Spanish Animation Company]   63
Sogecable/Sogecine/Sogetel/Sogepaq
   284, see also PRISA
Solá, Miguel Ángel (actor)   325, 336,
   351
Solana, Javier (minister of culture)   282
Soldevila, Laly (actor)   167
Soler, Llorenç (director)   333
Soler Leal, Amparo (actor)   167, 231, 249
Soliño, Norberto (distributor)   80
Sol(lín), Mauricio (director)   74
Sommer, Elke (actor)   165
songs   xiv, 47, 54, 56, 58–61, 66–70,
   83, 87, 103, 108, 124–6, 128–30, 153,
   159–64, 201, 210, 270–1, 299, 345–7
   blues   266
   boleros   300
   carceleras   10, 31, 56
   cuplé   24 n. 37, 141, 299
   Eurovision Song Contest   160, 188,
      201, 346
   fados   326, 349
   jazz   38, 96, 168, 193, 346
   pop   159–62, 183, 212
   rock   222, 307, 333
   silent films   6–7, 30–1, 47
   tango   108, 141, 251, 288, 325, 345,
      349

Soriano, Maruja (editor)   196
sound
   arrival of   40, 46, 50–5, 60, 63
   post-synchronisation   29, 38, 40, 42,
      51, 54, 151, 159, 213, 218, 233
   silent films   11, 19, 29–31, 40, 311,
      325
sound systems
   Chronophone   11
   Phonofilm   50, 53
   RCA Photophon   50
   Tobis-Klangfilm   57
   Western Electric   50, 54
Sota, Pedro de la (director)   243
Soto, Luchy (actor)   90
Soviet cinema   53, 60
Spain Today see Espanya al dia
Spains [two: Black and Red]   49, 152,
   180, 307
Spanish Film Conferences   36, 227, 256
special effects   6–10, 25, 38, 306–7, see
   also creationism
spectatorship   75, 82, 88, 105, 111,
   113–14, 119, 126, 152–3, 158–9, 181,
   194–5, 199–202, 204, 223, 226–8, 231,
   253, 255–6, 260, 270–2, 279–81, 285,
   303, 308, 314–15, 318, 324, 351
   escapism   25, 28, 54, 65, 71–2, 75,
      82, 84, 88, 93–5, 105–8, 114,
      124–9, 133, 140–4, 153, 181, 287,
      319–20, 340, 342, 349
   violent reactions, riots   35–6, 44–5,
      151, 194, 200, 214, 216
stage   46, 47, 67, 130, 267
   actors   15, 23, 94, 100, 137–8, 187,
      262, 267, 271, 283, 287, 299
   Serlian   9
   seventeenth-century   16, 19, 46, 94
   theatre/drama   17, 32 n. .10, 54, 64,
      102 n. 39, 104, 126, 149, 183, 205,
      211, 270, 286
Stamp, Terence (actor)   291
Storaro, Vittorio (cinematographer)   326
strikes   5, 24, 66, 71, 121, 140, 225,
   246–7
students   32–3, 71, 79, 137–8, 142, 144,
   156, 186, 233, 245, 268, 273, 287,
   293–4, 329, 332, 308, 340, 346, 348
Studio 28 see under screens
Studio des Ursulines see under screens
Studios   13, 18, 41, 54, 63, 109, 132–3

Bronston   172–3
CEA   57–8, 62, 66–7, 70–2
Charmatín Madrid   89, 143
Cinecittà   78, 82
Ciudad Lineal   57
Elstree   50
Joinville   52, 57–8
Madrid Films   41
Orphea Films   55–7, 62, 74, 84
Sevilla Studios, Madrid   124
UFA   78, 80–1, 91, 349
Suárez, Adolfo (government president)   225
Suárez, Carlos (cinematographer/ screenwriter/director)   260, 295
Suárez, Emma (actor)   285–6, 292, 335
Suárez, Gonzalo (director/screenwriter/ actor)   188, 192–3, 200 n. 2, 205, 212–13, 224, 260, 267, 287, 290, 320
Suárez, Julio (director)   174
Suárez de Lezo, Luis (director)   62, 124
subtitles   98, 291
Suchet, David   342
summer narratives   135, 145, 166–7, 191, 203, 211, 267, 293, 298–9, 330, 334, 347, see also rites of passage
Summers, Manuel (director)   185, 189, 196, 210, 213, 242, 270
supernatural see occult
surreal(ism)   42, 44, 64, 108, 192, 221, 281, 298, 342–3
suspense see thrillers
Switzerland, location   148, 329
synchronisation see under sound

Taberna, Helena (director)   292 n. 12, 326, 340
Tabio, Juan Carlos (director)   313
Tallafé, Manuel (actor)   346
Tamayo y Baus, Manuel (playwright)   101, 330
tango see under dance
Tapia, Gonzalo (director)   337
Targarona, Mar (director/producer)   311, 334
Tati, Jacques (screenwriter/director/ actor)   135, 166
Taurog, Norman (director)   121
Távora, Pilar (director)   230
Taylor, Lili (actor)   309
Taylor, Rod (actor)   273

Tejero, Fernando (actor)   332
Telerín Family   176
television   22, 144, 153, 163, 175–6, 195, 199, 201, 224, 227, 230, 248, 253, 255–7, 267, 269–70, 273, 283–4, 297, 302–4, 315, 333, 349
  funding for films   313, 315, 318, 320, 349
  on screen   129, 144 n. 41, 202, 230, 247, 267, 269–70, 285, 294, 295, 310, 318–19
  series   147 n. 45, 154, 163, 167 n. 14, 175–6, 234, 248, 252, 258, 260, 264, 273, 287, 297, 301, 318–19, 326, 328, 334, 344, 347
Tellería, Ernesto (director)   306
Temple, Ben (actor)   330
Temple, Shirley (actor)   61
Tercera vía [Third Way]   217–18, 229, 232
terrorism/terrorist,   198, 225, 231, 243, 255, 267, 274, 278, 292, 308, 317, 324, 340, 342
Thalberg, Irving (producer)   51
theatres/cinemas see under screens
theatre/stage see under stage
Thomas, Gerald (director)   165 n. 10
Thomas de Carranza. Enrique (DGCPE)   199
Thompson, Stith (folklorist)   115
Thous Orts, Maximiliano (director)   7, 83 n. 9
thrillers/suspense   96, 129–30, 137, 148, 161, 170–1, 192–3, 205–6, 212–13, 219, 221, 229, 236, 246–8, 262, 265–7, 272, 274–6, 278, 285–6, 288–92, 306–9, 311–12, 321–2, 333, 336–40, 343
  political   211–2, 235, 242–3, 291–2
Time Magazine   24 n. 37
Tirso de Molina (playwright)   104, 260 n. 6
Tobis-Klangfilm see under sound systems
Togores i Muntades, Josep de (director)   18, 21–3
Toledo, Goya (actor)   322, 346
Toledo, Guillermo (actor)   323
Toro, Guillermo del (director)   329, 350–1
toros   2, 5, 11, 13, 22–4, 28–31, 35–6, 56, 59–60, 62, 65–6, 80, 106–7,

127–8, 135, 139 , 142–3, 150, 161,
163–4, 177, 180, 190, 201, 211, 272,
306, 325, 342
Torrado, Ramón (director) 34, 65, 108,
121, 125, 140, 154, 159–60, 173, 201,
206
Torre, Claudio de la (director) 96, 105
Torrecilla, Rafael (director/producer)
124, 127
Torrent, Ana (actor) 215, 222, 232, 285,
292 n. 12, 308, 334, 337, 340
Torres, Ricardo (cinematographer) 78
Torres Ballester, Gonzalo (author) 248
Tosar, Luis (actor) 331–2
Tosas, Ramón 'Ivá' (comics' author)
252, 295
tourism/tourists 23–4, 33, 106, 144, 146,
149, 156–7, 159, 161, 164–5, 169,
175, 179–80, 183, 196, 203, 209, 218,
249–51, 280–1, 299, 310, 341
Tourneur, Jacques (director) 111 n. 50
Tracy, Spencer (actor) 121
trafficking see black-market
trains 2 n. 4, 4, 7, 74, 132 n. 18, 148,
177 n. 29, 222, 291–2, 298, 302
Tramullas Beltrán, Antoni (photographer)
11
Tramvia, Oriol (actor) 289
transnational cinema 265–6, 281, 286,
291–2, 298, 302, 315, 321, 323, 340,
345, 349–51
transsexual 235–7, 242, 324
transvestism/cross-dressing 179, 213,
236, 242, 296, 324
tremendismo 236–7
Trenet, Charles (singer) 168
Tricicle [Joan Gràcia, Paco Mir and Carles
Sans] (directors/comedians) 311
Trigo, Felipe (author) 258
Trilla-La Riva see under dubbing
Trincado, Joaquín (director) 295
Trueba, David (director) 160, 293, 329,
348
Trueba, Fernando (director/producer)
xiv, 80, 88, 233, 242, 262, 266–7, 270,
287, 293, 296, 303, 320, 348–9
Truffaut, François (director) 334
Turpin, Ben (actor) 28
Turquí [Turchi], Augusto (director) 23
Turtle, Frank (director) 52

Ucicky, Gustav (director) 37
UFA [Universumfilm Aktiengesellschaft]
see under studios
UK, location
Jersey 321
Liverpool 286
London 208, 298–9, 345
Oxford 309
Ulargui, Saturnino (entrepreneur) 50, 84
UN 327
Unamuno, Miguel de (author) 46, 104,
186, 205
underground cinema 220, 235 n. 14, 276
un/employment 70–1, 93–5, 112, 117–
18, 121, 128, 164–5, 178, 184, 190–1,
217, 233–4, 235–7, 247, 258, 282,
288–9, 305, 307, 315, 317, 332–3, 348
Ungría, Alfonso (director) 220, 244,
278, 289
UNICEF 327
UNINCI [Unión Industrial
Cinematográfica] see under production
companies
United Nations see UN
Universumfilm Aktiengesellschaft see
under studios, UFA
Urbizu, Enrique (director) 278, 287,
313, 337
Urgoiti, Ricardo (producer) 60–2
Uribe, Imanol (director/producer) 70,
241–2, 264, 267, 277, 280, 289, 292,
294, 303, 320, 330, 336
USA, location 41, 109, 143, 151, 232–3,
265, 296–7, 308–9, 323, 345
Ustinov, Peter 107, 143

Vajda, Ladislao (director) 87, 94, 109,
122, 126–7, 142–3, 148, 153–4, 182,
205 n. 14
Val del Omar, José (director/
cinematographer) 73, 151, 326
Valcárcel, Horacio (screenwriter) 330
Valderrama, Juanito (singer/actor) 142,
159
Valencia, location 21, 275, 277, 294,
302, 346
Benidorm 159, 203, 297
Valencian Cinema 13–5, 18, 238–40,
275, 277
Valentino, Rudolph (actor) 17

Valenzuela, Laura (actor)   167
Valera, Juan (author)   205
Valero, Antonio (actor)   270, 290
Valle Inclán, Ramón del (author)   138, 142 n. 43, 155, 205, 213, 259, 301
Valone, Raf (actor)   206
Valverde, Fernando (actor)   344
Valverde, Víctor (actor)   230
Van Parys, Georges (composer)   55
Vara Cuervo, Rafael (animation)   176
Varda, Agnès (director)   177 n. 28
Vatican   103, 123 n. 10, 152, 164, 268
VCE [Viejo Cine Español] *see under* comedy, popular
Vázquez, Ángel (author)   232
Vázquez Montalbán, Manuel (author)   228, 247, 291
Vega, Felipe (director)   273–4, 289, 295, 297, 347
Vega, Pastora (actor)   312
Vega, Paz (actor)   324, 346, 351
Vega, Vicente (actor)   95
Velasco, Concha (actor)   124, 156, 159, 163, 167–8, 209, 218–19, 260, 290, 319, 341
Vélez de Guevara, Luis (author)   100, 205
Velo, Carlos (director)   73, 79, 90
Ventura, Pere Joan (director)   327
Vera, Gerardo (director)   111 n. 49, 171, 336
Verbeke, Natalia (actor)   346
Verdaguer, Antoni (director)   276, 296, 301
Verdú, Maribel (actor)   262, 278, 285–7, 300, 304, 336–7
Vergano, Serena (director)   190
Vergara, Pau (director)   328
Vergés, Rosa (director)   310, 347
Vernon, Howard (actor)   174
Viance, Carmen (actor)   32, 35, 40
videos *see* DVDs
Vidor, Charles (director)   300 n. 16
Vidor, King (director)   172
Viejo Cine Español [VCE, Old Spanish Cinema] *see under* comedy, popular
Vilà Vilamala, Joan (director)   32–3, 66, 72
Viladomat, Domingo (director)   123, 145, 147 n. 44
Vilar, Antonio (actor)   100, 104, 109, 121, 132 n. 18

Vilar, Ignacio (director)   333
Vilarasau, Emma (actor)   335
Vilches, Ernesto (actor)   21
Villalonga, Llorenç (author)   249
Villaronga, Agustí (director)   89 n. 19, 262 n. 9, 276, 291, 320, 329
Villatoro, Ángel (director)   73
Viota, Paulino (director)   247
Visconti, Luchino (director)   184
Visedo, Irene (actor)   338, 346
Vivas, Miguel Ángel (director)   340
Vives, Amadeo (composer)   126
Vivó, José (actor)   215
Viyuela, Pepe (actor)   176
Vizcano Casas, Fernando (author)   239
Vodack, Vlacar (actor)   292
Vogler, Rüdiger (actor)   263
voice-overs   86, 99–100, 109, 111–12, 120, 123, 134, 138, 145, 187, 231, 240, 258, 267, 286, 301, 303
Von Sternberg, Josef (director)   55, 64, 266
Von Stroheim, Erich (director)   41
Von Sydow, Max (actor)   337
Voltaire (author)   102

Wagner, Richard (composer)   43
Waitzman, Adolfo (composer)   169
Wall Sreet Crash   46
Wallace, Richard (director)   50
Wallowits, Julio (director)   339
Walsh, Raoul (director)   23
war films
    Balkans   302, 339
    Carlist   4, 34–5, 149, 311
    Cine cruzada   89–93, 99, 330
    Civil War   72–4, 90–1, 96, 112, 114, 123–4, 155, 157, 170, 191, 200, 206–7, 214, 299, *see also* memory: recovery
    Cold War   91, 116, 122–4, 135, 155
    Cuban   4, 35, 90, 92–3, 112, 246
    Moroccan   4–5, 17, 24–5, 28, 31, 34, 52, 79, 95, 112, 220, 301
    Philippines   4, 92
    Six-Day War   299
    World War, First   xiv, 10, 34
    World War, Second   34 n. 18, 93, 95, 107
Welles, Orson (director)   74, 111, 171–2
Western Electric Co *see* sound systems

westerns/chorizo   127, 145, 157–8, 162, 170–4, 185, 196, 204, 207–9, 211, 219, 228, 305–6, 323, 330
  Spanish sets   172–4, 321
Whale, James (director)   222, 342
Wiene, Robert (director)   110
Wilson, Elsie Jane (director)   84
woman's emancipation   49, 59, 69, 226, 231
women   35, 40, 49, 56, 59, 76, 107, 113, 145, 168, 180–4, 196, 210, 230–1, 248, 254, 265, 273, 284–8, 298, 304–5, 308–9, 315, 324–6, 333–5, 339, 341, 344–7
  femme fatale   90, 108, 148, 162, 272, 287
  lesbian   208, 212, 251, 259, 310–11
  professional   69, 145, 164, 178, 202, 208, 230–1, 270, 272, 274, 284–7, 290, 293, 295, 307, 310–11, 321, 324, 335, 337, 340, 343, 345–6
  strong   71, 94, 102, 114, 124–5, 192, 212, 229, 231–2, 245, 251, 267, 272, 284–8, 295, 304, 307–8, 310–12, 323–5, 331, 334–5, 337, 340
  victim   35, 40, 60–1, 88, 111, 124–5, 138, 151, 157, 171, 174, 180, 197, 205, 216, 232, 265, 272, 284–7, 291, 293, 297, 307, 311, 322–5, 331, 334, 336, 339–41, 346
  virgin, mother or whore   183, 186, 286, 307, 322
Wood, Sam (director)   51
World Wars, First and Second *see under* war films

Wyller, William (director)   266

Xaudaró, Joaquín (animation producer) 63
xenophobia *see* race
Xirgú, Margarita (actor)   7, 15, 18

Yagüe, Jesús (director)   238
Yarza, Rosita (actor)   94
Ycobalzeta, Anna (actor)   346
Yegros, Lina (actor)   95
Young, Terence (director)   120
Yoyes (Etarista) [María Dolores González Katarain]   292, 340
Yuste, Josema [Martes y Trece] (actor) 305

Zabala, Carlos (director)   313
Zabalza, José María (director)   150, 174, 207, 228, 268,
Zacarías, Miguel (director)   126
Zambrano, Benito (director)   331, 350
Zambrano, María (author)   327
zarzuela *see under* musicals *and* songs
Zecca, Ferdinand (director)   11
Zola, Emile (author)   230
Zorrilla, China (actor)   350
Zorrilla, José (playwright)   104, 149, 262
Zorrilla, José Antonio (director)   247, 262
Zulueta, Iván (director)   212, 222, 251–2, 320